THE ATLANTIC WAR REMEMBERED

THE
ATLANTIC WAR
REMEMBERED

AN ORAL HISTORY COLLECTION

Edited by John T. Mason, Jr.

NAVAL INSTITUTE PRESS
Annapolis, Maryland

Library of Congress Cataloging-in-Publicaton Data

The Atlantic war remembered : an oral history collection /
edited by John T. Mason Jr.
     p.   cm.
   Includes bibliographical references and index.
   ISBN 0-87021-523-X
   1. World War, 1939–1945—Personal narratives, American. 2. World War, 1939–1945—Campaigns—Europe.
3. World War, 1939–1945—Campaigns—Mediterranean
Region. 4. Europe—History—1918–1945. 5. Mediterranean Region—History. I. Mason, John T., 1909–
D811.A2A73   1990
940.54′5973—dc20   90-43436

Printed in the United States of America on acid-free paper ∞

9 8 7 6 5 4 3 2

Maps: Morison, Samuel Eliot. *History of United States Naval
Operations in World War II.* Vols. 1, 2, 9, 11. 1947–57. Re-
print. Boston: Little, Brown, 1975.

I dedicate this volume to the fine group of men and women represented herein. All of them served their country with distinction in World War II. Many of them became my personal friends. That has proved to be one of the great privileges of my life.

CONTENTS

CONTENTS

ABBREVIATIONS AND CODE NAMES

AAA	antiaircraft artillery
ACV	auxiliary aircraft carrier
AGC	amphibious force command ship
AI	aircraft interception (type of British radar)
Anvil/Dragoon	Allied plan for southern France, 1944
APA	attack transport
ASW	antisubmarine warfare
Avalanche	attack on Salerno, Italy
AVG	escort vessel, aircraft; the *Long Island* was the only one; later vessels in this classification were designated CVE
AVP	small seaplane tender
B-36	U.S. bomber
BuAir	Bureau of Aeronautics
C & R	convoy and routing
C-47	cargo ship
C-4	cargo ship
CinCLant	commander in chief, Atlantic
CinCMed	commander in chief, Mediterranean
CNO	chief of naval operations
CO	commanding officer
COMLANCRABNAV	commander landing craft and bases, North West African waters
COMINCH	commander in chief
C-3	cargo ship with certain type of hull
CVE	escort aircraft carrier
CXAM	early experimental installations of radar
DC	U.S. airplane manufactured by Douglas
DD	destroyer
DSO	Distinguished Service Order
DUKW	amphibious truck
EDO	engineering duty officer
FFI	French Forces of the Interior

FX & FD	experimental and fighter director radios
Husky	Allied plan for invasion of Sicily
JCS	joint chiefs of staff
KCB	Knight Commander of the Bath
LCI	landing craft, infantry
LCIL	landing craft, infantry, large
LCM	landing craft, mechanized
LCT	landing craft, tank
LCU	British amphibious craft with rocket launchers
LCVP	landing craft, vehicle, personnel
LST	landing ship, tank
MIT	Massachusetts Institute of Technology
MP	military police
MTB	British patrol craft
NAF	Naval Aircraft Factory, Philadelphia, PA
NAS	naval air station
NKVD	Soviet secret police
ONI	Office of Naval Intelligence
OSS	Office of Strategic Services
Overlord	Allied plan for Normandy invasion, 1944
PBN	navy version of PBY patrol bomber
PBY	patrol bomber, amphibian
PB-ZM	unarmed aircraft
PDM	period delay mechanism
P-51	fighter plane
PG	postgraduate
P-party	British minesweeping unit
PQ-17	designation of convoy from Iceland to Murmansk
PT	motor torpedo boat
P-38	two-engine fighter plane
R-4D	Soviet Navy transport
RAF	Royal Air Force
RDF	radio direction finder
RNVR	Royal Navy Volunteer Reserve
SCR	Signal Corps radio
SeaBee	naval construction battalion
SEAL	sea-air-land (team)
SG	early radar installed on shipboard
Sledgehammer	proposed Allied landing on Cotentin Peninsula, France, 1943
SNJ	scout trainer plane, manufactured by North American

SOC	scout-observation plane, manufactured by Curtiss
SPAR	woman member of the U.S. Coast Guard; from coast guard motto "Semper Paratus"
Stuka	Axis dive-bomber
TBM	torpedo bomber, manufactured by Martin
TB-3	torpedo bomber plane
TODT	foreign labor force utilized by Axis forces in Normandy
Torch	Allied plan for invasion of North Africa, 1942
UDT	underwater demolition team
USNA	U.S. Naval Academy
VFR	visual flight rules
VS	volunteer specialist
WAAC/WAC	Women's Army Auxiliary Corps, later Women's Army Corps
WAVES	Women Accepted for Voluntary Emergency Service (U.S. Navy)
WPA	Works Progress Administration
WRNS/Wrens	Women's Royal Naval Service (Royal Navy)
XF6F	experimental fighter plane made by Grumman

MAPS

PREFACE

All Gaul is divided into three parts, wrote Julius Caesar as he contemplated the conquest of that ancient land, or so I learned in my Latin class. In like fashion World War II was divided into two parts, so believed the Allied powers. Still, as the war unfolded they learned to their consternation it became a global war of many parts. That conflict of parts proved often a hazard of great moment.

The war in Europe, the first half exploding in 1939 with the Nazi invasion of Poland, was soon a war of survival for Great Britain, France, and the lesser powers of western Europe. When the Nazis invaded Russia in 1941 the war in Europe added an eastern front, extending into the Balkans and the Mediterranean.

The conflict assumed worldwide proportions when Japan struck at Pearl Harbor in December 1941. This immediate threat to the United States made her an active belligerent while intensifying the conflict for the Pacific colonies of Great Britain, France, and the Netherlands. It became a truly global war when the United States and Great Britain invaded North Africa in November 1942 and followed that with invasions in Algeria, Sicily, Italy, Normandy, and southern France. Then one could say that hardly a portion of the civilized world (and even portions of the uncivilized world) remained untouched. The oceans, too, in a way greater than in World War I became a dangerous front demanding the attention and energies of the major powers to deal with the modern submarine tactics of the enemy.

This vast picture is important to an understanding of the staggering demands on the Western countries so engaged. It called for great wisdom to design the necessary stratagems, the allocation of materials, the priorities. No wonder that questions were raised by the major democracies and the Soviets. Great Britain saw the need for concentration on the European side of the conflict; the United States often felt she must devote the major efforts against the dynamic force of the Japanese on her western flank in the Pacific. Russia, when her forces faced imminent disaster on the eastern front, made insistent and strenuous demands that the Allies hasten an invasion of France to divide the military might of the Nazis. These demands were made at times when the Western Alliance lacked the men and the ships for such an enterprise.

All these problems are revealed in the frequent conferences of the major Western leaders. Their loyalties of long standing, their political ideologies, even their personal characteristics are revealed in their discussions, augmented as they were by the practical military advice of the highest rank in their respective countries. Great difficulties arose and were not easily resolved. Yet all three of the major leaders of the West—Roosevelt, Churchill, and Stalin—knew that the fate of Western civilization hung in the balance and they must persevere at all costs.

This is the background for some of the battles dealt with in the oral history excerpts that follow in this book. They are necessarily of major naval emphasis because they are taken from the naval history oral interviews conducted under the aegis of Columbia University in 1960–69 and at the U.S. Naval Institute in 1969–82. The navy in such a war had the primary initiative. Once an amphibious operation was decided upon it was the task of the navy, or the navies as necessity would have it, to carry the troops to land on the beaches; to supply the air forces with whatever they needed; and to provide a supply of equipment, ammunition, and food for all the armed forces on land.

It is a truism (sometimes a shocking one to those of us who lived through it) to realize that the events of World War II have now become a part of past history. So many of today's readers are unfamiliar with these events. Yet some people today comment on results of these conflicts in that present-day problems in the world often reflect the residual of that war. The Yalta Conference (February 1945) is a prime example. Rear Admiral Clarence Olsen, the U.S. naval attaché in Moscow at the time, has given us a vivid picture of the scene. He was delegated by the American ambassador in Moscow to supervise the frantic efforts to set the physical stage for the deliberations of the Big Three: Roosevelt, Churchill, and Stalin. The picture Olsen gives in his interview will help the reader to understand the possibility for error that crept into the decisions taken by the chief participants. Poor health and physical discomfort were bound to affect the results.

Once again, as in the preface to *The Pacific War Remembered,* I feel impelled to expound on some of the virtues of the oral history method. This is certainly true where pursued in a conscientious manner and with due concern for the historical facts. We entered into the interviews that follow only after extensive preparations on the part of the interviewees and interviewer. Then followed the inevitable checking of the transcript for accuracy on the part of both parties. In order to make the reading of the transcript flow more freely the questions of the interviewer have been eliminated, but the context of the question is invariably incorporated in the answer obtained.

Realism is apparent in these interviews. The subject of the interview is speaking directly. The personality stands forth. Strong points and foibles are likely to be seen. It becomes a verbal portrait.

I use as an illustration my interviews with Admiral Alan Kirk, the senior American naval officer at the Normandy landings. His words bring back to me even today the vivid personality, the sophisticated man of the world. He once asked me suddenly what I thought of him and I responded: "You remind me of Winston Churchill; you have a Churchillian manner—your decisiveness, yes, even the daunting nature of your intellect." He also brings back to me his oft-repeated respect for the American sailor and even his love. It was the inventiveness of that sailor and his willingness to perform in the face of great danger that became for Alan Kirk the bedrock upon which he relied so heavily when the going was rough.

In like fashion the gentle yet authoritative, hulking sort of man that was Admiral Kent Hewitt comes back to me with great realism as I recall eating a hamburger with him in a local diner in Hackensack, New Jersey, after a long morning of talk on his activities in World War II. His story as it appears in this volume is a detailed one, both wise and bold, as he shepherded his men and ships for the first of America's major amphibious landings, on the coast of North Africa. Another of Admiral Hewitt's amphibious operations is described in the section dealing with the south of France.

These men, Kirk and Hewitt and many others, live in memory and in history. That is truly a virtue of the oral history method.

The contents of some interviews in this volume are a departure from most in the earlier volume on the Pacific because they deal with subjects not directly related to battles. There is a short section devoted to an interview with Admiral Horacio Rivero on the subject of radar. Rivero was one of the very first men in the U.S. Navy to deal with the development of radar when it first came on stream to revolutionize the conduct of war at sea, in the air, and under the water. Rivero's account is augmented in part by information from interviews I had with Sir Robert Watson-Watt, the noted British scientist who was in residence for a time in Tuxedo Park, New York. It was there I discovered him and conducted interviews a number of times over two years. He told me much about his struggles to develop the idea of radar, sometimes under the most difficult of circumstances but just in time for use against the German Luftwaffe as they spearheaded the planned German assault on the British islands. The RAF, inferior in numbers, was able to withstand because they had the advantage of an early radar. Consequently the German attempt at invasion was forestalled and finally postponed indefinitely.

It is pleasing indeed to have in this volume a series of interviews with several women who contributed greatly to the war effort. Their work was not mentioned in the earlier volume on the Pacific phase of the war because women in the military were not a part of that conflict until very late. Only then did Congress make it possible for them to serve there. In this volume are interviews with Mildred McAfee Horton, the first director of the navy's WAVES; with Ruth Cheney Streeter, the first director of the Women Marines; and with Dorothy Constance Stratton, the first director of the Coast Guard's SPARs. Other women in the military, especially those in the army's WACS and those in the air forces, were not a part of the navy's story and do not appear here.

There is also a series of excerpts about the lend-lease program of the Rooseveltian period. This became an indispensable weapon in providing the wherewithal—the tools—to sustain the worldwide efforts of our allies in the battle against the Nazis. Some of these interviews focus largely on lend-lease to the Russians and some of the difficulties experienced there. Great Britain was the major recipient of this program and really the incentive for President Roosevelt to set it up in the first place. There are no special interviews on that phase of the lend-lease program but bits of the story come to light in many of the interviews that focus on specific battles.

The staggering complexity of the Normandy landings on the sandy beaches of France is spelled out in a brief summary in the preface to the accounts of that operation as well as in the reports of Admirals Kirk and Hall and the details provided by Admiral Sullivan in his description of the clearing of Cherbourg Harbor after the devastation left by the departing Germans. From all this readers can obtain an idea about the magnitude of this invasion and also get a sense of the fragile nature of this military gamble. A single violent storm, originating in far-off Greenland, came swiftly across the ocean and into the English Channel, delaying this beautifully coordinated landing by a day and disrupting the minute plans to land hundreds of thousands of troops from some four thousand ships of all shapes and sizes. The air forces, primed for the initial assault, were also grounded for the same period of time. All this is an unforgettable episode in the annals of history. Yet that effort and the sacrifices made were entirely justified, most men and women agree, by the lasting results obtained.

Naturally I want to express my heartfelt gratitude to various people who have contributed to what has gone into the preparation of this book. I am especially indebted to Ronald J. Grele, the director of the Oral History Research Office at Columbia University, for his blanket approval for my use of many excerpts from the Columbia Oral History Collection. It was the first collection upon which I worked and most of the interviews on the war in the Atlantic and the Mediterranean date from that time in the 1960s. I am grateful too for the individual permissions that have been given for other interviews appearing in this volume.

Once again I cite the help that has come from former colleagues at the U.S. Naval Institute during my period of service there when the balance of my oral history interviews on the navy were conducted. I am especially grateful to Tom Epley, the Naval Institute Press director, for his generous encouragement; to the late Marjorie Kerns for her outstanding kindness and willingness to help with my numerous calls; to other Book Department staff members for their assistance in many ways; and to Patty Maddocks, the director of the Institute's library, for her generous work in getting photographs, maps, and biographies—something only a professional like Patty can do with grace and effectiveness. Also I thank Agnes Hoover of the Naval Historical Center in Washington, D.C., for the assistance she gave Mrs. Maddocks in gathering the large requests for material.

Alice Creighton and her staff in the special collections department of the Nimitz Library at the Naval Academy are praised for all their courtesies in making life easier for me on my frequent trips to Annapolis. It goes without saying that I am always grateful to my successor as director of the Naval Institute's oral history program, Paul Stillwell, and his assistant, Susan Sweeney. Both of them are always at the other end of the telephone when I need help. I want to pay my respects to the manuscript editor of this book—to Marilyn Wilderson, who spent countless hours reviewing my text and leading me patiently and gently without rancor through the intricacies of lower case and upper case and all the rules of modern editing.

Best of all, I express a singular gratitude to my beloved wife, Elizabeth Branch Mason, for my introduction to oral history, for her constant encouragement, for her painstaking help with the manuscript, and the hours of typing she undertook to make the text ready.

THE ATLANTIC WAR REMEMBERED

The following excerpts from oral history interviews with Mildred McAfee Horton, Ruth Cheney Streeter and Dorothy Stratton are included in this volume for a particular reason. Mildred McAfee was the first director of the WAVES (Women Accepted for Voluntary Emergency Service), the women who served in the U.S. Navy in World War II. Ruth Streeter was the first director of the women marines (Marine Corps Women's Reserve) in World War II. Dorothy Stratton was the first director of the women's reserve in the U.S. Coast Guard, named SPAR after the motto of the coast guard—*Semper Paratus,* "Always Ready."

Thus they became the pioneers in the first major effort of American women to serve in the armed forces of their country. The U.S. Army of course had its well-known counterpart in the WAC (Women's Army Corps) under the direction of Oveta Culp Hobby.* Their illustrious record is not covered in this book for it is devoted solely to the navy and its related services. These women aided greatly in fostering a remarkable use of women in 1942–45, when the demands on our manpower were very great and the services in need of reinforcement. The theme that the women used—indeed, the general theme of all the recruitment in these new organizations—met with great success. Their powerful and pervasive slogan was: "Free a man to fight."

The reader of these interviews should keep in mind the vast contrast between the social customs and general mores of fifty-odd years ago as compared with those today. American women of 1940 were in a position different from the women of the occupied countries of Europe and of the United Kingdom. The frightful circumstances of a cruel war were already upon the latter and they had responded with dedication. The enemy had either already overrun their countries or was at their national gates. The citizens of the United States were only beginning to grasp the magnitude of the world conflict that burst upon them at Pearl Harbor in December 1941. That event proved to be a watershed of mammoth proportions. It

*The army's women's reserve was originally called the Women's Army Auxiliary Corps (WAAC). After 1943 it was designated the Women's Army Corps (WAC).

changed the attitude of Americans overnight; it aroused our patriotism and love of country as nothing else could. It even filled us with an unaccustomed fear—we could lose this war into which we had been plunged so precipitously. Now every man, woman, and child must do his or her part.

The impact of war almost immediately filled the ranks of the newly formed WAVES, the Marine Corps Women's Reserve, and the SPAR of the U.S. Coast Guard; it brought forth quickly the symbol of "Rosie the Riveter," the wartime woman of basic industry. Women performed not only clerical jobs; they did manual labor, they served everywhere. For many women it became the introduction to what had been largely a man's world where few had ventured before. And what is more significant, it opened the gates and led through the intervening years to the greater liberation of women in our society.

No clearer picture of this development can be found than in the careers of these three women: Mildred McAfee, the esteemed president of Wellesley College, an Ivy League school for women; Ruth Streeter, a woman of wealth and privilege; and Dorothy Stratton, the daughter of a midwestern clergyman and herself dean of women at Purdue University. All three took up their assigned jobs with enthusiasm and confidence. They learned the hard way, for not one of them received any special training in military matters before being thrust into their respective slots. All three services—the U.S. Navy, the U.S. Marine Corps and the U.S. Coast Guard—were considerably less than enthusiastic at having women join their ranks in uniform. All three of these women came without a real understanding of the rigid code of military rank that prevailed. They came into service with a middle-grade rank thrust upon them and with the plans for their new organizations already largely in place. They came without any real authority or designated responsibility, but they did not let that deter them. They earned high respect and a permanent place for women in the United States armed forces; they earned the success that came to them, and they received the grateful plaudits of their country.

THE NAVY WAS A MAN'S WORLD

CAPTAIN MILDRED McAFEE, WAVES

NIMITZ LIBRARY, SPECIAL COLLECTIONS

MILDRED HELEN McAFEE was born in Parkville, Missouri, on 12 May 1900, the daughter of a clergyman and educator who was for several years the secretary of the Presbyterian Board of Missions in New York City. Her grandfather was a cofounder and president of Park College in Parkville. Miss McAfee prepared for college at the Francis W. Parker School in Chicago and in 1920 was graduated from Vassar College with a B.A., having been named to membership in Phi Beta Kappa. After that followed a series of teaching assignments and church work in Illinois and Tennessee. She also undertook some graduate work at the University of Chicago, tutored at Bryn Mawr, and served for a five-year period as dean of women and professor of sociology at Centre College in Danville, Kentucky. In all this time she also attended summer sessions of the University of Chicago in 1929, 1931, and 1933 and Columbia University in 1924 and 1932, securing her M.A. degree from Chicago in 1928.

Miss McAfee was named president of Wellesley College in 1936. She served there for ten years with the exception of the period between August 1942 and February 1946, when she was on leave of absence to serve as director of the Women's Reserve, U.S. Naval Reserve (WAVES). Miss McAfee's story of her work with the WAVES during World War II is told in the segment of her oral history that follows in this chapter. As she relates this story we learn that at a high point some eighty-six thousand women (eight thousand of whom were officers) were enrolled in the WAVES, a powerful force that served at nine hundred shore stations in the continental United States and Hawaii. In so doing they released approximately fifty thousand navy men for duty afloat or overseas. Miss McAfee was married to Dr. Douglas Horton, a minister of the General Council of Congregational Christian Churches, on 10 August 1945, not long before her period of service in the WAVES came to an end in February 1946.

Her achievements in the scholastic world were not only noticed but honored by some sixteen universities and colleges who bestowed a doctoral degree upon her. Her service on various boards of schools, civic organizations and even foreign universities are too numerous to name—a remarkable career.

The U.S. Army began to take women into the service six months before the naval law was altered so that women could become eligible. My understanding is that the navy resisted very much the whole idea of having women in the service but that when they began to see that the manpower shortage might prevent their doing some of the things they needed to do without drawing on womanpower, they then decided to establish it on a little different basis from what the army had tried. The theory from the beginning, I understand, was that if women were going to be in the service, they were going to be *in* the navy and under the control of the naval officials rather than being an auxiliary corps that would run its own ship.

The idea of the WAVES was influenced in many of the details by the British experience with the Wrens.* Admiral Jacobs, the chief of naval personnel, went to Canada on a trip and viewed there some of the British and Canadian Wrens. The byproduct of that visit was his absolute insistance that the women of America in the navy must wear black stockings because they looked so handsome on the Wrens as they marched past him on review.

So we had to fight that battle, one of the first we fought, the battle of the black stockings. Several times he told me that his wife and daughter protested his attitude on our account. We were equally determined not to have black stockings because at that time they were not being worn by American women. I tried to buy some in Washington and could not find any except for the sheerest of sheer things, acceptable in a night club. In the WAVES they would have been worn out in half a day.

Finally at a dinner party Admiral Jacobs learned from his dinner partner that the same chemical used for dye in black stockings was needed for

*WRNS, Women's Royal Naval Service.

gunpowder or ammunition of some sort. So Jacobs relented rather than jeopardize the war effort.

Sometime during the winter after Pearl Harbor the personnel officer in Admiral King's office was working on the subject of women in the navy. He enlisted the help of Virginia Gildersleeve, dean of Barnard, and a Miss Reynard, who was a professor there, and asked them to consider the question. Miss Gildersleeve called a conference at Barnard of executives from a large number of women's colleges plus the deans from several coeducational colleges. I, as president of Wellesley, was invited. We were told at that conference that there was the likelihood that women would be admitted to the navy. The officer who talked with us at the conference was Paul B. Hartenstein, a professor at the University of Pennsylvania. He talked enlighteningly on the subject, the kinds of things women might be asked to do, and he asked us at the conference to encourage recruiting when legislation made all this possible.

Fairly quickly after this conference Miss Gildersleeve wrote me to ask if I would accept an appointment to head the woman's organization in the navy when it was established. It was right at this time it was explained to me that the navy had decided it was going to have somebody at the head of this organization who was not politically related or known. They had decided to try to get a woman's college president on the principle that the navy knew enough about the navy but they didn't know much about girls. Somebody who had been working with young women would be the kind of person they were looking for. Furthermore—and this was the real trick to it—the Congress had limited the rank to that of a lieutenant commander.

One thing we had been insisting upon at the meeting at Barnard (and the navy was in sympathy with this point) was that women should not have special privileges. They should conform to the existing regulations. This meant that the director to be was to be only a lieutenant commander and therefore must be within the age bracket of a lieutenant commander as the navy designated it. I happened to be the only one who was young enough to fall in that low rank.

Another definite theory was that in appointing anybody to be the head of this new organization in the navy, the authorities wanted to assure the parents and boyfriends of girls who thought of entering the service that they would be looked after. This was not going to be a wild show; it would be respectable, and the president of a woman's college was likely to meet the qualifications. She would be somebody accustomed to dealing with girls, and since she was in a position that had respect attached to it, she would enhance getting the right kind of persons into the service. [Miss McAfee was commissioned in August 1942.]

In her autobiography later Miss Gildersleeve was incensed with the trustees at Wellesley because they raised a question about releasing me

5

from my commitment there to respond to the offer. It turned out to be an error in understanding. The trustees thought that the navy might not buy the idea, since Miss Gildersleeve came in person to them. They thought the offer wasn't entirely official. Also, a son of a trustee said that he didn't think the college president should get mixed up in an organization where she would be only a lieutenant commander because that rank would not carry any weight.

Miss Gildersleeve thought the trustees were being unpatriotic, but when she talked with me I said I was willing to go to Washington and talk with the chief of naval personnel to find out what it was all about. I did go and I talked with Admiral Jacobs. I told him I knew nothing about navy ranks but that some of the trustees thought it debatable whether I really ought to leave a position with responsibility as president of a college for something at the rank of lieutenant commander. Jacobs said, "Why, think nothing of that. In the navy anybody who is in charge of anything is the ranking officer there. In a small boat it might be an ensign in charge but his word is law. It doesn't mean a thing. You'll be in charge and this will be your baby." Well, the fact of the matter was that for me and for many— for scores—of the women who came in, this matter of rank really didn't mean anything. It just didn't matter. We came to do a job and we didn't know enough about the navy to think that rank would make any difference.

But soon we were perfectly appalled by something in one of our first training schools. It was to be commanded by a male officer. There would be a woman executive officer, and there would be a woman officer in charge of actual instruction. These people were then named, but it turned out that the teacher outranked the executive by one day. The young man who had been assigned said, "We can't do this in the navy. We simply can't do this. The ranking officer with seniority has got to be the executive." And we thought it was just asinine, so silly. But I noticed that very soon people began to be sensitive about seniority—at first it just literally made no difference.

Almost immediately the issue came up of going overseas. One of the requirements of the law as written was that WAVES would not go overseas. It was hard on recruiting. A lot of women knew the army was sending women overseas, the Red Cross was sending women, nurses could go, why not WAVES? One of the reasons was the chairman of the House Naval Affairs Committee, Carl Vinson, a gentleman from southern Georgia. I got the very definite impression that he just wanted to protect these young girls. Senator David I. Walsh, the chairman of the Senate Naval Affairs Committee, entertained similar views. I think we all thought it was a little unnecessary to pick on us to be protected. We didn't think we were any worse off, in any worse danger, than any of the others.

Anyway, it was some time, certainly weeks, after I'd been there that suddenly I went to Admiral Jacobs and said: "It seems to me a little bit funny that we aren't finding out what people want women to do, instead of just getting women trained to do something." He said, "I think you're right. You ought to go round to these bureaus and find out what they'd like to have you do." And he arranged for me to go and visit the chiefs of all the various bureaus. When I got to Admiral Towers, head of BuAir [Bureau of Aeronautics], I was perfectly astonished at the violence with which he spoke: "Where have you been all this time? We've been clamoring for these WAVES and nobody's ever listened to us to know what we want." Then his bureau asked for the largest single number of all. Towers had not come directly to me because, you see, I was a lieutenant commander in the Bureau of Naval Personnel and this rank business, which made not one hill of beans difference to me, definitely made others recognize that as far as general policy was concerned, that was being done way up in some echelon that I never came in contact with. Admiral Jacobs's door was open to me any time I wanted it. But I've often thought he didn't make it very plain outside of the bureau. He was also more explicit to me than he was explaining to everybody else what the relationship of this strange new thing was going to be.

Now about the name WAVES. Since we knew the work was to be temporary for us we were the women accepted for volunteer emergency service and we weren't going to be there forever or stay there. There was a classification for officers called VS—volunteer specialist. They came right from civilian life into the navy. The question arose of course, what should the women be called in the service? I was extremely high-minded about this and I said, "I think they should be called by their ranks and just women in the service, in the navy." That was until I saw a headline in a Washington paper early in the summer (just after Congress had passed the enabling legislation). The headline in the paper said: "Goblettes come to town." Navy gobs. At that point I bought the nickname *Waves*. It had been going around the office as a possible name, *Women's Volunteer Service, WVS*. Those three letters could work into Waves, Wives, Wolves, or Woovs, and Waves seemed appropriate for the navy. And then it became: Women Accepted for Volunteer Emergency Service. In Hawaii, I am told, somebody came up with the thought Women Are Very Essential Sometimes.

After the legislation was passed there was an induction ceremony for me, very simple but very gracious and held in the office of Frank Knox, secretary of the navy. Admiral King was there and two or three other high-ranking officers. There was a press conference immediately afterwards but of course I had nothing to say. I had been in Washington for only a month before the legislation passed the Congress. It was well known that I was to be the commissioned officer in charge but it was very nebulous because I didn't have any status at all for the first few weeks. I had a desk and a civilian secretary. The theory was we were finding people who would be the nucleus of our organization, and that was done by way of naval districts.

Appointments were made in each naval district, often by a committee that had been named by Miss Gildersleeve to select a senior woman officer in the district. She was to be in charge of the recruiting office and program. Early in the game it was decided that all women would be enlisted or commissioned through the office of procurement officers, and not merely recruiting officers. That system caused some consternation at first, but it did one thing which we had hoped for: it brought in women to the offices who were very much more attractive, more appealing, than the post office recruiting station. In this we learned from the experience of the army. They had established recruiting offices and anybody could come without being cleared. We inaugurated a different system: applicants must write to the procurement office, give their name and age, their occupation, and if the basic facts looked promising, such an applicant was sent a form for further information with a date for an appointment for an interview.

We were fortunate to have women of experience to interview the applicants—people like a woman who had been director of personnel at Macy's in New York. We had another who had been dean of women at a college in Pennsylvania. There were many applicants who qualified as officers and were not needed as such immediately, and they just signed on as enlisted women. Of the first group of applicants who came in as enlisted women 75 percent were qualified to serve as officers when needed.

One of the most startling and really grim experiences for this first group was that Captain Underwood, the naval officer in command at Hunter College, decided that the way to train these women as officers was to put them through the kind of training a man would get at Annapolis in six weeks. They were to drill, to march, and do all the things that would be done on a naval station. So you got the dean of women at Purdue University, the director of the great housing development at Stanford University—people like that who had been accustomed to giving orders all their adult life. It was really excessively hard for them to take but they were sports and performed just beautifully. And then they went out to be the heads of all the other projects with that as background. These women were convinced that they were needed to get the thing off the ground. This was really a direct way in which they could help the war effort. They wanted to be in on it.

I stepped into one situation and said, "I just won't buy that." The public relations people in the navy sponsored a movie to publicize the newly formed WAVES. There was so much cheesecake in it, and it appealed to those who sought an adventure we couldn't possible guarantee. I told them we cannot have a movie that will make the applicants think they're coming in to get their man and to have a thrill. I was so convinced of the wrong nature of this that I appealed to Admiral Jacobs and he supported me in withdrawing this thing; it just completely misrepresented the direction of the WAVES and their service. This incident did much to convince the public relations people that this was not the way to go. It made it all quite clear that somebody was going to see to it that there wasn't going to be any riff-raff crowd in the service. But the real secret was that the navy, at no point, had thought in big terms. Well, eventually—I think I'm right—at one point we had eighty-six thousand women on duty at one time.

The authorities had not anticipated this great growth because, I really think, there was so much internal resistance to it. And the way it proved itself was something they could not have anticipated. You know, when a navy man in command of a station judges his own people they are always tops. "My people are wonderful." "We don't want WAVES in general, but my WAVES are fine." This possessive admiration of "My ship" and "My station" really meant that as soon as WAVES got out of training and on somebody's station, they were his girls, he was all for them. It really was simply fantastic. This is true of the old chiefs. The chiefs just died at the thought of having women and then their girls came along and the chiefs just melted. It was just part of the whole navy psychology that once they belonged, they were all right.

It was not a case of my undertaking to establish something outside of this framework. Every girl who went out to a station was under the command of the commanding officer of that station. We had a woman there who was liaison between the girls and the commanding officer but she wasn't in command. I think that once we had seven WAVES in my office and I was in command of them, but I had no command over the rest of it. I didn't want to command. It was very gratifying to be able to say, "We're not auxiliary, we're in the service." But it was hardly fair for me to get the red carpet treatment. It was a very painful position to be in—receiving all kinds of honors all over the place when really you knew that it was backdoor diplomacy if you had anything to do with it at all.

It was frustrating really not to be able to accomplish the things you wanted to except by very indirect methods. I may confess to a memorable experience when we were sensing the fact that we weren't getting anything much accomplished to speed things up. This was near the end of a year or two. We were accepted enough by then to feel the limitations of what we could do and accomplish. By that time we had a WAVE officer appointed to all of the navy offices to be a contact between my office and those offices. I had a coffee mess in my office every morning and all those officers came. They were my eyes and ears, and we talked about what we must get done and then they would go back and do it. This was subversive in the navy, in a way. So we sat there one day and I remember vividly that we solemnly agreed that we were going at this in the wrong way. We could go on having just as many ideas as we wanted to, but under no circumstances must they come from my office to all those other offices except indirectly. It would be the fine art of each of these young women to get the idea to the man in charge so he thought it was his own, never to say this was the combined judgment of all these women who came to my office for coffee daily.

I remember all of us felt positively embarrassed about this. How perfectly stupid to resort to this technique when we were there to do a job, how stupid! But we tried it, and boy it worked fine. We had a peaceful and lovely time from then on. The real fact was, all those offices were headed by people who were on their way up. We didn't care whether we went up or not, but these men knew that their professional careers depended on what happened in their command. If we had ideas that could work, that helped their careers, well and good. We didn't have a career and we didn't care. There was nothing noble about this. It was just a good technique. It worked fine.

For some of us who had been dealing with women's organizations it was an interesting experience to get into a man's world. We kept saying, we never had realized how completely the navy was a man's world. To the enlisted women, the young ones, the whole thing had a kind of exhilarating novelty to it. That didn't apply to the young officers as much as it did to the enlisted girls. The young junior officers comprised the hardest group from the point of view of achievement. For some of them there was enormous value in convincing people they could do things they had never done before.

One of our prize stories had to do with a certain station where the commanding officer needed a dietician (a mess hall director) and a recreation director. Finally a recreation director was sent out. The CO said, "I need a dietician much more than I need a recreation director, so you will run the mess hall." The WAVE said, "I've never done anything like this in my life before." He said, "You're in the navy. You do it." And she did it so well that when they sent a mess hall director out, the officer said, "We're very well pleased with what we have."

The first few weeks in the Bureau of Naval Personnel in the Arlington Annex were a muddle of complete confusion to me. I was tucked away in a little office somewhere. My first responsibility was the business of getting enough women there to start doing something. What they were to do was as vague to me as it was to all the rest of the navy.

I'm afraid it was a very unsystematic kind of thing because everybody was rushing around like mad as the war was expanding, and they didn't have time to brief me on anything much. I just stayed around and tried to see what was happening which affected women. For instance, one interesting little episode was the matter of uniforms. It was being handled in Admiral Jacobs's office by a young aide to the admiral. My memory is that I asked him what was happening about uniforms and he said: "We're having a showing of them this morning." I had not heard one word about it. It was with some reluctance that he said, "You can come and look at them if you want to." As though I wouldn't want to!

When I got there Mrs. Forrestal, the wife of the secretary of the navy, was there. She had been working with *Vogue* magazine and I think we must credit her with having gotten Mainbocher to design these uniforms. But my great contribution to the cause was that when I got there the design was basically the design which came through, but the stripes were red, white, and blue. It looked just like a comic opera costume. I struck. I said, "This we cannot do." Furthermore, there was a very pretty light blue colored shirt which was to go with this outfit, and we talked about the fact that it would be much better looking and WAVES would feel more comfortable in it as a working uniform and not as a show piece if the braid could be the same color as the shirt. At that point we were told emphatically that there just wasn't enough gold braid in the country and could never be during the war to let women wear gold braid. We said, "OK, we don't care," discovering later that this was a terrible slap in our face which we didn't even know enough to know was a slap in the face. We didn't mind a bit. All this was rather characteristic of the early stages. Everything had been gotten under way before there were any women around. It just didn't occur to these people in command to defer to us. But just by listening around and finding out what was happening we got ourselves into these things and eventually worked out the technique of the job. It really had to be that kind of overall consultation.

I remember when a young man from Marshall Field and Company in Chicago came to help reorganize the personnel bureau. I have a vivid memory of one session with him. He had the heads of all the departments in the bureau and of course I was the only woman present. Each man had written out a job analysis for himself. My job analysis consisted entirely of being in touch with these various departments to interpret what was happening there from the point of view of the women they were trying to incorporate in it. When all the job analyses had been read, Admiral Jacobs asked if there was any comment about overlapping, and so on. In all good faith but to the embarrassment of some, I said, "My only problem is that I'm supposed to be liaison with all these people and no one of these men has mentioned having any responsibility for seeing that I get information. How do I get it?" Jacobs said to them, "Each of you must write in that you are to keep the director of the Women's Reserve informed." This was rather par for the course: it wasn't in the thinking of naval officials to bother with trying to incorporate women into it. Subsequently, in the last years, it got to be very smooth. It was all understood.

One of the events which will always be riveted in my memory was the time we had something like 2,500 people in Washington. They were to celebrate our first anniversary. One of my officers organized a parade at the Washington monument where we had all the big brass speak to these women. I'll never forget the actual effect—the scene as we stood at the monument and saw these women coming from all over the city of Washington, marching, and forming a regular pattern of companies marching. This is the kind of thing that made them know they were a part of the navy. It was a very dramatic and exciting kind of thing which you couldn't do if you hadn't been trained to do it.

We always enjoyed the story on that occasion of the second ranking officer in command. I was with the powers that be up in the grandstand, but she had to be the person leading the whole procession. And she didn't know a thing about marching because she had never gone through this discipline. But she was flanked, right behind her, by a group of women who knew her well and knew the whole situation. On one occasion as they marched she said, "By the right flank," when it was quite plain that they had to go left, so they just went left and the whole procession followed after. We got along very well this way.

The prize story of this type had to do with Captain Underwood, our navy commander at Northampton. He had singled out Elizabeth Crandall to be the executive officer of the first group of WAVES training there. Elizabeth had been in charge of the very large women's residence at Stanford University. At Northampton she was in charge of this group as they marched back from the inn to their quarters two or three times. Suddenly Captain Underwood said, "Now you take these women back." The boys who were the instructors were waiting up at the inn and saw this. She had never conducted a drill in her life. Elizabeth got them started all right because they'd all lined up before and they marched up the main street. There was a car in the way. She knew they had to get around it but she didn't know what the word was for it. The men were out of hearing by that time and so she just turned around and said, "Ladies, use your judgment," which they did. They got around the car and from a distance it looked very fine. We adapted to situations like this.

In that early period the first day or two for most of the women was a perfectly appalling experience when suddenly they lost their identity and became just a member of this squad or that squad. But very shortly they began to develop a great sense of pride in the whole enterprise. People like Madame Chiang Kai-shek and others would come every two weeks to review the troops. This boosted a sense of the necessity for getting ready to do this kind of thing. Everybody recognized the fact that this was a big shift from the ordinary experience of girls. This was where the young officers picked them up when they fell down. They deliberately had a kind of personnel supervision which was not characteristic of the navy in general. Relatively few of the girls dropped out. Once they were there they were glad to be there.

The morale was helped by the fact that by and large the girls were given very good treatment on the naval stations. There was on occasion dull monotony—sometimes standing by without really enough to do. Sometimes it really wasn't unpleasant work. They really weren't assigned mean or difficult jobs except that often what they were doing seemed to be just meaningless, a routine something in an office or clinic. The air stations were usually very popular places because the WAVES were really doing things they saw were important. They were doing repair of machines or using the Link trainers. Here they knew they were really training pilots, and where there were so evidently important jobs, the morale was fine.

Rarely did it happen that WAVES were given work that was physically out of their league. One story was told, however, of two WAVES who were sent to a naval base inland to relieve two boys who didn't want to be transferred. The girls were assigned to a kind of warehouse and got there just before the lunch hour for the boys they were to relieve. "Look," said the men, "the job that you've got to do is to get these truck tires stowed away up in that loft." And they went off gleefully, chuckling to themselves. The girls looked around and when the men came back the tires were all up in the loft. "How on earth did you do it?" And one of the girls said, "We rigged a pulley, of course." They just established a leverage and pulled the tires into the loft and then stowed them.

There were sometimes administrative knots I had to try and untangle. There was one instance I remember, the business of determining what would happen about women who became pregnant in the service. They weren't allowed to become pregnant but some of them did without approval, and how to phrase the directives, how to work out the procedures by which this could be conveyed to everybody as to what to do in a specific case—that was the kind of thing that took a lot of time and consultation.

I remember one episode of hearing that there was rather lax discipline in the big barracks in Washington. I had no authority over it. There was nothing I could do about it except try to find out what was happening and why. I remember going down to the commanding officer of the Potomac River Command and saying I would like to go to a mast and hear how it was being administered. I had been perfectly apalled by the report of the episode where an MP had arrested a girl and a boy because they had presumably been having intercourse on the front lawn of some place or other in Washington. The captain at the mast kept staying: "Did you actually see this occur?" Then the poor little MP said, "Well, no, I didn't actually see it occur, but it's obvious that's what they were doing." And the captain said, "Well, then, we can't do anything about this."

I went storming back to the Bureau of Personnel and said: "Look, you couldn't hold her on that but you could certainly hold her on conduct unbecoming an officer." This was not being done. The way I had to do this was to see it, to hear it in action, and then get somebody topside to do something about it. They did, and it was straightened out presently, simply because the situation was beginning to get out of hand through this kind of literalism and unwillingness to involve any maintenance of standards. This in general was the way we did go about it, had to go about it.

We spent three years working very hard at such things, constant little needling things. One question we spent hours on during the first six months: What does a woman do about saluting? You don't salute in the navy unless you have your hat on. An officer takes his hat off when he goes into a house but a lady doesn't. What should she do when "The Star-Spangled Banner" was played? It was this kind of crucial matter in the navy.

We certainly had our discipline problems with the people that got in by mistake and weren't the kind of people we wanted to have around. But by and large it was an awfully good group and I used to be interested because there were a good many comments made to the effect that it wasn't quite nice for a nice girl to be in the navy. I mean, you know, a girl in every port for a navy sailor. I used to make quite a point in talking to a recruiting group that there was a kind of control over the girl in the navy which she never had in a factory, for instance. At war work in a factory a girl was really on her own, but in the navy there were standards of conduct and behavior. They were clearly explained and expressed for her. I never had any feeling that a girl was going to be thrown in with such bad characters that it was going to hurt her reputation. It is really true that bad actors were pretty quickly weeded out. Certainly the navy supported me very thoroughly and consistently in my insistence that coming to the navy was not going to stop these girls from being feminine and being nice girls. We weren't going to cheapen the thing to attract numbers. We never had to do that. We were never really down to the bottom of the barrel because we never had so many people that we had to take anybody who came.

14

This was a real problem in the army, where they really wanted so many people so quickly that they were encouraging and recruiting people to get in a lot of people. This was much harder to control than when they came in a few at a time. I remember when the Women's Army Auxiliary Corps was changed to the Women's Army Corps, and they came into the full army. I was present when Oveta Hobby was made a full colonel. I remember General Marshall saying to her on that occasion: "We can use 600,000 women any time you can get them for us." Well, that's an awful lot of women and it sort of put the pressure on the army to go out and get lots and lots of people, a much harder problem for them than the one we had. Our enrollment built up gradually. Altogether we probably had about 150,000 women who were involved at one point or another but never more than, I think, 86,000 at one time.

NO AUTHORITY AND NO RESPONSIBILITY EITHER

COLONEL RUTH CHENEY STREETER, WOMEN MARINES

U.S. NAVAL INSTITUTE

RUTH CHENEY STREETER was born on 2 October 1895 in Brookline, Massachusetts. She attended prep schools in the United States and France and completed her education at Bryn Mawr College in 1914–16. For many years Mrs. Streeter served as president of the Bryn Mawr Alumnae Association. In 1917 she married Thomas Streeter, who was a lawyer in New York City and later a rare book collector of national note. They made their family home in Morristown, New Jersey, where she became involved in a broad range of civic activities.

One of Mrs. Streeter's early interests was in aviation and the armed services. A favorite brother of hers was an aviator in World War I who was killed in Italy. Mrs. Streeter and her mother sponsored an annual Cheney Award for an outstanding member of the army air corps. This award is still given annually and Mrs. Streeter has been most often at the ceremony. In 1940 Mrs. Streeter began taking flying lessons herself. She earned a commercial license in 1942 and through the years made many flights in her own plane. Early in World War II she was active in the Civil Air Patrol and wanted badly to fly with the male members of that patrol as they sought out the German submarines off the New Jersey coast. Federal regulations of that period did not permit her this service so she donated her private plane to be piloted by other members of the patrol.

On 13 February 1943 a Marine Corps Women's Reserve was formally established by act of Congress and Ruth Streeter was named director with the rank of major. She was installed in her office by Secretary of the Navy Frank Knox and entered into this new service with great gusto and dedication. The Marine Corps Women's Reserve resisted being nicknamed (an improvement over the World War I term "marinettes") and was usually cited as WR. The reserve corps members were used in clerical and office work, communications, aviation support, cryptography, and machine assembly and repair, releasing thousands of male marines for duty overseas and combat. Trained at first in WAVES or SPARs camps and later in specific marine camps, the WR reached a peak strength of one thousand officers and eighteen thousand enlisted members by June 1944. Mrs. Streeter was promoted to lieutenant colonel in November 1943 and in 1945 to colonel. She retired in December 1945.

Mrs. Streeter was an activist throughout her years with the Marine Corps. She made many trips to marine camps throughout the nation and was most active in recruitment for the WR. She also visited the camps where they trained and often participated in some of the training exercises the women marines were exposed to. On one occasion she even participated in a parachute jump at a camp for men marines. Some of the events of her exciting career appear in the segment of her oral history that follows.

Mrs. Streeter was the mother of three sons who served in the armed forces in World War II and has always been proud of that fact. After the war she returned to Morristown and assisted her husband with his vast collection of books. After his death she supervised the auction of this collection at his request for he wanted other collectors to know the joy of obtaining some coveted book. She continues to live in the family home in Morristown, New Jersey.

A very old friend of my husband's and mine was Basil O'Connor. He had first worked in my husband's law office in Boston. When Tom, my husband, moved over to New York at the time we were married he suggested to Doc O'Connor that he come down and Tom would give him some of his business and see how he made out in New York.

Doc seemed to be doing all right for a few years, and one fine day we woke up and found that he was the law partner of the governor of New York, Franklin D. Roosevelt. The firm was then called Roosevelt and O'Connor. As Mr. Roosevelt went on and became president, he and Doc were still very good friends and kept in close touch with each other. Doc, I think, was his executor after the president's death and certainly was his attorney.

Tom was in New York on a Thursday in January 1943, and Doc asked to see him and then told him all about the formation of the women's reserve in the Marine Corps and the fact that they would like to suggest to me that I become director. It was a complete surprise to Tom and me. He came back to me in Morristown, our home, and told me about it and said they wanted me to go into the city the next day and be interviewed by Colonel Waller and Major Rhoades of the Marine Corps. Waller was then head of the marine reserves and had been delegated by the commandant, General Holcomb, to put into effect the plans the Marine Corps had for the women's reserve. Major Rhoades was Waller's attorney in civilian life. He had been an officer in World War I. As nearly as I can make out, General Holcomb said, "If I've got to have the women, I've got to have somebody in charge in whom I've got complete confidence."

So I was interviewed by the two of them the next day. The way it finally worked out was that since there was not time for me to go to officers' training school and since they wanted me to be commissioned and put to work within a month, then for about six months Major Rhoades was to be my "running mate." We had desks side by side. Rhoades was to advise me and tell me: "Now, if you want to get this done, this is the way to do it." Or, maybe, "this suggestion isn't the sort of thing we can do in the Marine Corps at all." I was trained in this fashion for about six months and was always very grateful for it.

The interesting thing, I learned eventually, was that when General Holcomb called on Colonel Waller to implement the plans for the women's reserve, Waller called on Major Rhoades, who had been a classmate of Basil O'Connor's at Harvard Law School. Rhoades knew that O'Connor was close to the president and was pretty well posted on things that were going on in Washington. So Rhoades had written O'Connor and told him about the plans for the marines and did he have any suggestions for a director. Apparently then O'Connor suggested me as a possible choice. Undoubtedly Dean Gildersleeve of Barnard and her advisory committee were consulted for they had been most helpful in choosing the three women named as directors of the other military services. Apparently I was very well looked into as to my previous experience, and so forth. They never asked me about it and I didn't know anything until the night before I was interviewed.

When I went down to be interviewed by General Holcomb I was introduced by Colonel Waller and asked a great many questions. The one question I was asked repeatedly was—Did I know any marines? As a matter of fact I didn't. I had no military connections with any of the services. When I was asked the same question again and again, I began to feel, I've lost my chance—I don't know the right people. But it turned out to be an advantage. They were afraid, apparently, that I would not be easily disciplined to go through channels if I had friends in the Corps. I would have been inclined to go to any friends I might have had to help me out. After the interview with the commandant, Colonel Waller said that if

I was appointed it would have to be approved by the secretary of the navy. I said in a wee small voice, "I don't think you'll have any difficulty there because Secretary Knox comes from New Hampshire, knows my mother very well, my father-in-law very well, and my husband used to be his personal counsel." Secretary Knox was kind enough to swear me in himself when I was commissioned.

The story, as I later learned, was that Dean Gildersleeve's committee at Barnard College did submit several names to the Marine Corps as possible candidates for director of the Marine Corps Women's Reserve. The Marine Corps then investigated the candidates, being open-minded as to whether or not to take a professional woman. If you do that you're bound to get somebody who has certain qualities that you want in a leader. But it is also true (and apparently this was the approach the Marine Corps used), that no profession at that time directly fitted a woman to operate in a military organization which does things very differently from what an ordinary profession or business does. So when they found that I complied with the qualifications as set forth legally but had a wide background in civic and state affairs and was not involved in one specific profession, that seemed to the Marine Corps to be an advantage.

Well, I was finally selected and installed as director on the thirteenth of February 1943.* I must say that from then on I had good cooperation from the press always. I think I had almost better cooperation than the other women's services. I think it was largely due to the prestige of the marines. They are a very colorful outfit and they were doing a particularly good job in the Pacific at the time. I always tried to be fair with the press and they were fair with me. Once in a while they'd ask me a question and I'd say, "Look, you know I can't answer that, so why do you ask me?" And they wouldn't be mad.

At the end of six months it dawned on me that none of the other women who were heading up the newly formed women's divisions in the WAVES, the WACS, or the SPARs had running mates. I didn't think it was a very dignified position to put me in under the circumstances. When I went to call on them they had their own offices. In those six months I had some training, and I felt that you can't stay in leading reins forever. So I sent up a memo to Colonel Waller and said I thought the Marine Corps wasn't getting its money out of me and that I thought it would be more dignified for them and for me if they felt I could take over.

---

*In her privately printed *Tales of an Ancient Marine*, Ruth Streeter tells us that after the swearing-in ceremony by Secretary of the Navy Frank Knox, "On the way out, General Holcomb looked rather bitterly at my shiny new oak leaves and said, 'It took me fourteen years to get those'; to which I replied, 'Yes, General, but you earned them first, and I have to earn mine afterwards.' " (p. 16).

About this time the heads of the other women's services, the three directors, came down to Camp LeJeune, our training center, so that we could show them our training program for the women marines who were going through down there. I had a chance to talk with Captain Mildred McAfee especially. She told me I should be very grateful for having had somebody advise me until I found my way around. She had not had that and was completely unprepared for the methods used in the military services and had been unfortunate in making certain mistakes in the beginning—entirely innocently—that had stirred up a certain feeling against her in the navy. I was very lucky, she told me, that I had had this teaching as I went along. I repeated this remark of Mildred McAfee to Colonel Waller and he approved my suggestion in the memo, saying, "Now you realize just what we were doing. We were trying to keep you from making those mistakes."

At the time, in World War II, having women in uniform was a new idea. It wasn't a completely new idea because the English and the Canadians had already had this system at work and some of these women were seen about the streets of Washington. They were known to be a valuable contribution to the war effort. Still it was rather difficult for a lot of people to take. We sometimes got mean or nasty remarks made about women in the military service.

I think it was very essential at that time for parents especially to think that there was some woman in each of the services who would keep an eye on the women's interests—the women's interests as distinguished from the men's interests. Today they are supposed to be indistinguishable. I'm not entirely sure that I agree with that point of view, but I'm sure it would not have been possible in 1942. None of the armed forces can operate without public opinion behind them. Public opinion had gone along with them as far as having women in uniform was concerned, but they still wanted to feel that if the girls had troubles they could go to somebody who would understand. And it was our job, the newly chosen directors of the various women's military organizations, to interpret the military to the women. It was our job equally to interpret the women to the military. We were a bridge of understanding between the two.

Of course we had women officers with the enlisted women; one of the things that we were very particular about in the Marine Corps was that women officers should be easily accessible to the enlisted women. This was done generally through the sergeant. I gather that the women's services have broadened their concepts the same as civilian people have today. In the 1940s they had not. I remember being stopped on the street in Washington one day by a woman, a perfect stranger, to compliment the women marines. She said, "You know, they have a certain dignity." They did. They had a certain reserve. They always looked well. They held themselves well, each one of them, not only the officers.

In recruiting I found that the parents wanted to think that somebody was keeping an eye out for their daughters. Of course I couldn't keep two eyes on twenty thousand people, but all the way down the line there was the feeling that you look out for your people. This attitude was of course very strongly held in the Marine Corps. It is one of their special traditions.

Maybe twenty years after the war was over I got a letter from a former woman sergeant who had gotten quite an important job in the Veterans Administration. Out of a blue sky she wrote: "I've never seen you or even heard you speak. But I want to tell you that I think the organization of the women marines was so much better than anything I've found since." I thanked her for her nice letter and heard from her again. This time she ended by saying: "I felt that you loved us all." This in spite of the fact that I was always concerned with discipline and had to be severe. You're not going to have discipline unless you react against certain things as well as in favor of certain things.

Well, I would never have dared show that comment of this woman to the Marine Corps officials. They would have thought that was sappy. I don't think you can treat women exactly the way you treat men. You've got to mother them a little bit—and it doesn't hurt the men any either!

In the very beginning I was helped greatly because the advanced planning for the set up of the women marines had all been accomplished. I didn't have to start any of it. I stepped into it. The Corps didn't make any announcement of the fact that they were going to take women until they had gotten the whole framework set up at headquarters. Then all they did was push the button. The wheels turned. One of the most helpful developments was that the WAVES arranged to take our enlisted training and our officers' training for the first three months. At the end of that time we set up our own training cadres down at Camp LeJeune, but since we had to have somebody to be in charge of them, it would have taken us three months or so to train enough people to run them. Our officers were trained at Mount Holyoke and the enlisted were trained at Hunter College along with the WAVES. They had male officers in charge and male drill instructors. When we were moved to Camp LeJeune we had our own officers.

I had a great shock early on when I made the mistake of going to Colonel Waller for sympathy over something or other. I said, "You know, Colonel, it's a little hard on me. I've got so much responsibility and no authority." He said, "Colonel Streeter, you have no responsibility either." That's right—I never did have. It was such a shock I nearly turned in my suit. It was such a blow to me. It was perhaps fortunate for me that nobody else besides Colonel Waller realized I had no authority. They were never quite sure how much authority I did have and this was quite a help.

This was one of Captain McAfee's problems in the WAVES. We were staff officers. We weren't line officers. We were used to being executives. If we were the responsible head of an organization, we had authority. We weren't used to being staff officers. And we had to adapt ourselves. It wasn't so bad after all. It took a little getting used to. But as Colonel Waller told me, "Now, look. You are never, in an organization like this, going to get to first base without the understanding and cooperation of a dozen other people at least." You know, things were always coming over my desk with an initial alongside. Every officer who saw it initialed it. If I wanted anything done, I had to clear it not only with my own people but with all the people on the side who might be interested too. It worked. I had no difficulty with it after I once understood the reason for it. You can't be a lone wolf in a military organization.

And then they have got this business of replacements. I once took a weekend off and flew when I was in the Marine Corps. I had sold my plane to the Civilian Air Patrol. I obviously wasn't going to be allowed to fly. I said to Colonel Waller: "I have a weekend off and I haven't flown for a long time. I don't want to lose my skill entirely. There is a place along the railroad out there where I could go to a little flying field. Would you have any objection if I went off Saturday and Sunday?" It was a weekend, I had leave. And Waller said, "No, why should I?" I said, "You spent a lot of time breaking me in to this job. Maybe you wouldn't like it if I broke my neck." He said, "Why should I care? The Marine Corps is set up to take care of people that break their necks. Go ahead." The Marine Corps always got a replacement.

I thought I had some bright ideas, very bright ideas, that were knocked out. But nevertheless you go along all right. I sent them up the line in memo form to my immediate superior in command. He either approved them or disapproved them or put them in the wastebasket. This system worked in World War II because of the tremendous motivation that every-body had in the middle of war. We were scared. At the time I went in we were licked. There was a tremendous fear and a knowledge that we had a long, long way to fight back before we were ever going to get the edge. And people just gave it all they had, which is something that anybody who hasn't lived through as severe a war as that probably has no conception of. As time went on I realized that this was a very cumbersome way and really that the position of director of the women's reserve, if it was going to exist at all, should have more status. But I wasn't going to fight about it in the middle of a war. I was doing pretty well. If I needed backing up, I was generally able to get it, and if not, it was probably because it wasn't a very good idea in the first place.

I once wrote that I tried to conduct my office with dignity, military efficiency, and humanity. I might say that in a military structure such as the marines there are very definitely certain things you can't do, no matter whether you think they'd be a good idea or not. But if you look around you can sometimes find situations that can be ameliorated. For instance, when they built barracks especially for women we had certain parts of the building that the men's barracks didn't have. We had a laundry. We did our own laundry so we always looked fresh and cool. We washed our uniforms every night ourselves. We also had built in two quite large reception rooms, one downstairs and one on the second floor. The reception room downstairs was for the women and their dates. The men could come and visit them there. The one upstairs was just for the women. They could lounge around there in their dressing gowns and relax if they had any spare time. Little things like that were a great help. We tried to think of them. They didn't cost much and they were just a little consideration.

When I visited around the camps I concentrated on the officers to see that they were looking after the enlisted women. That is what they're supposed to do. You don't do otherwise in the Marine Corps anyhow—jump over your officers' heads to go talk to the enlisted women, hardly ever. I always had to be very careful not to go outside the chain of command. I once had to relieve a company commander who persisted in going outside of her lieutenants and sergeants and having some of her own private mouthpieces around the outfit. There the whole morale of the company was bottom level as a result.

The first month after I assumed the directorship I made an extensive tour of the country, going to the West Coast and speaking in at least sixteen major cities and many minor ones. Yes, recruitment was the general purpose of the trip, but first I would tell the audience about the desperate situation the country was in, with our ships on the East Coast being sunk by German submarines within sight of Atlantic City. Recruits were much needed. This was no show, this was a vast necessity. And then of course I always used the theme: Free a Man to Fight.

It is significant that in the first eight weeks of existence for the women's Corps there were 2,493 enlistees. Within a year there were 800 officers and 14,000 others. The Marine Corps itself had not expected more than 6,000 as a total when they first opened up. I must lay most of that success to the reputation of the Marine Corps itself. I think perhaps I had a certain advantage, intangible though it was, over the other directors and also with the Marine Corps. It was known that I had three sons in the military service of our country. I think this helped me with the public. They knew I had sons at the front as many of them had sons at the front.

I later used the comment of the commandant of the Marine Corps when he said, "Without the women being in the Marine Corps the Sixth

Marine Division could not have been activated." The women's reserve was just about the same size, the same number of officers and enlisted personnel, as required in the Sixth Marine Division. This point I made and it made the women feel that they were necessary.

When I went to Pendleton in California I saw the marines preparing for embarkation to the war zone. I got an idea of the sort of training they were still going through. On one occasion I went up with a group of young paratroopers who were going up for the first time. I'm sure they were plenty nervous on this their first drop but they tried not to show it. I enquired afterwards if the Corps had any special recognition for first jumps and they said, yes, it was customary to let them have a case of beer. I said, "Will you please let them have a case of beer from me?" and I was popular with that group of paratroopers.

Later on at Camp LeJeune I participated in a version of the jump from a tower that young Marines were doing with a small parachute—a kind of preliminary form of parachute jumping. I also went in a training tank at LeJeune and again as a belly gunner in a mock-up training plane. It was quite an experience getting me out of that at the conclusion. I also witnessed and engaged in marksmanship training for ground troops. They had moving pictures of planes diving on you or flying over you. One had a machine gun that didn't shoot real bullets but dots of light so you could tell if you hit the plane coming at you. I also took part in a landing operation—climbed down nets in landing ships for beach landings. These were all experiences, if you want to call them that.

One of the most inspiring things as far as the women were concerned was their exposure at Camp LeJeune to viewing the kind of training the men were undergoing. When we had our recruit depot going full tilt we had three companies and each of them in rotation spent a total of six weeks at LeJeune. During that time they were given an arms demonstration by the male instructors who instructed the men. It began with hand-to-hand fighting, how you get a guy down and knife him; they had rifle shooting and they used grenades. They had bazookas. And it always ended up with a tank coming up a sand cliff onto the parade ground. The women sat in bleachers and witnessed all this. After things were organized we invited the other women directors to come down to one of these Saturday reviews. They wished they had something like that too for their trainees because it was so realistic. The hand-to-hand fighting was almost the worst to watch, but the point was not that our men were being trained to do these things but that the Japanese were also trained to do exactly this sort of thing, so our men had to face up to what the Japs were doing along exactly these same lines.

Our women were trained at various specialized schools. The jobs that were easiest to fill were clerical jobs. Many of the incoming women had such skills to begin with. The biggest demand was for them. Then we found that women could qualify for driving trucks and things of that sort. They were sent to quartermaster schools and communications schools, also noncommissioned officers' schools. They were even in secret and confidential files. That entertained me because it is often said that women can't keep a confidence. We had a large number of quartermaster personnel in aviation. We had airplane mechanics and Link trainers and a few operators in the control towers.

All this grew naturally as the supply and demands grew. Almost any employment was permissible except heavy lifting and combat. The women could try almost anything else.

In October 1944 I went out to Hawaii to see the lay of the ground and to help with specific arrangements for the women reserves we were to station there. These were our first outside the continental U.S. We sent only one contingent, about two thousand, with half going to the air station and the other half for the naval base. The base detachment fell heir to good comfortable barracks, for they had just been vacated by the Sea-Bees, who had built them for their own use.

Mrs. Streeter held the rank of colonel, U.S. Marine Corps Women's Reserve, in 1944. She was demobilized in 1945 and at the request of the commandant, awarded the Legion of Merit in 1946. She says she prizes highly the nice citation, "But it does embarrass me to some extent because it sounds as if I did everything, you know, when after all the nineteen thousand other women did quite a lot." ED.

GETTING THE DOOR OPEN

CAPTAIN DOROTHY C. STRATTON, SPARS

U.S. NAVAL INSTITUTE

DOROTHY CONSTANCE STRATTON was born on 24 March 1899 in Brookfield, Missouri. She graduated from Ottawa University in Ottawa, Kansas, in 1920. While teaching and holding administrative posts in public schools in Renton, Washington, and from 1923 in San Bernardino, California, she earned a master's degree from the University of Chicago in 1924 and a doctorate from Columbia University in 1932. In 1933 she was named dean of women and associate professor of psychology at Purdue University; she advanced to a full professorship in 1940.

In June 1942 she served on the Woman's Army Auxiliary Corps selection board for the V Corps. Later that year she enlisted in the WAVES and was given a lieutenant's commission. In November 1942 she was ordered to duty in the office of the commandant of the U.S. Coast Guard, where she developed plans and guidelines for a proposed women's reserve corps. Shortly thereafter she devised a name for the corps, taken from the Coast Guard motto, *Semper Paratus* ("Always Ready"), and with the rank of lieutenant commander was named director of the corps. That corps had been authorized by the Congress on 23 November 1942. She continued in that post, rising to the rank of captain, and separated from the service in 1946. In that period the SPARs grew to some ten thousand officers and enlisted personnel.

From 1947 to 1950 Dr. Stratton was director of personnel for the International Monetary Fund in Washington, D.C. From 1950 to 1960 she served as

26

national executive director of the Girl Scouts of America. From 1962 she was a member of the President's Commission on the Employment of the Handicapped and a consultant on vocational rehabilitation to the Department of Health, Education, and Welfare.

In retirement Dr. Stratton is back again at Purdue University in Indiana, where she makes her home in West Lafayette.

I was dean of women at Purdue University in 1942 when I got an invitation from Mrs. Oveta C. Hobby, the newly appointed director of the WAAC, to help recommend for selection the first officer candidates for the WAAC. It was my first experience with any of the women who began service with the military forces of the country in World War II. After that I was talking with Dr. Lillian Gilbreth, a member of the staff at Purdue University. She had been working with the navy and thought that this was something that was important to do and urged me to see if I could qualify. I was very much interested in women's services and the fact that women were going to be given an opportunity to serve. I felt pretty strongly that it was important that the United States join the Allies and help win the war. To put it simply it was important that we stop the Japanese and Hitler, and if there was any opportunity for me to do my little bit, I wanted to do it. So I went to Chicago for that delightful physical examination that one goes through. The president of the university thought it was the right thing for me and raised no objections. I was given a leave of absence for military duty.

On the twenty-eighth of August 1942 I was called to duty with the WAVES and commissioned as a senior lieutenant in the women's reserves. I was sent with the first class of WAVES to Northampton, Massachusetts, where training was under way. We had nothing to work with or any uniforms—no pillows, and hardly any blankets. In fact we didn't have anything except the shots we got, but we got along. My first reaction was that I thought I had made the worst mistake of my life. Of the four directors of the several services I was the only one who went through this period of training. Later I was glad I had because I knew what the other officers coming on were going through in their period of indoctrination. One thing—I didn't learn how to march because a senior lieutenant apparently doesn't march, or didn't then. So I had to do only one thing, which was lucky for me; I only had to say, "Platoon leaders, take charge." Only I said the first time: "Patrol leaders, take charge," and the commanding officer told me about it. After three weeks three of us were ordered to Washington. We had just got our uniforms the night before. As we walked through the train to go to the diner you could hear the whispers: "The WAVES, the WAVES."

We got to Washington. It was very crowded. I thought, Dear Lord, preserve me from ever being ordered to duty here during the war. But I was ordered there and hardly got out of it except for brief periods of travel during the next three and a half years.

Almost immediately I was assigned to the University of Wisconsin as assistant to the commanding officer (a navy commander) of the radio operators' school, the first one for women. Madison had seen no WAVES before. We were all just stumbling along trying to find our way, but it was a wonderful group of enlisted women and I enjoyed it greatly. I had no knowledge of the subject, but it didn't faze me because I had nothing to do with the instruction. It was my responsibility to see that the women were looked after—fed, uniformed, that sort of thing. That was not new to me, but when Sunday came I did have a new problem. The townspeople were very kind. They organized to come and take the WAVES for a drive, because it was the only time the enlisted women had free. They didn't want to be taken for a drive. When the second Sunday arrived the commanding officer ordered me to see that the local cars were filled. I had quite a time with that.

I was only in Madison for three or four weeks when I got a telegram from the Naval Office of Personnel telling me to report by the fastest transportation possible to Washington. So I did and was promptly taken to the Coast Guard headquarters, where I was ushered into a room full of admirals. I had never seen an admiral before in my life and here was a roomful of them. They asked a good many questions. It turned out they were planning to set up a women's reserve in the Coast Guard. I left them feeling I wouldn't hear anything for some time—maybe six weeks from next Wednesday I'd hear one way or another. But I heard almost immediately. So the navy lent me to the Coast Guard then. There was no legislation yet. Then I returned to Madison to wind up my assignment and came back to Washington to find a place to live—and there wasn't any place to live. Finally I found a sort of enlarged closet in the headquarters of the American Association of University Women on Eye Street. What I had was a very small room which had a window opening on a shaft. It was never possible to tell whether the sun was shining or it was raining or just what.

After we got the legislation enabling the Coast Guard to set up a women's organization on the twenty-third of November, I was sworn in on the twenty-fourth. I asked Miss McAfee (now head of the WAVES) if it would be possible to get a nucleus of the WAVE officers to start us off because it would save such an enormous amount of time. She said as far as she was concerned, "Yes," and the navy said, "Yes." So I went back to Northampton and made a plea to women who were there in training and got twelve of the WAVES who were getting their indoctrination to come to the Coast Guard and help us get started. Of course they were all volunteers. I couldn't have gotten them otherwise. Some of them obviously thought, "Here's a new service and it's a chance to help get this on its way." It saved us a lot of time.

Then came the question: What were we going to call this unit of the women's reserve of the Coast Guard? The WAACs had a name and the WAVES had a name, so what were we going to call the women's reserve of the Coast Guard? There wasn't anyone else except me to think about this. Everybody else had his mind on more important things.

So I tossed on that hard bed many nights trying to think what we'd call this organization. Sometimes when you just absolutely have to do something you do it. Suddenly it came to me from the motto of the Coast Guard: *Semper Paratus*—"Always Ready," SPAR. I proposed it to the commandant and his assistant. They accepted it and that was it. So that was one thing that I did.

A Commander Carroll, who was in charge of procurement in the Coast Guard, got me a desk and fixed me up. Of course there wasn't air conditioning and we had wool uniforms. We not only had them the first summer but the next summer as well. They never did have any air conditioning in my experience, but that was not very important in the total scheme of things.

Then we had to decide what the women were going to wear. The WAVES already had a very good-looking uniform designed by Mainbocher. Somebody (I think a man) in the Coast Guard had also designed a uniform for the SPARs. So which one was going to be chosen? With great solemnity a whole roomful of admirals sat around and decided which uniform was to be the one worn. The final decision was for the WAVES uniform with the Coast Guard's insignia. I very much approved the final decision.

The Coast Guard didn't really want women any more than the navy did. But the commandant, Admiral Waesche, was a very farseeing man. It was a little hard to hold out after the army and the navy had accepted women. And of course there were a great many jobs that could be done by women but the resistance was strong. I would say my biggest job at the beginning was to get some kind of acceptance. My first effort was to convince the Coast Guard if possible that the navy hadn't foisted off the worst they had, because the Coast Guard was pretty sure that the navy would give them the bottom of the barrel. So I first had to live down the fact that I had been in the WAVES before coming to them, even though it was only for a very short period of time.

In the brief interim period before the enabling legislation was passed in November, we knew we were going to use the enlisted women as yeomen, which is like our civilian stenographers, and as storekeepers,

29

which was in the field of finance—nothing at all like what the name implies. We were going to use them to man their own barracks. We were going to use enlisted women in galleys for the SPARs. But we couldn't foresee how much could be opened up because that depended so much on how much the Coast Guard was willing to accept the women. I don't think it was ever a question in the mind of Admiral Waesche, but it was a question of getting the service as a whole to accept them. The biggest job I had was getting acceptance, getting the door open so that the women could get a chance to do the jobs they were capable of doing. That was not easy. It took a great deal of personal contact, not only with the men officers but with their wives. We knew that was where part of our problem would be. If we could be accepted by the wives half our battle was won. That opposition of the wives was based on several things: some of the SPARs were to be commissioned as officers, perhaps as lieutenants j.g., when it had taken some of the men in peacetime maybe ten years before they got to be lieutenants. So that problem was built in right away. Secondly, the SPARs were going to be working directly with their husbands, the husbands of Coast Guard wives. This in itself was a threat. Then there was the question of why should women be in the Coast Guard anyway? This was a man's world, a man's job, and what were the women doing there anyway? Some of the key wives, who were enthusiastic, helped us a great deal. We just tried to make friends. But really that isn't any different from what it is in a university. If the president's wife likes you it helps a lot, and so it was in the services. I'll tell you who was a great help to us: Mrs. Forrestal, wife of the secretary of the navy. She sometimes flew up to the academy for the graduation of the women officers and this helped.

I might add that we had to make a decision almost immediately after our authorization as to where we were going to do the training of our women. The decision was made and we were the only service that trained the women officers in the regular academy. Mildred McAfee thought, and I agreed with her, that it would be a saving of the taxpayers' money and that it made sense to train the women together. So we agreed, and the first class of enlisted SPARs were trained at Hunter College with the WAVES.

Mrs. Streeter and I both found out that you had to identify the women with the service of which they were members. This had to be done because each service has its own tradition and is very proud. The services weren't unified in those days so, for the sake of gaining acceptance within the Coast Guard, we had to do our own training. And we had to find a place. By a stroke of good luck we got the Palm Beach Biltmore and made a training station out of it. I went down to look over the hotel property, and Admiral Donahue, chief of personnel for the Coast Guard, also came down. It proved to be very satisfactory and we took it over. It was a happy circumstance in that the owner of the Biltmore had ridden down on the train with us and wined and dined us. I think he made the original approach to the Coast Guard, at least that's my recollection. So we used the Palm Beach Biltmore until toward the end of the war. In the final days we used the Manhattan Beach Hotel.

Like all the other services, we had a lot of trouble in recruiting. This frankly surprised me. I thought that we'd have a rush to the colors, but as you know we didn't. From early on we had to fight the propaganda that women were after all just camp followers who weren't really in for any serious purpose. Now we did not get this from within the service, but from the public we had this to fight.

I remember Mrs. Hobby's saying to me the day that the newspaper stories appeared on the WACs, "I just thought I couldn't hold my head up. I just thought I couldn't hold my head up again. I talked to my husband and he said, 'Oveta, never pay any attention to anything that isn't true.'"

It was a subject that was hard to battle because, how could you? how do you? As Miss Lyon says in her book *Three Years before the Mast,* "If one SPAR got out of line, just one, then we were all like that." I wouldn't say, however, that it constituted a major problem. I don't think it was any more of a problem in the United States than it was in England, but it was part of our problem. It is true we didn't get the favorable newspaper stories that could have helped us. The newspapers would often look for the lurid story, but I don't think we worried too much about it. We were too busy trying to get on with the job.

I should say something about the motivation of all our volunteers. Most of them were very well motivated. They had mixed thoughts. There were those whose husbands had been called to service and who were lonely and wanted to get away from it all and do something different. There were those who genuinely felt that at any sacrifice to themselves they would come into the service to make whatever contribution they could. There were those who saw it as a way to "Join the Coast Guard and see the world." There were those who were just bored and wanted to do something different. Indeed there were a variety of motives.

Of course I discovered first of all, when I was on duty at the University of Wisconsin, that some of the women had hardly gotten in when they wanted out. The Red Cross was extremely helpful in such cases. They would get in touch with the families and make the necessary contacts. Often after they had done this they would either recommend to us, "Yes, the only thing to do is let this woman out," or recommend, "No, we can straighten this situation out and let's go on with it." Our SPAR rate of attrition was not out of line. I think overall we recruited about twelve thousand women and at peak strength we were about ten thousand. The rate of attrition was not too bad.

Miss Lyon in her book does raise the point that self-advancement was one of the motivating factors in volunteering. I think she was right in saying this. Remember that a lot of women were stuck in dead-end civilian jobs. Our advertising did say there were opportunities for advancement, and as a matter of fact there were. Another factor I think was more important: the women realized they got training in the services they never could have gotten in civilian life, technical training. This was a route to advancement not only in the services but in some cases at least after this period of service was over, just as it would be with a man who volunteered.

Of course we began recruiting with the navy. We had exactly the same problem there that I have described. The Coast Guard was sure that if there were choices at a Navy Recruiting Station the Coast Guard was going to get the little end of it. So we had finally to set up our separate recruiting stations and we really worked at it.

I often sought out Mildred McAfee in the early days of our organization. She once gave me a word of wisdom. "I thought," she said, "it was very important for me to keep the reins in my own hands until I discovered that there were no reins." I think she spoke a good deal of truth in that. Where we happened to have a commanding officer who was tough and unsympathetic, I found I had no command function any more than Mildred McAfee did. I could only try to persuade, so this was one, I would say, of the original basis decisions for our newfound organization. There were those who thought that the women's reserve should be set up as a separate unit with a command function with a director. There were those who felt it should be integrated into the regular service. And I think that was the better decision, both as I reflect on it now and as I thought it was at the time. It was better all around. While it made the job of the director a little more difficult, perhaps, I think it was much better. After all, if you can't persuade to your point of view, either you're not making a good case for it or you haven't got a good case to start with. If I had to face the situation again I would say that was the right decision . It gave the women much more of a feeling of belonging to the Coast Guard and the Coast Guard a feeling that the SPARs were part of the outfit than would have been the case in a separate unit.

Now with the advent of the SPARs we had to deal with some Coast Guard regulations that were designed primarily for men and now applied to women as well. One of the first questions came in that category. We solved it differently from the way the WAVES solved it or the WACs solved it. I don't say our solution was any better or worse. What are you going to call the woman officer? The WACs called her "Ma'am." The WAVES said, "Good morning, Miss Jones." We just decided that since women were in the service we would just say, "Good morning, Sir." So we used "Sir" for everybody, men or women. That got us over one very awkward hump. Nobody liked "Ma'am" and a lot of people didn't like "Sir" either, but you had to do something. So that was our solution.

On some of the Coast Guard regulations about solitary confinement, bread and water in the brig, and things like that, we had to soften things up a little bit.

Early on, the decision was made to train its SPAR officers at the Coast Guard Academy. It proved to be rough for the first group or two. The standards had all been set for the men and now here were women, too. A lot of them were in their thirties in our first groups and they were called upon to do all these physical exercises, learning to shoot guns, and doing all the things that they weren't going to be called on to do later.

I remember so well when I was dean of women at Purdue we had Catherine McHale, who was the only woman member we had on the board of trustees. She said to me: "Well, the important thing is to pick your fights. You can't fight them all. Which ones are you going to pick?" In fact, you had to be pretty careful which issues you were going to stand on. I believe, in spite of difficulties, it was a good decision to train our officers at the academy. There they got a feel that they couldn't have gotten anywhere else. If we'd had them in a hotel somewhere, they just couldn't have gotten that same feeling of the whole history and background of the Coast Guard. That was awfully important.

I made a point of attending every graduation of our women at the Coast Guard Academy. With any service you've got a personality that represents to the group what it is they're trying to do and what it's all about and I think it was very important to have a personal contact. I knew a lot of these people in civilian life. I wanted to show my interest and I wanted them to know it.

When you had to send women where the service wanted them to go and not where they wanted to go, it seemed to me to be extremely important to have some feeling of humanness and of individual interest. Furthermore, I enjoyed going. Of course I always spoke to the graduating class and I'd often take somebody, perhaps Congressman Margaret Chase Smith. She was very helpful. Often she would go down to Palm Beach with us to visit the girls in training there. Yes, we'd nearly always take a personality like Mrs. Smith or Mrs. Forrestal or somebody else.

We had a captain's mast, of course, that was a part of Coast Guard procedure, but I can't tell you much about it. I was never present at one. Of course I did have cognizance of disciplinary problems. I thought as a dean of women in a university that I'd seen everything but I hadn't. With the enlisted women we had all kinds of problems that I had never dreamed of. If the case was unusual often it would rattle along until finally it came to rest on my desk, not necessarily for a decision but for discussion or recommendation. It was the varieties of sexual problems that I guess were an eye-opener to me. I thought the services were pretty rough on any kind of sexual aberration. I thought that often we dismissed people that if I had had the decision alone or with the assistance of a psychiatrist I wouldn't have. I just think it wasn't very realistic to expect, any more than you were going to get twenty-twenty eyesight, that you were going to get everybody who was perfect in other ways. That's the thing that stands out in my mind on the discipline.

What I had to be concerned about was whether you were going to keep these cases or you weren't going to. I've watched how some of these people have gotten along in civilian life and they've gotten along very well. I must say I never cared much for those reports that came in from the intelligence service. I can't remember the name that we had for it. I just felt that we did an awful lot of snooping into personal lives that wasn't helping us win the war and that was what it was supposed to be all about.

The enlisted personnel were moved about in the service. The last groups of SPAR officers were all chosen from the enlisted personnel. They got chances to take specialized training. Then after they got such specialized training they got their new assignments. If they were yeomen they'd probably stay yeomen, unless they got a chance to be a SPAR officer. In other words they wouldn't be apt to change from yeoman to some other specialized rating like the loran.

Of course we had in the Coast Guard civil service employees. Working side by side, especially at headquarters, would be a civil service person doing a somewhat similar job to what the enlisted SPAR was doing. One was under certain regulations and getting paid a certain amount and the other was not under any such regulations and getting paid a different amount. There was a natural built-in questioning between the two because the civil service had been there first and the SPARs were described as Johnny-come-lately. We had a little smoothing out to do in that area. Usually after they got to know each other it worked out pretty well. Many times the civilian personnel could teach the rest of us a lot, if they were so inclined.

I would like to tell you one thing about how I got indoctrinated into the Coast Guard. I knew I didn't know anything about it and that this would quickly become evident so I asked to have a Coast Guard officer assigned to me. I could ask him anything I didn't know and he would go with me and keep me from making mistakes.

I was given the rank of captain on 1 February 1944, but it created no problem in terms of precedence. We were taught from the beginning that as far as any social courtesies arose when we were on duty the rank came first, not the woman. So I had no problem. I knew exactly where I walked and who got into the small boat first and who went into the elevator first.

Life was very easy. Occasionally there'd be an admiral who wouldn't use his rank. But by and large we all knew exactly where we stood.

You ask about the business of being a captain. I had a funny experience on Pennsylvania Avenue across from the White House. I was walking one day and this enlisted man in the navy came along. He looked at me, put his hands on his hips, and said, "Ha, ha, ha, a captain in the 'Hooligan Navy'" and then threw back his head and laughed. So I threw back my head and laughed and we passed each other pleasantly.

Of course some very funny things happened with the salute as well. I remember one time I was down in Norfolk. I had a SPAR driver, a very good driver, who never saluted. So the officer in charge had a little chat with her and said, "Look, this won't do. You're supposed to salute." She said, "Well, I'll tell you, I just don't care very much for saluting."

Did Miss McAfee tell you the story about the little woman on the railroad train on the way to the West Coast? She tells it and I tell it, so you can put it down that it happened to either one of us. The little old lady couldn't stand it any longer. Finally she looked across and she said, "Excuse me, but do you mind if I ask you—are you a WAC, a WAVE, or a SPAR?" That story stood me in good stead many times.

As soon as we got the legislation permitting the SPARs to go to Hawaii and Alaska we prepared. We didn't have any objections in the Coast Guard to the taking of this step. It was the Congress that insisted on protecting the women in the naval services and did not want them to go outside the continental limits. So as soon as we had the legislative permission we prepared to send our first contingent over. Four of us went by Pan Am clipper to make arrangements in Hawaii. We had a psychiatrist, the woman who was going to be in charge of the SPARs in Hawaii, the woman who did all the assignments of enlisted personnel at Coast Guard headquarters, and me—four of us went. We talked to the Coast Guard personnel there, looked into the housing problems, and tried our best to get things set up. The woman who was going to stay over and take charge of the SPARs stayed on.

I retired from the Coast Guard in 1946. When you're in the service everything is taken care of for you. You have your medical and dental care, you have the protection of the service. You don't have to worry about your clothes, you know what you're going to wear. You are taken care of, that's the only way I can express it, in a way that you're not in civilian life. So when we got out we all had to find new jobs or go back to jobs that somebody else had in our absence. I didn't go back to Purdue as dean of women, although I was still on leave of absence. I think it was easier not to, than to go back to where somebody else has been holding the job for several years. I don't think that would have been easy.

I recall that we women from the service didn't know what kind of clothes to buy. We made mistakes. We looked stranger than other civilians did, because we hadn't bought any clothes for four years. We were just sort of lost and it took awhile for us to find our way back into civilian life. The people who had given up their jobs had to go back and hunt jobs and they had a big adjustment to make. The women who were going back and hadn't seen their husbands in years had a tremendous family adjustment.

Shortly there was the Baruch-Hancock Report on demobilization and from this the Retraining and Reemployment Administration came into being. It was headed by General Erskine of the marines and I became his special assistant. We were supposed to coordinate all the activities of the federal government. We were supposed to coordinate the activities of all of the agencies dealing with retraining and reemployment. We didn't know as much as the people we were trying to coordinate. So we had a very interesting couple of years at that.

Quite a public relations program on reemployment was set up. Of course the veterans had preference for jobs. We had a field service which would go out and see how things were going. Actually we didn't turn out to have as big a reemployment problem as Baruch-Hancock had expected. There had been such a shortage of goods and material during the war that there was this buying surge. There was a tremendous upturn in the economy so people could get jobs. I thought that all ran surprisingly smoothly in view of what had been expected to be a tremendous reconversion problem.

I was with the Retraining and Reemployment Administration for eighteen months, and then I just happened to go to the right cocktail party and this led me to the International Monetary Fund. They were looking for somebody in the field of personnel so I came on to do that. We recruited economists from all over the world and from a great many nations. I had a Belgian managing director and had a pretty hard time to convince him that a woman could do anything. I didn't have anything to do with the "substantive" (as the United Nations calls it) work of the fund. I was supporting service to the staff, that's what I really was, and I stayed there for three and a half years and then went to the Girl Scouts, where I stayed for ten years. Again, my job had to do with personnel.

The Germans' extensive use of bombs and mines in their assault on the Allies in World War II leaves an indelible memory in the minds of those who lived through that war. The two excerpts that follow from oral history interviews with American naval officers spell this out in graphic form, especially the section of the excerpt from Admiral Draper Kauffman describing the year he spent in Great Britain as a reserve officer in the Royal Navy, during which he served continuously as a detonator of German bombs and mines. Winston Churchill's memorable phrase— "their finest hour"—delineates the ordeal of the British people and the price they paid. Draper Kauffman exemplifies all that in his story of the bombs and the mines that induced that finest hour.

Mine warfare was not new to our experience as a nation when we became involved in World War II. In the Civil War, mines were used, sometimes effectively. The history of World War I is replete with the use of mines, especially in the North Sea, as a bulwark against the kaiser's Grand Fleet. But World War II demonstrates the practical use of mines by both sides of the conflict in an offensive as well as a defensive way.

With the onset of the war in 1939 Britain took offensive action. She laid mines in the English Channel; she laid mines along the English east coast to discourage enemy submarine operations; she laid mines in both ends of the Irish Sea to exclude enemy subs from the area, and finally she laid a very large mine field extending to the north of England. It was protective for the homeland of course, but perhaps it was also responsible for the ultimate demise of the powerful German battleship *Bismarck*. In her exit from Norway she avoided the mine field north of the British Isles and went beyond to an area that was patrolled, where she was discovered and tracked down.

When the United States entered the war it too resorted to the defensive laying of mines to protect New York Harbor, Norfolk Harbor, and others along the eastern coast where German submarines operated freely.

But it was Hitler himself who boasted to the world that he had a "secret weapon"—an offensive weapon—that would win the war for him. Well, in truth it could have caused immense trouble and even the capitula-

37

tion of Great Britain if he had saved his "secret weapon," his magnetic mine, until April 1940 and then used such mines in quantity in all-out raids on the ports of Great Britain. In all probability shipping would have been denied the country for perhaps a month or more and the nation forced to its knees. Fortunately that did not happen.

Some have even observed that Hitler's failure to use the magnetic mines in force (when he used them only sparingly from September 1939 to April 1940) constituted one of his grave mistakes of the war. This period gave the British breathing time. It was an opportunity to recover one or more of these magnetic mines and work out countermeasures. Much of the value of a new weapon is found in its surprise introduction and extensive use before the opposing force can develop countermeasures.

Indeed in late September 1939 one of the first of these secret weapons parachuted not in the water but on a village on the banks of the Thames and caused great damage. Another was captured shortly afterwards; the alert British scientists claimed it and soon devised a countermeasure to deal with the menace. In fact, during all those terrible months of the frequent blitz attacks over the cities and ports of Britain, over London, Liverpool, Coventry, and the others, British experts became alert to all the nefarious variations in the bombs and the mines that the Germans showered upon them, and they came up with a series of countermeasures, some effective and some not entirely so. A historian today can discern in this a veritable duel of wits: the British perfecting countermeasures for the large number of German weapons and the Germans improving their weapons with clever additions. Timely intelligence often forewarned the British and helped prepare the way for remedies.

As the war went on the Germans continued to drop their magnetic mines in comparatively small numbers on British ports. The casualties in ships were very high in proportion to the number of mines dropped. For instance, in one weekend forty-five thousand tons of shipping was sunk by mines in the Bristol Channel. The sweeping required of the British was tremendous. It turned out that it was one of the major naval activities of the war. The British were forced to fit out and maintain almost one thousand minesweepers involving large numbers of personnel. Apparently the Germans had the same problem. They were observed to have used some fairly large vessels for sweeping. Those vessels might have been more useful to them in wartime coastal traffic.

When the Germans added a period-delay mechanism (PDM) to their magnetic mine it meant that the first time a sweep was made over the area of the mine the new gear prevented the weapon from firing. The delay was later extended so that six sweeps were required before the mine was detonated, which contributed to the need for greater vigilance and greater expenditures of time and equipment.

As both Admirals Waters and Kauffman point out, there is a different technique required in dealing with bombs and mines. When Kauffman returned to the United States and resumed a commission in the U.S. Navy he was put to work establishing a bomb disposal school in Washington, D.C. Waters and his associates were already at work with a school they established for mine warfare. They volunteered to help Kauffman in setting up his school but did not invite him to join them. The differences were too apparent at the time.

In light of the experience gained by all the Allied powers in World War II it must be acknowledged that mine warfare is an important auxiliary form of modern warfare. It can contribute effectively to the winning or losing of a war.

NOT FOR HEROES—MINE DISPOSAL SCHOOL IN WASHINGTON, D.C.

REAR ADMIRAL ODALE DABNEY WATERS, JR.

ODALE DABNEY WATERS, JR., was born in Manassas, Virginia, on 13 July 1910. He attended the Swavely School and Strayer Business College, Washington, D.C., before entering the U.S. Naval Academy on 9 July 1928. As a midshipman he was a member of the track team and was managing editor of *The Lucky Bag*. He graduated with distinction in the class of 1932 and was commissioned ensign on 2 June 1932.

Waters was first assigned to the USS *Augusta* in which he had junior officer duties in gunnery and fire control. His cruiser was flagship of the Commander in Chief, Asiatic Fleet. Waters served on her until May 1936, when he returned to the United States. In September 1936 he joined the USS *Downes* as torpedo officer. In 1938 he became a student in ordnance engineering at the Naval Postgraduate School in Annapolis. Then he was sent for six months as an assistant naval attaché at the American embassy in London. The experience gained there resulted in his establishing the first U.S. Navy Mine Disposal School after his return to the United States in 1941. He became officer in charge of that school in the Washington Navy Yard and operated it for the training of personnel until January 1943.

Waters served aboard the USS *Memphis* for a year and then in 1944 he was ordered as fleet gunnery officer and assistant chief of staff to Commander, Fourth Fleet. Then for a matter of months he was assistant operations officer and war plans officer on the staff of the Commander in Chief, U.S. Atlantic Fleet.

In June 1945 Waters assumed command of the USS *Laffey* (DD 724) and

40

remained in that command until October 1946, participating in the summer of 1946 in Operation Crossroads, the atom bomb tests at Bikini in the Pacific.

Later that year he reported to the Naval Ordnance Laboratory in Washington, D.C., as senior technical officer and mine development project officer. There he was also engaged in the design of atomic weapons.

In 1950 he was a student once again for a brief period at the Armed Forces Staff College in Norfolk, Virginia, leaving there in July to become ordnance and gunnery officer on the staff of Commander, Operational Development Force, for two years. He then took command of the USS *Glynn* for a year, spending three months of that time in sub-Arctic waters. For three years thereafter he was on the staff of the Supreme Allied Commander, Atlantic, and was concerned with strategic applications and policy. Then he took command of Destroyer Squadron Two and operated in the Middle East during the Suez Canal incident as a unit of the Middle East Force. In 1960 he was selected for the rank of rear admiral. From March 1962 to February 1964 he served as inspector general and then became Commander Mine Force, Pacific Fleet, and commander of the naval base in Los Angeles. His final assignment came in 1965, when he was designated oceanographer of the navy and commander of the Naval Oceanographic Office in Suitland, Maryland.

In retirement Admiral Waters lived in Sumner, Maryland, and then in Florida, where he died in 1986.

In the fall of 1940 I was sent over to England as an observer—actually I was sent over as an assistant naval attaché with diplomatic status. There were probably twenty-five naval officers attached to the embassy at that time to gain experience in various phases of warfare. I was sent over primarily to cover the advent of the magnetic acoustic mine that the Germans had just sprung as Hitler's secret weapon. By that time, the U.S. had concluded the agreement with Britain to turn over the fifty destroyers and for the ninety-nine-year leases on the several British bases in the Caribbean. So the exchange of information between the two countries was pretty free except for one or two things.

The one thing the U.S. would not exchange (and it stuck in their craw) was the Norden bombsight. We wouldn't give the British the Norden bombsight. Somebody high up in government decided we shouldn't give the British the Norden bombsight because it was such a great bombsight and they thought so highly of it. It had been developed by the navy for accurate pinpoint bombing. It wasn't nearly as great as everybody thought at the time but it was probably much ahead of anything that anybody else had.

When I got over there we were sitting around talking about new things and trying to get the lay of the land. Gus Wellings [John Wellings] was one of the officers assigned as an observer aboard British destroyers. He spoke up and said: "Now when you get around to the British navy there are a few things that you want to watch out about. One of them is the Norden bombsight. This is pretty much stuck in their craws. As a matter of fact, I don't see why they don't give them the damn thing. But," said he, "they will bring it up. There are various ways you can handle it when it does come up. I've developed a way that seems to work pretty well—at least temporarily—because it shocks them a little bit."

"What is that, Gus? What do you say?" "Well," said he, "you will be sitting around the wardroom and somebody will bring up the question of why in the hell don't you give us the bombsight? I always say, 'You know, I really think it's because we're pretty sure, or at least we think, you already have it.' And then they'll say, 'What do you mean?' and then I would reply, 'About two years ago one of the bombsights was stolen from the Philadelphia Navy Yard and we were always pretty damn sure the British stole it.' That shuts them up for a couple of days on this."

I think that was just somebody's poor judgment or an administrative error. After all we gave them destroyers. But the destroyers had the Mark 8 torpedo in them. Well, we knew very well that the only variation of that torpedo that we'd ever been able to make work was when you finally got down to the Mark 83D. A, B, and C didn't work. So what did we do but put the Mark 83A torpedos in them just because they were sitting on the shelf some place.

Well, one Saturday I was back in London and the senior technical officer was there, Commander P. E. Lee. We had a crisis because the British had attempted to fire the torpedos and the only thing they did was circle around and come back and almost hit the firing ship. They wanted to know what to do. So Commander Lee said, "I need a torpedo expert." Of course those of us there were seasoned naval officers and nobody spoke up. So he made the rounds: "Have you ever been a torpedo officer?" And the reply was consistently, "No, sir." But when he came to me I said, "Yes, sir." And he said, "You're my torpedo expert. Go over to the Admiralty and see Captain Jackson there and find out what the hell this problem's all about and then come back and we'll see what we can do for them."

So I went over and Captain Jackson was a sort of vaudeville type of an Englishman—a Colonel Blimp type. He wore a monocle and hemmed, hawed, and sputtered so that he was difficult to understand. I asked, "Are these the Mark 83A's?" I knew enough about them because they were the kind used in the old four-pipers. I had never fooled around with anything that antique, but I did know that you had to have the 83D for the torpedo to work. I came back to Commander Lee and told him what we had done to those poor people. I said, "I think the least we can do is to get all of the drawings over here for how you'd modify these things to be 83Ds and the spare parts or whatever you need and enough good navy torpedo men to help them put it together." So that's what they did and that solved the big torpedo crisis.

Before I came to London after my destroyer duty in the States I requested and was selected to go to PG [postgraduate] school in ordnance engineering. There were various sorts of subdivisions among ordnance engineers. Other than specific specialists the rest were what they called *general*. I was called *general* and was supposed to know it all. These German mines made their appearance early in 1940 and they were using them more and more. The first one was magnetic but then the acoustic came along. The only man in our technical office who was qualified to look after this new problem was an ED [engineering duty] officer, and he was also a naval constructor who was so busy studying the damage to British ships from bombs and gunfire, he couldn't cover it all. So he sent an appeal for two mining experts plus a civilian scientist. We were just completing the academic part of our course and were going around to various installations on a make-learn status. I had just started thirty-day leave when cancellation of my leave came through and I was told to report, not to the Bureau of Ordnance, but to Naval Intelligence. There I filled out forms, got a diplomatic passport, and was on my way to London with my classmate, Moe Archer [Captain Stephen Morris Archer]. We were really technical observers but had the status of assistant attachés. When we got to London we were told what the problem was and attached to the HMS *Vernon* in Portsmouth, the British main establishment for mines and torpedoes.

Shortly before our arrival the British had learned through intelligence that the Germans were going to plant this thing in the channel but the Brits didn't know whether it was magnetic or acoustic. The first of these German mines had been laid mistakenly on the tidelands at the mouth of the Thames where there is a pretty good rise and fall of the tides. It was exposed at low tide and everybody from Churchill down said: "Go get it." It was quite a feat. A British naval commander did just that. It was taken apart successfully and defanged at Portsmouth, where it had been taken. Then it was found to be magnetic and that started all of the magnetic minesweeping effort and the degaussing of ships. A later capture of an acoustic one caused them to develop a means of combating that. But it was obvious then that with this kind of sophisticated technical warfare the only way to really be able to cope was to have mine recovery teams trained to bring the mines back alive so they could analyze them and figure out a countermeasure.

That was what the British were involved in when we came on the scene, so we started working with them. They taught us all they knew about these things. We saw the actual mines, so Moe Archer and I started taking turns going with them to recover these things and helping them. By the end of winter we had written all our reports and had pretty well covered the subject. The naval attaché in London wrote back to the chief of naval operations what an important development this was and that the U.S. Navy should start preparing to deal with the problem. Since there were only the two of us, Archer and myself, who knew anything about the subject, we were stuck. So I came back to the States in April. Archie stayed a little longer in London.

I managed to catch a ride in a big British convoy coming across to Halifax and eventually got back to Washington, where I was told to sit down and start planning to start something that would enable the U.S. Navy to be capable of recovering and dissecting enemy mines. First of all I came up with a plan that involved a school for training personnel in this work and a plan for the manufacture and buying of tools for us to use. This required special tools based on research and development. I felt we were in a better position to do this because the British were living a hand-to-mouth existence and didn't really have time to check things out. My plan was approved.

Archer came back and we started our first class down in the old Naval Gun Factory in Washington in June 1941. This was close to the deep-sea diving school because we felt everyone in the business had to be capable of diving. You couldn't tell whether these things would be dropped under water or on land by mistake. We started in a building that had been a stable in Civil War days and eventually got over to Anacostia, where we turned out our first class some sixteen weeks after we started. We had a mixed class of officers and enlisted men—all volunteers. We were allowed two more regular officers on the staff and we also had a small core of Coast Guard men that were sent over to be trained and to work with the navy. The first groups we got were awfully good men, especially the enlisted men. They were old-time petty officers—first class, and chiefs, and so on—who were in the mine warfare business. They took very aptly to the training because they knew a great deal about it to begin with.

By the time of Pearl Harbor we had established strategical points covered by training units—two officers and two men to a unit—stationed in Pearl Harbor, Panama, and Manila. These were the important points for us to cover because of course the British had the European side to cover.

We also turned out some almost carbon copies of the German magnetic mines so we'd have them in our inventory. At the same time we worked at developing new techniques and new tools. We experimented with X ray in trying to develop portable X ray machines that would work on land and underwater. We developed several different methods for burning mines that we didn't want to recover but had to get rid of some way.

To satisfy this need for doing this development work and also to serve as a place where we could train people at the school in the use of demolition, burning mines, and countermining them—that sort of thing—we got a piece of land that the navy owned down at the powder factory near Indian Head—at Stump Neck, a little isolated peninsula sticking out into the Potomac River where we said we could go down in the woods and blow ourselves up in peace and quiet.

In the training of these techniques we did not use live mines—rather squibs so that if a man made a mistake he would get a little pop to make it dramatic. We did have a few casualties, a relatively small number but not nearly so many as was experienced in bomb disposal. The British particularly had to train people so fast that they gave them practically no training and put them out to dispose of those things. We went around and tried to get people to volunteer out of high school. It was rather an unusual process picking the people because we had learned in our experience in England that what we were looking for were intelligent people who were somewhat apt in a technical sense, who had some capabilities technically and could use their hands and handle tools and be smart enough to understand the circuits and what they were dealing with. But the thing we stayed away from studiously were the would-be heroes. We had found from the English experience that a man who wasn't really smart enough to understand how dangerous this work was and who was really sort of stupidly brave and was willing to risk his life and all those things just for the sheer glory of it was the person we stayed well away from because when you've got a person like that he's not only likely to blow himself up but several of his teammates as well. That was the philosophy we had in looking for people. I think it turned out pretty well.

Then of course the diving requirement always cut us down a bit because the people when accepted had to be physically qualified for deep-sea diving and this takes a little bit more than just a plain run-of-the-line physical exam. Then we found there was a psychological factor that in those days didn't necessarily show up in the physical tests. Every now and then there would be a man on the first day of instruction in diving when he was in the shallow water tank with the deep-sea rig on—when the instructor would close the face plate, closing him up in his diving helmet—he would say, "Let me out, I can't stand it." Claustrophobia.

I stayed on this job from June 1941 to January 1943. In that time I expect we turned out a couple of hundred men. More classes were graduated after that but lots of them were used as the nucleus of the underwater demolition teams that came along a bit later, taking them from the mine disposal and bomb disposal school graduates.

The bomb disposal school is sort of a sidelight to this story. Our experiences in England convinced us that during wartime particularly it's not possible to train people who can dispose of both mines and bombs. The problem is just too complex to train a reserve officer, particularly one who is in a hurry, to do all of those things, so we kept bomb disposal and mine disposal separate. But after we had got our mine disposal school going there was heavy pressure on us in the navy for the mine disposal people to undertake bombs as well.

We would have probably lost that battle except for the fact that there was a Lieutenant Draper Kauffman, who had graduated from the Naval Academy in 1933. He had gotten out, was in Germany when the war broke out in 1939, and was captured as an ambulance driver and finally set loose as a noncombatant. He went over to England, joined the Royal Navy Volunteer Reserve and was in bomb disposal. After a year he managed to get leave and came over to this country and shifted from the RNVR into the U.S. Naval Reserves and showed up with all this background. It was proposed that he come and join us at the mine school and we said "No." This solved our problem very neatly. We agreed that we would give him all sorts of help and advice on how to start his school of bomb disposal. That's a tough job in itself. That's what happened. He started the bomb disposal school and they stayed separate all through the war and were brought together as explosive ordnance disposal after the war. That is all right in peacetime, but I think it's a hard thing to cover all those things in a wartime situation.

Actually the Germans didn't use very many mines over here. Those that they did were very effective, but they had such a field day with their torpedoes that they really could accomplish more using torpedoes than mines, although you can argue that point. For example, in 1942 they closed the port of Norfolk for forty-eight hours with just a string of about half a dozen mines. They closed the port of New York I think about two or three times. Whenever they wanted to go to the trouble of bringing mines over in submarines and landing them they could do it.

When they mined the entrances to Norfolk in 1942 I was called there. We lost several ships in a convoy coming in and the minesweeps were out sweeping and one of them had snagged a mechanical sweep in something and turned it over to a Coast Guard cutter standing by holding the end of the line. They thought perhaps they had an unexploded mine on the end of it. So I arrived with a unit and we managed to pass the steel minesweeping cable ashore down at Virginia Beach and we hitched it up. We had a big six-by-six army truck there and we started pulling on it and the line got taut and nothing happened. We budged it a little bit and then we stood the truck right up on its rear wheels, pulling so hard, and nothing happened. We finally got a big army tank that we borrowed and put that on the end of the line and got down behind the dunes as this thing broke water. It was a great big old-fashioned wrought iron anchor that had been lost by some ship out there and had probably been there for a hundred years or so. It was still in very good condition.

There was another incident about that time. We were called down to Jacksonville at the mouth of the Saint Johns River, which was an assembly point for coastal convoys. A German submarine had been in there and had laid a stick of mines and according to our intelligence the minesweepers who had been sweeping monotonously back and forth there for about three or four months all of a sudden had mines go off underneath the tails of their magnetic sweeps. This almost shocked them to death. They swept four mines I think. Intelligence indicated that a German submarine at that time carried a stick of six so there were two unexposed mines according to the best calculations. We were sent down to try and get them back alive. We had a device that worked on a new principle of electric field—sort of a hydrofoil that you towed from a boat. It was a good idea but the thing wasn't well enough made to stand up in the sea. When the thing was working you weren't sure it was working well. We steamed around there. We had a diving team and this indicator device to try and locate the mines on the bottom and we'd get a strike, which was what we called it, from the indicator device and then we'd mark it with a buoy and put a diving party down and usually it would be an old tin can or something.

We worked down there for about a week not getting anywhere and one day the weather got so bad that we couldn't go out so we didn't have anything to do and I decided to go and talk to the shrimp fishermen who were there at the mouth of Saint Johns River. They were always getting in our way. There would always be a shrimp trawler right where you wanted to go with the indicator device. I went over and asked the fishermen if they had seined anything unusual in their nets and they said, "Sure, you mean those bits of metal we've been getting?" I went back and looked at them and they had enough pieces to make a whole mine. Of course these were the pieces of the mine cases that had been exploded by our sweepers. Just by looking at them and by looking at the markings on them we determined that they were the same old what they called an *S*-type German magnetic submarine-laid mine. We decided it wasn't worth expending any more effort on them and we used this good intelligence we got from the shrimp fishermen and came home.

I finally did what so many people do in the navy. I trained my own relief for I was anxious to get to sea. On January 1, 1943, I was relieved as officer in charge of the Navy Mine Disposal School by an excellent Coast Guard officer who had been a graduate of our first class in the training school.

VOLUNTEERING IS A DANGEROUS HABIT

REAR ADMIRAL DRAPER L. KAUFFMAN

U.S. NAVY

DRAPER LAURENCE KAUFFMAN was born in San Diego, California, on 4 August 1911. He attended St. Albans School in Washington, D.C., and Kent School in Kent, Connecticut, and was appointed to the U.S. Naval Academy from Ohio in 1929. As a midshipman he was a member of the lightweight crew and selected captain in 1933. He also served on the staff of *The Log* and *The Lucky Bag*.

Upon graduation from the Naval Academy in 1933 he was forced to resign from the navy because of poor eyesight. He was then employed by the U.S. Line Steamship Company in New York and in the company's European offices until 16 April 1940, when he joined the American Volunteer Ambulance Corps with the French Army. On 18 June 1940 he was captured by the Germans and held prisoner until August 1940. For his services with the French Army he was awarded the croix de guerre with star.

After leaving the prison camp he made his way to England via France, Spain, and Portugal and joined the British Royal Navy Volunteer Reserve, serving as a sublieutenant and lieutenant. From September 1940 to November 1941 he was a bomb- and mine-disposal officer in the Royal Navy. For his service in this position he was twice commended by the British Admiralty and on 29 March 1941 was commended by King George VI.

He resigned from the British Navy to accept an appointment as lieutenant in the U.S. Naval Reserve on 7 November 1941, was promoted to lieutenant commander on 11 January 1943, and to commander 1 March 1944. On 15 October 1946 he was transferred to the regular navy and eventually obtained the rank of rear admiral in July 1961.

Kauffman was ordered to duty in the Bureau of Ordnance in November 1941. Because of his previous bomb disposal experience he was dispatched on a quick trip to Hawaii to recover an unexploded five-hundred-pound Japanese bomb that was found at Scofield Barracks after the Japanese attack of 7 December 1941. He saved all parts of this bomb and it was used for study by the ordnance experts.

In January 1942 he was assigned the task of organizing a Naval Bomb Disposal School at the U.S. Navy Yard in Washington, D.C. He also assisted the U.S. Army in setting up a comparable school at Aberdeen, Maryland.

In June 1943 Kauffman was assigned the task of organizing the first navy demolition teams, which later became known as the UDTs, the Underwater Demolition Teams. He thus became the first commanding officer of the Naval Combat Demolition Unit at the Naval Amphibious Training Base in Fort Pierce, Florida. He also organized and became chairman of the Joint Army and Navy Experimental and Testing Board (JANET).

In April 1944 he was ordered to the Pacific Fleet and served at the Naval Combat Demolition Training and Experimental Base, Maui, Territory of Hawaii; as commanding officer of Underwater Demolition Team No. 5; as senior staff officer, Underwater Demolition Teams, Amphibious Forces, Pacific Fleet; and amphibious training officer, Pacific Fleet. This duty led him with his group in night reconnaissance of the landing beaches on Tinian Island and during assaults on Iwo Jima and Okinawa Gunto.

In February 1946 Kauffman was assigned duty with Joint Task Force One, Naval Operations, in the Navy Department. That group conducted the atomic bomb test at Bikini in the Pacific during Operation Crossroads the following summer. That fall he transferred to the Office of the Chief of Naval Operations as head of the Defense and Protection Section (against atomic warfare). He established the first U.S. Navy Radiological Safety School on the West Coast and later assisted the army in establishing a similar school on the East Coast.

After Kauffman attended the Naval Damage Control School in Philadelphia in late 1947 he was assigned to the USS *Valley Forge* (CV 45) and was aboard her during her cruise around the world in 1948. He then did a short tour at the Fleet Sonar School in Key West and then commanded the USS *Gearing* (DD 710) from December 1948 until July 1950, when he entered the Naval War College in Newport. He completed a logistics course in June 1951 and remained for two years as a member of the strategy and tactics staff. He then commanded a destroyer division and in July 1954 returned to the Navy Department, where he served a year in the Strategic Plans Division of the CNO and two years after that as aide to Secretary Thomas S. Gates (1955–57). Gates was first undersecretary and then secretary of the navy in this time.

There followed several short commands at sea, one of an APA and another of a cruiser; also he was on the staff of the commander in chief of the Pacific Fleet. Then in 1960 he became a rear admiral and took command of Destroyer Flotilla Three. In March 1962 he was assigned as chief of the Strategic Plans and Policy Division of the Joint Staff of the Joint Chiefs of Staff.

In July 1963 he was selected by the secretary of the navy to set up a new department of the navy, the Office of Program Appraisal, and this put him on the immediate staff of the secretary of the navy. Then in March 1965 he was named superintendent of the Naval Academy in Annapolis, Maryland. In July of 1968 he was named commander of the U.S. Naval Forces in the Philippines and served there until May 1970. His next command was to the Ninth Naval District with headquarters in Great Lakes, Illinois. This was his last command for he retired on 1 June 1973. In 1974 he became the tenth president of the Marion Military Institute in Marion, Alabama, but retired from this position in October 1976 because of ill health. Admiral Kauffman died unexpectedly while on a vacation trip in Budapest, Hungary, on 18 August 1979. He was buried in the cemetery on the Naval Academy grounds.

I came to graduation at the Naval Academy and June Week in 1933 and was without a job or a commission. They had raised the standards and I failed my eye exam completely. In fact they were in the process of executing a new law that would permit only half of the graduates of the class to be commissioned. It was in the depression years and the navy was cutting down rather rigorously.

With that as background I read an article in *American Magazine* which said you don't go out looking for a job. First you decide what type of business you want to get into. Write down why you've chosen that business and then look at several companies within that business. I believed this implicitly and so I spent the summer looking over various kinds of business. I picked the shipping industry and then visited quite a few companies. Then I chose U.S. Lines (then known as International Mercantile Marine Company), and after a considerable amount of difficulty I got in to see Mr. Basil Harris, a vice president of the company. As the magazine article had advised I had prepared a twelve-minute speech that I had rehearsed in front of a mirror, and I told Mr. Harris why I had picked the U.S. Lines, what kind of experience I hoped to gain by serving in various departments, and so forth. Mr. Harris hired me. He then followed that at three-month intervals with six more fellows who did the same routine.

From January to June 1939 I spent time in Europe, with two months in U.S. Lines offices in Germany, two months in France, and two months in England. I came home absolutely convinced there would be a war unless the United States made a positive pronouncement that we would enter the war and help the French and the British. I was convinced that if we did not do so there would be a war and both France and Britain would fall. I went to two meetings in Germany where Mr. Hitler spoke, and although I couldn't understand what he said I did feel the unbelievable emotion of the crowd; it was frightening.

I got back to New York and got on the free lecture circuit where you can go, if you have anything to say, and speak every night of the week if you desire. Four nights a week I went to these clubs and organizations. The gist of my speech was that the U.S. must come out with a positive statement that we would join Britain and France if Germany started a war. I've never caused such a large amount of boredom in my life. The apathy of my audiences was constant until Germany invaded Poland. Then I simply said we should get into the war immediately. Then the apathy of my previous audiences was matched only by the antagonism of the present ones. I didn't realize that people actually throw vegetables at speakers, but they do! The reaction of the women, particularly, was violent. I persisted in speaking although I knew I was doing no good whatsoever. Eventually I decided, well, all right, I guess they're right.

I then heard of the American Volunteer Ambulance Corps. They had agreed to be under the French Army, taking direct orders only from them. An applicant was supposed to buy his own ambulance at three thousand dollars and to take care of his own expenses while with the French army. I couldn't afford this amount but the ambulance corps head got most of the money from others to assist me. I had tried to join the naval reserve but could get only in a category four because of my eyes and that made me mad.

That is how I happened to make this weird decision to join the French army. There was no swearing of allegiance, but we were under the orders of whichever French military commander we met in the area that we were in. By the tenth of May 1940, when all hell broke loose, I happened to hit my frontline post. By that date the corps probably had forty drivers. It was an interesting coincidence because our area was a small pie-shaped area, starting with a base and then a *poste de secours,* they called it, in Sarre Union, which was about ten miles short of the Maginot Line. Then I went from there on the tenth of May, on a voluntary basis, to Neunkirchen, which was our advanced post and was about four miles this side of the Siegfried Line and about six miles beyond the Maginot Line. This was a very interesting spot because it was manned by a volunteer group from the French army. They were an extraordinary group—they were used to patrol between the Maginot and Siegfried lines. They were all carefully se- lected, a very elite, very prima donna corps of men, as brave a group as I've ever come across.

That very first night was when the cold war became the hot war. Our area was on the Saar River and neither the Siegfried Line nor the Maginot Line was strong there. It was the weak spot in both lines because the water table was very high and it was very difficult to build good emplacements.

51

I had a couple of experiences my first night there that certainly were the most physically frightening experiences of my life and the most horror filled. Driving an ambulance through a great deal of shell fire, then picking up freshly wounded men, bleeding like stuck pigs, in terrible pain. The two-week period at Neunkirchen—I can just think of two things, downright physical fear and deep, deep horror. Since then my respect for marine and army infantrymen has always been enormous. I fully understand when I hear people talk about a soldier freezing, and not being able to fire his rifle, or running. I can't tell you how close I came to running several times. That night when I volunteered for the first of these trips I was violently sick at my stomach after I got away from everybody. Then when I was just getting myself a little bit composed they came up and asked me to go back for another load. If I had not been an American working with the French I would never, ever have gone on that second round. But of course you can't let the people of one country see a guy from another country giving in.

My ambulance was not inviolable to enemy attack so we took to covering the red cross and the American flag with a blanket because the ambulance was such an easy target.

Without a doubt I would say that those two weeks in that area were the worst of my sixty-six years. I don't know how I stayed awake during that time. I just went out to the field, picked them up, and brought them back to the advanced post at Neunkirchen. Then the ambulance based at the *poste de secours* came and picked them up. We would let them know at the advanced post, they'd be there to meet the ambulance, and I could go back again. I had three stretcher bearers assigned but actually at the end I had only one man who went along, a Frenchman. I had done very well in French at the academy but in France I thought that I knew practically no French, but of course, in a situation such as I was in, you have a sense of urgency to bring it back somewhat quickly.

I had three extremely different two-week periods in succession. The first one at Neunkirchen, then I was sent to a place called Berig, where there was a large open hospital and where we made only about one trip a day and that was usually to hospitals farther back, so it was not a dangerous trip at all.

The war was going on all around us but it didn't touch us. Another driver and myself were billeted with a wonderful French peasant family, with lots of milk, bread, butter—all the things we wanted. But most interesting was the group we ate with—the junior doctors. They had the same status in the medical fraternity as our interns. There were four I got to know very well. They were very serious, very philosophical types. We used to talk and talk and talk. They thought about after the war; what had led France into its present situation—two weeks of solid philosophy, which sounds amazing in the middle of a war.

One night I remember the president of France came on the radio and announced that Italy had entered the war. At the end of his speech they played the "Marseillaise" and these men were on their feet before the music started—without doubt the most inspiring national anthem of any country. They talked a long, long time that night as they went from worry about ultimate defeat (this was really the first time this had come into the conversation) until they brought themselves to believe that Italy's entry didn't matter. It is too weak, they thought, and would not keep the French from winning out in the end.

The final two weeks of my assignment were characterized by the thought of despair and defeat. I had three extraordinary experiences in just six weeks.

Now I rejoined the corps d'armée that I'd been with at the beginning and it was obvious we were retreating. They used the American ambulances for the last-minute evacuation of any town on the route, and the last-minute evacuation of people from the hospitals. I was told by a French general that this was deliberate—while his troops were retreating, to see an American ambulance going back up to the front to get the wounded. The general thought this was good for morale.

A most devastating thing happened about this time. During a complete power blackout notices appeared on the town hall and all around the little town I was in at the time. Other ambulance drivers said the same thing had happened in other towns. The notices proclaimed that the United States had entered the war. It was perhaps almost thirty-six hours before this was contradicted. It was brilliant propaganda on the part of the Germans if they did it, because the enormous relief of the people was followed by an even more enormous letdown. Looking back I was interested in the reaction of the French towards us. They were wild with enthusiasm, but they didn't show resentment in the time after the truth was made known.

I shall never forget this small corps d'armée, which I now rejoined. We were surrounded and we retreated to the top of Mont Repos. The weather was beautiful and the scenery was just unbelievably beautiful. Four of us sat for about five hours watching the cavalcade go by. It wasn't just that the men were in tatters or that the horses were worn; it was the sag of the shoulders and the realization that they had really been defeated.

One other cavalcade at the beginning of this last two-week period I remember. I had gone to Saar Union to evacuate the hospital and the civilians had been given two days to leave. It was tragic to see these people. Only the very old and the very young being in carts, the rest walking and carrying what little they could. Of course they started out carrying more than they could handle and had to drop much of it along the way. Here they were, departing from their homes. For the older people this was the third time in their lifetime that they had had to evacuate their homes in front of the Germans, which is a terrible thing to think about. There was a bitterness in these people—bitterness past belief. It was towards the Germans but also against their own government for being so ill prepared. Of course the bitterness against the Germans was basic and so deep. There is bound to be in France still—so many years later—a deep-seated fear of the Germans even though it's without any reason whatsoever now.

These were probably as emotional and traumatic a six weeks as I have ever had except that it was broken in the middle by ten days in Berig. It was almost as though you were writing a play and said, "Now, let's put this character through real personal hell for a couple of weeks, then let's let him relax for a couple of weeks, and then put him through not so much a personal hell but let him witness a national hell."

Toward the end we were in a situation where we were surrounded with no hospital within our area. Our medical general sent for us, about ten of us, and asked for a volunteer to take some wounded through the French lines and the German lines to a French hospital that had been overrun. The particular wounded had been carefully selected in that they would not live if they didn't get to a hospital but probably would live if they did. So I loaded up my ambulance, volunteered to take the job, and at the last minute Lieutenant Steel decided to go with me. Theoretically we could take only four patients, but we rigged it up so that we could take eight.

Our object was to go through the two lines without permission from the Germans and then try to persuade them to let us come back again for another load. It seemed pretty dubious to me, unless we could manage to be blindfolded and have somebody else drive the car. We got to the forward French post and they said the forward German post was about two kilometers along this very windy road. I had Steel with me and he spoke German because he had been an area manager of the Coca-Cola Company in Germany. So we started those two kilometers and I don't think we went much more than that an hour, just crawling. We had a bell on the ambulance and I kept ringing the bell. We had a white flag in front and two on top and I had the door ajar. The distance we had to go to the hospital was about seven kilometers. It took us through very peaceful scenery. I remember the cows browsing; the weather was beautiful and the scenery great.

Finally we came around a bend and saw something move. With no bravery whatsoever I jammed on the brakes, jumped out of the car, threw my hands in the air, and like a grade-C movie, yelled "Kamerad." This sounds ridiculous now but didn't then. A dozen Germans came up and examined the two of us. They had two machine guns pointing at us. Then others got behind the ambulance with more machine guns pointed at this potential Trojan horse while we opened the doors. Then they examined and found that yes, there were really some severely wounded men. Steel tried to persuade them to blindfold us and to drive the ambulance with the idea of taking the wounded to the hospital and then coming back for more. But no—the Germans didn't have time for that. So they finally permitted us to drive on to the hospital. It was a hospital from which I had evacuated people only three days before. Steel attempted to persuade the Germans to let us go back after delivering our patients at the hospital, and at one point we thought he had persuaded them to allow this, but as soon as we heard some motorcycles charging up behind us we knew we'd lost that game. We were then taken to a prison camp. We finally landed at the prison camp at Luneville. Of course they would have been very stupid to have let us go through their lines and see everything we could see and then go back and tell the French. By international law they were allowed to capture medical personnel and by law they were to return them as soon as the exigencies of the war permitted.

We were taken captive on June 22, which was the day that the French and Germans signed the armistice at Compiègne. We were in the prison camp for only four weeks. They mostly left us alone but when they got mad at us they kicked us. (I am told the Japanese reaction was to slap their prisoners.) By the end of the week there were fifteen Americans in the camp and a few thousand French.

We had to fill out and sign questionnaires when we arrived, including the question "Have you ever been in Germany?" We were not in Germany at that moment; it was still northeast France. I don't know why but I checked "no." Well, one day the prison commander sent for me, stood me in front of his desk. I saw he had before him quite a large file and I could read my name upside down on the top page of the file. He said, "Have you ever been in Germany?" and I thought I'd better follow through so I said, "No, sir."

"I suppose you are not the Draper Kauffman who came here as a midshipman in 1929 and went to Hamburg and Berlin?" He flipped a page and that described another visit in 1936 and then my visit in 1939. He had incredible detail, including the fact that on Good Friday I was at the Four Seasons Hotel in Berlin; that I talked to the head porter, or concierge, and he got me a ticket to see *Parsifal* and I had said how wonderful to see *Parsifal* at the German State Opera house on Good Friday; that I came back afterwards and he asked me how I liked it and I said, "I hate to say so but I thought it was dreadful." That on Easter Sunday I had gone out to Sans Souci by bus and had gotten to know a couple—I knew the ones he mentioned—they had said they were from Iowa and that the three of us sat on a bench on a beautiful day and I had said, "You know, if I were a bomber pilot and ordered to bomb a place like this I don't think I could do it."

Every bit of what he read was absolutely correct. There was a little more evidence of my last trip. I simply marveled at the enormously detailed dossier. It baffles. Finally I answered "Yes, I had visited Germany." And the commander of the camp just laughed. He was just doing it to tease me and to show me the omniscience of the German Republic.

Then we Americans were given desks in an ordinary school classroom with blackboards. I remember they showed us a film that realistically showed the German air force sinking five British battleships. I really believed, until I got to England, that they had really sunk those five battleships.

Another interesting thing was to talk to the German guards, for a number of them did speak English. I am afraid I was the troublemaker in the group because I said such things as, "There is no way that you're going to keep the U.S. out of this war and as you well know when this happens it will be all over as far as you're concerned. We proved that in 1917–19 and it will be the same thing all over again." But the most interesting point was that these young guards absolutely believed that the world had reached a stage where it had to be run by one homogeneous group of people and that the Germans had proved that they were the only people capable of running the world.

The French on the other hand were terribly low. It's an extraordinary thing to see a defeated people.

I will talk about my release from the German prison—two people were principally involved. The first was an elderly woman who came to the prison gates one morning. We heard a high, shrill, obviously American voice berating the guards at the entrance to the gate. It was a hot day and yet she had on a long black dress, and she was giving those guards hell because she was an American citizen and had a perfect right to visit this prison camp. She spoke in English and of course the guards didn't understand much. Finally she took her umbrella and whacked it down on the helmet of a German guard and then marched past him and through the inner gate. We knew she couldn't stay long after that incident. But fortunately we had prepared a list of our names and our home addresses and we gave it to the woman. Our primary concern had been to get word to our families that we were alive. All our families knew of course that we were missing in action. The woman came in and sat down and the colonel came in and in no time started arguing with her. She argued back and from then on we dubbed the colonel "the little wet hen" because that's what he looked like as he began wringing his hands. There was nothing in his book of instructions to tell him how to deal with a female like that. She was either a Biddle or a Drexel from Philadelphia, we later learned. The colonel lost the argument evidently for he let her stay and he walked away.

She then asked us questions about ourselves and suddenly turned to Steel and spoke to him in perfect German. He was fascinated and asked why she had addressed the guards in English. She retorted, "Never, never speak their language to them. You lower yourself when you do. I can't think of anything sillier." Presently she left us but we learned that she was with the Morgan group, mostly an American group of women who were in France to help in some way with relief. Anyway, she got word back to our embassy in Paris. Admiral Hillenkoetter was the naval attaché and he had been in touch with my father. So I think that is why I got released. Anyway the day came when the fifteen of us were put in a cattle car. It took us two days to get to Paris with two guards in tow. Hillenkoetter received us from the German guards at the embassy and we had to sign statements that we would never again join any armed forces against the German Reich. The Germans kept our passports. Our embassy issued us new passports that were good for travel only through France, Portugal, and Spain en route to the United States. Another paragraph said specifically "not valid in the United Kingdom." The Morgan group of women were wonderful to us. They got us rooms at the Hotel Bristol and got a doctor. All of us had become very thin—I had gone from 165 pounds when I left America to 125 in Paris.

Then we left Paris and went down through France to the Spanish border. Then across the border to Lisbon—it took us eight days. In the harbor I saw a big American cruiser. I found out that Admiral LeBreton was in command of the task group and I went aboard and asked to see him. He welcomed me with open arms and had been expecting me because Dad had been overloading navy circuits to Europe in order to get some word of me. The admiral gave me a marvelous meal and we discussed my idea of going up to England. By the time I got out of prison camp I was even more violently anti-German. It took me years after the war to get my senses back. Then I went to see Sir Noel Charles, the British ambassador in Lisbon, and told him I would like to join the British navy when I got up to London. Did he think that was possible? Sir Noel said he would query the navy people. They said they would give every consideration to my application so Sir Noel asked how I planned to get to England. He then said he could put me on a freighter. He called in somebody and was told, "Yes, we can put you on a small freighter to England, but you will have to sign on in order to be legal." It turned out that I was signed on as a second pantryman. I slept in a passenger cabin but then it was found they needed a second pantryman badly and so I took the job. I learned there is a great social gulf between first and second pantryman—the second doing the pots and pans and peeling potatoes.

It took our ship forty-three days to go from Lisbon to Scotland via the South Atlantic and the mouth of the Amazon, then to Boston where our ship joined an assorted convoy back across the Atlantic. When I landed in Scotland I had some difficulty because of my passport, which stated that it was not valid for travel in Britain. But they let me go to London with instructions to report to the American consul and to the chief of police. I went to the consular office and said, "I have a mistake on my passport. Would you correct it for me? The passport says not valid for travel in Britain but I am now in Britain and so the statement is wrong obviously." So the girl gave me a new passport for travel in the United Kingdom for six months. She never questioned me. Then I was able to go to the office of the chief of police and everything was all right. Then I went around to the Admiralty and said I wanted to join the British navy. They wanted verification and so I got to Admiral Kirk, then our naval attaché. He put a note on my dossier saying, "I have known him all his life and know his family very well." Then I went back to the British navy captain in the Admiralty and he sent me for a five-minute physical exam, which proved my eyes were bad. By five o'clock that afternoon I was a sublieutenant RNVR (Special Branch), meaning you can't go to sea. You wore a green-felt stripe to show that you were a nonseagoing officer. So here was I, an American getting into the Wavy Navy between nine o'clock in the morning and five o'clock in the afternoon. Then I was sent down to Hove, near Brighton, to the school for new officers—the British equivalent of our ninety-day-wonder type of school in World War II. I am sure I would never have been given a commission if I had not been a Naval Academy graduate. It even helped me in France.

The shore station was named HMS *King Alfred*. We had about four hundred to five hundred officers at a time and a ten-week course. It was an excellent course. I was very happy there. At the end of two weeks they had an election in my class for the class officer, which I think meant class sucker because you had to do all the dirty work—and I landed it. At the end of your third week there you took a week's turn as vice president of the mess. On Thursday night, the formal evening, the "dining in" evening, the port was passed in exactly the right manner and all that sort of stuff. At the end of the meal the president of the mess (he was of course the captain) would stand up and say, "Mr. Vice, the king." And the vice president was to stand up and say, "Gentlemen, the king."

I went to the exec who was the sort of father confessor to all of us and I said, "Commander, would it be very bad taste of me—I'm supposed to do this tonight—to say in the toast, 'Gentlemen, the president and the king.' "

"Well," he said, "I don't know, Kauffman, but that's a very interesting idea. I have no objection if you decide to do it." I didn't know what I should do but when I got up I said: "Gentlemen, the president and the king." Bless their hearts. There wasn't a murmur and every single person said "the president and the king." But it was a very scary moment.

This story I know is true—because I saw it. There was a very wealthy private girls' school in Hove and men who were billeted there had a little sign over the head of their beds and a buzzer and it said: "Ring twice for mistress." This was the favorite joke of everybody around. You can be sure they guarded those signs with the greatest care.

I went to see Captain Kirk one day in London about something and Captain Hillenkoetter happened to be there from Paris. The secretary told Kirk I was in the outer office and he opened the door and said, "Draper, come on in." Then he turned to Hillenkoetter and said, "Hilly, this is Reggie Kauffman's son." "Yes, I know," said Hillenkoetter. "Draper, what in hell are you doing in a British navy uniform?" I said, "Well, sir, I am a lieutenant in the RNVR." And he said, "Do you remember that piece of paper you signed that you would never join any armed force against the German Reich?" "Yes, sir, I do, but it was signed under duress." Hillenkoetter answered, "That doesn't make any difference." But Alan Kirk thought that was funny as hell and took my side.

I was at the Princess Hotel and on a Thursday night the Germans dropped one of their first unexploded time bombs, right near the hotel. An army bomb disposal squad came over to dig it up and the thing went off and eliminated the bomb disposal squad. As luck would have it the next morning the school asked for volunteers for bomb disposal and got zero. At noon formation they again asked for volunteers and this time they got three. They wanted six. That evening they got none and the next morning they got seventeen of us. We were all interviewed. I was spending my time saying, "Good grief, Kauffman, what did you do that for?"

The captain started off by asking, "Young man, are you frightfully keen for this type of duty?" I said, "No, sir," and heaved a sigh of relief for I thought that left me off the hook. But it turned out that was the key question. Anyone who answered "yes" was crossed off the list immediately. Anybody who was crazy enough for this type of duty was too crazy to have it.

There were nightly raids at that time over the English coast. It happened that about 20 percent of the German bombs were duds. A dud bomb will go anywhere from ten to thirty-five feet into the ground. But as they were duds the people didn't pay too much attention to them and lived and worked around them. But then the Germans began to add a percentage of time bombs so that you had to pay attention to all of their bombs and clean a large area all around them. As a result London was within a week just about jammed. It took about eight hours, I am told, to get from one side of London to the other in an emergency vehicle because of all the area roped off. All bombs were off limits because you could not tell one from the other. Later it was learned that these duds were due to faulty ordnance.

One of these darn things goes down thirty feet and you then have to dig a thirty-foot-deep hole with shoring or it will collapse on you. Then when you get to the bottom you work on the fuse but 99 percent of bomb disposal is the very unglamorous job of digging a hole in the ground. By the end of three or four weeks of instruction, however, mostly in digging, the army had enough volunteers. I did a couple of easy bombs there in London, but before long the ruling was changed to a very obvious one that the navy people would do only unexploded bombs on ships and at naval stations. (An easy bomb was where it was easy to get to—ten or fifteen feet down—and the fuse was only an ordinary dud fuse.)

I suppose this is the time to mention the battle of wits that went on all during the blitz between the Germans and the British, the German fuse designers and the British bomb disposal people. The Germans started with the time bomb, and then, through British newspapers, they found that the disposal people would get down to the bomb and simply take the fuse out. So they put an antiwithdrawal device behind the fuse so that if you pulled the fuse out you set the bomb off.

That was our glamorous period because during that period we had designated bomb cemeteries everywhere, in places such as parks, where you could dump a bomb and let it go off with no harm to the war effort. Well, we would get down to the bomb, hoist it out of the ground, put it in a truck, race through town to a cemetery, and dump it there. There was always a police car that went ahead of us with loudspeakers telling everybody to get out of the way, bomb disposal was coming through. But the British were very much like Americans. As soon as they heard that they'd all come dashing round to see the truck go by. This was our glamor period.

After you had a certain number of bombs in a cemetery and they had another nearby, they'd close the one off and leave it, with nobody going near it for about two weeks. At that time two weeks was the longest timed fuse. Then they would send people in and actually detonate the bombs where they were. Then we found the next step in the game when the Germans reacted by putting in an antidisturbance device. This was a device that did not function for the first fifteen minutes after the bomb hit and from then on if you disturbed the bomb, a trembler would touch the side of the fuse and set the bomb off. Obviously you couldn't move it.

This required insertion into the fuse of a liquid, very gently inserted, a liquid that congealed and froze the trembler to keep it from touching the sides. It was a little tricky because you had to heat the liquid and you had to very, very gently drill two tiny holes at the top of the fuse and insert the liquid very slowly and carefully. If you were careful, drilling the hole would not be enough vibration to set it off. *

We were able to keep abreast of all these new techniques by our intelligence people. As soon as they knew about a new fuse they would tell us and then what to do about it. One fascinating thing was the Germans always printed a number on the outside of the fuse: a 5 for instance would identify a straightforward action fuse, a 7 was a time fuse, and so on. They never tried to fool us on that point. They used numbers because they frequently had to handle their own bombs—perhaps a plane crash in Germany, something like that. It was an enormous help to us, the bomb disposal people.

Anyway at the end of this period I was sent to the naval base at Holyhead. I felt that the chances of getting an unexploded bomb on the naval base at Holyhead were darned small. But just at that time the Germans came up with what we called a land mine. Basically it was a mine designed to be dropped in harbors such as London, Liverpool, etc. It was dropped by parachute and this meant a very gentle landing that permitted a thin light skin so that 95 percent of its two thousand kilograms was pure explosive as opposed to the normal bomb, whose weight was about half that, casing and explosive.

The mine fuses were beautifully machined and probably very expensive to make. The original fuses were designed so that the magnetic field of a ship passing over a mine as it lay on the bottom would set it off. Several months later acoustic fuses were added, which would be set off by propeller noises and even later pressure-influenced designs came into being. As these were mines they were the full responsibility of the navy's Department of Torpedoes and Mines.

They were designed for use in water but because accuracy was very difficult using parachutes some of them came down on land where they did not detonate or were not supposed to. But one day in late September one did come down on a small town on the banks of the Thames and did detonate, causing far more devastation than a comparable two-thousand-kilo bomb for two reasons. First it was 95 percent (not 50 percent) explo-

---

*Anthony Eden praises the bomb disposal squads in *Another World, 1897–1917:* "Of all the variants of courage there is one which in my judgment surpasses all. The bomb disposal squads, whether in London in the blitz or in Ulster more recently, are surely the bravest of men. In cold blood calmly to place your life at a desperate hazard in the hope of saving others can never be surpassed and rarely equalled by any deed of daring or even sacrifice in the heat of battle." (London: Allen Lane, 1976), 133.

sives and second there was no penetration of the ground, which causes ordinary bombs to lose much of their power.

This incident was played up by the British press with detailed pictures of the devastation. The paper reached the German embassy in Dublin the next day and within a month the Germans had added a new fuse to their mines, a bomb-type fuse. This new one was designed to go off seventeen seconds after impact unless by that time the mine was in fifteen feet of water. There were three little holes in the top of this fuse and water pressure exceeding that of a 15-foot-depth would stop this fuse from operating and allow the mine to act only as a mine. So you had a combination of a bomb and a mine. Consequently the mechanism was so complicated that it was easily subject to malfunction. As it turned out it malfunctioned 35 percent of the time. And since the disposal officer could easily disturb the mine in some way, it could free the stalled working of the fuse and it would start again, accompanied by the familiar buzzing noise. But with that resumption you had no idea when it had stalled originally. You may have one second or seventeen seconds to get away. This mine disposal effort was a much more sporting proposition than bomb disposal.

Late in November there was a major three-night blitz on Liverpool. Since Holyhead, where I was stationed at the moment, was only about a two-hour drive I went over early the next morning to see if I could help the bomb disposal unit. But that had very little business in terms of bombs so they referred me to the new mine disposal group, which was completely separate with its own commander and chain of command. I found they were pretty frantic because this was the first time land mines had been used in such numbers and there weren't enough disposal officers to take care of the situation. I was welcomed with open arms, to my surprise, and was sent to assist Lieutenant Riley on a job. Later that day Captain Currie of the mine disposal unit got through to my boss in London and got permission to use me. Lieutenant Riley, known as Mother Riley, was the group's oldest and most experienced officer and also an excellent teacher.

The first mine I handled that day was unforgettable. The mine had come down in a crowded section of Liverpool, its parachute had tangled around a chimney, and the mine, about eight feet long, had its nose resting comfortably in the seat of an overstuffed chair in the reception room of a rather fancy house of ill-repute. The fuse turned out to be accessible and Riley had the mine safe in no time. From then on I was on my own. We had lost a couple of men earlier that morning. A complete set of tools was made up for me from their belongings and I inherited from one of the men who had died that morning his petty officer, Martin, who was outstanding. For the rest of that blitz job Martin and I handled eight more mines. All of them were rather simple with no complications.

At the end of the show—about a week—I went back to Holyhead but took with me my set of tools, and Petty Officer Martin went with me. Captain Currie agreed to explain the situation to Captain Llewellyn, my boss, when he got back to London and also that he would try to get me transferred to the mine disposal group in Liverpool. Captain Llewellyn apparently resisted this but never said anything to me. So when the Christmas blitz hit Liverpool I went down again to help. I had quite a few mines to deal with on that occasion. The first one was on Christmas Eve. It was a hard-to-get-at one. We had something like a thousand people evacuated from their homes. It was in a slum area of Liverpool. We finally got the people back in their homes—with the mine made safe—about ten minutes before midnight on Christmas Day.

The next one was early Christmas morning. It was a very unattractive job because it had smashed up in the cellar of a house, explosives scattered over everything. Dermatitis is our prime worry in such circumstances. I finally found the fuses and eliminated them and then I got ahold of two fire departments, one on either side of the house, and the firemen burned the house.

My unfortunate experience took place in my own bailiwick of Holyhead. Mine disposal had gotten a little more sophisticated by this time because we had gotten nonmagnetic tools and there was fear that metallic tools would set off the magnetic mines. I personally didn't think that even a heavy socket wrench of pure iron would have set off these things, but the authorities were worried about it. Later when the Germans began using acoustic fuses on their mines they made nervous wrecks out of us because our rule was that you could not make any noise lasting more than half a second without ten seconds in between such noises. If you were to unscrew something, you could unscrew it a quarter of a turn and check your watch; ten or twelve seconds later you could unscrew it another quarter of a turn. I had doubts about this rule but it was an established rule, and I wasn't about to disobey one and experiment.

It was about the second of January that we did have an unexploded parachute mine right on the railway line into Holyhead. It was a bitterly cold day. I went up to work on it and had my chief petty officer, Martin, with me but at a safe distance in a sort of culvert. I did something—I think my hand may have slipped as I was trying to twist the fuse open—and I heard the bomb fuse start and it took off like a sky rocket. It blew me quite a distance. Martin claimed that he timed it at eleven seconds from seeing me jump to my feet and that he knew the exact distance I had traveled. He put it in his report. Captain Currie's official comment reads as follows (for I kept it with me even after returning to the States): "It is apparent that Lieutenant Kauffman accomplished the equivalent of a nine-second hundred-yard dash. This world record may have been induced by a sense of urgency." But that incident caused a real step-up in the feud between Captain Currie of the mine disposal group and Captain Llewellyn, my boss with the bomb disposal group, and I was sent to Oban, Scotland, to get me away from mine disposal work.

While in Oban we had a very interesting unexploded bomb in a merchant ship off the island of Mull. The crew had deserted the ship because of the bomb. It was not a very risky job because the bomb turned out to be an ordinary dud fuse. It was a dirty job nonetheless because the bomb had ended up in a coal bunker where it was covered by several feet of soft and shifty coal with just a bit of tail fin visible. The ship was listing and rolling in uncomfortably heavy seas. There is something rather eerie about being alone on a deserted ship under these circumstances. When I finally got the fuse defused I got Martin aboard and we hoisted it over the side. I looked and felt like a chimney sweep who hadn't had a bath in a year.

Several years later when I had returned to the U.S. I got an award for salvage. I didn't know British naval officers got salvage awards—we don't.

Then in March came the terrible blitz on Glasgow and once again I got permission to work on that—on the mines there—but I don't know how that was arranged. At any rate it was an emergency and I worked on at least twelve mines there. After the mess was cleaned up we had the usual very fancy dinner given by the mayor or lord provost. It was very sad celebrating, however, because we had lost two fine officers during the week, and one was a very close friend of mine. Immediately afterwards I was ordered to Plymouth as chief bomb disposal officer. I arrived on the first of May, just in time for the famous German blitz attack on the town. It lasted for five out of eight nights. It was really a stinker. I wouldn't say I got no sleep but it came near to that. I had been complaining of not having enough bomb disposal jobs to handle but I certainly had no complaints after that. I was given three squads, but really only one squad because there were only two other officers, so the only difference between the chief disposal officer and the other two was who would do what bombs.

But as you know the Germans stopped their blitz on England on May 10, 1941. So my war in Europe was exactly one year long. May 10, 1940 to May 10, 1941.

In June of that year the three services set up a committee to try and evaluate all bomb and mine disposal casualties and to come up with a reason for these casualties. I was on the committee because I was the only one who had a significant amount of both mine and bomb disposal experience. We found the number-one cause was carelessness and the number-two reason was fatigue. In many cases it was found that both were very much related. And of course there was the other category of operational—just a fuse goes off at the wrong time.

About now I got my long-awaited transfer to mine disposal so I reverted to sublieutenant for about six weeks. I sent my father a copy of the court circular—or whatever they called it—that had all promotions in it and noted my change of status to "temporary acting probationary lieutenant in the reserve." My father sent this over to his opposite number in the Royal Navy in Iceland, Admiral Sir Frederick Dalrymple-Hamilton. Dad underlined "temp," "prob," "act" and then slashed a line across the paper in red and wrote, also in red, "Cautious people, the British." I know this because when Dad died, Admiral Dalrymple-Hamilton sent me this. He'd kept it all those years and said, "I thought you would enjoy having this." I have shown it to hundreds of people since. The pay of an acting lieutenant then was $54 per month, whereas in the U.S. Navy it was $260. There were some advantages, however. You went everywhere in a car that had a very distinctive red nose and red stern. You couldn't walk into a pub and pay for a drink. I would start talking to people and they would learn I was an American and boy, the place was mine.

Then I had one last mine to do. We weren't sure whether it was a mine or a bomb, in southwest England. They had stopped the blitz but still made an occasional flight over. It was a brand-new gadget, what we later called a top-hat mine, or more officially a george-type mine. I was sent down to take care of it, made sketches and everything like that, and then went back and told the unexploded bomb committee all the details. A navy lieutenant commander was the guiding light of this committee. He had been the British amateur chess champion and his mind worked perfectly in dealing with mines of this sort.

I explained that I could find no fuse whatsoever but there was something that looked sort of like a top hat, bolted on to the rear of the bomb or mine. It was about one thousand kilos and the circumference would be no more than thirty-six inches.

I was told to go back and go down the hole, which was about thirty feet deep, and unscrew this top hat—unscrew the twelve bolts—lift it off carefully, and snip every wire I could find, and to do this in absolute darkness; then come out and leave it alone for the following day (or however many days) until there was a bright sunny day. Then go back and defuse it, the idea being they had been looking for the Germans to use a photoelectric booby trap and they were sure that was what this was. And it was! It was set so that, had we taken the top hat off with any daylight it would have set the bomb or mine off.

The interesting thing to me was that the U.S. Navy had several officers who were in the United Kingdom for several months at a time. They were here because they were setting up the U.S. Mine Disposal School and were drawing on the experience gained by the British. All three of these men had been friends of mine at the Naval Academy. Anyway, Moe Archer, one of them, got permission to join me on this expedition provided that he did not go near the bomb or mine while I was working on it. Well, Moe had a cold, so that while I was unscrewing these bolts all of a sudden I heard a cough just above me. There was Moe Archer coming down. So I climbed up. We were still working on the no-noise possibility of an acoustic mine, and I got him away from the hole and whispered to him, "You have to go back." Moe's argument was: "Now, look, Draper, if it doesn't go off we're perfectly all right and no one will know the difference. If it does go off, neither of us is going to get court-martialed." Well, I couldn't get him away so I let him come on down. He had brought a wrench with him and he helped me.

Of course I wore one of these phones, as I always did with anything other than very routine operations—a phone connected with somebody at a safe distance—and I would say, "I'm now about to unscrew nut number three a quarter of a turn to the right (or left—left actually in most cases), then another quarter of a turn." Not that you expected anything to happen but if anything did happen there's no point in the next guy making the same mistake.

Well, I found the wires I had been told about—there were ten or twelve, I guess—and I dealt with them very, very carefully, very gently, feeling around, coming across a wire and snipping it. I distinctly remember that in at least two cases I cut a wire twice. When I came to take the top hat off, it was heavy and very awkward, particularly down in that hole. It was far easier for the two of us to do this than one. Of course I should never have let Moe do it, but I could have spent the whole night arguing with Moe Archer, whom I'd known for many, many years.

Then we took all kinds of pictures and we took the fuses out for they could be seen then, and brought it all back to London for the experts to have fun with. By this time sunlight had no effect on it for it was wired with an external wire and connected with a lens externally—I mean external to the bomb body but inside the top hat so that by snipping it we made it inoperative.

This was the real end of the blitz on England with bombs and mines. The next was with V-1 and V-2 and I'm not sure how this fitted in with the missile situation.

It was a wonderful period to be doing what I was doing because I was constantly in an area that had been very badly hit. Churchill's phrase "their finest hour" was so conspicuous in a blitzed area. It was amazing how the people reacted. When Churchill would give a speech on the radio I always went to a local pub to listen to it and watch the expressions of the people in the pub when Churchill was speaking. In a very different way, but the same in quality he had the people in that country in the palm of his hand the way Hitler did his people. But as I say, it was different—different as night and day.

I saw Mr. Churchill one time when he reviewed the mine disposal group. He had of course been briefed by aides so he came to me. He knew I was an American and said, "How did you happen to join our navy?" This was difficult because I had to say, "Well, sir, after I got out of prison camp—" and he, "Why did you join the French Army?" He actually spent ten or fifteen minutes with me and that was a very long time.

To continue this story, I was very interested later when Dad was head of the Allied Antisubmarine Board set up by Churchill and Roosevelt. When Dad had lunch with Churchill after briefing him on the work of the board, Churchill said, "Tell me, Admiral, how did you feel about your son doing mine disposal work over here in England?" So his aides had briefed him again; good aides are a great help.

Well, in the early fall of 1941 I was given thirty days leave by the Admiralty and very generously, too, because the thirty days would start and end in Halifax rather than in England. I was sent home on the Canadian DD *Assiniboine*.

Of course I was not going home to transfer to the U.S. Navy. My father wanted me very much to do so but I was absolutely convinced— very, very wrongly because this was only a month and a half before Pearl Harbor—that we were never going to get into the war. So I felt that staying in England I would be doing something useful and if I transferred to the U.S. Navy I didn't see that it would be as useful.

But soon I got a call to see Admiral Blandy, head of the Bureau of Ordnance, and he tried to convince me I should transfer back to the U.S. Navy. On my second call on him—at his command—he showed me two dispatches from the U.S. Navy and the Admiralty, one asking them to release me from the British navy and the second a reply from the Admiralty in which they seemed quite happy to have me transferred. The fact that I was trained in bomb disposal work was a factor. Dad swore that he did not participate in any of this though I've always suspected him of it. It's probably the only case I can think of where I have not been completely confident in what my father told me.

Shortly I was marched down to Admiral Nimitz's office in the Bureau of Navigation. My rank in the Royal Navy at that point was lieutenant. Nimitz said, "Our present rules are that you would come in as a junior lieutenant." And I said, "Sir, I'd prefer not to be demoted." And he said to the captain present, "I don't see why he should be." There was some further conversation with the captain present and finally Nimitz said:

"Now we have a new rule. Officers in the British navy transferring to our navy may keep their rank." That turned out to be very important because it put me with year group 35. If I had gone back as a junior lieutenant I would not have asked for transfer to regular navy status after World War II. In any case I was to be desperately in need of that extra half-stripe very soon. For I was given the job of starting the bomb disposal school. Blandy wanted a bomb disposal school as quickly as possible. And starting a bomb disposal school in Washington, even with two full stripes, a lieutenant had problems. The disadvantages of junior rank in starting a navy organization are quite large.

It seems appropriate to include in this volume two selections from oral histories that deal with aircraft production and the problems of allocation and distribution, especially in the U.S. Navy. The reader will also find background information that explains the great success that finally led Secretary of the Navy James Forrestal to tell some prominent men in the manufacturing business in 1945: "You fellows are swamping us with your production. Engines, propellers, and airplanes are running out of our ears. The time has come to slow down." Two men prominently involved during World War II with aircraft, their production and allocation, are Commander Eugene Wilson and Admiral George Anderson. Biographies of these men precede their oral history selections.

Aircraft production came out of World War I as a struggling infant. It was Admiral Mahan, the great naval historian, who first made known to the world the decisive influence of sea power on history. It took two world wars to make clear a decisive parallel view of air power, not only on the sea but on the land and in the commercial skies of the world.

When aviation emerged from World War I, it was in a fragile state. Yet a small group of naval enthusiasts began to build industrial plants for manufacturing airplanes. They had vision. And they derived great support from the recommendations of the Morrow board, a group of men authorized by President Coolidge to study the aircraft industry and make proposals for its development in preparation for another emergency if ever that occurred. Thoughts about military preparation of any kind were at rock bottom in the decades after World War I. Pacifism and depression were major deterrents. Yet in spite of the currents against it, Carl Vinson, the aggressive chairman of the House Naval Affairs Committee, secured the passage of the Air Corps Act of 1926. This was followed by timely recommendations of Admiral Moffett, the venerable chief of the navy's Bureau of Aeronautics. Out of that act came legislation that provided for a five-year program for naval aviation. The army quickly followed suit, and the Post Office Department stepped in and inaugurated a program for contracting the delivery of mail by air, thus giving a real spurt to commercial aviation.

In the favorable climate that prevailed from these several developments, American aviation attained world leadership, which it held until the airmail contracts were suddenly cancelled by the postmaster general in the early days of the Roosevelt presidency. The record shows that in that action American aviation received a body blow from which it was slow to recover.

We find an illustration of that state in the record of Pratt and Whitney, the great airplane plant in Hartford, Connecticut. By 1939 their engine production had reached the end of the rope because of lack of work. They began first by laying off a large percentage of their highly skilled employees whom they had trained over the years. They were rescued, almost miraculously, as were others of the industry, by the desperate orders for aircraft from abroad—from England, France, and the Netherlands.

Admiral George Anderson, in the excerpt from his interviews, calls the condition of the aircraft industry in the spring of 1940 "grossly inadequate." In his valuable record of Roosevelt and Hopkins in their war years in the White House, Robert Sherwood describes the situation: "During the month of July 1941 when Hopkins was visiting London and Moscow and learning so much about the importance of bombing Germany the production of our four engined bombers in the U.S. achieved a total of two. The hopefully scheduled total for the five months of 1941 remaining was only 213."*

The attack on Pearl Harbor in December 1941 brought an immediate reaction from the entire industrial sector in the country. It was followed at once by the president's call for an almost unbelievable quota of fifty thousand airplanes. After the immediate shock of that call the aircraft industry buckled down to a stupendous effort.

Harry Hopkins confided in a friend just a short time before the Pearl Harbor attack: "I don't think that we can ever lick Hitler with a lend-lease program. Unfortunately it is going to take much more than that." Robert Sherwood, the man who knew the mind of Hopkins and the thinking in the White House, observed: "Those remarks of Hopkins were obviously not a complete statement of his feelings. He knew we could not have even an adequate production program until the automobile industry could be converted from a peace time basis to a war time one. Until the American people as a whole realized that production was not merely a matter of aid to foreigners, however deserving they might be, but a matter of life and death for their own sons."†

*Robert E. Sherwood, *Roosevelt and Hopkins: An Intimate History* (New York: Harper & Brothers), 410.
†Ibid., 410.

Of course there was much truth in that prediction. We see in the excerpt from the Wilson memoir following that the automotive industry was quickly involved once William Knudsen took over the Office of War Production in Washington. He saw at once that Henry Ford was persuaded to turn to the production of airplanes and General Motors followed shortly with their Buick and Chevrolet components. The spigots were opened and the flow continued unabated until the United States truly became the "arsenal of democracy." According to Wilson, an aircraft official described it this way: "The industry has been blown up like a balloon. Our present output (1945) is all out of proportion to our own meager resources." That of course led to other problems for the aircraft industry when the war was over—problems not unlike those after World War I, when surpluses had to be liquidated. Yet in this instance the airplane had become essential to modern life and the adjustment less painful.

A WONDER WORKER AND THE FIFTY-THOUSAND-PLANE PROGRAM

COMMANDER EUGENE EDWARD WILSON

COURTESY JOHN MONSARRAT

EUGENE EDWARD WILSON was born in Dayton, Washington, on 21 August 1887. He entered the U.S. Naval Academy in 1904, graduating in 1908. In 1913, while in command of the USS *Truxton,* Commander Wilson was appointed to the Navy Postgraduate school and received an M.A. in engineering from Columbia University. There he was profoundly influenced by Dr. Charles E. Lucke, an advocate of the social responsibilities of the engineering profession. In 1924 he was selected by Admiral William A. Moffett as chief of the Engine Section of the Navy Bureau of Aeronautics. Wilson became a strong supporter of the Moffett doctrine of employing air forces from mobile bases. At times he also served the admiral as a ghost writer for his speeches and articles.

In 1929 Wilson resigned from the navy with the rank of commander and in 1930 assumed the post of president of Hamilton-Standard Propeller Corporation, a subsidiary of United Aircraft and Transport Corporation. That same year he became president of Sikorsky Aviation and Transport Corporation. The following year he also became president of Chance Vought Corporation, holding these three presidencies simultaneously for a time. In 1940 he assumed the presidency of United Aircraft Corporation.

In 1943, Under Secretary of the Navy James Forrestal requested Wilson's help in obtaining the aircraft manufacturing industry's cooperation in the formulation of postwar aviation policy. As a result Wilson accepted the chairmanship of the Board of Governors of the Aeronautical Chamber of Commerce. This involved his major attention to general aeronautical industry affairs and caused him to step down from the position of president of the United Aircraft Corporation to that of vice chairman in order to free himself for more time with the Aeronautical Chamber of Commerce. In 1946 Wilson severed all of his business connections.

The last twenty-five years of his life he devoted to writing and publishing a number of books on aeronautics. He wrote some poetry and produced several motion pictures dealing largely with environmental subjects. Much of his time in those years was spent with his wife, Genevieve, on their handsome yacht, the *Salar IV.* This became a necessity, he once told this editor, because it was more beneficial to his wife's health to live on the water. The yacht was fully equipped and staffed, and the couple migrated from Essex, Connecticut, in summer to Annapolis, Maryland, in the fall and Hobe Sound, Florida, in the winter.

Wilson died in Hartford, Connecticut, on 10 July 1974.

When the United States became actively involved in World War I on 7 April 1917 the nation was almost wholly unprepared. Perhaps it was the least prepared in the field of aeronautics. There were no manufacturing facilities, nor even designs of airplanes or engines to go into production. We were involved in that war for only eighteen months but during that time industry performance was remarkable. Yet in terms of aircraft contribution it was a failure as one looks back on it.

Immediately after the end of World War I there was a noticeable revulsion in the United States—and indeed in the Western world—against anything military. The war, as the slogans said, was "a war to end all wars" and consequently few people were interested in the subject of national defense. Fortunately there was a small group of men within the aircraft industry who determined to prevent a recurrence of unpreparedness in case of another war. They were led by Frederick B. Rentschler. They organized a small engineering and manufacturing group called the Wright Aeronautical Corporation and developed it as the first company to produce good aircraft engines of American design. Later Rentschler came to Hartford, Connecticut, and established the Pratt and Whitney company with a small group of experienced men, and that became in time one of the largest aircraft engine manufacturing plants in the world.

The going was hard in spite of the enthusiasm and drive of this small group of aeronautically minded men. In the aftermath of war, as is usual,

73

a great amount of surplus war stocks swamped what little market there was. But they persevered and in 1926 they were rewarded, at least by hope of improvement.

Rentschler went to the secretary of war and secretary of navy and suggested they interest President Calvin Coolidge in the problem. The president responded by appointing an independent commission to look into the matter and come forth with recommendations he could act upon. The commission was headed by Dwight Morrow and was nonpolitical and nonpartisan. It included such men as Senator Hiram Bingham of Connecticut, a pilot himself; Carl Vinson of Georgia, the future chairman of the House Naval Affairs Committee; General MacArthur; and others. The secretary was Dr. William Duvand, a classmate of Admiral Mahan, who knew the whole background of military affairs.

The commission came out with a recommendation for a policy of integration in the form of an air program based on military, commercial, and naval aviation—a tripartite operation that would be cooperative and competitive and that led ultimately to Carl Vinson's Air Corps Act of 1926 and subsequent events that prepared the United States for World War II. Another recommendation was for the naming of three assistant secretaries for air—one for the War Department, one for the Navy Department and a third for the Commerce Department.

The Morrow board, after careful consideration and investigation, concluded that the development of a strong air force was vital to the national defense of the country; that a strong industry was a requirement of a strong air force; that this industry could be achieved only by a program of engineering development and expanding air power. The president accepted the report and put into being a five-year building program for the army and navy. This was carried out in spite of the cloud of pacifism that hung over the country in the decade of the 1930s and in spite of the worldwide depression that curtailed initiative. It had become an almost derisive term for anybody advocating national defense to be called a "merchant of death" or a "munitions racketeer." Yet, in the late 1930s, when there were signs of an emergency developing, a powerful nucleus became available for expansion.

In January 1939 we had concluded that we at Pratt and Whitney had reached the end of the rope; that there was no other recourse but to shut down the company for lack of work. We began by laying off 20 percent of our skilled engine employees whom we had trained over the years.

I should also add at this point that one of the basic principles we tried to establish back on the Morrow board was that a private aircraft manufacturing industry had to be in the forefront of technological development and capable of rapid expansion in time of war. We at United and Pratt and Whitney were really implementing that portion of the Morrow board recommendations when we actually organized in advance our own planning operation.* We included in that planning such problems as: Where could we locate new facilities? To what extent could we expand our own facilities without overstress? What type of building, what type of equipment, the architects, and more important, the source of supply of materials and partly finished or finished parts? In United Aircraft, from the very beginning, thanks to the wisdom of Fred Rentschler, we had never had any intention of manufacturing any entire product in our own plant. The plan was originally designed to provide for the production of major parts by specialists in that field. Whenever it came to matters involving steel forgings or aluminum forgings we looked to plants that could manufacture them. In some cases the president of a given company was a director of United Aircraft.

But at that time the situation in Europe deteriorated. France was utterly unprepared for war and that of course was an invitation for Hitler to invade. The reason was not only the unstable political situation in France but also socialism had moved in and taken over the French aircraft industry. That industry was practically nationalized and then all the planning went for naught and the French air corps rapidly deteriorated. In 1939 they were utterly unprepared for war.

To a lesser degree in England they were in much the same situation. There were a few saving graces in their situation, however. De Havilland Aircraft was still operating as a private venture but the rest of British aviation had been taken over by the Royal Aeronautical establishment and was operated by the government.

Then things began to get worse and worse for the industry in the United States. Hap Arnold and others went to the House Naval Affairs Committee, chaired by Carl Vinson, who had been the father to the long-term program that had brought the aircraft industry to a certain position by 1939. He [Arnold] urged the House to pass legislation to provide for the procurement of enough aircraft engines and aircraft for the different factories to at least keep them alive—keep the blood flowing. So it happened that appropriations were provided. That was most unusual because at that time most surplus funds were going to the WPA—the shovels and the leaf raking—and not much attention was given to the monies for the very equipment that would be necessary to deter a war, much less fight one. Token orders were then given to United, Pratt and Whitney, to Wright Aeronautical, to Douglas, and others just to try and keep us alive until something could happen.

*United Aircraft was the parent company for various units that produced aircraft engines and specific parts; Pratt and Whitney, for example, made airplane engines. Wilson's oral history indicates the interlocking relationship of the various entities under the United Aircraft umbrella.

Then something did happen for our company. A new situation appeared on the horizon. Jean Monnet, who later became the creator of the Common Market, came on the scene. He was a very patriotic Frenchman and at this crucial moment tried to take a last stand to try and save France in her crisis. He was very highly regarded in New York financial circles. The next thing we knew, Henry Morgenthau, the secretary of the treasury, summoned Don Brown, our Pratt and Whitney Aircraft president, and Guy Vaughn of Curtiss-Wright to Washington for a conference in connection with a contract to build engines and aircraft for the French government. Now that government was practically bankrupt, but this was some kind of a bank credit that had been established under which they were to buy American aircraft and American engines in defense against Hitler. Our arms embargo was still in effect and yet the secretary of the treasury was in the act of negotiating with American manufacturers for the sale of aircraft and aircraft engines to the French. Under the law, if Hitler wanted to stop the delivery all he had to do was to declare war on the French and make them combatants—and we would be prohibited from delivering the goods.

By dint of a very great effort on the part of all concerned, we finally emerged with a contract with the French government, not only for the construction of a lot of engines, which were to go into airplanes that were being bought from American airplane companies, but also for the construction of a brand-new factory.

Now the controlling factor in all of this is, the last thing we wanted was more factories. We had a good factory with plenty of facilities for any ordinary requirements. Not only that, for years we had been overburdened with excess facilities. That was true of the whole aircraft industry. All these facilities sat there and ate their heads off, because you had to charge depreciation against them and you didn't get any good out of them. No matter how good a job you did with your operating plant you had a great burden in losses. We'd had a terrific time trying to liquidate those excess surplus World War I facilities. So we were gun-shy on additional facilities, especially since this was the time just before the so-called phony war and nobody was sure that a real conflict would break out. To us the idea of going out and building tremendous new facilities just did not make any sense.

So United took the position that we had no funds of our own. The American banking interests might have been willing to lend us funds but there was no evidence that they would. We insisted that if the French government wanted us to build a factory—an eight-million-dollar factory—the funds would have to be advanced for that by the French government. But that was contrary to French law; for them the idea of putting government capital investments into a foreign country didn't make sense. The other provision was that in the event nothing happened, that factory would become the property of United Aircraft at the end of the operation. Well, as I say, a lot of hard work went into this deal, but it was finally settled.

Fortunately, having planned for that sort of thing, we had the drawings all made. All we had to do was move the cars off the parking lot and put the bulldozers in there, and almost within hours we were under way, building a new factory that was bigger than the one we had, for the French government. In the meantime we had all the orders and everything made out to the different machine tool suppliers for the tools for the work. These suppliers were made aware of what we were doing and they were prepared to move in. Since our own plant was still in operation we just started assembling and shipping at once under the terms of the French contract and we thus kept the pipeline going until we got the new factory in operation. There is a lot more to the story than just that because you can imagine the detail of building a new plant and bringing in new tools and getting new sources of supply.

About that time Don Brown fell ill and was taken to the hospital, where he died. With that event I fell heir to the presidency of the company. By that time the war was on and the government just violated its own Arms Embargo Act and continued to ship regardless of the provisions of the act. You can appreciate the difficulties of making judgments and plans under a phony situation like that where a law on the statute books that contains penalties for you is violated by the very government that is negotiating the contract with you. You knew that if anything developed politically you'd be charged with being a "warmonger" and you'd be holding the sack. The encouragement to deal with that sort of thing was at a minimum at that time.

We no sooner got the French job going along when—wham!—who should arrive on the scene but Sir Henry Self, who was a civil servant in the Air Ministry in England. Now, Sir Henry Self was a typical civil servant, used to kicking the British aircraft industry around over there, because private enterprise had practically disappeared in the aircraft industry. He came over with a very haughty mien, and he sat down with Secretary Morgenthau to negotiate the construction of a British factory.

At the same time there arrived an envoy from France whose name was Rene Pleven. He was one of the participants in the debacle that led to French decline. Well these two characters came in with a new attitude. They thought we were begging for business. We had been rejecting business and we didn't want any more than we had. We'd taken more than we wanted in the French decision. So we sat down and agreed in our company that we couldn't take any more business and overload ourselves.

Well, Henry Self made up his mind he was going to show the United

States how things were done in good old England, and we immediately got our backs up on him. Rene Pleven, on the other hand, was one of those slick customers, and he took the position that the contract that had been negotiated by Colonel Jacquin was a fraud—that we had overcharged him and that he was just a dumb soldier. The truth of the matter was that the contract had been negotiated in the Treasury Department, with Captain Harry Collins of the navy sitting in. Collins was the head of procurement in the Treasury Department and a very, very able man. Harry Collins and Don Brown, the president of Pratt and Whitney, and Colonel Jacquin had negotiated as fine an instrument of negotiations as I'd ever seen.

Obviously there were some politics in this, because Pleven and Jacquin were apparently on different sides of the French coin—if you could call it a coin. I guess it had more facets than that. What Pleven was trying to do was to put Jacquin in the hole. We made up our minds at United Aircraft that he'd been square with us and we were going to stand by him. By this time Don had died and I had been dragged into the negotiations. So when we were called down to the Treasury Department, in the first meeting with Mr. Morgenthau in the chair and Harry Collins nearby, Mr. Rene Pleven on one side and Sir Henry Self on the other side, we had our decision. Mr. Morgenthau stated the case. Guy Vaughn was there for Curtiss-Wright and he said, "What is your attitude on that?"—the general point being that the prices that we'd got from the French government were way too high and the price would have to come down and deliveries up.

I said: "United Aircraft has reached the decision that we are not interested in expanding our operations under any circumstances, and least of all will we accept any kind of order that is without some provision for accelerated amortization. Our procedure would be to insist that we be able to write off the cost of this factory over the shipments of the first contract." In other words, the first contract that was made with the British would cover not only the cost of the engines but the cost of the facility, so that when we were through that was written off. It was on nobody's books and it wasn't worth anything. Well, that was of course totally unacceptable to stuffy old Sir Henry Self, and we didn't care because we didn't want any part of it. At that point a little interruption occurred when Carleton Ward, who was representing Pratt and Whitney, interrupted and thought he would undercut the head office negotiations and take charge himself. The matter died right there.

I came back to Hartford to get busy on the French contracts. We were at home one evening when the telephone rang and the watchman at the factory said: "Mr. Secretary Morgenthau has arrived in his airplane from Cape Cod and wants to see you." I jumped in the car and whisked over to the factory. At that time the French plant was under way. Here was a great new facility. The brick and mortar were complete, the machine tools were coming in, the operation was moving. We'd only been at it at that time, I think, about four or five months, and certain of the operations were already under way. That was due to our advance planning and thanks to the planning organization we'd created beforehand.

I took Mr. Morgenthau around to show him this plant. He was visibly surprised that we'd gotten this far. Then when we got into my office he said: "Well, I'm up here in connection with this British contract. It's very important that you take this contract. We want you not to delay any longer." I said: "I'm sorry, Mr. Morgenthau." (I had already thought this little speech out on the drive over to the factory.) I said: "I'm awfully sorry, but we're totally unable to take that. We are a company that's already operating far beyond our capabilities with respect to working capital, with respect to facilities, or any of these other things, and we do have a sense of responsibility to our stockholders and to our own country. We are utterly unwilling to take this contract unless you can arrange to alter the provisions in such a way that we could write this facility off the books over the shipments comprising the first contract." Well, when Mr. Morgenthau saw we were adamant he said, "All right." Since he was Secretary of the Treasury I thought of course he could do this. He said: "All right, I'll promise that."

So we accepted the order and turned to and started to build a new addition for the British, which was bigger than the French addition and about half again as big as our own original plant. In any event, we were moving, and that was another one of those gay operations in which you moved the parking lot back, you put the bulldozers in, you dug out the basement. These contractors who had been putting up the other factory and the architects who'd done the other thing—they just put in some more elements of the same thing. The machine tool operators extended their production line, and we were going like a house afire. The result was that within nine months of breaking ground we were in full production. We did it in the French factory, we did it in the English factory, and then a little later in the American factory, which was as big as all the rest of them put together. That was the kind of expansion we did right there at Hartford.

Now I want to introduce another part of the story that deals with our particular problems with aircraft production at our plants, new and old, in the Hartford area.

When the president announced the fifty-thousand-plane program in January 1942 he knew, I guess—at least we knew—that we were in a box. The program was utterly and completely fantastic. Even the army and the navy people who were responsible for this sort of thing called it "the numbers racket." But if we refused to undertake that program and to promise to deliver those aircraft—that became the basis for a takeover by the U.S. government. At that time the whole tactics of it devolved on me; I had to do the operations in Washington.

So we couldn't refuse. I did the next best thing and agreed that we would accept this fifty-thousand-plane schedule but under three conditions. First, that Pratt and Whitney and Wright Aeronautical, which were under both the army and navy, would be consolidated under one or the other. I expressed no preference. I didn't have to. I knew the navy would sing out for Pratt and Whitney. But we had to have one company, one boss. This was so because the biggest problem we had when it came to deliveries was to get by army and navy inspectors who were competing with each other to see who could be the snottiest and who could reject the most goods on all kinds of pretenses.

The second thing we had to insist on was that whatever specification we manufactured—each type of engine, each class of engine—would have to be standardized. We could not deliver engines to specifications promulgated by the many countries for whom we were building engines. They had to take the same auxiliaries and to be a complete package. That was quite a problem because the army and navy couldn't even agree on some of the accessories of these things. Each service preferred this or the other for obscure reasons. But we got that agreement.

Then I said: "We must insist that the whole philosophy of inspection be altered: that the inspection in wartime must have regard for the urgency of delivery and be relevant to conformance with detailed specifications, many of which have no real fundamental merit."

Now that really was trouble and for a long time they were unwilling to agree to that. I said, "All right, United Aircraft's management cannot risk the stockholders' equity on accepting a set of requirements that are well known to be impossible in the beginning and after failing in them, being taken over by the government." So finally our third condition was agreed to.

In the meantime the decision with respect to consolidating the engine companies under one administration came to the desk of Frank Knox, the secretary of the navy. When I put the proposal up to the Navy Department it went through Admiral J. H. Towers, the chief of the Bureau of Aeronautics. Towers had as assistant, Gus Reed of the Naval Reserve. It seemed that Secretary Knox had balked at the proposal for the consolidation of the aircraft companies and probably because of orders from upstairs. Immediately we were in trouble, so Jack Towers, Gus Reed, and I went to Knox's office together to sell this idea. We met with the question of legality of the operation. As luck would have it the chief of the Judge Advocate's office was Admiral Woodson, an old friend, and he was called in. After some discussion the secretary finally gave in and it was agreed that Pratt and

Whitney would belong to the navy and Wright Aeronautical to the army. Without that arrangement we would have been beaten from the beginning. After that particular situation was cleared we began to move, but even then we never got away from this inspection problem entirely.

When I went to Washington in order to negotiate the contract with the government I found myself sitting across the desk from Commander L. B. Richardson, who had been my assistant when I was chief of the aircraft branch of the Bureau of Aeronautics. He was now the procurement officer.

Well, price was the important element and contract principles was the other important element. What was the basic principle? I stated it in the beginning. All of this was not just my opinion. It was the result of conferences with Rentschler and others before I left for Washington. In our meetings we had agreed upon what would be United's program. Then Rentschler wrote the memorandum for it and I took it to Washington.

We at United agreed to this: 1. Under no circumstances can the army or the navy accept any slightest inference that there has been any profiteering in connection with this war contract. We must avoid that at all cost. Now out of that principle comes this principle: 2. These contracts cannot be a cost-plus basis for obvious reasons. That means there must be a fixed price. "Now, neither you nor I," I told Richardson, "can arrive at that. We can draw our curves and we can get an estimate but not within the limits that are necessary to be sure that we do not open ourselves ever to any criticism of having profits."

This was all a public relations move having to do with the animosity that the government had shown against us in the airmail contracts. We had to do this, and in doing this we were only doing what Fred Rentschler had done back in the first Wasp contract, when he came to Washington to me and said: "We've made too much money on this contract, what do we do?"* My advice was: "You are going to have to relinquish the excess profit but not after you've once had it in your fingers—*before* it ever happens." So I said to Richardson: "We have agreed to this among ourselves. You fix the price. As far as I'm concerned the only thing I can do is give you my opinion. You fix the price. We will undertake then, either in writing or any other way, formally or publicly, to accept a fixed price contract at that price and to accept responsibility in case of any loss. In case of any incipient excessive profit, we will undertake to reduce the invoice price in advance of the shipment of the goods, to the point where we will never earn any excess profit."

Well, Richardson nearly fell over because that took him off the hook

*The Wasp was an early aircraft engine.

and everybody else. It was the basis on which we operated. Back of it was our real concern for the shop. With a fifty-thousand-airplane program if we ever got behind on production, Walter Reuther and some of his people were indeed anxious to take over the factories. They thought that if it was a government-operated show they would not have any trouble with private enterprise. They were waiting. So we were fighting. It was a matter of life or death, of survival, for us.

The essence of the whole thing then is that we tried to introduce new standards of social justice to the industrial organization—at the same time never missing sight of the fact that we were in a competitive process, wherein profit and loss were the key to our survival. In other words, enlightened self-interest motivated this whole leadership philosophy.

Yet, that wasn't enough. When the demands kept increasing, it was then that we went to Washington to see Bill Knudsen. The pressures were on us to build another factory which we were to manage in some other part of the country, having reached the capacity of our local facilities. We refused point-blank to undertake any bigger job than our management could handle. We were frank to say: "We've got our hands full on this. All you've got to do is to overload us with the creation of some facility of this kind in Columbus, Ohio, or St. Louis, and you'll break down the whole organization and we'll collapse." We believed that and I think it would have happened. Yet we knew that was not a good argument because there were some of them who were hoping we would break down. Any failure on our part would immediately justify the government moving in and taking over. Then the government would only be responsible to itself for deliveries.

It was quite a situation and finally, when the fifty-thousand-plane program came, I was sitting in my office in Hartford one day when Mrs. Dexter said, "Secretary Morgenthau's on the wire." I took the call and he said: "Could you come to supper at my house tomorrow night at 7 o'clock?" "Yes, sir," I said. He said, "Would you mind if I had a competitor there?" "Certainly not, but who?" "Guy W. Vaughn of Curtiss-Wright." "Well," I said, "he is one of my closest personal friends. I'll see you Sunday."

So I flew down to Washington and met Guy at the Carleton Hotel. I greeted him by saying, "What is going on here?" He said: "I've talked with Tommy the Cork (Thomas G. Corcoran, who was one of the New Deal boys). He tells me that the play is that the Treasury Department is going to take over all this airplane procurement for the fifty-thousand-plane program and it will be handled through the procurement office of the treasury, where Harry Collins is the head."

Well, the truth was that Harry Collins had been sent over by the paymaster general of the navy originally to be sure the treasury confined itself to those things that a central procurement agency could do—certainly not the production of aircraft that had to go through the armed services where they already had highly trained men and facilities for that purpose. This meeting with the secretary was intended to get us to agree to give them a license to build our engines in whatever facilities they might select. It was obvious that the chief requirement for these facilities was that they should be politically well located. They weren't inspired by any of the considerations that had to do with production as we were and Wright Aeronautical was.

Then Guy and I went over to supper with Mr. Morgenthau. He greeted us and then sat at a little side table with us and two or three other people whom I did not know. Obviously it was distasteful for him to sit down with such "warmongers" and "munitions racketeers," but he made the best of it and endeavored to go through with it. Finally he announced that "We're going to procure all these engines through the Treasury Department and we will insist that you license us to manufacture your engines." He then turned to Guy: "What about you, Mr. Vaughn?" Guy said, "We won't license; we'll fight you." Then Morgenthau turned to me: "What about you, Mr. Wilson?" I said, "We'll license," and he replied, "What's the catch to it?"

The truth was that under the contracts we had with the army and the navy, they had a perfect right to take the license. It was a part of the contracts. All they had to do was to exercise this particular option and they could have anybody build the engines—but the treasury didn't know that. So I said, "We'll agree to license," and Morgenthau said, "What will it cost?" My reply was, "A dollar an engine."

"Well," said he, "there must be some catch to it." And I said, "There is. The catch is that we must have the authority over who will build these engines. If we are going to accept the responsibility for the performance of those engines we will insist on the authority and control over the agencies that will manufacture our product." And Morgenthau replied: "That doesn't make very much sense. What do you mean, this responsibility?" And my reply: "Well, Mr. Secretary, as a pilot myself I naturally have a great sense of responsibility for the people who get killed with these engines. They have a habit of stopping at the wrong time. Now if you want to accept responsibility for all these kids that get killed because some of these government-manufactured engines break down, why you can have it. We'd just be delighted to see you take that over." You should have seen the secretary back-pedal out of there. He couldn't get out fast enough.

The next morning the Treasury Department thought they had better bring somebody in who knew something about the aircraft industry, somebody to counsel the treasury. Harry Collins phoned me and asked me about it. I named George Meade, a member of the National Advisory Committee for Aeronautics and a former chief engineer of Pratt and Whitney. I suggested to Collins—here is a man who knows the aircraft industry like nobody else. So the treasury took him on in an advisory capacity, and it didn't take George Meade more than about thirty seconds to tell the secretary what he wanted to hear: that he'd better get out of this procurement business as fast as he could in the Treasury Department and turn it back to the armed forces, who had the organization and the background and the familiarity with the whole thing. So it was then turned back to the army and the navy.

Well, the army and the navy hadn't worried too much about the fifty-thousand-plane program as long as the treasury was doing it, but when it became their job they were frank to say that they couldn't even think in those numbers, that they couldn't imagine needing that many airplanes. They had no plans for anything of that sort nor could they conceive of any use for that number.

In the meantime, Bill Knudsen had been appointed head of the War Production Board with Sidney Hillman as his "proconsul." Then George Meade was appointed as an assistant to Bill Knudsen. That was wonderful, because Bill Knudsen was a man whom we greatly admired—a manufacturer, a rugged, substantial character and a great patriot.

Then we from the aircraft industry were called upon. We sat there in a meeting which consisted of Knudsen and Meade, also a general from McCook Field who was in charge of this type of thing at the time and also somebody from the Navy Department. The problem before them was to get this procurement back in the hands of the armed forces who were competent to take care of it. The man from Wright Field, George Brett, was also there. He was very annoyed that they should even talk in terms of fifty thousand planes and was frank to say that the whole thing was nothing but a numbers racket and furthermore it was interfering with his golf game, and he departed.

In the meantime Fred Rentschler had sat down with Knudsen. They spoke the same language. Fred pointed out that we had gone ahead with the French addition and the British addition, and the American addition was in the immediate future. "Now," said Fred to Knudsen, "if you're going to need as many engines as you are talking about, then we've got to bring in the automotive industry." Knudsen said, "Now, who do you mean by the automotive industry?" "Henry Ford" was of course the reply. Knudsen had worked for Henry Ford and also had come down to Washington from the presidency of General Motors. So Knudsen said: "Don't you know what Mr. Ford has said—that he wouldn't do any war business if it was the last thing he did?" "Yes," said Fred Rentschler, "but you and George Meade are the only two people who can persuade him that this is his duty."

Poor old Bill sighed, but he and George Meade did go out to Detroit, and the next thing you know Henry Ford did agree to come in. His son Edsel was the nominal president of Ford Motor at the time but the actual kingpin was Charles E. Sorensen. Edsel and Sorensen then selected some key men as people who might head up the Ford operation. They were sent down to us in Hartford and spent several weeks working with our foremen to analyze the problems of engine production and see whether they could handle it. Then Sorensen and Edsel came to see Fred Rentschler and me. Sorensen stayed with us at our house.

The next morning after they had consulted with their people we met in Fred Rentschler's office. There Edsel and Sorensen agreed that they could undertake this proposition. "We will go ahead under these conditions. We must have complete cooperation and vigorous assistance absolutely; we must have the presence in our factory of leading men from your organization who can pilot our group into this new endeavor. We can't see anything in here that we can't do from a mechanical standpoint, except we see a totally different philosophy of production. We are used to separate big specialized tools to do a certain individual job and you are using a machine-tooled job with interchangeable fixtures." Then they said, "We have to have access to all of your suppliers." We said, "We can help you there but our suppliers are presently all overloaded—also our subcontractors' suppliers. You are going to have to create new sources of supply, but we will make certain that our subcontractors and suppliers collaborate with your subcontractors and suppliers."

Then Fred said something they didn't take to heart: "We must impress upon you that this is a very different business from the automotive business in many ways, but principally it is different in this: that precision is the key to the whole operation, and precision is machine precision, not hand fitting and that sort of thing. Furthermore, cleanliness and care are absolute prerequisites."

Well, they didn't take that into account, but they did move in. They got their operation going, but they couldn't get an engine past final test. They just had them all over the backyard, because they had neglected to take care of that meticulous detail that was essential to the aircraft industry. Our people went out and spent a couple weeks with them and put them back in order and then they were really going to town.

Then we moved out to General Motors, and there Buick was assigned to the job. Red Curtis was the president of Buick and he built a factory near Chicago in Hawthorne. I went out there once and dedicated the factory.

The next person who came in was George Mason of Nash Kelvinator. He was a good operator. He not only took on propellers but he took on Vought and Sikorsky. It was the refrigerator department that did a lot of this. He moved very ably in this direction and we had the closest relationships with that whole establishment.

Then as we moved along this requirement was made. They (the government officials) weren't satisfied with our progress. We were ordered to quit dragging our feet and go out and build a great big factory that was bigger than the whole of the East Hartford installation. This was to be in some place of our choosing. John Harner was manager of Pratt and Whitney at that time. He was a very able young man. He jumped into a company airplane and went on a tour, landing up in Kansas City. He reported to me: "There is a nice plot of ground down here south of Kansas City. I checked over all the other facilities. If we have to build this factory, this is the place to build it." Whereupon we moved into a completely new installation down there.

Well, they were forcing us to build a factory down there, and it must have been politically inspired because it took us into the corn country and we had to train a bunch of farmers and make production workers out of them. It was all right under the conditions we imposed. I took the position that we had no facilities, no funds, no nothing to take on an operation of this kind; that the most we could offer would be a small nucleus of management group—an experienced group who could give direction to an operation of this kind and that the financing would have to be entirely governmental. It would have to place funds at the disposal of whoever was operating that facility to take care of working capital. And we had one requirement: we would accept no profit from this program *and no loss*. We didn't care anything about the no-profit; the thing we were concerned about was the no-loss. Under the profit control arrangement we had set up with the Navy Department to stabilize our net profit at the twelve million dollars we had earned the year before we went into the big war effort, that was the fixed figure. That profit was on the sale of aircraft to foreign countries, France and England. The twelve million earned that year was conscionable, whether a profit on sales or working capital, or whatever. That was an earned equity and was fair to our stockholders and fair to everybody concerned, so we stabilized it at that fixed figure.

Well, everybody thought that was kind of crazy, but it wasn't, because from that time on they started introducing complications in the form of renegotiation of contracts, excess profits taxes, etc. The purpose of those things was to impress the public with the fact that the administration was making certain that none of these munitions racketeers or merchants of death were going to cheat the people. They ended up by cheating themselves, because if you started off with a twelve million dollar net return—

worked out with consideration of our cash requirements and our forecast—and if labor moved in and under government support raised the wages all over the country, that didn't make any difference—it just increased the costs. We just started off with the net and we put the cost in and if the government added 50 or 75 percent profits tax on that, it just had to be added to the price. Every one of those punitive measures that they took against us ended up only in increasing the price. The result was that when we got through, it just meant that much money went through our hands long enough to give it back to the Treasury Department, and it just inflated the whole financial operation without changing anything.

It was a boomerang in this way, that the vagaries of the accounting system are such that on the twelve-million-dollar fixed earnings the bigger the volume the lower the percentage of profit. Now the more they put on excess profits taxes and punitive measures and increased wages on top of that, the bigger the sales price was and the lower the percentage of profit of sales. We came out then with a net profit of a half percent on a billion dollars' worth of business—those are just rough figures.

SAVVY PAYS OFF IN AIRCRAFT PROCUREMENT

ADMIRAL GEORGE W. ANDERSON, JR.

U.S. NAVY

GEORGE WHELAN ANDERSON, JR., was born on 15 December 1906 in Brooklyn, New York. He attended Brooklyn Preparatory School and entered the U.S. Naval Academy in 1923. He graduated and was commissioned an ensign on 2 June 1927. He remained at the academy for the short course in naval aviation and then joined the USS *Cincinnati,* where he served as junior officer until 1930. In that year he enrolled at the Naval Air Station in Pensacola, Florida, for flight training. He was designated a naval aviator in October 1930 and ordered to the Atlantic Fleet for duty in the aviation unit of the USS *Concord* and later the USS *Raleigh.*

Between 1933 and 1935 Anderson was assigned to the Flight Test Division of the Naval Air Station, Norfolk, Virginia. He then had duty afloat with Fighting Squadron Two, based on the USS *Lexington.* He followed with orders to report to the Newport News Shipbuilding and Dry Dock Company where the USS *Yorktown* was building. He joined that carrier on her commissioning on 30 September 1937. From the fall of 1939 until early 1940 he was attached to Patrol Squadron Forty-four, Patrol Wing Four, based at Seattle, Washington. Then he was assigned to the Plans Division, Bureau of Aeronautics in Washington, D.C., where he participated in the formulation of the American aircraft program for World War II. He was again on duty with the USS *Yorktown* in 1943 as navigator and tactical officer and saw action in the Pacific against Japanese forces in the air, at sea, and on shore from 31 August 1943 to 15 August 1945. From November 1943 to March 1944 he had duty as Plans Officer on the staff of Commander, Aircraft, U.S. Pacific Fleet. On 28 March 1944 he reported as assistant to the Deputy Commander in Chief, U.S. Pacific Fleet and Pacific Ocean Areas.

In June 1945 Anderson became aviation officer in the strategic plans section of the staff of Commander in Chief (COMINCH), U.S. Fleet, in Washington, D.C. This also involved duty as deputy navy planner on the Joint Planning Staff. In 1946 he was ordered to the Office of the Chief of Naval Operations, Navy Department, and appointed a member of the Permanent Joint Board of Defense for Canada–United States. He also served with the Joint War Plans Committee of the Joint Staff.

In 1948 Anderson returned to sea for a year in an antisubmarine carrier and then reported to the National War College in Washington, D.C., for a year of study. In July 1950 he joined the staff of the Commander, Sixth Fleet, as fleet operations officer. In December of the same year he joined the staff of SHAPE (Supreme Allied Command in Europe) and remained there until July 1952, when he took over command of the USS *Franklin D. Roosevelt*. He was detached from that aircraft carrier in June 1953 and reported for duty once again to the Navy Department in Washington. From 1953 to 1955 he served as special assistant to the chairman of the Joint Chiefs of Staff.

Admiral Anderson then held key posts in the three major theaters of the cold war. In the Pacific he commanded the patrol force off Formosa (1955–56) and served as chief of staff to the CinCPac Joint Staff (1956–57) during a period of tense relations with communist China. Promoted to vice admiral in May 1957 he was chief of staff to the Pacific commander (1956–57).

In the equally tense Middle East, Anderson temporarily, and at his own request, reverted in rank to rear admiral in order to command Carrier Division Six (1958–59) in the flagship USS *Saratoga* (CVA 60), which supported the Marine Corps landing in Lebanon in July 1958. Again as vice admiral he fleeted up to be Commander, Sixth Fleet, and Commander, Naval Striking and Support Forces, Southern Europe (1959–61).

Anderson's appointment as chief of naval operations for a term of two years with the rank of admiral was approved by the U.S. Senate on 29 June 1961. He was sworn in at the Naval Academy on 1 August. He climaxed his career by leading the navy in the thermonuclear arena, especially during the Cuban missile confrontation with the Soviet Union in October 1962. He was relieved of all active duty pending his retirement on 1 August 1963. President Kennedy named him ambassador to Portugal in 1963 and he served there with distinction until 1966. The admiral also served as president of the Naval Academy Alumni Association from 1971 to 1974. Currently he makes his home in Washington, D.C.

In the spring of 1940 I got orders to report to the Navy Department in the Plans Division of the Bureau of Aeronautics—in a key job for a younger officer, called programs and allocations, a job that justified the appropriations for airplanes and allocated and assigned where they would be bought. Admiral Ramsey was head of the Plans Division. It was for him I was going to work. Admiral John H. Towers was chief of the Bureau of Aeronautics; Ramsey, as head of the Plans Division, had responsibility for formulating the aircraft programs and then supervising, through the regular matériel divisions of the bureau, actual procurement. By tradition I accompanied the chief of the bureau to the Congress in the justifying of all the papers and had to appear with him regularly before the House Naval Affairs Committee and the Senate Naval Affairs Committee.

The aircraft requirement desk headed by A. B. Vosseller would specify the requirements in quality, depending on the types of aircraft that were available or recommended by the engineering division of the bureau. I would formulate the number that we needed and reconcile that with the possibility of the appropriations. The cost would be given to us, including the spare parts, and we would go up eventually to get the appropriations. Then with the approval of the chief we would decide the orders, and they would be contracted for by the regular divisions of the bureau.

Two weeks after I reported, the Germans went through the Low Countries and France. As a result the whole situation and attitude of the Congress as well as the president were stimulated, and great expansion in our planning took place. The status of the aviation program at this time was a 2,500-plane program and was being, with a laborious amount of red tape, processed through the system to be increased to a 3,000-plane program. Shortly after that sights were set higher, and it was made up to a 10,000-plane program; later on it went to 15,000 and then practically unlimited.

The next major development was a very secret mission which was sent over by the British with some outstanding officers to do planning with representatives of the Joint Board—Army-Navy Board. My boss, Ramsey, was one of the members of the board. Kelly Turner was another member. What they did was formulate a joint plan that was ultimately called Rainbow 5, which would delineate the major objectives of the U.S. and Great Britain in the event that the U.S. became involved in the war. It did envisage a war against Japan and the Axis Powers, and of course, the major determining decision was that the first objective was to win against the Axis Powers and we would take a strategic defensive against Japan. This was put into effect basically, but it was locked in a safe on the Sunday when Pearl Harbor occurred and they couldn't get the safe open until Monday. In this development of the program every airplane had to be earmarked for a specific spot. Normally you would buy 50 percent spare aircraft, replacement aircraft, and spare parts to take care of the airplanes for the first few years of their life.

We didn't have too many planes of the type we ultimately needed in the war under development. We had the Grumman fighters, we had the

Douglas dive bomber, we had a torpedo plane, and the principal emphasis was on patrol seaplanes—Catalinas, PBYs and the Martin PMs—the emphasis being on patrol rather than the bomber role. We had no land patrol planes and we more or less took (with great difficulty in obtaining deliveries) the same type of training planes that were being ordered by the Army Air Corps. Originally we had done our primary training in seaplanes but it became apparent, even at that time, that primary training could better and more economically be accomplished with great volume in land planes.

Also, we were buying convertible land planes/seaplanes that were used in the cruisers and the battleships. They were being built by Curtiss at the time—SOCs they were called (*S*cout-*O*bservation and *C* for Curtiss). The air corps was in a better position. They had a wider variety of airplanes potentially available: fighters, bombers, training planes, the SNJs and basic training planes, transport planes, the DC, and the DC-4 was under development. They had a wider range although they hadn't had sufficient money to do what was necessary to build up a good base. They had some pretty good thinking behind their programs.

Then we were learning lessons from the war in Europe of the need for armored seats, for self-sealing fuel tanks. The planes we had in service did not incorporate those features so it was necessary to get those adjusted. Of course one of the big lessons was that we had to have more armament, offensive armament, in all of our aircraft. This required our aircraft manufacturers to redesign the planes we had, and the Brewster fighter, for example, just did not measure up.

The aircraft industry at the time was grossly inadequate. It required a tremendous expansion, but this expansion was facilitated by the lend-lease program. Also, valid orders had been placed by the Netherlands. They had a very good aircraft program in which they had envisaged getting all these new and modern planes coordinated with a pilot-training program and sending them out to the East Indies.

We also were involved in trying to bail out the French. They had called President Roosevelt and he promised assistance. We were told to turn over fifty dive-bombers to them—Curtiss dive-bombers. To get them we had to take them from the naval reserve stations. The French sent over to Halifax the aircraft carrier *Bearn*. We called up naval reserve officers and had them fly the planes to some central point—I think Buffalo. There the pilots were demobilized, put on civilian suits, and continued the delivery to the *Bearn*. The U.S. Navy identification was eliminated in this process. This was being handled by Curtiss for us and the aircraft were delivered on board the *Bearn*. Unfortunately, by that time it was too late. The *Bearn* then went down to Martinique and the planes remained down there for most of the rest of the war.

We had another case where the Greeks were in dire straits. We had some new Grumman fighters about to be delivered to us where they were badly needed. We were directed to provide those to the Greeks. Grumman jumped in and translated the instruction books into Greek; the lettering on the panels and internal markings of devices were all in Greek. Those planes were sent over to the western desert where, of course, the British took over after Greece had fallen to the Nazis.

Apart from the program side of this desk in the bureau (and this involved the actual direction of procurement, the planning for procurement), the allocation side reposed on this little desk also with the assignment of all the aircraft in the navy and the naval reserve to ships and stations and squadrons that were training and about to be commissioned. A tremendous amount of work was focused in the particular section of the Plans Division which today is handled by dozens of people and supervised by all the echelons of the Department of Defense and the higher civilian echelons of the Navy Department. I suppose also the Bureau of the Budget and the General Accounting Office.

The next side of this period was the evolution of further planning with the British, initially under the lend-lease program and later of course during the war. They formed a joint aircraft committee and Admiral Towers was on it and General Arnold, head of the Army Air Corps. There were two major subcommittees: the allocations committee, which was to allocate not only the production and assignment of new aircraft—and inevitably the need to expand aircraft production. The other side was the standardization.

We had arrangements of course to expand the aircraft industry, which really got under way before Pearl Harbor. We reached a tremendous peak and acceleration right after Pearl Harbor, when they converted the automobile factories for engines and air frames.

When the attack occurred on Pearl Harbor I went down to the old Navy Department on Constitution Avenue. Everybody was sort of shocked; nobody knew what the whole impact of it was. Secretary Knox was going out to Pearl Harbor the next day and Admiral Towers told me: "You know more about the aircraft situation than anybody else in the navy. I want you to report to Admiral Stark [chief of naval operations] in the morning first thing and stay with him wherever he goes all during the day. Stay with him as long as you can help him." I did.

Later on that morning I accompanied Stark to the first meeting of the old Joint Board, Army and Navy. It included General Marshall and Admiral Stark. General Arnold was out of town. Tooey Spaatz was pinch-hitting for him. General Gerow was in charge of army plans, and Sherman Miles I think was intelligence. On the navy side were Admiral Horne, Admiral Towers, and Admiral Kelly Turner. There they discussed what the situation was, what they knew, what they didn't know, and their apprehension of the situation that might occur.

It was very apparent that the outstanding individual in the room from the standpoint of calmness and judgment was General Marshall, who had his feet right on the ground. From a standpoint of good common sense there was my own boss, Admiral Jack Towers, who was also a relatively unruffled individual. Of course Admiral Stark was quite shocked by the tremendous losses we had at Pearl Harbor and the concern of whether further raids might be made on Alaska or even on the West Coast. There were various reports of sightings of Japanese ships or submarines threatening our Pacific coast and what they would do about the island positions—all the natural concerns that one would expect after a surprise attack.

After that was over I went back and Admiral Stark thanked me for my assistance and let me go back to my own job. Normally the role that I played in advising Admiral Stark on the aviation aspects would have been fulfilled by Commander Forrest Sherman, who was actually in the Plans Division of the Office of the Chief of Naval Operations. But he had made a quick trip to Ottawa to exchange information and tidy up plans with the Canadians, because before Pearl Harbor we had gone through the various stages of enforced neutrality yet at the same time doing our best to assist the British in coping with the submarine threat in the Atlantic. We had established a patrol force of the Atlantic Fleet under Admiral Bristol and he had assembled a very fine staff. What forces we had available had moved up into the Newfoundland area and were actually conducting these patrols in the western part of the Atlantic Ocean.

I kept feeding information to the office of the CNO almost directly. Admiral Towers had said to "cut the red tape and deal directly as rapidly as you can. You know what the job is to be done. Do it."

Admiral Towers was the first navy person to appear before the Congress after Pearl Harbor because he was scheduled to go up before the old House Naval Affairs Committee on Tuesday morning. So I went up with him and some of these congressmen were avid to get the information and, in some cases, throw the harpoons at the military. One congressman said: "Now Admiral, what do you mean about this backbone of the fleet having been sunk at Pearl Harbor?" He came back and said: "You're in error because the backbone of the fleet is in the aircraft carriers and they were at sea." Then the congressman said to me: "Now what do you want?" I said: "Well, I think we need five hundred patrol planes, PBYs; we need one thousand dive bombers; we need one thousand fighters; and we need one hundred transports, as the first thing—not pinned down to any particular billets, types, or to any particular assignments." This was just the first cut that would give expansion in our orders and therefore production ultimately and also provide replacements. It was a rough count but it was a tremendous help in getting everything going because that was fed into one of the bills that was already in process up there.

We were authorized to go out and get the additional assistance that we needed. Admiral Towers had set up a program to provide for air intelligence officers. They came largely out of Ivy League colleges and had been sent up to Quonset Point to an air intelligence school. All told we had wonderful people. We couldn't have done the things we did without that fine group of people who came in initially right about the time of Pearl Harbor.

Captain Radford was brought in and put in charge of the aviation training program. Our base requirements had been prepared before this period because we had an expansion program that was twofold. The first one was bases in the U.S. and the second one was bases that we acquired in the destroyer deal—the fifty destroyers we provided for the British in exchange for bases in the Caribbean. So we had the foundations laid for the building-up of Jacksonville, Quonset Point, Alameda. They were coming along very well. Then on the training program—this went back to early 1940. We had decided to expand into Texas—the Corpus Christi area as well as Pensacola.

Another interesting sidelight in this period: Admiral Towers had felt very strongly that we should have a program for women in the navy. Others in the department wanted this also. There was very, very strong objection from Senator Walsh of Massachusetts. He said never would they have women in the navy again (they did in World War I) while he was the chairman of the Senate Naval Affairs Committee.

Now Admiral Towers knew that I knew Senator Walsh because of his principal assistant, a relative of mine, so Towers said: "George, I want you to be sure that you can win over Senator Walsh so that he'll no longer object to having women in the Navy." Well, about once a week for a long period of time my friend, Joe McIntyre, would bring Senator Walsh up to my house on Upton Street and we would sit around and drink scotch and we'd talk about various things. I'd talk about the needs of the navy in aviation programs and each time the main objective was to persuade him of the usefulness of the role of women in the navy. Finally, one night Senator Walsh said: "All right, I'll withdraw my opposition on the assurance that the morals of these girls will be protected and never will anybody propose that they be sent to ships." I reported that to Admiral Towers and we got the doggone thing through. Actually, it was the aviation side of the navy that really carried the ball in the testimony because we really had as good a case for them as any part of the navy did at that time.

During 1942 it was quite obvious that there had to be a great expansion of aviation training. No longer could they train all the European pilots in Europe because of the deteriorating situation over there, so they had what was called an Allied training conference in Ottawa. I was told to go up with Captain Radford, who was the representative for the navy at that conference, because I could handle the aircraft side and advise him on that aspect. There were meetings with the British and the Canadians with some French around and of course the Army Air Corps. It was a tremendous conference.

Right in the middle of it I got a telephone call saying to come back to Washington—that Admiral Towers wanted me right away for something more important. I got back and he said, "We're leaving for England. Be ready to go tomorrow morning." This was just before the Battle of Midway. Hap Arnold had arranged the transportation over in a Boeing Stratocruiser. It didn't go very high in the air but it was one of the few long-range transports taken over from commercial usage.

We went over to Bolling Field and took off from there to go to Canada and Newfoundland and then over to Prestwick. I was with Admiral Towers and Major Hoyt Vandenberg was with Hap Arnold. Generals Dwight Eisenhower and Mark Clark were aboard also, and a British Air Marshal Ewell plus a few other people. We started off and we got up to Goose Bay. I remember at the end of a runway there was a big moose. We got in there to find miserable facilities. They couldn't make any progress with the base because there weren't enough nails to do the construction work. Admiral Towers told them whom they should get in touch with to ask for an urgent shipment of nails.

Then we started to fly across the Atlantic. We got about halfway and found that the winds were so strong we couldn't make it so we had to turn around and come back. We flew back about a hundred feet off the water with a load of ice on our wings and got into Gander. We had to wait there for a change in the wind and for the crew to rest up. That day I remember they went out and shot skeet and we played bridge and poker. Finally we got going again. This time the wind had changed but the driftmeter in the plane had stuck and about the time we thought we were going to see Prestwick it became apparent that we were way off course to the north and far, far east. We had to make about a 120-degree turn and eventually got back to Prestwick. There they reported that London was fogged in but we had to get down there because they were to meet with the prime minister the next morning.

We had to to down by train. Inasmuch as I was the junior one in the party, I was a lieutenant commander, I was entrusted with the responsibility of paying for the tea and biscuits in the morning—which was the equivalent of a Pullman fare. We were given the tickets except for the cost of the tea and biscuits. We were met at the station. Admiral Towers was the guest of the British navy and we stayed at the Dorchester Hotel. He was given a naval aide (British) named Tennyson. The aide had been given some money to pay the expenses that we might incur over there from the U.S. side. Since the admiral was always taken care of we entertained ourselves quite properly by using each other's funds.

The meeting was really to get an amicable allocation of aircraft between the U.S. and the British. Marshal Slessor had been over before and he had worked out with General Arnold, with Admiral Towers's participation, a broad allocation of aircraft which did not satisfy the desires of either the RAF or the Army Air Corps. They were the ones principally concerned because we were in reasonably good shape for the navy except in the case of training planes.

In any event, we met at 10 Downing Street with the prime minister, Mr. Churchill. He was pretty well briefed on everything. He went down the list, first on bombers, then on fighters. When he came down to transports Admiral Towers said: "I think Lieutenant Commander Anderson can probably give you the best information on that because he knows more about it than any of us do." And I said: "The simple problem is you say you want transports, you want bombers—you want your cake and eat it too. There are four-engine airplanes, four-engine seaplanes; if you want more four-engine transports you've got to give up some four-engine bombers. There are just not enough to go around."

Well, it worked out all right in the general allocation. There was no final head banging. As we got up old Winston turned around to me and said: "Young man, you realize I established the rank of lieutenant commander in His Majesty's Navy." We had been in the British Naval War Room and they had plotted on the board there all the deployments of U.S. ships. They had the *Lexington* up there on the plot. They didn't know that she had been sunk in the Battle of the Coral Sea. They didn't have the information on that.

Then we got called back home. President Roosevelt wanted Arnold, Towers, and Eisenhower back in Washington as soon as possible. On the way we picked up Lord Mountbatten, also Averell Harriman. The president wanted them back in Washington because the Battle of Midway was developing and he didn't know what was going to happen. Of course, no one did.

Going back to the immediate aftermath of Pearl Harbor, at Christmas time Winston Churchill and Lord Beaverbrook arrived over here. They were staying at the White House and they were going to resolve all the problems because they were particularly apprehensive that Admiral King and the Navy Department were influenced (by the indignation that the

American people had over Pearl Harbor) to put greater emphasis on the war in the Pacific than the war in Europe. Churchill was very anxious to pin things down at the White House.

The president was going before the Congress in January with a dramatic program to expand our aircraft production greatly and enunciating the requirements that we had. He wanted fifty thousand planes in 1942 and one hundred thousand planes in 1943 and this we were going to produce. This had started with what is the maximum capacity of the production facilities in the U.S. and they had added in production facilities that included spare parts and everything else and they wanted it rounded off to a round figure. This was fifty thousand and one hundred thousand but that included the spare parts. This evolved from a New Year's Eve conversation between Roosevelt, Hopkins, Beaverbrook, and Churchill in which they more or less had gotten together with Roosevelt over a good many drinks, I guess, to round out these dramatic figures.

A couple of days later these had filtered down to Admiral Towers's office and he sent for me. I looked at them and said: "My God, they've included the spare parts. It should be less." He said: "How much?" and I said: "I think ten thousand less in 1942 and twenty-five thousand less in 1943." He said: "Well, we'll get that word up there."

Well, what the hell did they do? They increased the numbers instead of subtracting! They increased it, but it still went in and this was the big objective that was presented to the world. It was really startling to all of us. This was then to be implemented. Fortunately, I don't think they ever got to those levels, but they spent an awful lot up there on this broad statement.

The demands from Russian sources started in the summer of 1941. After the invasion the Russian requirements were just extravagant. They came in not only for planes but for all sorts of military equipment and materials. For example, they would come in and want a number of PBYs that would have taken up our whole year's production. They had demands for rubber. It was just fantastic. All the way through we had to resist the pressures that were being put on us. Most of these pressures did not affect naval aviation as directly as they did the Army Air Corps, but we sort of supported the Army Air Corps in trying to resist this excess pressure. Resistance would appear in the various committees. They had a heavy supporter in Harry Hopkins at the White House.

There were other things where pressure came through on political sides. We were told that we were to produce a transport to be made out of stainless steel by the Budd Corporation. This included building them a plant. The plane really hadn't been properly designed. Stainless steel was a scarce commodity. There was no prospect of getting the airplane in time. I went up and told the boss who was handling this, actually Cap Davison, that this thing didn't make sense and shouldn't be approved. Well, a few days later I was told that this is approved and don't ask any more questions and don't raise any more fuss about it—there are other things you should take care of. And all the correspondence that had come up saying how inadequate and costly and unwise and not recommended the decision was—that subsequently was cleared out of the files. By the time I came back to check on it the files had been completely cleaned by somebody. It was done in a political operation directed out of the White House. Those things happen.

Looking back, there was a major policy conflict between the army and navy and between naval aviation and the Army Air Corps. It was partly due to the army's desire to expand greatly and get on with the war in Europe and not to get over-committed in the Pacific. Also, it was due in part to the Air Corps's attitude from the old Billy Mitchell days deprecating the aircraft carrier and their ambition to have a single air force which would take over all aspects of military and civilian air. This became apparent later on. But in spite of that we worked pretty harmoniously. At least I was able to work pretty harmoniously with my opposite numbers in the Army Air Corps.

On one occasion Grumman came down and they were developing the experimental XF6F, which was their next generation of fighters. There were two experimental planes on order. We'd order two at a time. In the wartime expansion you had to have an ace in the hole so you'd order two. They were originally to be equipped with the Wright 1820 radial engine, but Jake Swinbul, vice president of Grumman, came down to my office and said: "Look George, our airplane's not going to be any good with that engine. It would be a hell of an airplane with a Pratt and Whitney 1830 engine."

Admiral Dale Harris, then a captain, had relieved Vosseller in Aircraft Requirements. He came in and we talked about this situation. We agreed that we'd better try out a Pratt and Whitney in one of those aircraft, and then the question was (a) Can we get the engine? and (b) Can we get approval to do this thing fast because the airplane was more or less completed? I called my friend from the Army Air Corps, Lieutenant Colonel Langmead, and said: "I need an 1830 engine fast. We don't have one available. Can you divert one from the production line at Pratt and Whitney?" He said: "Sure, I'll get it on a truck right away."

So he had the engine on a truck down to Grumman that afternoon. I went in to see Admiral Towers, having talked to Swinbul of Grumman and Military Requirements, and I said: "Admiral, I want to change the engine in the XF6F, on one of them, from a Wright to a Pratt and Whitney." He said "What does engineering think about it?" and I said: "They don't know a damned thing about it." He said: "What does Military Requirements think?" "They agree." "What does Grumman think?" "They will make a great airplane." "Go ahead and do it."

It took two weeks before the Engineering Department of the Bureau of Aeronautics knew that the engine had been changed. They were mad but they were so relieved that the airplane had developed such phenomenal performance. We processed it through the chain of command to get the official change made. Then I had to go and work out in the Joint Aircraft Committee with the Army Air Corps to get the production engines for the plane, but at the same time we had Buick coming in and making 1830 engines along the same design, and with the cooperation of my friends in the Army Air Corps we got the engines for the XF6F and it turned out to be a hell of a fine airplane. It really saved the war in the Pacific in that next phase.

Also, you spoke of North American. North American had produced an airplane for the British, an old lend-lease order, in which the Army Air Corps was not particularly interested but naval air, from our observers in England, found out that this was going to be a hell of a hot fighter. I went to my friend Eddy Langmead and said: "You'd better get with your own operating people and get some of those aircraft because they're better than anything you've got coming up the line." It turned out to be the P-51, and as a result of the U.S. Navy finding out about the airplane, the production was expanded and the allocations were diverted so that the U.S. Army Air Corps got the Mustang P-51, which turned out to be a superb fighter plane for them. The other one that they were building was the P-38, which was a two-engine fighter. We worked hand in glove in helping them get production of that, which of course we wouldn't use at that time. I would say that our cooperation at that level and through the medium of the Joint Aircraft Committee was very good.

When war broke out in Europe in September 1939, Franklin D. Roosevelt was well into his second term of office as president. The attention of the United States Navy was largely focused on the Pacific for this had been the custom for at least ten years. Yet, with war clouds over Europe, things began to change. From January 1939 on, the navy gradually deployed some ships to the Atlantic. This became the nucleus of the great Atlantic Fleet that would develop in short order. Admiral Ernest J. King was ordered to command this fleet and he was as ever a man of action. Almost simultaneously, the first tangible impact of the European war was an order from President Roosevelt in September 1939 to organize a neutrality patrol. The announced objective of this patrol was to report and track any belligerent air, surface, or underwater naval forces approaching the coasts of the United States or the coasts of the West Indies. This objective was announced by Sumner Welles of the U.S. State Department to the foreign ministers of the American republics assembled in Panama in the same month. Our sole purpose, the Pan American group was told, was to defend the Western Hemisphere. Their approval of this organization of a neutrality patrol was given but only after considerable debate. This is known in history as the Act of Panama of 2 October 1939. It declared the policy of the Americas was to keep the European war from the new world.

It was obvious of course that few of the Latin American states possessed more than a handful of combat ships for such a patrol so the role became the burden of the U.S. Navy.

Out of the background of events came the genesis of an idea the president derived from an account of a British experiment with the conversion of a merchant ship to operate planes against the U-boat menace. In due course Admiral Duncan (then Captain Duncan) was called from duty at Pensacola Air Station to take charge of the conversion of a Moore-McCormick Line merchant vessel to a small carrier. After FDR had investigated the possibility of this experiment he gave the navy ninety days to accomplish the task. Duncan was called to Washington for an interview with the president and given all necessary authority to expedite the matter. Duncan was incidentally the brother-in-law of Harry Hopkins and so his qualifications were undoubtedly known to FDR. Duncan's story follows in the excerpt from his oral history.

102

TWO CELEBRITIES WITNESS A GALA PERFORMANCE

ADMIRAL DONALD B. DUNCAN

NIMITZ LIBRARY, SPECIAL COLLECTIONS

DONALD BRADLEY DUNCAN was born in Michigan on 1 September 1896. He graduated from the U.S. Naval Academy in 1917. In 1920–21 he was enrolled in flight training at Pensacola and was designated a navigator upon completion of his studies. Later he did postgraduate work at the Naval Academy in Annapolis. In 1926 he was awarded a master of science degree from Harvard University. Duncan's early duty at sea was largely in aircraft carriers. On shore he served in several capacities in the Bureau of Aeronautics. Later he became an executive officer at the Naval Air Station in Pensacola. In 1941 he took a special command—that of the USS *Long Island,* the first merchant ship converted to an aircraft carrier escort. This story is told in Duncan's words in an excerpt that follows.

In 1942 Duncan commissioned and became commanding officer of the USS *Essex,* the first of her class, and he participated in the attacks on Wake and Marcus Islands in the Pacific. As he moved up the ladder of command he served on the staff of Admiral King in Washington, D.C., on the staff of the commander in chief of the Pacific Fleet, and then as vice admiral he became deputy commander in chief of the Pacific Fleet. As the war drew to a close he had a tour of duty as deputy chief of naval operations for air, and finally as Commander, Second Task Fleet. Duncan retired in 1957 in the rank of admiral. He then became governor of the Naval Home in Philadelphia. Later he lived in Washington, D.C., and finally he took up residence in Pensacola, Florida, where he died on 8 September 1975.

I left the air station in Pensacola in March 1941 under orders to proceed and report to the supervisor of shipbuilding at Newport News as the prospective commanding officer of the USS *Long Island,* which I had never heard of and which I soon discovered was a merchantman being converted to an aircraft carrier. I was to be prospective commanding officer in connection with fitting out the ship. At the time she was called an AVG. That put her in an auxiliary class. That had a great deal to do with the way she was manned, curiously enough, for the Bureau of Navigation manned ships in accordance with the category they belonged in.

I had a letter not long after from the officer who had been ordered to be the executive officer. His name was James Barner and he was an old-time aviator, an ex-quartermaster in the navy who had trained under my aegis as a student when I was chief flight instructor at Pensacola. I knew him very well. He was a very able man and I was delighted to have him. He knew a lot of things perhaps that I didn't know about fitting out a ship and getting her ready and getting the crew assembled.

I got my orders not long before I was going to have to be up there so I didn't have a chance to find out too much about the ship. Shortly before I was detached from Pensacola we had a visit from the Chief of Naval Operations, Admiral Harold Stark. I told him I was about to go to command this strange animal and he said, "Well, we don't know whether that's going to amount to much or not," to which I replied, "Well, I'll soon find out."

Before I went to Newport News I stopped in Washington and called on a man I knew very well, Calvin Bolster, an aeronautical engineering duty only officer in the Bureau of Aeronautics. He was a brilliant man and was in charge of a section of the bureau that had to do with conversions, design, and so on. And I asked him, "What is this thing I'm going to command?" Then he told me some of the story of the initiation of that project.

At the time this idea was conceived, Admiral Pratt (then retired but a former CNO) was writing for *Newsweek* as the military editor of the magazine. He had read about the British putting an aircraft on a merchant ship as a one-shot business to fly off and help protect the ship against possible air attack or maybe even a submarine. Admiral Pratt wrote this up in *Newsweek* and said: "Why don't we convert a few merchant ships along the lines the British are doing?" without himself having any notion of just how this would be done.

Well, President Roosevelt read this article and sent for some people from the Navy Department and he said: "How about this? Here is Admiral Pratt saying we ought to do something along these lines. I think it has possibilities. I want you to work it out." Well, he didn't get much enthusiasm out of the Navy Department. And he didn't leave any doubt, within a very short time, that this was what he wanted done. He was not consulting; he was ordering them to get a merchant ship and convert it to an aircraft carrier.

So they started from zero. Calvin Bolster was the man that Admiral Pratt had come to as soon as the president had sent for him to ask what he was talking about—which he did even before he talked to the people in the Navy Department. Admiral Pratt had come to Bolster and said: "Look, I'm in the docks. I've got to tell the president how to build an aircraft carrier." So Bolster drew him a sketch on a piece of paper as to what he thought it ought to look like and said he thought it was perfectly feasible to build a small ship into an aircraft carrier without saying too much about how it would work or what could fly from it. That sold the president and he told the navy to build it.

He gave them ninety days to do the job. He said the shipyard could do it and they would have ninety days. By the time I got to Newport News the ninety days had begun to disappear and the ship had begun to look like an aircraft carrier. So they went ahead, four bells and a jingle, on converting this merchantman. They took a Moore-McCormack C-3 hull, a ship that was on a South American run, and sent her into Newport News as she was returning from a routine trip. I remember being told afterwards that the yard was ready to start work on her by the time she got in. They even had a tale they were passing around when I got there that after they tied her up and the master of the ship went to check in with the yard and take care of his paperwork—when he came back to the ship his cabin was missing.

The ship was a standard C-3 hull and she hadn't been in the passenger trade. She had a lot of refrigerator space for example. And she was diesel powered, which caused us many a headache. That was done because they thought they would have a problem with smoke from an oil-fired ship and the diesels wouldn't give that problem. It didn't work out that way.

When I stopped in Washington and talked with Bolster he gave me a blueprint of what he had drawn, told me how the design had progressed and what was being provided. After talking with him I felt the ship would be operable and useful. She had the three elements needed to make an aircraft carrier: she had a hangar space which could hold about a dozen airplanes; she had an elevator to get them up and down; she had a catapult to get them in the air and an arresting gear to get them back on deck. Those were the basic things, and that was it.

This was indeed the beginning of the whole business of the auxiliary carriers. That was how the ACVs began. She was the first one.

So, armed with that information and doing some talking at the Bureau of Ships I went down and took over. The crew had been assembled and consisted in large part of the reserve division of the naval reserve from Birmingham, Alabama. The officers—with the exception of myself, the executive officer, and a couple of officers in the air department—were all merchant marine reserve officers. We had about 300 to 350 men on board and we had sixteen or eighteen planes—six fighters and ten or twelve scouting planes. The ship's speed, on paper, was eighteen and one-half knots, but we never made her go faster than seventeen and one-half and that not too often. We were something like the old *Rangeley* in which we had to pray for a little wind over the deck when we were going to take off. On the catapults of course it didn't matter. We had one flush deck— hydraulic catapults. When I got down there to Newport News the flight deck supports were up and the flight deck was being laid. She had been named the *Long Island* after the battle of Long Island in the American Revolution. The shipyard really had an organization at work on it. They said they could do it in ninety days. Incidentally, the yard was pretty busy for they were in the process of designing and getting started on the con- struction of the *Essex*-class carriers at the time. But it was a project the president had said—"Do!"—so from the top down they were doing it.

After I had a chance to see what was doing, had a chance to talk with the supervisor of shipbuilding in the yard, to the inspectors, I found a number of things I thought should be done. I made frequent visits to Washington. Initially I got quite a lot of resistance from the Bureau of Ships. The officer in charge there of the project had the idea that this was purely experimental. She'd go out, launch and land one airplane, and that would be the end of that. I didn't approach it from that standpoint at all. I thought it was going to be an operating ship. I thought it would be useful and I wanted to have everything on it that it needed in order to operate aircraft. One example is that she had no parachute run, no place to pack and stow parachutes. They could just do it on the wardroom table, or something like that. That seemed to me to be completely out of order. A lot of things like that. And, of course, with something brand new, we had to invent things from day to day.

The flight deck was only 330 feet long, as they had designed it, and it ran from the stern of the ship up to and including the pilothouse where it ended. The forward hold of the ship had been worked open and some booms rigged to put boats in there, so that the full 410-foot length of the ship had not been utilized. Nothing could be done about that at that time, and she still was completely operable, because with some luck on the wind we could get our scouts off the deck and we had the catapult for the fighters. So I didn't do anything about that at the time. But there were a number of details where the air department and my executive officer and I felt that changes could and should be made while the ship was in work—and I always had a lot of trouble getting changes made. So I went to Admiral Towers, who was the chief of the Bureau of Aeronautics and told him what was going on. He said he would talk to the chief of the bureau who was Captain Cochrane, a very able man. He told Cochrane I was having some trouble and Cochrane told me that I wouldn't have any more. He got it fixed so I got a little better cooperation from the people at the bureau. The truth was very few people thought that this was a feasible and useful thing to do, and they were very busy doing other things.

About midway through the business of getting her converted, I had a telephone call from Harry Hopkins, who told me that the president wanted to see me and would I come up to Washington. Yes, I said, I'd be up the next morning, so he told me when to come. I flew up. I had an airplane which had been provided by the bureau for me to use while I was there. I went to the White House and they were expecting me so I was taken right up to the second floor to the president's bedroom. I found him in bed, having his coffee and reading his newspapers. He welcomed me very cordially and asked me to sit down and tell him about my ship. So I did, very frankly and completely, including my difficulties in getting a few things done.

After I had finished talking he said: "Well, that's fine. Is it going to be done on time?" I answered yes, and then he said: "Now this is the important thing. This is why I wanted to see you. Is it going to be operable and is it going to be useful? Can it get the airplanes on and off, and can they carry depth bombs, and will it be able to look for submarines?" That was the original idea—convoy business. Afterwards of course they became hunter-killer group carriers, but that was the president's original idea. So I said: "Mr. President, my answer to that question is an unqualified yes. The ship will be operable. It will be useful and that is the reason why I want to get everything on it that is needed for it to be a real carrier. We won't have any trouble operating the ship."

And he said: "That's what I really wanted to find out." He picked up the telephone and called Admiral Vickery, who was head of the Maritime Commission. "Vickery," he said, "about those eight ships—the C-3s that are building, that you told me about. I want them converted into aircraft carriers right away. That can go forward right now and we'll take care of all the paperwork and so forth." Then he hung up the phone and said: "Well, I wanted to find out what you thought about this. On the strength of what you say, you've just heard me tell them to make eight more of them. Vickery told me a few days ago that they had eight ships on the ways which were building as merchantmen, of the same general design of the C-3 hull, but steamships." I had told him I thought a steamship would be better, although I hadn't had experience running it yet. "I had to make the decision right now," the president went on to say, "because every day's work that goes on those merchant ships has to be torn out. Right now they're in the place where they can be turned into aircraft carriers with the least interference with what has already been done."

So I said: "I think that's a very wise decision. As far as I'm concerned, I think I can assure you that the ships will pay their freight. There may be a lot of people who don't think so, but I think so."

I've always looked back on that as a wonderful experience. I got a glimpse of how Mr. Roosevelt did some things at that time. That was the genesis of the G-carriers. I think the first one of that group of eight was the *Bogue*. She made a wonderful record in submarine warfare. As I left his room at the White House after that conference with him he said: "You go down to the Navy Department and tell the people there that I said you were to have anything on that ship you wanted and thought you needed, with no questions asked, with the one stipulation that it will not delay the commissioning of the ship." And that was the end of any troubles I had with the Navy Department on getting things done.

At the end of the ninety days the ship was completed, moved to the navy yard at Norfolk and we proceeded with the fitting-out period. Commissioning, fitting out, and a little shakedown took another month. At the end of the fourth month from the time the ship had arrived at Newport News we landed the squadron off the Virginia Capes.

Our initial assignment, after our shakedown period, was in the Atlantic patrols. At that time they had three patrol lines running across the Atlantic: one in the North Atlantic, one in the mid-Atlantic, and one in the South Atlantic which consisted of a cruiser and a couple of destroyers just to keep an eye on the sea lanes. We were assigned to one of the patrols that operated out of Bermuda so the first place we went was Bermuda. We made a couple of trips across the Atlantic and back with a cruiser, operating our aircraft and just making the trip. It was useful experience. We had with us all the instruction for convoy duty and the way the convoys were organized so that we were available to be taken off to that purpose. But we were never used for that while I had the ship. After I left (in six months) she went up to Argentia and became part of the convoy organization.

From the duty on which we went out from Bermuda and came back we were detailed to go back to the coast with one of the cruisers under the command of Captain Hewitt, a very understanding and able man. We went back with him and took part in an amphibious exercise off the North Carolina coast at New River. The amphibious forces of the Atlantic Fleet were getting organized and operated and trained. This was of course all new business for a small aircraft carrier. After this was over we got orders from the CinC, Atlantic Fleet, who was Admiral King, to proceed to Provincetown, Massachusetts, and operate in that vicinity to await further instructions. That was in the midsummer of 1941. On the third day we got orders to proceed to a point up in the North Atlantic 150 miles or so west of Argentia. The orders came from Admiral King to make a rendezvous with his flagship and to be prepared to operate aircraft. I didn't know just what this was all about but it was on the occasion of the return of the president from his meeting with Mr. Churchill in Newfoundland. The *Augusta* was the flagship. The president was in the *Augusta* and returning to the United States.

We received the order in the middle of the night and had some people on liberty ashore but we managed to rouse them and get them back very quickly. By the time she was ready to go we had the people back with few exceptions and we were able to get under way and start out. We got to the exact location on schedule and unexpectedly sighted the *Augusta* and her destroyer escort. We immediately got a signal to take station formation on the starboard side. We could see on the deck the people gathered to watch this demonstration. I could see the president sitting there on deck for we were only about five hundred yards away from the ship. Admiral King had them headed right into the wind and fortunately we were ready to go. We were told to launch aircraft and we started in. Again Mr. Hopkins was there and I got a message from him which said: "You had better do your stuff or you will be in Moscow."

Well, a very strange thing happened. We started launching our fighters that always had to be launched with the catapult. It ran diagonally off the port side of the flight deck at the forward end, at an angle of thirty degrees to the centerline. The first two aircraft went off in good form. I was down on the bridge where I couldn't see what was going on on the flight deck, but I could see the airplanes as they came off. I heard the engine of the third plane revving up. The next thing I heard, the plane started down the track and then a terrific bang which sounded as though it came from underneath the flight deck. And after what seemed like an eternity the airplane sort of staggered off the deck and started sinking towards the water. The pilot operated his aircraft with the greatest skill because he did not have flying speed when he got off the end of the deck but he gained it in his descent toward the water. He kept his wings level and his engine full down and before he got to the water he zoomed off in fine shape. By that time I knew what had happened. The hook on the underside of the fuselage had carried away right after he got his initial impulse. So he got a good start from the catapult, but he went the rest of the way on his engines and got off. It seemed to me a miraculous thing.

The flight-deck crew had gotten the additional fighters down below and we were ready to launch the scouts by flying off the deck, which we did with an incredibly short interval of time. The people on the *Augusta,* I found out later, did not even know we had a casualty that had put the catapult out of commission. Of course the catapult made a no-load shot and came up against the catapult machinery. The piston and all that came up against the stops with a terrific bang and just carried everything away and put the catapult completely out of commission. That meant we couldn't launch any more fighters. But we got the scouts off with no trouble and having seen us get them off, apparently Admiral King thought that was enough so he told us we were detached and to proceed back to our aircraft commander in Norfolk.

So I left the formation and picked up our aircraft. I sent a message to the bureau and to the navy yard in Philadelphia, which specialized in catapult business, and told them I wanted to get the catapult fixed and unless otherwise directed I was proceeding to the navy yard in Philadelphia to have it fixed. So that was the opportunity for the president to see his baby launching aircraft and it came very close to being a disastrous one. I can tell you that I don't think that airplane missed the water by more than six or eight feet. The distance from the flight deck to the water was very valuable to him.

Of course we built a great many of those little ships, not only the *Bogue* class, but the Kaiser ships, the converted oilers, cruiser conversions—and all of them took their beginnings from the experience with the *Long Island.*

Winston Churchill's well-known book *The Gathering Storm* tends to explain some of President Franklin Delano Roosevelt's actions in 1940 and 1941. To be sure, the administration was restrained by the provisions of the Neutrality Act of 1935, but around the fringes of its provisions the president could and did act for the welfare of the nation. Only in November 1941 was the Congress induced to amend certain provisions of that act, freeing U.S. merchant vessels to arm themselves against hostile attack and to travel in the war zone.

A historian can recall certain actions that fall within the limits of the Neutrality Act without doing violence to it. There was the Selective Training and Service Act of Congress in September 1940. It marks the first occasion when the United States adopted compulsory military training in time of peace. Also in 1940 was the notable destroyer-base deal. Great Britain was in desperate need of destroyers to shepherd her convoys in the Atlantic. America needed military bases for her growing responsibilities in Atlantic waters. In this agreement Britain gave the United States sovereign rights for ninety-nine years to provide needed facilities for naval, military, and air bases in the Bahama Islands, in Jamaica, Antigua and Saint Lucia, Trinidad and British Guiana. And all this in exchange for fifty four-stack destroyers of the U.S. arsenal dating from World War I.

There was the dramatic meeting between the president of the United States and the prime minister of Great Britain off Argentia, Newfoundland, in August 1941. Important decisions were made on convoys and for a future alliance of the two powers while the United States was still neutral. And there was of course President Roosevelt's declaration of an Unlimited National Emergency on 27 May 1941. In that he spelled out his reasoning that indicated a probable attack on the American nation. "It would be suicide," he said, "to wait until they (the enemy) are in our front yard. . . . Old fashioned common sense calls for the use of a strategy which will prevent such an enemy from gaining a foothold in the first place. We have, accordingly, extended our patrol in North and South Atlantic waters." And there was the president's inspired idea of a lend-lease program in 1941 to supply desperately needed arms and other supplies to a beleaguered Britain, and to Russia and others in due time.

Two other actions, among others, deserve mention because of their significance. Only three weeks after the Germans had invaded Denmark the local government of Greenland, a Danish colony, asked the United States for protection. There was a very real fear that the Germans would come in force and take over the island. They already had a weather-reporting station on the east coast of great value to the Luftwaffe. The United States responded to the Danish request by getting various departments of the government to assemble a South Greenland Survey Expedition to explore certain areas of Greenland with a view to the establishment of possible bases—weather-reporting stations, search radars, radio stations, airfields.

Following that in April 1941 the Danish minister in Washington (still functioning for his captive country in Europe) signed an agreement with the secretary of state. By virtue of this the United States became the protector of Greenland and became responsible for its supply and defense until Denmark was free once again from Nazi control. The agreement gave the United States the right in return to establish bases and facilities deemed necessary for the defense of the island or for the defense of America.

Inevitably there arose the question of Iceland, an independent island nation, but most importantly, a strategic island astride the convoy routes of the Atlantic Ocean. Great Britain, the premier maritime power of that time, was well aware of Iceland's importance in the titanic struggle against the power of the Nazis. As early as 1940 Britain had sent a military force to Iceland after the fall of Denmark and Norway to Germany. Iceland was fearful of the same impending fate and invited the British to provide protection.

But now in 1941 Britain was anxious to use its occupying troops elsewhere for the government's many obligations were obvious. Churchill in turn asked the United States to take Britain's place in Iceland. Roosevelt agreed to send a task force to the island, providing the government of that place would give him an official invitation. That invitation was not immediately forthcoming. The Icelanders seemed hesitant but Churchill applied some personal pressure on the prime minister and the promised invitation was issued. Strangely enough, because of this delay, the president had to order a task force to embark from the United States with a contingent of marines before the invitation had arrived in Washington. Consequently, the force of twenty-five ships arrived in the outer roadstead to Reykjavík on the same day the official invitation came and the same day on which it was accepted. The use of that island in wartime was of great help in convoy routing, convoy protection against U-boats, and general rescue work.

The oral history excerpt by Admiral Gallery that follows is an example of the practical use of Iceland made by both the United States and the British. Commander Daniel V. Gallery (later Rear Admiral Gallery) was ordered there in late 1941 to command a primitive fleet air base during a transitional period when the Royal Air Force was still active on the island. As Gallery says, at first he and his men were for all practical purposes an RAF squadron until a new U.S. base could be built by the U.S. SeaBees. His story of that period gives the reader a fine account of the effectiveness of such a base in conducting warfare against the marauding U-boats that plagued the convoys from the U.S. ports to the United Kingdom.

Later in 1943 the Gallery story shifts to a new assignment. Gallery's focus in Iceland had been on the convoys and getting them through; he turned now to a personal vendetta against the U-boats. He went to Astoria, Oregon, before his new command, the USS *Guadalcanal,* was commissioned and brought her from there into the Atlantic to wage all-out warfare against the German submarines. The *Guadalcanal* was an early Kaiser-class small carrier (sometimes called a jeep carrier) and was designated a CVE. Henry J. Kaiser was an American industrialist who conceived the idea of producing small escort carriers to be built to merchant-ship standards but built from the keel up as a carrier. He turned them out in very large numbers beginning in 1940 for the U.S. Navy and the Royal Navy on lend-lease. Much time was saved in their production for it was along assembly lines just as was done with automobiles.

The *Guadalcanal* was eleven thousand tons and could make nineteen knots. She carried a complement of 1,200 men and was armed with twelve TBMs (torpedo planes) and eight single-seater fighters. Under the resourceful leadership of Commander Gallery the *Guadalcanal* was highly successful in hunting and sinking U-boats in the Atlantic convoy routes. During the course of her career she earned a Presidential Unit Citation. Gallery was the first in the Atlantic to train his fighters for night flying and this technique certainly contributed to the success of the sinkings. He also achieved a long-standing ambition to capture a U-boat and he towed her into Bermuda, where she was taken over by the Naval Intelligence people and much was learned about German boats. She was the U-boat 505 and is today in the Museum of Science and Industry in Chicago.

U-BOAT WAR FROM ICELAND TO MURMANSK AND THE COASTS OF AFRICA

REAR ADMIRAL DANIEL V. GALLERY, JR.

NATIONAL ARCHIVES

DANIEL VINCENT GALLERY, JR., was born on 10 July 1901 in Chicago, Illinois, and attended St. Ignatius High School after which he was enrolled in the U.S. Naval Academy in 1917 and graduated on 3 June 1920 (he was a member of the class of 1921 but early graduation came because of World War I). Immediately after graduation he participated in the Antwerp Olympic games as a wrestler. There followed service in several U.S. battleships, cruisers, and destroyers, all with engineering training. Finally he had duty as a turret officer on the USS *Idaho* (1924–27), after which he had flight training at Pensacola, Florida, in 1927 to fly with Torpedo Squadron Nine out of Norfolk. Throughout 1930–32 he taught flying at Pensacola. In 1932–35 he studied aviation ordnance engineering at Annapolis and the Washington Navy Yard, reporting to Scouting Four on the carrier *Langley* (CV 1) in mid-1935. One year later he became the commanding officer of the *Langley* with the rank of lieutenant commander. There followed a tour as skipper of Observation Three with the U.S. Fleet's battleships in 1937–38 and then he headed the Aviation Ordnance Section of the Bureau of Aeronautics. In January 1941 he reported to the American embassy in London as assistant naval attaché for air. Early in 1942 he assumed command of the Patrol Plane Base Detachment in Iceland, directing his planes throughout the crucial period of the U-boat war. Promoted as captain in September 1942 he was detached in May 1943 from Iceland.

114

Then followed the exciting period when he took command of the USS *Guadalcanal* (CVE 60) on the west coast of the United States. Gallery took his new ship to the Atlantic and became the nucleus of a hunter-killer task group. It was then that he inaugurated night flying for his pilots and thus coordinated their fighting qualities with the habits of the U-boat commanders who surfaced at night. In early 1944 his carrier planes had great success in sinking German U-boats. Finally in June of that year the *Guadalcanal* captured the U-505, forcing her crew to abandon her on the surface off Cape Blanco, French West Africa. This became the first enemy ship captured at sea by the U.S. Navy since 1815. Her story follows in detail in the excerpt from Gallery's oral history.

In September 1944 Gallery became assistant director, Plans Division under the chief of naval operations (air), and in 1945 he was given command of the fast carrier USS *Hancock* (CV 19) off the Japanese coast. Later assignments included assistant for guided missiles in the Office of the Chief of Naval Operations (1946); commander of Fleet Air at Quonset Point, Rhode Island (1950–51); and commander of Car Div Six, flagship *Coral Sea* (CVB 43) in the Mediterranean (1952). In late 1952 he was Commander, Naval Air Reserve Training Command, and Commandant, Ninth Naval District at Great Lakes, Illinois. Finally his commands included the Caribbean Sea Frontier and the Tenth Naval District at San Juan, Puerto Rico, and also Commandant, Fifteenth Naval District. He was detached in 1960 and retired as a rear admiral in October of that year.

Admiral Gallery, noted as an accomplished raconteur, had begun to publish autobiographical books beginning in 1951. His commands in the postwar period gave him more time to write. By 1971 he had produced nine books, something of a record for a naval officer. Many of these books are a mixture of fact and fiction and certainly reflect his naval experiences.

Admiral Gallery in retirement made his home in a picturesque spot outside Vienna, Virginia, where he lived with Mrs. Gallery. The admiral died at the Bethesda Naval Hospital on 19 January 1977.

In January of 1941 I went to London as a special observer. I was there for three months attached to the embassy and circulating around among the various airfields in England and visiting the fleet. At the end of that time I came back to the bureau and was there just a very short time when I was detached and ordered back to England in connection with the building of the seaplane base at Loch Erne (about September 1941). We were build-ing this big seaplane base in Loch Erne and looking forward to the time we were going to be in the war. This was all undercover at the time, of course, because there was no assurance that we were going to be in it. We were building the seaplane base there and I was designated to be the commanding officer when and if we got in the war. I was over there for about three months on that job.

The role of the seaplanes was to take part in escorting convoys in the Battle of the Atlantic, which was one of the crucial battles of the war. At that time we were losing the Battle of the Atlantic hand over fist. This job as skipper of that base was really one of the plums, especially for somebody of commander rank, which was my rank then. We planned to have about four squadrons of seaplanes at the base. But then the Japs came along and knocked the whole thing into a cocked hat with Pearl Harbor, and they knocked me up to Iceland. Instead of having this nice plush seaplane base at Loch Erne I left as commanding officer of the Fleet Air Base, Iceland. This was a hell of a comedown because up in Iceland when I went there we had nothing but a bunch of abandoned Nissen huts that the British had put up and eventually abandoned. Things were pretty primitive.

Up in Iceland eventually I had a squadron of PBYs, the old work horse, PBY amphibians. We were escorting convoys past Iceland. We'd go out for thirteen-hour hops and pick the convoys up five hundred miles south of Iceland and escort them for three or four hours. If you'd pick them up at five hundred miles it took you about five hours to get out there and five hours back, and that only left three or four hours.

When I got there the fleet air base consisted of these Nissen huts that had been abandoned by the British. We had a squadron of PBY airplanes and an old four-pipe destroyer to sort of act as tender for them. The boys were really roughing it out there. Life was primitive, to say the least. But it was wartime and we'd just been knocked flat on our can at Pearl Harbor so we were willing to put up with some hardships. We were working very closely with the RAF and the Royal Navy. For all practical purposes we were an RAF squadron. Then we got to setting up our own fleet air base and that took several months. We had a SeaBee outfit up there who built the base for us. They brought in Nissen huts and all the necessary galley and living equipment and that sort of thing. Inside of about three or four months we had a very comfortable base, at least in comparison to what we had started with. That was right at the height of the Battle of the Atlantic and the convoys were catching hell. So we had a busy time.

When I first showed up there and met the British air commodore and the British rear admiral, I noticed that they were both rather reserved in their reception of me. Then after I got to know them pretty well and saw that they had a twinkle in their eyes, one of them remarked to me one day, "We were rather suspicious of you when you first came up here to take command because one look at your face, which is a map of Ireland, made us a bit suspicious that you might make things as difficult as possible for His Majesty's forces." So I told them, "No, I had no feelings of that kind whatsoever. As a matter of fact, I bear no ill will whatever toward the

British. I am eternally grateful to your ancestors for persecuting my ancestors so that I was born in the United States."

I had to exchange a lot of memos and correspondence with the rear admiral and the air commodore. Whenever you have any correspondence with a high-ranking British officer, he signs his name and he puts a whole flock of initials behind it—DSO, KCB, and all that sort of thing—indicating the orders and decorations that he had. I had nothing to put behind my name except "Junior," which made no impression whatever on our gallant allies. So after I got to know them better and saw the twinkle in their eyes, I began putting DDLM after my name, knowing very well that sooner or later one of them would ask me, "What did it mean?" And sure enough one morning the air commodore met me in RAF headquarters and after saying "Good morning, Dan, old man," he said: "I say, old boy, what does that DDLM mean that you put after your name?" I said, "Oh, that's the American equivalent of your KCB." (Knight Commander of the Bath is one of the biggest and best things they've got.) So the air commodore was duly impressed. He said: "Oh, that's splendid. I didn't know you Americans had any such things." Then I could see the wheels going around inside his head, trying to figure out what they stood for and finally he gave up. He said, "Just what do the initials stand for?" I said: "They stand for 'Dan, Dan, the Lavatory Man,' the same thing as KCB, isn't it?"

That was the humorous side. The other side of it was rather grim, the escorting of the convoys. This was at the height of the Battle of the Atlantic when the Germans were sinking seven or eight thousand tons a month. They were sinking ships faster than we could build them at that time and we were sinking very few submarines. Actually the fate of England was hanging in the balance then. There were times when England was within sight of starvation and surrender. That went on all through 1942. I believe it was April of 1943 that the tide suddenly turned. From that point on we were winning the Battle of the Atlantic. The tide turned very suddenly and dramatically and it was the result of four or five different things that came to a head at once.

One was the tremendous building program in the United States. Another was the advent of the long-range aircraft which could reach out into the middle of the Atlantic from bases, which we couldn't do prior to that. Another was the advent of the jeep carrier, which closed the gap in the middle of the Atlantic. And there was a new radar and better depth charges and homing aircraft torpedoes. All these things came to a head at once and when they did we slaughtered the U-boats for three months, April, May, and June of 1943, when we sank a hundred U-boats and just rocked the U-boat fleet right back on their heels.

In that early stage some of the convoys had a hundred ships. In some convoys we lost as many as twenty. On the Murmansk run, which was a brutal thing, the PQ-17 lost well over half. The convoy before PQ-17 had been very roughly handled. They had trouble with the crews of the merchant ships. They almost mutinied and weren't going to sail. But they promised them a tremendous naval escort as they sailed and this naval escort they were promised was comprised of the *Washington* [U.S. battleship] and the *King George V* [British battleship]. They were supposed to protect the convoy. Actually they tagged along about 150 miles astern. The convoy came under attack by submarines and aircraft.

I remember very well, on the Fourth of July of that year I was in the RAF headquarters and we were looking at the chart showing where the convoy was. It was up around the North Cape of Norway and it was having a bad time. We got a flash that the *Tirpitz* was coming out to attack the convoy. The air commodore and I just rubbed our hands together and said: "Boy, this is it. The *Washington* and the *King George V* will get the *Tirpitz* today." He said, "Boy, this looks like it's going to be the best Fourth of July since you blokes declared your independence."

Then about an hour later we got this message from London: "All warships retired at high speed to the west, convoy scattered."

Everybody just slouched out of air force headquarters and went back to their huts and either cursed or wept or both. That was the story of PQ-17. That convoy was slaughtered. The reason behind that order from London was that our battleships had been catching hell along about that time. We had lost our whole fleet at Pearl Harbor. The *Prince of Wales* and the *Repulse* had been sunk at Singapore. All the shipyards were full of battleships which had been damaged by either air attack or torpedoes. So the British were simply gun-shy, and they weren't about to risk any more big ships within range of either torpedoes or aircraft. And so even though they had the word that the *Tirpitz* was coming out, they recalled the battleships and told them to retire. As a matter of fact, when the *Washington* got back to Reykjavík, after that the boys didn't want to come ashore because they didn't want to face their friends there after turning around and abandoning the convoy.

It's a time that I look back on with no regrets whatever. It was rugged duty in a way, but in other ways it wasn't. And we could certainly feel that we were pulling our weight in the Battle of the Atlantic. We sank five or six subs which was quite a respectable score for one squadron.

We did all right for amusement. We had pretty good recreational facilities. We had a gymnasium there—rather it was a storehouse which we converted to a gymnasium. We played basketball. We had some red-hot basketball games there with the army. We had bowling alleys. We played a lot of softball. We had a lot of social activities with the local people—dances and that sort of thing. The Icelanders were rather cool to us in the beginning because they had been up there for about a thousand years minding their own business and keeping out of the world's wars and they did not appreciate it when we muscled in on them. They just wanted to be let alone and we'd moved in on them. But after awhile they got used to it.

The RAF Coastal Command was the outfit that I was working with and they were extremely effective. Their main mission was escort of convoys, antisubmarine warfare. And they were damn good at it and did a very fine job.

There is an interesting story in connection with our first kill. After we had been there several months we had several chances for attacking subs and we muffed them for various reasons: one, maybe buck fever on the part of the pilot, or maybe the bomb rack hung up and didn't work, or various things of that kind. We missed our first three or four chances. So I laid down the law to the boys and said: "From now on we're closing the bar in the officer's club until we get a sure kill," which was a cruel and unusual punishment. Anyway, we closed the bar.

Then a couple of weeks later this lad Hopgood went out and caught a German sub and attacked it with depth charges and damaged it so that it could not submerge. Hopgood was on the way to a convoy which was about a hundred miles from the spot where he attacked the sub. After he had expended all his depth charges he then saw that the sub was surfacing and couldn't submerge. He then flew from the spot to the convoy and told them about the sub and they broke off a couple of destroyers to go over and get the sub. He circled back and forth between the disabled sub and the oncoming destroyers, coaching them on. The submarine came across an Icelandic fishing vessel. They went alongside and boarded it, abandoned the sub, opened the scudding valves on it, sank the sub and headed for Germany with the fishing vessel. Hopgood saw all of this; he was circling around reporting it to these destroyers, and they kept coming. Eventually they came alongside the Icelandic fishing vessel and went aboard and got the whole German crew and took them prisoners.

Of course this was a very exciting time in all the RAF headquarters while all this was going on, because this report was coming in from out at sea. And so at all the RAF headquarters in England and up in Iceland the big wheels were gathered around the radio set listening to this very dramatic development out at sea. All of Hopgood's reports of what was happening were framed in very official language and coded, of course. Everybody hung on each report as it came in. Then at the end when the British destroyers took the Germans off the Icelandic fishing vessel, Hopgood's last report came in to me in plain English, no code, he said: "Sank sub, open club." And we did. We damn near blew the roof off the joint. At the height of the celebration that night we decided that we needed a

119

suitable trophy for this victory. So the most suitable one would be the skipper's pants: in other words, we'd caught him with his pants down. So I wrote a letter to the first lord of the Admiralty, who had been up there and had addressed our officers about two weeks before. I wrote to him and explained the American expression, 'caught with your pants down' and said we would like to have the skipper's pants to hang in the bar room of our officers' club. "In order to avoid leaving the skipper in an embarrassing position I am sending herewith a pair of my own khaki pants which you can exchange with him for his."

I got a nice letter back from the first lord of the Admiralty saying that he had turned my letter over to the proper authorities and I would be hearing from them before long. About two weeks later I got a very stuffy letter from the head of Naval Intelligence quoting the Geneva Convention on the business of humiliating prisoners and so forth and so on. And he said, "In view of this it is impossible to send you the skipper's pants." I didn't mind the malarky about the Geneva Convention so much as I did the outrageous fact that he didn't even send my own pants back.

I left Reykjavík about the first of June 1943 and after a month in the States went out to Astoria, Oregon, as prospective CO of the USS *Guadalcanal*, which was a Kaiser-class converted carrier, the so-called jeep carrier. It was eleven thousand tons built to merchant-ship standards and could make nineteen knots. By all navy standards these ships were just impossible, but actually they did a tremendous job in the war. The Kaiser ships were not converted merchant ships. They were built right from the keel up as carriers, but they were built to merchant-ship standards. They were just barely good enough, but they *were* good enough. And they did a tremendous job during the war in the Atlantic hunting submarines. There were only three or four of us that got into the Atlantic. The rest of them all went to the Pacific and they were used almost entirely for aircraft transports—that is, hauling replacement planes for the fast carrier task force.

On the *Guadalcanal* we had twelve TBMs, the so-called Turkey Martin torpedo planes. And I believe we had eight single-seater fighters. I tried to get rid of the fighters and get other torpedo planes to replace them but I never could sell that idea. The fighters were of no use to me at all. But they kept saying the Germans had got the Focke-Wulf, a very long-range plane which theoretically could get out more or less to a ship like the *Guadalcanal*. So they said we had to have the fighter planes to protect against the Focke-Wulf, but we never did encounter any Focke-Wulfs.

We assembled the crew for the ship while it was building in Astoria. The building of the ship, incidentally, was a complete innovation in the eyes of shipbuilding, inasmuch as up to that time each ship was built individually, you might say, the way a fashionable tailor makes a suit of clothes—each suit of clothes is a little bit different. In the case of the Kaiser-class carriers, these were mass-produced the same way automobiles were. Very large sections of the ship were built in various parts of the country and shipped to Astoria, where they were put on an assembly line. They'd assemble these sections on the building ways and weld them together and then slide the thing down the ways and into the water.

There were some wild rumors going around at the time that these ships were defectively designed and that they would break in two as soon as they got into a heavy seaway. There were a couple of the C-4 cargo ships that broke in two, which lends a little weight to this thing. I remember that I had to get my crew together and assure them that there was no truth to this whatsoever. Although I remember very well the first night that we got under way, when we left Astoria. It was rougher than hell that day. The ship was bucking and pitching. All along the hangar deck there were very thin plates which had nothing whatsoever to do with the strength of the ship. They were really just spray shields. But as the ship would sag over the top of a wave, and then hog and sag, these plates would oil-can in and out. That noise just boomed through the ship like thunder and it sounded like we were just about to break in two any minute. I'm sure that everybody on the ship thought of this business of breaking in two that night, but it didn't.

We had about 1,200 men as complement. I would say of that 1,200 maybe a thousand were on their first ship. They were absolutely green. Then we had perhaps two hundred who had experience on other ships. Some of them came from carriers which had been sunk in the Pacific (we had one or two of them). It was a completely green and inexperienced crew. We had a shakedown of sorts. We went from Astoria around to Norfolk. You might say that was our shakedown cruise. In a way, having a completely inexperienced crew like that has some advantages. One of them was that I had very high ambitions for this ship. So I was proposing to the boys right from the start that we do some things that to an old timer would sound a little far-fetched. In fact, an old-timer might say: "Well, this skipper is nuts. You just can't do this." But with a bunch of completely inexperienced kids, they said: "Well, if the old man says we can do it, we can." By God, they went out and did it.

One of the things was this business of towing a submarine home which I had in mind right from the beginning. That idea originated in a way up in Iceland right after Hopgood's exploit where this sub was surfaced and crippled. Discussing that around the fireplace in the officers' club one night, we got to letting our imaginations run riot, and we said: "Why couldn't we board and capture a submarine with a PBY aircraft?" You could land a PBY in fairly rough water—you couldn't get it off again, but you could land it. So then we'd send a message in to the base and tell them: "We have captured a sub—send out and get it."

Along about the time we had got into planning it was 1 o'clock in the morning and we all decided to go to bed and sleep it off. This was really where the idea of capturing a sub started and I still had it in the back of my mind when we were putting the *Guadalcanal* in commission. As a matter of fact, on our shakedown cruise I ran through an exercise that wasn't on our regular schedule of exercises but I wanted to do it anyway: to take a destroyer in tow. It was a very laborious job handling those heavy lines and the boys didn't like it a damn bit. I didn't say that the thing I had in mind here was eventually taking a U-boat in tow, but that is what I did have in mind. This gets back to what I said about an inexperienced crew at times being an advantage because they'll believe a lot of things that a bunch of old-timers would not believe. They'll not only believe them— they'll go out and do them.

On our shakedown cruise we went first to San Diego, where we picked up our air group and spent some time breaking them in. Incidentally, I made the first take-off and landing from the ship in an SNJ down at San Diego. I wanted to do that because I had rather ambitious plans for the air group too, and I wanted the people in the air group to know the skipper could do these things himself as well as talk about them, so I made the first landing and take-off. This would add credibility to what I was telling them.

We got up to Norfolk around Christmas time and we shoved off on our first cruise early in January. The way they worked it at that time you would sail about the same time as a convoy did but were not tied to the convoy. The admiral simply told us to operate in the vicinity of the Azores against submarines. Those were the orders and gave you plenty of elbow room to write your own ticket. We would go out and hunt submarines as best we could. Of course we relied very heavily on the daily broadcast from Washington from the Tenth Fleet: the estimate of the submarine situation in the Atlantic which they put out every day. And they would pinpoint the location of all submarines that they'd had reports on in the past twenty-four hours. They would estimate where other submarines were, that is, that they knew a submarine had been at a certain point let us say three or four days ago. They would estimate where he was going and where he was today.

There was a Commander Ken Knowles in Washington who ran this submarine estimate thing. He was just a soothsayer. He could put himself in the position of a German skipper and just figure out what the guy was going to do and where he would go. He was absolutely uncanny in his predictions. I treated this COMINCH daily estimate as Bible truth every day and we based our operations on it completely. One reason why I did was that the very first thing that happened on this first cruise was we got a special message from COMINCH from the Tenth Fleet saying: "There is going to be a refueling rendezvous of submarines off the Azores at a certain point at sunset on a certain day." It just gave us that information. We were going to be reasonably close to it so I laid off about a hundred miles from that point until about four in the afternoon. Then we launched eight torpedo planes to search that area. And right at sunset we caught the refueler with a sub alongside, hoses stretched across, and another sub standing by waiting his turn. We caught them and we blasted the hell out of the refueler and the guy alongside of him. We sank the refueler, an auxiliary tanker. The one that was taking fuel—we thought we got him too but we found out after the war that he was able to limp back into Brest. After that experience, just following the COMINCH estimate exactly, turning out the way it did, I believed everything that I heard from then on.

The night we made this kill, we made the kill right at sunset. It was about forty miles from the ship to the spot where the tanker was sunk, and I had eight planes in the air. There were only three, I think, that were in on the actual attack. The others were spread out, for that was quite an area we were searching. The others all heard the report of the attack. So each one of these guys figured it was absolutely essential for the war effort for him to get over there and take a gander at these Germans swimming around in the water. Up to this time nobody in the Atlantic had flown at night off the CVEs. The idea was you always got your plane back just before dark. It was an overcast day and I knew it was going to be darker than hell that night so we had to get those guys back. I kept screaming at them to get the hell back to the ship and land, but as I say they figured it was essential for the war effort to have a look at those guys in the water.

Eventually they got back to the ship and when they did it was damn near dark. The first three got aboard all right. The fourth one went off the side of the flight deck and nosed down in the gallery walkway. So we had to get this guy out of there. We were a brand-new ship then. We just got butter-fingered and clumsy that night and we couldn't get that plane out of the gallery walkway. We tried everything, but we just couldn't budge it. I even tried to flip it over the side by turning the ship real sharp and putting a list on it and then shoving it over but we couldn't get rid of it. I called the guys in the air—there were four of them—and I made a pitch to them and said: "Now, look, the tail of that plane sticks out a bit on the flight deck but not much. If you guys will land just the least little bit over to the port side you won't hit the tail." I got some very skeptical and reluctant "rogers" back from the air.

Then we started making passes and trying to bring those guys in. We were lit up like a barroom on a Saturday night because we had to. But it was black. And the boys had not done any night flying. They were jittery

123

and they made some of the wildest passes I have ever seen. We had to keep waving them off, waving them off. Meanwhile they were burning up their gasoline. So we finally in desperation gave one guy a cut and he came down, hit his wheels on deck, bounced in the air, rolled over on his back, and dove into the water. Our plane guard destroyer picked up all three of the guys in the plane and saved them. But that was enough of that. So I told the other three, "Now you land in the water. We'll have our destroyer turn the search lights on. We'll pick you up." They landed in the water and we did pick them up but that was what turned the tide for me on this night flying. I decided that we were going to learn to fly at night.

The first thing we did the next day—we took this turkey that had gone into the gallery walkway—by that time we had it back on deck again. For the next two weeks every day, morning and afternoon, we would take that plane and roll it off the side of the deck into the gallery walkway and the boys would drag it back on again. By the time they had done that about a dozen times they were real experts at it, and they could whip it out of there in a couple of minutes. By the time we got back to Norfolk they were damn sick and tired of it, so I finally let them give the thing a military funeral by shoving it over the stern end of the deck into the water.

Then when we got in from that cruise we got a new squadron aboard for the next cruise. The first thing I did was to get the skipper in and tell him that on this cruise we start flying at night. I proposed to start with a full moon. Then they would be flying each night with the moon getting a little smaller until eventually, in twelve days, there would be no moon. They'd be flying absolutely black. He went along with this idea. He said, "Okay, we'll have a shot at it." It was a new squadron and they were new at the job. They had done some carrier-landing practice ashore but they hadn't done any at sea. So with the first full moon we had we started them flying at night. It was pretty hairy because, what the hell, when you are breaking the ice on a brand-new business, it's bound to be hairy.

On the first half of that cruise, from Norfolk to Casablanca, we flew all day long every day, bringing the last planes in just before sunset. We never did get the kind of weather I wanted to start the night flying. The moon wasn't right anyway. Then on our way back things happened to break for us just right. There was a nice calm sea the night of the full moon and so we started our night flying. That very night we got the U-515. We caught him on the surface charging his battery and drove him down. Then we hounded him all night. Every time he'd pop up, we'd nail him again and chase him down again. Making a depth charge attack on a sub at night, or even in the daylight, is not a 100-percent thing. You don't get the kill every time, and especially at night you don't. We drove him down three or four times that night.

In the meantime we had broken off a couple of destroyers with my escort to get over there to that spot. They got there about seven o'clock in the morning—right over the spot where this guy was. From seven that morning until one that afternoon these destroyers were working this guy over. He was a hell of a sub skipper incidentally, Werner Hencke. He knew all the tricks of the trade. He was down at six hundred feet. He was squirming around and would do all sorts of tricks on us. Finally about two o'clock in the afternoon we shook him up bad enough so that he figured the gig was up. His battery was shot by that time anyway so he finally surfaced right in the middle of the task group. We blasted away with everything we had. He finally up-ended and sank. We picked up forty-five out of the fifty-five people in his crew.

This was the very first night we'd been flying. During that same night we made another contact, or thought we made another contact on another sub. So as soon as we got Hencke we sent out a search for the second sub. And we got him the next night. So we got two kills the first two nights we flew. We had gone three weeks before, flying in the daytime, with no kills at all. The subs simply did not come up in the daytime. They came up at night. If you wanted to do business out there, you had to fly at night. Of course when we came back from that cruise and reported this, all the other CVEs started night flying. But we broke the ice on it.

There was one interesting sidelight to the sinking of the U-515. That was the one that was commanded by Oberleutnant Werner Hencke, who was one of the U-boat aces. He had the Iron Cross with Oak Leaves. He was a very ambitious guy and he was out to get diamonds for his Iron Cross. In fact, his crew blamed his overweening ambition to get diamonds for the loss of their ship. They said that if he hadn't been so damn set on getting diamonds we wouldn't have got them and that he would have gotten away.

When we got Hencke and his men aboard the *Guadalcanal* we immediately separated them into three groups. We took all the nonrated men and we locked them up in one compartment, all the rated men in another compartment, and then we took the four officers and put them in the brig. We kept them separated as long as they were on the ship so that they couldn't talk to each other and give each other pep talks on security.

The day after we got these people Hencke sent word up from the brig that he wanted to see me. So I had him brought up to the cabin. He registered a protest about being kept in the brig. He quoted the Geneva Convention to me and said that he was entitled to an officer's stateroom and to eat in the wardroom and so forth and so on. I didn't have a copy of the Geneva Convention handy at the time but I told him that this was completely impracticable on this ship: "Among other things we've got a hell of a lot of new members on this ship who are of Jewish extraction and a lot of Poles. These lads might not be very polite to you if I gave you the run of the ship. You'll just have to do the best you can in the brig." So he went back to the brig.

And then about three days later my chief master at arms came up to me with this story. He had gotten acquainted with Hencke because he brought him his food and talked to him while he was eating. Hencke had told the chief master at arms that just before his ship had sailed on that cruise she was on her way out from Lorient and there was a propaganda broadcast beamed at the U-boat bases in which the British said they had just learned that it was the U-515 that had sunk the *Ceramic,* a big passenger liner, with a very heavy loss of life, around eight hundred people. It seemed that after torpedoing the *Ceramic* the sub that did this job had surfaced and picked up one soldier to bring back in as proof. All the rest were lost because there was a hell of a storm that came up right afterwards. They got this soldier back to Germany and put him on a broadcast to announce that he had been saved and that the *Ceramic* was sunk. The British announced on their broadcast to the U-boat bases that they found it was the U-515 that had sunk the *Ceramic* and said they had learned that the U-515 had surfaced and machine-gunned survivors in the lifeboats. Then the broadcast said: "If ever we get anybody from the U-515 we're going to try them as pirates."

Hencke denied this indignantly, the machine-gunning of survivors. And I believed him—I don't think he did. But anyway, that was what the British said in their broadcast and it was the story Hencke recited to my chief master at arms.

I meant to say that when Hencke had been protesting about my treatment of him—and this was just a shot in the dark—I said, "If you don't like the way I am treating you, we're going in to Gibraltar and I'll turn you over to the British." As I say, this was just a shot in the dark. We weren't going anywhere near Gibraltar. I didn't know about the British propaganda broadcast. And Hencke said, "Well, no, no, it's not that bad. Don't do that." And I replied, "All right."

Then I began putting two and two together. I began to wonder how far can I push this thing of turning him over to the British? So I drew up a statement on a sheet of official paper saying: "I, Werner Hencke, Oberleutenant German Navy, hereby promise on my honor that if I am imprisoned in the United States instead of in England I'll answer all questions truthfully when interrogated." I had a place for him to sign, for me to sign, and my exec to sign as witness. I figured this is something where I've got nothing to lose and a possibility of gaining something. The only thing that could happen is Hencke could spit in my face, which won't affect the outcome of the war one way or the other. But if he falls for it, maybe something good will come of it.

126

So I had Hencke brought up to the cabin. On the desk I had the chart of Gibraltar laid out with dividers and things on it as if I were looking over the anchorage of Gibraltar, because I told him that we were going in there. And he saw it. Then I had a phony dispatch from COMINCH, which I gave to Hencke. The dispatch said, "The British have required when you refuel in Gibraltar you turn over Hencke and his crew to them. In view of the crowded condition of your ship you are authorized to use your discretion." This was from COMINCH to me.

I handed this dispatch to Hencke. His face fell when he read it and he said, "Well, I suppose there's nothing you can do about it." I said, "There is. This dispatch authorizes me to use my discretion. If you make it worth my while I'll take you to the United States." So he said, "What do you want me to do?" I said, "Just sign this," and shoved the paper across the table at him.

This was sort of like a scene from a movie you might say. He read the thing and said, "You know, of course, that I can't sign this." I said, "Well, it's up to you. If you sign it, you go to the United States. If you don't, you and your crew go to England." So he thought that over for a minute or two. And then he picked up the pen and he signed it. So we sent Hencke back to the brig.

Then I had a photostat made of this thing Hencke had signed and passed that around among his whole crew. And I made a similar proposition to everyone in the crew, except specifying in much greater detail as to what they would talk about and asked them to sign it. So they all figured, what the hell, the skipper's talking, so why shouldn't we? Every one of them signed it.

Then when we got back to Norfolk, we turned these guys in, and I turned the papers in. ONI went to work. Hencke of course reneged on his agreement, as I was sure he would, and said it was obtained under false pretenses and duress and so on. He didn't talk; he didn't say a word.

But his crew didn't know that. They'd had no communication with him. We'd kept them separated. They all figured, the skipper is singing, why shouldn't we? And they sang like a bunch of canary birds. ONI got plenty out of them.

Then the finale to this thing was rather tragic; Hencke eventually found out that the crew had been talking and it preyed on his mind. Then ONI said to Hencke, "Either you talk or we're going to send you to England in accordance with your agreement." Hencke still wouldn't talk. So they got ready to send him to England. He was in a prisoner-of-war camp. The day before he was supposed to leave, Hencke just walked over to the fence and started climbing it. The sentry hailed him and called at him to halt, and he didn't halt. So the sentry shot him and killed him.

The next day we got the U-68. These two incidentally were old-time

U-boats. Between the two of them they'd sunk around 350,000 tons. We caught the U-68 right at sunrise, the planes coming in out of the west with the sun shining in the east. They caught them completely unaware on the surface with only three lookouts up on the conning tower when they hit. And we plastered them with machine guns, rockets, depth charges, and a homing torpedo. We broke the sub in two so down she went and left the three lookouts swimming around in the water. The planes that had made the kill dropped a life raft in the water for the men there and they radioed us. We were about sixty miles away. Then we kept one plane over the spot, circling, so we could see him on radar to guide us in. About four hours later we got over there and picked up the survivors. There were only two of them left by that time. One of them was dead but the other one was swimming around and holding his dead friend up. He was near gone when we got him. His name was Kastrup.

The next day I got him up to the cabin, and he was still in pretty shaky condition. And I asked him a few questions, which he had no business answering. I'll never forget this young kid. After I asked his name and his rate and so on and the name of his U-boat, which he answered, then I began asking some other questions about U-boat operations which he had no business answering. He just shook his head and said, no, he wouldn't answer that. I said, "Well, you should answer." The angle I worked on him was this: "Your skipper, when your sub was attacked, closed the hatch on you and the other lookouts and submerged, and left you up there to your own devices. In other words, he abandoned you. Therefore you should have no loyalty to him; you should talk."

I'll never forget this young guy. He looked me right in the eye and said, *"Ich bin Deutsche soldaten."* "I'm a German soldier." And he wouldn't say a damn word. And I've always had great respect for the guy. This happened on Easter Sunday morning. I send him an Easter card each year, and I get an answer back from him. He's living now in Essen, Germany.

That was the second cruise. The name of the skipper was Dick Gould. I recommended that squadron, which was the outfit that broke the ice for night flying, for the Presidential Unit Citation. I never found out whether they got it or not. But anyway, they opened up night flying because from then on it became routine in the Atlantic.

There was another idea that I had gotten from this previous cruise when we developed night-flying techniques. This one was rather far-fetched—towing a submarine home. This idea was born while I was in Iceland with the PBY base and it stuck in the back of my mind.

I was pretty familiar with the habits of submarines by this time and I knew that when you got one cornered and hammered him with depth charges and punished him so much that he figured he was finished and going to sink it was standard operational procedure for submarines to blow their tanks and come up and abandon ship, giving the crew a chance to get overboard so they could be rescued and then open the scuttling valves and sink the ship.

I knew this was the standard practice and I figured that in the heat of battle it was quite possible that a sub skipper would figure that he had it prematurely and that he would surface before he really had to and abandon ship and open the scuttling valves. If we could get aboard in time and close the scuttling valves we might be able to keep it afloat and tow it home. I was gambling on the human element and it was a long gamble, but of course the prize would be well worth the gamble. Among other things we'd get the submarine codes, the main thing we would be after.

At the departure conference for this cruise where I had all my submarine skippers together, I outlined this plan to the boys and told them that I wanted everybody to organize boarding parties and to keep a whale boat ready to lower. And that if we brought a sub up this next cruise, instead of immediately throwing the works at him and trying to blast him out of the water and sink him, we would just shoot a lot of small stuff at him to keep him away from his guns, discouraging him from shooting torpedoes, and to expedite his abandon ship rule so the skipper could get his people off of there and we could get our people aboard and try to close the scuttling valves.

The destroyers I had with me on this cruise were the same ones that I had on the previous cruise when we brought up the U-515. Then we hammered away at her for ten or fifteen minutes before she sank. In fact, I was beginning to think we'd have to ram her. So this idea wasn't too far-fetched to this particular group.

At the departure conference we always had a lot of outsiders from CinCLant, from COMINCH, from the ASW experts, and so on, just sitting back and listening. When we were discussing the capture business I saw some of these people look at each other and make circular motions with their fingers like, this guy is nuts, but they didn't say anything. So we agreed that if we brought a sub up on this cruise we would try to get aboard and capture him.

We shoved off and started our regular routine of round-the-clock night flying. It went fine; the boys took to it and could handle it. After about a month we were off the Cape Verde Islands and we were beginning to run low on fuel and were going to have to head for Casablanca. Then we picked up a broadcast from COMINCH on a homebound U-boat coming back from the Gold Coast in Africa. That was not too far away from us so we started hunting for him. We were on his tail for about a week. We got a daily report from COMINCH but that was just an estimate of where they thought he was. Those estimates, as I said, were uncannily accurate as we found. We followed our information daily and a number of times we got close to this guy. We got indications of a submarine: the disappearing radar blips and noisy sonar buoys and things of that kind, which you can't be sure of, but later on we were sure of them. But each time he'd get away from us. This had gone on for about a week.

Finally we were getting low on fuel. Our chief engineer was up warning me, "By God, we'd better get into Casablanca or we are going to run out of fuel." Knowing the chief I knew he always kept a little bit up his sleeve, so I kept pushing him and pushing him. Finally he said, "This is the last night we can possibly operate." We operated that last night and got more indications but again got no contact.

So the next day we were heading for Casablanca. We gave up the hunt and headed for Casablanca. Along about noon on Sunday our destroyers ran right over this guy [the U-505]. He had made a detour in toward the coast during the night and was on his way back out again and we were right over him.

We caught him completely by surprise. He was running submerged and a destroyer picked him up on sonar. We depth charged him. The first attack shook him up a bit but didn't do much damage. Our planes in the air could see this guy in clear water. This isn't often you can do this, but they spotted him running submerged and they were able to coach our destroyers right over him.

We dropped another depth charge which shook him up pretty badly, rolled him over on end under water and dumped everything into the bilges. They were just sitting down to their Sunday dinner and everything was dumped on top of them. He jammed his rudder hard over and it created panic among the crew. They came swarming out of the after torpedo room yelling that the pressure hull had been ruptured and that the after torpedo room was flooding. The skipper took their word for it.

So he blew his tanks and surfaced and abandoned ship. He came up and the crew went overboard and left the sub running at about seven knots on the surface with the rudder jammed hard over running in a big circle. The sub popped up almost in the middle of the task group. The destroyers immediately opened up on it with their small stuff—20 millimeter and machine guns and some 3-inch. Meantime we dropped our boats in the water. The boat from the *Pillsbury* was the first one to get there. Lieutenant David was in charge of the boarding party of ten men. They chased the sub around in a circle and finally caught up with it and threw a line aboard. A boy jumped out of the whale boat and tied it to the back of the submarine.

Incidentally, I was about half a mile away and watching this thing through the binoculars. I broadcast over the loudspeaker, "Heigh-ho Silver, ride 'em, Cowboy," when they got the line aboard. Then David and two other lads, Anispul and Wdowiak, were the first aboard. They beat it up to the conning tower, which was open.

We'd seen a number of people go overboard but we were by no means sure that everybody had gone overboard. It was a good chance that there were still people on board waiting for intruders down there to greet them with a machine gun. But David, Anispul, and Wdowiak plunged down the conning tower and found to their amazement that the sub was all theirs. That is, she was all theirs if she didn't sink or blow up. She was completely abandoned, the skipper and everybody gone.

But she was in almost neutral buoyancy by this time, just about ready to up end and go down. Water was pouring into her and as far as I knew there were booby traps all over her. They soon found the place where the water was coming in, which was the bilge strainer that had the cover knocked off. Then one of the men found the cover lying right there on the floor plate. That was lucky for us. If the thing had gone down in the bilges where he couldn't find it, we wouldn't have been able to save the sub. But he was able to put the cover back in place and set up. There was a lot of pressure of course to overcome, but he had a lot of incentive too to get it back. He screwed on the nuts and stopped the water just in the nick of time.

Then the *Pillsbury* came up alongside her to try to take her in tow. Instead of taking her in tow astern she tried to take her in tow alongside, but the big bow flippers on the sub stick out in the water and they cut into the side of the *Pillsbury* and ripped a long underwater gash in her and flooded the two main compartments, and she had to back clear. I thought we were going to lose her because she had flooded the two compartments. The *Pillsbury* radioed to me that she didn't think a destroyer could do this towing job. So I said, "All right, destroyers stand clear, I'll take her in tow myself." I took the *Guadalcanal* over and backed down and put the stern up close to her bow and got a towline over. By that time we had maybe twenty of our people on board the sub.

While I was lying there with the bow of the sub not more than twenty feet from my stern I said sort of a short prayer: "Dear Lord, I've got some young lads on board that submarine. Please don't let any of them monkey with the firing switch or torpedoes." Well, they didn't, and we finally got her in tow and started to haul her away. It soon developed that she sheared way out to starboard until the towline was as taut as a bow string—but anyway we were able to drag her along because the rudder was jammed. We were able to tow her all that afternoon.

But by this time I was in a spot where I couldn't get to Casablanca. I didn't have enough fuel left so I sent a message to CinCLant saying we had boarded and captured a sub and that I didn't have enough fuel to get to

Casablanca and requested permission to take her into Dakar. I got an answer back from CinCLant almost immediately saying: "Nothing doing on Dakar. Take her to Bermuda (which was 2,500 miles away). We'll have a tanker rendezvous with you with fuel." So that got me off the spot with the fuel.

I was denied Dakar because that port was infested with German spies. If we had taken her into Dakar the Germans would have known about it immediately. The threat of running out of fuel almost won a place in naval history comparable to the foolish virgins who ran out of oil. When I sent my message to CinCLant I added a postcript saying: "I've got a captured sub in tow," and my situation was all right then. It got me off the hook.

Here's one little interesting sideline on this thing. We had a custom on my ship of having the padre say a morning prayer every morning on the loudspeaker. When we were getting ready to put the *Guadalcanal* in commission I had been reading the reports of the battles out in the Pacific and in several of them I noticed that the skipper of the ship told about having the padre get on the loudspeaker just before the battle started and say a prayer. I discussed this with my chaplain and we both agreed that this would be bad psychology as well as rather shabby theology to wait until you're looking down the enemy's gun barrels before you ask God for help. So instead of that we said, "We'll do it every morning as a matter of ship's routine."

Every morning the padre would get out the colors and the boatswain's mate would ask for attention to the morning prayer. Everybody would stop what they were doing and face the colors and the padre would say a short nonsectarian prayer to which everybody could say amen.

Incidentally, I hope the Supreme Court doesn't hear about this, because if they do they may declare everything we ever did on that ship unconstitutional and make us give that sub back to the Germans.

That evening just at sunset I was up on the bridge looking aft at this thing we had in tow, still hardly believing it. Father Weldon came up to the bridge. I said to him, "Well, Padre, it looks like your morning prayer worked this morning," and he said, "Captain, it sure does."

And then he told me a story about the bishop of Dublin. It seems the bishop of Dublin was driving down the road one Sunday morning and he came across one of his flock who had a flat tire and was pulled off on the side of the road trying to change it. The flat tire was stuck on the rim and Pat couldn't budge it no matter how hard he heaved. He was painting the air blue with a lot of bad language while he was trying. So the bishop stopped and took him to task for his bad language. He said, "Now, Pat, instead of cursing and swearing like that you ought to try prayer." So Pat said, "Yes, Your Worship, let's do that." So the two of them bowed their heads and said a short prayer. Then Pat spit on his hands and got ready to heave again, and just the instant he touched the tire it popped right off in his hands, whereupon the bishop said, "Well, I'll be God damned." And Father Weldon said to me: "I feel exactly the same way when I look aft at that thing we've got in tow."

By that time in the evening we had the boarding crew back on the *Guadalcanal* because we were afraid the sub was going to sink. We weren't at all sure she'd stay afloat, so I didn't leave anybody aboard during the night.

As soon as the sun went down, our lookouts, our sonar operators, and radar operators began to let their imaginations run away with them. They were all worked up because of the excitement of the afternoon and they began seeing hobgoblins all around us. The sonar people were getting firm echoes, the radar people were getting disappearing radar blips, and the lookouts were sighting periscopes. It sounded like we were completely surrounded by the German U-boats and they were closing in on us. So I towed the thing a little bit too fast and busted the towline. Then we had to circle it the rest of the night.

The first thing in the morning we got out a bigger towline and got that aboard. While we were getting it aboard I went over to the thing myself to try and get the rudder amidships, because the boys had reported to me that the rudder was jammed and they could not move it with the electric steering gear. The door to the after torpedo room was closed, which was where the hand steering was, and they said it had a booby trap on it.

At the departure conference from the ship I told the boys: "In case we encounter any booby traps that's my pigeon. I'll take care of that," because I was an ordnance P.G. [postgraduate] and I knew something about fuses and that kind of stuff. I was just itching for an excuse to get over there myself anyway.

So I went over and we went back to the after torpedo room and the watertight door was closed. The main panel on the door had an open cover of a fuse box lying across it so that you could open the door without closing the cover to this fuse box. This was what the boys thought was a booby trap, because there were a lot of electrical connections in the fuse box. They thought, "Maybe if we close this thing it will set something off."

I looked it over and I decided that it was not a booby trap. So I closed the cover to the fuse box. One of the nice things about that sort of business is that you find out right away whether you were right or wrong. And I was right, nothing happened.

Then we opened the door to the after torpedo room. We had to do that very carefully because according to the Germans it was flooded, and we didn't want to flood the rest of the boat. So we had to crack it very carefully and make sure that no water came out. And it didn't; it was dry.

We got back in there and got at the hand steering gear and connected it up and brought the rudder back amidships.

Incidentally, while we were back there it occurred to me that here we were on a U-boat which was down by the stern about fifteen degrees and almost neutral buoyancy ready to up end any minute. I remembered that one of the ways that submariners have of trimming their ship is to send a number of people all the way forward or all the way aft. Here we were, four of us, all aft on this thing which was down by the stern fifteen degrees. Again we got away with it, but as soon as we got the rudder amidships I said, "Let's get the hell out of here," which we did.

I should add that one of the main things I was relying on in terms of possible booby traps on the sub was the fact that the crew had been taken quite by surprise in our initial attack and didn't have time to do anything about booby traps. They probably figured it was going to be on the bottom in another couple of minutes so they didn't set any traps. Not only there—they had thirteen five-pound demolition charges set along in the keel and they had a switch up in the conning tower which could be set on anything from a few seconds to three or four minutes. We knew this was sort of a uniform installation and that this had it so the first thing we did when we got aboard (we didn't know where the switch was or how it worked) was to run along and look down in the bilges and we could see the five-pound charges. We reached down and got hold of the wires and yanked them off. In the first few minutes aboard we had found twelve of those things but we knew there was one more. We didn't find that for two weeks.

In the meantime, a day or so later, we found the switch that operated these charges and we found that it was left unset. The Germans were so sure that when they abandoned ship she was going to the bottom in a couple of minutes, they just neglected to set the firing.

After the rudder was righted the sub towed very neatly from the stern and everything was fine. I towed her for three days, I believe. We were right in the middle of a submarine operating area at the time so I figured we had to protect ourselves. We had to keep our planes in the air, so we resumed flight operations with the sub in tow. At the time I couldn't tow more than eight knots; that was as fast as I dared go. And at times we had only ten knots of wind across the deck. You should have twenty-five knots wind to fly off one of those baby flattops but we did it anyway and the boys were able to handle it. It goes to show that when the chips are down the boys rise to the occasion.

Three days after we got her in tow we rendezvoused with a tanker. She came alongside and filled us up and filled our destroyers up. Then we proceeded to Bermuda towing this thing.

We had one destroyer with us that could make three or four knots more than any of the rest. Among the things we got off the sub were the operations code books and their cipher. We put them in a sack and put them on this other destroyer and sent her on ahead of us. She rushed this thing to Bermuda where it was picked up and flown to Washington.

There they immediately put a watch on U-boat frequencies and for the rest of the war we read the traffic of the U-boats. Of course the Germans had periodic changes that they made about every two weeks in the code, but the key to all the changes was in the code books that we captured so we could follow the changes right along.

The Germans did not learn of the capture of their sub until the end of the war. And that leads me to what I think was probably the most remarkable part of this whole remarkable episode—the fact that we were able to keep it secret. This was very important on account of the code books. If they had known they were captured they would have thrown away the old code books and put in completely new codes and we wouldn't have been able to read their stuff. So it was very important to keep the capture a secret.

But when we were towing the thing to Bermuda here I had 2,400 young lads in my task group, all of them just bursting with the best story of their lives. I had to get them together and explain to them the vital necessity of keeping their mouths shut. They couldn't say a word to anybody when they got home, not even their wives, mothers, sweethearts—nobody. That's one hell of a big order. So I'm proud of the fact that the boys did keep their mouths shut and the Germans didn't find out about this capture. I think that speaks very highly indeed of devotion to duty and sense of duty and responsibility in the average young American in bell-bottom trousers.

We towed her into Bermuda and we left her in Bermuda. When we arrived, of course, there was a large delegation of experts from the Navy Department to take over and inspect it. She was kept in Bermuda for the rest of the war and her crew were all interned in Bermuda in a special camp all by themselves. They left the sub in Bermuda because it is an island and the British had very tight control over everything going out by mail, telephone, radio, and press. And they were able to clamp an iron-clad lid on the thing so word couldn't get out. If we'd brought her into Norfolk or any other place in the U.S. it would have been out in no time. Also the fact that the crew was kept separate from any other German prisoners meant that there wasn't any word getting back to the homeland that way through the mails.

Incidentally, in the original skirmish the skipper had been hit in the leg with a 50-caliber gun and he eventually lost that leg. When we got him aboard my ship he was down at sick bay and he hadn't actually seen us take his ship in tow.

I went down to see him in sick bay the next day and told him we had his ship in tow and he didn't believe it. So I sent over to his cabin and got a picture of his wife and kids off the desk and gave it to him. Then he believed it and then he kept shaking his head and saying, "I will be punished for this, I will be punished for this." I tried to reassure him that they had already lost the war, that Hitler and his mob would be thrown out at the end of the war, and that they'd forget about it but he wouldn't believe it. He kept shaking his head and saying "I will be punished for this."

As a matter of fact, when the war was over in a way he was punished for a while because the Germans have a very elite society now composed of survivors of the U-boat fleet with headquarters in Hamburg. Only about 20 percent of the active U-boat fleet survived the war. They had 80 percent casualties, which is a terrific casualty rate. The skipper of the U-505 was barred from membership in this society on account of the capture.

When I heard about this I wrote to Krutchmer, who was the number-one ace-of-aces and the head man in the U-boat survivors fraternity. I wrote him and said I thought it was unfair to bar Lange from membership because he was simply the victim of circumstances. He had done everything that he should have done, and he had done the same thing that 780 other guys had done but nobody had ever tried to board their subs before. I pointed out to Krutchmer in my letter, "The same thing could have happened to you, Krutchmer," because Krutchmer too was captured by the British. A British destroyer had laid alongside his sub for fifteen minutes and then the sub went down. They could have gotten aboard his sub in that time and probably saved it. I got a nice letter back from Krutchmer thanking me for my letter and saying that he agreed with me and that they had lifted the suspension on Lange and he was allowed to join the fraternity.

Eventually I got to be good friends with Lange. I looked him up about seven or eight years after the war when I was in Germany—in Hamburg. I wasn't sure that he'd be glad to see me because I hadn't been too polite to him that day we first met. But he was. He took the whole day off from his business and showed me all around Hamburg. He took me to lunch at his club, to dinner at his home, and to the theater afterwards.

That's a funny way to make friends with a guy—you shoot his leg off and take his ship away from him, but we got to be good friends.

136

When Germany surrendered the navy brought the U-505 to the United States from her anchorage in Bermuda. She was used in a war bond–selling trip along the eastern seaboard and then relegated to the Portsmouth Navy Yard, Kittery, Maine, where she remained for about ten years without maintenance of any kind. The navy several times planned to take her out and sink her in the Atlantic Ocean, but each time Admiral Gallery put up a fight. He knew there was some thought of taking her to Chicago for permanent display, and when Gallery was assigned as commander, Naval Air Reserve Training, in Glenview, Illinois, there began to be some action. The Navy League chapter in Chicago became interested; the *Chicago Tribune* took up the cause, and a mayor's committee was named to handle the matter. The navy was persuaded to give consent and did so with the proviso that the money for the submarine's transport, and so on, would be raised from private sources. An act of Congress was required to transfer ownership from the U.S. Navy to the Museum of Science and Industry in Chicago. Finally she was transported there where she is on display today.

Sometime during the 1970s, Admiral Gallery came to my office in Annapolis and spent several hours with me while we played a tape he had brought from Chicago dealing with the ceremonies surrounding the arrival of the U-505 at the museum in Chicago. I shared with him in that time some of his joy and his memories of that notable event in his illustrious naval career. Dan was a fine officer, a man of sensitivity and notable humor—and above all he was a fine friend. ED.

137

The development of radar as a major force in the waging of World War II is a subject too vast to deal with in a brief introduction to what follows in the story of Admiral Rivero. His straightforward account tells of the early development of radar in the U.S. Navy. But any account of the original development, be it succinct or lengthy, is only half told if one avoids mention of the development of radar in Great Britain. It was there that a particularly brilliant scientist named Robert Watson-Watt came to the fore with his studies that ultimately produced radar just in time to give the RAF the necessary tools to win over the German Luftwaffe in the Battle of Britain—a major victory that has had repercussions throughout the world.

Watson-Watt first became interested in electrical engineering after graduation from a Scottish university at the outset of World War I.* The War Ministry observed that his talents were such that he could better serve the war effort by weather watching than by weapon wielding and so he was given a place in the meteorological office of the Royal Aircraft Establishment. It was the aircraft establishment that wanted the Meteorological Service to work on the possibility of giving timely thunderstorm warnings to the aviators of the infant RAF (then the Royal Flying Corps). Such a research effort had been offered to the war office by the head of the Meteorological Service but his offer was rudely refused by a staff officer of the war office in a blunt question: "Do you think the British army goes into battle with umbrellas?"†

At any rate, the task assigned the young scientist was to aid in the unraveling of the story of radio "atmospherics" or static. These two names (neither justified nor appropriate, according to Watson-Watt) had been given to the naturally occurring electromagnetic waves that interfere with the clear and faithful reception of the man-made radio signals that are sent out as carriers of information. A one-time head of the Air Ministry later

*The following discussion of Watson-Watt's work is taken from *The Pulse of Radar: The Autobiography of Sir Robert Watson-Watt* (New York: Dial Press, 1959).
†Ibid., 20.

said that Watson-Watt's study of thunderstorms was his first step towards his subsequent development of radar. As his work began to come to fruition in the middle of the 1930s he concentrated most importantly on the development of radar, which would be especially useful in combating the Luftwaffe, for that was seen as playing a major role in any invasion of Britain. Such invasion thoughts were beginning to be a matter of concern in certain areas of the military, if not among the populace at large.

By the year 1936 matters seemed to have progressed sufficiently that Watson-Watt moved his workshop to a coastal manor, Bawdsey, near Felixstowe, and he went on an energetic search to recruit a group of young academic physicists. This move marked the creation of the Air Ministry's radar laboratory. Watson-Watt went into all parts of the kingdom, "requesting, demanding or wheedling" the release of high-grade research men. The recruits, as he observed, resembled an Oxford or Cambridge college more nearly than a government research laboratory. When assembled the men lived together in the manor house and ate together in a large wood-paneled hall. Some of their most fertile discussions took place in true common-room style around a fire in the evening. In 1936, through some influences at Winston Churchill, Watson-Watt was transferred to the Air Ministry staff and appointed superintendent of the Bawdsey Research Station with no retired brass, as had been threatened, above him in the administration and operation of the station. The first RAF officer to be fully inducted into the secrets of radar (later Air Marshal Raymond Hart) was attached to Bawdsey to found a new school to instruct RAF personnel who would operate the earliest chain stations along the eastern coast of the United Kingdom. The personnel shared in discussion about "our hopes, our partial successes and our temporary failures," said Watson-Watt.*

A point made by Admiral Rivero in his interview was that the greatest weakness in the U.S. development of radar was that those in charge failed to organize and prepare for training people to operate and get the most out of the marvelous invention. The British were perhaps more farsighted although they too maintained strict security over the development of radar. Watson-Watt says: "We in our work were acutely concerned to ensure that we found good operators, trained them well and gave them equipment which was as convenient and comfortable to use, and as good as we could devise. All this seemed to us to be as necessary as any more strictly technical excellence." It was fortunate that the British used this foresight because when the Battle of Britain came about in the summer of 1940 their defensive efforts were strained to the utmost in defending the country from invasion.

*Ibid., 119–120.

Lord Swinton, who was secretary of state for air, said in that time: "I felt that in our Ministry with all the new possibilities in the air we needed a much closer relationship with the scientists than we had even on our Scientific Committee. I felt that I had got to get the ablest scientists I could and make them an absolutely integral part of the Operational Staff. Scientists had been here as advisers before but I wanted these men to be at the absolute heart of all operational planning, and so I said to the Chief of Staff: 'I want no secrets held from these men; they will be as much a part of the Operational Staff as you and your staff are.' "

The reader will find it useful to realize the speed at which radar developed in Britain with the threat of invasion a growing probability. In time for the Battle of Britain, which began in August 1940 and ended 15 September, when Hitler called a halt to further efforts, the British had erected fifty-seven radar stations, many with standby and supplementary mobile equipment, in uninterrupted watch over the British Isles. They also had over four hundred AAA gun-laying radars in operational use. By the time the first factory-built SCR (Signal Corps Radio equipment—U.S. terminology) appeared in the United States, the United Kingdom had produced more than a thousand radar transmitters in all.

Admiral Morison, in his history of U.S. naval operations in World War II, reports: "President James Conant of Harvard, with a number of fellow scientists visited England during the Battle for Britain and returned convinced that one of the main factors which saved England from destruction under the long sustained assault of the Luftwaffe was a group of 'operational' scientists. These men not only invented and developed, but aided and abetted the operation of coastal aircraft-warning radar. The instruments, spotted along the coasts of the North Sea and the English Channel, picked up incoming waves of bombers at what then seemed an immense distance. Thus the Royal Air Force had sufficient time before a bombing attack to get the Spitfires on the backs of the German bombers. A small group of these scientists worked closely with the RAF fighter command to coordinate coast warning radar with defending fighter planes. Results were so favorable that similar scientific groups were organized to help other branches of the RAF including the Anti-Submarine Coastal Command."*

Dr. Lee du Bridge, an American physicist and one-time director of the radiation laboratory at MIT (1940–45) said that his radiation laboratory itself was founded on the basis of information brought to this country by the British and it depended heavily during the early years upon British ex-

*Samuel Eliot Morison, *History of United States Naval Operations in World War II*, vol. 1, *Operations in North African Waters, October 1942–June 1943* (Boston: Little, Brown, 1975) 220.

perience, both operational and technical. He continues by saying: "The British ideas were the guiding influence of the initial group of our physicists who had, for the most part, never before heard of microwaves or of the detection of aircraft by radio. The British laboratories were a continual source of new ideas and new techniques which were generously shared with the Americans and which were promptly embodied into American practice."*

Even before the Battle of Britain took place there had been afloat in the United States an unconditional disclosure and unilateral proposal: that all the British then knew about science and war should be shared with the United States. There were some doubts and hesitations in London about giving "our treasured secrets" to a still neutral country but they were not shared by Winston Churchill; Lord Lothian, the British ambassador to the United States; the famous physicist Sir Henry Tizard; and others. Informal disclosure was not possible, but arrangements then were made for a military interchange of information in an aide-mémoire signed by President Roosevelt in July 1940. A British military mission was then accredited and there followed action elsewhere in U.S. defense-science circles. Out of this arrangement came the National Defense Research Committee in the United States.

Admiral Rivero in his interview makes it clear that he pursued as a specialty the development of radar to revolutionize fire control on ships. That fits in neatly with a remark of Admiral Fraser of the Royal Navy: "Radar brought the greatest revolution in naval tactics since the change from sail to steam."†

---

*Watson-Watt, *Autobiography, 276.*
†Ibid., 149.

NAVY ENSIGN IN CHARGE OF THIS THING WITHOUT A NAME

ADMIRAL HORACIO RIVERO, JR.

U.S. NAVY

HORACIO RIVERO, JR., was born in Ponce, Puerto Rico on 18 May 1910. He was graduated from Central High School in San Juan before entering the U.S. Naval Academy on 20 June 1927. He graduated from the academy with distinction (third in a class of 441 members) and was commissioned ensign on 4 June 1931. He then served on the USS *Northampton* and the USS *Chicago*. From May 1933 to June 1934 he had duty on the staff of Admiral J. M. Reeves, and later when Admiral Reeves was named Commander in Chief, U.S. Fleet, Rivero served on the flagship USS *Pennsylvania* as the assistant fleet communications officer until his assignment in June 1936 to the new DD USS *Porter*. After his return to the United States he received instruction at the Naval Postgraduate School in Annapolis and then continued his course in ordnance engineering at the Massachusetts Institute of Technology in Cambridge, Massachusetts. He graduated there in June 1940 with the degree of master of science in electrical engineering. There followed duty at the Naval Gun Factory, the Naval Proving Ground at Dahlgren, Virginia, and a tour of duty in the Bureau of Ordnance, where he had the first fire-control radar desk in that bureau as well as the first one in the Bureau of Ships.

After the United States entered the war Rivero was ordered to duty in the new USS *San Juan* (CL 54). When she was commissioned he became her assistant gunnery officer, participating in the landings at Guadalcanal-Tulagi, a lone raid on the Gilbert Islands, and the battle of Santa Cruz Islands. In 1943 and

143

1944 he continued duty on the USS *San Juan* when she participated in the South and Central Pacific campaigns. The *San Juan* became part of a covering force under the command of Admiral Halsey. This involved raids on Bougainville, the capture of the Gilbert Islands, carrier raids on Rabaul, and attacks on Kwajalein in the Marshall Islands.

Rivero returned to the United States in 1944 to assist in fitting out the USS *Pittsburgh* (CA 72) and served in her until the end of the war, first as gunnery officer and later as executive officer. The *Pittsburgh* operated in this period with both the Fifth and Third fleets, participating in the Iwo Jima and Okinawa campaigns. The *Pittsburgh* was heavily damaged when a severe typhoon struck the Third Fleet. She lost her bow but proceeded to port under her own steam. Rivero was awarded the Legion of Merit for "his timely direction of the heads of departments of the ship and his immediate inspections of damaged and flooded portions of the ship under extremely hazardous conditions."

Later assignments of particular significance began in March 1949 when he was one of the original members of the Weapons System Evaluation Group, Office of the Secretary of Defense. For a year he commanded Destroyer Flotilla One, from July 1957 to October 1958, and then became director of the Long Range Objectives Group, Office of the Chief of Naval Operations. In December 1960 he reported as deputy chief of staff and deputy chief of staff for Plans and Operations to the Commander in Chief, U.S. Atlantic Fleet. In October 1962 he assumed command of Amphibious Force, Atlantic Fleet, serving during the period of the Cuban missile crisis. In July 1964 he became vice chief of naval operations and served until February 1968, when he reported as commander in chief of the Allied Forces, Southern Europe. He retired from this assignment and from the navy on 1 June 1972.

Admiral Rivero assumed a difficult job for his country when he was named in 1972 as U.S. ambassador to Spain in the latter days of General Franco. Rivero brought honor to this service in many ways. In one matter he distinguished himself in a way no other ambassador from any nation had ever done in Spain: he visited and conferred with officials in all fifty provinces of the country and did it within the space of his first year in office, at the same time conducting his normal work as a knowing and forceful U.S. ambassador to the Spanish government. He resigned as ambassador when President Ford assumed the presidency in 1974 and retired to his home in San Diego, California, where he now lives.

It was 1940 and we were starting to get worried about the war. I was sent to the Bureau of Ordnance to the Fire Control Section—Section L, they called it. The head was Captain Fin France and the man in charge of the main battery was Freddie Withington. I was put in the Fire Control Section. I was Charley. Captain France said to me: "Now there's something going on at the Naval Research Laboratory. I want you to go over and see whether we have any interest in that." He didn't tell me what it was. They didn't have a name for it. And he said, "You go down and talk to Deke Parsons in Dahlgren because he knows all about it." Deke had been involved in that somehow in his previous duty in Washington. Not many people knew about this subject and there was nobody in the Bureau of Ordnance that was involved. It was the Bureau of Ships, the Bureau of Engineering business, and that of the research laboratory. But somehow Deke Parsons got an interest in the experimental work going on there. He was a natural scientist. So I went down to Dahlgren and talked to Deke and said that Captain France asked me to talk to him before I went over to the research laboratory.

I remember Deke sitting down and explaining the radar equation: what happens when you put out a beam of electromagnetic radiation and then it bounces back. And he showed me the equation and then I went back, armed with that information, to the Naval Research Laboratory and saw some of the experiments going on and I thought, "This does concern me. We could use that in fire control." And then I became the fire control officer in charge of this thing which didn't even have a name yet.

When I had been at the Massachusetts Institute of Technology they didn't know about the development of radar but not long after that something was done there. Anyway, I was then the first man in charge of radar in the Bureau of Ordnance. In the Bureau of Ships there was an organization of at least three or four people whose head was Jennings Dow. He had been to England. He was a radio engineer and he had been sent to England to become familiar with the work the British had been doing on this by Robert Watson-Watt. He had made the trip in 1940 and with him was Sam Tucker. So I teamed up now with Sam Tucker because he was a radio engineer and my interest was to see how this could be adapted to the ordnance part of the navy. The army was doing some work then and they were very secretive. However, I remember going to Fort Monmouth to see some of it. I think we called it RDF and the British called it RDF—radio direction finder. The army had developed a search radar and an antiaircraft fire control radar and they were very crude.

In the navy by 1941 we had already built ten radar sets which we put on ships. It was called CXAM, with a big two-hundred-megacycle mattress thing for an antenna. I went over to a couple of ships where it was installed to see it. I remember that I went aboard the USS *Chester* and talked to the captain about how the thing was working. But it was all very secret. Only the captain and one other officer on a ship where it was installed would know anything about it. And the officer didn't know much about it anyway because not many had learned about the theory.

After I got into the Bureau of Ordnance the first fire control radars were developed by the Bell Laboratories. I think we bought ten of the first set. It was a console type. We put it in the plotting room of the ship. It was around 400 megacycles. About that time the magnetron had been invented by Oliphant.* He came over to the U.S. in 1940 or 1941. I remember going to the meeting in Washington where he presented his paper on the subject.

We had set up by this time the Office of Scientific Research and Development with Vannevar Bush and James Conant and under their aegis the radiation laboratory at MIT was created using an awful lot of British work but also creating their own. I remember seeing up there one of the British AI radars, the aircraft interception radars. It was a ten-centimeter radar, the first one ever made. I think the British made the first one because the magnetron made it possible to get to that high frequency. Actually, there was a lot of interchange between the British and the U.S., particularly after the radiation laboratory at MIT was created, but it was mostly in connection with the airborne radar.

In the Bureau of Ordnance I was the officer in charge of radar and I passed on the design from the fire control point of view and I helped try to figure out how we could get it broken up into boxes so we could put it in the directors of the old battleships and the cruisers. That was the first set of stuff that we actually bought for the gunnery part of the navy. It was fascinating because I was the only guy at the beginning of it. I remember seeing the chief of the Bureau of Ordnance, I think Admiral Blandy, and trying to explain it to him. He said: "Now you go ahead and do what's necessary. I don't understand that. You're in charge." I was a lieutenant.

Its potential wasn't realized at that time. I remember the captain of the *Chester,* who said, "Oh, that's a big mattress, a big sail that I've got on top of my mast." He was *agin* it. He wasn't interested either. Nobody knew much about it but a few of us knew what could happen. The officer assigned to the *Chester* didn't have much concept either. He was a radio engineer, a radio postgraduate, but he didn't know anything about this particular kind of business. I remember his saying that he had used the radar to follow the anchors down to the bottom. It isn't possible. Radar doesn't penetrate water, not in those frequencies anyway.

But I was very lucky. I was the one in the business in the Bureau of Ordnance. I had no one to talk to in the bureau that could understand the language. The only fellows to talk to were Sam Tucker over in the Bureau of Ships and Jim Smith, who was an engineer on loan from Bell Laboratories. And the three of us traveled everywhere together, to witness all the

---

*A magnetron is an electron tube for amplifying or generating microwaves with the flow of electrons controlled by an external magnetic field.

146

experiments, all the tests. I got involved in both the Bureau of Engineering side and the Bureau of Ordnance side. I had additional duty in the Bureau of Engineering. So I very easily coordinated with myself for getting approval of both bureaus in a particular thing that we wanted because I didn't have to ask anybody. I gave approval because nobody else would understand what I was talking about. My job was to get it incorporated into the fire control system. I helped the design of how the boxes would have to fit into the fire control system of the director. I thought that instead of having the damn thing down in the plotting room it should be put right in the director by breaking it up in little components. That they did. So we had to design the thing so it would fit. There were so many different kinds of directors, from the old *Florida, Arkansas*-type of battleship down to the later ones. It was interesting work.

I think we bought about eight or ten of the first ones, of the earlier design, for fire control, but it was at too low a frequency to really be very effective. It was all in one console which went into the plotting room of some of the cruisers. In the meantime a development was going on at Bell Laboratories primarily on the so-called FX and FD radios, Mark III and Mark IV, which were the first ones really that were effective and went into series production. I was the one who passed on whether they were satisfactory or not, on the basis of one experiment, breadboard type, which I saw done at some place up on the Jersey coast where the Bell Labs had an experimental site. And on the basis of that experiment I said, "All right, we'll go ahead with production." I didn't have to ask anybody.

Then when the contracts were coming in I didn't wait for the final development before production. I remember sitting in the conference room of the Bureau of Ordnance one day, a lieutenant, with Dr. Lack, who was the president of Western Electric, the manufacturing people for the Bell system, and I gave the approval. I had a lawyer from the contract section with me. I gave approval for the purchase of practically all the fire control Mark III and Mark IV radars that we fought the war with. I was a lieutenant, and this was maybe $100 million in cost, or something like that. I said, "All right, we'll buy two hundred," or whatever the number was. They were still developing it. The antenna hadn't been developed yet. The final form of the thing hadn't been decided but we went ahead in order to start manufacturing.

You see, we saved time. I was aware of the urgency of this thing. War was coming on us. France had fallen and everybody knew that we were going to be involved in it sooner or later. So the idea I had was that we must get this out, get it on the ships. It took a long time to get it on the ships. What I used to do: I would get word when a set was being finished in Chicago where they were building them. I would call the factory or the

Western Electric men that I dealt with and I would say: "All right, serial number 3. You have it at the airport on such and such a day. We'll have an airplane which will take it to Bremerton." And I assigned what ship they would go to and where, serial number by serial number. It was on the basis of the availability of the ship. I didn't want to have the sets sit around so I wanted every set as it came out of the factory to go immediately to some ship and have it installed.

The Bureau of Engineering people would take care of the installation. They had to have special engineers borrowed from some of the companies involved—General Electric or Bell Labs—to really walk it through for installation. There wasn't any real training program. That's one mistake we made. We didn't think that far ahead. Unfortunately we didn't capitalize on the fact that we had it early in the war against the Japanese (who didn't have it), because not enough people knew about it. That was one of the mistakes we made—that we didn't organize and prepare, through this tremendous secrecy, for training people to operate and get the most out of radar.

One thing I did at the Bureau of Ordnance when I was making all these decisions and spending millions and millions of dollars approving development projects and selecting the equipment and so forth. I had read about the congressional investigations after World War I so I thought I'm going to be ready for the one after this war. I kept a complete file of everything I did, telephone conversations, decisions, whom I talked to, and so on. I left this behind when I left the bureau. I guess it disappeared because I tried to get hold of it later on without success. It may be in the archives. I had the whole story right there. I was very careful. Every day I would write down everything. It was almost like a diary. I never had so much authority in my life.

Then in December 1941 I left the Bureau of Ordnance. I finally got myself sprung and ordered to report to the new cruiser *San Juan* and helped put her in commission. Before I left I arranged to have SG radar, serial number 1, sent to the *San Juan* because I knew what radar was worth. And by golly, they actually got it out to the Navy Yard. I think they either started installation or completed it when somebody on Admiral King's staff found out about it and arranged to have the damn thing taken off and sent to the flagship in Philadelphia, the *Augusta,* which at that point wasn't going to go anywhere. So then I got serial number 2 for the *San Juan,* and it was the only SG radar available in the Pacific for quite some time.

Before I left the Bureau of Ordnance in 1941 the bureau had been reorganized under Admiral Blandy into maintenance, production, research and development, and one other—so there was to be established a radar section in maintenance, a radar section in production, a radar section in research and development. In the beginning I was all three, but when I left the thing had grown so that three people relieved me. But of course before I left I'd been doing all the dealings in research installation, maintenance. I wasn't so much an expert as I was the guy with all the strings in my hand.

So I was sprung in December 1941. I wanted to go to the war. That's what you become a naval officer for.

The story of Operation Torch benefits greatly from an outline of the events that preceded it. It was one of the first amphibious operations of World War II and the techniques for such landings had not been perfected as they were to be later. It is fascinating therefore to read the account of Admiral Hewitt as he related it in interviews. The cooperation of American military forces was in an early stage but the reader can see the unfolding of techniques because of urgency.

France had collapsed in the face of Nazi might. It was a body blow to both British and American thought. The United States was not yet a combatant, but in 1940 the president and the military at least were aware of the inevitable involvement. American citizens had not yet been alerted to the prospect. Isolationism was still a factor to deal with, especially in the middle area of the country. This made it difficult for President Roosevelt for he had to tread with caution and yet keep a watchful eye on European events. With the fall of France the British nation stood alone, and the thinking of the American government was that we must not let her crumble before the Nazi might.

The French collapse uncovered some frightful questions for the Western world. What would be the fate of the French navy? What would be the fate of the French Empire, particularly that part of it in North Africa and on the borders of the Atlantic Ocean? The consequences were great, especially because the government of that part of France still under the control of French officials was unpredictable. Marshal Pétain, a French hero of World War I, was elderly and without strength to resist Nazi demands. Pierre Laval, a longtime French politician who served with Pétain as vice-premier in the newly formed Vichy government, early on pursued a policy of collaboration with the Nazis. President Roosevelt, with acute awareness of the dangers inherent in this situation, engaged in a diplomatic act of great importance. He named Admiral William Leahy to the post of ambassador to Vichy France. Not only had Leahy had a career of great significance in the U.S. Navy, but he also had served in various diplomatic assignments and proved quite able to deal with the events in France. As a navy man he could talk with ease to Admiral Darlan, the commander in chief of the French navy, reported to be a close advisor of Marshal Pétain.

Leahy had instructions to cultivate close relations with Marshal Pétain to try and prevent the Vichy government from taking any steps that could be harmful to the United States. One other instruction to Admiral Leahy proved to be of the greatest importance. That was to assist the French authorities in North Africa to support the economic status of that part of the French Empire.

Leahy dispatched his counselor of embassy in Vichy, the Hon. Robert D. Murphy, to North Africa where he in short order drew up an agreement with General Weygand, the current overall commander of French North and West Africa. This agreement provided that the United States would supply North Africa with some American products (paid for by blocked francs in the United States) that were necessary to the North African economy. British consent to the shipment of supplies was necessary because the Royal Navy controlled a great portion of the Mediterranean Sea and under the exigencies of war the government had to issue navicerts to the ships bringing the supplies. The British readily acceded to this arrangement, providing the United States sent adequate control officers to see that the goods brought in to the French did not fall into the hands of the Germans. Murphy immediately named thirteen control officers to carry out the task and he himself took residence in Algiers to oversee their duties. In time he came to exert considerable influence over the French officials.

Meanwhile the British had pursued a different policy from that of the Americans with Vichy for they began to encourage and support General de Gaulle, who had fled to London. In doing this they helped him to keep the French underground (the resistance movement) alive and effective in the occupied country. Thus the two allies, Britain at war with the Nazis and the Americans still neutral, exercised a dual diplomacy to the ultimate benefit of the Allied effort.

About this time the Royal Navy was having considerable difficulty in maintaining communications with Egypt and the Suez Canal for the Germans had acquired airfields on both sides of the eastern Mediterranean. There was also increasing concern that the Germans would now begin to infiltrate French North Africa in the area between Bizerte and Dakar and perhaps even break down the earlier refusal of General Franco to permit them to cross Spanish territory to the Straits. Hitler was also pressing Marshal Pétain to permit German troops passage through part of unoccupied France to French North Africa. Pétain had refused but he had little power to prevent it.

Admiral Darlan had a conference with Hitler in May in his aerie at Berchtesgaden and this caused immediate concern. President Roosevelt, ever sensitive to such movements, issued a public statement in Washington warning the government of Marshal Pétain not to deliver their North African colonies and their Atlantic coasts of Africa to the Nazis for it would involve the peace of the western hemisphere. Both the British and the Americans feared this as a possibility because there were reports that Pétain's government was weeding out certain army and colonial officials in North Africa, and this did indeed seem ominous.*

Meanwhile Murphy was busy building up a nucleus of French patriots who would be able to assist the Allied forces when the time was ripe. Marshal Pétain was pressed to discontinue the Murphy-Weygand food agreement because the Germans realized the effectiveness of this policy. Pétain refused but he did recall General Weygand from North Africa and named others in his stead.

In May 1941 Admiral Darlan signed a secret agreement with the German ambassador in Paris in which he agreed to support a rebellion in Iraq against the British (thus endangering the Suez Canal), to the use of the port of Bizerte in Tunisia, and to the right to base submarines, warships, and planes at Dakar. When this was learned Admiral Leahy and several of the senior officials still in French North Africa applied pressure on Pétain to prevent the agreement from going into effect. An immediate break in relations with the United States was also threatened. With this Pétain discarded the Darlan agreement and the immediate crisis subsided.

The denouement to this drama of deceit and disappointment with the Vichy government was nearing. The United States was plunged into the real war with the attack on Pearl Harbor in December of 1941. General Rommel began a new offensive in January of 1942 and Mr. Murphy discovered that Admiral Darlan had been supplying the general with food, trucks, and gasoline from North Africa. Admiral Leahy, although discouraged when General Weygand was recalled to Vichy, stayed on in his post for a while longer. But when the arch advocate of cooperation with Germany, Pierre Laval, came back to office as prime minister under Pétain in April 1942, Roosevelt immediately recalled Admiral Leahy and left only a small staff in the Vichy Embassy. It was now determined that some military action was necessary on the part of the Allies. Even so, that resolve was slowed by lack of a common objective between the British and American military.

The first step had been taken when Churchill visited the White House at Christmas time in 1941; he and Roosevelt agreed that a major military operation against Germany must be attempted in 1942. The problem of when and where was turned over to the chiefs of staff. They had their first

---

*Robert E. Sherwood, *Roosevelt and Hopkins: An Intimate History* (New York: Harper & Brothers, 1948) 296.

meeting in January 1942. The president suggested to them—indeed, he urged them—that a simultaneous landing in Morocco and Algeria should be made, but the chiefs ignored this suggestion and on 3 March called for the invasion of northern France, the Cotentin Peninsula. This idea had been proposed before and had been given the name Sledgehammer. Churchill did not favor this proposal now nor had he favored it in the past.

There followed several meetings of the combined chiefs of staff (British and American) in London and Washington, several trips by Churchill to Washington, and some events that forced the North African invasion back on the burner. Mr. Molotov, the foreign minister of Russia, made a special trip to Washington in May of 1942 to paint an alarming picture of Russia's military state on the eastern front. Germany had been concentrating most of her forces on that front and Russia was in danger of collapse. The Russians blamed this in part on the failure of the Western Allies to open a front on the continent of Europe to draw off some of the German military forces. Could the Russians hold out? Could the Western Allies divert some of the German might from the east? Roosevelt promised he would do his best to bring about a North African or European front in 1942 and issued a press statement to advise the country of this urgent need. Churchill came to Washington shortly afterward with some of his staff for a conference. Tobruk in the African desert had fallen to General Rommel and he was advancing into Egypt. Matters of the gravest concern now were the danger of Russian collapse on the eastern front and the danger of Rommel's advance on the Suez Canal, the lifeline to the Indian Ocean. "It was a very black hour," said General Marshall. At this moment came a ray of hope: General Montgomery was able to stop Rommel in the battle of El Alamein, in part because the Americans came to his rescue with a shipment of four hundred Sherman tanks to replace those he had lost at Tobruk.

Disagreement between the British and American military figures did not subside until an ominous development began to be apparent. Churchill reported in *The Hinge of Fate* that the American chiefs of staff were in a "fish or cut bait mood." The thought was: if the British won't or can't do Sledgehammer in 1942, let us leave the European theater and concentrate on Japan. There was no evidence that either Marshall or King harbored this idea, but there was a strong sense of feeling in the powerful second ranks of the American staff. The president was convinced the two allies had to join forces and fight against the Germans in 1942. Where then could this be but in French North Africa? This was, said Henry Stimson, the American secretary of war, the president's secret war baby.

The president also stated in instructions he put forth to Marshall, King, and Harry Hopkins as they met with the British in London in July 1942: "Our common aim must be defeat of the Axis powers. There can be no compromise on this point. We should concentrate our efforts and avoid dispersion. I am opposed to an American all-out effort in the Pacific against Japan with the view of her defeat as quickly as possible. It is of the utmost importance. The fall of Japan does not defeat Germany. American concentration against Japan this year or in 1943 increases the chance of complete German domination of Europe and Africa." Churchill commented: "This is the most masterly document on war policy that I had ever seen from his hand." And it had results. The combined chiefs made their final decisions on North Africa on 25 July 1942 in London. When word came to Roosevelt in Washington, his relief over the decision was manifest: "Thank God."*

The interviews that follow deal with the naval phase of the military action against French North Africa. They treat the organization of the vast convoy that departed from Norfolk, Virginia, and contribute to the historical record. The interviews with Admiral H. Kent Hewitt present a straightforward story of the invasion in the operation known as Torch. The admiral was a very intelligent man, a meticulous man who took pains in dealing with all aspects of the preparatory training, indeed of the training even before he was made aware of the pending mission. First it was simply training for an amphibious operation, but when Torch was revealed to him, his impressive organizational skills were used to the fullest. His story speaks for itself.

Admiral James gives an interesting account of the Glassford Mission to Dakar. It is a supplement to the Casablanca landings and vastly important in rescuing that African port from the Germans. It also reveals the great amount of shipping that fell into Allied hands at a moment when shipping was at a premium. Incidentally, it gives a brief picture of the Casablanca Conference that occurred a short time after the invasion. Churchill and Roosevelt were present as were their top military leaders, and James happened to be there with his boss, Admiral Glassford.

Admiral Whiting, as Captain Whiting, was skipper of the new battleship *Massachusetts,* the momentary pride of the U.S. Navy. Whiting tells the story of her initial failure to carry out a successful mission against the new French battleship *Jean Bart* when the 16-inch shells on the *Massachusetts* failed to detonate.

The brief addendum of Admiral George Dyer follows at the end. Captain Dyer at the time was intelligence officer to Admiral King, the COMINCH of the U.S. Navy. Dyer's story provides the reader with an understanding of the heavy cloak of secrecy that surrounded preparations for the North African invasion. That proved to be useful because the enemy was taken largely by surprise.

*Winston S. Churchill, *The Hinge of Fate* (Boston: Houghton Mifflin, 1948) 440–41.

OPERATION TORCH— LANDING IN FRENCH MOROCCO

ADMIRAL H. KENT HEWITT

U.S. NAVY

HENRY KENT HEWITT was born on 11 February 1887 in Hackensack, New Jersey. He graduated from the U.S. Naval Academy in 1907. After six years at sea he reported as a mathematics instructor at the academy. In July 1916 he took command of the USS *Eagle* and engaged in survey work in the Caribbean area. The *Eagle* also had the duty of protecting American life and property during the Cuban revolution. In July 1918 he became commanding officer of the USS *Cummings* based at Brest, France, and received the Navy Cross for this work. He then had a brief tour as commanding officer of the USS *Ludlow,* after which he returned once more for another year of teaching at the Naval Academy. From 1921 to 1923 he was gunnery officer in the USS *Pennsylvania,* and then became head of the gunnery section, Division of Fleet Training in OpNav. In 1928 he enrolled in the senior course at the Naval War College and remained there on the staff for two years.

In 1931 he became commander, DesDiv, and a year later was ordered as operations officer for commander of the Battle Fleet. This was followed by three years as head of the Department of Mathematics at the Naval Academy. He then assumed command of the USS *Indianapolis* but in July 1937 was appointed chief of staff and aide to Commander, Cruisers Scouting Force. From there he went to command the Puget Sound Naval Ammunition Depot.

He was raised to rear admiral in 1940. His World War II service really began

156

in April 1942 when he was transferred to command the Amphibious Force, Atlantic Fleet. In October of that year he assumed additional command of the Western Naval Task Force—the great flotilla that transported the troops under General Patton for the invasion of Morocco. For that service he received both the army and navy Distinguished Service medals.

In February 1943 Hewitt was put in command of the Eighth Fleet, with headquarters in Algiers under the supreme Allied command of General Eisenhower and the naval command of Admiral of the Fleet Sir Andrew Cunningham, RN, Commander in Chief, Mediterranean. In July Hewitt commanded the American half of the invasion of Sicily and followed with support operations. He then commanded the Allied Combined Forces, which in September 1943 established the Allied army under Lieutenant General Mark Clark at Salerno and supported his subsequent operations. In February of 1944 he provided Eighth Fleet forces for the assault landing of the Fifth Army at Anzio. In August of the same year his Allied Forces established the Seventh Army in southern France and assisted in the capture of Port de Bouc, Marseilles, and Toulon.

In April 1945 Admiral Hewitt was back in the United States, where he had special duty under SecNav in connection with the Pearl Harbor investigations. He was at the Naval War College in an advisory capacity in September 1946 and the next year was the chief of naval operation's representative on the Military Staff Committee of the United Nations Security Council. Admiral Hewitt retired from active duty on 1 March 1949 and lived with his wife, Floride, at The Foretop, Orwell, Vermont. He died after a brief illness at a hospital in Middlebury, Vermont, on 15 September 1972 and was buried in the Naval Academy Cemetery in Annapolis.

Early in 1942 I received radio orders to command the Amphibious Force of the Atlantic Fleet and reported by plane to NAS at Hampton Roads, Virginia.

The mission was the preparation of training and also planning. The amphibious training involved not only the training of the transports and the landing craft that had already been assigned to us but training officers and crew for the large number of larger landing ships and craft which were under construction at the time—the LSTs, the LCTs, and LCILs.

Then we had to carry out military training of troops in amphibious landings and all the necessary joint training of shore parties, involving, for instance: navy beach battalions, navy beach master units for the naval part of the work on beaches, army engineer units for the army part of the work preparing roadways, putting down mats and doing everything of that sort on the beaches. Also joint army and naval communications, bearing in mind that on the beach forward you have army communications and that from the beach back to the ship on amphibious operations you have

157

naval communications, both aerial and visual signals. Somewhere they had to be linked up and we found out that the Army Signal Corps people knew very little about naval communications and vice versa. So one of the things we had to do was establish joint communications schools.

Then there was the question of transport quartermasters—instruction in how to load transports. There was the question of army supplies and equipment having to be loaded into a naval transport. Naturally the military and naval people had to work together very closely on that. The ordinary army quartermaster knew practically nothing about loading a ship, particularly combat-loading it.

So we had a transport quartermaster school with a joint staff of army and navy. And there were a number of other features of that sort. Even some of the medical units had to have some joint training because casualties coming back from the front line to the beach had to be taken over by naval medical people at the beach and taken out to the ships. So there was quite a big program ahead and we had a great deal on our minds. Of course we had been working with the marines but the marines had been taken away from us and sent to the Pacific, all except one marine colonel I was allowed to keep. So I had to get a military staff to handle the military end of it. I asked the War Department for assistance and they detailed a number of very good senior army officers who had recent Naval War College training. So I was able to set up a military section of my staff as well as a naval section. I think it was probably one of the first joint staffs formed. I was reasonably well acquainted with the general staff organization of G-1, G-2, G-3, and G-4 and liked the general principle of it so I organized my naval staff also in four sections and labelled them N-1, N-2, N-3, and N-4. That worked very satisfactorily. On any joint program, for instance in intelligence, the N-2 and G-2 people would work close together; in operations, N-3 and G-3 would naturally link together. If they had a problem that was purely naval or purely military they worked right down through the military or naval section staff. I had one army colonel and I made him my army chief of staff; Captain Johnson was my naval chief of staff.

Since the navy had previously been carrying out a great many simple landing operations with the marines off Solomon's Island near the mouth of the Patuxent River we continued doing some training up there. In fact we developed a little amphibious training base up there where we could eventually put in some of the smaller amphibious craft. We had a boat repair place right at the town of Solomon's Island itself. Also we took over a little harbor right along the beach between Cape Henry and Norfolk proper, a small inlet really, that could accommodate quite a number of landing craft. There were some beautiful beaches adjacent to it and stretching all the way from there to Cape Henry. We took over the whole area and proceeded to develop it as rapidly as possible.

Unfortunately for the training of crews in beaching craft and the soldiers in landing, most of it had to be in smooth water. It would have been more desirable to have gone out to the open sea and have landings on the open sea beaches. That of course was impracticable then because there was the problem of enemy submarines off the coast. We had a complete lack of suitable escorts. Yet with our base at Little Creek we were able sometimes to send some of our landing craft around outside the cape and carry out some exercises off Virginia Beach itself.

What we had that summer were some of the smaller landing craft. They were designed to be carried by the assault transports and assault cargo ships—the LCVPs with ramps and the larger LCMs (to carry a small tank, a small truck or land vehicle).

When this business first came up I think the army wanted the navy to handle the whole thing but the chief of personnel said he could not get enough men so the army was forced to start some of that on their own. They had Camp Edwards on Cape Cod where they began to train army boat crews. To do that they took away some of our best Coast Guard officers who had been instructing our crews in landing. The army put in such a plea to the Navy Department that over the protest of the commander of the Amphibious Force some of the best Coast Guard instructors were taken away from the navy and devoted to the training of these army boat crews. The difficulty was the navy was not using the draft. They were taking volunteers while the army was drafting people. It was unfortunate all around. At the very time we were trying to get suitable officers and people for the larger landing craft we had to compete with such things as an advertisement in the New York paper which I cut out one day, a big half-page advertisement: "Join the Army's Navy." It was addressed to yachtsmen, fishermen, and everybody of that sort. There should not have been an army's navy at any time and there should not be in the future.

Along in June [1942] I was ordered by Admiral King to make a trip to England with the purpose of seeing what the British were doing in their combined operations. Lord Louis Mountbatten was their chief of combined operations in amphibious work. We were there for about two weeks and visited almost all the training bases of combined operations. We also attended the landing exercises on the south coast that later turned out to be the raid on Dieppe.

I returned to the States on the Fourth of July and shortly after that began to hear about plans for operations in North Africa. I think it was around the twenty-fifth of July that the decision was finally made to go ahead with that operation.

While in England we chose some of the places for training in preparation for a cross-channel operation. I even recommended a deputy, Captain A. C. Bennett, to go over and start work for me.

In fact, we had been working on a number of plans—the seizure of Martinique, for instance—because Admiral Robert, the French naval commander, was rather a thorn in the side of the administration. He had some ships there and so there was always the thought they might fall into the hands of the Germans. There was a plan for landing in the Azores, to use that as an advance aviation base. Then we worked on a plan for a possible seizure of Dakar. All of these were worked on before we were given the go-ahead on Casablanca and Morocco.

I met General Patton shortly after he was designated the military commander for the Moroccan landing. He was brought in from the desert out in California where he had a tank command. He came to the War Department in Washington and I met him there, but it was some time before I could persuade him and his staff to come down to Ocean View. We tried to get them down in the beginning but they always felt there were so many things to be taken care of in the department. We tried to convince them that daily personal contact between opposite numbers of the staff and the commanders was very important but we could not prevail. So planning members of my staff and his staff had to do a lot of traveling between Washington and Ocean View. They didn't get down there until the last week or so before the departure. Then we had rather hurried rehearsals for the operation, carried out in Chesapeake Bay. General Patton and I got together on those. The last week or so we managed to get several senior naval and army commanders together to work together but they didn't have a long enough time.

I should add that while training for Torch we were still carrying on the other training program of preparing crews for the new landing craft under construction. We had a dual problem.

The main difficulty for the Moroccan landing was the availability of the troops and the shipping. Some of the transports we were to use were held until the last moment; some of the troops weren't on hand. The Third Division which formed the main part of the force for the landing at Fedhala had had some amphibious training on the West Coast. They were given some of the rudiments there but it was unfortunate in some respects because they knew just enough about it to think they knew it all and they didn't. They had to be trained in our methods. Two regimental combat teams of the Ninth Division which took part in the operation had received prior training. They had at least one landing and weren't so bad. The armored division of General Harmon (the Second) had to come down to be trained in landing. We had to learn something about landing those tanks ourselves. They brought a few specimen tanks ahead of time for experiment to see how to do those things. There was always a lack of time and facilities but above all the serious lack of any opportunity for landing in the surf, in the open sea.

About a week or ten days before we were due to leave Hampton Roads I received word that my presence was desired in the White House the following morning. I debated whether I should go by car or by plane and finally decided on the plane because it was quicker. I checked at five in the morning and was told that there was no indication the weather wouldn't be satisfactory for the flight. But the weather did shut in and I had a disturbing time getting to Washington for the appointment. When I got to the Navy Department about ten I was informed that General Patton and I were both to appear and that we were to be introduced in the White House by separate entrances to meet in the president's outer office, the idea being that reporters would not see us at all and certainly not together. Consequently they would not form any conclusions as to our being connected to certain operations.

General Patton and I did meet outside the president's office and were conducted in. We wondered what he had to tell us. I had not seen the president since I had taken him to South America on the *Indianapolis,* and General Patton had not met him at all before. Consequently I greeted the president first, said I was very glad to see him again, and presented General Patton. Then the president lolled back in his chair and said: "Gentlemen, what have you got on your minds?" He knew perfectly well we had plenty on our minds, but that sort of broke the ice and we carried on quite a conversation for half or three-quarters of an hour about the operation and the possibilities. We both assured him we would do our utmost to carry out our part of the task. Then we left the White House and I went back to Hampton Roads and got on with the final work. General Patton moved down there shortly afterwards and that was very fortunate because a lot of last-moment items had to be settled.

A day or two before the final departure from Hampton Roads we assembled most of the senior officers of both the army and navy groups to go over their final plans. I think most of them learned for the first time what their destination was to be. It was a general briefing and a discussion of the plan before everybody parted company and went to their appointed tasks; about 150 took part. We did not know at the time whether the great efforts at secrecy had been a success. There were quite a number of things we thought might indicate a leak but subsequent developments revealed that the whole operation was a complete surprise to the French and the Germans. They seemed to think that any attack at all might be off Dakar. I think it's on record somewhere that some German diplomat or agent in

Spain made the report that he thought the landing might be made in Morocco but apparently no weight was given to that by the German government.

It might be well to go back over some of the general considerations. There were really two days of departure from Hampton Roads and there were other days of departure by the other units.

We had knowledge of the French naval forces at Casablanca. We also had knowledge of those at Dakar. The French forces at Casablanca could interfere very seriously with the landing. They had the *Jean Bart,* a partially completed battleship with one quadruple turret completed. We did not know for sure whether she was mobile. Then there was a French light cruiser and quite a number of large destroyers and other craft. A particular menace was the submarines, for a number were known to be in the harbor at Casablanca. We could provide defense against surface forces by our own cruisers and destroyers and battleships, but defense against the submarines based so close to where we intended to land was a very serious matter. The only protection we had was our destroyer screens and our air. To provide means of containing the French surface forces we had assigned to us a group of ships which I organized into a covering group under Admiral Giffen. That was composed of the battleship *Massachusetts,* a couple of cruisers, and the necessary escorting destroyers. We had sufficient gunpower to take care of everything in Casablanca, however, and also anything that might move up from Dakar. For the submarines, we could only lean upon our air group. There was the *Ranger,* our only fleet carrier in the Atlantic at the time, and various CVEs, the escort carriers. The latter of course were of minimum speed but under some conditions were quite effective. The Air Force was given the job of bombing the submarines if they made any attempt to leave the harbor—a move that would be considered hostile.

So we had various groups. Admiral Giffen's force, the covering force, was up at Casco Bay, Maine, the base it had been operating from on other duties right along. In order to train the air outfit with some degree of secrecy we advanced the air group to Bermuda, an island where all communications were under British control. It was a very secure place. We also sent there the three old destroyers which were to be cut down and converted for the special purpose of landing a specially trained troop outfit at Safi, and also the one that would carry a troop unit into the Sebou River at Port Lyautey. Had the work been done on those ships in Norfolk yard, a great many people would have to see it and would have wondered what was going on. So that was done at Bermuda.

Then the number of transports that had to depart from Hampton Roads after being loaded with troops was so great that it would have been difficult to form them into one convoy in daylight without involving too much loss of time and running the special risk of attack by enemy submarines which might be watching the mouth of the Chesapeake. There is shallow water for some distance out of the Chesapeake Capes and there was quite a long swept channel. All of those ships going out of the channel, single file, on reaching the end of the channel, one by one—if they were to wait around while this tremendous convoy was being formed—would have made especially good targets for any enemy submarines that happened to be there.

To avoid that we planned to send the transport ships out in two groups. The first group was the northern group, to be landed at Port Lyautey. The southern group was to be landed at Safi. The southern group was sent out twenty-four hours ahead. To kill time and also to gain some deception, they had orders to turn south towards the Caribbean. Also as a cover plan, very secret inquiries had been made some time before of the Haitian government to obtain permission for amphibious exercises in the Gulf of Gonaives. The hope was of course that security in the Haitian government wouldn't be as good as it might be. Then of course that southern group was supposed after a night of southerly course to turn back to the north-eastward and join the second group that came out. The second group was accompanied by the task force flagship, *Augusta*. We went along with that. General Patton was with me. He was of course in command of all the embarked troops, but he had no responsibilities as far as the operations were concerned until the landings actually began.

Tactically the design was that the Fedhala force would form the center column of the task force. When the first group joined up, they would be able to open out so that the northern force would be on the left flank and the southern force on the right flank. The center group would come right in between the two columns, and then they would be formed up. Then of course off the Moroccan coast where they were to separate to go to their various destinations each of those groups would be on the proper side of the convoy and able to peel off without any difficulty. Of course all these rendezvous had to be thoroughly published and known to all the commanders beforehand and there had to be alternate rendezvous in case there were any failures. It was absolutely essential that complete radio silence be kept.

The first rendezvous came out all right and the covering group under the command of Admiral Giffen, which had left Casco Bay in time to make about the same rendezvous, took stations ahead of the transport group. The *Augusta* was in position ahead of the center column of the main convoy so that she would be in a position to control the whole force by the use of visual signals. And there was a linking ship, one of the cruisers, I think the *Brooklyn*, which was placed between the *Augusta* and the covering forces up ahead. Of course the covering force also had the

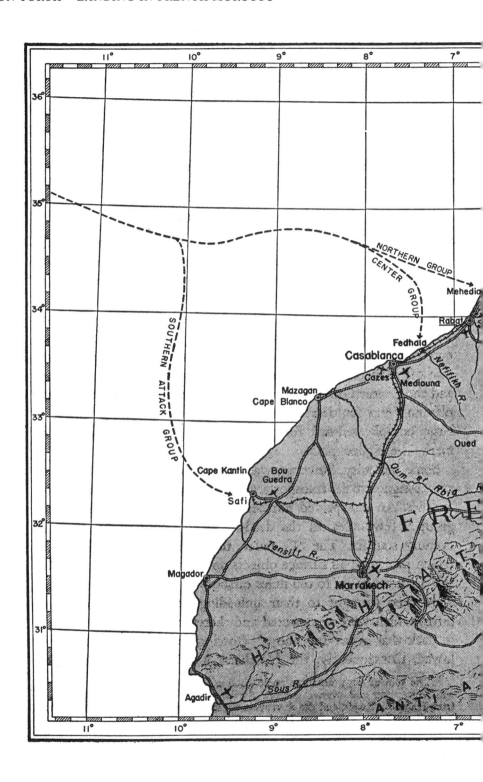

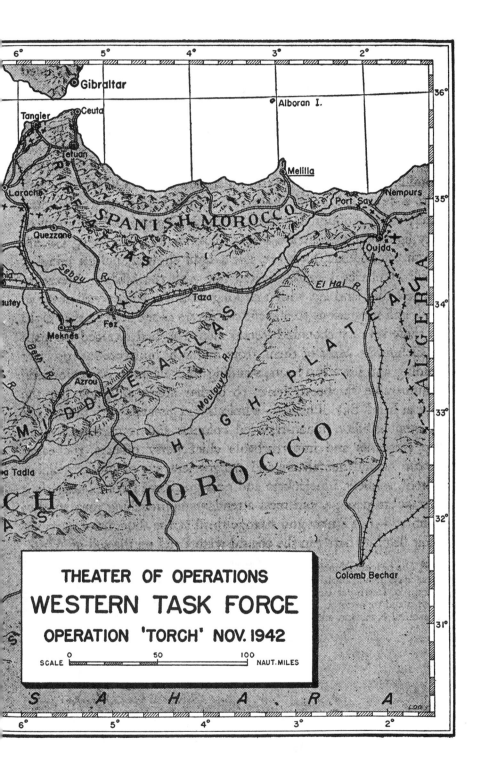

THEATER OF OPERATIONS
WESTERN TASK FORCE
OPERATION 'TORCH' NOV. 1942

SCALE 0   50   100   NAUT. MILES

duty of preventing any interference with the convoy by any German cruiser raiders or anything of that sort which might happen to get to sea.

That whole force initially moved in the general direction south of Halifax and Newfoundland, as if they were bound for the British Isles. South of Newfoundland they turned southeast in the general direction of Dakar and went along on that course. The final rendezvous was made with the air group plus the three old destroyers which had come out from Bermuda under Admiral McWhorter's command. The air group formed upper stern of the main transport convoy. So that was the size of the force, well over one hundred ships that had to be formed and maneuvered entirely by visual signals. They did very well, considering that many of the ships and officers and crew were green. My flag lieutenant, B. H. Griswold III, who was responsible for the signaling, was making his first cruise in that sort of capacity. He was a reserve officer and by dint of great application he had studied up the signals so that he handled the job like a veteran.

The time of leaving had been made early enough to provide for certain contingencies that might arise, such as very bad weather or breakdowns, things of that sort, which might not have been unexpected considering the greenness of many of the crews. Then the extra time available could be used for taking deceptive courses. There was always until the last moment the chance that if there were unexpected delays we could cut the corners and still reach the destination on time, which of course is the major consideration.

The movement southeastward toward Dakar was continued until after nightfall, when we were south of the Azores, at which time the convoy course was changed to the northeastward toward the Strait of Gibraltar as if the convoy was going to enter the Mediterranean. Most of these changes were made at dark whenever practical. This was to shake off any submarines that might be trailing and also to conceal the new movement as long as possible. As a matter of fact, it was customary to make a couple of changes of course, some of them minor, during the night. One was to shake off submarines and one probably later on during the night was to bring us more toward the direction we wanted to go. All these signals had to be made by flag. There was a method of flag signals by which you could direct changes of course at a specified time, and those were always sent out before dark. After that, no further signal was made. Everything was carried out exactly on time.

There was always the danger that some unit might not get the signal and then become lost, but everything worked all right.

The weather situation was one of our big headaches from the beginning. We knew about surf conditions off that coast. We knew from past experiences that there was probably only about one chance in six of having weather on a particular date that was suitable for carrying out a landing. That was one of the calculated risks. If we had not found suitable weather we would have been faced with having to wait for it—cruising up and down off the coast. This would involve the further chance of discovery and of making ourselves a further target for possible submarines—also running down our fuel which wasn't too much in the first place.

We had been making a study of weather conditions all along, as soon as we knew what our objective was to be, and our amphibious force meteorologist, Lieutenant Commander Stewart, had been making a very careful study of the relation between weather conditions in the North Atlantic and surf conditions on the Moroccan coast. The bad surf on the coast was caused by swells which were generated more or less in the North Atlantic and which swept down southeastward and broke against the African coast. Before we departed we made arrangements to get all possible weather reports and to receive special predictions of surf conditions from the Navy Department. The army also had arranged for broadcasts from the War Department.

We got these each day as we went along. The decision as to whether the landing would be carried out on schedule had to be made by daylight on the seventh because at that time the different forces would have to break off and proceed to their destinations off the Sebou River, Fedhala, or Safi, as the case might be, or the covering force covering the entrance to Casablanca. Most of the night of the sixth/seventh was spent going over these reports, particularly by our aerologist, Lieutenant Commander R. C. Steere, and by daylight I was naturally up going over these reports with him. The reports from the War Department were particularly discouraging. They predicted surf conditions which would make the landing absolutely impracticable. The report from the Navy Department was not so discouraging, but it wasn't too optimistic. The aerologist had made up his weather map from the reports he had received and had been looking over it very carefully. He told me that in his opinion the surf would be low enough to make a landing practicable. He said he was sure of one thing—that the surf conditions on the ninth would be much worse than on the eighth.

Based on that and on the great desirability of making the landing on time with no delay, my decision was to take the chance. Of course, it was always possible having put the attack plan into effect, to call it off at the last moment if our later reports indicated that the landing would be impossible. Of course, that would have to be made by radio.

I have not mentioned the force of observation submarines which had been sent ahead to observe conditions off the Moroccan coast and at Dakar. One submarine was assigned off the Sebou area, one off Fedhala, one off Casablanca, and one off Safi. They were to observe any unusual occurrences and report them if necessary, to report any particularly bad weather if necessary, to take positions off the chosen land areas at night and maintain these positions, and then to shine a light seaward to act as a guide position light for the approaching transports. This is what they did. Then two submarines, if I remember rightly, were sent to observe off Dakar. That was primarily to let us know promptly of any movement by the French surface forces at Dakar. The orders for these pilot submarines, after they had accomplished their function, were to proceed southward and to form a scouting line against any possible advance of the French forces from Dakar.

Well, we went ahead on that decision and, as is known, the landing was carried out on time. The troops were able to get ashore. There were many landing craft lost and smashed up due to the surf and lack of experience, plus inadequate training of the crews. By the next day the landing craft were unable to land within the harbor of Fedhala. The surf had gotten much worse. And it is a fact that for some sixty days after the eighth of November there was no day on which the surf conditions were as favorable as the day on which we landed. It was an act of divine providence, I think, that we were able to get ashore at the appointed hour.

Perhaps I should say a word here about General Patton. He didn't sound too optimistic at the final briefing in Hampton Roads. He said he didn't expect to land anywhere near where we expected to land and nowhere near the right time. But knowing General Patton as I do know him I know that was just said for effect. He didn't really believe that at all. Of course, he also said—whenever and wherever we landed them, they'd go ashore to fight. The general was a great reader. On the journey over he amused himself as best he could. One of the things he did was to read the Koran. He wanted to get some insight into the character of the native Moroccan population. One of the objections he raised, from a military point of view, to a landing in that particular area (Casablanca) was that the troops would have to advance through and thereby defoul a native burying ground. This might have aroused the native populations, something we were most anxious to avoid.

I would like to add a word about communications because I made arrangements for an hourly situation report to be broadcast to the supreme Allied commander in Gibraltar when the landings began and we broke radio silence. This was the responsibility of the intelligence section of my staff. I saw these intelligence reports as they were drafted. So there was a constant flow of information going out. They went out through our communications and we had adequate communications. There was no reason to suspect that they were not transmitted as they were supposed to be. But it so happened that these were not received by General Eisenhower or Admiral Cunningham in Gibraltar. They were so much concerned about the lack of information from us that they eventually dispatched a destroyer down there with Admiral Bieri to find out what was going on. One message, as I remember, that we had made the landing did get through to General Eisenhower but nothing after that.

The only explanation I can make is that the British communications on the rock must have been so overloaded that they were not able to take the messages in or decode them and deliver them.

And now a word about Vice Admiral Michelier, the French admiral who was in command of the Casablanca sector. My first meeting with him was on the day of the armistice in the Morocco area, November 11, at a luncheon in a brasserie in Fedhala with General Patton. When I first arrived and met the admiral we shook hands a little gravely, perhaps. Then I said: "Admiral, we are very sorry to have had to fire on the French flag in order to carry out our operation. We always considered the French our friends and we still want them as our friends." He looked at me and smiled and said: "Admiral, you carried out your orders. I carried out mine. Now I'm ready to cooperate with you in every possible way." And that's what he did. He leaned over backward to cooperate with us.

One of his first operations was to form on his staff what he called the American bureau, whose duties were to see what we wanted and to arrange for it. Later on he personally offered the torpedo net which had been around the damaged *Jean Bart* for the protection of the *Augusta* when we were in Casablanca harbor. Michelier was a very fine and very able naval officer, and very conscientious. It was just unfortunate that he felt it necessary to carry out his orders so blindly as to overlook the importance of the primary task of defeating the Axis which was the enemy of France as well as the United States.

I stayed long enough in Casablanca to make sure that everything was going along all right, all the transports and the other forces had departed from the various areas—Casablanca, the Sebou River and Safi—and formed different convoys proceeding back to the United States. Then I proceeded in the *Augusta* at high speed without escort back to the United States myself.

DAKAR YIELDS VALUABLE TOOLS FOR THE ALLIES

REAR ADMIRAL RALPH KIRK JAMES

COURTESY JOHN T. MASON, JR.

RALPH KIRK JAMES was born on 26 May, 1906 in Chicago, Illinois, where he attended various schools including the Armour Institute of Technology before entering the U.S. Naval Academy. After graduation from the academy in 1928 he transferred to the Naval Construction Corps and in 1933 received a master of science degree from Massachusetts Institute of Technology. Subsequently he served at the Puget Sound Naval Shipyard and then aboard the tender USS *Whitney,* attached to the destroyer forces of the Pacific Fleet.

James was on duty in the Bureau of Ships in 1942 when he was named a member of Admiral William Glassford's State Department mission to French West Africa. On that mission James surveyed the Allied shipping interned in Dakar harbor, reviewed damaged ships in Casablanca's harbor, and surveyed Allied ships in the port of Algiers. In January 1943 he accompanied Admiral Glassford to the Casablanca Conference where he recommended the disposition of French naval ships in Allied hands. Following that he was given duty with the commander of the South Pacific Fleet. At headquarters on Espiritu Santo he was responsible for the coordination of all fleet repairs in the area. In 1944 he was transferred to the staff of Commander, Service Squadron 10, headquartered at Manus in the Admiralty Islands. There he became the maintenance officer responsible for repair work on damaged ships. In 1945 he returned to the United States and became commanding officer of the new Ships' Parts Control Center at

170

Mechanicsburg, Pennsylvania. From that wartime command he went to the Bureau of Ships as comptroller and then in 1955 became commander of the Long Beach Naval Shipyard in Long Beach, California. He was promoted to rear admiral in 1956 and returned to the Bureau of Ships as assistant chief. In April 1959 he was named chief of the bureau and served four years in that capacity. He retired in June 1963.

In retirement Admiral James became executive secretary of the committee of American Steamships Lines, representing shipping to the major ports of the world. After retirement from that job he came to live in Annapolis, Maryland, where he still resides.

In late November 1942, I was launched on one of the more exciting phases of my career. Up to that time I had been engaged in the preparation for and fighting of the war in its early stages. I was limited to desk work in the bureaus of C and R and Engineering in Washington. For one who aspired to do a little more in the war effort this was a rather dull, though necessary assignment. Then I was told in 1942 that I had been selected to go on a special joint State Department–navy mission to Africa. The estimated time period was about three weeks; it turned out later to be more nearly three months. I was told very little about the nature of this mission. I did know that the composition of the group was to include a naval architect, a naval engineer, and a naval aviator, with Rear Admiral William Glassford as head of the mission.

I met a few days later with Admiral Glassford and the other members that were to become our mission group. Glassford explained that we were going into French West Africa, specifically into Dakar. His description of the mission was very limited. But it became apparent later on as things began to unfold that the reason was we were to be the major supporting side function to the launching of Operation Torch, a landing on the beaches of North Africa. That Torch mission was kept quite secret and had not yet been launched when we left the United States by air and proceeded with stops in the West Indies and Brazil. We were carrying all this time while en route two very large and heavy boxes, the official responsibility of two aides, one with General Kibbler of our mission and the other for Admiral Glassford. The two aides carried these boxes en route like the man with the box that triggers the bomb does today.

Finally the boxes were opened and the material was passed around to all the members of our mission. It became crystal clear what our function was in French West Africa: our objective was to bring the French forces there under the banner of Allied forces attacking North Africa. To achieve this we had fountain pens and .45-caliber revolvers as our sole instruments for bringing about such a result. The information we were given contained the full and complete story of the invasion of North Africa (already under way while we were en route). We were told the forces involved, the schedule dates of the several landings, who was in command, what the French opposing forces were expected to be, and a very comprehensive examination of the French West African areas and of the headquarters of the French then located in Dakar.

Our mission was expected to get a treaty with the Free French forces in Dakar—if indeed they proved to be Free French and not hewing to the Vichy French line. Our mission included Maynard Barnes of the State Department. He later became the consul general at Dakar. We were to be joined in Dakar by Colonel Julius Holmes, who was serving General Eisenhower as his counselor along with Ambassador Robert Murphy. We were also to be joined by Air Force Brigadier General Cyrus R. Smith, president of American Airlines. Captain Benny Haven and I were designated to make a survey of all French naval units in the harbor at Dakar and to do what we could to ready them for participation in the war, assuming we succeeded in negotiating a treaty. I also had the task of reviewing the merchant ships in the harbor. There proved to be over eighty of these, largely French and interned at Dakar. They had all been deprived of one or more key pieces of equipment by the Germans and so were stranded in the harbor. At least ten other nationalities were represented in this group of ships. The crews had been interned by the Germans at the outset of war. We found there were about sixty naval ships at Dakar, including the battleship *Richelieu,* the largest and newest although not yet finished 16-inch-gun battleship that the French had been building when war broke out.

The *Richelieu* and her sister ship, the *Jean Bart,* in Casablanca harbor were truly magnificent new warships of the era. The *Richelieu* was completely crewed (she was 90 per cent completed) and a Captain DeRaymond was her commanding officer. He was a very delightful person with whom we had immediate and continuous association.

Upon our arriving in Dakar we started off with the usual amenities where we met the governor, General Pierre Boisson. He was an old retired army general who had served with distinction at the battle of Verdun in World War I. He had lost much of his hearing and was managing at Dakar with a large box containing battery cells of a very large size that were wired to his desk. By now the batteries were dead, but our OSS people had learned of this beforehand so we carried in our baggage a set of replacement batteries to present to the general immediately upon our arrival.

It is interesting to record that as our seaplane, which flew us from Natal to Dakar nonstop, was making the first landings of Allied planes at the French seaplane ramp there, another seaplane was departing two or three ramps away from us, filled with German officers who were evacuating Dakar. Our one exposure to the enemy on that occasion was glaring across a hundred yards of open water at the handful of Germans who were embarking as we disembarked.

We didn't arrive in Dakar until December 19 but the greatest part of our delay was because we had been dallying in our different stops en route while awaiting French approval for our arrival in Dakar with a guarantee of not being attacked when we came in for landing. We went over in a PB2M, a completely unarmed aircraft. The total weaponry on board consisted of a .45-caliber pistol in each of our briefcases.

Our official contacts developed immediately after we arrived. Through General Boisson we were put in touch with all the navy and army commanders. These officers made available all their staff and their various other functionaries but denied us any contact with them socially. We were given very pleasant quarters in what was known as the governor's guest house, but we were more or less isolated there and I don't doubt that we were under constant surveillance while we were there. One of the interesting memories I have is as we walked along the street at night (there was no automotive transportation available for us except when we made strictly official visits), people would pop out of the shadows and come up and give us an affectionate greeting in French to reflect the fact that in Dakar, notwithstanding the presence and the influence of the Germans, there were still many French who were very eager to see the triumph of the Allied arms in Africa and the restoration of a Free France. This was due in part to the fact that the influence of the Germans was still very strong there and people were still fearful that the Germans would succeed in war and they would be headed for extermination if they were seen fraternizing with the Americans.

Then on Christmas day there was an eventful occurrence in Algiers when Admiral Darlan, the premier of the Vichy French, was assassinated. This immediately caused speculation as to what our own future might be. This loss of Darlan caused a complete change of alignment of French loyalties in French Africa. There had been a distinct loyalty to the Vichy government in Dakar and a distinct belief that maybe the American force of arms would fail. So the French felt that they had better play it cozy and not be caught out on a limb by lending support to us. It was serious for us because if the pendulum had swung to a revulsion by the French to the assassination of Darlan we could have been considered interlopers and dealt with accordingly. The American vice consul who had been in Dakar during the German occupation had been interned in Timbuktu. He was released only a matter of days before our group had arrived. He was all filled with the fact that we had better get our bags packed, pack as much loot as we could for survival and be ready to go any time Christmas day when the gendarmes came around to collect us. But as it turned out the death of Darlan apparently freed a lot of the inhibitions of the French in Africa and greater support for the Allied effort was immediately apparent. Now there was a tremendous effort on the part of the French in Dakar to embrace us socially. Almost immediately invitations were sent to the group to appear at the French Naval Club, the Naval Officers' Club, the Army Club, the Diplomatic Club, and all places that we had been denied.

Admiral Glassford, whom I considered to be a consummate diplomat, received all of these invitations and returned all unopened with the same flourish and flair that they had been delivered, using his two aides to do this. Among the invitations was one from the local Rotary Club, as there was one from the governor general, the commander of the naval forces, and so on. Glassford sent an acceptance to the president of the Rotary Club of Dakar stating that he and his staff would be pleased to attend their dinner meeting in downtown Dakar. Undoubtedly he meant it pointedly to make clear to all who had ignored us that he too was capable of the same game. We had not been ignored by Rotary. It had no military connotation and therefore he felt that by accepting he showed our desire to communicate and fraternize, but that we weren't going to let the slights of the previous days go unremarked.

The night of the Rotary dinner we dressed in a completely non-reg uniform of white trousers and blue coats and walked together to the hotel, not using cars or transport, which had suddenly become available. I guess we walked a good three miles down through the city in loose formation but in formation nonetheless. And there were more and more cries of "Vive la France" and "Vive l'Amerique" from the population as we walked. Admiral Glassford, who spoke impeccable French, commented upon our pleasure and delight in being there. Official invitations continued to flow at a great rate and after the first rejection of all of them we accepted others.

The fundamental job I had to do was to examine all of the ships of the French navy and determine the extent of the damage they had suffered—especially the battleship *Richelieu*. She had been attacked by a Free French force aboard British ships on September 25, 1940. General de Gaulle had tried to become the rallying point for the Free French after the fall of France. He had convinced the British that if they mounted an operation into French West Africa with him on board and a large number of Free French volunteers the mere presence of this British naval squadron off the port of Dakar would cause the French there to come along and join the Allied cause.

Instead, the British naval force was brought under fire by the French ships, including the battleship *Richelieu*. She had been completely outfitted with her main battery and her secondary battery but they had never been test fired. When she opened up with her 16-inch guns, before long they had tremendous explosions on board from her own powder. As a result at least three, maybe five, of their 16-inch-gun batteries were completely crippled.

The battle raged on. The British attacked the harbor in general and did quite a bit of damage to the shipping and the naval ships there. The battle essentially was concluded right there in Dakar harbor. The *Richelieu* was so badly damaged that they very cleverly disguised her incapacity by carving out of tree trunks replacement barrels for the guns. In a very short time, to all appearances, at least air surveillance, the *Richelieu* was still in full fighting form. But when we came aboard it was quickly pointed out to us she had limited capabilities. They wanted us to get her over to the United States along with the other ships for she had great potential if we could replace her main battery.

Haven and I toured every ship that was in the harbor. We talked with the captains of each ship and learned of their problems to get the ships back in full service. We completed our task in a month and a half and prepared a rather extensive list of things to be done, assuming that a number of them would be returned to the United States to have the work performed.

Early in our stay we called on the commander of the dockyard. He was an old crotchety engineer who was completely in support of the Vichy French. He proceeded immediately to deliver a lecture to Haven and me on how the French had their honor destroyed when the Germans took over their country for a second time in his lifetime. It was a tragedy, but after some time France had learned to live with the German invader. Then he said, "Now you have come in and landed on the coast of North Africa. You have told us you are going to free the French. I, for one, am free and don't want your kind of freedom. You are meddling." With that sort of tirade, after we had come in preaching our dedication to the French people, it was a rather large pill to swallow. As we were entering the dockyard on the morning of our first visit a very unpleasant experience occurred.

A truckload of French soldiers came out of the dockyard just at the moment that the vice consul, Dumont, and myself were entering the dockyard. They spotted me in my uniform and apparently identified Dumont as being an American also. As the truck passed someone spat a large wad of spit that hit me right smack in the chest. It was an obvious attempt to reflect their personal feelings about the Americans. Happily my instincts were strong enough so that instead of acknowledging this insult I was able to keep my head high and walk through the gate. That was a reflection of the attitudes of many of the people in Dakar at that time.

The previously interned merchant shipping was a very impressive group of relatively modern ships of varying tonnages: dry cargo ships, bulk carriers, and tankers. They had been immobilized by one means or another by the French navy. I was given the task of getting these ships back into service and into the Allied shipping pool at the earliest possible date. They had a senior captain who met periodically with the captains of the other ships. I began a series of meetings with them and we were able to get on with the listing of the things they needed to get out of the harbor. Working with this group and with the French Navy I was able to get the parts that had been removed from the ships put back on board, the crews to rejoin their respective ships, and to assemble the manpower to make essential repairs.

The likelihood was that soon we would be able to get at least a half dozen ships released immediately and soon increasing numbers until finally in a couple of months I expected all of the ships would have been out of the harbor. Soon it became too much of a burden for me, because my other work was to review all of the naval ships so Admiral Glassford sent off a request to get assistance from the War Shipping Board for somebody who was experienced in merchant ship problems of insurance, licensing, crew sizes, cargo booking, and all of those aspects.

While we were in Dakar the intent of President Roosevelt to meet in Casablanca was related to Admiral Glassford. Others of us had guessed as much because we had a message that said, "Prepare a ramp of such and such specifications and have it available on the air field at Dakar on such and such a day." I had just dealt with specifications of such a ramp before I left the bureau in Washington. There we had been involved in building a ramp for a destroyer for the visits at sea of President Roosevelt. So when I read this I said, "The president is coming to Dakar." Everybody poo-pooed this. I went around and told Admiral Glassford. "I've just read this message and I can tell you I'm sure that is a ramp to accommodate President Roosevelt and his infirmity. We can expect him to be here." Glassford knew this all along and he said, "You big nosey type. You shouldn't be so damned smart. That's supposed to be a super-secret matter."

He then told me that I was to join him in a flight to Algiers and later to Casablanca to join in the Casablanca Conference and to present the report on the French ships in Dakar, Algiers, and Casablanca. I was a lieutenant commander in those days and this was just flying in super-elevated circles of grandeur. I couldn't have been happier with the opportunity to go. Glassford and I and one of his aides flew out of Dakar early on January the seventh. We flew to Casablanca, where we stayed for a few days, and then flew into Algiers. Our purpose was to meet with General Eisenhower to outline the character of the work being done by the Glassford mission, the development of the treaty relationship, Glassford's judgment of the forces, and the effectiveness of the Free French and the total French forces now in Dakar. My particular job was to present the status of the French naval forces and examine the situation on American ships in Casablanca that had been brought in after their attack on the harbor. Also I was to judge what to do with a few of our American naval ships that had been rather badly damaged in the attack and to continue the kind of work that I was doing down in Dakar for the French ships in the harbors at Algiers and Casablanca.

AN INCONCLUSIVE DUEL

VICE ADMIRAL FRANCIS E. M. WHITING

NIMITZ LIBRARY, SPECIAL COLLECTIONS

FRANCIS ELIOT MAYNARD WHITING was born on 10 February 1891. He was appointed to the U.S. Naval Academy and was graduated with the class of 1912 and proceeded to sea in the USS *Delaware*. Later he had submarine training and then served on the staff of the commander of the Atlantic Fleet, for which he was awarded a letter of commendation during World War I. He then had duty with the recruiting bureau in New York, after which he was appointed as aide to the commandant of the Third Naval District. In 1921–22 he served with the Washington Limitation of Arms Conference. Then he was ordered to the USS *Pittsburgh* as first lieutenant. Other sea duty included command of the DD *Bulmer* with the Asiatic Fleet, command of the yacht *Sylph,* and service as aide to the assistant secretary of the navy. Just before World War II he was assigned to duty in the Bureau of Navigation and was commended by the chief of the Bureau of Yards and Docks for work in the organization of the SeaBees.

When hostilities began in World War II Captain Whiting was ordered to fit out and take command of the USS *Massachusetts*. She was commissioned in May 1942 and later sailed for the invasion of North Africa on 8 November 1942. She came under fire of the French battleship *Jean Bart* and returned fire with the first 16-inch shells directed by a U.S. ship against a European Axis power. Whiting was promoted to rear admiral and given command of the Southeast

178

Pacific naval forces. He was cited for his leadership at the battle of Leyte Gulf, became naval commander at Saipan, and accepted the Japanese surrender on Marcus Island. He retired in 1947. Among numerous awards he was given the Legion of Merit three times and a Bronze Star medal on two occasions. Admiral Whiting died on 7 June 1978.

In March 1942 I reported to the Bethlehem Steel Corporation as prospective commander of the USS *Massachusetts*. The period of commissioning and later in command until I left before Christmas 1942 was probably the most interesting period of my naval career.

The *Massachusetts* was a thirty-five-thousand-ton battleship with nine 16-inch guns and twelve 5-inch antiaircraft guns and a number of other smaller guns. It was difficult to grasp the strange feeling of enthusiasm to get that ship going. I had about four hundred regular navy and a crew of two thousand was assembling. I had about twenty regular officers and eighty or ninety reserves. Their enthusiasm and willingness to work and learn and to see things done was simply amazing. It would take your breath away. The same was true of the workmen at the Fall River shipyard. They wanted to get that ship out to sea in order to do her part. I never had any trouble with that end of things. When we had a conference with representatives of the navy yard, with operations and with men from the shipyard at Bethlehem Steel, I expressed the thought that the ship could be commissioned about the fifteenth of May and sail about the first of July the way things were going. There was considerable difference of opinion. We finally compromised on the fifteenth of May for commissioning and the first of August for sailing. As a matter of fact we commissioned on the thirteenth of May and sailed on the third of July. This shows what can be done when you have willing workhorses.

We started drilling as soon as the ship was commissioned. We had a dock at the naval annex. We'd go through the motions of drilling. As soon as the engines were gotten ready we tied her up very securely. The outboard engines we'd run one-third ahead and the inboard engines we'd run one-third astern so there wouldn't be too much strain on the lines. We did that for twenty or thirty days so that by the time the ship was ready to leave we knew how to handle the boilers and the engines.

Things shaped up very well so far as antiaircraft drills were concerned. We were right across the bay from the Boston airport, which operated twenty-four hours a day so there were plenty of planes flying overhead. Whenever planes would go over, the antiaircraft boys would work on them—not fire guns, of course—but sightings and things like that. The only reason we didn't sail on the first of July was because of bad fog and because we did not get ammunition in time from Hingham, Massachusetts. So great was the enthusiasm of the crew that when we sailed on short notice, there was only one absentee.

To show you how civilians were interested in our progress, Howard Johnson came aboard to check on our galley arrangements. He was there to watch us serve a meal. His observations were based of course on experience with his restaurants where a cafeteria style of serving was used.

Another point of interest was radar. Very few people in the service knew anything about it. In 1940 when I had a destroyer division we came east to go with the Atlantic Fleet. The battleship *Texas* was a unit of that fleet. On top of her mast was this big bedspring which nobody seemed to know anything about. It was the first I ever heard of radar. One day I was going through the after end of the chart house just astern of the bridge when I came upon a man with a large piece of paper with circles drawn on it. He had earphones and was plotting an airplane. I asked him what he was doing and he said, "That's radar." I became intensely interested as he explained what it was. That was all I needed to know to realize that I would get going on radar as fast as I could. I never had formal training but I acquired knowledge by watching these kids and asking questions. As soon as we got to sea I began operating it and watching it work.

During the time we were getting ready to go to sea, the battle reports started coming in. It was quickly evident that we on the *Massachusetts* were sadly lacking in antiaircraft defense. It was necessary to get some 40-millimeter quads but they were in short supply. We decided we did not need any boats except one whaleboat. We removed the cranes and we put quads on top of the crane stands. We took off all our boats except the one whaleboat and we removed both cranes. Of course we had plenty of rafts. So by the time we finished our shakedown period, we had 102 or 103 anti-aircraft weapons. We had about fourteen or fifteen quads and sixty 20-millimeters in the space where the boats had been. This of course entailed a much larger complement of gunners—about 2,400.

The ship was organized into three watches, which was an innovation. It was due largely to the fact we had only three turrets. I consulted with our doctors after having decided to organize the ship into a watch in three. The command would have the four-to-eight watch in the morning and the four-to-eight watch in the afternoon. The men having the mid watch would have the twelve-to-four watch and would stand that watch for the duration of the cruise. That was done in order to avoid having to change their physical habits. We, by doing this, voided the old naval custom of having a dog watch where a man went to sleep at a different hour every night on those long cruises. It showed up well as a practice because when we went into Casablanca we had only three men in sick bay—one with a broken arm, another with jitters, and a third with appendicitis.

In the area of damage control we had the latest equipment for that time. Our damage control people were taught by the Boston Fire Department how to go into a hut blazing with gasoline fire and put it out. They helped us in modern equipment and we got that equipment for the ship. It wasn't regulation but the Boston Fire Department used it and they knew more about such things than I did. So we would always go out and buy such equipment.

We had cooperation from everybody from the governor down. He had a house near the tennis club and one day my six-year-old boy came upstairs and said: "Daddy, the government is downstairs." It was Governor Saltonstall. He had come over to pay us a call. He said: "Of course you live on the wrong side of the tracks. We have a nice swimming pool. We hope your kids will come and use it."

The first time I went to sea with the ship the governor and Charles Francis Adams, the former secretary of the navy, came on board and made the trip with us from Boston to Casco Bay and back. The governor wandered all over the ship. Mr. Adams took a station on the starboard side of the bridge and never left it for the five hours we were under way. I went over to him once and said: "Mr. Adams, I want to do some 16-inch firing here today. We have a southwester blowing. Do you think there is any chance of it clearing up?" We had four or five thousand yards visibility. He said: "No, it will blow for a couple days."

The people of Massachusetts were interested. They were going to see that ship was all right one way or the other. The Advertising Club gave us a beautiful set of colors. The school children raised a number of thousands of dollars and it was turned into something useful for the crew.

I had no idea of our first assignment at sea until we broke with the shore. The summer months had been occupied with training, much of it in Casco Bay. We went down to the Chesapeake for bombardment work and antiaircraft training. Once we went to Norfolk for the degaussing station was there. But when we broke from shore on duty we joined the armada that was going to Casablanca thirty-six hours later. They were coming up from Norfolk and we were in time to rendezvous. We got over to Casablanca without any worry. And in time the signal came to "Play ball"— the signal to commence firing. We had about sixteen thousand yards range, the range we had decided upon to be the most effective because the *Jean Bart* [French battleship], our principal problem, was moored behind the dock. She was not mobile but the firing turret was mobile to start with and did fire. We couldn't tell whether we hit her or not. She was only in thirty-five or thirty-six feet of water. If we hid hit her, all she did was sink a little bit to the bottom. There were a number of French destroyers and one cruiser—the *Primauguet*. There were submarines and at least one came out. We used an awful lot of ammunition because we couldn't tell.

After it was all over we were informed by dispatch that went to the chief of naval operations and the Bureau of Ordnance that we had hit the *Jean Bart* five times. We did hit her firing turret but the shell had not penetrated. It had bounced off because the angle wasn't right—it ricocheted. We did not receive this dispatch until about four or five days after it was all over when we were well on our way back. The dispatch was a terrible blow to me because it announced that all of our shots were duds.

When I got back I went to Washington to see Spike Blandy, head of the Bureau of Ordnance. He had sent experts to look into the matter. He said that when the Sunday dispatch arrived it was the most harrowing day in his life because everybody from the president down wanted to know what it was all about. These 16-inch shells were all duds. I had a very nice letter from Blandy a couple of months later after a thorough investigation. It was determined that every one of the shells performed its function all right. One of them went through the boiler room and out the side of the boiler that was not functioning. The shot that had hit the turret put it out of business for twenty-four hours before they could get it going again.

The *Augusta* with Admiral Hewitt and General Patton on board had moved in a little bit and became a target but the shells missed her by about five hundred yards. With that she retreated very quickly. I was then given authority to expend additional ammunition. I had been limited in the amount I could use because there was another French battleship down at Dakar, the *Richelieu,* and they didn't know whether she was in operation or not.

During the first afternoon there were a number of sorties by French destroyers. The *Primauguet* started out too but she was quickly holed. One of their subs came out also and aimed four torpedoes at the *Massachusetts,* but they were avoided without any trouble. We turned toward him for that was the best way to avoid him. I was always worried about my stern because that was the vulnerable part of the ship. If you got hit in the bow you could manage well enough, but if in the stern with those two rudders you were in a bad way.

We were hit three or four times by shells but with little damage. I was walking aft to look over the place that had been hit. One little kid about nineteen years old reacted typically of the unseasoned crew. He started to salute but instead of saluting he hit me on the back and said: "Hi, Captain, we did all right." That was the spirit of the ship.

We got back to Norfolk and reloaded and went up to Boston. My wife didn't know that I was back in the country but the governor telephoned her. He said: "The *Massachusetts* is just rounding Cape Cod. If Whiting is using the same speed he usually does he'll dock in two hours and ten minutes." That is just an example of the interest. She was down at the dock to meet me. I said: "How did you know about this?" "Guv called me up." That was a very fine thing on his part.

ADMIRAL KING'S "MAN FRIDAY" COMES UP WITH SURPRISING DATA

VICE ADMIRAL GEORGE CARROLL DYER

ED HOLM

GEORGE CARROLL DYER was born in Minneapolis, Minnesota, on 27 April 1898. He graduated from the U.S. Naval Academy in the class of 1919 (graduating in 1918 because of wartime exigencies). He commanded his first submarine at the age of twenty-one and was on duty in the Philippines and Chinese waters while his submarine was a unit of the Asiatic Fleet.

During the next decade he took postgraduate work at the Naval Academy Postgraduate School in Annapolis and followed that with a course at the Naval War College in Newport, Rhode Island. In that same period of time Dyer had a tour at the Naval Academy, where he taught seamanship and navigation. He also qualified for deep-sea diving at the Naval Diving School.

In 1941 Dyer was serving as executive officer aboard the USS *Indianapolis* at Johnston Island, 700 miles southwest of Hawaii when Pearl Harbor was attacked by the Japanese. He then returned to Washington, D.C., where he served as intelligence officer for Admiral King and in the Plans Division for the U.S. Fleet. Dyer relates an incident from that period, and just before the invasion of North Africa, in an oral history excerpt that follows.

In February 1943 Dyer persuaded Admiral King to release him for sea duty and he went as chief of staff to Rear Admiral Richard L. Conolly, who was in charge of amphibious bases in Northwest Africa. Dyer saw duty in the Tunisian,

Sicilian, and Italian amphibious landings. He was wounded by a new type of German flying bomb in the Salerno landings and was returned to the Naval Medical Center in Bethesda for recuperation.

Dyer was given command of the light cruiser *Astoria* and saw service in the Philippine, Iwo Jima, and Okinawa campaigns in the Pacific. In 1945 he became special assistant to the deputy commander in chief. He was promoted to flag rank in 1945 and became chief of logistic plans and then general plans in the office of the CNO.

Dyer was made deputy commandant of the National War College in Washington, D.C., in the early days of its founding before the Korean War. He then became deputy commandant of the United Nations Blockade and Escort Force of more than one hundred ships that came into being with the Korean War. His last active command was that of the training command for the Pacific Fleet and commandant of the Eleventh Naval District with headquarters in San Diego, California. He retired in February 1955 after several strokes. He made his home in Annapolis, Maryland, where he died on 24 June 1987.

Admiral Dyer was a former president of the Naval Academy Alumni Association. He was the author of *Naval Logistics,* a standard textbook; *On the Treadmill to Pearl Harbor;* and *The Amphibians Came to Conquer.*

When we started planning for the landing in North Africa it was of course a highly secret operation. As far as the Navy Department was concerned, it continued to be a highly secret operation. Very few people down on working level knew anything about it. They knew we were getting ready for an operation and certain things had to be done, but where it was going to be, they just didn't know. Then reports started coming in. Young fellows would come by and say: "My army counterpart—or Lieutenant John Jones, or something like that—tells me we're going to land in North Africa." This alarmed Admiral King just tremendously. I told him about some of this and said, "The army is just spreading this news all over Washington." He and General Marshall and General Arnold got together as the joint chiefs and came up with a directive telling the army and the navy to establish a security officer for their respective departments. One of the side tasks was to find out how many officers in each department knew something about the North African landing. That became my initial task. I was terribly embarrassed when I took my report to Admiral King— that some sixty-one officers had knowledge of the proposed landing. He just raised Cain with me.

About twenty-four hours later Admiral King sent for me again and said, "Do you know what the army number is?" I said, "I don't have any knowledge, Admiral. I'll bet it's close to six hundred." "Six hundred," he exclaimed. "It's 1,342! You can forget what I said yesterday."

Of course we in the navy went around patting ourselves on the back. We had so few who knew about the plans for North Africa. The army then really tightened things up. They tightened them up with a thumbscrew. One thing that most people don't appreciate is that in the early days of the war very few people gave a great deal of thought to logistics. When you talk about logistics you're talking about a multiheaded endeavor. It really cuts across lines everywhere. When you have to start shipping things in June to be in Africa, or Australia, or Sicily, in September, you have to tell a lot of people. You have to establish a time schedule and a deadline. It really got to be a tremendous chore and a very difficult one.

Admiral King issued a strong order almost immediately after the above events. He called for very tight security in the entire department. One of my tasks at that time was to report to the Navy Department before dawn, visit the secret dispatch room in Naval Intelligence, gather up the relevant dispatches that had come in during the night from European sources, and proceed to summarize them for use in the War Room of the secretary of the navy. The secretary usually came for a briefing around 9 A.M. But with Admiral King's order I was deprived of my daily source material. Confusion resulted but in a day or two a solution was found. I had clearance of course for handling material through Top Secret. Now it was decided that I would be assigned a special officer who met the COMINCH requirements. That officer collected the dispatches, met with me, and read the dispatches aloud to me. I then took notes, wrote out my report for the War Room, and work proceeded as usual. ED.

An adequate preface is a prerequisite to the unusual and dramatic story that follows from an oral history given by Admiral Jerauld Wright. His account involves the initial invasion of North Africa by American and British forces in November 1942: the question of French military leadership in North Africa, the possible French resistance to the invasion, and some of the personalities involved in all these.

The story actually begins with the recall of General Maxime Weygand from his post as commander of French Military Forces in North Africa in November 1941. It was a recall forced upon Marshal Pétain, the head of the Vichy French government, by the Nazis, for they threatened to occupy all of France, let the French starve, and the Germans live off the products of the country unless Weygand was recalled. On the day on which Pétain took action Weygand delivered the same message to Robert Murphy, the ranking U.S. diplomat in French North Africa. Weygand also gave Murphy a copy of the statement he planned to read to Pétain upon his return to Vichy. In it he said he had moved to North Africa after the British proved in 1940 that they could stand up to the Nazi aerial attacks on them. In his opinion the move and his command of French forces in North Africa increased the potential importance of the area.

France now held a trump card in that her relations with the United States had been strengthened by the agreement Weygand had achieved with the Americans. The latter promised to supply food and other necessary supplies to the French in North Africa. On the other hand, if the French colony had fallen into the hands of Germany the Nazis would have been able to draw on the riches of North Africa and that would have enabled them to continue the war for ten years if necessary. In the doing Germany would have been able to force its will on all of France and its colonies without the risk of reaction.

When Weygand was recalled, North Africa was left with no overall military commander. The position had been especially created for him and was abolished when he departed. Admiral Raymond Fenard was given the title of delegate general and took over part of Weygand's functions but he was given no military authority. This left a vacuum that Murphy and the authorities in Washington decided to try and fill in their own interests. Could they find another senior French officer or officers who would possibly support an American/British operation in North Africa?

Murphy had been assigned to the U.S. Embassy in Vichy when President Roosevelt sent Admiral Leahy there as ambassador. Leahy had sent him on to North Africa to engineer the food arrangements with the French. Murphy made many friends among the French officials and established himself in Algiers on something of a permanent basis. One man whom he had hoped to bring over to the American side was the five-star-general Auguste Nogues, the resident general of Morocco. Nogues was perhaps the most influential military figure in French North Africa. Murphy reported that he had been "warily friendly" but had always refused to budge from his proclaimed policy that French North Africa would be defended from attacks by any sources whatever—the Nazis or the Allies.

When plans for the invasion were shaping up in Washington, Murphy decided to make still another try at persuading General Nogues. He told him about American success in building its industrial plant after the Japanese attack on Pearl Harbor and then posed a hypothetical question: If the United States by chance should be in a position to send an invasion force of one-half million men fully equipped with planes, guns, and so on, would Nogues be induced to join forces? The general exploded in indignation. "Don't do that! If you do I will meet you with all the fire power I possess." Murphy had not mentioned Great Britain as a party to such an invasion because he knew that most of the French military were Anglophobes of long standing.

Admiral Jean Charles François Darlan now comes into the picture. He too was a five-star-admiral and commander of all the French military forces. He had resigned himself to the defeat of France in 1940. Pétain then made him minister of marine. Darlan became known as an opportunist. Admiral Leahy considered him dangerous and ambitious. In the American and British press he was vilified in that time as a "black opportunist," perhaps because at one time he was known to have visited Hitler in Berchtesgaden for a private interview. On the other hand he told Leahy that if the Allies landed in North Africa with force he would not oppose them.

When Pierre Laval came back to power in the Vichy government in 1942 Admiral Leahy resigned his post and returned to the United States to serve as chief of staff to President Roosevelt. Before he left Vichy, however, he called on Darlan and was told by the admiral that he was still in command of national defense under Pétain, and Darlan pledged to Leahy that the French fleet would not be used against the United States. He did not wish to have relations with the British, however. His animosity against them was great and went back a long, long way to the Naval Conference in 1922 when standards of size for national navies were established.

Darlan now began his efforts with Robert Murphy in Algiers. His agent in this capacity was Admiral Fenard, who made his first visit to Murphy only six days after Admiral Leahy had left Vichy for the United States. Murphy learned from him that Darlan still retained top authority over the entire African military establishment. Fenard then went on to propose that the United States should regard French North Africa as a separate unit from France proper and one that could and would resume hostilities against the Nazis "at the proper time" but only when the Americans were able to provide the matériel that made such action effective. Darlan was wary at the same time about the United States making a misstep for it might provoke a German invasion of North Africa. Most of the military in North Africa entertained a similar fear. The defeat in 1940, the disruption in French relations with their colonies and especially North Africa made them fear that in the postwar world there would be native movements toward independence from the mother country, indeed the breakup of the empire. Of course that proved to be the case.

For about six months after Fenard's meeting with Murphy he kept up his contact. He was also joined by Admiral Darlan's son Alain, a young naval officer. Alain Darlan seemed to be ardently pro-Allies and joined Fenard in begging Murphy to believe in France's friendly attitude towards the United States in spite of deceptive appearances in Vichy, due to the pressure of the Germans. Murphy responded by saying that the United States would have a greater tendency to believe this if Darlan had been more forthcoming with our ambassador when he was assigned to Vichy. Young Darlan then told him that his father did not believe the Americans could keep secrets and cited examples of leaks in the British and American press and on the air.

Young Darlan fell victim to infantile paralysis sometime afterward. Word got to President Roosevelt and he sent a message of sympathy to the admiral. That was followed by a trip by Admiral Darlan and his wife to North Africa to visit their son. Eventually Alain was given a visa for the United States and went to Warm Springs for treatment at the behest of the president. After the assassination of Admiral Darlan on Christmas Eve 1942 the president invited Madame Darlan to visit her son in Warm Springs at the expense of the U.S. government.

When Weygand was removed from the picture and Darlan proved to be unreliable (at least in the eyes of Mr. Murphy), another possibility was sought. Various people recommended General Henri Giraud. Both Churchill and General de Gaulle had praised him over British radio as a true French patriot, and Murphy, who knew him, felt he was the right kind of leader, who might bring inspiration and hope to the French people. He had a brilliant record as a young officer in French Africa, knew the terrain and the people—also the Arabs, who had respect for him. He had been a prisoner of Germans in World War I and escaped from their prison; he had been a prisoner in World War II and again escaped from their prison, so he had never been forced to give his oath that he would not serve again against the Germans in World War II. This had been a stumbling block for many of the French military. They had given their oath and it was one of binding honor. Giraud also had not given any pledge to Marshal Pétain and his government in Vichy so he was entirely free to organize French resistance to the Germans.

At that time Giraud was living under cover in the south of France. Murphy had no problem getting in touch with him through a trusted French businessman who had shown friendship and allegiance to the Allied cause. This man held several interviews with Giraud and finally got him to consent to make the trip to North Africa and to participate in a possible campaign against the Germans. Giraud laid down several conditions: it should be an American operation only—not with the British; the Americans should land simultaneously in France proper; and he—or another French officer—should be given the overall command. Murphy avowed that this seemingly arbitrary demand for overall command was not a matter of personal ego or ambition. That was something Giraud never demonstrated but he insisted on this point because it would guarantee French sovereignty in North Africa and it would demonstrate to the Arabs and the Berbers that the United States accepted this premise. When Murphy told General Eisenhower of Giraud's conditions he merely said: "The question of command must wait." As a matter of fact the question still waited undecided as far as Giraud was concerned when Murphy informed him of the approximate date of the invasion only a few days before the troops actually landed at Casablanca.

Soon after Giraud had consented to come to North Africa he named General Charles Emmanuel Mast to represent him in Algiers. Mast was deputy commander of the 19th Army Corps stationed in Algeria. He was also the first French general officer to commit himself decisively to the support of the proposed United States expedition.

Murphy said that when he returned to North Africa from a trip to Washington he was confronted by General Mast and Admiral Fenard, the Darlan representative. Both these men seemed to sense that some decision had been made about a campaign in North Africa and both made encouraging overtures to Murphy. He duly reported both conversations to the White House and got an immediate reply from Admiral Leahy authorizing him to initiate any arrangement with Darlan that Murphy felt might assist the forthcoming military operation. Murphy also advised General Eisenhower, and the latter came up with a formula to have Giraud and

Darlan work as a team and divide the command between them. This plan was approved unofficially in both London and Washington but it went nowhere before the invasion forces landed.

Murphy was not allowed to inform General Mast how soon the pending operation was to commence, but he was authorized to give assurances of American support for the French cause. Mast then urged that the time had come to instigate talks between the French and American military leaders. Murphy discussed this with General Eisenhower in London, and the general approved, asking Murphy to arrange a secret meeting somewhere along the North Africa coast. The American delegation was to arrive there in a submarine to insure secrecy, for the coast was heavily policed by Vichy and Axis authorities. This was the reason for the meeting in the farmhouse on the coast near a place called Cherchell. The French delegation was headed by General Mast and the American delegation by General Mark Clark, deputy to General Eisenhower, and General Lyman Lemnitzer, another staff member of Eisenhower's; Captain Jerauld Wright represented the U.S. Navy. Wright's account of this meeting follows, as well as his additional account of the rescue of General Giraud in a British submarine, captained by Wright, an American. This became necessary because Giraud would not come out from France in a British submarine. Wright compromised by acting as skipper of an Allied submarine, which was the only one available.

A TRUE CLOAK-AND-DAGGER ATTEMPT AT INTELLIGENCE GATHERING

ADMIRAL JERAULD WRIGHT

NIMITZ LIBRARY, SPECIAL COLLECTIONS

JERAULD WRIGHT was born in Amherst, Massachusetts, on 4 June 1898. He was a member of the class of 1918 at the U.S. Naval Academy but due to wartime schedules he actually graduated on 28 June 1917.

As an ensign he spent World War I on the gunboat USS *Castine* in the patrol force out of Gibraltar while his father, Major General William Wright, commanded the 89th Army Division in the Meuse-Argonne offensives of 1918. From 1918 to 1924 young Wright saw duty in succession on destroyers *Dyer, Reid, Breese,* and *John D. Ford.* From 1924 to 1926 he was assigned to duty on the presidential yacht *Mayflower* and also served as naval aide to President Coolidge in the White House. Then from 1926 to 1931 he saw duty in the Bureau of Ordnance in Washington, D.C. and also served as naval aide to President Herbert Hoover.

As a first lieutenant he saw duty on the USS *Salt Lake City* and then went to the executive staff at the U.S. Naval Academy, where he served from 1931 to 1935 and then returned again in 1939–41. Between these assignments at the Naval Academy he served as aide to the assistant secretary of the navy in 1935–36 and had duty in the Bureau of Ordnance in 1936–37. In the period of 1937–39 he was commander of the USS *Blue.* Following this he was executive officer on the battleship *Mississippi* from 1941 to 1942. He was then assigned to the headquarters of the commander in chief of the U.S. Fleet and to the staff of commander, Naval Forces, Europe. He then followed with duty on the staff of the British Admiral of the Fleet in 1943 and later in the same year was assistant chief of staff to Commander of Naval Forces, North West Africa.

In 1944–45 Wright commanded Amphibious Group Five at Okinawa and later commanded Amphibious Group Six in his flagship USS *San Francisco* (CA 38) in Chinese waters to superintend the surrender of Japanese forces in Korea. For the next three years he headed the Operational Readiness section of the Office of the Chief of Naval Operations. In 1948–50 he followed as Atlantic Fleet Amphibious Force commander with a promotion to vice admiral and he was appointed to be deputy U.S. representative to the Standing Group, North Atlantic Treaty Organization. In February 1952 he reported as deputy commander in chief in London of U.S. Naval Forces Eastern Atlantic and Mediterranean.

Admiral Wright became Commander in Chief, Atlantic Fleet, and Supreme Allied Commander, Atlantic, in the rank of admiral in April 1954 with headquarters in Norfolk and directed all NATO naval forces during the Russo-American cold war of the Eisenhower era until his retirement in 1960. Then he worked for the Central Intelligence Agency in Washington during 1961–63. Admiral Wright now lives in Washington, D.C.

I was on the COMINCH staff in Washington in the summer of 1942 when I was informed that I would proceed to London to join the staff of Admiral Kirk, who was then naval attaché. I sailed for London on the fourth of July. I knew I was going to be a planning officer and involved in naval planning for anything the navy might be called upon to do. One of the contingency plans was for Operation Sledgehammer, a proposed landing on the Cotentin Peninsula in France to fulfill our agreement with the Russians that we'd open up a second front. The United States was keen on a channel-crossing at that time, but the British were opposed, and Harry Hopkins was sent over as the head of a planning delegation. As a deputy of the president, he was to consult with the prime minister and make the decision on the next move.

In the meantime the British had conceived and executed the Dieppe raid against the French coast. The terrific losses in that raid, which gave an aura almost of disaster, convinced the planners that an operation against the coast at that time with the forces then available was not feasible. The decision was taken to plan for and carry out Operation Torch, which was the invasion of North Africa. This fitted in with Mr. Churchill's thoughts. He was very much in favor of an operation in the Mediterranean, with Allied entry into Europe by means of the "soft underbelly" of the Balkans and Italy and southern France. His objective was to use the Allied invasion of North Africa as a stepping-stone toward further operations on the southern coast of Europe.

The planning took place in Norfolk House on Norfolk Square with a large contingent from the American and British armies and from the Royal Navy. Very few American naval officers were included, but I was one. Admiral A. C. Bennett was another, and Admiral Bernard Bieri came over from Washington to represent the chief of naval operations in the employment of whatever U.S. ships might be involved.

It was decided there would be three components to the landing: one, consisting of British and American troops, would land at Oran; another would land in Algiers. The third contingent was made up entirely of U.S. army and naval forces to be assembled in Norfolk, Virginia, from whence they would proceed across the Atlantic Ocean toward the coast of Morocco for a landing in the Casablanca area. The overriding purpose of the operation was to maintain control of the Mediterranean Sea and to prepare for eventual operations into southern Europe through the Mediterranean, Sicily, Italy, and southern France.

The French were not brought into the planning and the plans were never disclosed to the French military or political people in London. These people were under the leadership of General de Gaulle, who was a very gallant and a very fine officer but who had surrounded himself with a staff that was suspect from having been responsible for a large number of important leaks. One of these was the raid on Dakar in the spring of 1942, with a force of British and French troops under General de Gaulle. The raid was a complete flop and it was probably so because the plans had been disclosed beforehand to the Vichy government and the Germans. The failure on the part of the Allies to impart any knowledge of Torch to the French in London resulted in considerable ill feeling later on. They had reason to believe the Allies were planning some operation and were trying to learn by any means what we were doing. Directly across Norfolk Square the French rented a large apartment building that faced Norfolk House. Every night the windows framed a Frenchman with a pair of binoculars trying to determine what the hell was going on across the square.

Counterintelligence and secrecy were in the hands of the British because the planning was being done in London. Consequently they engaged in deception that was designed to deceive the French particularly as to what our plans were. They had a cover plan that involved a landing in Norway. In order to execute this they sent a whole bunch of newspapermen to northern Scotland and had them trained in the use of skis and snowshoes so that when they landed in Norway they would be able to accompany the troops. Naturally this stimulated a lot of curiosity on the

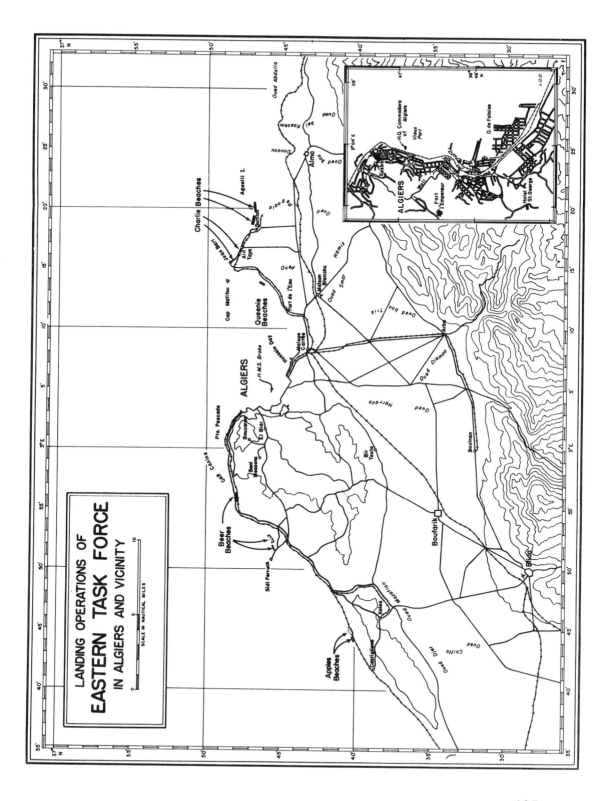

LANDING OPERATIONS OF
EASTERN TASK FORCE
IN ALGIERS AND VICINITY

SCALE IN NAUTICAL MILES

ALGIERS

Charlie Beaches

Queenie Beaches

Beer Beaches

Apples Beaches

195

part of the press. They accepted the plan in good faith but it was just the opposite of what we actually intended to do.

Our planning in London proceeded rather hectically because the time was short. The date, I believe, was determined principally by the surf conditions and weather conditions on the Atlantic coast. The third part of the plan, the landing in the Casablanca area, was under the command of Admiral Kent Hewitt in Norfolk, Virginia, where he set up the Western Task Force. General Patton was his army commander, and the two of them jointly commanded the task force. Plans for the other two task forces were formulated in London: the Central Task Force to land in Oran and the Eastern Task Force to land in Algiers. There was considerable discussion about having the Eastern Task Force land in Tunisia instead of Algiers because Tunisia was threatened by the Germans. This didn't develop because the only base we had to support such an operation was in Gibraltar, and fighter aircraft based at Gibraltar could not provide air cover or reach Tunisia while they could provide cover for a landing in Algeria.

Malta was so very badly battered by the Germans and Italians it was impossible for the Allies to depend on any degree of support from the meager air facilities there.

Our intelligence on North Africa came entirely from our astute consul general there—Bob Murphy. He was a very remarkable man. Not only was he very fluent in French but he traveled extensively in North Africa and had assembled a corps of military and diplomatic personnel in Algiers. They provided invaluable information on French activities and French military personnel. He made many trips to Washington to acquaint the military planners there on the policy-making level with what was going on in North Africa and to apprise them of the capabilities of the French, the French affiliations, and the French activities and loyalties.

Murphy had a great many clandestine meetings with the French in North Africa whom he had identified as being sympathetic to the Allied cause. He proposed that before the operation took place there should be a meeting between Eisenhower's military planners and the French military in North Africa who were sympathetic. His idea was to enlist French assistance in the landings and not have to fight our way in but get their cooperation. This was agreed to on the president and prime minister level, and it was decided to do it about mid-October (D day being in early November), so the time bracket was very short.

The decision to go ahead was made in Norfolk House one Sunday. Mark Clark was to be in command as General Eisenhower's deputy. At first the French had wanted Eisenhower himself to go, but that was obviously impossible, so he nominated his deputy to be the senior U.S. military officer in the outfit. Clark selected Lemnitzer, chief of plans on Eisenhower's staff; Arch Hamlin, who was chief of logistics; Julius

Holmes, who was a political adviser and very familiar with French politics and fluent in the French language; and me as representing the U.S. Navy. There were no British other than three young commando officers skilled in walkie-talkies, guns, lassos, and daggers and folbots and all the clandestine activities that would be associated with this operation; the commandos were to join us in Gibraltar.*

Finally we shoved off on a Monday morning in two B-17s. Clark was in one plane, Lemnitzer in another; I was with Clark. They gave each of us a money belt with about three hundred Canadian dollars in gold and about the equivalent of three hundred dollars in French paper francs. We had also a little knapsack filled with a toothbrush and personal accessories. The money was in case we got stuck and needed money to buy ourselves a boat or buy ourselves a policeman or anything we might need under conditions of that kind. They had to go to the Bank of England on Sunday afternoon to get the gold coins because that's the only tangible currency when you are in a position like that. French paper didn't do any good, nor did British paper or American paper. French gold louis were shunned because of the grave risk that the operation might be disclosed as something in which the French would be interested.

We got into Gibraltar that night and landed on the runway although it was very short for that type of plane. Immediately we went to call on General MacFarland, the British governor general of Gibraltar. He invited us to the governor's palace, where we had a few drinks and dinner. He had a large group of Royal Navy officers present and a group of British army officers. We discussed our plans. All of them were very unenthusiastic about the operation we were about to embark on. They didn't think it would work. They thought it was dangerous and would disclose everything; they thought it was very foolish, very ill conceived, to go into the coast of North Africa in the heart of Vichy French activities and under the conditions we had set up. Clark was a very determined fellow and said, "Whether you agree with it or not, we're going and that's it. Let's not discuss the risk involved. This is what we're going to do."

We did get a lot of sympathy from one young fellow, a lieutenant in the Royal Navy named Bill Jewell—N. L. A. Jewell. He was in command of HMS *Seraph*, a submarine into which we were to be embarked. Jewell didn't have any qualms about being able to get us in, land us, and get us off. That was a source of considerable consolation to General Clark. We also had the three British commandos, army officers specially trained in clandestine operations. One of them was a man named Livingston, another a fellow named Courtney, and the other a fellow named Foote.

Folbot is a portmanteau word, abbreviating "folding" and "boat"; it is the English version of the German word *faltboot*.

197

Courtney's nickname was Jumbo and it was well placed because he had plenty of guts and was kind of big and clumsy. Livingston was nicknamed "Dr. Livingston, I presume," after the famous meeting in Africa. I forget what nickname we had for Foote, but they all knew their stuff. They were all skilled in clandestine radio communications, particularly in the use of infrared lights for the purpose of signaling to another person who had only binoculars and was qualified to read infrared signals. So we had infrared transmitters and infrared receivers and we could transmit with each other without any danger of anyone else reading the transmissions who didn't have infrared equipment.

The other item of important equipment was what the British call "folbots"—a folding boat of stout canvas, stretched on a frame in the form of a kayak. A kayak has a jointed framework that you can break down and put into a suitcase. You can pass it through a torpedo hatch on a submarine. These folbots have been used extensively by commandos and others in the Mediterranean for trying to get ashore from a submarine. Our commandos were familiar with the manner of setting them up. The folded frame was passed down through the hatch; then the skin came down later. When you wanted to embark in it you then pulled the whole on deck, opened the framework of the kayak and then stretched the canvas over it. We had four of these folbots. Two men could ride in each one. We embarked them at Gibraltar with all of our infrared signaling equipment and our clandestine radios and weapons. Each of us had one of the army's new light carbines that were more accurate than a pistol; each of us had an infrared transmitter and a pair of binoculars that enabled you to read infrared signals. The infrared equipment was intended for communication only with the beach and from the beach to the submarine. The first night out we decided to have a rehearsal. It was a rather dark night some miles off the coast. Everything went all right. We got the boats out, got into them and paddled around the submarine. Then we got them back aboard and took them down and restowed them below.

Eventually we got opposite the selected landing site—a place called Cherchell on the coast of Algeria. The meeting was to take place in a French farmhouse with a large square structure on top, something that stood up over the tree line on top of the cliff. There was a single window in this square structure. If it was safe to land, Murphy, his young consular assistant, and several French confreres would exhibit a light in the window. Actually this was a deserted plantation house made of stone with this tower structure on top. It had been used for smuggling. Murphy and his people had selected this as the most likely place where we would be undetected.

We were supposed to land about 8 o'clock and conduct our discussions with the French and get off before sunrise. That was the plan. We got in about two miles from the beach and there wasn't any light. We could see the tower in the moonlight and we could see the configuration of the hill, but there wasn't any light. That didn't show up until about three or four o'clock in the morning. Then there was a big scramble to get the boats out and get the hell to shore as fast as possible. The way it was planned, Julius Holmes and his commandos would go in first and then he would signal out to us if everything was all right. I was instrumental in deciding what the signal should be: we would use the Morse signal *O* for "OK" and *F* for phoney. Julius paddled ashore, landed and consulted with Murphy, who met him on the beach, then sent out an *O* for "OK". The rest of us scrambled around and got in the boats. The second boat that went in was Mark Clark with Jumbo Courtney, the commando. Jumbo stepped on the gunwale of the boat and busted it. So they had to pull that kayak back, and they dragged Jumbo and Clark out of it and took over one of the other kayaks. Clark and I got in that, with me in the front seat and Clark behind, paddling to beat hell to get in to the beach. We got ashore all right and there was complete calm—no surf, nothing. Then the rest of them came in. We took the boats and carried them up the path to this farmhouse. There was a path leading down the cliff and through the brush. We carried the boats up that path, took them into the farmhouse and stored them in a great big kitchen which was full of enormous cooking vats that had been used to prepare food for a large number of laborers. We stuck these kayaks in the kitchen, stacked up on top of each other, and locked the door so nobody could get in or see them.

The Frenchman who was the owner of the house had had a lot of Arabs in the house—employees, gardeners and so on. When he was told that we would land there and have these consultations, he told the Arabs to walk into the hills and forget about their association with the house. They disappeared into the hills, not very far, just far enough to see what was going on. And they saw us towing these big bundles, folbots, up the path and stowing them in this house. They immediately concluded it was a smuggling operation and that they would get a considerable reward from the Vichy police if they disclosed it to them. So they went to the police station and told the Vichy police what was going on, and that was the basis of what became the attempt by the police to break the operation up.

Well, this all took time. We landed at four or five in the morning. There were no French there—nobody came out from Algiers or Oran or anywhere. Only Murphy, his assistant Ridgeway Knight, and several Frenchmen whom Murphy knew were there. They got on the telephone and got word to the Frenchmen in the delegation that we were waiting for them. They came in driblets, two or three at a time. Among them was a General Mast, a prominent army general in North Africa. He was chief of staff in North Africa to General Giraud who was in France. Mast headed up the delegation that conducted our conversations. The subject was: what assistance would the French offer in case we land? Mark Clark was not permitted to disclose either the time or date of the landing or the place. He just had to put the thing on a supposing condition—suppose we did land, what would you be able to do? It was rather frustrating from our standpoint. Of course the French were extremely anxious to know about it but we couldn't tell them much of anything.

Even so the conversations lasted through lunch until mid-afternoon, when the telephone jangled. It was a spy whom Murphy had arranged to be placed in the Vichy police headquarters. He disclosed the fact that the Arab servants who had been in the house before we arrived had seen what they assumed was a smuggling operation and had gone to the Vichy police, who were now going to raid the place. Well, naturally, all hell busted loose. The Frenchmen disappeared through doors and windows, got into their cars and got the hell out of there as fast as they could, leaving just the five of us, our three commandos, Bob Murphy, and Ridgeway Knight to handle the situation. It would not have done to have the French police find us all there, so the eight of us were shunted into an empty wine cellar, a trap door was pulled over the wine cellar and a piano crate was shoved on top of the door. Murphy and Ridgeway Knight stayed on the ground level because there had to be somebody to handle the French police.

There was a vent, a ground-level vent, in the wine cellar that opened up into the yard and faced the gate in the wall. So we heard Murphy talking to these police. They wanted to know why he was there—Mr. Consul General, what are you doing? Why are you down here? "Well," Murphy said, "we had a little party down here. We had some girls, a little liquor, and food. Everybody's left now but I can assure you that no harm was done. If you want to inspect the house, go ahead and look it over." They took him up on that and did inspect the house. They found the table where we'd had lunch covered with wine bottles, half-eaten food, and a lot of dirty glasses and plates around the place. So they assumed his statement was correct that he had had a party there. Fortunately we had gathered up all of our papers before we headed for the wine cellar. The police looked over the building rather carefully but didn't go into the kitchen. Nobody knows why, but they never stuck their noses into this kitchen where all the kayaks had been stowed. Clark was a little nervous in this wine cellar. Then this guy, Jumbo Courtney, developed a coughing fit and Clark took off his undershirt, stuck it over Jumbo's mouth, and sat on it. That sort of calmed him down a bit. What a time to have a coughing fit with an open vent leading right out in the yard. We all had our arms there and we were instructed, if any Frenchman stuck his head in that trap door, to give him the works, which we were all prepared to do. Then after some further interrogation of Murphy, some laughter, some jokes (I don't know enough French to know what it was all about), they finally left and said they were coming back tomorrow morning to give the place a good going over. This took place in the early evening.

Well, in the meantime, I had become suspicious of the weather and went up in the tower (this was while the conversation was still going on with Murphy) and to my dismay, I noticed that the surf instead of being dead calm as it had been all the previous night and day had mounted up to waves several feet in height. An onshore breeze kicked up these waves. I was a little apprehensive as to how the hell these kayaks were going to get through this surf but there was nothing to do about it.

We decided we'd better get the hell out of that wine cellar as fast as we could, whatever our chances were on the beach, so we pulled the kayaks out of the kitchen and trundled them down the pathway to the beach. Jumbo, the clumsy commando, convinced Clark that the original plan to take Clark in his kayak should be carried out, so he and Clark got into the kayak (it was bright moonlight) and shoved off. They got as far as the first breaker. It smacked them and turned them around sideways, upending the kayak, the commando, the radio, and the lasso—the whole works rolled up the beach. You can't get into a boat like that and go through the surf just by saying you want to do it. You've got to do the thing properly like the Coast Guard does when they launch a boat through the surf, but it was obviously impossible to get through the surf with these kayaks, the surf being as high as it was. We went back into the bushes, stacked all our boats, and hid at the base of this cliff for three or four hours. We were very apprehensive that some Arab would come wandering down the beach. It was skimpy cover we had and we might have to lasso him and strangle him. We were ready to do it if we had to but fortunately none of them showed up. We hid in the bushes for about four hours. Just at the first sign of dawn I got hold of Clark and said, "Let's walk down the beach a few hundred yards and pick out a spot where the surf isn't as active."

We walked down to a place that looked a little bit calmer. We sat there, and I figured out that if we handled the situation in a proper seagoing fashion, we could make it. I proposed to Clark, "You go with me. I'll get us a boat. We'll get everybody else lined up on the sides of the boat, three or four on either side (there was Murphy, Holmes, the commandos, and the Frenchmen), and I'll watch the waves and when there is an appropriate interval between two big ones, I'll give the word to go, and everybody will rush and go through the surf as far as they can and give the boat a great big rush." If we did that between waves, the chances were it would ride over the next big wave. If it did, we'd be all set to go on from there. Well that was what we did. It worked. The others followed suit. For the last boat there were only about three people to shove it off but it worked all right. We got back to the submarine by means of our infrared signaling devices.

When Mark Clark got into his boat for the first comic failure he decided in true army fashion to take off his pants because he had a well established feeling that if he had to swim, his pants wouldn't do him any good. He had them bundled up on the seat of the kayak, and after it was rolled up on the beach with the commando, the general with a gun, radio, lasso, pistols, and everything, the pants were missing. Everybody tore around the beach. Find the pants. Find the general's pants. Well, I'd been in the navy for quite a while and I knew damned well you could get back to the ship without your pants, because many sailors have, but you couldn't get back without your paddles. So I said, "To hell with the pants, find the paddles," and that was recorded historically as one of the quotations of the era: To hell with the pants, find the paddles. We never did find the pants, but they found the paddles and we all got back to the submarine safely.

The last boat to make the submarine was Julius Holmes's boat. When he was trying to get aboard they had the kayak tied up alongside the submarine and a wave hit one side, went over the deck, landed in the kayak, and wrecked it. Well, they just cut the kayak off and let it go, and the submarine got the hell out of there as fast as possible. Then we suddenly realized that in Holmes's boat were a lot of clandestine communications giving the names of loyal French officers and all sorts of contacts in Algiers. So it was a matter of great interest to find the kayak and recover those papers, otherwise the whole operation would have been compromised and a lot of good Frenchmen probably would have been bumped off. We sent back word to Murphy, who stayed on the beach. He organized a search. I think they found the general's pants, but the papers and the kayak never showed up.

We were in the submarine congratulating ourselves on various aspects of the operation when Clark decided to write a report and transmit it to General Eisenhower. He said when we were threatened with disclosure to the Vichy police we hid in an empty wine cellar. My only contribution to that report was to change it to say "empty, repeat empty." That's what was finally reported. We got back to Gibraltar without any further incidents.

A DRAMATIC ESCAPE AT NIGHT FROM FRANCE

ADMIRAL JERAULD WRIGHT

In all our planning for Operation Torch, the invasion of North Africa, it was evident that we must get the cooperation of the French in some way. The French military forces in North Africa were in considerable strength and would be capable of offering effective resistance. And not only their participation in a military sense but also in a political sense. At the clandestine meeting in Cherchell under the guidance of Robert Murphy and General Mark Clark, in our meeting with General Mast, it was determined that Giraud would probably be available as a commander of French military forces and under whose leadership the French would respond. Mast had been Giraud's chief of staff on previous occasions. He spoke with some authority regarding the willingness of General Giraud to participate with the American forces. So it was decided by General Clark and Bob Murphy that we would make overtures to General Giraud about the possibility of his participating in our military efforts in North Africa. He had been a prisoner of the Germans in Spandau prison but had escaped and was in hiding in Vichy France when this decision was made.

After our return to London from the landing and conference in North Africa, the possibility of getting the assistance of General Giraud was discussed by Eisenhower's staff in some detail. Participating in the discussions were General Clark, Prime Minister Churchill, General Eisenhower, and others on his staff. The Allies were in communication with General Giraud through French resistance communications circuits terminating in Vichy France. It was learned in this way that General Giraud would not under any circumstances leave France in a British submarine. This was because of the considerable animosity on the part of the French over the recent British actions in Mers-el-Kébir, where some of the French ships in Oran harbor were sunk.

As an alternative, it was suggested that a British submarine be placed under American command, without disclosure of this fact to General Giraud. Accordingly the proposition was submitted that I should go to Gibraltar and board a British submarine to conduct this operation. I contacted Admiral Bieri, who was the American representative of the U.S. Navy in all our planning activities in London, and he suggested that I go down to Gibraltar immediately and he would advise Eisenhower and Cunningham the next day of my presence there. The time limit was extremely short. It left only a few hours of preparation for my departure. In order to complete arrangements I manned a telephone in General Eisenhower's office and got immediate response from his aides and assistants to my requests—first for air transportation to Gibraltar and automobile transportation to the airport that was to start me off on my flight.

Accordingly I departed by car from headquarters and went to the airport and there embarked in an aircraft that was being ferried to Gibraltar by a civilian crew. They were British civilians. The pilot stated he had no room for me in the cockpit but offered space in the bomb bay. I was given a very heavy flight suit and stuffed into the bomb bay where there was absolutely no room to move in any direction. It was rather cold but my flight suit kept me reasonably warm, but being unable to move any limb in any direction, the conditions were extremely uncomfortable.

We landed in Gibraltar in early daylight on October 27. I went immediately to the headquarters of General MacFarland, governor general of Gibraltar, and explained my mission. Fortunately Admiral Bieri had sent a message the night before from London explaining the purpose of my visit. MacFarland called in Admiral Collins, the British naval CinC in Gibraltar, and they discussed our trip. A submarine had been designated and was tied up at the dock waiting to depart. I think my presence in the submarine and my mission were undertaken without the complete knowledge of the British high command in either Gibraltar or London. But the British in Gibraltar were most cooperative and readily agreed to my taking command and bringing the French general off the coast of France.

It was the same submarine, the same crew, and the same group of commandos with which Clark and I and others had landed in North Africa a week or so before. In Gibraltar we had conversations with certain British reserve officers who had been picking up stranded pilots off the coast of Spain and southern France. They were familiar with clandestine operations in the area. Still we left Gibraltar without any detailed knowledge of where we would go or how the operation would be carried out.

General Giraud had been contacted and arrangements had been made to withdraw him from the coast of France at a place called La Faucette, just inside the Hyères Islands. This negotiation had taken considerable time, for communications with him had been conducted through the medium of a clandestine unit in France which formed a link between communications out of London and Gibraltar and the general in France. The clandestine radio operation, of course, was done against the knowledge of the Vichy police. I understand later, as a result of the rather massive traffic that was involved in this exchange, the clandestine unit was discovered by the police and all the participants in it were executed.

Meanwhile, the submarine had departed from Gibraltar and we were laying to in the Mediterranean awaiting instructions. Our wait lasted several days in which we were submerged in the daylight and surfaced at night.

I neglected to add that in my rather hasty departure from London I had discovered that General Giraud knew no English and it was necessary therefore to get an officer to go with me who was fluent in French. I contacted Colonel Julius Holmes and asked him to accompany me, but he said that his duties in London prevented him. He suggested that I get Colonel Bradley Gaylord to accompany me. Gaylord was stationed in Gibraltar as air force liaison officer with the British. Gaylord expressed a willingness to go along but I later discovered that his French was extremely limited and did, I think, little or nothing to clarify the situation to General Giraud when he finally embarked.

After several days of waiting in the Gulf of Lyons we received the necessary information as to the time and place for the meeting with the general. We were to enter the harbor of La Faucette on the surface, lie to in the harbor, and establish contact with the general at night by means of signal lights. Then he would come out in a French fishing boat. There was considerable delay in this operation but by use of shaded signal lights we were in touch with him. Submarines of course have very large underwater hulls and this bulging hull extending out from the submarine makes it difficult for any small boat to come alongside. This fishing boat came alongside and landed on the submerged hull. The general had to make a jump to get aboard during which he landed in the water. But the water between the surface and the bulging hull was only about knee deep so we pulled him aboard by the scruff of his neck, dusted him off, and he was none the worse for his experience.

There were three others in his party: his son, who was his aide; his bodyguard, who had been with him throughout his incarceration in Spandau prison; and his chief of staff. After they were all aboard we immediately departed with all possible speed toward the open waters of the Mediterranean. The one anxiety that we had was that motor torpedo boats in Toulon harbor would have been advised of our presence and might have interfered with us there. Apparently though our presence was unknown except to the general and his French fisherman who brought him off even though we were surfaced but awash in the harbor for a matter of four or five hours.

As soon as we cleared the coast of France General Giraud broke out a suitcase he had brought with him. In this, he explained, were the plans for the invasion of North Africa. He said he had prepared these plans in great detail and that they represented his views of how he would conduct them when he had been placed in command. We transmitted these views to Gibraltar by radio and received instructions back from there explaining that we should make no concessions whatsoever on command but would be very pleased to know what General Giraud's thoughts were. At this point the radio went dead. The transformer which converted the main power of the submarine into power for the radio set had burned out and completely removed any possible chance of further communication with Gibraltar by us. We could receive, however, and got a rather frantic appeal to know what had happened to us. Finally we were advised that a New Zealand flying boat would be sent out from Gibraltar to circle the Mediterranean and search for and contact what they assumed would be the remains of the submarine because they were convinced we had been lost. About the second day off the coast we spotted the flying boat. He landed nearby and transferred us and the general and his party to the aircraft, which flew us in to Gibraltar. The submarine then went on its way and returned later. When we arrived in Gibraltar I think it was about D minus two or three—very close to the invasion date.

There followed a long and acrimonious debate between Eisenhower and General Giraud. The first thing I did after landing in Gibraltar was to personally take General Giraud to Eisenhower's office. It was a room about eight feet square buried in the rock and the furniture in the room consisted of one table and three chairs. General Eisenhower and the general occupied two chairs and I wasn't invited to leave so I occupied the third and happened to be the only one present during the initial confrontation between Giraud and Eisenhower relative to his claims for command. Eisenhower had a fair understanding of French, adequate to know what Giraud wanted and to tell him in no uncertain terms that there wasn't a chance of his acceding to his demands. Giraud's position was that North Africa was French territory and any military operation conducted there must necessarily be under French command. He was the one to assume that command and he had the plans for the invasion in his briefcase ready to be implemented. Eisenhower explained that the plans for the invasion had been prepared; that he had been placed in command of the operation by actions of the prime minister and the president; the vast majority of the forces involved were British and American, and he had no intention of acceding to the demands of Giraud that he be placed in overall command.

He told Giraud that the invasion forces were all ready embarked; the plans were completed, the forces were approaching the Strait of Gibraltar and were to land in North Africa in a period of days. Any transfer of command and any accession to command by anyone other than himself was absolutely out of the question.

Giraud's reaction was typical. He was obstinate, demanding, and insistent that any operation on French territory be commanded by a French officer. The whole situation represented the traditional immovable object and irresistible force between the two men and no agreement could possibly be made. The meeting finally adjourned after about two hours of demand and counter-demand. It was left to future negotiations in which other members of Eisenhower's staff, the British governor general of Gibraltar, General Clark, and others participated. When Giraud saw the extent to which preparations had been made and carried out and saw the inevitability of Allied success, he capitulated on his demand for command. He was given command of all French forces participating in the operation. Of course they were very meager, those that were allied with us, and amounted to practically nothing.

On D day reports came in indicating the success of all three landings and indicating also that Darlan, who was head of all the French military detachments, was in Algiers. The presence of Darlan was a considerable surprise to Eisenhower and his staff. Darlan was the political and military head of all the military forces of France. He was in an extremely important position to control French military actions, for he was minister of defense in Vichy. On D plus 1 it was decided by General Eisenhower to send a delegation to Algiers to demand an armistice by the French military forces. The delegation was headed by General Mark Clark and consisted of Julius Holmes, several members of Clark's staff, and myself. I was sent along with specific instructions to render such assistance as possible to General Clark in getting the French fleet out of Toulon and turned around to be in a position of assistance to the Allies.

We took off from Gibraltar in a B-17 and landed on Maison Blanche airfield in the neighborhood of Algiers. In our landing we were greeted by an air raid by the German air force. Several Stukas came over but did no serious damage either to the field or to our efforts to get out of the plane and make our way to the George V Hotel, the headquarters of the French military commander of Algiers, Admiral Moreau. Clark's immediate mission was to negotiate with Darlan to get an immediate armistice and stop the resistance of the French forces to our landings. General Clark met with Admiral Darlan and General Juin and Mr. Bob Murphy in the Hotel George V on D plus 2 for the purpose of demanding that Darlan sign an armistice and direct the cessation of hostilities by the French forces. The American conversations were translated into French by Julius Holmes, with Bob Murphy assisting. I made copious notes of all the conversations, word for word, but unfortunately these notes were sunk when my effects were returned to America—sunk in the Atlantic. So my only comments in this case are just from memory.

General Clark demanded first that Darlan sign an armistice directing French forces to cease hostilities. Darlan refused on the grounds that he was subordinate to Marshal Pétain and the Vichy council of ministers. He couldn't take such action until both Pétain and the council approved of what he was doing. He was extremely hostile, not to the point of open hostility, but very resistant to everything we demanded on the ground that he was loyal to Marshal Pétain and he could do nothing without his approval. The conversations consisted of demands and resistance for a rather lengthy period of time. There was a clearcut impasse. Clark stated that the Americans had withdrawn recognition from Vichy France and didn't recognize Marshal Pétain as having any authority whatsoever over North Africa, and that he, Darlan, was the only man in the French government who could sign such an armistice with any assurance it would be carried out.

Finally Clark said to Darlan: "If you don't issue this order for surrender I'll get someone who can," meaning Giraud, although Darlan had said that the French forces would not under any circumstances obey Giraud's order because he had no position in the government of France. But Darlan continued his refusal. Finally Clark said that if he didn't sign the proposal he'd send him down to the headquarters ship in Algiers and transport him to Gibraltar where he could sweat it out on the rock. Darlan acted like a little kid. He was irritated, nervous, and uncertain as to his actions, but he was insistent. Marshal Juin, on the other hand, was more understanding of the need for it. Finally Juin said to Clark: "Give us five minutes by ourselves and we'll talk it over." Well, we all filed out of there, leaving the two behind to discuss matters. Five minutes later Clark looked at his watch and said, It's time to go back in. We went in and Juin said—not Darlan—Juin said, "We will sign." And Darlan actually did direct the subordinate commanders in all of North Africa to cease fighting and return to their established billets.

Franklin Delano Roosevelt was reelected to the presidency for a third term in November 1940 and almost immediately went for a cruise in the Caribbean on the USS *Tuscaloosa*. It was a favorite means of his for rest and relaxation. He had begun to brood over a problem that grew daily as the news of Hitler's successes on the continent of Europe became more ominous. Roosevelt's government was faced with developing some plans to aid the British, who now lived under the immediate threat of invasion by the Nazis since the French army had collapsed. He took his closest advisor, Harry Hopkins, along on the cruise. It was not to be all pleasure.

The president knew that he had a formidable obstacle to the development of aid for Britain in the legislation that the Congress had written into law some time before. It had been fashioned because of strong isolationist sentiment in the country. Many feared that the United States would be drawn into another European war such as that of 1914–18.

The legislation on the statute books required that warring countries who came to the United States for supplies were required to pay for them in cash and carry them away in their own ships. Lord Lothian, the British ambassador to Washington, had returned to his post on 23 November, announcing to reporters: "Well, boys, Britain's broke; it's money we want."

In the face of this Roosevelt was still determined to get some rest so he told Henry Morgenthau, his secretary of the treasury, and others who were involved with the question of aid to Britain to think about the problem in his absence and "use your imagination." But the problem would not wait. On 9 December a navy seaplane arrived alongside the *Tuscaloosa* with an urgent dispatch from Winston Churchill, the prime minister of Britain.

Churchill was firm and confident in his message: France had fallen to the armies of Hitler; Britain would fight on. She would rely on her navy and the Royal Air Force to defend the homeland and to hold at bay the Nazis in the Mediterranean and the Middle East. But, he warned, our merchant shipping losses are excessive—and alarming. So he hoped the United States could perform a "decisive act of constructive nonbelligerency by making ships available to Britain through gift, loan, or supply."

At this juncture Harry Hopkins favored sending supplies as a gift to Britain. Roosevelt stood for lending the supplies, and he used a simple figure of speech to illustrate:

> The U.S. was like a man whose neighbor was asking to borrow his garden hose to put out a fire. Common sense and decency recommended lending the hose before his neighbor's house was destroyed and the fire spread to his own. When the fire was out (by the use of the hose) the neighbor could return the hose or replace it.

On 17 December 1940 Roosevelt presented his lend-lease formula at a press conference. The United States, by enlisting private enterprise and building new government plants, would embark on an all-out military and naval defense program but lend or lease as much production including food as could be spared to Britain and other countries fighting the Axis. Secretary Morgenthau testified before a congressional committee on the same day. He told the Congress that Britain was "actually scraping the barrel."

Both the House of Representatives and the Senate soon had bills before them to consider the president's lend-lease proposals. The debate was lively but when it was certain that Congress would approve the proposal, a preliminary agreement with Britain was signed at Washington on 23 February 1941. The Lend-Lease Act of Congress was signed into law on 21 March. Roosevelt was eloquent in his recognition of this act: "This is the end of any attempt at appeasement in our land; the end of urging us to get along with the dictators; and the end of compromise with tyranny and the forces of oppression."

In early January 1941 the president in a press conference had announced that he was sending Harry Hopkins to Great Britain. Both British and American ambassadorial posts in these countries were vacant at the moment and Roosevelt wanted to dispatch a special observer who knew his mind and who was able to bring back an overall picture of affairs in Britain—one who could get a pretty precise estimate of Britain's needs for ships, airplanes, and munitions. The president urgently needed this information to deal with forthcoming British requests and to override any attempts by American governmental departments to whittle down these requests when presented. The president's thinking was that it was all in the interests of the United States and at the same time would enable the British to withstand the assaults of the German offense.

When Russia was dealt a sudden, treacherous blow in June 1941, Roosevelt immediately promised aid. Russia was truly staggered by the attack and it was by no means certain she could withstand. The first token

210

shipments were dispatched in the fall of 1941 and the first official act to guarantee lend-lease aid was signed in Moscow on 1 October 1941.

The shortest and most hazardous route for sending supplies to Russia at that time was for escorted convoys (a British responsibility) to gather in Iceland and sail from there under perilous circumstances up through the Barents Sea to the ice-free port of Murmansk. It was a journey of some ten days from Iceland and subject always to interception from German naval forces hidden in the fjords of Norway or from Luftwaffe aircraft based along the route.

The longest route was through the Persian Gulf in the early months of the war until the Mediterranean was opened to British and American traffic. Up to that time ships had to sail around the Cape of Good Hope, a matter of seventy-six days.

Still another route was available. Supplies were picked up by Russian ships from American ports on the Pacific Coast and sailed to Siberian ports—a long route but fairly safe as long as Russia remained a neutral partner to the struggle against Japan.

A vivid account of lend-lease shipments to Russia follows. Admiral Samuel Frankel, an American naval officer fluent in the Russian tongue, was dispatched early in the conflict as the navy's resident officer in Murmansk. His principal duty was to receive lend-lease shipments and disburse them to the Russians. Frankel served for almost four years in this capacity and performed a notable task.

A second segment follows from the oral history of Admiral Clarence Olsen, the U.S. naval attaché in Moscow in the time of Ambassador Averell Harriman. Olsen, because of his official status, was allowed some freedom in traveling about the country. In so doing he learned much about the Russian attitude toward American lend-lease and how large the expectations were for countless items not immediately needed in the war. Olsen and many Americans like him in Russia did their best to function as honest allies to bring about victory over the enemy. They were frustrated by a lack of trust.

A third oral history segment follows from Captain (later Admiral) Harry Donald Felt, who went to Russia during Ambassador Harriman's period of service. He was the first naval aviator from the United States in Russia, and he was to be attached to the Military Mission of the embassy. His mission was to travel the Soviet Union as best he could within limitations, view airfields and other installations, and report on the general wartime situation. Matters of lend-lease were certainly within his purview and add to the stories of others who also reported on these.

The fourth man to report on lend-lease and the Russians was Commander Herbert Riley (later vice admiral), who deals with a prolonged encounter he had in Washington with several Russian representatives who were intent on getting Navy Catalinas, called PBNs, from the Naval Aircraft Factory in Philadelphia. Their motives, as it turned out, were twofold. Not only did they want the PBNs, but they also hoped to have an opportunity to study the functions of the aircraft factory. Riley understood their unspoken motives. In a most astute manner he dealt with the matter, got the planes assigned to the Russians, made facilities available for the training of their pilots in the use of the aircraft, got them off on the homeward journey to Russia, and all without granting their desire for an inspection of the aircraft factory. It was done without unpleasantness or disappointment to anybody.

Lend-lease with Great Britain is not dealt with in this book as a special subject. Some references are made in a secondary way in the interviews. Those who wish to pursue the subject in any depth will find details in various American and British reports. An inkling of the magnitude of this aid to beleaguered Britain can be dramatically measured by a single statistic. From a table dealing with vessels built for the Royal Navy in the United States it is stated that more than 2,500 landing craft of nine different designs were delivered to the British during the war. These craft were the most useful of all naval vessels for the amphibious operations.

A NAVAL DIPLOMAT IN MURMANSK

REAR ADMIRAL SAMUEL B. FRANKEL

SAMUEL BENJAMIN FRANKEL was born in Cincinnati, Ohio, on 14 July 1905. He enlisted in the U.S. Navy in January 1924 and was honorably discharged to enter the U.S. Naval Academy on appointment at large in June 1925. He was graduated and commissioned ensign on 8 June 1929. Upon graduation he was assigned to the USS *Trenton,* flagship of Light Cruiser Division Two, Scouting Fleet. In August 1930 he reported to Managua, Nicaragua, for supervisory duty with the Electoral Mission. In August 1931 he joined the USS *Houston* on the Asiatic Station until October 1933, when he was transferred to the USS *Augusta,* flagship of the Asiatic Fleet for duty as communication and watch officer. He returned to the United States in June 1934 to serve on the USS *Chester* until February 1935 and then as communications officer of the USS *Chaumont.* In May 1936 he was sent to Riga, Latvia, where he was a student of the Russian language until June 1938. After his return to the United States he served briefly at the Naval Gun Factory in Washington, D.C., and then assisted in fitting out the USS *Ellet* in Kearney, New Jersey. When the USS *Ellet* was commissioned he served first as her gunnery officer and then as her executive officer. He was detached on 1 July 1941 and ordered to the U.S. embassy in Moscow, USSR, where he served as assistant naval attaché and assistant naval attaché for air in Murmansk-Archangel until November 1944. Frankel received the Distinguished Service

Medal for this duty. His citation reads: ". . . duty of great responsibility as Assistant Naval Attache in Murmansk and Archangel . . . he displayed extraordinary initiative and tireless energy in the direction of repairs to damaged U.S. vessels, in salvaging of stranded and abandoned vessels and in the supervision, rescue, hospitalization and repatriation of survivors of sunken vessels."

In November 1944, Frankel returned to the U.S. Navy Department, where he served until July 1945 in the office of the commander in chief, U.S. Fleet. He next had brief duty as chief of staff to commander, Task Force Seventy-One, taking over the remnants of the Japanese Navy at Tsingtao and removing Allied prisoners of war from Mukden, Manchuria. In December 1945 he joined the staff of the commander in chief, U.S. Pacific Fleet, as officer in charge, Joint Intelligence Center, Pacific Ocean Areas. In 1946 he served for a short time in the Office of the Chief of Naval Operations (Intelligence Division) after which he was assigned to the Central Intelligence Agency in Washington, D.C., until March 1948, when he was sent as naval attaché to Nanking, China, where he stayed for a year after the Communists had taken over, returning to the United States in May 1950. He then served as director of the Naval Intelligence School for three years.

In June 1953 he reported as assistant chief of staff for intelligence on the staff of the Commander in Chief, Pacific, and Commander in Chief, Pacific Fleet. In March 1956 he was ordered detached with assignment to the Joint Staff Office, Joint Chiefs of Staff, Washington, D.C., and in April 1958 became deputy director for security in the Office of Naval Intelligence, Office of the Chief of Naval Operations. In May 1960 he assumed the duties of deputy director of naval intelligence. He was chief of staff of the Defense Intelligence Agency, Washington, D.C., from September 1961 until relieved of active duty pending his retirement, effective 1 July 1964.

Admiral Frankel was awarded the Legion of Merit for exceptionally meritorious conduct as chief of staff of the Defense Intelligence Agency from 30 September 1961 to 30 June 1964. His citation reads:

> As one of three general flag officers selected by the Secretary of Defense to activate and establish a new integrated intelligence agency, Rear Admiral Frankel was responsible for coordinating the planning, organization and operation of the agency from its initial inception to its present status as the principal intelligence instrument of the Department of Defense. Exercising brilliant leadership, outstanding professional competence, and a vast knowledge of intelligence and its national functions he was eminently successful in carrying out the extremely sensitive and important assignment as Chief of Staff, meeting every demand of his office in spite of constant pressure from the highest level of government, short and inflexible deadlines and agency personnel with diverse backgrounds . . . through his distinguished service during this period he contributed immeasurably to the successful establishment and operation of the Defense Intelligence Agency.

Admiral and Mrs. Frankel make their home in Rancho Bernardo, San Diego, California.

Suddenly I got orders to report to Washington. It was just before we became involved in the war. When the Germans, the Russians, and the British became involved it was decided we ought to go through the IBM cards to find officers who spoke Russian and get them over to Russia as soon as possible. So of course I was picked up.

I was to go to the USSR as one of the assistant naval attachés. There was a question of how to get there. While all of this was being worked out I was brushing up on the Russian language. It was decided that a Captain Boswell would go as assistant military attaché, and a yeoman named McGinnis would go as a member of the staff. We were all to go as supercargo on a freighter in convoy. We were not at war. We could go as Americans but not as passengers and not on an American ship. After a time of waiting we were told the name of our ship—the *Ville d'Anvers,* flying the Belgian flag. (A week earlier it had been the *American Banker,* flying the American flag.)

I went aboard and introduced myself to the skipper, a little Englishman, a very gamecock type of bird. The ship was filthy. The captain said he didn't know when the ship would sail. Day after day they postponed it. Finally the day came. When we got under way I learned there was a crew of fifty-two representing twenty-three different nationalities. None were Americans. Another assistant naval attaché, George Roulard, was on a second freighter in a convoy bound for Iceland. That convoy was attacked by German submarines and several ships were lost. We had no such difficulty and got safely to Iceland and waited for the Arkhangelsk convoy to be formed. The crew of the *Ville d'Anvers* settled down by this time. A few wanted to leave the ship after they found out where she was going, but the skipper handled them all right. In leaving the States he had told the crew he would countenance no trouble and would treat anybody who didn't carry out his orders as a mutineer.

We anchored in Havalfjordur to await enough ships to assemble to make the run to Arkhangelsk. I checked with the skipper, who said there was no indication when we would be sailing. It would be perfectly safe for me to visit an old friend, the U.S. consul general in Reykjavík. While I was there with him the convoy set sail. I dashed down to the port, got hold of a motor boat to take me to my ship, but it was too late. The consul general came to my rescue and spoke to the naval officer in charge there. He assigned a destroyer to take me out and intercept the convoy. We reached my ship the following dawn. They lowered a rope ladder and I clambered aboard.

This convoy out of Iceland bore the number one designation, the first really large organized convoy, although I think it was actually the second convoy on the route. The date was in August 1941. We saw nothing on the way. We ran into snow flurries but there were no alerts. It was a good thing. We had in the *Ville d'Anvers* nothing in the line of armament for defense, except two rather unique objects. On top of one of the deckhouses was a steam-operated grenade thrower. The idea was to put a grenade in this thing, throw the lever, and the steam would eject the grenade some three or four hundred feet in the air where it would explode. The theory was to wait until an enemy plane came over, shoot the thing, and it would knock down the plane. We were to test it with a potato each morning. The skipper had been a bit concerned about this weapon and while waiting in Iceland had obtained two Lewis machine guns, one on each wing of the bridge. There was another weapon on board—a rocket launcher on each wing of the bridge. This was also an ingenious device. These rockets would be set off. They would go straight up, carrying with them wire which was in a coil. These rockets would go maybe five hundred feet trailing this wire. Any plane attacking the ship would have his wings sheared off by the wire that ran between the rocket and the ship.

These weapons were perhaps psychologically a small factor for safety but otherwise they didn't amount to anything. There was no armed guard on board. The crew would operate these things and we were to help. Actually the Germans had not yet established themselves on the tip of Norway or in Petsamo in Finland, so we saw no evidence of air and no evidence of submarines. We had just a minimum of British escorts until we got close to Arkhangelsk, when a couple of Russian destroyers came out. It wasn't really an organized escort group.

We got to Arkhangelsk and went up the long run to our berth. There was a tremendous amount of activity there. You could see the long line of lumber-loading wharves, for lumber was the chief export of that area. That very night I was invited ashore to be the U.S. representative at a meeting between the British Ministry of War Transport and the Russian Assistant Commissar of Foreign Trade. They were having the customary Soviet dinner, which meant it was more than half liquid. I sat down and being a late arrival I was encouraged to catch up. We sat and toasted each other. Though I had been accustomed to handle vodka during my stay in Riga this was a little bit different. I found I did very well while seated. At least to my own ears my Russian was coming back by leaps and bounds. I found that when I started to get to my feet I wasn't doing too well. But I did get back to the ship under my own steam.

We waited in Arkhangelsk for our further orders. When they came we were to report to the senior naval attaché in Moscow. Some of the ships had been in Arkhangelsk for a long time. The facilities for unloading the types of cargo these ships carried were nonexistent. So they had to do a lot of Mickey Mouse rigging to get some of the heavy things ashore. Murmansk was not open yet. It didn't have the facilities.

We found we could get a train to Moscow, but we waited several days until the train formed. The captain and the crew loaded us with sacks of provisions, for we were told there was no way of knowing how long it would take to get to Moscow. We didn't have any money. Actually we signed chits and borrowed money from the British, who had money there. As the train got further south we saw refugees coming north. The stations were crowded—lots of women with children who were in pretty bad shape. We gave them quite a bit of our food. We just felt sorry for them. We occupied hard-class compartments on the train—wooden benches. Hot water was furnished and you could buy things at the stations. Peasants came up largely with hard-boiled eggs and black bread. Farther south it became more difficult. The supply was inadequate so prices went up, as much as a dollar for one egg and other things accordingly.

When we got close to Moscow we learned the city was practically under siege and the embassies had left the city. We were never told just where, perhaps along the river, maybe in Gorki much farther down. At the station north of Moscow I decided that we had better go to the local NKVD and tell them about our predicament. The official there was very cooperative. He said we should shift to the river from the railroad. He would see that we got transportation on a river boat. We did get on the first steamer. It was crowded, jammed full. Normally it carried something like six hundred. We had fifteen hundred on board and alongside the steamer was a barge that carried about eight hundred youngsters from the Boy's Technical Training School that they were moving away from the area. We were given two cabins with two bunks for the six of us. They provided blankets and a mattress. We were certainly well taken care of with what was available and treated like princes relatively.

A captain of the Soviet navy was aboard with his family. I'm sure he had been directed by the NKVD to look after us. He was of great service and arranged food for us. He'd go ashore when we came to a port and come back with provisions. He was really marvelous. Not until we got near Kuybyshev did we find that the embassies were in fact located there.

The acceptance of the Russians in a joyful spirit of the hardships was really a pleasure to observe. They sang. There were lots of accordions and guitars around. So it was really an excursion trip except there were four or five times the usual number on an excursion trip. It took four or five days on a trip of nine hundred miles.

We hitchhiked up to town from the river and found our embassy located in an old schoolhouse. We came in completely as a surprise, but crowded though they were they were very helpful in getting us settled.

There were a lot of American correspondents in Kuybyshev living in the so-called hotel. They named it *Nichevo nyet* ("there is nothing"), a reference to the menu from which nothing was available. So a lot of them did their own cooking. The British were fine with whiskey. There was vodka and beer and marvelous mineral water. Food was short but it was all right. This was now the capital of Russia and every effort was made to supply the capital with whatever it needed.

After awhile word came to the ambassador from the British in Arkhangelsk that they were having trouble with crews in ships that came from the United States. They had no control over them. Would we send an American representative up there? So I was detailed to go and see whether this was feasible and desirable. This was a trial run just to see, really an inspection and examination. The Soviet navy was ordered to escort one of us up there. I was assigned an escort. We were given space on a plane. We flew to Arkhangelsk, inspected the port, then went to a place called Molotovsk, which we were considering as an auxiliary port to Arkhangelsk. It was a naval shipbuilding yard. With great reluctance the Soviets decided they would throw it open to merchant vessels. Then we came back to Moscow for by that time the city was safe.

I got back to Kuybyshev and reported it would be a good idea to have somebody there to represent the U.S. Our people were used to facilities that the British had never given their people or had curtailed in time of war. It was decided that the War Shipping Administration should send a rep but since that would take time, one of us who spoke Russian should go. I was the one to go. I could take a yeoman with me. I was to go up alone at first and the yeoman, McGinnis, would follow later. There was an old TB3 available, a low-winged monoplane with a flying speed of about eighty-five knots top speed. We were to fly from Kuybyshev to Moscow. Then I would take the train north.

It was fifty-five below zero on the ground. They had an awful job starting the plane. The captain didn't want to fly as it was foggy and conditions were very bad. But he was ordered to get us to Moscow (myself and two British naval officers) and so he did. The pilot sat up on top. I don't know if it was an open cockpit or not. We were told we would be given the best place in the plane, the bombardier's cockpit, the bubble up front. There were three seats and also a little stand. A machine gun was mounted there, with a gunner properly garbed in his flying suit.

I had my cipher codes with me in a briefcase. I had seventeen boxes of odds and ends, office supplies, scattered throughout the plane. There were some seventeen passengers also scattered throughout the plane. My garb was standard U.S. winter gear. I was in uniform with the normal cap and overcoat and I did have galoshes on.

As soon as we left the shelter of the airport I started getting cold. Pretty soon I was a little bit numb because it was open to the wind. The gunnery hatch was up there. We could see we were flying in fog. We were flying low in order to do sight navigation. There were no aids to navigation. The pilot was following along the railroad. We came out of the fog and then things began to happen. We came to a station. The ceiling was very, very low. He started to circle the station. There was a patch of fog. As we came out of it there was a parked freight train right there. I had time to think—maybe I did say—"hold your hats, boys" and we hit the train at the station. I could feel myself being thrown around, blinded by snow in my face. Suddenly everything was quiet. "I guess I've had it," I said, "I must be wherever I've gone." Then I could hear some noise and I started to stir. I realized I was all right. I called to the two Britishers in front of me, "Are you all right?" I saw one of them was bleeding about the face and he said to me: "You've got blood on your face." "Let's get out of here," I cried. I was so stiff and cold I had an awful time, but we got out.

There were the local gentry around. One of them with a pitchfork in true partisan style. The Russian passengers were there, including a general. They were all dressed in winter garb with no distinguishing marks. I recovered my cap and put it on my head. The general said in Russian: "We're your people." The fellow with the pitchfork said: "Maybe so, but you'll need documents." We found out later what they thought.

The pilot said he came out of the fog and knew he was too low but he couldn't pull out. The plane had fixed landing gear that hit the train, knocking over a freight car filled with pipe. There was a lot of snow and it saved us. A wing was sheared off by a telephone pole and we started spinning and continued tail first for a couple of hundred yards. The pilot said he had cut the ignition as soon as he knew he couldn't make it so there was no fire. The local gentry thought a German plane had come over and dropped a bomb and the resultant blast had knocked the plane down.

We scrambled, picked up the seventeen pieces of baggage including my bottle of Grand Marnier, and were taken into the station, where they gave us some borscht. Meanwhile a doctor came. I think he probably was a vet. He made me strip. I had been sitting in line with the propellers and since they were wooden they shattered and some of the pieces hit me. They did a little damage. The doctor put on bandages but not very well because when I stood up, the bandages on my legs fell down. Nobody else was hurt. When a hospital train came along we were put aboard, fed, and given a place to sleep. In Moscow they offered me a truck to carry the stuff to the embassy.

After a few days rest at the embassy I went up to Arkhangelsk by train. It was crowded and conditions were difficult but I had food and a little sterno stove. In Arkhangelsk I stayed with the British. Since the winter was bad, Arkhangelsk port was closed and they were bringing ships into Murmansk. So I was flown into Murmansk in an old C-47, Russian version. The plane was carrying detonators. As we approached somebody came dashing out of the front cockpit and gave me a little tommy gun. He pointed out the window to a plane way up in the sky. Shoot if you see it. Luckily it was a Russian plane and we were not attacked. We landed and I came into a place called the Arctic Hotel, where I was given a room and bath. There was also a restaurant.

Since there was a convoy in at the time I got in touch with the skippers and offered to help in any way—consular work. I got in touch with the British and with Admiral Papanin, a rear admiral in the Russian navy and head of the North Sea route that had its western terminus in Murmansk. He was an interesting fellow, an Arctic explorer and one of the early Heroes of the Soviet Union. A very revered character, he ran his organization like a feudal chieftain. When anybody was in trouble they could come to him and he would take care of them. We got to be on pretty friendly terms. I told him I couldn't operate out of a hotel room. American ships were making up the bulk of the convoys. I just had to get organized so he gave orders to the man in charge of logistics to give me a flat in a building being put up for the Soviet navy.

In a short time I did have the apartment—a so-called flat. There were four rooms, a bath, and a kitchen. It wasn't finished completely or properly. I remember the way you would check on whether your electrical wiring system was being overloaded. There was no fuse box or circuit breaker in the apartment but feed wires within reaching distance. When you cut something else in on your system you would feel these wires. If they were getting too hot you would pull the plug on this latest appliance.

We had running water most of the time. We had electricity most of the time. We had hot water once a week. We didn't have any windows left after a little while. They were all knocked out. So I got some plastic, ordered some from the U.S. and it came out on one of the ships. We had radiators and most of the time they worked. It never got really cold in Murmansk. As they used to say, "We have nine months of winter and three months of bad weather." The Gulf Stream terminates just east of Murmansk on the Kola Peninsula. That was the reason it was so important. The Kola inlet never froze. It might get a skim of ice, no more than a half-inch thick at the most. The only time we got cold in the winter actually was when there was a wind from the south or southwest. It was always around freezing, so it never got bitterly cold. In the spring they'd have occasional fog. That made it very difficult because there wasn't much pavement—a short stretch of paved road, the main thoroughfare.

During the time I was living at the hotel, McGinnis came up by train with the rest of the gear. He and I then ran the thing on our own for a good part of the early years.

In the meantime there had been several raids on the city of Murmansk. At first there was no defense for the city. The planes would come in and down over the port very low, maybe six hundred to one thousand feet and drop their bombs with considerable accuracy. The town itself was not damaged in the early stages. It was a town of maybe six or seven thousand at the most. Most of the residents had been moved out; only the working people and a few of the families were there. Some new buildings had gone up. Most of them were made of wood or stone with brick chimneys. That was about all that was left of the bulk of the town later on.

At first we had no transportation. Then we had two cars shipped out. Unfortunately the ship that those cars were on was sunk. Finally I asked through the commissar of foreign trade if I could have one of the jeeps assigned to me. We were shipping many of them up there. But prior to that time I just walked all over the place, down to the port, everywhere. The jeep was a big help. After awhile I got more people. I got three more people. I finally had a staff of five, including a mechanic who took care of our boat so we could go around. We serviced the ships. We would go down and visit the ships and endeavor to get return cargo for them, cargo or ballast so that they could go back safely. We had a little trouble with the Soviets on this because they had great demands on their transportation. I finally convinced them (Admiral Standley helped considerably on this) that these same ships of ours would have to bring out more cargo. If they didn't get back home safely, if we lost more ships because of inability to keep the sea, the convoys couldn't be enlarged. Finally I told the representative that if we couldn't be assured of ballast we'd just stop unloading. When the convoys formed to go back, the ships would go back with parts of the loads in their bottoms, mainly steel rails. That's where they used to put the heavy stuff, down in the bottom where it would act as ballast. It would be a shame after they'd come all this way if they couldn't unload this stuff, but I had to be assured they'd have return ballast. Ambassador Standley backed me on this. We actually never did send cargoes back, we always off-loaded everything. But I had to use this as a leverage.

Actually I had a very good relationship with the Soviets up there so that if any ships suffered damage which could be repaired locally the Soviets really gave us first priority. They had difficulty because their commissariats are quite autonomous. The head of the fishing industry up there had control over certain shipyards, certain wharves, and certain materials. The navy had other areas. The shipping of foreign trade had other areas.

In one case we had a ship which had a big hole under her counter. The yards were crowded. The crew said they could fix it if they could get the material. We had about a sixteen-foot tide there so we put the stern up on the beach and the bow would float up and down but this hole would be clear above the water most of the time. They needed some plating and some welding equipment. I got the plates from one shipyard. They didn't

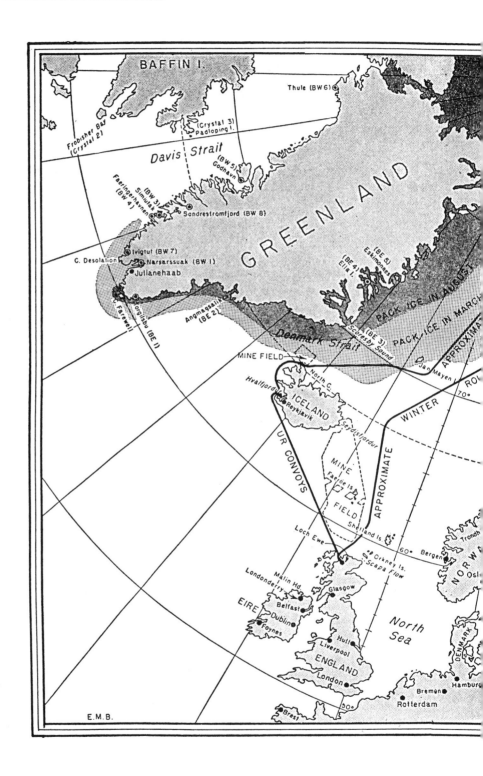

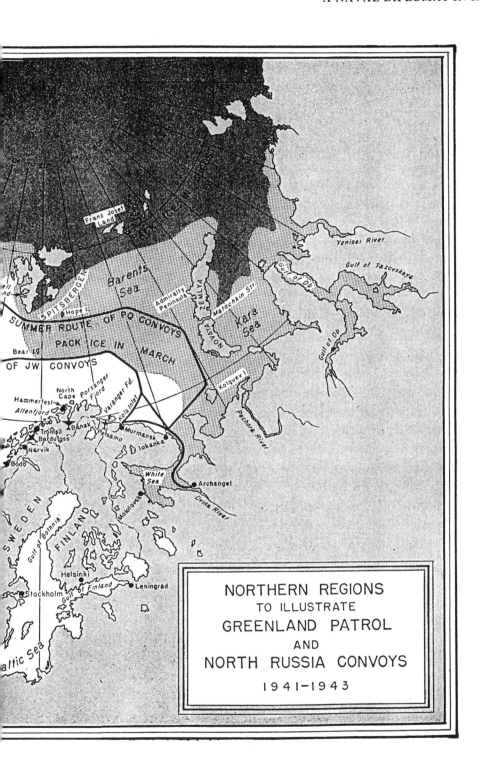

NORTHERN REGIONS
TO ILLUSTRATE
GREENLAND PATROL
AND
NORTH RUSSIA CONVOYS
1941–1943

have any welding equipment so I got that from another place. We didn't have any gasoline to run the motor for this thing so I got the gasoline from another. I signed chits back and forth. One company couldn't go to another without a great deal of red tape and time consumed. I was sort of the broker to a certain extent—the go-between among these people. The Soviets didn't meet the standards that some of our people expected but I knew they were doing more than the best they could because it was to their advantage. Papanin was a big help on this and was all for it.

My concern was generally for between twenty and twenty-five ships in an incoming convoy. We were very fortunate in that not a single American ship went to the bottom there in the inlet. Some of them were hit but they were all saved by various means. The British did lose seven or eight ships right there in the inlet.

The Germans did move aircraft up into the northern tip of Norway. These were mainly to intercept convoys. For attacks on Murmansk the Germans established an airfield at Petsamo, about ten-minutes flying time away. You could actually see them circle to get altitude and then they would come in, so that you had very little advance notice, except that they were quite regular. After a while it got to be a pattern. A photographic plane would come over. Then two hours or so later they'd make the raid. This was pretty much standard.

I remember on one occasion I was aboard a ship which had been involved in an air attack off Normandy previously. The skipper was paying, giving the men some rubles to take ashore. They had just 50-caliber machine guns on board. There was an air alert and in came the planes. They were Stukas and Junker-88s. The Germans used to attach whistles to these planes and they'd make a terrific racket, just like howling demons. A plane came diving down on us, and since I happened to be there I manned the machine gun. He came down and you could see him. I thought I was hitting him, but of course I wasn't because he kept on. He dropped two bombs and actually straddled the ship. In the meantime the skipper didn't know what to do, so I told him to just stay below and this would be over.

In raids of this sort the Germans would not have many planes— anywhere between four and ten at the most. Then the Soviets brought up antiaircraft and their own planes, mostly Air Cobras and Tomahawks. Sometimes you'd see dogfights but generally the action was hit-and-run. Finally the Soviets had plenty of antiaircraft guns ringing the city so they forced the Germans to go up higher. With that of course they weren't so accurate so they were dropping occasional bombs on the town. The main port was roughly a half mile away. From an altitude of ten thousand or eleven thousand feet that wasn't much of a miss. Later on they actually went for the town.

While we were living in the apartment building they had a fire raid which we had word was coming off. They destroyed more than half the town in one day. It was a horrible thing to see. Except for the section of the town where we were, all the buildings and homes were made of wood. After the raid all you could see was what looked like a graveyard of tombstones—the chimneys of these places that had burned down. The firebombs were dropped in large containers that would open up on the way down scattering these small phosphorus bombs with magnesium casings. You could handle them by putting sand on them, or water, if you got to them soon enough. Except that the Germans learned a cute trick. They would put explosives in them at random so you never knew when you were approaching one if it would explode or not. So that kept you away from them. They were small bombs; they weighed maybe two or three pounds, very light. They just rained down. It looked like a bunch of silver snowflakes coming down and just blanketed the town.

Whenever Arkhangelsk opened up we would shift down there because there was very little air damage. The German planes had a long way to go so there was an occasional air raid but very, very seldom. Arkhangelsk would be open after the ice spate in April through to November. Then we'd send most of the ships in there, but if it was crowded we would still send some ships into Murmansk. We didn't like to because of the knowledge that they were subject to constant air raids.

The Soviets had facilities at Murmansk for ready transport out of the cargoes by rail. There is a line from Moscow to Leningrad and on to Murmansk. The line was cut when Leningrad was under siege, but they ran a line across a very boggy area to connect with the Moscow-Arkhangelsk line. The road bed was so soft you could stand on the rear car and could see the rails come up again after the train had passed over it, but they kept it open. On the way down from Murmansk they had trouble because the Germans were practically on the railroad tracks. You would sometimes wait for a day or two for what they called good weather— which means foggy weather. Then they could rush on through. They kept repairing the lines with whole sections of rail. They had replacements for every bridge right alongside so they kept it open. Materials went out from Murmansk very fast. There were times of course when the port was jammed. Later on the Germans realized that they should use firebombs and they did. As a result a lot of material was lost.

I was given a place in Arkhangelsk—a log hut—and moved down there when the port was open and we weren't using Murmansk. The White Sea area was very predictable as to its use. When the ice first started to form you could get ships in there with the aid of icebreakers, and through a mild winter you could use the facilities if there were sufficient icebreakers. But when the spring spate started there was a period of time when nothing could get through. The spring flow would cause ice shelves to build on top of each other, perhaps to a depth of forty feet.

During the winter our trouble was sometimes due to the nature of the ships we'd send through. Most of our ships used bronze propellers. They are easily damaged by ice. The Soviets on the other hand used cast steel propellers on any of the ships that were likely to encounter ice. We didn't actually change our type of propellers but no ship was held up because of damage of this kind. They would either straighten out a damaged propeller or cut off the damaged part. This would not reduce the speed very much.

I always had a problem shifting from Murmansk to Arkhangelsk after the spate had gone through in the spring. There was one occasion when the ice had gone out and we had ships in Murmansk. I was told there was very little cargo of ballast available at Murmansk. The Soviets asked if I would send the ships around to Arkhangelsk to pick up cargo. "Has the place been swept for mines?" I asked. "Oh yes, we do that automatically as soon as the spate is through so we can get any mines that have been dropped." "Can they get there and get loaded up in time for the returning convoy?" "Oh yes, we guarantee that." "All right," I said, "are you sending any ships around?" "Yes, we're sending three of our ships." "Fine. You put those three ships first in line going around and we'll follow right on through." They didn't. They hadn't swept. They would take a chance with our ships but not with their own.

But I had a very good arrangement with them actually. At first they used to complain and I could understand why. The first time I was asked to do something they said: You do this, whatever it was, and we'll do this and everything will be fine. I agreed. It was some small thing and they didn't follow through. So when the next proposition came up I followed the standard procedure which they accepted. I would break down the cooperative job in two columns: one I would do, followed by one that they would do. Two that I would do, followed by two that they would do, until we got down and got the job done. The first time I'd do the first thing. On another project they'd start off doing the first thing. So we followed through that way. It worked out very nicely. We had respect for each other. No promises were made idly, otherwise we wouldn't go through with it. Actually Mr. Mikoyan (Ministry of Foreign Trade) complained to Admiral Standley (U.S. ambassador) one time about this thing. Admiral Standley said, "Frankel's in charge; work it out with him."

I had a meeting with Mr. Mikoyan one time when he complained to the ambassador about cargo tonnages and the discrepancy between my figures and those of his people. The figures his people gave him were not the same as the figures I gave to General Faymonville, the head of the American mission in Moscow. I kept him advised of all the things going on up in

Murmansk, including what they were doing with the material we turned over and how fast we were moving. I came down to Moscow one time and Admiral Standley said: "Let's go over to see Mr. Mikoyan and get something straightened out." I did the interpreting and found out what was troubling Mr. Mikoyan. He was getting confusing reports. My figures would show that a ship still had two thousand tons aboard, and his figures would show that it was empty. I said: "It's quite simple, Mr. Mikoyan. If you want to take their figures, we'll send the ship back with 2,000 tons. You will have gotten five thousand tons, but you really haven't. You've only gotten three thousand tons because there are still two thousand tons aboard. You wouldn't want that." "How do you account for these different figures?" he asked. "It's quite simple. I tell how much a ship has discharged by a simple mathematical formula. I know what the depth of the ship is and I know that every inch is fifty tons off. So when you find ten inches less draft, five hundred tons have come off the ship. When it gets down to where it shows that the ship is empty, then it means the cargo is off."

He said: "How do my people tell this?" I said, "It's quite simple the way they do it. They take a look and they see a fifteen-ton crane coming off and it's shivering and shaking. They say, that must be at least twenty tons on there and they mark down twenty tons coming off. They see another one coming and they see a five-ton crane shivering and shaking. That must be at least six tons coming off." So I explained that they do it by estimating these things and they overestimate. Naturally everybody does overestimate. The result is they're discharging the thing by their system, at about twice the rate of the actual discharge, which is shown by my system. "If you total up the reports you get every day or every week or whatever it is about how the convoy is being unloaded, you will find that when they finish the job they've unloaded twice as much cargo as came in the ships." "Ah, I see," said Mr. Mikoyan. "We'll take your figures." This is the way they did it from then on.

Admiral Standley, our ambassador in Moscow at the time, was a fine naval officer and a fine gentleman. He approached his job there as a wartime job. He was quick to get down to the heart of problems. He made no bones about telling the Soviets when they were falling down on the job and demanded they do something about it. He was gentle in manner, but forceful in words. He was the first one to accuse, and justly so, the Soviets of storing up material—that they were not using it. He got this, a good part, from us. We were watching the stuff being unloaded and being moved in a direction that indicated it was not being used at the front or being stored for future use—this sort of thing. He was assigned to do a job to expedite our policy at that time with the Soviets and to ride herd on any agreements which had been made. He was quite right because early in the game he realized that as far as good will goes, you can't put that in the bank with the Soviets and draw on it later. You've got to play for the present, not bank on the future, because the Soviets will only do things that benefit the Soviets. They feel no moral obligation but will fulfill the obligation if by not doing so they are a net loser—which is understandable if not admirable.

I used to be too democratic for the Soviets. At times I was told about this. Admiral Papanin told me so one time. After I'd gotten my flat, which was attributable mostly to Admiral Papanin's intercession and my friend Mr. Gregorian, who was responsible for this sort of thing up there, I decided I would have a little party. I assembled some goodies from the ships, tinned hams and things of that order. And I got some whiskey and wine that I could get locally. I sent out invitations to the captain of the port; the secretary of the Communist Party; the admiral of the Northern Fleet, and his chief of staff, Admiral Golovkov; Admiral Papanin and his staff. Then I sent an invitation to the head stevedore, who was quite an important person because he controlled the loading and unloading of ships. I sent invitations to the interpreters. They had girls who worked on bills of lading, translators, a good group of kids. They learned English in school and were very amusing sometimes in their translations. So I had a cross section of everybody with whom we worked, not the people who manned cranes and things like that, but people with whom we worked. What I thought was a reasonable semidemocratic level.

I made the invitation from 5 o'clock on. I made it a little humorous, "food and drink for man." I didn't say beast because I thought they might misunderstand. Promptly at 5 o'clock in came the junior group, which would be those girls who did the translations. They came in and had a sandwich or something and a glass of wine, and they went off. A little later the next senior group came in. They came in groups. The chief of staff and all the British came up from Polyarnoya. The admiral of the Northern Fleet sent word that he was unable to make it because he'd been pressured because of the convoys and escorts and so forth. I could understand that. Then Admiral Papanin sent his regrets with his chief of staff. He said, unfortunately Admiral Papanin wasn't feeling well and couldn't make it. I realized that something was wrong.

The next morning I had some oranges there and something special I had gotten off a ship. I went over, without calling in advance, to see Admiral Papanin. I used to go and see him occasionally on problems. I came in and said: "Sorry, Admiral, that you weren't feeling so well yesterday. I thought I'd bring you some things here since you're off your feed." He said, "Sit down a minute." So I sat down. We called each other by our patronymics. He was Ivan Dimitrovich and I was Samuel Ivanovich. He said, "You gave a party yesterday." "Yes, I'm sorry you couldn't make it. Admiral Golovkov couldn't make it. I understand that you were not feeling well." He said: "You didn't give the right kind of party. You should have asked me and I would have told you what to do." "What would you have done? What would you have recommended?" And he said: "These people whom you invited—they don't mean a thing. They can't do anything for you. They're not important to you. You should have had a nice dinner with Admiral Golovkov, his chief of staff, me and my chief of staff, and the Ministry of Foreign Trade representative. You would have had a good bang-up time. These things would really have counted. You spread your entertainment over people who really don't count."

Of course he knew whom I had invited. He was told. When I sent out the invitations I said, those of you who have worked with us, I wish to show our appreciation and so forth. Now that we have a place to entertain, I'd like to have you to entertain. He was a pretty shrewd guy.

Referring to the ill-fated Iceland-Murmansk convoy PQ-17—we lost twenty-three out of thirty-one ships on this particular run. We were in Arkhangelsk at the time. We had lots of survivors in there with very little place to put them, but again the Soviets came through. Most of these men went in the water without shoes on, so we had a demand for something like three hundred pairs of shoes for these people. Some of the lend-lease material that had come in was shoes. So I prevailed on the Soviets to part with some to give to these men. These were Endicott-Johnson shoes, which the Soviets promised to pay lend-lease for, something like six dollars a pair. These shoes were sold by the Soviet Union for forty dollars a pair. I eventually got a bill for these shoes for thirty dollars a pair—again a different Soviet organization, but they had to account for them. Anyway it was all resolved eventually.

I had a little trouble with some of the merchant seamen from the convoys. Those who had been on the run before were all right but some of the new ones complained, especially about food. They wanted a choice of ice cream for dessert. Most of them were given what the Soviets themselves didn't have enough of—dried codfish, plenty of bread, tea, occasionally a sweet of some kind. Some of them were up there for almost nine months, unable to get back. It was during the summer months and we had to wait for the convoys to be resumed, for whenever it got so that we were losing more than 25 percent of the ships it was decided it was uneconomical to continue with them. So we had a long stretch of time when we had no convoys. The authorities were thinking over the situation—should we continue or should we not? We did try to get some of the men back on a British cruiser, but unfortunately it was sunk. So they came back to us again. They were rescued and came back.

The men put on a skit one time which was very funny. One of the scenes featured somebody who was supposed to give a sample of blood and all that came out was clear liquid. He said: "What did you expect with the stuff they've been feeding us?" The men were mostly good humored about things, but we had a couple who were really troublemakers.

There certainly was a morale problem, especially in the early stages of the war. Bonuses were given, very good bonuses for seamen. They had all sorts of clauses in their contracts. If a bomb exploded within a certain distance they got an extra bonus or if they went through certain areas they got extra bonuses. It got so an ordinary seaman might be getting the equivalent of five or six hundred dollars a month where normally it would be in the area of one hundred dollars a month at that time. The men who were there in the first runs didn't quite understand the many problems and were not too sympathetic to the making of sacrifices in behalf of the so-called common effort. Those who repeated the run were quite different. They realized what it was and they were inspired by more than the money involved because they could have gone to other places with almost the same return and certainly much more safety guaranteed. It got so that the union representatives—and there were two generally on each ship—would speak for the crew. They would come up with certain demands. They wanted this or the skipper wasn't doing that. They wanted to go down to Moscow and take a trip. It was very unusual in that those who carried Communist cards (there were some who were members of the American Communist Party) were sure that they were going to be met with red carpet treatment, flown down to Moscow to talk to Joe Stalin, and all these imaginary sort of things. The Soviets were very cold to these people. In fact some of them came to me, at least three of them, and said: "We want you to witness the tearing up of our cards. We don't think the Communist system is a good system!" A great number of these people were communications people.

When they actually got in trouble and the ships were being attacked they had the sense of being heroes of course and had good stories to tell when they got back. For the most part they were a good bunch, they were an excellent bunch. They helped out the armed guard people. They gave up some of their bonuses which they got from the Soviets. The armed guard couldn't accept them but they sometimes made purses for the guards at the end of the run and gave them money because the guards were getting around seventy-five dollars a month and the people who were running below deck when trouble started were getting five hundred a month. The relationship was very good with the exception of a few people. Some of them were terrorizing the rest of the crew. I had to send some people home.

I remember two brothers on one ship. They were not the representatives of the union. I asked them to come and talk with me and they did. I

230

think I asked them to stay for dinner. I found out they were completely recalcitrant. They were threatening the captain. He was scared of them. So I had these men picked up and sent back under guard. They raised hell when they got back. One of the columnists wrote about these fellows. They were fighting heroes during this run and Captain Frankel up there in Murmansk had sent them back in irons and thereby lost their valuable service to the merchant marine—stuff like that.

Then we had other people who just got scared—survivors. I put them across the Kola Peninsula in a place where they weren't subject to bombs. It was a camp sort of thing. They thought they were missing the sights and jollities of Murmansk and they complained when they got back. They criticized and said they felt like lepers. The War Shipping Administration, on one of my trips back, asked me to talk to union officials if I would. I said, "Sure, I'll talk with them." They immediately saw the light—that I was really protecting these people and safeguarding them by putting them out of the way of danger. When I showed them some of the pictures of Murmansk with the place destroyed, they said, "Sure, we'll tell these people off—not to complain."

THE BEAR'S VORACIOUS APPETITE

REAR ADMIRAL CLARENCE E. OLSEN

U.S. ARMY AIR CORPS (LADD FIELD)

CLARENCE EDWARD OLSEN was born on 27 October 1899 in Aloha, Michigan. He graduated from the U.S. Naval Academy in 1921. He spent his first six years after graduation in various ships at sea and then he returned to the Naval Academy for enrollment in the Postgraduate School. This tour was followed by one at the Naval War College in Newport, Rhode Island. He served at sea again until June 1934, when he was assigned to the ROTC unit at Northwestern University. From June 1936 to July 1941 he served on the staff of commander, Base Force. After two sea assignments he took command of the USS *Arctic* and was in this command when the United States entered World War II.

In 1942 Olsen was assigned to Headquarters, Commander of the U.S. Fleet, serving in the Navy Department in Washington. In 1945 he became chief of the Naval Division of the U.S. Military Mission to the Union of Soviet Socialist Republics in Moscow. He was awarded the Legion of Merit for this service. An account of this is contained in the excerpt from his oral history included in this book. This interesting duty was followed by his command of the USS *Baltimore* and then another tour in the Navy Department. From May 1948 to March 1950 he was in command of the U.S. naval base in Norfolk. There followed his command of Cruiser Division Two and in September 1951 he took command of the Newport naval base. In 1953 he was in command of the blockading and

232

escort force of the U.S. Pacific Fleet and in 1954 took over his last active command, that of the Fourteenth Naval District and as commander of the Hawaiian Sea Frontier. Admiral Olsen retired as a rear admiral in July 1959. He then lived in Hawaii with his wife and died at Bethesda Naval Hospital on 11 November 1971.

I came to Washington in 1942 from duty on the West Coast to serve as a member of the planning staff under Admiral Cooke. Suddenly in 1943 I was informed that I was to be given the rank of commodore and would be sent to Moscow to take over the assignment as naval attaché under Ambassador Averell Harriman. The switch in plans was sudden because Admiral Standley (who had been serving as our ambassador to Russia) had come home on leave and was certain he would not be permitted to return. He had forced the Russians to admit that they were getting all these lend-lease materials from the United States but had been changing the labels on the packages when they arrived and had been telling their people that these goods were from the U.S. but that they had been forced to pay a high price for them. In other words, Standley had forced the Russians to lose face so when he arrived back in the United States, he had a firm conviction that he wasn't going to be allowed back.

At any rate when I came into my shop on Monday my buzzer rang, and when I went in to Admiral Cooke he got up and said, "Congratulations, Commodore." I said: "You can't do this to me. I'm going to the Pacific." He said: "You've got three days to change your uniforms, pack your bags, and go with the ambassador to Moscow." I got absolutely no briefing. Fortunately Admiral Duncan (who had been with Admiral Standley in Moscow) was in town and I got ahold of him for a few wise words about clothing, supplies, and things like that—how to handle your money affairs and so on. But I had no time for any real briefing of the circumstances in Russia. I went in cold. Then Admiral Duncan came back over there and was with me for two weeks. That was a great help. It was my real indoctrination. Later I traveled to learn more.

Of course we had Sam Frankel up in Murmansk as our senior representative there. He was a crackerjack. He spoke fluent Russian and they all liked him. He liked the job and he did very well in handling those ships that came in convoys with lend-lease materials. We can't blame the Russians too much for the way they looked at things because they were in desperation all the time. They had practically nothing and they didn't have great leadership. They didn't have anybody who had any idea of organization or planning. They just drove ahead and did the best they could with what they could get their hands on. They were also suspicious of foreigners, but they were always there with their hands out for more. Sam Frankel was great in helping them out all he could. I think that he got as much from them as was humanly possible under the circumstances. And he was up there for almost four years.

I went up to Murmansk and surrounding areas at least three or four times. Twice I was there in winter months. It was very rugged because the train service was bad and part of it we had to finish in one of their propeller-driven snow sleds because the train got stalled. Temperatures were always below zero, five or ten degrees below zero most of the time. I visited a number of the ships that were tied up at the dock and talked with the skippers. I saw the kind of labor they got—all prison labor being marched from barracks to dock at the point of guns and at the end of bayonets. They were political prisoners or helpless people who were being forced to do the labor of unloading. Of course they were all starved, emaciated. All they had on their bodies, outside of a few clothes, was a tin cup lashed to their belts. They ate and drank from that and washed their teeth—if they ever did. It was not uncommon for them to be carrying, say, a case of lard down the gangway of the docks and they would inadvertently drop it so that it would burst wide open and a can or two would burst out. They'd all dive in with their hands and dig it out with their fingers, eat just plain lard cold, as fast as they could to get the fat, get the grease. Men and women were all involved in this. In one case when I was there the ships were all frozen in. Of course they emptied their garbage out through the slip shute on to the fantail, right out on the ice. One of the prisoner-workers couldn't stand it when he saw all this bread and potato peelings and like things going down on the ice. He just jumped out of ranks, jumped onto the ice and began to scoop it up with both hands. A guard just picked up his gun and shot him through the head and left him there. Sam Frankel had a hell of a time then for it took him many days persuading the Russians to remove the body. They just wanted it to stay there as an example to the rest of the troops that were working on the docks.

Both the American and the British seamen who manned these ships were thoroughly disgusted by some of the treatment that they witnessed. I heard repeatedly that the sailors were so disgusted they swore they would never go on another convoy to Russia. Trouble with recruiting developed because of the stories our sailors brought home.

I think the convoy duty was the worst convoy duty in any war we've ever had. They were sitting ducks going up around the North Cape, targets for the German submarines and the German aircraft. Some of the convoys came in not decimated but almost obliterated. Half of them would be sunk or destroyed and others would be just crippled to the point where they could barely creep in. I don't remember exact numbers but I'd say an average of about half of them got through.

I don't think the Russian officials had any understanding of the psychological effect these hardships had on our sailors. I don't think it meant anything to them. Lives to them meant nothing at all. They're just absolutely cold-blooded. This was exemplified all through the war, the way they piled bodies up in front of cities and drove their people in over the minefields in order to clear the way for the troops coming afterwards. This just meant nothing to them. Their objectives were what they were after—no matter how many lives were lost. It was always to gain the objective!

Other ports for receiving our lend-lease shipments to Russia included Arkhangelsk and Molotovsk. We had a small group of men there under a lieutenant. We also had a small staff in Vladivostok, where Commander Roulard was stationed with a chief yeoman and his interpreter. Later in the war some of the shipments of relief stores came through Vladivostok and on by train to Moscow.

After Ambassador Standley got tough with the Russians about labeling lend-lease items properly, as far as we knew everything was sent down marked with U.S. shipping labels and signs just as they had come into port. We never had any words with the Russians about this. We were then sending in everything in the world that you could think of: all kinds of ammunition, food, medical supplies, trucks, automobiles, airplane parts. The list they would give us for requests was almost unbelievable. As a matter of fact, at times it was ridiculous.

We of course through our lend-lease office in Russia had to screen a lot of these things to try and cut them down to something normal. For instance, when the cruiser *Milwaukee* came in to Murmansk (she was the only large ship we gave them under lend-lease) they gave us a list of replacement parts that would sink the ship. We pointed out to them that the ship had been completely overhauled in New York before it came over there. They had all modern radio and radar equipment, the latest allowed for that type ship. The storerooms were full with a year and a half of supplies. Three months later they were requesting enough supplies to sink the ship. It was obvious they wanted to winterize the ship—they said—and build houses over it. Well, you can't keep a man-of-war in shape by putting everything under cover. But they claimed the ship wasn't built for the cold-weather service that they had up there, which was just another of their "come-ons." It was quite obvious that they weren't interested in rebuilding or supplying the *Milwaukee*. They were just interested in an excuse to get everything they could lay their hands on for other purposes. It was just a blunt demand for a lot of things.

In fact, at one time, Admiral Kuznetsov, the commander in chief of the Russian Navy, had me in for a conference as he wanted a number of minelayers assigned to the Russian Navy. I believe the number he asked was 144 and I said, "Well, Admiral, that is a large request." He said, "We have a great requirement in all of our areas for these minelayers." "But, Admiral," I said, "I think that you know obviously from the number that you are requesting that it includes the entire shipbuilding program in that category of the U.S. Navy. Only one third of it is complete now, and the rest of it won't be complete for another year or more." He said, "But we have need for every one of them." And I replied, "There are only about seven other battle areas that need them also and it is the duty of the joint chiefs of staff to determine how many go to each area." "But we need them—they don't need them in the other areas like we need them here. The bear has a voracious appetite." I said, "I agree with you on that. I'm sorry I can't agree with your request for 144 minelayers." And he responded, "We want all we can get." I said, "I'll transmit your request to the joint chiefs of staff with my recommendations." I think I recommended five or something like that. They had no hesitancy in asking for the impossible. That was only one instance where they did that.

In another they requested that I get for them detailed plans and specifications of all our types of navy ships, from carriers on down to harbor craft. I almost laughed at them (but you can't do that to a four-star admiral) and so I asked why they had a need for that information. They said, "well, we're going to build." I said, "But you can't build any of these things during the war years so that's a postwar requirement and not a current requirement." But they said, "There will be great efforts made to increase our navy after the war and we need these plans." I said, "Admiral, you haven't got a chance in a million to get those plans because you have no current need for them. If I submit this request, I'm afraid that my CNO will just laugh at the whole thing, but if you wish I will send it in." I sent it with my own recommendation and of course nothing ever came of it. That was the character of their requests. They would demand or request unlimited things without any reason or logical backing for it.

Our army ran into the same thing. General Spaulding and General Faymonville before him had a very difficult time screening out what was reasonable and what was unreasonable. (Generals Spaulding and Faymonville headed up the lend-lease end of the program in Russia.)

Our lend-lease effort to the Russians in this time was such that they never could have accomplished anything to speak of in comparison to what they did. But even so, they never admitted to their people that they had gotten any successful great help from the United States. Yet it was absolutely evident everywhere you went. General Deane had more opportunity to see this up at the front than any of us because we were never allowed to go up to the front. He did on several occasions with army generals—with General Antonoff, I think, and Zhukov and others.

Another part of my job was to have an exchange of weather information. This was not very hard to achieve since we supplied all the equipment, and in the China area we provided personnel to help them install the equipment. They would never allow us to man the stations, however. Supply all the equipment, yes, and give the instructions, but they insisted on doing all the rest. And they were quite capable. They did help us out a great deal because we were able to feed weather information to our fleet in the Pacific and this helped in our flights from the various stations in the fleet up into the Japanese area. We had no other sources of weather in that part of the Pacific. I would evaluate their assistance in that as a very helpful service.

It is worth noting that the Russians didn't want anybody, any foreigner there for any reason at all. We were only in Moscow on tolerance. But they did not want foreigners in their country. That was almost a positive rule. When we set up the three airfields in the south of Russia to facilitate straight-over bombing from England and Italy—straight across Europe and the oilfields of Romania especially, with plans for landing in Russia for refueling and rebombing and then flying back—we had a very difficult time justifying our personnel. They realized our efforts would help the war effort but they were always suspicious that we had an ulterior motive. The suspicion that goes on in their minds is something unbelievable.

Our operations were always handicapped because we would give them information freely, all that we had that was going to be helpful. We on the other hand would have some things we wanted assistance on. We'd go into a conference with them and have this all written out, laid it on the line, said we would like this and like that, in order to facilitate such and such an operation. And the answer would always be, we will take it into consideration and let you know in a day or two. Then you would have to prod them into another meeting because you wanted the answers as quickly as you could get them. Finally after several delays they would call you into a conference and tell you that what you asked isn't necessary because "we've already done this." They would have implemented everything they could to forestall having to do anything more with us. It happened time and time again. Of course it served a purpose in one way in getting some things done but it also blocked us in a thousand ways in getting information we needed to carry out our part of the operations. Again it was their suspicious attitude. They didn't want us to take credit or get credit for anything.

Another example: I was there in Moscow as head of lend-lease when Deane went to England at the end of the war. Our troops were crossing into Germany. They had an agreement with Eisenhower that our troops would go up to the Oder River and the Russians would meet us there. Well, actually our troops overran the river by about forty-odd miles, and during that time we were trying to make agreements on signals and signs so that the Russians would recognize our tanks and our troops as American rather than German. We were collaborating quite closely with them. Then Eisenhower sent a dispatch to General Antonoff saying that after contact was made with the Soviet troops moving westward, the American troops would move back to this agreed river line.

I delivered this dispatch to General Antonoff and his staff about 2 o'clock in the morning and he just looked at me and asked that I read it over again. I agreed, through an interpreter, of course, and then he looked at me and said, "Did General Eisenhower send this?" I said, "Yes, of course he sent it." "How do you know he sent it?" I replied that I had no question in my mind that he had sent it. He said, "Would you go back to your office and send and ask General Eisenhower for a confirmation of this statement?" They wouldn't believe that anybody would be so foolish as to back down forty miles over captured land. As a result I went back and sent a message to General Eisenhower and told him General Antonoff requested confirmation of dispatch so and so. It came back almost immediately and at 5 o'clock in the morning I was back there with the confirmation. Antonoff thanked me very much, then they went ahead and did what they wanted to do, moving their troops forward to meet ours and pushed back to the river.

On first delivery, the Russian mind just could not believe that any advancing general would give up captured land, which again is characteristic of them. You know perfectly well if the Russians had gone forty miles the other side of the river towards us that they never would have backed down. We'd have had a hell of a fight with them to make them back down.

TO RUSSIA ON AN UNSTATED MISSION

ADMIRAL HARRY D. FELT

U.S. NAVY

HARRY DONALD FELT was born 21 June 1902 in Topeka, Kansas, but moved to Washington, D.C., when ten years old. He entered the U.S. Naval Academy in 1919 and graduated in the class of 1923. He then served five years in battleships and destroyers before reporting for flight training at Pensacola. He was designated a naval aviator in 1929 and flew naval aircraft regularly for the balance of his career. Immediately following his designation as naval aviator he had a series of normal tours of aviation duty both aboard ship and ashore.

Pearl Harbor day, 7 December 1941, found Lieutenant Commander Felt in command of a carrier-based dive-bombing squadron. Shortly after that he was assigned as carrier air group commander aboard the USS *Saratoga* and participated in the first offensive action of the war, the occupation of Guadalcanal. For this action he was awarded the Distinguished Flying Cross for achievement in aerial flights against the enemy. A little later he was awarded the Navy Cross for leading an attack by his air group on Japanese forces at sea. Then he went back to the United States for about a year training combat pilots. This was followed by a year in Moscow as a member of the U.S. Military Mission to the Soviet Union. He was the first naval aviator to serve in this capacity. He then returned to the Pacific in command of the carrier USS *Chenango* and took part in the Okinawa campaign and the occupation of Japan.

After the end of World War II Admiral Felt served in several capacities on the staff of the chief of naval operations. He also attended the National War

239

College. He commanded the attack carrier USS *Franklin D. Roosevelt* and later served as commander of the Middle East Force in the Persian Gulf area. As a flag officer he commanded an antisubmarine carrier division and an attack carrier division and held the post of vice chief of naval operations, where he served for two years until July 1958, when he was designated Commander in Chief, Pacific Fleet. He served in that capacity until 1 July 1964, the date of his retirement.

Admiral Felt has lived in Honolulu with his wife since retirement. Their son, Donald Linn Felt, is retired as a rear admiral and lives in Arlington, Virginia.

I got a telephone call one day from my good friend Duckworth on Admiral Cooke's staff saying, "How would you like to go to Russia? No, don't answer that question. You are going to Russia." So that was the end of that. I was going to Russia. So I started to try and prepare myself to go to Russia and Kathryn helped me a lot. We had no concept of what life would be like, but she went down to the dime store and bought me lots of lipsticks for all the girls that I would meet in Russia and things like that.

We got in the car and went up to Jacksonville and there I left Kathryn and our daughter on their own, told them to head for the West Coast and make out the best they could. And I went to Washington. I was having a heck of a time finding out about Russia and what it was all about. Then one day I ran into Wu Duncan in the corridor and he asked me what I was doing and I told him, and he said, "Come over with me and I'll help you." And he dug out files and reports that gave me some idea of what to expect. I could expect no laundry so I loaded with soap. I loaded with a whole raft of paper collars. In those days we were wearing stiff paper collars. I got some heavy clothes of course and did the best I could to learn a little bit about Russia. And one day, I was going in to old Main Navy—that's where everybody was in those days—and out in front of the building was Admiral McCain (John Sydney), who was chief of BuAir then. He was fumbling around and it was quite clear he wanted to buy a paper. So I said, "What's the matter, Admiral?" and I bought him a Sunday paper.

He looked at me and then said, "Oh, yes, you're that fellow who's going to Russia." And of course I said, "Yes, you're right." Now it was Admiral McCain who made the decision to send a naval aviator to Russia, the idea being that there was no naval aviator over there and they thought it would be a good idea to have a naval aviator serving on the Military Mission in Moscow. Then he looked at me and said: "Well, I don't think you're going to accomplish anything." That was my send-off! In fact, nobody had any idea of what I might achieve. I was only in Washington for a few days but finally somehow or other I joined up with another fellow who was also being ordered to the mission. This was Zondorak (Chas. J., Captain). He had been one of a small group of youngsters who years before had been over in China and had been given a Russian course. He could speak Russian and I thought this was great.

So we loaded up and I had a great big wooden box which they allowed me to take plus my hand baggage and the last thing that happened before departure was a call from either the medical center in Bethesda or the hospital saying, "We've got a crate of white rats we want taken to Moscow. They're all inoculated with all the horrible diseases, each with a different disease. All you have to do is deliver them." By the time we made a stop in Africa the crate was commencing to smell pretty high, and the crew put it way back in the tail of the airplane. In Cairo we made another change and took off for Teheran. There a navy medical unit took the rats off my hands and cleaned the crate and gave them back to me. Finally I managed to deliver about half of them in Moscow.

In Teheran it was quite interesting to see how the Russians behaved, completely disciplined, segregated unto themselves. It was also interesting to see how the community water system worked, particularly the system of flooding these deep gutters from the mountain streams, one by one, and learning that these people believed that water having flowed over three stones was pure and then watching how they used the water. Finally it was arranged for Zondo and me to go up to Moscow in a Russian airplane.

We got there early at the airfield. Nobody was around and there was the airplane sitting there. Finally the pilot showed up and he went around kicking various things to check the airplane out. Zondo pointed at the flat tire on one of the wheels. The Russian shook his head and cursed a bit and went in and got a bottle and pumped the tire up. They had no spare tires; he just pumped it up, kicked it again and said something. I asked Zondo what he said and Zondo translated: "Oh, that goddamned American rubber."

Then we watched them load the plane full of people, one of them being a woman who had been the interpreter at the Teheran Conference. She could speak some English. It was just flabbergasting to see the way they loaded that airplane. There were bucket seats and everybody had big cartons of everything under the sun and a heck of a lot of vodka that they were taking from Persia up to Russia. Nothing tied down—nothing. We knew doggone well when that plane landed that tire was going to go flat again. It happened. The tire went flat but fortunately the pilot controlled the airplane and none of this stuff started to rattle around inside. But there we were—at Baku. Again no spare wheel, so we were stranded.

We went into the operations building and got the usual cup of tea. While there a Russian general showed up in his airplane. He was going to

241

Moscow, having been on duty some place in North Africa, and was senior enough—a lieutenant general—to have been provided an airplane. He said, "All right, I'll take you." So we climbed aboard and here again, as in the early days of my flying across country, in Russia—this was in 1944—there were no aids to navigation, all VFR and all daytime flying. Our first stop was Stalingrad. This was shortly after the Russians had successfully defended Stalingrad from the Nazis. The general took us on a tour right away and we saw what had happened to Stalingrad. Again, being a typical American, I wandered off the beaten path and into the field with everybody screaming at me—"Watch out for the mines." I did pick up a key—all rusted and burned—and I have it yet with my medals. I have called it my key to Stalingrad.

That night I was introduced to the standard way of holding a Russian meeting. A chair like this I'm sitting in, a long table with a red cover on it and chairs along each side, the head man sitting in this chair, and here comes the vodka treatment, which I'd never experienced. The idea, I'm convinced of and learned later, when vodka is available to a Russian there's only one objective and that is to get drunk. If there's an American around get him as drunk as you are! I was exposed to this "dodna" (bottoms up). Well, that went on—I think we had something to eat but it was a pretty gay party. Nobody was feeling any pain. It was time to go to bed and we went into a great big open room just with army cots, wooden, canvas type. Then the general and I got into an argument. He gave the woman interpreter the cot next to his. And I said, "No, sir, General, I don't trust you. She's not going to sleep in that cot." Apparently after arguing a bit I went sound asleep.

The next day we went to Moscow. It was May Day. I think it was a Sunday and again, thank goodness, I had Zondorak along because there we were. Nobody meeting us, just lost. Of course we had our papers and the Russians weren't bothering us any, but they weren't helping us any, either. Zondorak knew enough to get on the telephone and finally somebody came out and picked us up.

We were put into a hotel and first of all the bedding and beds were something I'd never seen before. It took a little time to figure out how to handle all those big pillows and the way they made a bed up. Secondly, hospitality was offered immediately of the kind we didn't dare accept and there were knocks on the door. Thirdly, eating was difficult. The meals you got in the hotel were very meager and right soon it was agreed that Kemp Tolley and his wife, Vlada, were to take us in for breakfast in their apartment in the American Embassy. That tided us over. Soon after that Tolley was ordered out of the country, and Zondy and I with another fellow who'd shown up—Denny Knoll, an aerologist—took over Tolley's apartment and there we had a cook and a maid. Then I found out that living wasn't as rugged as I'd been taught at the Navy Department. The cook washed all the clothes in the bathtub every day and the maid cleaned up. We had the privilege of buying at the Russian store. Well, we had one egg every morning for breakfast. That was quite a privilege. We were allowed to buy vodka and things like that also. The cook was a German refugee who came to Moscow from the Ukraine. Kemp had employed her and we inherited her. She had to report to the NKVD every week on our activities. She occupied a little cubby hole off the kitchen where she slept and the only time she dared go out was when she'd meet some friend on the street. That was the only place where Russians could talk openly. Our phone was tapped. We knew that. Every time we'd pick it up we'd hear all the connections being made by the fellow who lived in the hotel next door. The apartment may have been bugged. We didn't know and we didn't much care because we had a little game going on of having conversations saying what we thought about certain things, hoping that it would be taped.

Now of course when I arrived in Moscow I wanted an interview with a Russian authority, naval authority, as soon as I could get one. This was put into the paper mill. Meanwhile, shortly after I got there, Admiral Olsen, the naval attaché, had been invited to go up and visit the Russian fleet at Leningrad and he asked me to come along. It was a trip in one of these international coach jobs, with private rooms and bunks and a wash-room. The only thing provided was a samovar that the train people provided. We had to take our own food; you prepared it on one of those little burners, the train crawling along about the pace of a fast jog on the railroad that had been put together after the Germans had practically destroyed it. Quite a long trip getting into Leningrad, going to a hotel, and then meeting a wonderful guy—a commodore, Russian naval officer—our host, who took us next day out to visit the fleet all along the Neva River.

We visited a submarine, all red-carpeted, no torpedoes on board, shined up to beat the band, a destroyer, watched them go through a gun drill, a gun battery ashore firing into Finland, and lunch on the old battleship that was established there with the admiral in command. I asked the commodore if I had his permission to take pictures. I'd never known anything about photography, but before I left Moscow the boys provided me with a camera and gave me instructions. The commodore said, "Sure, anything you want." So I had a ball. I pushed the right button and I changed the film, took two rolls of film and included all the ships being built in the ways along the Neva River, the beginning of their modern navy.

The next day we went sightseeing and I took pictures again. Two things were outstanding—the museum they've set up depicting the attack on Leningrad and going to some palace outside Leningrad. And yes, we visited an aviation unit. Somebody discouraged me from trying to fly one of their airplanes, and I was never sure whether they meant it when they said I could. When we got back to the hotel after the second day of touring all of the pictures I took on sightseeing day came out nicely developed but none of the pictures I took on the previous day came out. What I had done, like a stupid neophyte, was I had left the film in the hotel room. That was intelligence gathering that didn't work.

The other thing I was introduced to for the first time was the manner of gorging their guests through that Intourist agency. Four meals a day was minimum and each meal was the same, a big spread of all kinds of Russian food, including vodka all the time. We finally made a plea to knock off some of this. We'd have breakfast, we'd have lunch, we'd have a meal at I guess British teatime and then after going to the ballet or something at night, another meal about 11 P.M.—all the same, this great spread. A dozen items on the menu and many courses—overpowering.

I guess the principal reaction I got from that visit to Leningrad (not then knowing much about the history of the Russian Navy during World War II) was first, the successful defense of Leningrad and while defending it, still producing; the factories though badly damaged were still producing. And the other lesson was the complete ineffectiveness of the Russian Navy, having been bottled in, after trying to break the barrier, the mine barrier.

My request for a meeting with a senior Russian naval officer finally came through thirty days after my request was filed. Meanwhile I'd been turning over in my mind what I was going to say to this fellow and others—how can I make an approach that might attract them. I finally hit on this: to tell them that I had been impressed with the way they used their aviation in support of troops and to tell them, if they didn't know it, that this was exactly our U.S. naval aviation concept—amphibious attack, the support of troops. By golly, that caught on. Not too long after that they offered me a trip and provided (I learned later) the only transport aircraft the Russian Navy owned, an R-4D, I think it was, with a Hero of the Soviet Union to go along as escort and a Russian crew for the airplane.

We went down to the Crimea, to an air base called Taganrog, right in the center of the peninsula where I was welcomed with the news that they had a hot bath ready for me. I had another officer along with me, a U.S. naval reserve officer, born of Russian parents and very good with the Russian language. They couldn't believe he was an American; he was great. We were taken to a barracks building, a long narrow building. On the right, as you entered, was the kitchen; on the left was a head (and if you haven't seen a Russian head you haven't seen anything); then into the living spaces—a dining room and individual rooms. We were put up in there and immediately taken over to a bathhouse. The attendants were

244

there, the towels were there, the hot water was on, and I had a quick shower and everybody was amazed, disappointed, because they thought Americans bathed at least an hour long and wanted the water steaming hot. So you see they didn't know much more about Americans than we knew about them.

After the bath I guess the next thing to do was to have a meal; it was the same kind of Intourist-provided meal. In other words, the commanding officer had been provided funds and Intourist put on this kind of a spread. We sat down at a table, a group of men. Meanwhile I learned that the commanding officer had a wife there and I said, "Where is your wife?" and he said, "Oh, she's back in the other room. Would you like for her to come and be with us?" "Of course," I said, and that livened up the meal from then on.

I flew with the commanding officer in a Stormovik, which we'd heard so much about. I went out in a transport-type plane, having examined their torpedoes and having been given a ground demonstration of how they put the torpedoes on and what not, and watched them drop these torpedoes. With this tactic they had just panicked the Germans. The torpedo went floating down under the canopy of a parachute, hit the water, and took off in decreasing diametrical circles. Apparently they had the German ships just running crazy with this torpedo running crazy around them.

just after the Germans had been cleared out and before the Yalta Conference. We got into Sevastopol and saw what had happened there. The harbor was completely deserted. Here I got an explanation of Russian defense, which was to throw the troops in and take the casualties, "mass 'em and throw 'em." All the time we were taking pictures of this man's wife centered in the pictures because she was a kind of pretty girl.

Then we got to Yalta. It's a lovely place, really, all white buildings, villa-type. Unannounced, the Hero of the Soviet Union did two things immediately. He picked out the villa he wanted us to use and went in and commandeered it—just moved whoever was in it out. We moved in, got ourselves established somewhat, and decided we'd like to go swimming. Meanwhile the Hero had been to the beach and had observed that the Russians were down there bathing in the nude. He cleared them all off the beach because he knew the Americans wouldn't like that. I suppose you have seen a beach like this: nothing but smooth rocks with a problem. Here we are in normal clothes—how to get shifted into a pair of trunks? My young companion, the fellow who spoke such fluent Russian, and I resolved it by just sitting down and changing—that was all. The Russian woman with us just took off all her clothes except her undershorts and her undershorts were typical Russian red. And we enjoyed the water. Meanwhile the commanding officer and others with him began to acquire a horrible sunburn. They rummaged around and found some wine which the Germans hadn't discovered and brought it to the beach and we started to drink. Again, in typical Russian fashion, water glasses full of wine, locked arms, drink it down. No moderation or pleasure out of it. I finally demurred and asked if they'd ever taken the time to taste that wine. It was beautiful wine. They said no, and were puzzled why I would ask such a question. "Well," I said, "let's try it, just sip." They thought, "Gee, that's pretty good," never thought about tasting it before.

The night we were at the Stormovik training center we also went to a dinner party—men and women, toasts, of course, as happens at all these parties. A Russian commissar present, of course, made a typical commissar-type speech and Felt maliciously made a different kind of speech. There were presents for the hostess, chocolate candy and things like that. It was very successful, very friendly. Questions were asked: "Well, can we visit you?" "Well, sure, we'd be delighted if you ever get to Moscow." And we were asked, "Well, where do you live there?" "In the American Embassy." "Oh." That was the end of that. They wouldn't dare try that.

There was another trip I made to the area where our American prisoners of war were encamped, way down in the southern corner, an area of vegetation and groves. This was Tashkent. The idea was for me, an army doctor, and again a Hero of the Soviet Union as escort to fly down to take medicines and playing cards and paperbacks and anything we could think of. Now these prisoners-of-war were our people who had been flying out of Alaska to the Kamchatka Peninsula area. If they got into any kind of a combat situation they would run out of gas. They were truly extended on these operations and had to force land in Kamchatka. The Russians would pick them up there and send them down to this place, far removed from any Japanese eyes, because, remember, Russia and Japan were not at war at this time. These were our navy pilots and personnel. The Air Force personnel had gone down in the Maritime Provinces area around Vladivostok.

We went out to the camp, after checking into a hotel, and just barged in and you've never seen expressions like those on the faces of these fellows. I wore my naval aviation green uniform with my wings on it and of course the doctor had his army uniform on. They just couldn't believe—this was an apparition. Well, the doctor inoculated everybody. There was a Russian woman doctor in attendance there, but she had very little to work with. We distributed supplies, ate with them, talked with them, watched their recreational activities. They had organized softball by taking an old soccer ball and making a soft ball out of it and cutting a limb off a tree to make a bat—things like that. They taught the Russians how to play softball while at the same time they were being beaten badly at volleyball by the Russians, who are expert at that. We left the camp with an understanding that an arrangement would be made for these people to escape. This was something that Stalin agreed to. Only one man in the whole group was to know this, but the word would be put out suddenly one day by the Russians that they were gong to shift the Americans from this camp to another one. All right, get your belongings, climb in those trucks, and the route taken by the trucks was right along the northern border of Persia. Suddenly there'd be a little breakdown and the convoy would come to a halt and the one man in the know would say: "Hey, that's Persia. Let's go." And off they would be. That was all agreed to. They'd been over there six months already.

But what happened? Drew Pearson learned of this and he published it in a Washington newspaper, about the plan. It showed up the day these guys were on the road. Stalin learned about it and countermanded the order. The convoy turned around and those guys had another six months back in the camp.

I am reminded that one of my first trips out of Moscow was going down to Poltava to be present when the first American bombers landed in Russia. This arrangement had been made whereby the American bombers taking off from Italy and bombing the airfields in Ploesti (Romania) and thereabouts would continue on, instead of turning back, and land in Poltava. It was a good idea. I remember the takeoff from the airport in Moscow very vividly. I had heard a lot about Russian pilots' contempt for ordinary safety precautions such as we took. I'd heard that they never warmed up their engines before giving them the gun in below-freezing temperatures. I didn't realize they took off down wind, however. I was put up in the bow, in the gunner's bubble, of a B-17, standing in there. They turned the engines up, gave it the gun, and took off downwind. All I could see coming at me was the forest. We fortunately pulled up just clear. Well, I watched the bombers land at Poltava, met some of our people, stayed there that night. I watched them disperse the bombers and service them. I was particularly interested in how the Russians would protect these planes while they were on the ground. Asking questions, I was told that the Russian fighters would take care of that. "That's interesting," I said. "I would like to see some of that." About that time two of the fighters landed with women pilots. That was the fighter defense of Poltava, I was told.

I went back to Moscow the next day and shortly thereafter the planes at Poltava were destroyed by the Germans who came in, having of course spotted the whole operation and apparently knowing full well the defense would be inadequate. They really raised havoc and that was the last of that operation. It was not repeated again.

It was interesting to learn how the Russians cleared the airfield at

Poltava of the mines. For the Germans had dropped little mines all over the field. The Russians did it with human beings. They just formed a scrimmage line—you might describe it—as such—with a lot of people and just swept across the field, blowing up the mines. These people were of course from the military.

It so happened that my roommate, Zondorak, went to the one and only night club and found there these airmen from Poltava, American airmen. And at another table were some Japanese. At this time Russia was not at war with Japan. Well, one of the American lads apparently got a little high and he pulled out his .45, pulled the clip out, counted the bullets, and then with a finger, looking over at the Japanese table, counted one, two, three, four, and so on. It was quite obvious what the man had in mind. Zondorak went over and put a stop to that but I've often wondered what might have happened if this really had come about.

There came a time when Admiral Olsen realized that this wasn't a fifty-fifty shake between the Americans and the Russians on this matter of seeing and visiting places. In America the Russians would come over with authority to go into all of our factories, carrying their notebooks, making sketches—there were practically no restrictions; whereas in Russia, other than these couple of things I've mentioned, like the trip down to the Crimea, it was the arranged red-carpet treatment. Everything staged. Then Olsen decided that he'd better go back and talk to Admiral King and recommend that we not ask for any more trips. This was done and then we had the problem of what are we going to do with ourselves. We can't just have parties and go to the ballet and all that sort of thing. We've got to be active some way or other. So we decided to plan, plan on the problem of whether the Russians could whip the Japanese out in Manchuria and the maritime province area, the thought being that the Japanese would make their last defense on the mainland. Now, this was a mistake. There was one officer there in Moscow in the military mission who had a reputation at least of knowing the Japanese mind. It's always dangerous if you rely on one man who says, I know. Anyhow he said that the Japanese would make their last stand on the mainland of Asia and not in the home islands.

On this basis was generated the thought that we'd better get Russia into the war, so we started a plan to see how it might come out. We thought we had little or no intelligence, but as it developed it came out that the Russians would have no problem really.

Now, to make that story a bit shorter, came the Yalta Conference, at which Stalin was enticed to come into the war—at a price, it turned out. He made a promise that—I believe it was thirty days after VE Day, or thirty days after some date—he would attack the Japanese. The thirty days was necessary for him to group and get across on the TransSiberian Railway and then launch his attack.

248

When we started on this planning project, Ambassador Harriman was present with us quite often as we'd brief and critique some of these things. Our problem, as I have stated, was to study the question whether Russia should be brought into the war; would they be able to handle or defeat the Japanese? At first it looked to us that they'd have a very tough time of it, but as we studied the problem more and more it became clear that the Russians could do it hands down. That is, as a matter of fact, the way it turned out.

While still on duty in Moscow I was detailed to travel up to Archangel (Arkhangelsk) and temporarily replace our man stationed there to deal with the lend-lease shipping into that port. The job involved a routine checking of the waterfront, going aboard ship, meeting with the ships' skippers, who were mostly British during my brief stay. The ships came in convoy, of course. There would be a party for the skippers on the first night, hosted by the Russians. I was present at one of these parties. It was very strange to witness the attitudes. The British skippers would be off to one side and the Russians off to another. The Russians were hosting the party with no communication between them and the British. It was clear to me right off the bat that the merchant ship skippers, in the eyes of the Russians, were inferior to Russian naval officers. The impression I got here was a sort of class distinction.

I might comment a bit on lend-lease as I observed it while in Russia. The Russians always seemed anxious to get everything they could get regardless whether they could use it at the moment or not. Just what the object of acquiring all this stuff was not quite clear in my mind because things would come in bulk and sit on the side and just deteriorate, never be used, never be assembled. Of course there was a lot of dishonesty in this thing too. I say "dishonesty."

Red Cross supplies would come in and they'd be confiscated immediately and it would never be shown to the people in Russia that they were American Red Cross supplies. They showed up in the stores that were available only to the members of the Communist Party and to senior officers. Locomotives would come in with the markings on them: "Made in the USA by so-and-so." All of those would be eliminated and Russian things would be marked on them.

One of the things I recall so vividly was that we provided them with P-38 airplanes—that's a twin-fighter, I believe. As I recall it, they were assembled and test flown in Teheran and then turned over to the Russians. They started killing themselves in that airplane, to the point where they had to come to the Military Mission in Moscow. We had an air force colonel on this mission, and they had to request assistance. We had to send some pilots over there to teach them how to fly them. That was pretty amazing.

But almost immediately after I got back to the U.S. from my tour in Moscow I became aware of what seemed to be the long-range objectives of the USSR. They seemed to be going out 100 percent for technical education. Every boy and girl wanted a technical education, and if their family qualified under the Communist system they were getting that kind of education. When I left there it almost seemed they couldn't put a piece of machinery together but I had to qualify this thinking—this might change with all these kids being educated in technological subjects.

At a party one night while still in Moscow I was talking with the head of the Russian air force. We had just learned a short time before that one of Hap Arnold's most modern bombers—I think a B-36—had gone down out in the Russian Maritime Provinces. He said, "I've flown that airplane." And I said, "Now, wait a minute, General, don't try to kid me like that." And he said, "Yes, I have flown it."

I found out that what he said was true. He'd gone all the way out there when he heard about it. The plane wasn't badly damaged apparently, and he'd flown it. I said, "Where is it now?" and he said, "It's coming here to our research and development center." "What are you going to do with it?" "We're going to tear it apart, piece by piece, and examine it, and then we're going to build one of our own." And that is what they did. I countered with, "Why do you do that? Why don't you say to the U.S., 'Look, we've got one of your airplanes—how about giving us some more?' We're giving you everything you ask for!" "No," he said, "I've got longer range plans."

I left Moscow in Secretary of State Stettinius's airplane just after the Yalta Conference. I had got a set of orders from Washington to take command of a small carrier in the Pacific. After we left Moscow the secretary asked me to come and sit with him and talk with him. He talked about the Yalta Conference and how successful it had been. The Americans were elated, just absolutely elated. They felt they had accomplished everything they wanted to accomplish—that was to get the Russians to come into the war.

A YOUNG NAVAL OFFICER KEEPS HIS COOL

VICE ADMIRAL HERBERT D. RILEY

U.S NAVAL INSTITUTE

HERBERT DOUGLAS RILEY was a ninth-generation Marylander born in Baltimore on 24 December 1904. He was a graduate of Baltimore Polytechnic Institute in 1923 and of the U.S. Naval Academy in 1927. After two years in the USS *New Mexico* he completed flight training in Pensacola in July 1930. He then served in various naval aviation squadrons and participated in initial long-distance flights with VP-10 and in the National Air Races at Los Angeles with VF-3 in 1936. In one tour at the naval air station in Anacostia he was a test pilot with additional duty at the White House as naval aide to President Roosevelt.

With the advent of World War II he had duty as an operations officer with Commander, Fleet Air, West Coast. He was involved in air operations at Guadalcanal and then saw service as section head of the aviation Plans Division of the Navy Department.

In 1944 Riley took command of the USS *Makassar Strait,* a CVE, and took part in the Iwo Jima and Okinawa operations. In 1946 he was on the staff of Commander, First Carrier Task Force, and that same year was named deputy airborne commander for the atom bomb test in the summer on the Bikini atoll. He then returned to the Navy Department after the tests and two years later became assistant to Navy Secretary James Forrestal and then in succession aide to Secretary of Defense Louis Johnson. From July 1949 to July 1950 he attended the National War College. He then joined the staff of CinCLant Fleet and two years later transferred to the staff of SACLANT. He followed that by taking command of the USS *Coral Sea* and then became Chief of Staff, Carrier Division Two. In January 1954 Riley became assistant director and shortly after director of politico-military policy in the Navy Department. He then became commander of Carrier Division One, with duty in the Seventh Fleet and Chief of Staff, Pacific Command, from 1958 until 1961. Then he was named deputy chief of naval operations for fleet operations and readiness. His final position was director of the Joint Staff of the Joint Chiefs of Staff (1962–64), in which capacity he served during the Cuban missile crisis.

Vice Admiral Riley retired from active duty on 1 April 1964. He died at his home on Kent Island, Maryland, on 17 January 1973.

When Admiral McCain came in as head of the Bureau of Aeronautics succeeding Admiral Towers, I had been designated as relief for Commander George Anderson. McCain had me designated as his alternate on the Munitions Assignment Committee (air) of the Joint Aircraft Committee. For ten months I attended all the meetings for the admiral until finally he decided I might as well be the member and not just an alternate. It was a very nasty situation for me to be in as a commander for I did not have the rank nor stature to sit with men like General Hap Arnold and General Barney Giles of the Army Air Corps.

While I was in allocations I didn't have anything to do with the testing of new planes. But I would consult with the test pilots on different things we were working on with the manufacturers. Of course they also kept a very loose liaison with the manufacturers directly, not through us at all. I did fly all new types of planes as they came out and consulted with chief engineers of the companies.

Sometimes in wartime there were blocks to effective production of planes and so we used devious devices at times—to get around these blocks.

We were very dubious about the Soviets. We didn't think they were in this war for anything more than they could get out of it, and they weren't in the Pacific war at all. Of course technically they did get into it, but they weren't any help in our war in the Pacific. They were handling one side of Germany and doing it pretty capably at that, but that was remote from our Pacific interests and what we thought was the best use of our airplanes. But they were allies and had a seat at the table to bid for U.S. production out of lend-lease.

This was a time when we were trying to get all of the airplane production we could get out of the manufacturers. Particularly in the case of Catalinas, the PBYs, we had three different production lines turning them

252

out. And then a fourth line came into the picture. The Naval Aircraft Factory wanted to get into the aircraft business. They'd been doing experimental work for a long time, but they didn't have a very good reputation for production efficiency. It was often said of the Naval Aircraft Factory: they should close it up and save millions by contracting for the work that they did with commercial sources. That was a moot point into which I won't go any further. They did manage to wangle a contract for building some of our PBYs and they did have a facility there capable of turning out a few—not very many—but they could turn out a few without expansion of their plant. To keep them happy the navy let them go ahead and produce a few airplanes.

They called their plane the PBN, the Naval Aircraft Factory version of the PBY. A contract was executed—I think it was for something like twenty-eight airplanes in the initial contract—a drop in the bucket. It didn't match the production of the Consolidated Factory for one month.

The first thing that they did was to take the blueprints of the PBY and see if they couldn't improve on them. They did a mock-up job and without any word to the Bureau of Aeronautics or to us in programs and allocations or anyone else, they decided to improve the tail of the PBY. And sure enough, what they did to it was an aerodynamic improvement of the tail of the PBY. But that also made it a bastard that we couldn't use any place because parts weren't interchangeable between a PBN and all the hundreds of Consolidated PBYs that we had, nor those which came out of the other production facilities. All others were standardized, but the PBN was a beast apart. It was a perfectly good airplane but NAF had exceeded their authority. They had been properly dressed down for it but there we were. Twenty-one of the twenty-eight had been built—by the time the story got out. They hadn't been delivered. They were still working on them at the Naval Aircraft Factory.

About that time it was decided that there would be a meeting of the Munitions Assignment Committee (air) to go over the annual production and the promises that would be made to our allies. Much to everybody's surprise, the Russians demanded one squadron—they didn't say how many planes that was but they demanded one squadron of PBYs. Well, we needed our PBYs and all of our allies did except the Russians. We had no idea of what they were going to do with the planes, and the Russians never will tell you anything. The only thing we were told was that they would take air delivery of these planes; they would have their crews pick them up and ferry them to Russia. That's all we knew, and we didn't like it much.

Then I got an idea. Here was our solution. Let's say they wanted one squadron and let's say they use eighteen planes in a squadron. They have to have spares. That would bring them up to say twenty-one, twenty-four;

we've got twenty-eight of these PBNs, perfectly good airplanes, not a thing wrong with them, but they won't fit any of our customers. We can't put them in with PBYs because the spares are not interchangeable.

So I decided right at the outset that this is how I would deal with the Russians. They wouldn't have to meet with the other Allies. They wanted entirely private meetings anyhow. They didn't want to meet with anybody—just for their senior representative to meet with our senior representative. They wouldn't meet with the others because they wanted to be different. We couldn't find any reason behind anything but one thing: we found out eventually why they wanted the airplanes. As to their maneuvers to get them, we didn't understand.

The meeting between the top men was between their top Washington man and Admiral McCain. It lasted about ten minutes while they had a cup of coffee. Admiral McCain convinced the Russians that as far as airplane allocation was concerned, he didn't know anything about it and wasn't about to deal with it and they would have to deal with me. They could pick a representative and he could come and see me any time he wanted to, and we would work this thing out. Admiral McCain said that he would accept any deal I arranged.

The Russians saw they weren't going to get anywhere with him, so a Russian captain came to see me. I was a commander, so he had to be a rank senior. He made an appointment to see me and said, at the outset: "If you have seen our correspondence, you know that a tentative agreement has been made between the White House and Moscow that we get a squadron of seaplanes." I replied affirmatively and said that we were prepared to talk business then and there. He said it was Catalinas we were talking about. I said, "You didn't say how many airplanes you wanted. You said you wanted a squadron and frankly I don't know how many planes you have in a squadron. I guessed at eighteen." He said, "That's exactly right. We do have eighteen, we want eighteen airplanes." I said: "Well, obviously you're going to have to have some spares. You can't just take eighteen and operate without some backup behind them." With alacrity he responded: "Oh, yes, yes. What would you suggest?" I said, "You have to have a minimum of three spares, twenty-one total and you'd be safer with six—twenty-four. But since this is a long haul and you've got to ferry them to Russia and then operate in rugged conditions (they were going to operate them off Murmansk—that's all he would tell me) you are going to need plenty of backup. It just so happens we've got, or will have, twenty-eight very fine, modernized Catalinas." I put it that way. Actually the tail was good—the whole plane was good; it just wasn't any good to us. I thought this would be a good chance to get rid of the PBNs and get them out of our hair forever, by giving them to the Russians. I said, "We'll round this off; I'll give you twenty-eight." He just couldn't believe it. He came there to argue with me to get eighteen, and here he was going home with twenty-eight in the pocket. He was a cinch to become an admiral. He was very pleased.

He went back wondering what the hitch was on this, why this great generosity, and of course his superior immediately called Admiral Mc-Cain and said what a highly successful meeting he had and what a fine representative had met with his man and worked out all the details, that everything was set. All we had to work out was the timing, when the crews would get them and so on. That became the subject of the next session. When it came to the question of the timing of the crews for their checkout—they had to be taught to fly these airplanes, in order to take delivery themselves and fly them on to Russia. Our responsibility ended when they left the country.

I had flown out of the Naval Aircraft Factory, from the river there, with a seaplane. It was just murderous to take off and land with all that debris floating around and all of the river traffic. The aircraft factory had a tiny field, but its seaplane facilities were very, very limited; it was a gingerly operation at best. I thought that to bring this bunch of Russians to Philadelphia to take delivery of all these airplanes would be pretty much of a mess. Quite sincerely, from an operational point of view I thought this was no good. But we had a good seaplane facility down at Elizabeth City, North Carolina. It was a small air station not being used at that time. It had barracks and all sorts of facilities and they were not in use. So I made up my mind to use it for the delivery point. We'd have our pilots ferry them out of the aircraft factory and fly them down there. In the meantime, I'd beat the bullrushes by messages to get qualified Russian interpreters, because we had to be able to talk to these people and check them out. I knew we would never get enough pilots to do this but just interpreters to go along with our pilots that we had checking the Russians out. This was so that they could manage these new planes, fly them out of Elizabeth City, and get them out of the country. Ideal operational conditions did prevail at Elizabeth City.

Another representative came over to make arrangements for the Russian crews and said: "Our people haven't seen any of your big cities and so we're going to give them a little bit of a break. We'll just bring them in about ten days ahead of time to Philadelphia and just put them up in hotels in town. They can make their contacts with the Naval Aircraft Factory and then go into their training. We estimate that the training will take about a month for all of our people. Then we'll get under way."

I said: "Well, there's just one thing about that. You can take your crews to New York or Philadelphia or any place you want to see something of the country, but when the time comes for delivery, we've got a place down in North Carolina that's ideally set up for it. We have Russian-

English interpreters down there right now. They are ready whenever your people arrive, and as to the airplanes, twenty-one of them are there now and the others will be before your crews get here. Soon we will have twenty-eight airplanes at Elizabeth City ready to operate for training and checkout. We even have, in your cockpits, all the signs in Russian and English. This is all set for you."

He thought that was all fine except he didn't know about taking the crews down to Elizabeth City. He didn't think that was any good at all. His understanding was that they would take them from the Naval Aircraft Factory. After a little questioning, it came out that they thought the Naval Aircraft Factory was the very top "hush-hush secret place" for the development of everything that was done in naval aviation, and that all the advanced development that the Navy tested in any kind of any airplane was done at the Naval Aircraft Factory. If they could just get some people into it for a month's duty, they would be able to find out everything that went on in the aircraft factory. This was the primary reason they were so happy to get the Naval Aircraft Factory's airplanes and didn't hold out for the standard Catalinas. This all became very obvious.

Then everything became tied up in a knot. "No, our agreement was the aircraft factory," said the Russians. No agreement said to take delivery there—agreement that the PBNs were allocated, yes, but not where training, check-out, and delivery would be effected. That would have to be done where practical and it was not practical to train pilots at Philadelphia. He said he couldn't accept that; he would have to go back to his superior. He went off, a bit upset. This was the first time I had seen him get in a huff.

Of course, I immediately got to Admiral McCain to tell him about this development. He knew about the Elizabeth City plan, the whole set-up, and knew that it was just perfect. He had underwritten the whole plan. He said, "Well, we will take care of that. You know what will happen. He is going to go to his top man, who will call Moscow. Then Uncle Joe Stalin is going to call FDR, and before we know it we will be delivering them out of Philadelphia regardless of the physical handicaps, limitations, and so on. We don't want any part of that, and neither do we want a couple hundred Russians on a snooping job at the aircraft factory, even though it isn't what they think it is." He said, "We'll fix that." He picked up his telephone and called Admiral Leahy, who was chief of staff to the president. Going all the way back to the *New Mexico* days, Leahy had been skipper of the New Mex when McCain was exec, when I came aboard as a fresh-caught ensign. He called Leahy and said: "I'm going to send Herb Riley, an old *New Mexico* shipmate, over to see you and talk to you about something. You'll think it's pretty funny, but we need your help fast."

Leahy said, "Send him over right away." I went to Admiral Leahy's office. I hadn't seen him since the *New Mexico* days. He came in, was very cordial, and I told him the story as quickly as I could. I told him I was afraid there would be a telephone call from Stalin to FDR. He said, "I think we can handle that."

He left his office and when he came back, he said, "Come with me," and took me into the president's office. He said, "Tell the president the story you just told me," so I did. FDR threw back his head and roared. He thought this was the funniest damn thing he'd heard in a long time. He said, "Okay, I'm briefed. If Joe calls me, I'll tell him it's all set, don't worry about it. Elizabeth City's where they will get the aircraft."

Sure enough there was a telephone call from Stalin to the president that night and the president nipped the Russian complaint in the bud. He told Leahy about it. Leahy of course told McCain—who told me. The next day my Russian counterpart was back in my office and said that he had found that Elizabeth City was quite all right as the training and delivery site.

This is the sort of thing that happened. Almost unbelievable sometimes, but true and interesting, when you consider the people concerned— the characters in the cast.

They said they were going to use them in Murmansk. We never found out how much if any they did use them. We do know they ferried them over the northern route to take them to Murmansk, and I think they lost two of the planes. They didn't lose the crews, but they crashed up two of the planes in landing. None of our people ever saw the planes, and we could never get any report or confirmation that they were ever used. Neither did we ever receive any request for additional spare parts.

The funniest thing about the whole incident was that when the crews arrived in the United States not one of them had a suitcase. They didn't have a toothbrush. They didn't have a spare pair of shoes. They had what they were standing in and nothing else. When asked about their flight gear they said: "Oh, lend-lease, we get everything lend-lease." Lend-lease was the only English words that they knew. Everything they wanted was to be lend-lease—their clothes, every piece of equipment they received, everything that went into the airplanes and all supporting gear. They knew about lend-lease well enough!

The Casablanca Conference was held in January 1943. Both President Roosevelt and Prime Minister Churchill attended with a full panoply of military staff. The record of that meeting gives the impression that things were less frenetic than were some of the meetings that followed. There were reasons to be confident. The invasion of French North Africa and Algeria had been carried off with success. The Americans were beginning to meet with some gains in their struggles against the formidable foe in the Pacific. The initial fear of a Russian collapse on the eastern front, where the Nazis employed some 180 divisions, had lessened. The collapse had not materialized and hope had taken the place of despair.

To be sure the military leaders discussed with vigor such things as the long proposed invasion of the Continent from English shores, but the real progress that came from the Casablanca Conference was certainly the firm decision to launch an attack on Sicily. Sardinia had been proposed as an alternate because it was thought to be less heavily defended, but that idea was quickly abandoned and Sicily was chosen as the target with the strong backing of Admiral King. He argued that the Allied forces would have to take that island sooner or later because of its strategic location, so why not concentrate on it now with so many of the Allied forces still in the Mediterranean? This decision viewed Sicily as an end in itself, not tied to any thought of an invasion of the Italian peninsula. Churchill did say, however, that the conquest of Sicily would open new opportunities for more thrusts against the "soft underbelly of the Axis." Such remarks of Churchill were often construed by hard-headed and practical Americans to be romanticism without stable reasoning. In fairness to the grand old man of Britain, his colorful language often carried a sense of truth not yet discerned by more practical men.

Hanson Baldwin, the military authority of the *New York Times,* wrote: "The Sicilian campaign, the largest amphibious assault of World War II (a 38-day conquest) represented the end of the beginning in the long Allied road to victory. Sicily was a strategic compromise, conceived in dissension, born of uneasy alliance—a child of conflicting concepts and unclear in purpose. The campaign was fought because something had to be done."*

Several advantages were seen as possible in the invasion of Sicily. In victory the line of communications through the Mediterranean would be secured. This in turn would save on ships and men now employed of necessity on the longer route around the Cape of Good Hope and into the Indian Ocean. The invasion of Sicily itself could cause the Germans to divert some of their forces now employed on the eastern front. At the same time it could also apply pressure to the Italians and perhaps hasten their withdrawal from the war. Lastly, it might cause a situation wherein Turkey could be persuaded to come into the war on the Allied side and thus strengthen the situation in the Middle East.

It should be noted that military strategists on the Allied side from General Eisenhower on down the chain of command viewed Sicily in all probability as a "mighty bloody affair" (as expressed by Admiral Kirk, one of the Allied commanders named to take part in the invasion). Defenses of the island were believed to be very strong. The landing would be difficult because the topography of the beaches differed greatly from that of the North African coast and some of the small landing craft now in use were thought to be unsuitable.

It was good that the decision for Sicily cleared the air for the time being. The landings in French North Africa in later 1942 in reality began to make less urgent the belief that the Allies must land on the Continent in mid-1943. So what were they to do with the military forces now available in the Mediterranean? They had to be employed. It was not possible to sit still. In war you're either winning or losing and you have got to keep going. You've got to keep fighting and crowd the enemy; otherwise, the enemy will build up reserves and become impregnable. The excerpts that follow give some idea of the nature of the amphibious landing.

Phil Bucklew and his Scouts and Raiders proved of great assistance to Admiral Conolly, especially in the training of personnel in handling landing craft on the beaches of Sicily. It was all a kind of preparation for much more difficult operations to come at Salerno and Normandy.

Admiral Conolly's story is a solid account of meticulous preparations for a landing on an island that was thought to be heavily defended. It also gives ample evidence of the admiral's military skills, for which he was noted, and it reveals the disappointment he experienced in the lack of air support, as well as the surprising lack of defense by the Germans and the vigorous role of General Patton.

Commodore Sullivan (later rear admiral) was dispatched to Palermo

*Hanson W. Baldwin, *Battles Lost and Won: Great Campaigns of World War II* (New York: Harper & Row, 1966), 188.

260

on a hasty mission to repair the damage to a shattered port in order to facilitate its use in an anticipated need for military supplies. Instead the reader is given a clue to the speed with which the Sicilian campaign was accomplished. Even before Sullivan's salvage operations were begun in the harbor it was becoming useless to the Allied forces. Their thoughts were turning rapidly to the Italian peninsula and the possibilities for use of the great harbor at Naples. Suddenly the campaign on the Italian peninsula, the boot of Italy, became a much larger objective.

Admiral Alan Kirk's brief account is both pithy and succinct. It conveys the opinion of a talented admiral who had been led to believe that the conflict was to be a pretty bloody affair. In a very few words he analyzes the reasons for the short campaign. In the doing his sense of humor shines through.

The development of the Scouts and Raiders is an illustrious story in history. They are a group that came into being with the concept of amphibious warfare and became a mighty adjunct to that type of warfare as it blossomed in World War II. The idea had origins in the World War II program of the former heavyweight boxing champion Gene Tunney. Phil Bucklew, one of the first men in the Scouts and Raiders program, was a native of Ohio. He had played football in high school and college, became a professional in the early days of that sport, and finally organized a team of his own. They were on a barnstorming tour of the nation and had reached Los Angeles on 7 December 1941, when the United States was catapulted into the war. His team was disbanded immediately and most of the men qualified for enlistment in the navy. Bucklew stayed on the West Coast and saw a notice of Gene Tunney's program of physical education. Later Bucklew termed that program "primarily a calisthenics drill that was preparation for boot training." He enrolled in the Tunney program and completed the course, staying on as an assistant instructor.

During that period a call was issued for volunteers to enroll in a special project called "amphibious commandos." Ten of the men, including Phil Bucklew, answered the call. They were inducted into the navy in mid-1942 and were joined almost immediately by approximately one hundred enlisted men who had come directly from boot camp. The initial program was generated out of Norfolk, Virginia, but soon moved to an area on the Patuxent River where the Naval Air Station is now located. At Patuxent there was a small commercial boatyard. With the advent of these amphibious commandos it became the assembly point for the first landing craft the navy had. Transports would come into Norfolk, embark some marines, and sail up the Chesapeake Bay. Then the amphibious commandos came out in landing craft, anchored alongside the troop ships, debarked the marines who came down the nets, and landed them ashore. It was early training for the marines to prepare for future amphibious assaults as well as a period during which the ships were being rigged with davits to carry landing craft, something they had not had before.

Training was not formalized when the original group of amphibious commandos assembled at Patuxent. They had not operated boats until then but they learned under the direction of four Coast Guard chiefs who were tough, knowledgeable, and good. Bucklew says of that period: "It was the most practical training that I experienced. In fact, it was the best training I ever had in the navy. The whole theme was—if you smashed up a boat or the engine quit, all the chief said was: 'Fix it!' I recall one time when I was having a little trouble. I said, 'Chief, it's not working so well. After chow I'll be back down.' 'No,' said he, 'you'll have chow after you fix it.' "

These early amphibious commandos (the name was probably inspired by the commando raid by British and Canadians on the French port of Dieppe in 1942) soon became known as Scouts and Raiders with the landing of our troops in North Africa, and they continued to bear that name well after the landings in Normandy.

The experiences of the Scouts and Raiders were variegated as time went on. In mid-1942 some of them trained with the British forces operating out of the submarine base in Malta in preparation for joint Anglo-American landings on Sicily. Bucklew's account of their Sicilian experiences is the first in the series of oral history excerpts on that campaign.

Their early training began with boats at Patuxent. Then they learned the handling of weapons—the 50-caliber types, the small arms, then demolitions—and when they worked with the army commandos they picked up more knowledge, rope tricks, and assault tactics. Gradually they converted to rocketry and before Normandy they engaged in demolition work with the early UDT groups that were preparing to deliver and cover troop landings on the Normandy beaches. It was there that the UDTs suffered heavy casualties amounting to as much as 40 percent of their personnel.

After Normandy, when the European conflict was coming to a close, the Scouts and Raiders began to develop new units under a new name: "Amphibious Roger." This was an ambiguous title because such units were intended for service in the Far East and for operations in the jungle. Their training at this time was at Fort Pierce in Florida. Phil Bucklew himself was put in command of this training period.

The far eastern phase of this story is not included in this book. Their service in China, Korea, and Vietnam was just as profitable as was the earlier contribution in the European theater. Bucklew continued as the leader in most of these operations. In his last and senior period of service in Vietnam, Captain Bucklew became head of the Special Operations Support Group, made up of small command groups such as the SEALS, the UDTs, and the Boat Support group.

Portions of Captain Bucklew's oral history are included in later sections of this book, sections that deal with the Allied invasions at Salerno, Italy, and the assault on the Normandy beaches.

It is fitting that this description of the Scouts and Raiders include a reference to the dedication of a special building named the Phil H. Bucklew Center for Naval Special Warfare on 21 January 1987 at the Naval Amphibious Base in Coronado, California. It is a handsome recognition of all those military personnel who have served and now serve in what is categorized as Naval Special Warfare.

NEW HELP FOR THE ADMIRAL

CAPTAIN PHIL H. BUCKLEW

U.S. NAVY (COURTESY PHIL BUCKLEW)

PHIL H. BUCKLEW was born in Columbus, Ohio, on 18 December 1914. He attended public schools including high school in his home town. It happened that the family residence was adjacent to the playing field of Ohio State University. Young Bucklew became so fascinated with the football practice he observed there that he determined to be a football player. This ambition grew to the degree that in high school he was soon recognized as a gifted athlete. Another ambition of his was to attend Ohio State University. Unfortunately the university required him to attend a prep school for a year or so before enrollment and his family demurred. But Xavier University in Cincinnati had heard of his prowess in football and was anxious to build a team of its own, so the authorities there offered a scholarship and he accepted. The result was that he remained there for four years and earned a degree, to be followed by another two years as the coach of their football team. While at Xavier he also enrolled in the naval reserve and was initially faithful in attendance but gradually gave up the relationship.

Then he received an offer to play football with the Cleveland Rams (later the Los Angeles Rams), but after two years he was tempted by an offer from the Detroit Lions. Friends intervened, however, and urged him to set up a team in Columbus instead. Bucklew went to Lexington, Kentucky, and obtained a franchise from the fledgling American League and went back to Columbus to discover that the local paper had announced the formation of a team to be coached by Bucklew. There followed the usual struggle for finances, but Bucklew organized a barnstorming tour with the players he had assembled, toured the East Coast and the West Coast, and met with success in such places as New York City, Boston, and Buffalo, as well as Los Angeles, Seattle, and Hollywood.

The team happened to be playing a game in Los Angeles on 7 December 1941 when news of the Japanese attack on Pearl Harbor was announced in the stadium. The crowd began to leave and the game came to a sudden end. The players adjourned to a local bar and one of the members suggested that all of them volunteer for service. Bucklew, because of his former relationship with the naval reserve, suggested they consider the navy. The next day thirty young men presented themselves at the enlistment office in Los Angeles.

Bucklew discovered that he wasn't in shape for the service. He was very much overweight, but he very soon saw a notice of the new program in physical fitness that the heavyweight champion Gene Tunney had inaugurated. Bucklew enrolled and finished the course, then stayed on for a short time as an instructor. Soon he saw a notice in the press asking for volunteers to become amphibious commandos. Bucklew and nine others were accepted.

They were sent to Patuxent Air Base on the Chesapeake for indoctrination. He said later that it was the best training he had in all his years with the navy. These new amphibious commandos were introduced to the first landing craft the navy had, a rather primitive forerunner to the later models.

Later that summer these men, now with a new name, the Scouts and Raiders, found themselves on the USS *Leedstown,* a transport that joined the convoy forming in Norfolk and elsewhere for the invasion of North Africa. Their transport was sunk off the North African Coast and the survivors were sent back to the United States. Bucklew had applied for a commission a few months before and became an ensign in 1943. His buddies were already en route to Fort Pierce in Florida and he managed to get there, too, thus keeping them together for what was to be an eventual record-setting four years. Once again back in the Mediterranean they managed further training with the British for combined operations, mastering many of the standard assault tactics.

Bucklew was then assigned to the staff of Admiral Conolly for the landings in Sicily in July 1943, and after that again with Admiral Conolly for deployment at Salerno in September 1943. The next major operation for Bucklew was the Normandy landings in June 1944, specifically the beach surveys and German defenses before the actual landing of troops. This part of his story is told graphically in the oral history excerpts that follow.

In December 1944 Bucklew and his small group of one-time volunteers were once again at Fort Pierce in Florida. They were now called the Amphibious Rogers, preparing for jungle operations in the Far East. This mission was designed to gather intelligence for Rear Admiral Milton Miles, who made his headquarters in Chungking with Chiang Kai-shek. This kept Bucklew in China until 1946 and afforded him an adventure of great danger, an intelligence-gathering mission on the China coast off Amoy. It required him to make a trip on foot for about one hundred miles through the mountains disguised as a Chinese coolie, constantly dodging Japanese soldiers.

From 1947 Bucklew was back in the United States and from September 1947 to June 1951 he was engaged in graduate work at Columbia University. He also served as assistant football coach to Lou Little, the noted coach at Columbia. Bucklew did a certain amount of scouting for the Columbia team, and as a professor of naval science he was advisor and administrator for one hundred or more freshmen students in NROTC.

Between June 1951 and April 1956 Bucklew was commanding officer of Beach Jumper Unit Two, organizing and maintaining a Tactical Deception Unit of 240 men.

In June 1956 Bucklew became intelligence officer on the staff of the U.S. Naval Forces, Korea, and adviser to the director of Naval Intelligence in the Korean Navy. July 1958 found him the officer in charge, Amphibious Intelligence School, in the training command of the U.S. Pacific Fleet. He left this job in July 1961 and until June 1963 served as intelligence officer on the staff of the commander of Amphibious Forces with the Seventh Fleet. This was followed by duty as executive officer at the U.S. Amphibious Base in Coronado, California.

From November 1963 to December 1967 Bucklew was Commander, Naval Operations Support Group, Pacific, the headquarters command of five component naval special operations: two Underwater Demolition Teams, a SeaAirLand (SEAL) team, a Beach Jumper Tactical Deception unit, and a Boat Support unit.

In January 1967 the captain was back in Washington as head of the Special Operations Branch, Strike Warfare Division, on the staff of the chief of naval operations. His final tour of duty came in March 1969, when he was representative of the chief of naval operations on a special project sponsored by the chairman of the Joint Chiefs of Staff to document historical data and effectiveness of selected activities in the Vietnamese conflict.

Captain Bucklew retired in 1969 and makes his home in Fairfax, Virginia. He has been the recipient of numerous citations from the navy and from foreign countries. A signal honor came to him in recent years when a building was named to recognize his long service in the field of amphibious warfare. It is located at the Amphibious Base in Coronado, California.

We joined the British in Malta as part of their Combined Operations Group to perform submarine and beach reconnaissance on the coast of Sicily. We participated with and under them. The Royal Navy was tasked with submarine responsibility in the Mediterranean. Their favorite type of submarine was of medium size, about 150 feet in length, more maneuverable, and for Mediterranean use a very practical assignment. These were also used for reconnaissance purposes as well as for attack—going in to the beach, releasing the scouts in kayak canoes to go on in shore, making the beach reconnaissance, and then homing to the submarine. Most of the work involved determining beach gradients and changes in the beaches, looking for shoals, taking soundings, and making any sight observations and specific checks.

We worked with the British until I returned to Algiers, probably about June. That was prior to the Sicilian landings. From there I was assigned to Admiral Richard Conolly, COMLANCRABNAV at Bizerte. Sicily was to be the first landing ship operation—a new experiment for the Mediterranean—with a small staff headquartered afloat and ashore. There I had with me one of my original group, Rip Howe. We got our boats together on my arrival and with a nucleus of crews from our Scouts and Raiders, commenced building a new outfit. Admiral Conolly gave me a pretty blanket backup on how many men we needed, how many men I should get. We sent out calls for volunteers from both army and navy. They were training people like mad in the States but not for the tactics needed here. Conolly said: "We are not taking any more from the States. I want the men trained here for the job as we decide to do it." We did everything there from road work—every morning we were out running a couple of miles—to swimming, kayak canoe work, and were just getting into rocketry, mortars, and that sort of thing. Our basic task was advance reconnaissance in order to assure that the troops were landed on their designated beach targets.

I learned a lesson there from Admiral Conolly. He worked in a very informal way. I could assign and train my own people and I did until one day he said: "Tell me, who are you going to assign where? How are you going to do this?" I had chosen a spot, Green Beach. It was kind of a tricky thing with a narrow channel entrance. He said, "Who is going to handle it?" And I said: "I'm going to take it." And he said: "Now wait a minute. Why?" My reply was: "I think I have the most experience and that's a tricky one to get into." He said: "There are fifteen thousand troops going over Red Beach and that's where you are going to be." I said: "That's an easy one, Admiral. I'd give that to Rip and I'll take the other." He said: "You give Rip Green Beach. Now let's get something straight. You know I ask a lot of questions but don't ever forget, I still make the decisions here." This is where I began learning a few important things.

Our special mission was to identify the exits, the roadways. You had to get the troops in and make certain they are not off one hundred yards or whatever—off target—or else the army is piled up and becomes very vulnerable. On land they may go charging to take a foxhole and they do it rather blindly; in amphibious landings you had to make certain they hit the beach exactly where their little charts said. Their job begins from where we land them and their intelligence targeting is specific in charging known foxholes, gun emplacements, and so on. We had to check it out and be as certain as possible. Admiral Conolly gave me quite a lecture that day that I never forgot. He said that the objective of such a landing is to save as many lives as you can: "I concede you are the most experienced person, but where the most troops are is where the most experienced person will be." And I said, "Aye, aye, sir." And that was the way it was, although it wasn't the toughest one.

Our procedure as we approached our task was that we would come in advance of the landing force—maybe it was about an hour in advance of the landing craft embarking troops from the ship. We would go in as best we could by identifying shoreline silhouettes. In the case of Sicily it was difficult because the shoreline was all as flat as could be. The reconnaissance procedure commences in the middle of the night to around one o'clock in the morning and you usually work under the quarter moon so as to have protection of full darkness as the troops approach the beach. You try to center your beach. Then you make your passes on it to locate your flanks. In most cases you have something like a pillbox on one flank and some tangible, identifiable object on the other. After you center, you normally make a full sweep one flank to the other. It requires dropping a man off at each flank. By flashlight signal, whatever code you are giving, he then locates himself at that flank with another scout at the other flank. You then back off your boat until you receive the flank signals and then you can estimate the accurate center of the beach. Then, as the landing craft come in, you have to make them come down the alley. It is a very simple procedure.

It did get tough, however, at Sicily. Whatever happened, they turned airfield searchlights on and it looked like Broadway. You learn from experience in working from the water or from a boat that regardless of how bright the searchlights are, you are still difficult to be seen. You feel as though you are stark naked there in making your runs, but experience teaches that powerful aircraft searchlights over the water provide a glare for the observer also. You may be scared but you are protected on the water.

The opposition at Sicily was not the roughest. I feel that some of the Germans there—I was pretty well convinced they were going to surrender. I put my flank men ashore and got my two signals from my flank men, both of them army types. One performed one of the most heroic actions I had seen and he was later awarded a Silver Star for it. He was amazing. From the flank the enemy opened fire. It was almost the same spot from where I was receiving my flank light signal. I was getting the flank signal with machine gun fire coming right over it and it was steady fire. I found my sergeant, the flank man, on the beach next morning and said: "What the hell were you doing?" He said: "Well the pillbox was occupied. I felt the safest thing to do was to get my back right up against it." They were firing over his head. And he was sitting there safe with a shielded light. He was right under their fire.

So we landed the troops. But as I say, I felt they were going to give up because I had an 88 working me over from the shore. The Germans could do more with those 88s. They handled them like a 38-caliber gun and they chased me from one end of the beach to the other. They just kept laying it in my wake. I would swing around and come back and the gunner would make me back off. I knew he would hit me if he could control it that well. So I thought he is playing something here and not playing for keeps. He is going to quit. As the troops came in the Germans folded fast.

This was the section where Patton landed—Whiskey Knoll. I did not lose a man in the operation. That was a fairly easy one. We went back to Bizerte then and trained for Salerno. It was a much rougher operation, much more difficult, much heavier casualties.

LANDING THE THIRD INFANTRY DIVISION AT LICATA

ADMIRAL RICHARD L. CONOLLY

U.S. NAVAL INSTITUTE

RICHARD LANSING CONOLLY was born on 26 April 1892 in Waukegan, Illinois. He was a student at Lake Forest Academy from 1906 to 1909 where he received a B.S. degree. He was a member of the class of 1914 at the U.S. Naval Academy and entered active duty in the Mexican crisis of 1914 aboard the battleship *Virginia* (BB 13). He was then sent to the armored cruiser *Montana* (ACR 13) for instruction in torpedoes during the summer of 1915 and then to the battleship *Vermont* (BB 20) as torpedo officer the following spring. He was assigned to the destroyer *Smith* (DD 17) in 1916 and spent World War I on escort duty out of Brest, France.

From 1918 to 1920 he served as executive officer in succession on the destroyers *Foote, Worden,* and *Hunt.* He was then enrolled in the graduate school at the Naval Academy, to be followed by work at Columbia University, where he earned an M.S. degree in 1922. Conolly then had battleship duty in the Pacific, and from 1925 to 1927 he taught electrical engineering at the Naval Academy. There followed destroyer duty in the Atlantic and the Caribbean area. From 1931 to 1933 he was a student and then an instructor at the Naval War College. After further sea duty Conolly returned to the Naval Academy to teach seamanship and navigation and electrical engineering, part of the time as acting department head.

As captain he then commanded Destroyer Squadron Seven and after that Destroyer Division Six, which were part of Admiral Halsey's escort force during the early months of the Pacific war, including the Doolittle raid on Tokyo in April 1942. He then joined Admiral King's staff at the Navy Department and was promoted to rear admiral. Early in 1943 he reported to the Atlantic Fleet Amphibious Force and was in charge of Landing Craft and Bases, Northwest African Waters. In May of 1943 he moved in his flagship USS *Biscayne* from Algerian ports to Bizerte, Tunisia, in preparation for the invasion of Sicily.

Admiral Conolly began his amphibious combat career in July 1943 when he commanded Task Force 86, one of the three invasion transport forces at Sicily and then amphibious elements under British command for the Salerno, Italy, assault in September. The next month Admiral Conolly was transferred to the amphibious forces in the Pacific Fleet. He boarded his new amphibious command ship *Appalachian* (AGC 1) at San Diego late in November as Commander, Group Three, Fifth Amphibious Force. As such he led Task Force 53 in the capture of Kwajalein in the Marshall Islands in 1944. Then redesignated Commander, Group Three, he landed and supported the marines at Guam. He then landed army forces at Leyte in October and at Lingayen Gulf in January 1945. His next task was to begin the plans for the invasion of the Japanese mainland, but he was directed to the occupation of northern Japan in October.

Conolly was promoted to vice admiral in December 1945 and served briefly in the Navy Department in several different commands. In 1946 he went to Europe to advise Allied foreign ministers at Paris and London. In late September he took command of U.S. Naval Forces Europe and became commander of the Twelfth Fleet in the rank of admiral. There followed several shifts in commands in the European theater until finally he was named Commander in Chief, U.S. Naval Forces Atlantic and Mediterranean, where he remained until mid-1950. Then Conolly reverted in rank to vice admiral in order to become president of the Naval War College from 1950 to 1953. He then retired from active duty as a full admiral again on 1 November 1953.

Both Admiral and Mrs. Conolly met tragic deaths in an airplane crash at La Guardia Field, New York City, on 1 March 1962.

The reason we couldn't entertain a concept of withdrawing forces to Britain and letting them stay there while training for the invasion was if we'd taken the pressure off the Germans, and they'd had free, full range to prosecute the war against the Russians, they probably would have licked the Russians. Stalin was crying bloody murder all the time, claiming that he couldn't hold the Germans unless we put counterpressure on them. He wanted the landing immediately on the Continent, whether we were ready to make it or not, just to take the pressure off him.

It didn't necessarily imply going into southern Italy if we invaded Sicily. We couldn't go north of Salerno because we needed air coverage, and the British didn't have sufficient base in aviation to tip the scales. In

1948 I discussed this with the then General Eisenhower. He wanted to know what use the carriers were. "Well, suppose you had had eight fleet carriers at the time in the Mediterranean, each with a hundred first-class fighter bombers that could operate continuously. How would you like to have had that before the battle of Salerno?" I asked.

He said, "It would have changed the whole character of the operation. We wouldn't have landed at Salerno. We would have landed further up the peninsula," which of course we would have. That would have been a complete neutralization of German air power in Italy. We would have bombed the hell out of their airfields and kept their air out of commission continually.

Thought was given to other possible operations besides Sicily, namely Sardinia and Corsica. Sardinia was the real alternative to Sicily. I didn't favor Sardinia. I preferred Sicily at the time, because it would open up the whole Mediterranean and it gave you a much greater freedom of action than if you'd gone into Sardinia. Both navies favored Sicily. Sardinia would have allowed the Germans to have a quicker means of concentrating their forces in the northern part of the theater of operations. I don't think it would have been as successful. I favored the invasion of Sicily at the time, and the way it was done, on the southern coast.

Consideration had not been given to going into Greece and other southern sections of Europe, until after Sicily. Only the Sicily operation made it possible to consider other courses of action.

I wasn't involved in the choice of landing places in southern Sicily. Originally the landings had been planned for the northwestern corner of the island, around Palermo, and I don't know why they abandoned that. I think one of the considerations was mine fields. Another consideration was the fact that there were supposed to be heavy shore batteries there, which usually impressed the army a lot more than they impressed the navy. The mine fields impressed the navy. It was judged, from our intelligence, that the mine fields ended down at Empedocle, just west of Licata, and that's why the landings were made where they were. The mine fields ended at the next port to the westward of us. Just between Empedocle and Licata was where the eastern end of the mine field turned out to be. Our intelligence was correct on that. So we made the invasion further to the eastward than was expected, and it was, I think, the best possible place to make the landing. The British at the same time made simultaneous landings on the east coast. It worked all right, in the end.

I had more responsibility as a task force commander than merely the landing of the Third Infantry Division, reinforced at Licata, because I had to prepare all the landing craft and the amphibious bases at which they trained and prepared for the movement, and I had to serve up all of the landing craft, not only my own task force, which was entirely landing craft, but those of Hall and Kirk for their operations. I not only had to prepare them, organize, and equip them, but I had to sail them and serve them up on a silver platter right off their beaches, which annoyed me at the time. I still think it was an imposition on me and my staff. We protested about it and were assured we wouldn't have to do it, but in the end, we did it.

There were other things we had to do. I never had so little time to prepare for a landing, and I never was so pushed for time as I was in the Sicily landings. There were several things. One of them was this matter of making the LSTs useful for landing heavy equipment like tanks, for which they were primarily designed, rolling stock of all kinds, which you could not get ashore past these sand bars without some special equipment. This point came up just before I left headquarters in Washington, and I went over to see my friend and classmate Ned Cochran, who was a design officer at the Bureau of Ships. I asked him what he had for unloading LSTs over beaches. He showed me three or four different things they'd been working on. None of them looked very good to me—not to him either. So then I canvassed the Navy Department and came across these pontoon cubicles that had been developed by the Bureau of Yards and Docks, by another classmate of mine, a fine fellow too, named Laycock. He had really been the inventor of these cubicles and had developed them. I said, "What are the prospects of using these things?"

Then I came across a little plan that was labeled "Project Goldrush." The project consisted of loading an LST with some aviation landing gear—that is, carrier arresting gear and catapult gear, that they could put on a small island—with the idea of making it a fighter base. You could move in an LST, land this in a hurry, set up catapults and the arresting gear and you'd have a little stationary aircraft carrier. Very clever arrangement. One of the features of this that I seized upon was the fact that they had a pontoon pier that they carried on deck and launched over the side. Then they ran it ashore, made a pier out of it, and then they landed their material on it. So that gave me an idea that eventually resulted in the whole pontoon causeway project.

So I got over to Algiers, and I was met by Admiral Hall and Jerauld Wright, who was then a captain and had been persuaded to be Admiral Hewitt's assistant chief of staff. He and a couple of yeomen were the embryonic elements on which Admiral Hewitt built his whole organization. The first thing they asked me was, since the landing at Algiers, what had been done in the Navy Department to solve this problem of landing the heavy rolling stock from LSTs. And I said, "Well, they haven't solved it, but I think I wrapped up all the lore there is available before I left."

They said, "What are they going to do about it back there?"

SICILY
1943

Heights in Feet, Soundings in Fathoms
Nautical Miles

Statute Miles

KEY

Principal roads
Railroads
100-meter contour, marking edge of plain
50-fathom line

274

I said, "I came over here expecting to find that you fellows had the whole thing solved." They said, "No such thing. This is worrying everybody."

I said, "I'll tell you what I'll do. I've got an idea," and I told them about using these pontoon cubicles. I'd thought this over far enough so that I thought it ought to result in a test being made. So I laid down the specifications and condensed this into a one-page dispatch. This was under Hall's title, making a query to certain divisions in the Navy Department. By this time I knew the organization of the Navy Department like a book, and I knew just where to push the buttons. So I sent this back: "Attention so and so, please have Admiral Farwell arrange to conduct tests; we want two pontoon causeways built, two pontoons wide and fourteen long." We figured if they could put two 175-sections together, we could bridge this gap to the beach. And it turned out that this was always more than adequate, to bridge the gap across the sand bar, across the runnel to the true beach.

So I sent this back, and they actually conducted the test at Prudence Island in Narragansett Bay. They had this big center of Yards and Docks up at Davisville, so that this was duck soup to them. They conducted the test and actually ran a medium tank to shore over the thing. They then reported the results of the test, and I said, "There it is."

But then the question came up: How are you going to carry these pontoons to the objective? Well, we wanted the best way of doing this. I used to work on this in my off hours all the time I was over there; right up to the Sicily landing we were working on getting this damn thing ready.

While I was still in Oran, before I set up my headquarters in Arzeu, a British officer had been told about this in a conference. The British officer was a captain in one of the big British steam-driven LSTs that were the forerunners of our construction. He came over with the very ingenious scheme of string and cardboard, showing how to raise a pontoon causeway up along the side of an LST. I thought it was sort of a Rube Goldberg contraption, which it was, but there was the germ of a good idea in it, and I wasn't going to drop it until I had found out whether or not it would work. It was essential to have the ship bring in the causeway and the side-carry method would save valuable deck space for pay load. So I sent a dispatch to Morocco and asked them to send up a young naval constructor, a lieutenant commander. We got the British officer in, the commanding officer of the British LST, and said to the naval constructor, "What do you think of this? Could you hinge these things on an LST and raise it up? Would the LST be seaworthy with these things on her sides?" That was the main thing.

He looked it all over and he said, "Sure, it could be done. The LST would be more seaworthy, and they could be secured so they wouldn't break loose in a seaway."

I said, "All right, now you sit down and you design these hinges, and you design a workable scheme of hoisting these alongside, with portable purchases and whatever else you need. You work this whole thing out, show where you put the pad-eyes and the fittings that have to be welded to the deck of the LST, how much space it would preempt in loading the LST after you get them on, and then when you get that done you can go back to Morocco."

So he got this worked out in two or three days, and we put the tender to work making these fittings, and we fitted up an LST. We found we could do it. But before that I had them send up some pontoons. I got them to send up a lot of spare ones they had down on the Moroccan sea frontier, ship them up on the narrow-gauge railroad that ran down to Arzeu. Finally a couple of hundred of them arrived down there. By that time, I had a construction battalion down there, so I put the SeaBees to work putting these things together and they built two causeways.

Meanwhile the Allied Force Headquarters had gotten hot on this issue, and they issued orders. I saw the written orders, signed by General Eisenhower, to General Clark, who had his headquarters up in the mountains, to get busy and solve this problem. So the army turned hell bent on this thing. They put two regiments of engineers to work on it. They built a lot of wooden pontoons and really went at it by the brute force method. They tried out everything. Finally they decided the most promising thing would be to drag all this stuff (the heavy equipment, rolling stock) through the runnel, and then dry it out and rehabilitate it on the shore. Well, that didn't sound too good. You can't fiddle-faddle around with a tank that's drowned out or a jeep that won't run if you're under enemy fire. That's a poor time to be loaded up with a lot of drowned-out equipment, at a beach landing. This was the best the army could do.

They called on General Harold Alexander, who was in command of all the land forces there, and asked him to come up to Arzeu to witness this test. I was politely invited too. So I gave them a ship for a test, and they brought it in on the beach and grounded it on a sand bar, and they dragged all this equipment through the water, and they were busy working on this thing, when my LST (and this was completely unintended) by a fortuitous coincidence, arrived. I had lost all track of this thing and just what stage the project was at, after two or three days. Our ship didn't even carry the pontoons on the sides but just towed the pontoon causeways alongside. They landed the two causeways, connected them together—it took them quite a while.

All the time as Alexander was watching this test of the drowned-out equipment, he kept casting his eye up the beach. And finally there came a tractor out from the bow of the LST and fished the ramp on the end of these two causeways which they'd finally got harnessed up. Then it went over the ramp and landed on the beach. Then we waited for a minute or so. Meanwhile nobody was paying any attention to the army's experiment. General Alexander had his attention fixed there on our ship. A medium tank came waddling out and went over this causeway and landed on the beach, whereupon General Alexander broke into a run up the beach to see this at close quarters. We tailed along with him—Michael O'Daniel and myself—and Alexander said, "How long have you had this working?"

I said, "This is the first time we've been able to do it here. It's been done back in the States." Then I told him about the project, and the pontoons on the side of the ship, and that we'd gotten that worked out to our satisfaction, and this was the first time we'd been able to actually use the gear in a simulated combat landing. We put the ramp on the end, and we had the crew working on that so that it could be permanently fitted and we wouldn't have to fiddle-faddle around. A lot of these things could be worked out in the course of the next month. Having witnessed this test, I could say it was an assured thing, that it could be done. Now the only question was getting it done. I said that I would immediately send dispatches, "Ship me enough pontoons and assembly crews so I can go into production."

He said, "Do our chaps know about this?"

I said, "Yes, there was a representative of Admiral Ramsey's who was up here, but he went back last Monday." Admiral Ramsey and his command were on the same level as Admiral Hewitt, and he was preparing the British part of the operation. He had his headquarters in Alexandria. "This captain has gone back to Alexandria, and the Admiralty has said that they can't carry these on the sides of the ships because it will make the LSTs unseaworthy." So I said, "We part company on this feature. But there's no reason you can't use the causeway, tow them in by tugs or something of that sort."

Pretty soon, having recorded the success of this operation to the CNO, I got orders to manufacture so many for ourselves and the other American task force commanders and so many for the British. Whereupon I told them that it would not be practicable to manufacture them for the British, and said they had better facilities than we did and more men, and I recommended that we divert the LSTs that came over loaded with these things to Bougie, where the British could set up an assembly yard of their own and build their own. I had to do so. It was a pain in the neck and a lot of trouble, and they were using my ships to get these things to the British, but we got them to them. I sent assembly crews up there and taught them how to do it, how to put them together. We gave them brains and equipment and everything else and set them up in business.

Meanwhile, when we went up to Bizerte, I set up another assembly yard up there, so we had two assembly yards grinding out pontoon causeways for the Sicily operation, one at Bizerte and one at Arzeu. By the time the operation took place, we had nine complete causeway kits assembled that could be carried on LSTs, and three others that we towed in with tugs. The British towed all theirs in, about four or five, as I remember.

Of course, before Sicily there was a storm, and we apparently had better luck with our tugs, because I think all of theirs were adrift in the Mediterranean and were a menace to navigation. We had two tugs that brought the things in, and we got them there, although they were awfully late. The ones that were actually used in combat landings were the ones that were carried in our LSTs. We had to parcel them out. Each of us, Hall, Kirk, and myself, had three of these pontoon causeways. Of course, by the time of Salerno we had plenty of them. We needed them at Salerno too. All those beaches were the same in the Mediterranean, both north and south, so we had good training around there in the Gulf of Arzeu and the surrounding territory. The beaches were all just like they would be in Sicily.

Even in the training period we ran into some difficulties with the army, because we considered it a naval responsibility to get the troops ashore, and yet they insisted that they be landed in rubber boats, and the nearest thing they had to a rubber boat was these rubber pontoons we used on the Treadway causeway. They wanted these launched from the deck of an LCI, which is a small ship. They were dead set on a secret landing at night. Now, actually we made a secret landing at night in Sicily, but we got away with murder, and, only due to the storm, with a tactical surprise. We considered a tactical surprise as being absolutely impossible, and yet they insisted that we use these rubber boats with the idea that they'd sneak in on the beaches. This thing did not come to a head until we finally had a conference at Port au Poule, in the Gulf of Arzeu, which was presided over by General Patton and Admiral Hewitt. We were given a chance to speak our minds on how progress was going. Hewitt said that neither Conolly nor Hall was satisfied with the use of rubber boats in the landing. Whereupon the army demanded the floor, and they were going to get into a real hot argument about this. General Patton just slapped them down, literally—said, "Sit down! I'll settle this. Once and for all, the navy is responsible for getting you ashore and they can put you ashore in any damned thing they want to."

So the next morning Mike O'Daniel called me in and said, "Well, of course you're going ahead with rubber boats, aren't you?"

I said, "No, General, I'm not. You heard what General Patton said."

He said, "Yes, but I hoped in spite of that you'd go ahead with the rubber boats."

I said, "No, we're not going to use rubber boats. They're completely out. From now on, we'll train in LCVPs."

Luckily, by that time I had assembled enough LCVPs so that we could set up a training unit. This was a problem in itself. We'd had to ship them over, the original group in the *General Chase,* which was a transport. They began sending LCVPs over on LSTs, deck-loaded. They'd send an LCM with an LCVP inside of it or an LST with several inside.

So they began to arrive over there in quantity, and immediately I set up a training unit ashore, a shore-based training unit for LCVPs. We didn't have any ship that could carry them at that time. In the end I trained all the LCVP crews for Hall's transports and for my own LST transports as well. He sent the transports over there and we supplied the boats and trained boat crews. Also I had to train my own boat crews for the LSTs.

That brought up another business. What were we going to do about landing the Third Infantry Division in LSTs instead of transports? A transport will hold a battalion of troops. An LST can embark a company. There are three companies to a battalion, so you have to have three or four LSTs for every APA that you would have in a normal battalion combat team. Eventually we had to have something like thirty-six, to get all the rifle companies of the Third Infantry Division into there. They had to have a lot of other things. They had to embark their tanks. Half an armored combat command was part of the reinforcement of the Third Infantry Division. I think the Second Armored Division split, half of it to the Third Infantry Division, half to the First Division.

We had to find a way of lifting the rifle companies, embarking them, and it took six LCVPs to do it. An LST normally carries only two. I said I thought it would be practical to fit extra davits on an LST. I sent this dispatch back and asked my friend Admiral Farwell, who was Admiral Horn's matériel man, and asked him if he had enough davits kicking around, and he said he did and could equip LSTs with them. Pretty soon these LSTs began arriving in the Mediterranean with their boats, complete with six davits. That solved the problem of lifting the whole infantry division across. Luckily we had them embarked in such large landing craft. Of course an LST is a small ship, actually, but they served very well as transports. I brought those in to the objective myself. They were part of my tactical command, when we sailed.

Those are the two very serious technical problems we had to surmount. One of them was a matter of getting tanks and so forth on the LSTs, and half-ton trucks loaded to the gills, for the operation. We had to get ashore fast, with ammunition, food, water, gasoline, and everything to keep the troops rolling over the pontoon causeways. The boat situation was a matter of getting the davits to carry the boats. This was all complicated by the dispersal of command and the dispersal of bases. We were under some enemy attack, too.

Our work was not seriously interfered with by the German air force. It was just a nuisance. Now and then they'd pull off something, but they didn't interfere seriously at all. You'd lose a lot of sleep, but I would say the general effect was insignificant. They were a nuisance. I believe they caused some delay, but it never held us back. It never kept us from doing what we really wanted to do.

I had to organize my own intelligence service. I had George Dyer, who was my chief of staff and had been Admiral King's intelligence officer. He and I knew more about the operation of intelligence than almost anybody you'd find anywhere. I'd made a study of it, and so had he, and we were old friends and classmates at the Naval War College. So I'd say we realized the necessity then of combat intelligence work better than almost anybody around. We assembled quite a strong intelligence group.

When we went up to Bizerte and started to plan with the Third Infantry Division, I took over the whole submarine base there, installed my headquarters in a building, and got the general's planning staff in there with us, messed them over in the former French submarine officers' mess, and they worked right there with our people. We set up a whole room, nothing but intelligence, my intelligence people and General Truscott's intelligence people. Sometimes we surprised them and turned up with something that would be useful to the army, and very often they would turn up something that would be useful to us. And we got all that came in from British sources. So I would say the intelligence was very good. I was very much pleased with the support we got from intelligence and so were the generals. We had everything that was available in the theater and sorted out what would be useful to us and that was available to the commanders and the planners.

By the time we got there, the choice of target had been decided upon in Sicily. As to D day, they kept postponing it. I think originally it was set much earlier, but they had to postpone it because the shipping just wasn't available. Some of the landing gear hadn't been built. They'd get them right hot off the assembly line and jam them in a ship and ship them over. It would take the LSTs about sixteen days to get over there.

The storm that came up created quite a few difficulties—more for me than for anyone else, because I had to get these landing craft where they were going, and some of these landing craft were not really seagoing ships by any means. We dispersed first along the coast of Africa, then to Tunisia; after we sailed we had to detour to the south, and then at various times pass through certain points, and all come in together on the night of the landing.

I had tactical command of the group comprising the LSTs. Meanwhile I took a destroyer and a squadron commander whose ships had been detailed—and I put him and his destroyer in charge of this group of LCTs. And as the weather got worse, I sent one of my own men with an escorting destroyer three times up to him during the day before, diverting him from a southeasterly route to something just south of east, to something east, and finally to something north of east, in order to get them there in time to be of any use at all on the morning of the landing.

I was disobeying rigid orders that came right from the commander-in-chief, but I was satisfied that under the circumstances he would want me to disobey them. On the other hand, there was risk that this convoy would be detected by the scouting planes from the shore. I didn't dare divert them very much, or point north of east until it got almost nightfall. When nightfall came, there was a strong wind blowing. He was headed towards his objective. I passed him, just at nightfall, and I sent the destroyer over and told him to steer nothing to the right of north all night. He steered north all night instead of 020 and he hit it right on the button. That's what I estimated would be the effect of the storm on these light ships, you see. I just made a rough guess and said, "That'll have to be it."

We had to make more preparations for the navigation, and General Truscott kept emphasizing to me in all the months I was working with him, "This is something that always worries me, the navigation." I said, "General, don't let that worry you. That's my problem. That's my worry. Now, set your mind at rest. I'm qualified for this job. There's no guarantee that you'll hit everything right on the button, but if anybody can do it, I think I can, because I served fifteen months as navigator of a battleship. I know my vessels. Furthermore, I've had a lot of experience in navigating yachts and small craft, and I know how to do that. I know that and all the factors that enter into that, which is of the essence in dealing with landing craft." For you can be a good battleship navigator and still not know how to do this. I said, "I know my vessels."

He got to know me better, and he never mentioned it again until the night before the landing. I had made provisions so that you couldn't miss on this, and we had rehearsed it again and again. It was lucky we did. It looked like an over-refinement until the storm came, and then it was of the very essence.

About fifteen minutes after we passed Malta and it was getting dark, I knew I was in the groove. So I took two cruisers and put them up right ahead of us, side by side, two light cruisers. I put them up ahead and told them the exact speed to maintain and the course we wanted to steer. Then I tailed in behind them in my flagship. My flagship was the *Biscayne*, which was a converted AVP, a tender. It was a little bigger than a frigate and probably displaced about 1,800 or 2,000 tons. It had been converted to my use with radar and radio and all the other things we needed. It was nothing like an AGC that I had later on all through the war, but very good for the purpose.

This navigation system I laid out consisted of this. Off each one of the landing areas they had a British submarine. These established themselves fifteen miles offshore, in this case off Licata Head. Then they lay on the bottom during the day. At night each surfaced and anchored, after dark. Then we had to make contact with him.

I sent in a destroyer to make contact with him. I told the destroyer to anchor right in the same place and relieve him. Then the destroyer took a masked twelve-inch searchlight, directed it, kept it directed to seaward, and he flashed a signal continuously. Then I had three of these patrol craft, PCs. They came in and took departure from him, and went in and anchored off their beach and stayed there. By the time we arrived (we had split up our convoy) they were making signals to bring in their own task group.

Meanwhile, I had another destroyer. He went on ahead, and as soon as he picked up the destroyer that replaced the submarine, ten miles further out, he kept him under a given bearing, and he flashed signals seaward. It was his signals that I got just as I passed Malta. So we had a regular lighted street to run up, until we got to the destroyer that was holding down the submarine's position, and then the task force split, fanned out, each with his own outfit. These patrol craft, these PCs, were anchored off each individual beach, in the center, a certain distance from shore. They'd taken their departure from the position marked by the destroyer which had replaced the submarine.

By the time we split up, I took in two of these outfits that had the bulk of the landing in them and we went right in. The Blue and Yellow beaches were right alongside of each other, so I brought in the task groups that were going to the Blue and Yellow beaches.

That system was absolutely foolproof, even in the rough weather that we encountered, and it was reassuring. Of course I think Truscott had in mind that I'd be up there "shooting the stars" and everything else. But that's the way we brought them in. It was piloting, actually, with our own self-established navigation marks.

We didn't send minesweepers in first. Intelligence had actually sent people in to investigate the beaches ahead of time. A British submarine had put a fellow ashore in a folbot. We had destroyer escorts as submarine defense, but we weren't too much worried about it. The activity in the Mediterranean had been troublesome, but we weren't too much worried about submarines. The rough weather, of course, protected us from them.

I don't know that any of the boats were swamped by rough weather before we started the landing operations, but I know that Admiral Cunningham was ashore in Malta, and he said that he talked to General Eisenhower about the possibility of calling it all off on account of the weather. He said they finally decided to go through with it. You would have had a hell of a time calling it off, I want to tell you that. Once the storm came up and we were committed, we were in the groove, and a lot of those little ships didn't have any radio or anything else, and there would have been a hell of a debacle if you'd tried to call it off. Some of them would have punched on through and been left high and dry.

Actually, as we got closer in to shore, we got some lee protection from the island, and the storm did start to abate, too. As we got in close to the island, it was not too bad. And when the boats went ashore, considerable surf had been kicked up but we had surprising success. I had some darned good boat crews, and they landed the troops and came back off. To all practical purposes, the Licata landing, strangely enough, was a tactical surprise. Here's what happened. When we came in there, I wanted the *Biscayne* to serve as an additional link in guiding the boats ashore, and we also wanted to supervise the operation. So we went in there and anchored. Meanwhile, the fortifications turned a searchlight on this little picket boat I had on shore. He had orders if he were under fire, or were detected, to up anchor and steam around and come back and anchor again, which he did. Then pretty soon they turned the searchlight on the *Biscayne*. I told the captain to sit tight. "If they open fire on us, why, shoot up that searchlight. Meanwhile, sit tight."

So we just sat there. Meanwhile the boats were going in, going past us. Pretty soon he turned off the searchlight. It was five or ten minutes we sat there with that damned thing—and real sweat running down us—as if you were under the klieg lights. Then he turned it off. No fire. Pretty soon our troops were ashore, and they overwhelmed this fortification. Apparently he never saw the boats. There was still a good breeze blowing. So I'd say we did get 100-percent tactical surprise, in spite of the fact that the guy was a little suspicious. He was suspicious enough to turn on the searchlight, but then apparently they all went back to sleep again.

General Patton used to say, "This is the advantage of the offensive against the defensive. Imagine yourself sitting there on those defenses on the island of Sicily. Hell, they'd been there for four years. This was 1943. They've been there four years. They can't keep alert all the time. We're going to land there and all of a sudden we'll be on their necks. That's the advantage. They don't know when we're coming."

I'm satisfied we got a 99.5 percent surprise. They had been a little suspicious. The same was true of the other landings. I think as a matter of fact Kirk opened fire on the beaches. He was bombarding the beaches down there while this was going on. The beaches weren't mined at Licata. From our intelligence reports we had expected mines, from the looks of a certain regular pattern on one of the beaches, but it turned out to be these concrete structures to hold the sand down. It was a bathing beach.

We landed on both sides of the town. Actually, the landing in the town was made by a little task group that were landed in a little cove and then went up the hill and seized the fortification over the city. By the time we were landing, they were seizing these fortifications and got them in no time at all. The whole thing was very successful. Well, we were a little behind schedule at the time, but as far as planning went, it was all coordinated, and the fact that my task force all came in together coordinated our landings as to time also.

I was left there in charge of all three beaches. Hall sailed first, then Hewitt told me to go down and take over from Kirk, then Hewitt went back to Algiers.

Then we began to get air attacks, although they were nothing like they were at Salerno during a similar period. There were no logistics problems in keeping the beaches open at that time. Of course we were using the little port of Licata and Gela and by that time Empedocle. I had some difficulty with minesweeping at Empedocle. A minesweeper hit a mine and had to be towed off. The *Brooklyn* got in one of the minefields we laid ourselves to protect the anchorages off Gela, but got out with no damage.

When I was still up at Licata, our air force brought out their aircraft over the harbors, and we shot down one plane. They weren't blown off course. They had orders to come out over these particular places, which was where all the ships were concentrated and all the troops, the defended ports. That was the plan they had for coming out, coming off the beach. It was the worst place the air force could possibly pick. They came out while we were in the middle of a red alert. We'd had an enemy attack on the port, and they were engaged at that time in bombing an LST convoy which had sailed at dusk. This American plane came over. The Third Infantry Division had a battery of guns on the mole, and it flew right over the mole at low altitude. I had eight LSTs in there, armed with 20-mm antiaircraft, and this fellow came over at low altitude, right over the mole. All the ships shot at him and the 40-millimeter battery shot at him and brought him down. I got reports that they'd shot down a Ju 88. Of course everything was a Ju 88. Both army and navy claimed the kill. They could see it was a good-sized plane, a two-engine plane, so it was a natural assumption. I had a boat in there from the *Biscayne* and ordered him out to see if there were any survivors in this Ju 88. He got out alongside the

plane and took off the crew. There was a little matter of identificati͡ꞈ
between the crew of the boat and the crew of the plane, because the
coxswain of the boat was of Italian extraction; and of course the Americans in the plane thought he was an Italian, an Italian-American, or an
American of Italian extraction; and the people in the boat thought the
plane crew were Germans. They finally got that ironed out and got them
all off and on board. Of course it was a C-47. That was the only American
plane shot down in that sector.

As a result of that, I reported to Admiral Hewitt that I considered the
air plan fatally defective, in that the exit routes were in just the wrong
places. I think all of them that were lost were shot down coming out.

I had this problem presented to me, when I was at Salerno, and they
were bringing in reinforcements by air to the airfields down at the American sector, the American beaches, and landing them on the airfields there
at that famous ruined temple, Paestum. I was working with General Clark
at headquarters. They were going to bring in troops between such and
such an hour and such and such an hour, so I said, yes, they could. And
the only way I could assure him they wouldn't be fired at was to give all
ships orders that they couldn't fire at any plane unless the plane were in an
attack position, threatening their own ship and positively identified as a
enemy plane. Otherwise they couldn't shoot at all. In other words, we had
to declare a moratorium on antiaircraft fire during the time they were
bringing these people in. It's a very serious matter. If we got an enemy air
attack, hell, they might sink a big ship and kill more people than all the
planes were carrying.

There's a responsibility that you have to take, and that's the only way I
could be assured that they were not going to be shot down.

There was an investigation of this thing at Sicily. One of the conclusions was that the air command had not been coordinated with the information of the command of the troops or of the ships—and it hadn't. They
didn't get the air plan until ten minutes before they sailed when it was
delivered on board, and neither Admiral Hewitt or General Patton had had
anything to do with coordinating it or formulating it or anything else. That
I know to be a fact. This is a good instance in which lack of coordination
caused trouble, and it wasn't due to separation of headquarters, either. If
they'd gotten into a plane and come up to Algiers they could have ironed
out a few of these things in half an hour; but they had either not bothered
to do it or didn't see the necessity of doing it, or refused to recognize the
necessity of any coordination at all. That whole air drop was a botched-up
mess. It was a damned disgrace. Really scandalous. We weren't prepared
to do it. The pilots were inexperienced. A lot of the pilots of these C-47s
were kids that hadn't even finished high school. In addition, these C-47s

were service planes, utility planes, and not combat planes at all. They were used for this air drop. It was a very ill-considered operation. Neither planes nor pilots were up to the job, in any shape or form. The thing was a scandal in my opinion.

As far as the amphibious assault landings went, this landing in Sicily was the biggest in the war. We landed six reinforced divisions in the initial landing. The follow-up was something else again. In Normandy the follow-up was tremendous, but we only had a front of five divisions. Of course we landed the airdrop of several divisions in Normandy, and at Sicily we had an airdrop of two divisions. The British landed one and we had one.

The lessons in tactical technique that I drew from the landing were these. In the first place, the chance of achieving a total tactical surprise by making a night landing was slight. It turned out to be successful, but this was entirely due to the fortuitous weather situation, not the inherent possibilities. The site of the landing, if they'd had proper air reconnaissance the day before, could have been very well worked out by the enemy, and the tactical surprise would not have been possible. We had good luck on that and nothing else. At Salerno this fact was borne out. We made a night landing and yet the Germans knew exactly where we were going to come in and were prepared.

Attempting to achieve a tactical surprise in a large amphibious operation is infeasible. We were straining for something (the army particularly demanded this) that was not practical of achievement in a landing on the scale of the Sicily landing. We did achieve it, but only due to good luck. At Salerno we did not.

As far as the effect of air power on the landings, I would say it was nil. The previous months of bombing had scarcely any significant effect. They may possibly have reduced the air power that the Germans could bring to bear, and possibly neutralized some of it. That's the only way I can think of that they achieved anything. But as far as any direct support of the landings themselves, it was nil.

Of course the difference between strategical and tactical bombing in air force parlance is something else again, because they would never accept our close air support concept, which General Truscott kept asking for. He had had close air support from carrier aircraft when he was a brigadier in charge of a regimental combat team that landed in North Africa and captured Port Lyautey. He had never forgotten that, and he kept clamoring for this. He kept asking me when we were going to get a U.S. carrier in there to support him. I kept telling him he wasn't going to get any. When he finally came to realize that, he went to the air force and tried to get them to give him some Mustangs, but they never got a thing.

Zero, he received—no close air support during the landings or operations ashore. We took out enemy batteries with naval gunfire, not with any bombing or strafing by the air force planes.

At one point, the German tanks tried to push the invading troops back and were prevented only by naval fire. Without the naval fire I don't think it would have been disastrous, but I do think they'd have had a tough time there in the center of the First Division. General Patton did bear that out in the testimony he gave on the effects of naval gunfire. These 6-inch batteries on the cruisers were terrific for their effect on the tanks or any kind of artillery or any kind of an enemy strong point. I recall our troops were held up momentarily at Licata on the left flank, and General Truscott got concerned about it. He wanted assistance and said, "We're under fire from some batteries up here."

I said, "Show me on the map where those batteries are." He did, and I said, "All right, we will have the *Brooklyn* shoot at them."

I had the *Brooklyn* shoot at them for five minutes. Then I decided just for good measure I'd give them five minutes more, and my chief of staff said, "My God, Admiral, do you know how many rounds of ammunition those guns will fire in five minutes? The *Brooklyn* has fifteen 6-inch guns, and the ammunition is right underneath the guns, and they'll fire probably something like ten rounds per gun per minute, and that much from fifteen-guns—that's more ammunition than the Third Infantry Division would use for their artillery for probably two days or a week." We just threw it right in there. We got the report back, the whole valley was full of dust and smoke, and no more gunfire out of that area. Those who were able pulled up stakes and got out. A lot of them got a terrific barrage of fire into this area. I told the *Brooklyn* to sprinkle her fire around all through that area. For ten minutes they got ten rounds per gun per minute from fifteen 6-inch guns. A standard artillery piece in the army is a 105-mm and that is a 4-inch gun. Fifteen 6-inch guns, shooting, tactically, an unlimited supply of ammunition at a terrific rate of fire is the equivalent of a regiment of army artillery of every caliber. We think a 6-inch gun is a small gun in the navy. In the army that's a big gun.

We had another case where they had some railroad batteries on the mole at Licata, and I had the *Brooklyn* fire in there. It turned out to be pea-shooters but they were mounted on railroad cars. We slammed the hell out of them. I don't know that they were even manned, but the troops that landed up on the hills were concerned about them. Our only problem was that we just didn't have enough targets. We could have done a lot more if we'd had the opportunity, and the ships were just itching to use their guns. I heard Admiral Hall tell about an incident at Gela where they knocked out the enemy tanks. The Germans didn't understand what the hell hit them. Some new type of artillery that they had never been up against before. The rate of fire just smothered them. Those are several of the lessons I learned. One of them was that it would have been very nice to have some close aircraft support; another was that the naval artillery was very potent.

There were no logistics problems encountered in supplying troops after landing. I never heard of any, at least. The shortage of supplies and ammunition usually takes place the first couple of days, while they're getting the beaches organized and unloading the ships. But by the sixth or seventh day, it's an army problem. They've got plenty of stuff on the beach; it's a matter of whether they can keep their roads in operation and find enough trucks to get them up there. They apparently did at Sicily. That Third Division I landed there—they were up and over the hills and far away. They reached their first day's objective line by about 11 o'clock in the morning! They went right on to Palermo. Of course, they had a very enterprising general.

An amphibious operation, in order to succeed, you've got to roll; it's got to grow. If you get sealed off on your beachhead, you may be safely ashore all right, but you're not going anywhere. You haven't done anything except establish a little island in the midst of hostile territory. That's what they did at Anzio. Later on they were able to come in and connect up with it, but by that time it had lost much of its significance.

Where General Truscott's command began and mine ended over the troops at Sicily was more or less laid down in the fundamental orders. Naval commanders were supposed to get the troops ashore. Initially, before we had trained together and before the final orders had come out, I had always understood that the naval commander was in command until the general established his headquarters ashore. The general was always my principal subordinate and always in direct command of the troops. After he was established ashore I turned over command to him. That is, whatever command I had I exercised through him over the troops. I didn't tell any troops directly what to do. I always told the general, "I think we ought to do this," if it came to that. Actually the plans were so well formulated that the thing just rolled. It was cut and dried what they were to do during the first days of the battle. When they needed direction, the general was ashore and was able to give it.

There was one thing that came up that we had to settle when the landing was made, and that was the organization of the beaches. Truscott had a brigadier that he took ashore especially for the purpose of organizing the beaches. Yet the communications between the ships that were unloading and the beaches were not what they should have been, due to the fact that the shore party and the beach party were inexperienced. The shore party was army and the beach party was navy. I knew they were having some trouble on the beaches and a certain amount was expected.

There was always disorder and confusion on the beaches. A massive amphibious assault is that kind of an operation. In other words, you can't carry it out by the numbers. But the whole test is in how effective you are in getting stores ashore and getting them off the beach.

It wasn't working to Truscott's satisfaction. He'd already gone ashore, and he came back and said, "Admiral, this thing isn't working." He had the brigadier with him, who was practically out on his feet, and he was a pretty tough fellow, too. Truscott said, "What can you do?"

I said, "I've been studying this thing and I'm prepared with an answer. I don't think your shore party is much good and I know damned well our beach party isn't. Here's what I'll do. I've got a lot of regular officers here who know their stuff, and I will put three of them ashore and three of them afloat—one on each beach and one off each beach. They'll be in communication with each other, and you tell the fellow on the beach what you want brought in. The whole trouble is that soldiers are trying to tell sailors what to do, and they don't talk the same language and they can't get any communication with them."

We set that up in a matter of two or three hours, and it worked wonderfully. Then the fur began to fly. The fellow on the beach had a little tent and a radio set, and he'd talk to his opposite number off the beach, who was in an LCI. He'd say, "Send in such and such, the army says they're loaded in such and such a ship. Get me some ammunition out of this or that ship." In nothing flat the thing really began to work. I knew it couldn't fail to work, because you had a line of communications, and you had one naval fellow talking to the other. Now, that doesn't mean that the navy took over the beach, by any means. All it means is that we didn't have a lieutenant colonel trying to talk to a commander and tell him to bring in such and such a ship. We had a navy commander telling a lieutenant commander off the beach to get busy and roll in these things. He was doing what the army wanted him to do but he was giving the orders. In other words, we were supporting the army. This provided a link that hadn't been there before.

Admiral A. B. Cunningham's headquarters was on Malta, and Eisenhower was there with him. I believe General Alexander was too. This didn't cause communication difficulties on air support. We simply didn't get any direct air support. After the troops got ashore and started operating in battle, I have no doubt they received some tactical air support. General Patton could request that some bridge be taken out. He had a liaison officer on his staff for that. But there was no support of the landings and no close support of troops whatever.

I stayed in command off the beaches until sometime about the twenty-third of July. Then I asked permission to leave, because I wanted to get in on the succeeding operation. I had a chap in there whom I had organized to be in a position to actually operate the ships, with the idea that I could turn it over to him. I went up to see General Patton and told him that I thought my service had come to an end, but that I would gladly stay although I didn't see any point in it. At this time he had headquarters outside of Gela somewhere. He didn't say anything in reply. I had lunch with him and he happened to be going that afternoon to fly down to Malta. He told Admiral Cunningham he wanted me to stay for three or four more days, so Cunningham told me I'd have to stay there.

By that time there were no air attacks or anything of that kind going on. It was cut and dried, all organized, and we were rolling forward. Patton was about to uproot his headquarters and move up to Palermo right from there.

I did make arrangements for an expedition under Captain Wellborn, a squadron commander of destroyers, to organize an expedition of mine-sweepers, gave him a lot of craft. We had organized this expeditionary force to go up to Palermo and open it up. I made arrangements with the U.S. Air Force colonel, the liaison officer on Patton's staff, as I recall, to give us air coverage on this expedition around to Palermo. He said they were going up to establish themselves up there and they'd provide these ships with air coverage. Somewhere along the line the plan was changed and by the time the ships got there they didn't have the air coverage. They had the hell bombed out of them. Hit two of Wellborn's destroyers and the Germans bombed the mole and killed a lot of personnel.

I immediately sent a dispatch directly to CinCMed asking him who would provide air coverage. Which was the agency that was supposed to be providing air coverage for these forces? He knew they were there. In fact, CinCMed directed that they be sent up there. It turned out that they'd transferred this sector to the Royal Air Force Coastal Command for protection from air attack and they were supposed to be providing air coverage, when they got established.

About that time I got back to Bizerte, and I met my old friend Hugh Pugh Lloyd, who was an air vice marshal in command of the fighter command for North Africa. He was in charge of the fighters that they would put in for protection, but he didn't have any shipping. I took four LSTs that I had had under overhaul, and before anybody gave them any orders, I turned them over to Lloyd and we loaded them and sent them over there. Then I caught hell from all and sundry. So did he.

Meanwhile, these LSTs were over at Palermo unloading the British fighter aircraft so they could set themselves up in business. Both Lloyd and I caught hell for using those four LSTs. All the LSTs were supposed to be earmarked for the use of General Sir Harold Alexander, reinforcing Sicily and getting ready to ferry Montgomery across the Strait of Messina. But we got the fighter aircraft established in nothing flat, due to this gentlemen's agreement between Lloyd and myself. Neither of us was considered a gentleman at the time.

After that I went back to Bizerte. The next morning I got a plane and went up to Algiers and talked to Admiral Hewitt. I told Hewitt that I didn't like the way things were going, that they were shuttling all of these reinforcements, troops, and matériel into Sicily, and I said, "A lot of these troops will never get there in time to fight, and we're shipping in ammunition and supplies that will still be there by the roadside a hundred years from now. This thing is caving in fast, and we shouldn't send another soldier in there."

He said, "I've just been talking to Admiral Cunningham, about this, this morning. I wish you'd go in and talk with him."

So I went in. I'd built up quite a head of steam on this. He said, "Well, I'm glad you mentioned this."

I said, "Admiral, if we land now, if we make a quickie, take some of these troops that are being earmarked to go to Sicily for reinforcements where they are not needed—if we act now and just scoop up what troops are available, get this regiment and that division, we can put them over the docks in Naples."

He said, "I couldn't agree more."

"We'll go right in over the docks of Naples, and we'll be fighting Italians; whereas if we wait three weeks, by God, it looks as if we're going to be fighting Germans."

He said, "All right, I will send for Eisenhower's G-3." And he did. It was General Rooks, a brother of a classmate of mine who was killed on the *Houston*. Rooks came down there. He was a major general and G-3 on Eisenhower's staff—and I went into my act again. I was sure that he had the shipping; if we'd just utilize it to dump troops quickly into Naples we could capture Naples.

"Well," he said, "Naples is mined."

I said, "Yes, and so is the Gulf of Salerno."

We hadn't gotten that plan then, but we were talking of it. I said, "So are the other positions that are being considered for future landings. But if we do this now instead of planning the whole thing out—hell, with the experience we've had, all you have to do is tell me to get the lift for one division or two divisions, and we can wrestle it out. The landing craft will be marvelous; we'll go right in over the mine field and destroy it. We know where the mines are. That's a naval problem."

The admiral said, "Yes, don't worry about the mines. We can take care of the mines; don't worry about that part of it."

But Rooks said, "No, it's all been gone into very clearly and we've decided not to do it." General Eisenhower decided that Patton was still calling for reinforcements and they were going to give him everything he asked for. This couldn't have been more wrong. I had the pleasure to hear General Marshall, six months later, address all the flag and general officers who were present in Pearl Harbor at the time. And I heard him say that they should have proceeded faster after the landing in Sicily to exploit strategically the victory, and that if they had proceeded faster they could have landed well up the peninsula instead of having to go in at Salerno.

The landings in Sicily took place July 10. The island was taken in less than a month. However, the Salerno operation didn't take place until September. August was taken up in planning, staging, concentrating. I've forgotten what the units were, but they landed the Ninth Division in Sicily, and I don't think the Ninth Division ever got into combat. I recall saying, "They're sailing reinforcements out of Bizerte pell-mell as fast as they can. Hell, you'd think they needed reinforcements. The thing's in the bag, it's a matter of two or three days!"

We used "leapfrog tactics" at Sicily more than once. They were very successful, too. My friend Charlie Wellborn was in on both of these and I believe commanded both operations. They loaded the troops into LSTs and then landed them behind the enemy, along the beach on the northern coast of the island. It was extremely successful.

We had one amusing incident in this connection. We sent six LSTs up there for that operation. One of the Third Division company that had been loaded in one of these LSTs for the initial leap happened to be assigned to the same LST for the second one. Here came the company commander and the captain of the LST. It was like old home week. They were loaded right into the same LST and down the coast and made the landing. In each case, the main force that was driving down the coast made contact with the others almost immediately. It wasn't so far down the coast that it could be sealed off, like Anzio, but the main force came driving through, and of course this softened up the opposition. They were bombing the troops in behind them, and they pulled out as fast as they could. The thing worked twice. Patton was very enthusiastic about it.

From the German point of view the withdrawal from the island was quite successful. Of course, Morison has criticized that, and I do too. I don't think we should have permitted that to happen. And if we'd had good coordination between the naval forces and the air forces at that time, it could have been prevented. I'd hate to think that the U.S. Navy couldn't have stopped that thing, if we'd had aircraft carriers. By bringing ships with air cover in there, we could have threaded a needle through the strait with a mopping-up force every evening, and in the day kept them plastered with bombing and strafing.

I was there at the time the decision was made not to intercept them in the strait; I don't know what happened there. But I know Admiral Cunningham was a very enterprising naval commander, and I think only the consideration that his ships would have been entirely exposed to German air attack, without any fighter cover or effective protection, could have influenced him.

I agree with Morison that something drastic should have been done at Messina. I think the reason it wasn't done was lack of proper air support for the Royal Navy. I think the Royal Navy could have done it—stopped the German troop movements across the Strait of Messina.

A MAJOR TASK CUT SHORT

REAR ADMIRAL WILLIAM A. SULLIVAN

U.S. NAVAL INSTITUTE

WILLIAM ALOYSIUS SULLIVAN was born in Lawrence, Massachusetts, on 27 August 1894. He attended Phillips Academy in Andover, Massachusetts, and graduated from the Massachusetts Institute of Technology in 1917, having studied both engineering and naval architecture. He received a commission as lieutenant, j.g., in the U.S. Navy in the same year and was stationed at Portsmouth Navy Yard in Kittery, Maine, from 1917 to 1922. There followed varied assignments in ship construction and repairs in various navy yards in the United States to Cavite in the Philippines, including three years as supervising constructor in Shanghai, China.

In 1938, while Sullivan was at the model basin in the navy yard in Washington, D.C., he began a serious study of problems involved in the salvage of ships. This was followed by two years as an assistant naval attaché in London for knowledge of British methods of salvage (1940–41). Sullivan worked very closely with Captain Doust of the Royal Navy in this period and continued a working relationship with Doust through many years to the benefit of both in their professional lives.

Upon his return from London, Sullivan became the head of the salvage section in the Bureau of Ships (1941–42), with additional duty as head of salvage in New York City in March 1942. There he became head of a special commission to study and make recommendations for the salvage of the USS *Lafayette* (the former French passenger liner *Normandie* that had been sabotaged in New York harbor and became immediately a hazard to shipping there). Sullivan also directed salvage operations on the East Coast of the United States during the German submarine campaign of 1942. That same year he went to Casablanca immediately after the capture of that port by the forces of Admiral Hewitt in November 1942 and organized a harbor clearance force and supervised work there and in Port Lyautey. Meanwhile, Sullivan was named commodore and assumed the job as chief of navy salvage in the Office of the Chief of Naval Operations in Washington, D.C.

In the Mediterranean Sullivan joined the staff of Admiral Sir Andrew Cunningham, Royal Navy, commander of Allied Naval Forces in the Mediterranean in 1943. Sullivan was placed in command of Task Force 84 during the Sicilian campaign and later the landing at Salerno in Italy. He directed salvage operations at various ports in the area while so occupied.

Salvage operations at this time assumed a frenzied nature, for the Allied naval and military forces were making rapid advances in several areas and salvage became a necessary clean-up job. Sullivan supervised the clearing of the badly damaged port of Naples after its occupation by Allied troops; he commanded Task Group 122.2 during the landings on the coast of Normandy in 1944; he entered Cherbourg harbor with the occupying troops and directed harbor clearance there as well as at Le Havre, Rouen, Brest, and other French ports. These ports were of immediate concern to Supreme Allied Commander General Eisenhower, for it was through them that supplies must be poured to nourish the Allied armies on their rapid advance to the Rhine.

In February 1945 Sullivan was in the Pacific, where he reported to Admiral Thomas Kinkaid, commander of the Seventh Fleet, and to General MacArthur. He entered the badly damaged harbor of Manila with the army troops and assumed the task of harbor clearance there with the help and cooperation of the Army Corps of Engineers.

Sullivan left Manila in August 1945 and returned to Washington where he retired from the naval service in the rank of rear admiral on 1 May 1948. He had some business interests in the Far East in the postwar era. He and Mrs. Sullivan retired eventually to their home on the New Jersey coast and finally to La Jolla, California, where the admiral died in September 1985. Burial was in the Arlington National Cemetery in Arlington, Virginia.

There seemed to be no reason why I should stay in Sicily. I had nothing to do there now so I left Sicily in an LST returning to Tunis. It took a day and a half. The next morning I paid a courtesy call on Admiral Dickens, the son of Charles Dickens, then caught a noon plane for Algiers. I arrived in Algiers tired and very dirty. I went to the apartment, had a bath, and got into clean clothes just as Admiral Hewitt's aide called. The admiral had heard I was back and wanted to see me so I went up to his place and didn't get back until 1 A.M. Admiral Hewitt had intimated that we might find Palermo on our hands much sooner than we expected. I hoped to write up a report of my observations on the Husky operations. I had a lot of suggestions about how landing craft salvage should be handled; also about better cooperation between the army and the navy on loading ships for amphibious operations and on having information readily available for fire fighters and for salvage. However, I had much other work to do in the immediate few days in the office.

Then came word that Palermo was about to be occupied and that I should leave at once. Arrangements were made for me to fly with General Cannon to Palermo. I brought Doc Schlesinger and Bob Helen along. When our plane landed the field had just been secured. We were the first U.S. plane to land. The air force had a car to take General Cannon away. We were left standing on a practically deserted airfield with our luggage. There was nobody to even talk to.

Then I found a British truck. Using my credentials as the staff officer with the British CinC staff, I impressed the truck to take us to the waterfront. We had trouble getting there because of the damage to the city by aerial bombing. We finally had to leave the truck four or five blocks from the waterfront and carry our luggage over the ruins of the city. We could not see even where the streets had been. It was my first experience with such complete devastation. Even London after the German air raids was not to be compared with this place.

We found a spot in the debris where it looked safe for us to leave our luggage and then sent the doctor out to find some shelter and food for the night. Bob Helen and I decided to take a look around the harbor. The whole area seemed absolutely deserted. We were all alone in a scene of the most horrible desolation. The harbor was pretty badly battered up. Ships were sunk not only in the harbor but also alongside quays. Many did not look like they would be salvage jobs. A great deal of the masonry quays were badly smashed. I wondered how much use the army really wanted with this port. If any great amount of tonnage was to be handled we had a most difficult job.

We met Doc Schlesinger towards evening. He had bummed some rations from some soldiers he had met wandering around. He had also found a room in a house that was not completely destroyed. So we gathered up the luggage and made our way to our lodging before dark. There was no furniture so we sat on the floor and ate rations and drank cold coffee made from the water in our canteens by flashlight. We slept on the floor. In the morning we noticed a strange smell around the place. It was very cold and the mosquitoes had been terrible during the night. We hid our luggage in the closet and went back around the waterfront. I hunted up the army and tried to get a jeep but nothing doing. General Patton sent an officer to find me. He wanted an estimate of what I thought of the harbor situation. I said I did not know—I had only been able to see a small portion and needed transportation. Then I could expedite our survey. There was no reply to my request.

Then we continued around the waterfront with our survey. With no boat and no transportation we only covered about a third of the harbor by dark. Then we bought some onions from a solitary Italian peddler that we saw walking around and bummed some more K rations from some soldiers who were just poking around. They all seemed to have K rations, which they readily gave us. Then we went back to our room and found that the smell was worse. Early the next morning the *Tackle,* our salvage boat, arrived. She went alongside an unblocked pier and unloaded a few jeeps. Helen and I then quickly completed our survey and the *Tackle* started unloading gear while the doctor arranged a party to look for billets. That night we went back to our room, but by this time, we had cots, blankets, and mosquito nets. The smell was so bad now that we investigated and found a dead horse in the courtyard.

The Doc had found a building which was quite suitable to be fixed up as a billet for the men from the *Tackle,* but he had located nothing for the officers. I set the *Tackle* to clearing out a warehouse near the berth and to patching up some holes blown in the masonry—all so that we could have some security for our salvage gear. We needed trucks to move the gear from the ship's side to the warehouse. I said I would get the trucks we required from General Patton but in the meantime get the *Tackle* unloaded in case someone tried to chase us away from that berth.

Helen and I went to contact the army to find out how the engineers intended to work, so that we could work with them. I did not want to start clearing berths if the roads leading to these berths were blocked and not scheduled for immediate attention by the engineers. We met five colonels that morning. Each one of them thought he was in charge of the port, and none of them had any idea of what it was all about. I contacted the naval base, which had nothing, knew less, and badly needed help and advice. Then Helen and I took another look around. He came up with a most remarkable suggestion—one we put to use not only in Palermo but to a very considerable extent in Naples, Cherbourg, Le Havre, Manila, and all of our other ports. He suggested that instead of trying to raise some of the large ships that had been sunk alongside of quays, that we build bridges from the quays to the decks of these ships; cut away the masts, the deck machinery, and the deckhouses; stiffen up the decks; and use the ships for unloading piers. Then we could bring a ship in, tie it alongside of this wreck, dump the stuff on the wreck, and the trucks would take it away. In fact that system saved three-quarters of our time or more. A number of the damaged ships alongside the quays in Palermo were so badly wrecked that the only way to remove them was to cut them up and lift them out in sections. That would have taken an enormous amount of time.

We got to the naval base section of the harbor and found an Italian destroyer had capsized in the graving dry dock. The caisson had been blown and the resulting rush of water into the dry dock had bodily lifted the destroyer up and over a spare caisson that had been docked ahead of it. The destroyer had fallen over on its side, knocked the spare caisson over, and the forepart of the destroyer was on top of it.

The buildings of the naval base had been damaged by bombing. Some had not been as badly wrecked as was much of the waterfront elsewhere. I was amazed at the tremendous amount of naval stores around—hundreds and hundreds of tons of shipbuilding plates and many other kinds of materials.

Later in the afternoon the Doc drove up in a beautiful four-passenger Fiat, a very deluxe job. He said he had found it abandoned and all it needed was a key and some gas. He also reported he had found a very fine house that had belonged to some Fascists who had fled. It was large enough for all of the officers. The Doc had already moved our luggage in. The place was undamaged and ready for occupancy. It was tremendous, with seventeen bedrooms, six toilets, and so on, and with a beautiful library full of books, two reception rooms, two dining rooms, a solarium, music room, hothouse, and bomb shelter. It was fully furnished except for mattresses, mosquito nets, and silver. We did not invite anyone else that night but got a bucket of water and cleaned up. Then we had a meal under candlelight in a very formal dining room. The Doc had found some candles and we set them in some silver candelabra. The meal was of K rations with some rather warm champagne for the Doc had found a wine locker in the basement.

The next morning I tried to contact the army again for I wanted to find out how badly Palermo was needed. What kind of ships were to be brought in for unloading? How many berths were needed and what priority was to be given to opening the various size berths and the various sectors of the harbor? I could obtain no helpful information. The army expected us to clear away all sunken ships, period. I could not get anyone to listen to my problem. Actually no one at this time in the army knew exactly how much use was to be made of Palermo. Also there was confusion in the command arrangements, not only among the engineers but also among the transportation people. It was clear to me that any work by us in clearing up the wrecks in some sections of the harbor would be wasted effort unless the army engineers could make a major effort to get the roads leading to these berths cleared and repaired and to repair the blown-up masonry quays. While we had everywhere extensive and complicated work, the engineers did also.

We met some Italians who said that most of the damage done around the harbor was done during some air raids late in May. One ammunition ship exploded when hit by a bomb, and the blast was so great that the waves created washed two ships right out of the water and up on the quays and the waves tore huge sections of masonry out of the quays. I was told that seventeen thousand Italians were killed.

I realized that the army could not come to much of a decision about the work that they should do until the number and location of the supply dumps could be determined and the roads selected to connect these dumps to the Palermo waterfront. It would then be possible for them to give us some idea of the priorities we should follow in clearing the harbor. In the meantime, I said: "Let's get the *Tackle* completely unloaded. Then let's take a look at the few wrecks that are not alongside the quays but which will limit the movement of ships in and out of the harbor." I had made another attempt to locate General Patton. I had run into one of his staff who handled transportation, a very nasty lieutenant colonel. He absolutely refused to recognize our claim for trucks and other motor vehicles. He said the navy's job was at sea; we had no use for trucks. Furthermore, the army was moving along the northern coast towards Messina and needed every possible truck they could get. So I told my officers to put the navy items on rollers and manhandle them from the dock alongside the *Tackle* into the warehouse. It would be good experience. Then I overheard some comment about myself and how I was selling out to the army. I had a little disciplinary problem. I ordered the officers to get busy and work with the men until this job was finished.

Then we had an urgent job come up. The destroyer *Mayrant* was hit by a bomb just offshore and was being towed into port. A message was sent in stating that both engine rooms and both fire rooms were flooded. I did not believe this for according to the information I had about the stability of destroyers, no destroyer could possibly remain afloat if both fire rooms and both engine rooms were flooded. But when the *Mayrant* was brought in I found the report was true.

I had it brought into a slip where it would receive maximum shelter from the wind and the sea. A small minesweeper was brought in and tied up alongside to furnish light and water. I had divers make an examination at once. The port side, in the way of the after fire room and the forward engine room, was badly smashed. There were three diagonal gashes each about ten feet or more in length and twenty inches in width, in addition to a great many other holes. The wretched condition of the shell where the damage was the greatest made the use of a conventional salvage patch impossible. The shell plating was too badly damaged to resist the pressure that could develop as we pumped out the ship around the edges of such a patch unless we did considerable shoring inside. I would not send any man inside to work with the precarious stability and buoyancy of the ship. Perhaps even a very moderate patch would also cause it to capsize.

The area of the port side in the way of the forward boiler room and after engine room was not so badly smashed, and except for one hole under the bulkhead between the two engine rooms, there were no holes in the shell leading into these two spaces that could not quickly be plugged up. It was evident that the best way to save this ship was to recover the buoyancy of the forward fire rooms and after engine rooms.

I started the divers plugging the small holes in the side by conventional wooden plugs, timber patches, secured with hook bolts. I had four ten-inch pumps and four six-inch pumps moved to the quay alongside. I could not possibly put a pump on the ship, for the additional weight might be all that was needed to sink it. I arranged for the pumps to be put on the side of the pier as close as possible to the ship and to carry the pump suctions over and drop them down through holes in the deck.

I arranged with the captain to send as many of his men as possible over to the salvage crew's billet and for some of his officers to move out to our house. I told Doc to make the necessary arrangements. I wanted to get as much of the crew off the ship as possible to reduce the amount of moving around. I asked the captain to get some of the readily removable topside weight off the ship but to be particularly careful in doing so—no sudden shifting of weight which might cause an inclination to one side or the other—and to have an officer supervising everything and no unnecessary work being done.

I decided the crew's mattresses and pillows offered the quickest solution to the problems of plugging the larger holes, and as soon as the pump suctions were placed below decks and the pumps started up slow speed, I had divers down stuffing mattresses in every big hole they could see. Some mattresses stuck in place, but some were sucked right through the holes. When this occurred, I had timbers placed to bridge the gap, then more mattresses stuck in. The timbers were secured with hook bolts and they furnished a shoulder to hold the mattresses. To accomplish this we took all the mattresses off the ship and we went around gathering others from Italian ships—any place, any kind of old mattress.

At first there was no change in the water level inside the ship, but we persevered in working on the holes in the shell in a hit-and-miss fashion, and gradually the water level started to drop.

When we got a foot differential between the inside and the outside level we began to have trouble with the mattresses giving way for the increased outside pressure was sufficient to force some right through the holes. Then we had to throw more mattresses in; all together we used more than one hundred.

I concentrated on the *Mayrant* and sent Commander Helen over to talk to the army officers who were now ready to talk sense. They had some idea of how much need the army had for Palermo so that an intelligent schedule of work for opening up the port could be developed. Helen's plan to utilize the wrecks of the ships lying in the unloading berths as piers was accepted, and the work of fitting bridges to these ships from the shore so that the trucks could move back and forth—and cutting away their topside structure so that the main decks could be used as platforms for unloading—this then was made the objective of a joint venture. We were able to do a lot of this work because we had cutting and welding equipment, and we were able to cut away parts of some of the sunken ships to act as steel in making up the bridges.

We agreed also to go ahead with the work of removing a few wrecks from the middle of the harbor that limited the movement of ships in and out of the slips. Helen also agreed to start at once the removal of a couple of dozen small wrecks that blocked some berths.

The sunken ships in the the middle of the harbor—some of them were too badly damaged to be floated. They had to be further reduced by explosives and lifted out in sections. One of our first tasks therefore was to salvage and rehabilitate a couple of floating Italian cranes around the place.

In the naval base we had spotted some submersible pontoons for raising sunken submarines. It was interesting to see that these pontoons were approximately if not exactly the same dimensions as those developed by the U.S. Navy for raising sunken subs. They were useful in raising small craft as well as sunken subs. I believe Helen put them to use after I had returned to Algiers. Later we had them taken to Naples, where they were very useful.

We worked all night on the *Mayrant* and in the morning it was possible to get into the fire room and look around. I took off my uniform and waded around in my underwear. We could see the holes in the transverse bulkheads through which most of the water had come to flood the end compartments. Only a few of these holes were readily accessible for patching. The other holes were behind machinery which had been secured to the bulkhead or the debris of machinery or other structure. I had to send men in to patch the accessible holes and to remove the debris required to make the other holes accessible. This work was done mostly in the after fire room and forward engine room, so that the patches could be put on the pressure side.

One of the long gashes in the side projected under the port bilge and under the bulkhead between the two engine rooms. I had divers go down in the after engine room, and after they had removed some of the machinery which blocked off the foot of that bulkhead, place a concrete patch

302

that would plug up the part of this gash that extended aft of the transverse bulkhead.

By nightfall we had made considerable progress but were not yet ready to try and dry out the two end compartments. I had been on the job now since the early afternoon of the day before so I thought it advisable to get a night's rest, not only for myself but for the men who were doing the work. Some of them also had remained continuously on the job. So I left a young officer in charge, told him to keep the water levels inside the ship more or less steady, not to pump too much for some of the patches might be sucked in, and not to let the water level rise for some of the patches might wash out. I also did not want pressure on the newly laid concrete patch at the foot of the bulkhead.

I had dinner at the house and found Doc had hired an old lady as the cook. She said she had been the cook for the previous occupants. Doc agreed to pay her the equivalent of five dollars per week. Jokingly I told him he would be paying too much. It turned out I was right. He had gotten mixed up. She had only wanted five dollars per month, but now she had a whole lot more guests to handle. We had eighteen or twenty officers in the house and later there would be more. I went to bed early, very happy at last to have a mosquito net and clean blankets. About 4 A.M. I was awakened by a terrific explosion. I realized an air raid was under way, and from the sounds of the explosives, it seemed that the bombs were dropping nearby. I dressed and went to the basement where the previous occupants had put in a very substantial shelter. By flashlight I took a count of the officers there but could not find Bob Helen or the officers of the *Mayrant*. Someone said they had gone to the harbor in Helen's jeep as soon as the raid started.

The Doc volunteered to drive me to the harbor in his jeep. He started off. We had to make a detour to get there. Then we had to abandon the jeep and walk. I found the *Mayrant* firing away with its entire main batteries as well as its machine guns. A fire was burning on the quay across the slip from the ship and another on the same quay as the *Mayrant* but further out. I was told that abandoned Italian army supply dumps were burning and that the explosions were from small-size artillery ammunition.

I found the salvage officer I had left in charge of the job on the pier where he should be, but the pumps were not running. He said the gas drums on the pier in which gas had been kept for operating the pumps had been hit by shrapnel and the gas lost. He said the pumps had just stopped and that he had sent some men out to try to get some more gas. Bob Helen had been there and had gone and said he would get gas. The *Mayrant* had none.

The battery on the *Mayrant* opened up again as another plane passed over. I could not see any particular reason why the *Mayrant* should be firing. There was a cruiser in the harbor and some other destroyers, and the army had set up AA batteries. The shock of the *Mayrant*'s firing would certainly loosen the mattress patches. With the pumps inoperative the ship would fill up again. Any additional flooding which might readily occur would certainly sink the ship. I communicated this idea to the bridge and was brusquely told to mind my own blankety-blank business and get my blankety-blank pumps working. Bob Helen then showed up with a can of gasoline. He had found a supply of gas about a mile away in jerry cans. He and I went back with as many men as were available around, and we each brought back a can. The air raid was continuing. I wondered how long this newly discovered dump would be available so when we got back I arranged for more cans to be taken away from the dump and deposited in various places so we would be sure to have a supply left.

At daybreak the shouting and the bombing died away. The pumps were running, but to keep the water levels at the same differential we had to operate the pumps faster than previously. It was apparent that some of our patches had loosened up, but which ones? I sent a diver down. His report did not seem reasonable, so I sent another one down. Some confusion. So I took off my uniform and in my underwear put on a diving helmet and went down myself to take a look around, and then decided a little more pumping to put some more outside pressure on the patches might produce better conditions. The water outside the ship was covered by a dirty scum, largely fuel oil. Consequently, when I came up my underwear was filthy. Nearby on the quay were the ruins of a former guardhouse. Three masonry walls were all that remained. They, however, provided some shelter from the shrapnel resulting from the occasional explosions of shells in the burning ammunition dumps nearby. The *Mayrant* officers had built a fire inside these three walls and were having a coffee break. I went inside to dry off and get some warmth, for the morning air was still chilly. I was filthy in my underwear but no more so that the young exec of the *Mayrant*, the one who had told me to get the blankety-blank pumps working. He was Lieutenant Commander Franklin D. Roosevelt, Jr. His shirt was sticking outside his trousers and the front of his shirt and his trousers also were soaked with blood. A bomb hitting the quay had knocked a huge hunk of masonry through the screen alongside of the *Mayrant* bridge and taken the legs off a quartermaster. Young Roosevelt had applied a tourniquet.

Before I was dried off we had visitors: General Patton and General Alexander. Patton, as always, all shined up; Alexander not so shined up but quite clean. All others present were more or less dirty but none so disgraceful as I, the senior naval officer present. I beat a hasty retreat outside and put on my uniform. General Alexander came out to have a few minutes' chat. Then he and Patton left. No chance to talk to Patton about my trucks. I never saw him again.

Two nearby dumps kept burning all day. This hampered our work somewhat. So also did the lack of trucks to move equipment.

The *Tackle* had been busy during the raid the night before. She received a report that a number of soldiers were marooned on the end of the quay to which the *Mayrant* was moored. Because of the dump on fire they could not get off the pier. Could the *Tackle* take them off by boat? The *Tackle* got a boat in commission to do this job just as a bomb hit a small British coaster that had come into port the afternoon before. This ship was loaded with ammunition for the army. It disappeared in one big bang. That was apparently the noise that woke me. The explosion sank a barge containing high-test gasoline for the air force. The gas released from this sunken barge caught fire on the surface, and the *Tackle*'s boat was prevented from getting to the pier by a huge blaze on the water. It went back to the ship and took on a high-pressure fire pump. A powerful stream of water broke up the blaze on the water so that the boat could get through to the pier. Seventeen men were rescued.

The fire fighters on the *Tackle* went down to some other ammunition dumps which had not been hit. I told Helen to start the harbor clearance work—see what he could do about the trucks—and I would concentrate on the *Mayrant*. That day we worked on the transverse bulkheads. I wanted to get these two bulkheads secured so we could pump the two end compartments dry. This would reduce the draft of the ship considerably, and with the buoyancy and stability that we recovered the ship would be safe for all intents and purposes. Until that was done the ship might sink any time.

Late in the afternoon we were able to pump these two end compartments almost down to the floor plates. I knocked off until daybreak, keeping a watch to maintain pumping sufficiently to overcome leakage. In the morning we resumed work.

The naval operating base, just established, notified me that the dry dock should be cleared soon, for the services of this dock were urgently needed to repair U.S. destroyers. This was a fine graving dock. We found the caisson in place, pretty badly smashed up, but we could not tell whether the sill in the way of the caisson was damaged or not until we got that caisson out. Another complication was that three small vessels were sunk outside the harbor in places that would prevent the use of this dry dock. They had to be salvaged also. This was a job that should not be undertaken unless there was a positive need for the dry dock, and providing we had no other harbor clearance work coming up. I went back to the *Mayrant,* where the work was starting to make progress.

The next day another destroyer was hit by a bomb dropped from a German plane. The bomb wrecked an engine room. The *Shubrick* was brought in but the work, while similar to that of the *Mayrant,* was not nearly as extensive. We soon had this ship secured so that it could be moved to Malta for further refit. The *Shubrick* was hit by a bomb that blew up inside the engine room. The *Mayrant* was not hit by a bomb. It was a near miss; it went off in the water and blew the ship's side in. And with a small ship, a near miss can be a hell of a lot more damaging than a direct hit.

When we had the after engine room and forward fire room of the *Mayrant* dried out, the ship had recovered sufficient buoyancy and stability so that there was no reason to worry about it sinking or capsizing as long as it was not hit again. It was not, however, sufficiently seaworthy to be moved to Malta. Much more of the badly damaged shell was accessible for inspection and attention inside the ship. I decided to place some concrete patches inside the ship—to put the concrete right on top of the mattresses. The men welded the ends of one-half-inch diameter rods to the shell plating on the inside wherever it was accessible and around the holes, which were plugged with mattresses. Other rods were then tied across these short rods in such a way as to act as steel reinforcing for the concrete patches. Down in the bilge it was impossible to get anything dried out because of the leakage, so we took some bags and filled them with mixtures of sand and cement and poked them in places so that after they were submerged the sand and cement mixture would harden into concrete. That gave us the lower edge of the form. On the sides we put timber forms, and I rigged some pipes in there to try to take away as much of the water leaking in as possible, and then we just poured concrete mix in and hoped to luck it would hold, which it did.

The *Mayrant* job was interesting because each part of the shell was a different problem. We really had no unified method of fixing it up. It was just—here's three square feet that has holes in it, fix it up one way—the next, fix it up another way. Get the damned thing tight and if it only lasted a week it would be good enough.

The day after the big raid I had a very dandified lieutenant colonel come to see me with a very meticulous salute. To me there was something disgraceful about an officer so dolled up when we were all existing under such difficult circumstances. He said he came with General Patton's compliments. The general would like a couple of hams. I thought he was looking for someone else, so I asked him who he thought he was talking to. He said, to Captain Sullivan. I said, "Well, there must be some mistake. We have no hams. There must be some other Captain Sullivan. Perhaps some army quartermaster." "No," said the colonel. "The General said Captain Sullivan, Navy Salvage." I blew up and said we had no hams but wished to hell we had so that I could say he could not have them. I told him to go back and tell Georgie that and to ask him when he was going to return our trucks? In about an hour the colonel was back, said the general knew I had hams and insisted on two as he had to entertain the Cardinal of Palermo. I really blew up this time. I said I did not give a damn how palsy-palsy Georgie was with any fat cardinal but that I wanted our trucks. Perhaps I would go out and steal a few hams if I had a truck, but first I would have to find a ham. All we had was K rations and Spam.

I saw the Doc soon and told him about my talk with the lieutenant colonel. I was still pretty boiled up. The Doc looked concerned. He said Patton was right about the hams, only that I did not have any—only the divers had hams. They were all quite worried that I might find out about it.

The divers had gone into the warehouse next door to our warehouse and taken a few Italian rifles which the MPs had been putting in there. The MPs had been cleaning up all of the loose military equipment around town. At night the divers had taken a boat out to the ships waiting outside the port to get in and had swapped them off as souvenirs for hams and butter.

When I had gone over to see the dry dock that morning with Helen the boys were taking the time to have some ham sandwiches. Patton had taken this time off to drop in and see me. He always liked to talk to the divers. They gave him a ham sandwich. He said it was delicious—the first ham he'd had for a long time. The Doc said he felt sure that the army would trade a truck for a ham and we had hundreds of rifles next door to trade for hams. "OK," I said, "see what you can do." I heard no more from Patton about the hams, but we had our trucks back quickly. In fact, we had six back the next morning. I was waiting for a chance to tell Patton about the deal and to rub it in, but, as I said, I never saw him again.

Helen got the harbor clearance work organized quickly and everything progressed smoothly. He ran into unexpected trouble. One of the ships in midstream that had looked undamaged and which we had assumed to have been sunk because the crew had opened the seacocks, turned out to be a much greater job. A bomb had gone through the hatch and exploded in the rock bottom of the harbor, blowing back through the bottom a number of rock fragments. It was another job like the ships at Casablanca but on a much less complicated scale.

The commandant of the naval base was insistent on our taking on the rehabilitation of the dry dock. He had a very screwy idea as to how the Italian destroyer could be lifted upright by requisitioning all the army mobile cranes in the area. He was a difficult person to talk to; once he got an idea he would refuse to listen to anybody else. One morning I went over to have a cup of coffee with him. He was still hopped up on using army mobile cranes. Suddenly a tremendous explosion rocked the whole area. There was a great gusher of water in the harbor just where we had a diving crew working on a submerged wreck. The crew was working for an officer named Clark. The other officers called him "One Stick Clark." He had acquired a particular skill in underwater cutting up of ships, using explosives. He had been reported several times for using excessive and dangerous amounts of explosives. When questioned he always very seriously said: "Honest to God, Captain, I only used one stick."

I went down to the area. Apparently no one was injured but we lost a diving barge and some equipment. Clark said he had run a hose filled with explosives along the side of the wreck at mud level, had removed the barge well away in accordance with orders before he closed the circuit. We sent another barge out and dropped a diver down. He could not see anything of the ship, only a big hole in the stone bottom of the harbor. I decided the wreck had been that of an Italian ammunition ship which had sunk without exploding, and that Clark had not used sufficient care when he started work. He should have had his divers make a more thorough investigation of the inside of the ship.

Well, I don't know. I blamed him for it. But it may also have been that there were six ammunition ships altogether that had previously blown up in Palermo harbor and it's my thought now that when an ammunition ship blows up, all of the ammunition isn't detonated at that time. Some of it is thrown out into the water. There were pretty strong currents around Palermo bottom and the whole bottom was more or less flat. It was rock, but it was covered with two or three inches of very, very light mud, a kind of slime. And it may have been possible that a lot of this undetonated ammunition was rolled along the rock surface until it hit a wreck, and then would just pile up in there, and at the same time be concealed by the mud coverage so that the divers didn't see it. And when they set off this blast, they may have set off that. But whatever it was, there was at least a hundred tons of explosives that went off. This was just something terrific. As no one was injured and as the one blast had eliminated more than ten days of work, I said nothing more except I hoped it was a good lesson for Clark to investigate a little more.

However, I heard more about this later in the day when I met Admiral Lyal Davidson. He was very wrought up, said the blast had rolled his flagship, the *Philadelphia,* over at least 25 degrees. No damage was done except that his aide, who was leaving the ship, fell off the gangplank and had to swim. I had to laugh at this. I did not mean to do so. It was probably a question of relief that the aide wasn't injured. Anyway, the admiral, who was invariably a very calm and phlegmatic person, got very, very sore and gave me hell.

The *Mayrant* was hardly prepared for sea when I was called back to

Algiers. I went back and was briefed about the next stages of the war—Salerno and the occupation of Naples. Palermo was only needed to support our forces in Sicily and for a U.S. naval base. As soon as all hostilities in Sicily ended there would not be much need for unloading military supplies at Palermo, although some ships were still en route for that port. Salerno was to be another amphibious undertaking, but the British and Americans were to strike at adjacent beaches. Admiral Hewitt would be in command of the combined naval forces. Naples was to become our chief port in the Mediterranean. Consequently we would have much more clearance work to do there. The Germans would no doubt smash it up well before leaving.

My decisions in Palermo were approved. However, if we could do anything to recondition the dry dock at the naval base we should. The French had now taken over salvage in North Africa. Wroten had left with his last officers and was en route to Palermo. I told Admiral Hewitt about the difficulties of getting an understanding in Palermo about what harbor clearance work was required and about the priorities of the various projects. He asked me to prepare a memorandum on the subject, but I never got around to doing it. I had a lot of other work in the office.

BREVITY—THE SOUL OF WISDOM AND WIT

ADMIRAL ALAN G. KIRK

ALAN GOODRICH KIRK was born in Philadelphia, Pennsylvania, on 30 October 1888. He attended the U.S. Naval Academy and graduated with a B.S. in the class of 1909. He spent the first two years in the Atlantic on the battleship USS *Kansas*. From 1911 to 1914 he was on the Asiatic Fleet gunboat USS *Wilmington* (PG 8) and as gunnery officer on the armored cruiser USS *Saratoga* (ACR 2) as she sailed off the coast of war-torn China during the Sun Yat-sen revolution that overthrew the Manchu dynasty.

Kirk returned to the United States and boarded the USS *Utah* (BB 31) for duty in the Atlantic until 1916, when he was ordered to the Naval Proving Ground, Indian Head, Maryland, and served there as proof and experimental officer for the balance of World War I. He then served in the Atlantic on several battleships as a gunnery officer, part of the time returning troops from Europe. He became executive officer and navigator of the presidential yacht *Mayflower* during the final months of the second term of President Wilson and the early months of the term of President Warren G. Harding. From 1922 to 1924 he was on duty in the Bureau of Ordnance in Washington, D.C., centralizing records and also serving as naval aide to Presidents Harding and Calvin Coolidge.

Beginning in 1928 he spent one year at the Naval War College in Newport, Rhode Island, as a student and two years on the staff. From 1933 to 1936 he was in Washington as the assistant director of ships movements division in the Navy Department. He then served in the Atlantic, performing several duties with ships of the Atlantic Fleet. From 1939 to 1941 he had duty at the U.S. embassy in London, where he served as naval attaché and attaché for air. He served for a brief period in 1941 as director of Naval Intelligence in Washington, following that with a short assignment as commander, Destroyer Squadron Seven, with the Atlantic Fleet's amphibious force.

In May 1942, now rear admiral, Kirk was again back in London as naval attaché but also chief of staff to Admiral Harold R. Stark, the U.S. naval commander in Europe. In February 1943 he became Commander, Amphibious Force, Atlantic Fleet, and with his flag in the amphibious command ship *Ancon* (AGC 4) he led Task Force 85 in supporting the army in its assault at Scoglitti, Sicily, in the summer of 1943. In November he became senior American naval commander under supreme British naval command in the planning for the Normandy landings, which began on 6 June 1944. The admiral flew his flag in the *Augusta* (CA 31) as Commander, TF 122 (Western Naval Task Force). In July, following the capture of Cherbourg, Kirk was relieved of this command and then became Commander, U.S. Naval Forces, France, and naval commander to General Dwight D. Eisenhower, commanding naval units in the advance into Germany.

Detached and promoted to vice admiral in July 1945, Kirk served on the General Board until his resignation and retirement in the rank of full admiral the following March 1946, to enter diplomatic service. Skilled and experienced in this work, he was named U.S. ambassador to Belgium and Luxembourg (1946–47), ambassador to the Soviet Union from 1949 to 1952, and to Nationalist China (Taiwan) in 1962–63. Admiral Kirk died at the Presbyterian Hospital in New York City on 15 October 1963.

The Sicily operation, called by the code name of Husky, was looked upon by the planners in London and the planners in Washington and some of the planners on Admiral Cunningham's staff and General Eisenhower's staff—they thought that was going to be a pretty bloody affair. It was looked upon as one of the real trials of strength.

The original plans called for landings at Palermo, where I was supposed to land; at Licata on the west end of the island, where Conolly finally did land; at Syracuse, as the British call it; and at Gela, also on the south coast. But Monty Montgomery was put in charge of the operation, under Eisenhower, as the land commander. Cunningham was the naval commander and Tedder was the air force commander. Montgomery said that we would be defeated in detail, that this was not the way to land in Sicily, the positions chosen were not mutually supporting; we'd have to revise the whole plan. He was right. We revised the plan. The British took what you might call the southeast coast, from Syracuse down to the cape; and we took the south and southwesterly coast, from Licata eastward. That made everybody supporting everybody else. It made the problem of supply simpler, protection against aircraft and submarines better and easier. Then that plan was carried off. That was correct. We would have had trouble if we'd done it the other way, I think. It was the first big amphibious operation of the war, as a matter of fact, including the Pacific. Although the North African landing had taken place, that was one thing, but this was an organized affair and went very well.

Then at once, with Patton's indomitable drive, our forces, the Seventh Army, moved right across Sicily, over the mountains, the mountain chain, and came down the north coast towards Messina, catching Palermo on the way. It was a very sound strategic insight of Patton's. It was very good and of course Eisenhower let him go, let him have his head.

We got back to Oran. We had taken about six hundred of the officers of Rommel's army. They were lined up on the dock. I went down and took a look at them. Boy, they were lean, tanned, hard in the face. They were tough babies!

One day soon after I was at sea, it got kind of rough, and I signaled to the captain of the ship that had these men on board. I said, "How are the *herrenvolk* doing?" You know, the American navy doesn't have much of a sense of humor when busy. They're always so damned serious. I never got an answer. Another time I sent a message to Davidson (Vice Admiral L. A.) when we were approaching the landing at Sicily, through the storm and waves. I sent him a signal: "Jolly boating weather." No reply, no response, none!

312

The invasion of the Italian peninsula at Salerno proved to be difficult. The struggle to get agreement on launching such a campaign by the Allies was in many ways more difficult. Both the Americans and the British had strong opinions about strategy that went back to their earliest conference in World War II. The British had as background experiences from a long series of colonial wars. Unforgettable too was the memory of Gallipoli in World War I, when the British military forces learned sadly about the difficulties of making landings in a hostile land that was prepared with strong shore-based fortifications. More recently there was the terrifying Dunkirk experience that cost the British nation dearly. From that time on the British had been examining the possibilities of a return to the continent, as the Americans and the Russians consistently demanded in order to stave off defeat of the Russian armies by the Nazis.

Churchill, as the chief British strategist, was thoroughly aware of the difficulties inherent in that action without the utmost preparation in advance. It is Harry Hopkins, the shrewd advisor to President Roosevelt, who said: "In trying to figure out whether we could have got across the Channel successfully in 1942 or 1943 you've got to answer this question: Could Eisenhower, Bradley, Patton, Montgomery and the rest have handled the big show as they did if they hadn't had the experience fighting the Germans in North Africa and Sicily first."*

In hindsight, Churchill was correct in resisting the enormous pressure that Russia and America had applied for what amounted to a premature second front in order to take some of the burden from the Russians.

At any rate, in 1943 strong differences of opinion persisted as Allied forces faced a need for new decisions and new directions. Then it was that Churchill persuaded President Roosevelt to call a meeting of the combined chiefs of staff (CCS) in Washington that May. Operation Torch, the invasion of North Africa, had been successful in late 1942; a decision had been made to invade Sicily in 1943 and preparations were under way, but

*Quoted in Robert E. Sherwood, *Roosevelt and Hopkins: An Intimate History* (New York: Harper & Brothers, 1948), 807.

the final determination on an invasion of the European continent was still undecided.

Churchill was strongly of the opinion that another Mediterranean action was necessary first, once the Sicilian campaign was over. He wanted the Allies to exploit the conquest of Sicily with a further effort to knock Italy out of the war, to obtain a foothold on the Italian peninsula and at the same time put a drain on the German military might. General Marshall and Admiral King were strongly focused on the defeat of Germany. This was the primary objective; all others were secondary and could only be accomplished by an invasion that came to grips with German might. They were suspicious of British motives in that the British had opted for the invasion of North Africa in 1942, then Sicily, and now for Salerno. Churchill had argued forcibly on a number of occasions against precipitous action across the Channel, but he had never weakened in his determination to reenter Europe at an appropriate moment.

At the May 1943 conference in Washington the atmosphere was rife with suspicions. But fortunately Admiral Leahy was present as he had not been at the conference in Casablanca. Now he was chief of staff to President Roosevelt. He was a strong man of wisdom and opened the conference the first day. Perhaps one can speculate that he was imbued with Roosevelt's belief that agreement with the British was more important than promoting any particular strategy.

Leahy began the discussion with some trenchant advice: they must discuss a global strategy before getting into specifics about the next campaign. This included a review of the entire Pacific campaign as it had developed to the present point. Leahy seemed to be a stabilizing force and finally the impasse was broken. But not before General Marshall went so far in saying that if the postponement of the invasion of the Continent was again delayed he felt that planning for that operation should cease and the United States should redeploy its main military, naval, and air forces in the Pacific. Churchill, on the other hand, argued strongly for the invasion of the Italian peninsula, as he wrote to his friend Field Marshal Jan Christiaan Smuts of South Africa: "I shall make it a capital issue. I will in no circumstances allow the powerful British forces (in the Mediterranean) and others controlled by the British to stand idle."*

But finally the deadlock was broken because both sides wanted to get on with the cross-channel operation. Churchill even agreed to set a target date of 1 May 1944, but the Americans refused to agree upon any specific invasion of Italy. The British prime minister got an important concession,

*Winston S. Churchill, *Closing the Ring,* vol. 5 of *The Second World War* (Boston: Houghton Mifflin, 1951), 36.

however, in that General Eisenhower was directed to begin planning for a possible invasion and when his plans were formulated they were to be examined by the combined chiefs. The general was told, however, that he could use only the military forces then under his command.

Finally on July 26, Avalanche (code name for Salerno) was authorized and planning got under way.

SKIPPING SALVOS OFF SALERNO

CAPTAIN PHIL H. BUCKLEW*

That was a very sticky operation. My own experiences were more humorous I suppose—frightening to me—but humorous as I look back on them. Based on my experience with the British working out of Malta and before Sicily, it was decided that we would go in to the beaches at Salerno in kayak canoes. My young bos'n's mate and I operated our canoe at the head of the task force in the belief we would be less detected in a canoe than with a powerboat. Before we went in we had had photographic reconnaissance. Then we had to go in and identify landmarks that provided exits. Roadway exits were the main problem there, it being mountainous terrain. The troops had to be in the right spot to exit their way up the hills and out.

On this particular operation we did not have physical reconnaissance to go by. It was discussed much with Admiral Conolly but was decided against as we took submarine photographic reconnaissance. This gave us a certain silhouette picture, and then we ran a few aircraft over the area. It was a combination of all these we had to work with.

Our operation began about two o'clock in the morning. Ordinarily when you have a mountainous background, it is very difficult to get much of a silhouette; however, in this case the shore fire made it pretty certain. In response to the British bombardment, the enemy were starting their repeat firing so we knew where their gun emplacements were. Also we could identify our own position as the middle of the beach from where an enemy pillbox was working on us and from the flanks in the different

*For biographical information on Bucklew, see pp. 264–266.

316

areas. We were a little frightened perhaps but not hurt, and we got the troops in.

As I said, we did not have live reconnaissance on the beaches. That was one reason for caution and for the approach being taken by a sneak craft rather than by a powerboat: to get a person to the beach in a kayak to see how it looks and to signal our estimate as to the best area for initial landing. There were many things I didn't know were scheduled to occur although Admiral Conolly had discussed some detail with those on the operating level when we were preparing for Salerno.

One thing I was completely unaware of was the use of a rocket ship. This was the introduction of a rocket ship. So to me this became a very "hot" night. The first thing that occurred began with the bombardment by British ships. They lacked radar and fire-control instruments. I was aware of the shore bombardment that would occur over my head as I was in there in advance of the troops, but I had been assured that they would fire long; they would fire long and reduce their fire toward the beach. But it didn't happen that way. They fired short and skipped them in. Ray King, my bos'n's mate, and I had quite a sensation with this naval bombardment by the British destroyers—skipping in the water and over us in our kayak canoe. A shell coming at you in that salvo looks like a big ball of fire and it looks like it is going to hit you right on the nose. It either goes over or it doesn't—they were skipping. We had a bit of a thrill with that, you might say. We were the sole kayak in this area. We had come in by a landing craft to an area of about three miles offshore, had debarked in our kayak, and gone on in while our mother craft, the LST, lay dead in the water. It was our intent that we would return to her.

After the first shock of the salvos, and as things were expected to quiet down, the next thrill came. We didn't know what it was, but it turned out to be a British amphibious craft, an LCU that had been converted with about fifty rocket launchers. When they laid their barrage—and we were looking it in the eye—it was more like a battleship salvo. The rockets went over our heads. They had a tremendous roar and went with a swish, swish. We didn't know what it was. The next moment I was hit—hit in the chest—a good thump that took my wind away and I thought: well, that's it. It doesn't hurt too much but that's it. So I called over my shoulder to my bos'n's mate, "I think I took a hit so you will have to take over." About that time my life jacket began to smoke and smolder. I hadn't taken a hit but I had taken a piece of a rocket that was burning the kapok in my jacket. I was kind of embarrassed. My bos'n's mate let me hear about it quite a few times afterwards. He would say: "Boss, tell me about that hit you took." So there was some excitement and it was humorous in retrospect. But there was nothing humorous about the landing. We got in off the beach and we identified the target landing area from about fifty feet back on the beach. By light signal we brought in the first landing craft and the waves thereafter—but they took an awful beating.

The deepest defenses were far stronger than anticipated, for the Germans had not withdrawn and were well placed up in the hills. It was our first encounter with the German 88s mounted on flatcars. They would come in and out of caves and then open fire and withdraw. Actually they had held off the task force for about a week's time. And finally on D plus 5, a conference was called and it was decided to withdraw our forces. Admiral Conolly made quite a dramatic speech and asked for one more try: "If we withdraw we will lose our whole landing force; they are not of the capability and training and experience to evacuate a force. We have never done this. We have landed offensively. Let us utilize all our naval gunfire." (I did not hear the admiral's speech, but I knew of it from outside.) And for a three-day period the navy peppered those mountains and really poured it on. Everybody fired everything they had and they finally cracked an exit and the troops could move from where they were bogged down on the beaches. I remember the cruiser *Philadelphia* burnt out the bore of all of her guns. It was just a horrible mess, I recall. We had about a thousand casualties on the beaches. I helped withdraw some casualties in the earlier part until I was pulled back to the flagship and ultimately to Bizerte. With my boat and crew, I could operate from the *Biscayne*, which was the flagship of Admiral Conolly.

There was just one funny incident after another. Captain Dyer called down to me one time and said: "Buck (there was a Jewish fellow, skipper of an LST, I think his name was Greenberg but have forgotten now), Greenberg's in trouble over there. Take a run over and see if you can be of any help." So in my small boat I came alongside the LST. Of course we all knew each other well—we worked closely together in our training—and I hailed him. He was on the bridge and said: "Yes, you can help me if you can get me a chart of this area. I thought this damn thing was going to sink and I did like the book says and threw everything over the side." Well, you can't sink an LST easily and though he had a gaping hole in it, they were all right and they ultimately got back to Bizerte. His LST had been rigged not only to carry troops but they had rigged it with a flat top to use a Piper Cub–type plane for reconnaissance work. But once you rigged that so-called flight deck, the tank deck wasn't good for troops so they had a load of jackasses—mules—that they were going to use up in the mountains as they progressed. I happened to beat him back to Bizerte, and I was there when he came into the harbor. As you pass your casualty report to Harbor Control, his came in as: "One over-age Jewish skipper ready for survey; hole in the side of the ship; tank deck full of manure; flight deck beyond use." That became kind of a classic message. There was a lot of humor even under rough circumstances.

318

ITALIAN SURRENDER AND GERMAN RESISTANCE

VICE ADMIRAL GEORGE CARROLL DYER*

During the period before the final determination was made to go into Salerno there was considerable discussion of alternatives. My boss, Admiral Conolly (I was his chief of staff), was very strong for going into Gaeta. It is farther up the Italian coast, thirty miles north of Naples. One thing I believe influenced him greatly in his effort to get us to land at Gaeta was that the bay there wasn't mined while the bay at Salerno was mined. That meant that for Salerno we had to sweep for mines ahead of the amphibious craft, the LSTs and LCTs. And it meant that the landing operation would consume a great deal more time and give the enemy extra hours to react to our assault.

The other thing I believe influenced Conolly was that we had such inadequate air support from the army air force at Sicily. The cry to land at Salerno was based on the fact that the air force could provide a certain modest amount of air support at Salerno, but Conolly's position was that the army air force had supplied so little air support at Sicily that it really didn't make any difference whether we had it or we didn't have it. Therefore, let us go into Gaeta, which had advantages from the point of view of getting to Naples more quickly. The land between Gaeta and Naples was much more favorable for the army to advance over.

The army air force said flatly they could not provide any air support at Gaeta because it was roughly fifty miles—air miles—farther north. They claimed they could only spend twenty minutes over Salerno. It was the

*For biographical information on Dyer see pp. 184–185.

319

maximum their planes could spend flying out of Sicily and Gaeta was out of the question.

The determination against trying Gaeta was finally an army decision. In any amphibious operation the navy is required to land the army where the army wants to be landed if at all possible from a navy point of view.

There was still another factor to be considered. The landing was to be made in two major subdivisions. The American troops were to be landed in the southern half and the British troops were to be landed in the northern half. The landing craft under Admiral Conolly's command were landing British troops and specifically the British 46th Division. The U.S. Army commanders insisted there would be no preliminary gunfire bombardment. The British army and navy command also opposed such preliminary bombardment, but they were much less stubborn in their position. And of course General Eisenhower had an order that said—*you couldn't shoot until shot at.* To illustrate: there was British destroyer gunfire support up in our area but it was designated *UNCLE* and that meant it could only be fired when the German guns opened up on us.

The Salerno area was considered by the army to be more advantageous on another point. They felt the gunfire support after the landing would be more effective than at Gaeta because of the contour of the land where all the ground defenses had to be gathered into the level beach area. The Salerno-Agropole area is sort of like the inside of a cup on its side. About three miles from the beach to the east are the first row of hills backed up by two-thousand-foot mountains. The white sand beaches provided thus a very lovely landing area. The physical geography around Gaeta was in no way the same.

We have to remember that the British army and the navy experience at Gallipoli in World War I made a profound impression on them. You could hardly find any Britisher who would argue that it was possible to make a successful assault landing against alerted and prepared beach defenses. They had known a very bad experience. But in our navy and Marine Corps there was increased confidence in being able to land against strong defense because of what we felt we had mastered and the British had not: the art of adequate gunfire and air support. We had several examples of success in the Pacific to point to. Landing on Tulagi in the Solomons in August 1941 against a prepared Japanese defensive position, we did take the place after considerable initial delay. And another—while we were planning the Salerno landing in August and September 1943 our Southern Pacific Amphibious Force had just completed landings in New Georgia. It took us six weeks to take a strongly defended Jap position on Munda (one of the islands), but we had the idea we could make it and we did.

We had less than four weeks to plan the Salerno operation from the date we left Sicily and returned to Bizerte and the date the landing craft had to sail for Salerno from Bizerte. It was about a three-day sail with LCTs and LSTs from Bizerte up to Salerno. In truth the planning operation certainly was not a planner's dream. It really was a planner's nightmare. It depended a great deal on the Sicilian campaign, since General Alexander who was the senior army commander under General Eisenhower, was strongly opposed to the Salerno landing before he had cleaned up Sicily. To complicate the matter further there were high negotiations going on in regard to the surrender of Italy and the resulting question of coordination of the surrender with the assault landing so that the landing would be able to take the maximum advantage of the surrender. I learned secondhand that there was a considerable difference of opinion between our negotiators and the Italian negotiators. And there was a great unwillingness on the part of the Allied negotiators to accept the fact that the Italians were negotiating in good faith. We just didn't believe it, on our working level, with the result that progress toward the Italian surrender was up and down.

Salerno had three hazards. The bay was mined. The air cover promised was slight. There was to be no preliminary bombardment in the southern half of the area. Fortunately the British had now accepted and were willing that there be a limited amount of preliminary bombardment in the northern half where we were doing the landing. Admiral Conolly was in charge of the landing of the British troops.

Under the circumstances there could not be any surprise. German and Italian planes had been flying air reconnaissance over the whole North African coast. We were at Bizerte with three hundred amphibious craft plus a few other ships. It was quite obvious that the major sailing of the smaller craft was going to take place from there. All they had to do was to scout us when we left. Admiral Hewitt said that all the enemy had to do was to take a pair of dividers and swing them from North Africa and from Sicily and figure where the limits of the air cover would be. Also our problem of air cover was being discussed in the press at the time. The enemy could realize that we'd have to land at Salerno if we were going to land anywhere in Central Italy. Italian planes tracked us all the way up to Salerno and made attacks on us all the way. There could be no element of surprise in any way, shape, form, or description. There was no element of strategic surprise or of tactical surprise.

We had only destroyers in our area to provide the gunfire support in the first twenty-four hours of the landing. But on D plus three we had moved three cruisers into the Bay of Salerno. Of course in the northern sector where I was, the Royal Navy supplied most of the naval vessels and supported the operation. Very few U.S. naval ships were in our sector providing gunfire support. It was supplied by the British. I had a feeling that the British gunfire support was much less generous than that of the

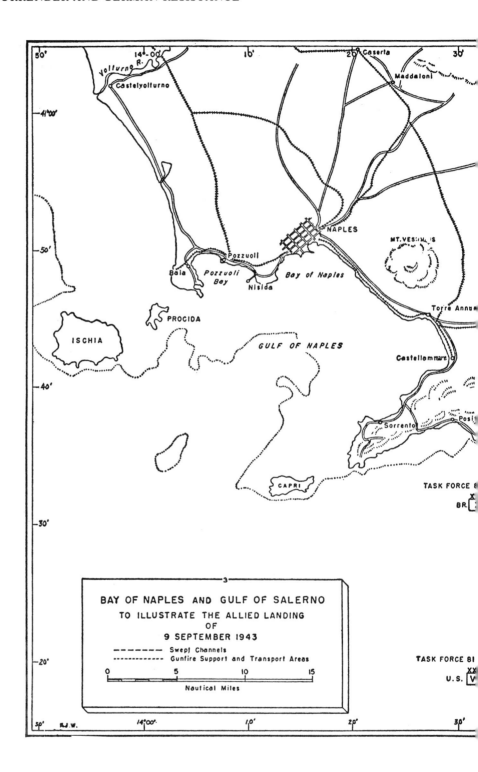

BAY OF NAPLES AND GULF OF SALERNO
TO ILLUSTRATE THE ALLIED LANDING
OF
9 SEPTEMBER 1943

――――― Swept Channels
············· Gunfire Support and Transport Areas

Nautical Miles

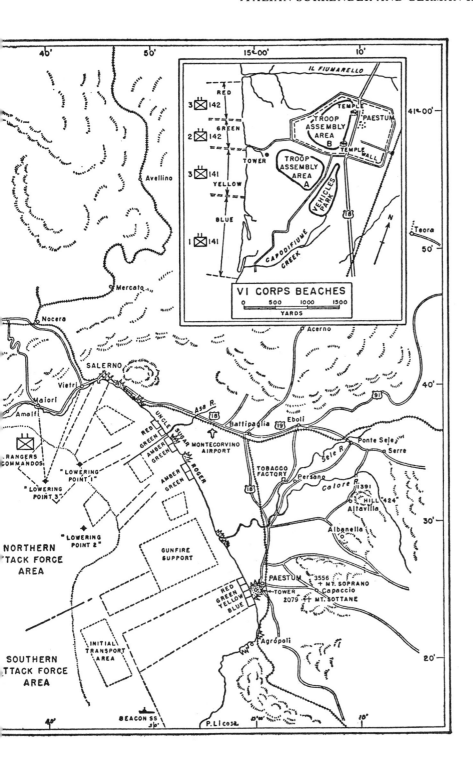

VI CORPS BEACHES

U.S. Navy. The Americans just poured it on but the British fired a limited number of salvos and then quit—that was it! They had provided their support. But they were fighting on rations and they had to be careful.

Admiral Hewitt was with the Southern Attack Force and Admiral Hall was the amphibious commander under him. He landed General Mark Clark and we to the north landed British Lieutenant General McCreery. While we were still at Bizerte there were many air raids and every time that happened some of the officers would come out and stand in the vicinity of the shelters that the Germans and Italians had left there. Our purpose was to watch the bombs falling. It was probably one of the most asinine things I ever did. The British General Horrocks (Sir Brian) was standing in the same group with me watching the air raid. Suddenly he was machine-gunned right through his shoulder and his chest area at an angle. We thought he was dying but he lived long enough to be sent home to Britain. He was replaced at once by General McCreery.

When McCreery arrived in Bizerte he was given a copy of our plan of action. Then he had a conference of all the senior officers of his corps. Conolly and Dyer were invited. This was four or five days before we were due to sail. The general stood up on his feet with a little short whip such as British officers carry (a swagger stick), whipped it against his legs and said: "I have read the plan. I don't like it, but we are going to do it. It's too damn late to change it." And it was. I was relieved because if he wanted to change the troop landing plan we'd have had to change all the amphibious-craft and landing-craft schedules.

As you perhaps know, the Sele River was the dividing line, or the boundary line, between the British landing and the U.S. landing. This had both its advantages and disadvantages. The disadvantages of it were made clear one day when the German tanks used to come down to the beach area to run over the Allied landing areas. The German tanks did this in the immediate area where our naval beach groups were located. After their attack was over, Admiral Conolly told me to go ashore and reestablish the beach control organization because the beach was in pandemonium. We had provided some slit trenches. Some of our people got into them but quite a few of them didn't. The tanks had just raised Cain with everyone that wasn't in a slit trench. I'll never forget the Sele River.

In my opinion the landing was made with only partial gunfire support but I don't know of any later difficulties that were directly related to that partial gunfire support. By and large on the southern half of the landing the American troops advanced fairly rapidly until they had really conquered the whole plain level back to the hills. On the northern half of the landing the British made fairly slow progress right from the very start. We landed some Raiders north of the British divisions and they had a fairly easy time in the early part of the assault landing but the British met with strong opposition almost immediately. They suffered quite a few casualties and another thing, a lot of their people surrendered for they found themselves in positions that were deemed untenable and surrendered. So everything was not the way it should have been.

The army had been subjected to severe criticism after the Sicily assault landing because of the terrible performance that the Army Air Corps had put on during that affair. This criticism had appeared in the press in a number of places. One I remember appeared in one of Hanson Baldwin's articles in the *New York Times*. All these articles had indicated, in a soft way, that there had been certain deficiencies in the Army Air Corps's support of the Sicily assault landing in the views of the other services. One thing I know is that General Eisenhower's headquarters appointed some kind of a new air commander for the Salerno landings. They also changed the air support system considerably from that effective at Sicily in that the British Coastal Command was given the chore of providing the air cover for the fleet. The U.S. Army Air Corps was relieved of that responsibility and it was turned over to the British—to the people who had been in the Fleet Air Arm but who were not part of the Royal Air Force. During the assault landing at Salerno there were planes from British carriers supporting the landing. They had two big carriers and some smaller carriers present in the area and they provided some of the air cover and they also provided some of the air support. Yet it seemed to me that the enemy air force was very active in the Salerno Bay area. In the craft scattered along the bay we were subjected to a tremendous number of air raids. We lost some ships and amphibious craft and some merchant ships.

The Germans had a new air-controlled flying bomb. They would fly this bomb over and a German plane would fly above it. Then the control plane would match images on a radar. When the radar image of the ship below was in a certain position in connection with this bomb, the bomb would tip up vertically and down it would come at tremendous speed. There wasn't anything you could do about it except watch it come down because you couldn't shoot it down with your anti-aircraft guns. It was beyond our air control capabilities where you had such a complete change of course and change of speed. You continued to shoot at it with the man-controlled guns but that was ineffective. They came in at about eight to ten thousand feet, then the bomb turned to the vertical and came down at a tremendous speed. We lost a number of merchant ships carrying supplies.

Admiral Hewitt's report summarizes the situation fairly well: "Enemy's regular and persistent bombing and strafing attacks effectively interrupted unloading activities." The going was pretty rough.

One thing that has disturbed me in the period subsequent to the war is that I read a book by General Mark Clark in regard to the Salerno landings. In this book he denies that he ever seriously contemplated evacuating the beaches at Salerno. My memory is quite different.

Along about D plus six or seven, Admiral Conolly called me into his office and said that the chief of staff of one of the army's divisions and a lesser staff officer from General Mark Clark's headquarters had come aboard. They had said that they desired that the navy plan immediately for an evacuation of the troops from the beachheads. That was almost impossible. When you land you run an LST or an LCT up on a beach at a good speed. It's fully loaded with a lot of momentum that carries it where you want it to go. Then you unload the craft and back off with a very lightly loaded craft. That is one thing but when you are up on a beach in an LCT or an LST in an unloaded craft or ship and then you reembark troops and their equipment, you put a tremendous number of additional tons in the craft. These craft have a very small engine-backing power with which to get off the beach and they just can't do it. An engine always has twice the power to go ahead than it does to back. So that evacuation from a beachhead means that you can take aboard only about half the load that you actually put on the beach from the same landing ship or craft. So since we had just finished a landing of two reinforced divisions down there in the southern part of the beachhead and Clark wanted to take them back on board ship and craft, we had an impossible situation insofar as the navy was concerned. As soon as the amphibious craft were unloaded we had started them to Bizerte to pick up additional stores to bring back for the troops' use. This had been going on for about five days. We didn't have a lot of empty ships sitting around in the Bay of Salerno just waiting to do something like an evacuation.

Logistic support for an army corps is a big proposition. When you are going to suddenly say, I've got to evacuate, you just don't have empty landing ships and craft available.

With such information as we had and knowledge of such landing ships and craft that were available to us, I, Stanley, and Buchanan of our staff worked all night on developing the naval aspect of this Op plan for evacuation. We gave it code name Brass Hat. I will never forget. I hated the name and still dislike it.

As soon as Admiral Conolly had been advised of General Clark's desire he sent a dispatch to Admiral Hewitt advising him. Hewitt got in a British DD—HMS *Hilary*—and came dashing back up from Algiers and brought along with him General Alexander and a number of other officers of his staff and the army staff. They got back up there some twenty-four hours after this thing had been decided by Clark and we had been told.

Admiral Conolly was the senior officer present off the beaches and that is why Clark sent his representative to him. The others had gone back to North Africa where they had their own things to do. Also it was desirable to get some of our ships out of the area and away from the German bombing attacks.

So the conference on Brass Hat was held in the *Biscayne,* Hewitt's *Ancon* being back in North Africa away from the German air assault. We had built in our ship before the Sicilian operation a so-called war room on the topside. This in fact made her top heavy. Into this crowded war room were put General Clark's staff, the corps commanders' staff, the two division commanders of his divisions, representatives of General Mc-Creery and his two divisions, General Alexander and some of his staff, and Admiral Hewitt and some of his staff. The first thing was that General Clark's representatives presented the situation as they saw it ashore. Then Admiral Conolly's representatives, in which I as chief of staff and others, presented the situation as we saw it from a seagoing point of view.

This I will never forget. General Alexander had not said a word during all these presentations. When they were finished he got up and walked to the front—only about three paces because it was so crowded. He turned around, took his little swagger stick, cracked his leg with it and said: "There will be no evacuation. Now we'll proceed from there."

The result of the conference was that everybody made more effort. A lot more air support was brought in. General Eisenhower evidently applied the whip up there in Algiers. Things they said they couldn't do before they did now—air support. It was a crisis and recognized as one. They loaded craft in Algiers with new troops and they loaded them in Sicily. They brought them up in everything that would float and run. They got them to Salerno and landed these additional troops. The army held on and the tide of battle turned. A German panzer division with a competent general in command had given our boys the devil and he almost won. In fact he had announced he was going to win. He had our troops on the run, he said, but wiser counsels prevailed.

I would say that General Eisenhower's announcement on the radio the night of our landings that Italy had surrendered had tremendous psychological repercussions on the troops. They could hardly go ashore determined to do or die when the enemy had just turned in his suit. The fact that the Germans hadn't turned in their suits was not readily apparent to the GI until somebody shot at him. So I think the GIs did a wonderful job of picking themselves up from a period where they were just walking ashore and raising the flag to where they had to fight for everything they got.*

*It is interesting to compare Admiral John Hall's story of the same events, taken from his oral history. The editor interviewed Admiral Hall in 1963. Here is Hall's account:

General Mark Clark was a very capable man, a fine-looking soldier. The Fifth

The reaction of the Italians to their country's surrender was just instantaneous. The night when we anchored the *Biscayne* in Salerno Bay, my admiral said the *Biscayne* must be the closest ship to the beach. We had dropped anchor about three-thirty in the morning and as soon as first light broke out came a small boat from the beach with four or five Italian officers in fresh uniforms. Up they came and on board, flying a white flag. They had one officer who spoke quite good English. I met them. My heart just went out to them. I couldn't do anything except treat them with the greatest courtesy, because they were in a terrible position. There were professional soldiers as well as naval officers amongst them.

Army had been built up as the great combat outfit, and they'd never been in combat as far as I know before Salerno. I think that Mark was so disappointed when it began to look as if we were not going to attack Salerno that I think he did all he could to speed things up. I think he rather expected to march into Naples and Rome. They were all a little surprised, I believe, at the resistance they met.

I have always laid the immediate resistance on the beaches to the fact that we had been negotiating with the Italians for an Italian surrender, without General Clark knowing about it. Certainly I didn't know about it and I was the attack force commander of the American attack force. Admiral Hewitt didn't know about it. We were landing at two or three o'clock in the morning. The afternoon before we got a dispatch from Allied Headquarters telling us to listen on a commercial radio broadcast frequency at six o'clock. General Walker, the landing force commander, and I were to have dinner in my cabin at six o'clock so I had them bring in this radio set. Here it was—General Eisenhower telling us about the armistice with Italy.

It alarmed me. I thought we were going to meet Italians on the beaches. I knew darned well that they couldn't have had a conference with the Italians over a period of ten days without the Germans knowing about it. I said to General Walker: "General, this means to me that we're going to meet a lot stronger resistance than we had expected. I'm going to send a signal to the force to that effect. I'd like to add that the commanding general of the landing forces concurs, if you agree with me." He said, "I do." So I sent that message out. But the commercial broadcast had been heard all over the ships by the whole force in all the troop compartments. So the hand grenades that an infantryman sticks in over and above his equipment when he's going in to battle—they were thrown down on the deck. In the officers' bunkrooms in the transports the extra clips of ammunition were thrown away. "We won't need them."

The immediate reaction—everything was quiet. But there were going to be a lot of people killed tonight. Immediately after that broadcast it sounded like a ladies' pink tea. Yap-yap-yap, a lot of conversation, you know. The tenseness was gone. I thought it was a very unfortunate thing. I know that we met a lot more strong resistance than we could have met. There were new fields of fire out there on the shore and tanks lined up opposite the beaches. Without the announcement about the Italians they would have been in charge of the beaches and the Germans would have been in reserve. The announcement changed this.

I'm not criticizing General Eisenhower, who was the overall commander. From his point of view I suppose it was fine, and from the national point of view, fine to have Italy fading out of the war. But I wish they had some other way to announce it a few hours before I was to land on enemy shores.

The first thing I told them was that I wanted the information on the mines that were in the area. The Italians produced this map. If we'd just had a Xerox system it would have been just wonderful. But we didn't so I turned it over to the staff chief quartermaster and told him to make a couple of copies of it right away and to get one to Admiral Hewitt, who at that time was in the Bay of Salerno. We then analyzed the Italian map and put out a signal to all ships present showing where the lines of mines were. Although we had swept through the mine fields and buoyed the channels where we had swept, it was favorable information to know where the mines were that hadn't been swept.

One of the Italian army officers who came aboard had a list of where all the guns in the hills were. They brought forward a lot of useful information. I then sent them down to the wardroom and gave them coffee and tried to make them feel a little bit comfortable.

I might comment further on the mines in the harbor and our efforts at sweeping. When we started our sweeping efforts prior to our landings and when we started to pick up mines we established certain lines on our charts that seemed to be indicated by the mines that were being swept. So we had, I would say, 10 or 20 percent of the mine information when the Italians handed us their chart. But what we had of course was not intelligence information but rather operational intelligence. It was something we deduced from the mines found. It was an educated guess.

About three days after the initial landing I went ashore into Amalfi harbor because we were looking for places where we could land craft without having to beach them. You can unload some types of craft much faster alongside a dock than you can on a beach. The British had announced that they had captured Amalfi harbor so I went ashore and toured the docks and harbor area. The Germans had blown up the docks to some extent but our army engineers immediately went to work to restore them. As a matter of fact we made quite good use of this small Amalfi harbor.

That was the only time I came close to any of the Italian population. I rode through a part of the town and also got out and walked around, but since I couldn't speak Italian and they couldn't speak English all we could do was just to look happy and wave at each other.

Perhaps you may have wondered why we had no American carriers or battleships involved in the operation at Salerno. The answer is that we had no carriers available in September 1943. The U.S. Navy and Admiral King had opted for the Pacific theater and everything our navy did in the Mediterranean was done reluctantly, in my very humble opinion. We had some old battleships in the Atlantic where they were escorting our troop convoys and protecting them from German raiders. They had all done some gunfire work in the war period but they were not peeled off from their escort chores and sent into the Mediterranean. The British of course did have carriers and many other elements of the fleet in the Mediterranean.

I thought the Salerno operation was an extremely good operation so far as the navy was concerned. Also I might add, our cruisers and destroyers that supported the Southern Attack Force landing did a tremendous job under very difficult circumstances. The army was quite happy about that.

The whole operation came to a precipitous close for me personally and I will give you a little background on that.

On the flag bridge of the *Biscayne* there was on either side and directly opposite the chartroom doors two 50-caliber machine guns, one on each side. Manning one of these was a great big brawny machinist's mate.

When the ship was in Bizerte the Germans used to send over their Stukas to make air attacks. When they did we used to lay a tremendous amount of smoke and the result was you could see little if anything. On the occasion of a particular raid I was on one side of the bridge when I heard the Stukas coming in on the other side in a dive. You could place where they were by their noise. So I was going from my side of the bridge and moving to the starboard side where the planes were coming in. In the narrow passageway connecting the two wings of the bridge I met this great big gunner who should have been at his gun but instead he was moving away in fright. When those Stukas came in they could certainly frighten you. So after that whenever we had an air attack I would station myself right behind the gunner and coach him because he was not a good gunner. He was a machinist's mate and was there at this station because the ship didn't have the ratings which an ordinary ship had—a ship that was equipped to fight antiaircraft battles. In a very limited way it was a command ship.

On the *Biscayne* Admiral Conolly was on watch twelve hours a day, from seven in the morning until seven at night. I then took over for the night shift—from seven in the evening until seven in the morning. On the particular day of my injury I had got up after watch, shaved and showered, and eaten a meal. Then I immediately went up to topside to read the dispatches because that was the thing I wanted to do—to learn what had happened while I was asleep. I went into the chartroom and was reading the dispatches when the general alarm sounded.

On the far side of the low hills that surrounded the Salerno plain there were a number of enemy air bases which our planes had bombed and rebombed but the Germans were still operating planes out of them. They would fly very close to the ground until they'd get to these hills and then they'd come up and over and bomb and strafe our ships. We had a minute or minute and a half to actually start shooting at them when they attacked.

On this day when the general alarm sounded off I rushed out to get

330

behind the gunner. I was just going through the door of the charthouse to my station when zowie—I got hit in the left leg and cried out, "I'm hit." They laid me down on the deck, then got a hospital corpsman and took me back aft because some other people had also been hit. The doctor came along with his great big needle and I said, "Don't put that in me. I want to know what's happening." The next thing they did was to put me on Admiral Hewitt's flag ship to receive attention, but the staff on the *Ancon* decided they couldn't handle me because my leg bone was somewhat shattered so they put me aboard the *St. Andrew,* a British hospital ship.

There I learned that two nights before the Germans had come over and bombed a British hospital ship. They had two there, manned by the merchant marine. On that night the Germans bombed one of the two ships, all outlined in lights with a big red cross on the top. It was no mistake. The bomb had gone down into the doctors' quarters and about a dozen doctors were killed.

Sometime after I had been settled on the *St. Andrew* one of the nurses came in and she was hysterical. "The master will not turn out the lights on the ship." It was beginning to get dark. Now when I had come aboard they had told me that I was the senior patient on board. So I said to the nurse, "As the senior patient on board, will you ask the master of the ship to please come down to see me?" So he came down and I said to him: "Sir, you are playing war according to the rules but the Germans play without any rules. You have seen what happened to the other hospital ship, the *St. Albans.* You should turn off your lights." But he said he would show me he had an order not to turn out his lights and I replied: "I've been in the navy about twenty-five years and I believe in obeying orders also. But there are times, if you're really bright, when you don't obey orders literally. You carry out their intent. The intent is to save you from being attacked in error. The Germans have shown they are not attacking a hospital ship in error. They are attacking intentionally and they'll be back here." There had been an air raid two or three hours before and that had been established as a pattern they seemed to be following. So I said further to the master: "They will have gone back and will load up their bombs and then they will come back. This time your lights will be on and you'll be bombed. I've been wounded but I have no desire to die. I just think you ought to go up and turn out those lights."

But no, he wouldn't do that. When he left I told the sad news to the nurse who had come back to me and I said to her, "Can you get me the senior doctor on board?" He had already been in to see me once but he came back. I told him what I had done and suggested that he go up to the master of the ship and argue the matter with him and then ask him to come down here again and tell him that you and I will talk to him. And the doctor was happy to carry out the plan.

The master came back down shortly. He was a Scotchman and very determined. I kept looking at my watch and figuring what time the German planes would be back again. They were very regular.

"What will it merit you," I said, "if you die defending what in effect is a foolish order at this moment, not a foolish order in general but a foolish order at this minute, because the other fellow isn't playing according to the rules? If your enemy is playing according to the rules you obey your order, but if he isn't, you use your common sense. Keep your lights on until you're clear of the task group that's scattered around. Then turn out your lights."

The next thing I heard the ship was under way. Still the lights were not out. I could see the glow on the water. But after he got out there he turned out his lights and we were not bombed.

The hospital ship took me to Bizerte and there they put me in an army field hospital where they set my leg for the first time. One day not long after in walked Admiral Conolly. "I'm flying back to the States either late this afternoon or tomorrow," and I said, "How about taking me with you?" and he sent a dispatch to Admiral Hewitt asking authority. Then it was New York and and finally the Naval Hospital in Bethesda.

All told I spent four months and thirteen days in the hospital for my leg bone was somewhat shattered. And then I got orders to sea in the *Astoria* for duty in the Pacific—the fulfillment of my desires.

In preceding prefaces to the several landings in North Africa, Sicily, and Salerno, there have been background summaries of the political and military discussions that took place before the events. Most of them were acrimonious to some degree and always there was a proviso that stood in the way of a definite decision on the capstone of all—the massive invasion of Northern France to strike at the heart of Nazi Germany. Churchill was often accused of blocking the way to that ultimate decision. Yet if one can believe the various references to his mind-set he was sound in his conviction that the Allies must undertake such an action, *but only* when they had sufficient men, armament, and landing craft to bring about a victory. One can guess that the disastrous British / Canadian raid on Dieppe in August 1942 had taught the British to be cautious about an assault on the Continent without overwhelming strength. Certainly the several Allied offensives in the Mediterranean that were carried out drained Nazi resources and men and at the same time gave the Allied forces experience in conducting amphibious operations. Admiral King and General Marshall, on the other hand, always argued for a massive frontal attack on the continent of Europe and sometimes without too great regard for the forces to back them up. In lieu of that major assault they proposed a token invasion in France through the Cotentin Peninsula, an operation called Sledgehammer. In this they were strongly driven by the repeated demands of Marshal Stalin for a second front to lessen his problems on the eastern front. This operation was finally abandoned.

There was another delay in the Allied plans for the grand assault on France. That was in the hands of President Roosevelt. At the Quebec Conference in August 1943 both the president and the prime minister, with the backing of their military advisers, decided that the main Allied effort in 1944 should be Overlord (the name for the invasion of France) and that the target date of 1 May should be confirmed. The supreme commander for this operation was to be an American and his selection would be made by President Roosevelt. The logical choice lay between General Marshall and General Eisenhower. Unfortunately, American political considerations got involved, the press was vocal, and a delay resulted.

This greatly hampered the planning for Overlord. It had been under way under the able direction of Lieutenant General Frederick Morgan, who had been named in March 1943 as chief of staff to the supreme allied commander yet to be named. Decisions had to be made on the size of the armies required for this great invasion, the proper time and place for training, what planes and landing craft would be required and how many, what would be expected of American factories. It was necessary, American planners knew, to have target dates. Factories had to retool in many instances; flotillas of beaching craft and planes had to be shifted from the Pacific in some cases to the Atlantic scene. It seemed to boil down to a somewhat rigid schedule on the part of the Americans versus a more flexible one on the part of the British.

Finally things began to jell. On 30 November General Sir Alan Brooke announced that the combined chiefs of staff had agreed to launch Overlord in May 1944 and to mount a supporting operation against the south of France. Churchill and Roosevelt were meeting with Stalin in Teheran that December, and Stalin provoked a decision on the naming of a supreme commander. He asked the president about the delay in naming one and was told that it had not been decided. To this he responded: "Then nothing will come out of these operations." Apparently this goaded the president to action for on 3 December he announced the appointment of General Eisenhower while the combined chiefs of staff published a short time later their directive to the supreme commander:

> You will enter the Continent of Europe and in conjunction with the other
> United Nations, undertake operations aimed at the heart of Germany
> and the destruction of her armed forces.

The Allied naval, army, and air commanders had already been designated. Admiral Sir Bertram H. Ramsay was the Allied naval commander, Expeditionary Force, while General Sir Bernard Montgomery of North African fame was in command of the ground forces, and Air Chief Marshal Sir Trafford Leigh-Mallory was the air commander. Rear Admiral Alan G. Kirk was commander, Western Naval Task Force, the key American naval figure in Overlord. He had been the U.S. naval attaché in London at the outbreak of war in Europe, was chief of staff to Admiral Stark in London in 1941 and quite conversant with British ways, problems, and personalities. He was also quite familiar with amphibious operations: he had been commander, amphibious forces Atlantic Fleet, and had been a part of the amphibious operation against Sicily. The other senior American naval officers were Rear Admiral Don P. Moon in charge of TF 125 Assault Force U (for Utah) Beach, and Rear Admiral John L. Hall, in command of TF 124 Assault Force O (for Omaha) Beach.

Both Kirk's and Hall's accounts of the landings follow. As naval com-

334

manders they were responsible for the landing of the troops and had command of them until they were deposited on the beaches and their military commanders had taken charge. The U.S. Air Forces and the Royal Air Force constituted a different matter. In both the Mediterranean operation and the Normandy landings the two air forces operated under their own commands and were not beholden to the naval commanders. This is brought out clearly by Admiral Hall, who felt strongly that a closer alliance was needed. The almost total lack of cooperation by the U.S. Air Forces in Sicily was a matter of grave concern to the naval and army commanders.

Many preliminary operations were engaged in before the main landings on the Normandy beaches. The RAF was most useful in obtaining photographs of the landing beaches, enemy gun emplacements, and troop concentrations. They had been engaged in this for almost a year before D day. The U.S. Scouts and Raiders contributed much to the knowledge of German beach fortifications and exotic obstacles on the beaches of Normandy; they took samples of sand depths to help prepare for the use of tanks and LSTs on D day. They in fact engaged in intelligence of value in several areas before the actual assault landings. Their tasks were dangerous and heroic. Captain Phil Bucklew's reports on Normandy (and Sicily and Salerno) as they appear in this volume are interesting adjuncts to amphibious operations.

Admiral Kirk gives us an account of the differences in practice in the Royal Navy and the U.S. Navy in the matter of advance planning. The British method, as exemplified by Admiral Ramsay, the overall naval commander for the landing operations, was to prepare a detailed operational order of some 1,100 printed pages, vastly specific and issued in advance to the officer personnel. Admiral Kirk tells us that he and other American officers found this somewhat confusing for their training had been quite different. They were accustomed to issuing broad directives to the lower echelons of command who then in practice were encouraged to work out their own details. "Our greatest asset," Kirk maintained, "was the resourcefulness of the American sailor." Kirk described the British method of their operational plans as something of a set piece, like a fireworks display. It was somewhat rigid, not subject to change except in extreme emergency. The American, on the other hand, had been trained in operational orders to be told what he was supposed to do—and then commanded to go ahead and do it. In this, imagination and resourcefulness often proved their value.

One of the most difficult problems confronting both navy and army for the Normandy assault was the timing, now pushed back from May to June. It required the careful selection of D day and H hour. A daylight landing was desirable—long experience told us that. Yet, since the channel is narrow and surprise was an element, it was thought the initial landings should be made during darkness—but how, when in that latitude the problem was to get enough darkness. It began to grow light at 0300 and by 0430 day had broken. But perhaps the most unusual factor was the tide. On that coast the average range is eighteen feet and the maximum is twenty-five feet. The army wanted the landings at an hour close to high water; the navy wanted a low-water landing so that their landing craft could ground outside the beach obstacles and land men to clear them before the tide rose. High water would lessen the time for the army to land troops and give the time required for troops to cross the exposed beaches. The army wanted a second high tide on D day to land the follow-up forces. And the aviators—they wanted a full moon for their initial endeavors.

"O what is so rare as a day in June" once sang the poet James Russell Lowell, "then if ever come perfect days." The weatherman told General Eisenhower, who had the burden of decision, that in that June at least there were only two groups of three days each that would fulfill all the desired conditions, and if they waited for the rare and perfect day the operation might never come off.

Since the weather was the first factor of importance, General Eisenhower was most alert to that fact. From the first of June on he met twice daily with his task force commanders and others in London to hear the latest weather forecasts. These were provided by a group captain of the RAF who headed a meteorological committee that gathered all the weather data available from all parts of the United Kingdom. By the third of June the forecasts began to be alarming. Westerly type weather of a cyclonic nature over Greenland and the Azores was moving across the Atlantic to the British Isles. On the fourth the prospect appeared completely hopeless. A low ceiling was certain for the fifth and this would prevent the air forces from getting into action. Furthermore the heavy seas forecast would swamp the landing craft. Certainly the Channel would be too rough for small ships.

Because of their distant location in various parts of the island, some of the assault vessels had to begin moving to their destination off Normandy at least six days before D day in order to meet accurate timing. Every available berth for shipping was filled in every port from Felixstowe on the North Sea to Milford Haven in Wales. Others were moored in rivers like the Clyde and the Humber, and at Belfast. The exact number of the ships involved is difficult to state. It depended on what was counted. The Admiralty reported that 931 ships sailed for the Western Naval Task Force and 1,796 for the Eastern Naval Task Force. That number included everything that crossed the Channel on its own bottom. Then there were the landing barges and the landing craft carried on ships. This brings the

336

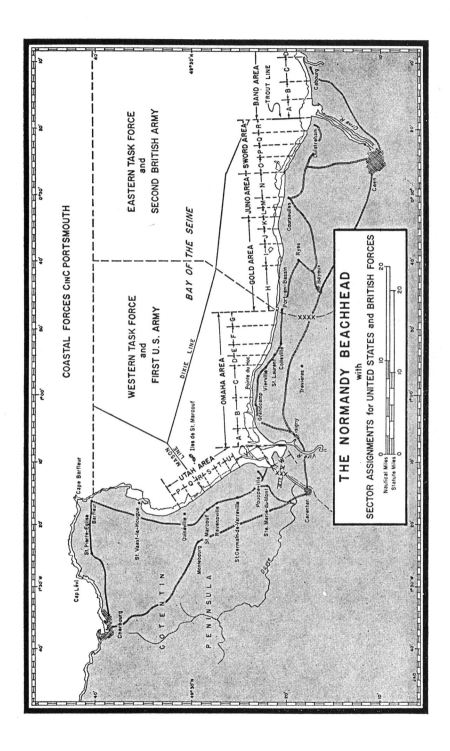

THE NORMANDY BEACHHEAD
with
SECTOR ASSIGNMENTS for UNITED STATES and BRITISH FORCES

337

totals to 2,010 for the Western Task Force and 3,323 for the Eastern Task Force.

Of course the planners had devised a contingency plan in case of bad weather. This was put into operation immediately on the evening of 4 June. It entailed most of the ships returning to their berths, and where distances were great, those vessels had to engage in stalling or other means of impeding their progress towards the destination. Hence matters of refueling, sailing speeds, and so on became major concerns. Finally at 0415 on 5 June General Eisenhower made the decision to resume the assault operations: "O.K. We'll go!" and Admiral Ramsay issued a special Order of the Day to every officer and enlisted man of the two navies:

> "It is our privilege to take part in the greatest amphibious operation in history. The hopes and prayers of the free world and of the enslaved people of Europe will be with us and we cannot fail them. I count on every man to do his utmost to ensure the success of this great enterprise which is the climax of the European War. Good luck to you all and God Speed."

Any account of the naval efforts at Normandy would be remiss without mention of Mulberry. It was brought to the attention of General Morgan and his planners in July 1943. A major problem for them as planners had been how to provide the assault forces with ammunition, supplies, and reinforcements over the beaches once a beachhead had been established. It was known of course that Cherbourg Harbor was the nearest and the most suitable, but it was strongly defended by the Germans, and as it turned out, heavily mined. It was known too that fair weather seldom lasted more than a few days at a time in the Channel. A prolonged landing operation could not succeed without fair weather. The only answer was to provide areas of sheltered water off the beaches. British brains and energy supplied that answer.

Impetus was given to the implementation of Mulberry by army members of Morgan's planning group for they insisted that Overlord could not be launched unless the army was assured of the use of a major port within a few days after landing. Cherbourg was indeed that port but Admiral Sullivan, the salvage master for the U.S. Navy in World War II, tells us in his oral history interviews that clearing of the port was tedious and quite prolonged. The Germans, in departing, had wrecked all port installations, sunk a number of ships in the harbor, and mined it extensively. General Eisenhower made a special trip to check on the harbor clearance. It was of the utmost importance to him.

In the final form, we are told, two artificial harbors were produced and built by British labor. They were designated as Mulberry A for the American beaches and Mulberry B for the British sector. Any ship ap-

338

Within the shelter made by the floating breakwaters—the sunken block ships and concrete phoenix units—these pierheads for Mulberry A were designed to ride up and down with the tide. From the pierheads a bridgelike causeway, floating on reinforced concrete pontoons, was created to make a roadway to the American beaches at Normandy. Photograph of a watercolor by Lieutenant Dwight Shepler, U.S. Navy combat artist. (National Archives)

proaching a Mulberry would first meet a floating breakwater composed of "bombardons," floating steel structures to break up wave action. Next came the breakwater, 2,200 yards long and composed of thirty-one concrete caissons called "phoenixes," each as tall as a five-story house, to be towed across the Channel and sunk in place. The phoenixes formed a seawall on two sides of an artificial harbor about two square miles in area, equal to that of the harbor at Gibraltar and big enough for seven Liberty ships and twelve smaller vessels to moor. Within each harbor were three pontoon-section runways anchored on their seaward ends to the pierheads and designed to rise and fall with the tide. This combination was to enable LSTs to unload at any stage of the tide and provide their wheeled cargoes with a one-way road for rolling ashore.

Then, in addition to the ingenious Mulberries there were the Gooseberries. Old ships in a line were sunk parallel to the shore in about three fathoms of water. They were intended to provide sheltered water for landing and for other craft at the beachhead. Each of the two American

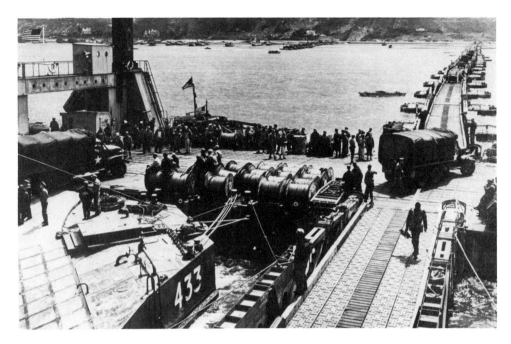

Trucks roll off LSTs on the runway toward the American beaches at Normandy in the artifical harbor called Mulberry A. (National Archives)

beaches and all three of the British beaches were provided with a Gooseberry. More than seventy ships were sunk in setting up the Gooseberries. About 132 tug boats were collected from British and American sources and were used in towing the Mulberries to the Normandy shore. Captain E. J. Moran, USNR, was in command of this vast tugboat fleet. He was the owner of a well-known tugboat company in New York City. He shepherded a convoy of tugboats and ferryboats across the Atlantic before D day. Many of them were used in the Gooseberry project.

Many references have been made to the effectiveness of these British inventions for use on the Normandy beaches. Some are full of praise but others are quite critical, including Admiral Hall, in command of the Omaha beach landings, in the excerpts from his oral history interviews that follow. His remarks are based on his experience at Omaha Beach during the great storm of 19–22 June, the worst storm reported in forty years of Channel history. The Mulberry A installed on Omaha Beach disintegrated at that time and no attempt was made to repair it. Mulberry B suffered far less damage than A because it was protected somewhat by outlying rocks. Most of the breakwaters of sunken ships at both Omaha and Utah held firm and so protected several hundred landing craft from destruction.

By the nature of things, in every amphibious operation, the navy carries the first burden. It is the landing from the sea of the ships loaded with men, protected overhead by planes and the guns of the warships off shore. So it was with Normandy but the amphibious landing was on a bigger scale than ever before. By the end of May the United States alone had gathered over one and a half million troops in the United Kingdom. Britain had a commensurate number. The navies employed almost three thousand ships in those initial landings. It was the stated task of the two navies with some assistance from Allied navies in exile. There you have a rough picture of things on that D day in June 1944.

Once ashore, the next step was immediately with the men—marines, army, or both. It was to consolidate their positions on the beaches and form a continuous front, preparatory to moving on under the direction of their own military commanders. The function of the navy had changed. Now it was to shepherd adequate supplies, the food and guns and other essentials. The need was constant as long as military action continued on land. Admiral Kirk summarized the transition when he said in an interview: "Maybe I didn't do any good in terms of knocking out the enemy, but after all Cherbourg was captured the next day by Joe Collins's army and I went up to London to report to Admiral Stark and then returned to the U.S. My job was done."

PREPARING FOR THE BIG PUSH AT NORMANDY

CAPTAIN PHIL H. BUCKLEW*

We came in then to Falmouth. We had a naval base there, right on the tip. Andreason [Lieutenant Andreason, a beach jumper who had worked out of Oran in the Arzeu area of North Africa in that campaign] and I, as soon as we arrived, reported to the admiral. He said that he understood we two were about the most experienced men they had in reconnaissance. "You will be joining the British for reconnaissance on the French coast." This was early in December 1943. Then he said: "Now I don't know much about reconnaissance but I imagine the first thing that you should do, since we have a command room here, you ought to spend a day there going through the plans we have." Well, we knew better than that. These were the plans for Normandy—Overlord, as they existed at that point. Reconnaissance people very seldom get complete information on anything. If they are captured the less they know the better. There are certain specifics that you are looking for in certain areas, and normally the charts that you use on reconnaissance of a naval type wouldn't even have markings of longitude and latitude. Others would guide you in part to where you are going and you work it from there in order not to reveal, if you are under pressure, any unnecessary information. Andreason and I knew that, but through interest and boredom we spent, fortunately, only one day. We did go through the Overlord plans and got the general drift and retained quite a bit of it. This was fine. Next, the admiral said: "You need a little leave. Why don't you take a few days off, go to London." We did that.

Soon after, higher command planned the preparation of a landing zone

*For biographical information on Bucklew, see pp. 264–266.

342

for the training of American troops. I think Colonel Thompson, an army training type, was to be in charge. They wanted an area similar to the northern French coast and there Thompson trained his troops under live fire. He had some trouble with it because in pulling a lot of people up from North Africa, from Sicily and Salerno, who had been living under live fire—they did not think that was the way to train. You do that on game day only.

Andreason and I were sent to do beach reconnaissance for this training area to determine if it was suitable for landing craft, etc. Slapton Sands was the name of the place. It is on the British east coast north of Falmouth. We stayed in a little hotel and got ourselves a boat and went out and checked gradients, talked with fishermen regarding tides, currents, obstacles, and developed a basic report without much hardship.

One day we got an urgent call to get back to Falmouth. It seems the area we were working was all mined and they had just found that out. Communications would often come a little late on such things but since we did not know of it, we did not have any problem.

We were still under the command at Falmouth but we were separate, we were different, we were reconnaissance types and did not do routine duties. When they needed us we were on call. We were not overworked but they kept us fairly busy with things they were setting up.

Then we were called up to London. By that time Admiral Kirk had set up the London command, the naval component of it. General Eisenhower and the various joint commands were already settled there. There we met the captain we were under following our original volunteering for "special duty." He was Captain Ted Wellings, at that time the operations officer on the staff of Admiral Kirk. Andreason and I were to be assigned for reconnaissance of Normandy, operating with the British from the Isle of Wight.

But in some manner the British learned that we had seen the Overlord plan for Normandy and said they could not use us for "We can't consider people who have been exposed to such knowledge." I believe they learned through the admiral at Falmouth who casually and innocently commented on the fact. Andreason and I were probably the only ones from the U.S. naval staff who knew reconnaissance enough to know that you do not do what we did in looking at the plans—but we were also the only U.S. Navy people with experience that were available at that time, so a compromise was made with the British to include us but first we would have to go to their Escape and Evasion School. We did that. They put us in a school which was conducted in a castle near London and we were isolated throughout our time there. Most of the students were going to be air-dropped in France. We were required to eat with knife and fork, European style. (Eating was considered the most revealing of American customs.)

Every instructor in the school was an escapee from the mainland. They had actually done it. Some of their tricks and gimmicks were unique.

Our classes were conducted in English. In the bar they served drinks freely but you never spoke English. They worked us, Andreason and I, over well because American pilots had a bad reputation for some of the things they had inadvertently done by speaking too freely: coming into an area in France and asking "How do I get in touch with the underground?" and that sort of thing. In any event, we completed the course and they accepted us for the coastal reconnaissance work. The course lasted about two weeks. We had a lot of briefings and debriefings. As an afterthought, I feel they overloaded us with a lot of inconsequential things to confuse us. If so, it was done very tactfully. I think they very discreetly brain-washed us, knowing that in the limited time we had with the plans for Overlord we did not know very much. Later as my part in the Normandy operation developed I knew a lot more.

We reported to the Isle of Wight. It was another pleasant experience, the same as I had previously on Malta with the British. They do a lot of singing and they have a pretty good bar in their mess.

Prince Philip was there with us on the Isle of Wight. He was under the name of Lieutenant Phillips and was a good naval officer. He was one of the boys. I do not know really what activity he had but we had a lot of fun in the mess and in the wardroom. He was really a good fellow as long as somebody did not slip up and call him Prince, for then he would leave the room immediately. If he was just Phillips or Lieutenant he was one of the boys.

There we were learning the British type of reconnaissance. For the coast of Normandy they had outfitted small landing craft, a closed bow type, with electronic instruments. There was no identification as to where you went. You were brought in on poles electronically, in a small boat. They towed you to a reasonable distance from the Normandy coast, ten or twenty miles from the coast. Then you were released from the British-type PT (which is called an MTB) and you were on your own, without knowledge and without any markings on your chart.

The purpose of our reconnaissance was to obtain sand samples from the Normandy beaches, which were (as it later developed but I did not know at the time and wondered about it) passed to the laboratory. The texture of the sand told them what kind of matting to put down to take the weight of tanks and heavy equipment. It was like racks of test tubes really. We took soundings of different depths coming on in. The tide is rather extreme there and we were at the point of low tide. The way you do it on depth is to use a sounding lead with the bottom hollowed out and filled with tallow so that when it hits the bottom (and you have to have the lead to get it down there) it picks up the sand. I imagine the greatest depth must have been fifteen feet at low level tide. This was accomplished, how successfully and what they got out of it you do not know. They had other boats at different times doing the same thing.

Our equipment on the beach looked like a rack of test tubes, a specially built rack, some with the sounding leads, most all of them with tallow. They were set up in a prearranged fashion—one to use at one depth and the next at another as you worked your way in to and from the beach. On the beach itself we had to come back with a bucket of sand.

On one occasion I was in the boat with two British Navy men and an enlisted man operating. We were doing very well when all of a sudden everything cut loose—flares from the beach, etc. Of course you never know what has been discovered, whether you are discovered or something out to seaward. The rocket flares in this case told us it was time to get out. Fortunately there was some offshore fog but we didn't have the faintest idea where our MTB was. We were working our way out slowly and were outside the coastal range and the flares when we ran right into a German coastal convoy. That convoy was running parallel to the coastline—about a six-ship convoy. The only thing to do was to cut our engines and lie dead in the water. The convoy passed right alongside us and went on. It was kind of scary. In another half hour we ran into our MTB and were towed back to the Isle of Wight. As the Britishers put it, "a jolly good evening."

The sand operations were in January or February, I do not recall, but it was about six months before the actual landings. I do know where we were because I was there again on D day. The Vierville church steeple was in the background and we were targeted on that steeple. It was a visual target though we did not know what it was. On D day it happened that it was my beach again, an American beach completely, Omaha Red Beach, and I remembered that steeple before the dawn and knew where it was.

Of course, during the intervening time between our sand operations and D day the Germans had added many beach obstacles. For them, an invasion was coming but the major question was, just where? They probably expected the attack closer to the Brest harbor area.

The beach defense preparations were a very interesting thing and very thorough—the obstacles and the pillboxes. Frankly, had the Germans had their full manpower strength that we bumped into elsewhere I think it is very questionable whether we could have made it in spite of our back-up strength. The beach obstacles were topped with Teller mines and we had a very difficult time getting in. We had to blow the gaps. Even on D day the UDTs took a full day to clear a single gap and we lost a lot of personnel; nearly 40 percent of UDTs were casualties. As illustration, I was sent ashore, probably D day plus seven or eight. Admiral Jimmy Hall had the actual assault command at Omaha Beach. His flagship was the *Ancon*. I was to accompany a German sergeant, a prisoner of war, who had offered to take us through the mine fields and identify the live and dummy fields. He explained to us that General Rommel had planned the defense and personally inspected it.

The German spoke some English but we had an interpreter. Rommel had made complete personal inspections of these mine fields and he would threaten to withdraw if certain areas weren't mined. If it wasn't done his way, he wouldn't play. So there were innumerable dummy mine fields, all with barbed wire and big signs with skull and crossbones and "Auf dem minem." My job was to go ashore with this sergeant who had told this story. He would go "stomp, stomp, stomp" right through all these mine fields and believe me I was going behind him trying to step in every foot step that he made. He often said, "dud field," but how did I know it was a dud field? I felt, what does he have to lose? The purpose was to mark the fields on the chart. This could clear and expedite an awful lot of things. The troops had to move through these areas. Of course they were bogged down in the beginning until you got exits cleared. It took the first full day of D day before you could get exits blown in beach obstacles, get landing ships in and then when they started to move you had mines everywhere which didn't mean that you had free wheeling through them. The army procedure was, of course, once they start they have tape going behind them like gauze and that's the path to follow. If they get through or it's blown, they zigzag, but where the tapes go, troops have moved.

Another illustration: Andreason and I were together on the *Ancon* after we were assigned to Admiral Hall. One time they called me to the admiral's cabin and I thought, "Oh, what did I do now?" and there was Commodore Sullivan. "We've got a problem; we'd like to send you in to see what you can find. We need safe havens for our flat-bottom craft. We are going to be hit by weather—we're pretty certain of it—and we want to find out if there are any rivers or streams that are large enough so that we could pull in landing craft of LST size to protect them against the weather. How much water is there in a given stream? Can you turn the ship around? Would you get stranded?" We had to look for these things in the area.

We had a very interesting experience during that one. We came to a German pillbox holding twelve Germans and they surrendered to us. We were on foot and going out on a dike-like structure and thought it had been cleared; our troops had moved on, but they had obviously bypassed this pillbox and these Germans came pouring out with their hands up. There were two of us—what were we going to do? There was no problem; we just steered them down and turned them over to some MPs. They were half drunk, really. They had some wine and had drunk the last of it and just surrendered without a shot being fired.

I had one disappointment that day. We went into the pillbox and we were cautious about it as it could have been booby-trapped. Here was a huge silk Nazi flag. It must have been ten feet by ten feet, beautiful silk, red with black swastika. We had work to do so we stuffed it away. I wanted to give it to Admiral Hall but when we came back that night it was gone. Somebody else had come across it.

We never went back to doing any special reconnaissance of the several different beaches, similar to what we had done before the invasion. Major amphibious type of intelligence was taken over by the air force—American or British or a combined operation. They developed a technique which was the first time it had been employed in determining gradients and the like. The procedure is to make a run on the beach on the hour and then the overlay of the photography will tell you as much about the beach and a lot more than you can discover by physical reconnaissance. It was a quiet spell for the coast as the main build-up occurred and the troop levels were increased.

COMMAND FROM THE FLAGSHIP *AUGUSTA*

ADMIRAL ALAN G. KIRK*

We got back to Hampton Roads Air Base and then it became a question of organizing staff for Normandy and getting away. I made some radical changes in my former staff, the ones who had gone with me to Sicily. I took Dick Craig as flag secretary, McGeorge Bundy—a first lieutenant in the army—as my army aide. I got as my chief of staff Arthur D. Struble, a most important post in an operation of that scale, and a finer man one couldn't have chosen. The Navy Department was very helpful in allowing him to go because he was a pretty important man to them. They realized this was going to be quite an affair. I wanted this man and they gave him to me.

I had a large voice in the overall planning for the invasion of France. I say that with some slight hesitation because I had seen the plans in Washington, the broad plans as mapped out, but when I got to London I found that the planning was done on quite a different basis. The plans had been agreed to in Quebec by the politicos, where it was to be, in the Bay of the Seine. I knew that, but everybody was aware of the fact that it was going to be a very tremendous and difficult operation and it would have certain hazards that could only be dimly foreseen.

It should be stated that while General Eisenhower and General Bedell Smith were in London in 1942 there had been considerable pressure for an early invasion of the Continent. That was the point of view in Washington of President Roosevelt and General Marshall. It had to be looked at most carefully with a very hard and cold eye to make sure we weren't going to make ourselves into a mess.

*For biographical information on Kirk, see pp. 310–311.

The British made a small landing at Dieppe in the summer of 1942, where they learned a good deal about what not to do and how strong the German defenses were and what accidental hazards would arise to upset a well-laid-out plan, such as the unexpected appearance of a tug with a lot of tows right through the landing area in the early dawn hours—which gave away the show.

The operation that was urged by Washington on the British—on Mr. Churchill and the British chiefs of staff—contemplated the seizing of the port of Cherbourg. That would involve a serious effort in great strength to capture the port in 1942 and hold it. The plan really fell down because it was soon obvious that nobody's fighter planes at that time could make the flight from bases on the south shore of England, get over Cherbourg, and remain there longer than twenty minutes. That was not long enough to insure command of the air over the fortress. And of course in 1942 the bombardment of England was still taking place, German bombers escorted by German fighters. So that was the basic reason that wasn't pushed through, plus the fact there were not enough landing craft. The LST (Landing Ship Tank) had not been really developed and all the other kinds of landing craft we had in 1944. We had a few in 1943 in Sicily but they weren't ready. We weren't ready. It was very reluctantly that the idea was given up but it would have been abortive. It would have been a disaster. If captured, the fortress of Cherbourg would have been very hard to hold, so the plan was given up in spite of the pressures from Washington.

So I got my Normandy staff together, turned over command of the Amphibious Force, Atlantic Fleet, and took off for Europe. We landed at Prestwick and proceeded down to London. I had an early meeting with Admiral Stark.

You must remember this was early November 1943. Things were uncertain at that time. On the eastern front things had gone quite badly for the Germans. Our work in Sicily had begun to be effective, followed as it was by advances into Italy. For a period there it looked as though the Germans might withdraw from France back into Germany, throw the weight of their forces over to the eastern front to give a final knockout blow to the Russians. The American forces would then have to make a quick entry into France, regain control of France. All this was based on the fact that should the Germans make this big retreat out of France to the eastern front a peace would be signed whereby the Germans would relinquish France but hold control of their own territory in the west of Germany with strong forces in the east. It seemed the Russians would be compelled then to make peace, for the Soviet armies could not have withstood the full might of Germany since we, the Western Allies, were expected to make a separate peace with Germany. That idea was taking a little bit of the juice, the zip, out of the planning for the Normandy invasion because you had to play two hands at one time: what we would do if we really did have to go into the valley of the Seine and Paris, and on the other hand, if the Germans concentrated on the eastern front.

At the same time I was given to understand that the naval planners in Norfolk House had become something of an irritation to Admiral Stark. It was expected that my staff would supersede and displace these other naval officers who were in Norfolk House with Admiral Ramsey. So I realized there was sort of a troubled atmosphere and I would have to play my hand carefully with cards close to the chest. We had a slight arm's length position vis-à-vis Admiral Stark, who perhaps quite reasonably felt that he was the person who should command the American side of the invasion and not somebody else who had just come up from a lower echelon. Then we had this friction between the planners in Norfolk House and Admiral Stark's chief of staff. We had also to play this double hand—the operation to assume control of France and yet at the same time to go ahead with the long-range planning for Normandy. There were always little things— there were some undercurrents running around. I was surprised. I suppose that's what happens in big war commands just as I suppose it happens in business, in big organizations; apparently people looking for advancement and getting more power to themselves. Frankly, I was really upset and annoyed that this kind of undercurrent feeling should be allowed. I was surprised that Admiral Stark had allowed it to exist.

Then we had to make contact with Admiral Ramsey. Here is where I was really a little less than diplomatic, shall we say, because recalling our very friendly relationships in terms of golf games the year before, I suggested, couldn't we have lunch—which he declined. He didn't think he could lunch with me now. Then I thought to myself, I made a mistake. I really should have gone over formally and reported to him as the American naval commander under his exequatur, which was the Allied Naval Commander of the Expeditionary Force for the Invasion of Europe. So with good grace I accepted his excuse for not being able to lunch and hightailed over to see him right away.

At that stage it was not contemplated that the American navy should do very much in the invasion of Normandy. The plan called for three British landings on the west of the Seine River—actually the Orne that flows into the sea at Quistran. Then we would have just one landing, what later became Omaha Beach. In other words, the right flank of the whole attack would rest on the river that flows through Carenton to the sea at that point, with the bluff that later became so famous, Point du Hoe. I was expected by Ramsey and the chief of staff, George Creesey, to be advisor on this staff for American naval operations and that the actual task group of Americans that landed was to be under Admiral Ramsey completely.

350

That wasn't to my taste and I was certain that we would have to do more than land on one beach. I was sure that the American side would insist on fuller participation and eventually the U.S. Navy would have to send a good many more forces than they had originally outlined for it.

I think the British felt: after all it was from England, it was control of the British Channel, which they had lost control of when the *Scharnhorst* and *Gneisenau* went up the Channel (spring of 1942). Their amour propre was at stake, in a sense, and they just said they were going to run it. Then I went down to see Admiral Cunningham who had come back from Washington where he had been the British representative on the Joint Chiefs of Staff, Navy. He was an old friend of mine. He was very cheerful, very nice, very kind and said: "Of course you'll be with Admiral Ramsey in a big bomb shelter on the south coast of England." I said: "Oh, no, I don't expect to be there at all. I expect to be on my flagship off the coast of Normandy." This was perhaps a little pert on my part because at that time there was only one beach assigned to the U.S. forces. He smiled indulgently and let it go at that. Actually, of course, it turned out that I insisted and presented the case.

Bradley was there. He had been with me on my flagship at the landing in Sicily, an old friend. On his staff were people, some of whom I had known in the Sicily area. Right away I called him Brad and he called me Alan. My staff and his staff appreciated what was a very friendly understanding between the two top guys. That seeped down awful fast so there was no nonsense between the sailors and the soldiers about who was going to do what and this and that. It was strictly business with no backbiting and carping about this and that.

The naval contingents assigned to this operation in Europe were only sparsely seeded with regular navy. Almost all the sailor boys were almost invariably naval reserve laddies who had come from Iowa, Kansas, and so on. Those were the boys who when they were told to put their boats on the beach *put* them on the beach, whereas those retired chief bos'n's mates of long standing and chief quartermasters would not do it. They'd always inch up and then they would never put the ramp down on the land. They would put it down in the water and make the army wade through up to their necks. So I must say, I have a high feeling of regard for the willingness with which these newly trained young men (and they were awful young, you know, gosh, twenty, twenty-two, twenty-three) accepted this as doctrine and they carried it out.

Then I went visiting the various places where some of the amphibious operations were being conducted—down in Devon, in Dorset—to the few bases we had down there. It was still to be one American front. Eisenhower had not yet been nominated as supreme commander. Stalin had always complained, as we knew, and as the world learned later, that he never would agree that we British and Americans were serious about an invasion of western Europe because we never named a supreme commander.

When I left Washington to come back to England to take my part in the invasion, I first called on General Marshall, who at that time was very secretly, very sub rosa, expected to be the Allied supreme commander. I realized in talking with him that I wasn't getting what you might call as close concentrated attention as I thought I was going to get. Of course he knew even then that he wasn't going, that the president would not allow him to go, but we had to go through with this little act, this show, pretending that I was going to be the naval commander and he was going to be the supreme commander. We let it go at that. Then before Christmas Montgomery was nominated to be the principal military commander. We had Allied Naval Commander, Allied Military Commander, Allied Air Force Command and yet to be named, Supreme Commander, who turned out in due course to be Eisenhower. Montgomery came back to England from the Mediterranean. He examined this plan with the same kind of care he'd examined the plan for Sicily and he saw that it was not going to be satisfactory. He had caused the plans for Sicily to be adjusted, so he now said: "This is not strong enough. We haven't got enough troops, weight of metal, and weight of armor. The port of Cherbourg is vital to the further support of the American armies in France and to some extent of the British armies too. The port of Cherbourg has got to be captured as quickly as possible." To do that it was necessary to make a further landing to the westward in the Bay of the Seine, to cross the Cherbourg Peninsula at its base and cut off the Germans north of the line and resist reinforcements coming from the south of that line, and then proceed to assault and take Cherbourg as quickly as possible.

That modification was forced upon the authorities; I put it that way on purpose—forced upon the authorities. Then the question came up from my angle as the American naval officer in charge of the Western Task Force of the invasion: Could we make a successful landing on the Cotentin Peninsula? the Cherbourg Peninsula? There were large sandbanks off the eastern side of that, the so-called Mercour Isles. Behind that the water was of some depth but parts of it were almost bare at low water. The question then arose, could we have a transport area to seaward of these sandbanks, and could the landing craft get across the banks? So we had to get out the charts and hassle around with that. I agreed it could be done but of course that would call for more naval forces, not only men-of-war but also LSTs and LCIs and all the various ferries and what not we were organizing for that port, as well as the artificial harbor.

Well, it was then agreed there would be a second American front. Admiral Ramsey's staff greeted that with, I'd say, less than a cheerful attitude, because they saw at once that I had been correct in my earlier insistence that I would have to be afloat off the beaches with two task groups, exercising my command over them, instead of down in a bunker on the south coast of England. It was a very logical thing to do. The more closely you examined the problem the more reasonable it seemed to be. Then of course, in Washington, it was necessary to assemble the extra troops for that: men who had some amphibious training, and some of the landing craft, and for me, the gunfire support vessels necessary for the operation.

So my staff got to work. They studied it very thoroughly. Under Admiral Struble's direction a letter was prepared to the Navy Department telling them just what, in my view, was the proper support that would be necessary to make the landing a success. It so happened that the letter was actually signed on Christmas Eve, December 24, 1943. It went off to Washington. I wrote to Dickie Edwards, on Admiral King's staff, and told him this was it; that's what we had to have and that's what we ought to have, but we were going to go anyhow on whatever the date was to be, spring or early summer. But if they didn't want to have the thing look rather dubious, they'd better assemble the ships.

You know, I never heard from that order until the end of March, two months before we sailed. Action was finally taken. But one division of DDs arrived two days before D day. We threw them into the pot all right and they did dandy. In the interim the letter had been received in Washington and I said, "By God, they know what they ought to do and let me do it." And they did, finally. True they sent Savvy Cooke over from King's staff in March to examine the whole position, especially about the number of LSTs we needed for the landing of troops. That incidentally brought in the men-of-war for gunfire support. Cooke was an old friend of mine. We discussed my request. After he got back to Washington the orders began to trickle through that these ships were coming. But one division arrived on the fourth of June for a landing that was originally intended for the fifth of June but was postponed until the sixth.

Eisenhower was appointed as supreme commander in January. I had known him in London, in Sicily, in Washington, and I knew Smith, his chief of staff. Patton came over. He was put in cotton wool out of sight because they didn't want anybody to know that he was going to be in the battle because everybody thought—all the Germans thought—he was a Sherman and a Sheridan combined in one. We wanted to keep it dark that he was there. He was also in a rather dubious position after that incident in the hospital (after Sicily) when he slapped some wounded soldier in bed and said he was a coward. Well, that was smoothed over.

My staff and I then ran into a situation that was most difficult. The whole War College system of training for our navy was carried out by

Hewitt in the Mediterranean, by me under Hewitt in the Mediterranean, by all the fleets at sea in the Pacific under Admiral Nimitz. It always gave broad directives from the top to the principal commanders, who worked out their plans and submitted them to the topside fellow for approval and then passed it downward. Each fellow then did the details with his staff. Well, the British didn't do that. All the planning was done in Norfolk House by Admiral Ramsey and his staff in the minutest detail. These orders would come to me and would have to be sent down the line. It was really quite a mental adjustment. It didn't bother the naval reserves; hell, they'd never had another system of training, but it did bother the regular navy officers, especially those who'd been trained and brought up not just in a War College doctrinaire way but had seen those things actually carried out in all the peacetime maneuvers of the fleet and also all the operations of the war until this. It was really quite a problem. My staff officers would from time to time make comments: "We could do it better this way or that way" and these were never accepted by Admiral Ramsey's staff. In fact, we got some rather tough little comments back, directed at me for allowing these younger officers in their turn to speak out against the voice of the commander in chief. It got to be a little bit touchy, a little bit awkward.

The British Admiralty has always controlled the operations of their fleets in home waters. They controlled the Battle of Jutland from the Admiralty in a great sense. The famous PQ-17 convoy to Murmansk was controlled from the Admiralty. It was the Admiralty that ordered away all the escort ships, including the division of light cruisers and the destroyers. The search for the *Bismarck* was controlled by the Admiralty. Mr. Churchill interfered in all theaters of war with his ideas. Even in Burma they started to interfere but General Slim repudiated them and slapped them back.

Everyone knows that we had flung a very heavy bombardment over an area of France. In order to confuse the Germans it was necessary not to concentrate the bombing on the areas where we were going to land. So the rule was something like this: for every one bomb dropped in the landing area there were two bombs dropped elsewhere. The area around Calais and Dunkirk had a heavy bomb treatment and of course Le Havre—and the same with the bridges. By that time the Germans had been pretty well knocked out of the air on that front. They were occupied with the Russian attack and the Italian campaign. The Americans and the British had gained what you might describe as complete mastery of the air over the south coast of England and the north coast of France. We had occasional air raids but none on the big areas of concentration of shipping. So our aerial control over the whole northern coast of France in terms of fighter patrols was ever so much better than at the time when we were urged from

Washington or the British had been urged from Washington to make an assault on Cherbourg in 1942.

We were worried about mines. Minefields had been known to be laid in the Channel. Also we could perceive that Rommel, who had been transferred to command of the whole western coast, had shown considerable activity. That was learned from the system of OSS boys and what they had done in their contacts with the French. We could see from our aerial photographs that the Germans were building obstacles, putting them on the beaches, and obviously preparing the flat landing areas, the farmlands, with obstacles against airplanes landing. Gliders at that time were not unknown and they were taking precautions against them. It was a very curious thing that no one knew very much about the beaches of Normandy in spite of the fact that many British and some Americans had spent their vacations at Hougat and other fashionable places along the French coast. But nobody really knew very much about the actual composition of the beaches. Were they flat sand? Did they have runnels, holes, channels? Was there quicksand? Would landing craft be sinking into soft mud or what?

Of course we had maps in terms of depth of water and the rise and fall of tides and the strength of tidal currents. But there is quite a lot of difference between warning ships not to go inside a fifty-fathom curve or a ten-fathom curve, and knowing that if you do want to put your little boat on the ground itself on the land or the soil, what it is that you're putting it on. Is it on sand, or rocks or quicksand? Is it level or is it scarred with runnels and runways with the tide escaping back and forth? Quite different.

So we sent what we now call frogmen—mostly by the British but with some on our side too—to go in by submarine and swim ashore and walk around and take soundings and give a fairly good report on what it was like. They operated always at night. It became very dangerous as the Germans were always stringing mines across obstacles on the beach. Not many of the frogmen were lost. They were very, very careful, and of course we did not want any dead bodies recovered.

There was considerable concern on our side about the German E-boats known to be in Cherbourg harbor. They were pretty active, dashing out and around in the sea-lanes of the channel itself. They appeared to be practically the only naval menace to our flank, the western section.

We got to thinking about these E-boats. We knew they were in shelters inside Cherbourg Harbor. We had the *Nevada* with her new 14-inch guns. After Pearl Harbor she had been rebuilt and put together and had these marvelous 14-inch guns with the long-range, the high-angle fire.

I proposed that we take the *Nevada* out to sea off Cherbourg, give her a heavy screen of destroyers against possible submarine attack, give her adequate fighter cover (which it was perfectly simple to do), and have her go out one bright sunny day with what we call "airplane spot"—putting a trained naval spotter for gunfire in different planes to watch where the shots fell in Cherbourg Harbor and tell the ship what to do to correct the range or the deflection to hit the target. My staff and I worked this out. We felt that a moderate amount of ammunition could be expended on that and might really do quite a bit of damage to these nests where the E-boats were sheltered in the night.

Well, it caused quite a bit of furor because this paper got in the hands of my friend General Bedell Smith before it got to Admiral Ramsey, the Naval Commander Expeditionary Force. Our meeting was rather a heated occasion in which the British admiral threw this idea out of the window and only by the grace of God was it possible for me to say really that the proposal had gone forward more directly into the supreme Allied commander's hands than normally would have been the case. Ramsey would have returned it to me with disapproval, or whatever he wanted to say, but probably would not have forwarded it at all to Eisenhower. It would not be wholly truthful not to confess that steps were taken to make sure this got into the hands of the chief of staff of General Eisenhower before the British admiral who had become very testy and very difficult about the American effort. In any case, it was called off. We didn't do it.

I and my staff found the differences in the British and American approach to naval command a very complicating feature in dealing with Ramsey and his staff. The Normandy operation, the landing, became in the eyes of the British what they termed a set piece. In other words, no initiative was possible. It was like a fireworks display. You set off a little wick at a certain point and certain things begin to burn, lights go off, and what not. That was their idea of what this was to be—a somewhat formalized affair. I always had maintained that the resourcefulness of the American man, man or boy, was such a great asset that we should have told them—if you wanted to take a certain hill or a certain beach or landing place for the reason to get on farther, we should say: "This is what we think is the best way from our studies. When you get there, if you should find it different from that, disregard the 'how.' You know what you're supposed to do and why you are supposed to do it, and you do it!" That is what they did in Normandy, in Sicily, what the army did all through France and all the whole campaign in western Europe. It was the initiative of the American man, boy—soldier, sailor—whatever. His resourcefulness was an asset which we have and have had and I hope we always will have.

We had a meeting at St. Paul's School in London toward the very end shortly before we were ready to make the invasion. His Majesty the King was there; Churchill was there; Marshal Smuts was there; Eisenhower and all the commanders were there. We each had to make a presentation. It took all day. In my remarks I raised one question about the responsibility for the eastern corner of my sea area. It was necessary to draw some kind of a line from the coast of France out to sea which became the invasion area. I had supreme command of my part and Philip Vian of his part—the eastern part. Ramsey was of course to be on shore in Southampton. Well, the western end of this line of demarcation did not go quite up to the northern extremity of the Cherbourg Peninsula. If the E-boats came out— and they did—they were supposed to be attacked by the forces of CinC Plymouth and not by me. I felt that at that point there would be some question of who had the full responsibility. That caused a little bit of flutter which annoyed the prime minister and Admiral Ramsey but it was smoothed over. We just agreed to let it stay the way it was.

There were two interesting points we had to consider in connection with the landings. Our Russian friends had to be considered and when the landing was to be. They had pressed pretty hard for an earlier landing in Normandy than we were prepared to make. The timing of the assault had to depend on the assembling of the landing craft necessary, because when the second beachhead (Omaha) opened on my front that called for an additional number of LSTs particularly and some other craft and more transport types and all the small auxiliaries to go with it. They had to be drawn from the Med. The naval gunfire support ships, battleships, cruisers, and destroyers also had to come partially from the Med and partially from the U.S. That delayed us from April into May. Stalin was pressing all the time we take the pressure off his armies for they'd had a rugged time with the Germans almost into Moscow and almost into Leningrad and way down in the Caucasus. How heavy the strain was on the Soviets no one knows because they've never written any accounts of their operations that anyone's ever seen. There is no authentic account of what happened.

Now the question of the day. It was controlled by a number of factors. First of all the tidal conditions and the tidal range—the height to which the water rises between dead low water and top high water. On the coasts of Normandy it was 22 feet so that at low tide the beach was exposed nearly half a mile but at high tide that water was right against the sea wall or the cliffs. So the question was, what do you want? You wanted a rising tide so you could get your landing craft right up as close to the enemy positions on the firm land, the cliffs and the seashore but also you wanted time enough to destroy these obstacles that were on the beach so that the landing craft could get in, because if you tried to override them, water-borne, your boats would get snagged on these obstacles and blown up on the mines and then you'd have to put your soldiers out in water that was up to their necks and rising at the rate of two inches every ten minutes. You had to move awfully fast. That was the point of view of the soldiers. Then we had to take into consideration the point of view of those who used the naval guns against the German positions. In daylight they could see what they were shooting at. If they couldn't see themselves from their ships we'd have aircraft to tell them. That required daylight.

Then we had the question of the paratroopers, the airborne divisions, British as well as our own. We had the 101st Airborne, which was to land on the neck of the Cherbourg Peninsula and they had to have light to get down and see where they were—in other words, they wanted moonlight.

So you had the tide, you had the moon, you had sunrise, and you had weather—meaning general weather, not rain, not storms, not high winds.

Well, hereby hangs a very famous story. They were arguing back and forth whether it should be April or May and so on. You realize that tide changes every two weeks and the moon changes every month, the inconstant moon. So these various factors had to be reconciled.

Mr. Churchill held one of his after-midnight meetings in Number 10 Downing, where were present himself; his own chief of staff, General Ismay, popularly known as Pug Ismay; and there was Eisenhower and Bedell Smith; Montgomery and his staff; Ramsey and his chief of staff; Tedder and his chief of staff; and Bradley, who commanded the whole American army; and the general commanding the British army. I was not there.

They were arguing this back and forth around the table in the dining room or conference room at Number 10 and nobody could get anywhere. They were arguing also that the landing had to be after the March equinox and before the September equinox and we also wanted to be sure we got ashore in France while the fields and the lands were still dry and before all the crops had come to harvest so we wouldn't have the problem of waving grainfields.

In other words, as early after spring equinox as possible. What should be done? Finally Mr. Churchill lost his patience and he smote the table and said: "Well, what I would like to know is, when did William cross?"

The accused stood mute. No one could remember. He was obviously talking about William the Conqueror. Finally Pug Ismay, standing behind Mr. C., coughed into his hand and said: "Sir, I think it was 1066." Whereupon Mr. C. smote the table with his fist and said: "Dammit, everybody knows it was 1066. I want to know what month and what day."

And there was no one in that room, all those trained officers of many schools, British and American, army, navy, air—nobody could tell him. No one had the answer. So Mr. C. in effect said: "Class dismissed," and they all went home and got out their little history books and their railroad guides and every other thing, and do you know when William crossed? He crossed on the eighteenth of October, three weeks after the autumnal equinox. And he crossed with his horses and his men in armor. So when that was discovered, then we had to modify, and we agreed that because of the arrival of the ships that were expected, we couldn't go in April, we couldn't go in May. We would then go in June. It was worked out that it would be the fifth of June, because the phases of the moon and the tide and so on were right on the fifth, the sixth, and the seventh. It had to be one of those three days.

Now you read in the books of a dawn landing. They talk about landing at dawn. But when is dawn? What's your definition of dawn? Is it when the birds first begin to chirp in the trees? When I can see across the street? How far can I see? When there's light in the sky? When is dawn?

Finally it was agreed that dawn, in terms of H hour, should be what is known as nautical dawn, which is an astronomical phenomenon: when the sun is two and a half degrees below the horizon. Rosy-fingered dawn begins to shed a little more light than before when Mother Nature has covered the stars, has covered their faces by the light of day. That is dawn. At any rate, that was dawn from our point of view. Now, actually we were keeping summer time, and actually dawn was about 3 o'clock, summer time. And H hour, with the tide, had to be 6 A.M. so the whole coast of France was in plain sight. The sun was up at H hour but the moon was still shining for the airborne troops on our front of course and on the British front as well—forty, fifty, sixty miles apart, and they came over just after midnight.

That night in 10 Downing Street was really quite an occasion. I've always been sorry I wasn't there. That really was a priceless story. "When did William cross?" and nobody knew. I must confess frankly I didn't know either.

More of the St. Paul's School meeting. King George made a very simple and nice speech, impressed us all with the fate of the Empire and the free world. Churchill made one of his usual powerful speeches, of which I don't suppose there's any record. It didn't leave me with any lasting impression like any one of those great speeches during the war— "blood, sweat and tears," and so on. In my remarks I had said: "I know this is going to be embarrassing." I also said that this vast machine once set rolling couldn't be stopped. It had to go on and it had to succeed! We had to get them ashore and we would get them ashore. We would use all the power of the navy to make sure that the army did get ashore and stay there. I paid tribute to Ramsey's staff work by saying that the details had been worked out with such care that what the army needed would be provided. In that connection there was a nice, rather interesting point.

Bradley and I fell to talking one time about the supply of ammunition. Bradley said he wasn't too sure that he'd get it from the normal supply ships. In other words, lifting the ammunition out of the holds of the ships with a derrick, lowering it over the sides of the ships into boats and taking it ashore, and then getting it to the front. He very wisely suggested that he might be in real trouble if we got in difficulties with the ship-to-shore movement of ammunition or if the weather got so bad that the little boats that were supposed to take it in couldn't carry it. He said: "What do you think of the idea of getting some car ferries from the Eastern Seaboard, to be towed, heavily loaded to the gunwales with ammunition, towed over and just landed up on the beach, to be available?" I said I thought it was a fine idea, so we commandeered from the New York Harbor and Boston Harbor and Baltimore Harbor these car ferries. They are not used very much anymore anyhow. We had about eight or ten of them. They were towed across the Atlantic. I think they lost a couple of them on the way that broke loose and were never recovered. We loaded them with what the army called "units of fire"—so many rounds of small arms and so many rounds of machine-gun ammunition, ammunition for antitank guns and antiaircraft guns, and 105s and howitzers and bazookas and 155s and so on. Each barge was loaded with some of each kind of ammunition. The whole thing was what they called "combat loaded" for each type of gun. We towed those over right away, not on D day but D plus one and stranded them high up on the beaches, out of the way of the regular landing spots. So this reserve ammunition was available and by God, when the great storm came, it saved our bacon! A very well-conceived idea of Bradley's and very well executed.

The Luftwaffe hardly appeared at this time. The only instance of trouble with the Luftwaffe came when they did bombard Portland Harbor on D minus three or D minus four—a night attack and they dropped a few bombs. There was no real damage, happily. Their aerial reconnaissance was very poor because we had control of the air all the time. They couldn't poke their noses out. They did get some pictures of the artificial harbors. They were baffled as to what they were seeing–didn't know what it was. Just didn't know.

The planning, the British planning system, as I have already said, was different from ours. They prepared the plans for the landing in the most meticulous detail. Their stack of plans was about two feet high all carefully drawn and illustrated where appropriate. And they had to be delivered to the units concerned, not just the bombarding ships but the transports and the LSTs and the LCIs and all the way down the line. They were in great detail and they were good. They were a set piece, which is an organized job, and it was very well thought out I must admit. I do think it was well done. You must keep in mind, of course, that the main features were left to the two task force commanders. Getting on shore and getting established on shore—that was an individual job. We had to do that ourselves, work out our fire support plans, the waves in which the boats would touch down, what beaches they would go on, and so on.

But what I have in mind principally is the marvelous detail that was worked out for complete supply of these armies when they were on shore. That the British had learned from their sad experience in Gallipoli twenty years before. We too had progressed a great deal in our landings in Sicily, Salerno, Anzio, and some of the Pacific experiences as well. This seemed to me a beautifully worked-out plan.

You see, there was formed an artificial harbor on the coast of France by sinking a lot of old ships, some of them men-of-war, right on the bottom of the sea, in depths of water so that their decks would be well above high water—six or eight feet of freeboard. That was to form a kind of L-shape with the shore end of it; in my case, eastward where the rushing out ebb tides of the channel were strongest. The western end was also barricaded, but with a big opening. Ships could get in.

Then we had these phoenixes, which were great caissons, designed by Dickie Mountbatten's group in London quite some time before, and they were sunk. They were as big as houses, as a city house. They were sunk, towed over, put in position, and valves opened, filled with water at the bottom. Then, above that, they had living quarters for the little crews that were on them, who also manned the anti-aircraft guns. They were butted end to end to make a barrier. Outside of them was a row of what we called bombardons, anchored, and they were tremendous steel piles floating. This was to break the wave motions before they hit against these caissons. Then inside the harbor itself, we had a pier, and the pier came out from the shoreline to a depth of water, at low water, where a merchant-type ship that didn't draw over fourteen feet could go alongside, and the float, alongside of which the ships lay—LSTs or merchant-type or whatever they were—rose and fell with the tide just as it does in any ferryboat landing.

We had what we call a tide bridge, which goes up and down with the tide. To do that, these floats were looped to four enormous pillars which were sunk in the sand and had chains and counterweights to take the weight of the float loaded. So as the tide rose, these weights would lift the float up, and down as the tide went down. The counterweights would let the float back down and always keep it level with the water or at a certain height above the water proper for landing.

Then we had another device. We had a flexible hose to bring gasoline across the Channel from England to the tanks and the airplanes. It was laid on the bottom of the Channel, unreeled from great drums and brought across. Of course, the flow was not very great but it worked and it took the place of the supply of gasoline that had to come in tankers later on.

The emplacement of a phoenix in the artifical harbor Mulberry A off the Normandy beaches is shown in this photograph of a watercolor by Dwight Shepler, U.S. Navy combat artist. (National Archives)

Inside this harbor we had to have provision made for the berthing of the crews. We had little ferryboats where they served chow to the crews of the boats who were there all the time, working back and forth. We had little bunks for them to get some rest in. We had a little hospital base in there. We had it all worked out in great detail. I must say, the staffwork of the British was splendid on it, perfectly splendid. The detail of that was amazing.

Now every fellow, every landing craft coxswain and every LST skipper, didn't have to know all the details of this stuff. He had the general idea of it. But the people who were in these little boats had to know all this and have someone in charge of it. And that was so.

In late April 1944 I went down to Plymouth and hoisted my flag in the *Augusta,* took my staff down there, and we set up the headquarters command, the admiral's flag and his flagship, in Plymouth Harbor. I visited the various types of ships that were in there, and went to London from time to time, flew up in an airplane that I had, and discussed points that needed to be discussed, and we arranged all our plans. Then I went to see Admiral Ramsey at his headquarters near Southampton, near Eisenhower's own headquarters, and made final preparations. I think that it was obvious that things were going all right. The whole southern end of England was literally stuffed with the American army coming down from their training centers, with all their equipment, across the lanes and highways. A bulldozer very often had to go ahead and move, widen the roads here and there, but the British took it very nicely. There was never any complaint about that.

We were all ready to go on Monday, the fifth of June. On Sunday, the day before, Lady Nancy Astor asked Bradley and me to lunch at their house in Plymouth. So we went over. She had just come from a review of Girl Guides or something in the town of Plymouth and she said: "Next Sunday we're going to have a bigger and better parade," and would Bradley and I come and sit with her in the stands and take the salute? We told her very nicely and politely we'd be very glad to, knowing we were going to sail the next day.

The only thing I might add here is, I found they had very good tennis courts in the dockyards, in the officers' area of the dockyards of Plymouth. I used to go ashore from the *Augusta* every day and play tennis, from about 4 o'clock and come back about half past six. That was equivalent to Old Man Drake with his lawn bowls.

We came back aboard the ship and then it began to blow, southwest and fairly strongly. It looked a little bit dubious about Monday the fifth of June, which had been set for D day. Of course the units belonging to my Task Force 122, the Western Task Force—some of them had already started from Belfast and some of the Welsh ports and ports at the mouth of the Severn. I'm not quite sure whether it was very late afternoon of Sunday the fourth or in the evening that an urgent telegram came through for me to go ashore and talk on what was called the Green Line, the scrambled one that was supposed to be the safe telephone line to Ramsey, who was in his headquarters at Southampton. Of course, I went at once. He said: "The weather is so bad, the predictions are so bad, the forecast for Monday is so bad that we feel we'll have to delay one day. Can you hold up?" meaning could I take care of the change of plans. I said, "Yes, Admiral. We have an annex to the main plan—what to do in the event that we are delayed. Yes, we can."

I understand from reading some books, now that the war is all over, that Ramsey thought I was perhaps a little lighthearted about agreeing to his change of plans. In fact, one of his writers said that Admiral Kirk with his usual élan accepted the delay, the postponement, without any searching questions.

Here again is a difference between the American system and the British system. We had a plan, Annex George King, or whatever it was, that explicitly said what was to be done in the event we had to delay. To my mind it was perfectly clear that our naval forces, and roughly the American system of command, could put Annex George King or whatever it was into effect without any question. It never occurred to me there'd be any problem about it—to do what we should if the message got through. So I returned to my flagship and had the proper signal sent out to all the forces under my command, putting into effect Annex H with Operation Order so and so. No doubt it was a pretty tricky maneuver because ships that had started from Belfast or from the Bristol Channel or wherever had to do some careful calculations about how many hours they would steam on the reverse course and to turn about and come back so that on June sixth they would be where they should have been on June fifth, having already started on the fourth to be where they should be on the fifth. For the big ships that was not too difficult. They had chartrooms; they had navigational facilities; they knew precisely where they were; they knew how to calculate it. But the little ships, the little ones, the LCIs and the LSTs and LCMs and the Rhino ferries—to this great mass of miscellaneous craft—to them it was a problem.

Well, I may say that it was pretty rough. The wind was blowing about force 4 to 5 to 6. In the shallower waters of the Channel it was pretty rugged, not for the big transports or the battleships, but for the smaller craft it was a bit tough. When we put the annex into effect I may say that it did cause confusion but on balance everybody did exactly what he was supposed to do. Jimmy Hall in Portland Harbor had a mass of ships, small craft, and so on, that had to come back and take shelter there. He had to straighten them out, not only his own small craft but those that belonged to Moon that were going to Utah Beach. Everybody got the word except one small group of ships. They were steaming blandly towards the coast of France and Hall had to send a destroyer out to bring them back.

Well, now the interesting part about this is that forces of that size, that magnitude, that number from so many different parts of the south coast and west coast of England headed for France. I'm speaking now of the American side, let alone what was going on on the other side, the British side on the eastern end of the Channel. With all this, the Germans never saw or detected anything. They had no air reconnaissance, no cover. They never saw, never realized that we'd started and turned back, which is a great tribute to the command of the air that we exercised at that time. The Germans never saw it. The weather was bad. It wasn't very good flying weather. They had no ships out, they had no planes, nothing. So many ships had begun to move from various parts of the English coast. German reconnaissance aircraft could have detected movements along a very broad sector of the British Isles but they did not.

I sailed on the *Augusta* on the afternoon of Monday the fifth, headed eastward to the Isle of Wight, where there was the big circle we call Picadilly Circus. All the shipping arrived and fanned out in five lanes, three British and two American, for the coast of France. We had to go at a moderate speed—ten or twelve knots—to keep our proper place in the arrival time at the assault area. But we went by all these different types of ships—and that they were! It was sunny, it was windy, it was rough, choppy, but these little boats were going along. And the Rhino ferry was made up of a mass of these pontoons which we used on the beach itself to make a landing across the sands and the water. It floated at high tide but was grounded on the beach at low tide—by which soldiers could get ashore, by which gun carriers could be taken ashore, and antiaircraft guns. There they were, just like Robinson Crusoe. They had an outboard motor on the stern, chug-chugging along, and they had a little bonfire going. They were warming up their soup and lapping up their coffee. Really it was a most spectacular sight—thrilling!—to look out and see all this thing beginning to move. I had remarked at St. Paul's School Conference that this was a kind of juggernaut. When you started it you just couldn't stop it. There it was—and you could see it right in front of your eyes, rolling down the Channel and bringing us across to France!

The *Augusta* turned south, west of south, into our channel heading for Omaha Beach. It was dark. It began to be dark around half past ten at night but by 2 o'clock in the morning it began to be daylight or dawn. A little after midnight, let's say 1 A.M. on the sixth of June we began to see the German reaction to the airborne divisions that were landing. Our 101st and the 82nd airborne divisions were landing on what was called the base of the Cherbourg Peninsula to hold that line so that the Utah Beach forces, Joe Collins's Seventh, could get across and straddle that peninsula and prevent reinforcements coming from Brittany or from the Valley of the Loire to reinforce the garrison of Cherbourg because we had to capture Cherbourg in order to gain a deep-water port for great big ships, liners that drew thirty or thirty-five feet of water. It was there you had the unloading facilities on the piers and the rails, the railhead itself not only to Paris but perhaps the whole railway network of France. The army had to have this when we moved forward.

All that was spectacular. There were bursts of antiaircraft fire, red and green and white, like a tremendous Fourth of July celebration. And there were the flares which our own aircraft dropped so the parachutists themselves would have some chance to see where they were going. The wind was quite fresh, blowing from the southwest or west southwest. This forced the aircraft off course, with their gliders towed astern, and where they landed they didn't know. It isn't criticism; it was just that the wind, the darkness, and frankly our inexperience with this kind of thing caused our lack of precision. The Germans were caught completely by surprise. Nobody knew what was going on. At dawn the *Augusta* was almost in a position to fire her share of the bombardment of the beaches. I remember

365

distinctly seeing two parachutists drawn in this high wind eastward. They were tangled together. You could see the ropes tangled around the two men and the parachutes flying off at a tangent. Obviously nothing could be done about it. I don't know where they finally came to earth. I'm sure they were lost, either in the sea or on the German side. So it was not all duck soup for those fellows. Another thing happened that was rather too bad. The cold front coming across not only had high winds but it brought a cloud cover, a broken cloud cover so uneven that the great aerial bombardment of the beaches—Utah and Omaha—was interrupted. The pilots were so afraid that they'd drop their bombs on the landing craft coming in with the soldiers on board and the tanks that they dropped their bombs well behind the shoreline. It had been planned to drench with bombs the beach defenses so as to destroy the German morale. Now the bombs actually fell so far behind that they had no effect at all in softening up the beach defenses.

The naval gunfire began at 6 o'clock, H hour being 6:20, 6:25. That began on schedule. The bombarding ships came in quite close to the shore, having due regard for depth of water, the tidal range of twenty-two feet, and so on. They did a good job. All these things could have been better done had we had our own airplane spotters in the air over the beaches, but at that stage in the invasion we didn't have them. We didn't have any airplanes to spare for that. We did have the shore fire-control parties who went in with the troops and then talked back to their ships—how to direct the fire correctly, the range, the effects. But in the preliminary bombardment of the beaches we could only surmise where the beach defenses of the Germans were. This came of course from the best intelligence we had and from the maps of the shoreline. That wasn't what you'd call closely directed fire, firing from a map and your own position on the map at sea.

Curiously enough my own reaction as we neared H hour and began firing from the *Augusta* and all the other ships was one of—I hardly like to use the word—it was one of letdown. I couldn't say it was disappointment. That would be wrong, but it seemed to me again just like Sicily. There was no heavy German gunfire against the ships, against the transports. Now we all know the resistance on the shoreline at Omaha Beach was very intense. The point I make is that we had devoted quite a lot of attention to areas where we thought the Germans had heavy guns in the naval sense, 6-inch or bigger, and there weren't any. There was no gunfire. Nothing. Nor were there any German air attacks. We'd expected that. We'd assumed that the transport area would be under heavy bombardment. It was just amazing. Because we supposed there were 6-inch guns at Point du Hoe and other places, Admiral Hall anchored his transports roughly ten miles off the shore to be outside the range of what we

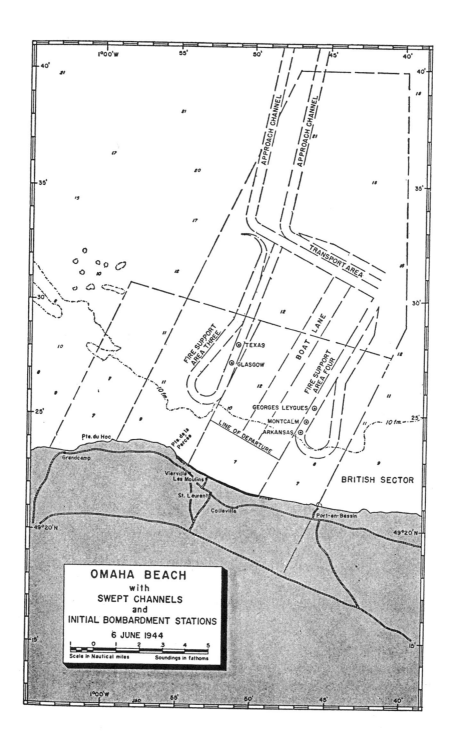

OMAHA BEACH
with
SWEPT CHANNELS
and
INITIAL BOMBARDMENT STATIONS
6 JUNE 1944

Scale in Nautical miles   Soundings in fathoms

called the accurate range of defending guns of that caliber. The same thing pertained to Admiral Moon over on his beach. He had taken into consideration the guns of the great fortress of Cherbourg. They did actually fire, ineffectively happily, not on his forces but did fire on the beach itself.

When the rocket-launching ships came in on the beach you could see the tracers from the base of their projectiles going up, over, and landing on the beach and you could see the dust and smoke. Of course, as always happens, some houses caught fire and that put smoke on the beach itself. But if you are in a landing craft, with a freeboard of six or seven feet height of eye looking toward the shore, the coast of France from ten miles away, you don't see the beach at all. That is one reason why the landing craft got lost. They couldn't get in close enough to see exactly where to go and then the smoke of burning houses and the smoke of gunfire obliterated the landmarks they had expected to see. This is not by way of being an excuse for the navy, but it's just one of those facts of life that when you're in a tiny little boat like a skiff or a row boat on the surface of the sea and you're ten miles away—say you're headed for Boston Harbor or Nantucket—you don't see it. You don't see the shoreline.

The guide boats, the leading boats, were supposed to take them accurately where they were intended to land, but—well, you know—"The best laid plans of mice and men gang aft agley."

At Omaha Beach the rough sea and the waves (not big ocean waves but the kind of waves you find on a shoreline, three or four feet high) are pretty hard to get out into when you're up to your waist in water and you're carrying a gun and ammunition and a gas mask and all the paraphernalia a poor soldier boy had to carry. They had a tough time. The demolition parties that were supposed to blow the obstacles and the mines away suffered under crossfire from the German emplacements on Omaha Beach—suffered heavy losses—so instead of clearing obstacles over a wide front they were only able to clear a few pathways through. So the assault on Omaha Beach was bogged down for practically twelve hours.

Now the curious thing about Omaha Beach was that our intelligence estimate (based on army, navy, and air intelligence) had not known that several weeks before D day the Germans had moved on that beach a field division brought back from the eastern front to be rehabilitated and retrained in western France before returning to the eastern front. As an exercise in short defense work they had been given this sector which we called Omaha Beach. So instead of coming up against a composite group made of Hungarians or Poles or Luxembourgers, nondescript in military terms, though they might be perfectly nice guys themselves, instead of something like that here was a hard-bitten, battle-scarred division. That was very tough.

It is now stated by several authors, Sam Morison in particular, that this information was available but nobody realized that they had it. I believe the French Resistance maintained that they had tried to send that information through and it had not gotten through. In any case, from 6:30 A.M. on the sixth of June until practically midafternoon, the successful attempt even to get a foothold, let alone a beachhead, on Omaha had been—I won't say had failed—but had been delayed.

In the early afternoon the Fifth Corps commander had got ashore and telephoned back on the walkie-talkie: Couldn't the navy put some gunfire down on the German position? Now this requires a little explanation because the task assigned the destroyers in particular (they were not very deep draft and had the 5-inch gun, which was awfully good for rapid fire)—they had done their bombardment, and then had gone outside the transport area on antisubmarine patrol—was to guard against attack by German submarines.

Well, when this appeal came to me that the general on shore wants gunfire, I ordered the officer who had command of the distinctly supportive naval forces, to send the destroyers in at once. They went in so close that they darned near stranded themselves. They had only about thirteen feet of water. On this long shelving beach they had a chance of running aground and if they'd stuck there and the tide had run out, they would have fallen over on their sides and caught fire. On the other hand, they did go in as close as they deemed possible and they fired very accurately. In fact today on the beach at Omaha there is a German pillbox with a very heavy machine gun (it was raising Cain with our landings on D day), and there is the impact of a naval 5-inch shell smacked by the blessing of the good Lord, I suppose, or let's say the accuracy of the gunfire, right smack in the slit in this armored turret where it blew the guns to pieces and the men to pieces. The army can never claim they had a gun on any boat going ashore of that type that could knock that hole in it. So it's a memento and a monument, and a happy one, and I applaud and approve its presence there. But it was done by the navy of the United States!

We were worried: I was worried, Bradley was worried, about Omaha Beach. We weren't too concerned about Utah Beach. The reports there were pretty good. But at Omaha the delay in the movement there meant that all the follow-up forces coming in from across the Channel—the next division, the tanks, the merchantships full of ammunition and stores (we had two hundred of them anchored off the beach at nightfall on D day, the sixth of June)—were piling up. Ramsey came down in a British DD. I went over to see him. He was perturbed about this and I said: "We'll straighten it out, don't worry!" He gave me a drink of whiskey, the only drink of whiskey I had from the fifth of June to the fourth of July. I was disturbed too, frankly, but I assured him we'd get it straightened out and by golly on the seventh of June all those ships had been discharged; their

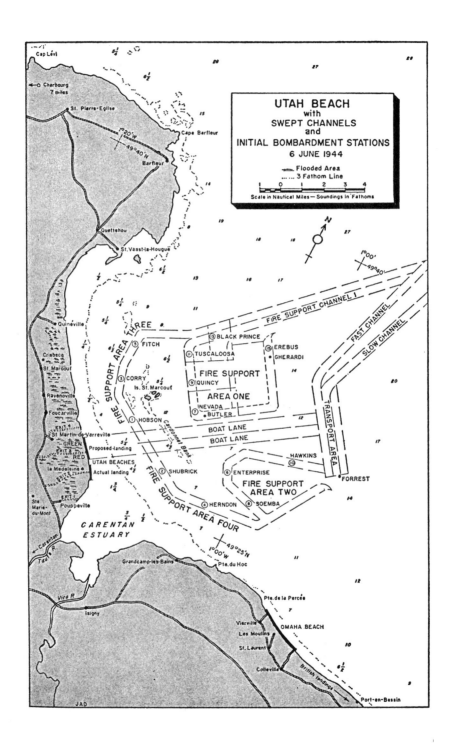

cargoes all had been landed. The reason—the beachhead had been enlarged from a toehold on the shoreline to a depth of several miles.

Then we began also to bring in this barrier of old ships to form a breakwater inside the artificial harbor. The Germans did have some aircraft that came over once in a while. They saw men-of-war, British, that we had sunk designedly to make a barrier and they reported to the press of the world that they had sunk two battleships off the beaches, never realizing that this was a planned operation on our part. We had air raids several nights, mostly on the British sector. They came out from the eastward, let's say from around Calais, and of course everybody opened fire. You were in more danger from falling fragments of your own shells than you were from anything they dropped. It was just pandemonium. It was a thing you really couldn't control. There were too many merchant ships and they all had these 20-mm Oerlikon guns. Add to their efforts the naval ships, the destroyers, and whatnot—everybody opened up. It was a perfect Fourth of July celebration and couldn't have been more picturesque.

The German high command was not convinced this was the real invasion of the Continent. They thought this was a feint. The real invasion would come at Calais, near Dieppe and Calais itself, where the British had an abortive episode in the summer of 1942. In fact, that was where our deception plans were most effective, because we had various signals, we had feints of one kind or another. We had little boats going over there with wonderful records imitating the sound of a ship dropping anchor, and the chain rumbling through the hause pipe, and the creaking of davits, and the squeaking of the men as they were supposed to be getting in the boats to go ashore. In fact, it's quite diverting. This thing was really planned by my friend, Douglas Fairbanks, Jr., who had worked with me in the amphibious force in the Atlantic Fleet and during Sicily. He perfected this thing and planned this operation.

On June 17 we began to get warnings of the big blow that lasted for three days. It has been written about and discussed in great detail. What happened was that it was an unusual situation of a clear storm, a storm without rain but with high winds, blowing from the east northeast. That created a swell on the sea and it was very, very bad. The British beaches were somewhat protected and the wind didn't blow directly on them. Of course they had some swells and some bad weather. We got the full brunt of it. At Utah Beach the wind was practically normal. It was the sand bars that protected that beach from serious wave action. But at Omaha Beach the wave motion got very, very high. It was so strong that it drove our bombardons against the caissons of the great outer bulwark itself and pierced their sides. They flooded and were pretty well wrecked. The same was true of the line of ships inside to form the main breakwater where we had billeted a great many of our personnel having to do with the provision ships, the meal ships, the hospital ships.

Now one of the things that caused the Omaha Beach to crumble was the fact that this wave motion scoured the sand out underneath these caissons, these great concrete structures, and they settled lower and lower in the sand. They were pretty nearly awash, which disrupted the batteries using their antiaircraft guns for antiaircraft defense and they had to be abandoned. The beautiful pier that had been built was wrecked and the shoreline, after this thing was over, was really just ghastly. All over landing craft were piled up on the beach, LCBPs, scout boats, the provision boats, LCMs—no LSTs, happily, or LCIs. The shoreline was just a shambles. It really was depressing. And this point was where the carfloats that we had loaded with ammunition to meet an emergency came in so well, because it was the one thing that supplied the army with its ammunition, not only for the soldiers, the infantry, but also for the artillery and the antiaircraft and the tanks.

We lost a number of sailors. We lost very few of the army because they couldn't come over. But we were certainly delayed and the army movements forward were delayed.

Bradley came to see me on about the twenty-second or twenty-third of June, asking if it would be possible to use the naval gunfire against the Cherbourg defenses, particularly those behind Cherbourg. The German artillery was placed behind the hills and firing over the hills. Our own artillery ashore at that time did not have enough of the howitzer type, the 105 and 155 howitzers. The shells would skim over the top of everything and then miss the target behind. So Bradley's idea was, could we help out? He knew it was imposing a rather onerous task on the naval command to bring men-of-war up against the seaward defenses of Cherbourg in order to let Joe Collins's troops take advantage of this gunfire against the German artillery behind the crest of the hill. So I said to Bradley, yes, we would do it. I suppose there was the old tradition of the American navy where Admiral Farragut rammed the forts of New Orleans and Mobile Bay and where David Porter's flotilla came down the Mississippi against Island Number 10 that means that you accept that as something that might be done.

At this time most of the men-of-war had been withdrawn and sent over to Portland to replenish before going down to the Med for the operation against the south of France. I felt sure we could help. I felt sure we could divide our men-of-war into two groups, the longer range ones and the shorter range ones. Then we could use the shorter range ones to subdue the fire of the batteries along the seacoast, the breakwater of Cherbourg Harbor, and so on, while the longer range ones could fire over into the backside of the hills where the German artillery was bothering Joe Collins.

So I sent a signal to Portland to organize the expedition. The immediate response was rather reluctant because of the time element. We had to get to Cherbourg awful fast. We couldn't keep on tying down the Seventh Corps south of Cherbourg any longer. So I suggested that if it was not possible I would go down there with the *Augusta* and destroyer escort and we would do our best with our 8-inch guns. That produced a result and a proper attack was organized on the forts. We used the *Nevada* and several of the older battleships like the *Wyoming*. One or two of the British cruisers also had long-range guns.

Well, here I know in fact I actually stepped completely on the toes of the British Naval CinC and the CinC of the Portsmouth area because those sea areas did not belong to me. Ramsey, having been present in the Gallipoli affair, like many British men of that vintage, was nonplussed at the thought that we should now begin to take on shore batteries in this modern world with naval ships. Nevertheless, he did not interfere, did not intervene, did not veto it. My order had been so phrased that it was almost impossible, because I said "in order to support the First Army at the request of General Bradley" we were going to do this.

When my friend Pete Quesada, who commanded some of the fighter units of the Eighth Air Force, heard about this (the air force had not been an actual addressee of my order) he organized and ordered a fighter patrol over the operation. At the same time he did another most wonderful thing. He had some naval gunfire spotters in his command who had been used here and there as necessary but not very well. This was their golden opportunity. He put them in our fighting aircraft, assigned them to their proper ships to control by airplane-spotting the gunfire—and to phone the results of the shots up in the hills back to their own ships. We were very grateful.

Mind you, our ships didn't go in close to the shore. The long-range ships were seven or eight miles away from the shore so that their guns would shoot 24,000 yards or so, and the shorter range ships were again about five or six miles off the shore, out in deep water where if there had been mines they'd just have gone to pot. They spent the day over there. The German shore batteries returned the fire but there were very few casualties, and then they withdrew without any loss of ships. The bombardment probably wasn't very successful, but at least it gave the Germans something to think about and it gave our navy a chance to participate in an action of a different type from what they had ever gone through before. Ramsey rushed down from Portland to see the ships as they returned, very nervous about what had happened, but he never made any comment to me, one way or the other, either approving or disapproving.

Maybe I didn't do any good in terms of knocking out the enemy, but after all, Cherbourg was captured the next day by Joe Collins's army.

After this I sent the *Augusta* back to refuel and return to the U.S. We sent the other men-of-war back and I transferred to a destroyer with some of my personal staff. It was time to turn over the beach to Admiral John Wilkes, who was in charge of that under the basic plan, the combatant ships having left and the situation being as nearly stabilized as one could expect. I returned to Portsmouth on the Fourth of July. One of my own staff group met me there and I went at once and reported to Admiral Ramsey in his office. Pretty chilly interview it was—grim! It was rather too bad because he was a decent guy and we had been rather good friends up until the Normandy operation. I think he was among those British naval flag officers who had no real conception of the power the United States Navy had developed. And if they began dimly to perceive that, they were unconsciously or subconsciously rather resentful. Why not? After all, they'd had command of the sea for centuries, and they were being displaced by a greater naval power, and they did not really quite like it.

Then I went up to London to report to Admiral Stark—to report and return to the United States. The job was done.

SOME DIFFICULT PROBLEMS AT OMAHA BEACH

ADMIRAL JOHN LESSLIE HALL, JR.

JOHN LESSLIE HALL, JR., was born on 11 April 1891 in Williamsburg, Virginia. He graduated from the College of William and Mary in 1909 with a B.S. degree and membership in Phi Beta Kappa. He then entered the U.S. Naval Academy and graduated with the class of 1913. At both schools he excelled in athletics, receiving a sword for general excellence at the academy. His first sea duty was in the USS *North Dakota,* followed by assignments in the USS *Reina Mercedes, Hannibal, Utah,* and *Illinois,* where he trained engineering personnel. In 1918 he helped fit out the USS *Philip* and then had shore duty at the Naval Academy. Further destroyer duty followed before being ordered as aide to the Commander, Destroyer Squadron 12, and then similar duty with the commandant of the Sixth Naval District in Charleston, South Carolina. He then had command of the USS *Childs,* a destroyer, until ordered once again to the Naval Academy in the Department of Physical Training with further duty as graduate manager of athletics and director of football.

Sea duty followed in several heavy ships before he took command of the gunboat *Asheville,* the station ship at Shanghai. In 1937 he attended the Naval War College before joining the staff there for two years. He followed with command of the USS *Arkansas* and later served with the Commander, Battleships, Atlantic Fleet.

Early in World War II he was ordered to the North African campaign to become Commander, West African Sea Frontier Force, and Commandant, Naval

Operating Base, Casablanca. In early 1943 he was given command of the amphibious force in the Mediterranean and commanded the attack groups in the landings at Gela, Sicily, and Salerno, Italy. For this he was decorated with the Legion of Merit as well as being appointed a Companion of the Order of the Bath by King George VI of England. Thereupon he was transferred to command the Eleventh Amphibious Force in England in training for the cross-channel invasion of France. In this duty he commanded the assault elements of the Fifth Army Corps on Omaha Beach. For this he received the Distinguished Service Medal of the U.S. Army, the Distinguished Service Order by Great Britain, and the Légion d'Honneur as well as the Croix de Guerre by France.

In late 1944 he was ordered to the Pacific theater as Commander, Amphibious Group Twelve, and took part in operations against the Japanese-held island of Okinawa. He later took command of Amphibious Force, Pacific Fleet, comprising some 3,000 ships and 550,000 personnel.

Admiral Hall retired on 1 May 1953 and died on 6 March 1978 in Scottsdale, Arizona. He is buried in Arlington National Cemetery.

I was very sick for several weeks aboard my flagship in the harbor at Algiers. I had been accustomed to go ashore and take long walks in the afternoon with some of my staff. So they said my illness might be sand-flea fever. I was worried because about that time I had gotten orders to go to England to take command of the Eleventh Amphibious Force preparatory to the invasion of Normandy. Of course I was very happy about that but also I was afraid that if they found out I was sick they would cancel my orders and somebody else would get my job. I couldn't eat anything; I couldn't drink milk or coffee.

I got to England the third or fourth of December 1943. I was still sick but my trip up—ten days at sea—was a joy to me. I had started to get my strength back; my temperature had left me. I was convalescing. I was well enough, however, to go up to London and still anxious to keep anybody from knowing I was still not recovered, for I knew that if they found out in Washington I had been sick they might cancel my orders. They had so many men who would have liked to have my job.

Well, the first job I had in England was to arrange practice landings on the beaches just outside of Dartmouth, where the British Naval Academy was located. The area is known as Slapton Sands. Mr. Churchill had required families who had lived for a thousand years on or near Slapton Sands to evacuate their homes in order that we could have an impact area where we could fire live bombs and live ammunition in training for combat. They wanted me to arrange a landing of some elements of the Fifth Corps under Major General L. T. Gerow (USA) to be held on New Year's

Day, 1944. Well, I begged off and held it on January 2 because I wouldn't have been quite ready on January 1. Later on Admiral Moon reported to me. He was to command a group of my forces and his assignment was to land the Seventh Corps on the Utah beaches to close in on Cherbourg. Well, in one of his rehearsals the German E-boats got active in the Channel and sunk an LST under his command and killed some of his troops and some of his naval ratings. So we did operate under some threat of enemy attack in our training exercises on the south coast of England.

I went to London and reported to Admiral Ramsey and to General Eisenhower. Admiral Ramsey took me down to see the First Sea Lord, Admiral Cunningham, who had been my commander in chief in the Mediterranean, and he showed us the blueprints and the drawings with the plans that had been made in Quebec for the artificial harbors in France and the plans to pump fuel oil across the Channel in pipelines—all these engineering projects that had seemed to be so important. And Admiral Cunningham said to me: "Hall, as one destroyer sailor to another, what do you think of these things?" I answered, "Admiral, anybody who's ever stood on a beach in French Morocco and has seen the sea toss about 150-ton concrete blocks as if they were pebbles and has seen the arrangements the French had made for pouring 150-ton concrete blocks to replace the defenses of Casablanca would laugh at these engineering projects that are to be put on the coast of France. One storm will wash them all away." Admiral Cunningham said, "I agree with you, Admiral Hall," and Admiral Ramsey said, "I do not agree with you at all." Well, since Admiral Ramsey was to be my new boss, I spoke up: "Admiral, I'll promise you that I will succeed in spite of them." But I did think it was the greatest waste of manpower and steel and equipment that I had seen planned for any operation in World War II. I did think that sinking the old ships off the coast to form a lee for landing craft might have merit (the Mulberries), but the phoenixes and all their plans for fancy landings for LSTs to unload the tank decks and the main decks simultaneously I thought were foolish because LSTs were built to land on the beaches. I said: "Admiral, I can land 150 or 300 of the LSTs and unload them on one tide and you're asking me to believe in a long-winded plan to unload two at a time off some fancy dock that you're going to build on a weather shore. I don't think it will last any time." Well, that's the way it turned out.

These ideas came from Mr. Churchill and Mr. Roosevelt, who were looking for some fancy way to win a war. I was on the lower level, a fighting man who knew that fancy engineering projects didn't win wars; it took fighting on the level at which I operated to win battles. I can't imagine why Admiral Ramsey embraced the idea, because I think he was a good seaman.

I can remember very well standing on the bridge a few days after the attack on the Omaha beaches and seeing all this wonderful work of un-loading supplies that was going on—twenty thousand tons per day per infantry division and saying, "I wish I owned a lot of real estate on these fine French beaches." A few days after the first storm you could have sold all the real estate you had for five cents because everything was wrecked. All the British LCTs were wrecked on the beaches, everything was wrecked. We had no business thinking that anything like our artificial harbors (the phoenixes) would contribute much to such an assault.

I was at another conference in London before the actual landings with Admiral King's chief of staff, Admiral Cooke, and two or three other American flag officers. I banged my fist on the table and said: "It's a crime to send me on the biggest amphibious attack in history with such inadequate gunfire support." Roosevelt and Churchill had agreed at some conference—Quebec, I believe—that England would furnish the naval gunfire support for the Normandy landings. Well, I didn't give a darn what they'd agreed on in conference. I wanted to give my troops the proper support. I fought like hell to do it. Finally Admiral Cooke said, "Hall, you've got no right to talk that way." I said: "Who had a better right to talk that way? If you're threatening to get me detached from my command, I know you can do it, but I don't think you would do that. I don't think you have the right to tell me that I have no right to talk this way. All I'm asking you to do is to detach a couple of squadrons of destroyers from some transoceanic convoy, give them to me, give me a chance to train them in gunfire support for the American army on the Omaha beaches." And I got them. Thank God I did!

Before I had attended this conference I had been informed they were giving me the British battleship *Warspite*. She had been hit so often she had only one turret operating. Her speed was reduced to ten knots. She was given to me to support the landing of the Fifth Corps and the Raiders on the Omaha beaches, and I had the old battleship USS *Arkansas* plus a few small British destroyers, plus two French cruisers, plus a Dutch gunboat. It can be recalled of course that the U.S. Navy at that time was very partial to the needs of the Pacific campaign.

If you read any army accounts of the landing on the Omaha beaches and particularly anything about the First Infantry Division they'll give full credit to American destroyer gunfire support for making it possible for them to get across those beaches. For those beaches were the strongest defended by the enemy in World War II. At some of our landings on little islands in the Pacific our forces had more ships shooting in to the beaches than we had on the total extent of the Normandy beaches.

It is a commentary on high-level civilian planning of military strategy. I can think of another example which was almost ridiculous. It was called the Pluto project. It was agreed upon at Quebec and was suggested by some engineers, whether civilian or army, I don't know. It was to pump fuel oil across the English Channel in pipes. I think they finally pumped a few gallons. Think of the difficulties. In the first place, you've got to have a beachhead on the enemy shore for the oil tanks in order to pump oil into them. Any fellow who knows anything about physics could figure out quickly what a tough job it is and what a slow job, to pump oil across the English Channel in a pipeline, compared with pumping it out of a tanker that you could sail into the channel and pump the oil from it into a tank on the shore. That you can do if you have a beachhead. You've got to have a beachhead in any case. They finally pumped a few gallons across by pipe just because the decision was made at Quebec.*

Without the assistance of all those fancy projects, we landed on the beaches in the Bay of the Seine between June 6 and August 6, 1944, over two million troops, four hundred thousand vehicles, and heaven knows how many millions of tons of stores, because we had learned how to do it the hard way. We did not have the assistance of all those wonderful projects that engineers and politicians at these conferences at Quebec and Teheran had given us to work with. They were impractical schemes, most of them. I never talked to Admiral Ramsey about it afterwards. I do recall his writing letters to tell us how important it was that we have our operation plans so clearly written that everybody could understand them.

Well, just before World War II, I had been head of the strategy section at the Navy War College, where my chief duty was to help instruct U.S. naval officers in how to write operations plans so that they could not be misunderstood, and I'd never seen such complicated misunderstandable operation plans as the British wrote. We, in America, had gradually come to the kind of plans that the old German general staff had developed way back in the days of the Prussian general staff, and I think we still adhere to a lot of what Clausewitz and others had enunciated. A plan that can be misunderstood will be misunderstood. We had gradually gotten to accept the principle that you must tell people what you want in terms of accomplishment rather than in terms of operation and movement: that if you paint a picture of what you want the battlefield to look like after you have finished your work, you paint that so that your subordinates understand it. Then they'll be much more able to accomplish their task than they would be if you tell them in terms of operation and movement what you want. The objective is the thing—what you want the picture to look like after the battle is over.

We really used to laugh at the long-winded operation plans that would

---

*See also Admiral Sullivan's comments on his work in clearing Cherbourg Harbor, pp. 410–419.

come out of Admiral Ramsey's command. We thought we knew a lot better how to let our subordinates know what we wanted to accomplish. I don't want to be misunderstood as running down the British. I think they're a great fighting race and I am very happy to have been associated with them in many joint operations. Their naval service was not as well prepared for war as we were. Admiral Sir John Tovey, commander in chief of the Home Fleet back in 1942, remarked that the U.S. Navy was much better prepared for war than they were, materially and in training and in the operation of ships.

I recall about that time a young officer came down from London and reported to my command for temporary additional duty as a member of my staff. He was sent down by Admiral Stark, who commanded U.S. Naval Forces in Europe. I asked my chief of staff, "Why did Admiral Stark send this young officer?" and he said, "He's to be the public relations officer on your staff." I said, "Well, bring him in and let me meet him." So he brought him in and I said, "Why were you sent down to my staff without my knowing about it?" "Admiral," he said, "Admiral Stark says that your command is not getting any publicity and he thinks you should have a public relations officer." My reply: "Do you know that it's top secret that my command has been transferred up here from the Mediterranean? I'm going to send you back to London as temporary additional duty completed and you can resume your regular duties because I don't want anyone to know that my command is even in England." So I did. I sent him back and I've often thought since that's one of the mistakes I made in my career. Maybe that young fellow could have done something to perpetuate us in history, which was something we couldn't do under the circumstances. I never got any repercussions from Admiral Stark, but I did get some from my own officers. They thought I was perhaps a little unwise to do what I did. I think they wanted a little more recognition than they were getting. But I took quite seriously the instructions that we were not to keep diaries—we were not to do anything except try to win the war. As far as public relations was concerned, I never worried too much about it.

Then about in March (1944) Admiral Ramsey put out an order directing the task-force organization for the actual attack on Normandy to go into effect. That in effect took out from under my command some amphibious forces in the United Kingdom—the Eleventh Amphibious Force, Admiral Moon and his task group—and put them under the direct command of Admiral Ramsey. I told Admiral Ramsey I thought it was a mistake and that I could help those people if he kept them in my force, but I was overruled. I think it's interesting that Admiral Moon, when he had problems with General Collins of the Seventh Corps, or when he had any landing exercises, would request that I attend the planning conference and the critique, which I usually did. I had a good deal more experience in amphibious assault than any of these others had, but my only comment to Admiral Moon after some of these exercises was that I thought he was trying to do too much himself. I thought he should recognize the fact that in a command the size of his he would have to delegate more authority than he was doing. Later on, after the Utah Beach landings and after the Normandy landings were over, he went down to the Mediterranean, and he became sick just before the landings in Southern France. I've always attributed it to the fact that he had not learned to delegate authority as much as one has to do in a situation of this kind. If you try to do everything yourself, the human mind and human body just can't stand it. Maybe I shouldn't have brought this up, but he did die down there.*

At this point my flagship was in Plymouth, and my naval gunfire outfit was working up at Dartmouth with the artillery forward observers and the army people who would have to call for naval gunfire support. We were running these schools; we were running underwater demolition training off the British beaches, working with the army. We were training transport quartermasters, and we were running all the kinds of schools you have to run for a joint amphibious operation. And I had to go to London quite frequently, at least once a month or maybe oftener, to attend conferences with the First Army and occasionally at General Eisenhower's headquarters.

I remember once when General Eisenhower sent for me and got me to go down to General Montgomery's headquarters at St. Paul's School to explain to them how we were adapting the United States attack to the reduced shipping that we would have to use. We didn't have as much shipping as we thought we needed, so we had to adapt our attack plans to the shipping we had. General Smith, chief of staff to Eisenhower, gave me a young colonel named Bonsteel from the First Army to go down to Montgomery's headquarters with me to explain how we were going to do it. When I got there I met with General de Guingand, Montgomery's chief of staff, for Montgomery was up in Scotland speaking to the troops. The first thing de Guingand told me was, "General Montgomery would not accept a reduction of that nature." So I said, "Well, General, apparently you misunderstand the job that I've been assigned. I'm down here to tell you how you would do it if you had to accept. I'm not sympathetic with your statement that General Montgomery wouldn't accept the situation, because in my business if I told my commander in chief that I wouldn't accept an order that he'd given me, there are so many finer U.S. officers who would like to have my job I'd be afraid to say that. So I'm not going

---

*Admiral Moon committed suicide. ED.

back and tell the commander in chief that you say your commander will not accept it. I don't accept that at all. I'm here to tell him how to do it." And then I turned to Bonsteel: "Isn't that correct?" "Yes, sir," he said, "that's correct." So that was from where we proceeded. I never did go back and tell Eisenhower that de Guingand said Montgomery would not accept what he was told to do because I thought Montgomery had his staff bluffed a lot more than he had me bluffed. It was amusing to see how cocky some people can get when they've been told they're great men.

We had to land on the Normandy beaches with smaller shipping accommodations than we had expected. It was because of the requirements for the pending invasion of Southern France that we didn't get ahold of things we were supposed to have. It's like the need for artillery ammunition. There's never enough artillery ammunition for a commander in battle. He'll always want more than exists. In the same way there just isn't enough shipping to do all the things that people want to do. They like to send every little unit in a separate ship, but sometimes you've got to adjust your loading to the existing situation.

I recall very shortly before the Normandy landing I attended a conference at St. Paul's School in London, General Montgomery's headquarters. It was a briefing by all of the principal commanders of the plans for this attack on the Normandy beaches. After the briefing was over General Eisenhower; Sir Winston Churchill; His Majesty King George VI; and Mr. Smuts, prime minister of South Africa, all got up and made speeches to us. I don't remember General Eisenhower's speech very well, but I remember Mr. Smuts very well because he told us that we were attempting something that had never succeeded in history and he doubted whether we would succeed. I often wondered why they let him talk to us.

I remember His Majesty since I had met him in the Home Fleet when I was chief of staff to the American force with the British Home Fleet in 1942. I remember so well this occasion when he stood up before us and with a slight quivering of his chin, which indicated the stammer he had been afflicted with earlier but had overcome so well, telling us in a very sincere and earnest way that he had great confidence because God was on our side. I enjoyed him. I enjoyed Mr. Churchill. I recall my thinking on that occasion that one bomb could have killed every principal commander that had any part in the Normandy landings there in St. Paul's School.

General George Patton, commanding the Third Army, with his chief of staff was sitting right behind me. When one of the Canadian generals got up and went into much more detail than any other general or admiral presenting his plan, George Patton got quite bored and whispered in a loud enough voice so I could hear, "If that so-and-so doesn't shut up, I'm going to do so-and-so"—both terms very vulgar. I started snickering and General Montgomery's chief of staff in the front row heard Patton and got up and whispered in the ear of the Canadian and he shut up right away. I was a great admirer of George Patton, although not in all ways. As a man and as a great master of quick tactical movement of troops ashore I thought he was outstanding.

The plans for the Normandy attack and the training for it are things that have never been adequately described. All this underwater demolition stuff. We had teams of army and navy working on beaches for months before the attack. We knew the terrible problems that existed. We finally decided the best we could hope to do would be to clear through each of every one of the seven battalion beaches on the Omaha landing in Normandy two-yard lanes to let the troops get through, and that's what we attempted to do. The naval gunfire support was inadequate compared with the tremendous strength the navy had in the Pacific for their landings. We had the forward fire-control parties and the naval gunfire liaison officers meet the gunnery people of the ships that were to support them; we had them work with them on actual gunfire on targets on Slapton Sands and also up in the Clyde where we had another impact area. We had all these people work together so that they actually knew each other, and when they called for gunfire during combat they were calling on people they knew.

Admiral Wilkes, who commanded the landing craft and bases of the Eleventh Amphibious Force, worked very intimately with all of the army logistics sections in the build-up and follow-up for the landings. Since there were about twenty thousand tons per day per division that had to be sent in as a follow-up to an amphibious landing, that required very extensive and detailed planning and execution. We worked very closely with the army for several months in preparation. That phase of the operation is something that I don't think has been adequately covered in any army or navy history of amphibious combat, and it's very important. Without it you land a bunch of troops on the beach and they're through. They can't exist without the backup just as Cornwallis couldn't exist around Yorktown when the French fleet came in and cut off the supplies that he was accustomed to getting by sea.

Admiral King came over two or three times during this training period. He sent Admiral Cooke over several times also. And of course we were in daily contact by dispatch. Admiral King had given Admiral Kirk and me complete freedom of action, almost anything we wanted except ships. I couldn't get enough ships until very late. It didn't make me feel at all secure about the gunfire support we were getting in the landings.

When the authorities made their decision to land on the Continent it was quite open for awhile when to land, even what year to land. Finally I think the U.S. probably forced the British into this operation a year before they thought they'd be ready for it. And finally they did. Mr. Churchill had promised that since the U.S. Navy was so vastly committed in the

Pacific, the Royal Navy would furnish the gunfire support. That was my difficulty at first because the Royal Navy simply was not equipped to furnish the kind of gunfire support that I thought we needed in an operation of that kind. They had given me the HMS *Warspite,* as I indicated previously, and a few Dutch, French, and British ships, including some destroyers. But their destroyers could not give the efficient accurate close gunfire support that American destroyers could give because they didn't have the directive system our ships had where you could feed into the directors the effect of the current, the effect of speed, the effect of various elements that affect the interior and exterior ballistics. They simply were not equipped for that accurate firing so we ended up with, thank God, a squadron of destroyers that I'd been told I couldn't have. They were the destroyers that furnished the really efficient, well-directed gunfire support that made the landings on the Omaha beaches successful. We trained both the French ships and the Dutch gunboat over gunfire support ranges off the entrance to the Clyde. They also had aboard American naval gunfire liaison people who worked with the artillery ashore for they had been trained in that kind of business. The American ships had been trained back in the United States, but we gave them refresher training and additional training in the Clyde.

We were pretty well trained in the use of radar by that time. But radar is no good unless you've got fighter planes to vector on the target after you discover it. In this we never did approach the efficiency of joint command that existed in the Central Pacific because the RAF was never willing to be under our command, and the U.S. Army Air Force was never willing to be under our command. They just cooperated. In my opinion any system that doesn't let the fellow who's responsible for winning the battle have the aircraft under his command is just like a man trying to fight without his right hand.

The first few days of the invasion we lost a lot of men. I lost a good many of my beach battalions. The army commander lost a lot of his. He had maybe twenty-five or thirty thousand troops in the shore parties and in the logistics support outfit in on the beaches. A lot of them were killed in and after the landings so that the system of checking in supplies fell down.

A few days later General Bradley and Admiral Kirk came out on the Omaha beaches, and I went ashore to meet them. General Bradley was very much concerned about the shortage of artillery ammunition and other supplies and food. I was amazed that he would have that shortage, so I said, "General, I think it's an imagined shortage rather than a real shortage. I think that your trouble is that your checking-in system has fallen down because a lot of people have been killed. I've had no ships sunk that were loaded with ammunition so all the ammunition that you planned to come over is here somewhere. Now it's up to you to find it. It's not a naval responsibility to know where the dumps are, where it is; that's your business." Well, it turned out that was true; a lot of these invoices that were supposed to come to me off the beaches were being sent over in Coast Guard ships, and they were being sent down to some of the British beaches by some army mistake in the rear. Things like that happen in combat. That was one place that I was told Admiral King got a little upset when he came to London shortly after that. He heard that Bradley had berated me on the beaches for a shortage of ammunition, and nobody had been able to tell him why until I told him why. I think it disappointed Admiral King so just after that he put me in charge of the whole show and everything went smoothly as far as I know.

I do think that some of our operations over the Omaha beaches were in the dark because we had a good many people killed in the assault phase of the operation. Even the beach battalion and the naval shore end of it had some difficulties. I did think that some of Admiral Wilkes's people (he was my landing craft and base commander back in England) had been brought in on the planning to take over from my combat assault people a little too early. So I had to stop that and put Captain Sabin (later admiral) in place of Admiral Wilkes's command for that phase of the operation because I didn't think things had progressed far enough to turn it over to Wilkes's command with the logistics in support. It was more of an immediate battle situation where Sabin, who had been with me for a long time, was more able to handle it. That seemed to please Admiral King and General Bradley.

About a week later I went over to General Bradley's command post. I was concerned at the number of casualties I had and that the army had under my immediate command in the early part of the attack, particularly the First Infantry Division, the twenty-ninth, and the Raiders. Bradley showed me his casualty list. The rest of them had gone way past my people by that time so I felt a lot better about it—that we had not paid more than we should have paid to get the foothold that we got on the Normandy shores. You've got to pay; war cannot be waged without running risks; you can't fight without losing lives. It makes you feel bad, but you've got to accept it. I used to wonder when I was a child how when you lost ten thousand at Antietam or Shiloh—I wondered how it affected a man of such deep sensibilities as Lee or Jackson. I learned the hard way. I was at Okinawa for two months after Easter Sunday in 1945 when we first attacked there and we lost five thousand naval killed—more than the army and the Marines added together fighting ashore. Most of them were from kamikaze attacks. Certainly the navy paid its way at Okinawa. I'm very proud of the navy.

The night before the attack I had an opportunity to talk to the young officers who were the heads of the underwater demolition teams for the

Omaha beaches. I knew they had a very tough job and I wanted to be with them. I went in and told them I'd like to go ashore with them but I couldn't. I told them that they were being supported by the greatest air support in history because I had been told that ten thousand aircraft were supporting my forces. I was sucker enough to believe it. I don't believe it now, but I did then. The aircraft were not trained the way I like to see them trained to support an operation of that kind, because they wouldn't come down through the clouds; they didn't drop a bomb within three miles of my beaches. I put that in my official reports, so I'm not saying anything that isn't known. The aviators didn't know how to do it in those days. With our navy pilots you could talk to them in the air and you could almost point your finger at the target and say, "That's what I want you to hit." But you couldn't do that in those days with aircraft that had to be briefed before they took off from the fields in England. You couldn't talk to them in the air and tell them what you wanted. I did have on board my flagship one of the two air amphibious squadrons in existence in the U.S. Army, so I was much more able to handle them than any other organization in the U.S. Navy, but since they were not under my command I couldn't talk to them; I couldn't tell them what I wanted, and I couldn't be sure they'd do what I wanted if I told them what to do.

It's a sad commentary on the lack of readiness to fight that existed in the United States prior to World War II. That's the reason why we've got places like the Armed Forces Staff College, the National War College, and these joint colleges. I trust that they're doing the job they're supposed to do.

But to go back to talk of my conversation with the underwater demolition teams before the invasion. I told them they had this job to do. I didn't think it was too difficult because they had the greatest air support in history and the finest naval gunfire support. Furthermore, if enemy artillery started banging on them I could close it off with smokescreens. I just expected them to lead their teams in and to do what they had been trained to do for the past several months and God bless them and good luck to them.

I did the same thing in talking with many other elements of the force in various ways at various times. I hope that it was a factor in building morale. I also briefed a number of correspondents who were to be with the military. In fact my principal job was doing that before the assault. I think all of us in those days were pioneers in joint operations. In the days before World War II the navy was trying to run some amphibious training in the Caribbean. The army couldn't get money from the War Department to put in army elements to participate. There was no joint planning, no joint effort, no means of joint action. There was a book called *Joint Action of the Army and the Navy*. It's really pitiful to read it today. It's always been a matter of getting enough money to do the things we ought to do. The budget for the armed forces in peace time is cut, cut, cut until they just can't do the things they want to do jointly. I'm afraid that will always be the case.

After the landings over the Omaha beaches the troops advanced rather fast and they had to dig in—the First Infantry Division, perhaps the Second, and the Twenty-ninth and some of the other follow-up troops had to dig in before St. Lo while the British caught up on the left around Caen.

It was during this time that I went up to General Bradley's command post and Bradley told me about the status of casualties in the First Army. I was so glad to see that the units which had taken heavy casualties in the landings at Omaha Beach had not lost many more troops afterwards. Most of our losses were in the initial assault because then they got in behind this German Fifty-second Division and cut them to pieces—the First Infantry Division, Twenty-ninth Infantry Division, the Second Division, and the Raiders. There were no more enthusiastic advocates of naval gunfire support than those troops who landed in assault around that part of the world.

The big storm that is inevitably connected with the story of the Normandy landings caused the phoenixes to be completely wrecked, and everything except for the hulks (the Mulberries) that had been sunk for the military harbor. The beaches were full of the wrecks of the pontoon causeways, and even a great many British LCTs that had come in on the follow-up were wrecked on the Omaha beaches. The value of real estate went down considerably. The port was no longer a port.

I was considerably concerned of course that we were not getting enough food and ammunition and supplies and so on to the troops. But we were, for during the three-day storm period we continued to land supplies. I don't remember exact details but within the two months over these open beaches we landed millions of tons of supplies, four hundred thousand vehicles, and over two million troops—the ships of my force alone. So historians say. I couldn't make any accounting of that.

I shouldn't say that the storm was any great surprise to those of us who had been skeptical of the planning for these pontoon causeways (the phoenixes). I had been used to watching the sea toss a 150-ton concrete block around at Casablanca. I'd seen the condition of the beaches there. It was far worse than anything we could encounter in the Bay of the Seine. In other words, the sweep from the sea was not enough to build up the tremendous seas that piled every day on the northwest coast of Africa with the whole range of the Atlantic Ocean in which to build up. So I don't think it was a very unusual storm or anything that you couldn't have expected to happen. You just thanked the Lord for the good weather that we had just before that and just after.

I think it was during this time that I decided to anchor some of the coasters in fairly close to the beach and let the tide run out and dry them so that the workers could go out and unload directly from the coasters. That was the thing we did. The coasters were of course quite different from the LSTs. The coasters were the small coastal steamers which had been loaded in England to be unloaded on our own boats alongside these coasters, so that when we needed food or some of the cargo of the coasters badly enough I would take a chance and have them anchor and dry out so that the army unloading teams in their trucks could go alongside them and unload directly from the coasters instead of having the coasters unload into the landing craft to land on the beaches. We never had one damaged that I know of. Although I would have had to lose some if necessary to have the troops have ammunition and food and the supplies for combat.

It was a twenty-four-hour tour of duty. Occasionally things would quiet down and you'd get a little sleep. You were usually interrupted by reports of various kinds from members of the staff. I know, later on at Okinawa, where the kamikaze planes were coming in every night, I remember the deep bass voice of my chief of staff waking me to say: "There are thirty-two separate raids on the screen. This is one of the biggest attacks we've had." All I could say was, "Make smoke," because making smoke was the best offense I know against enemy air opposition at Omaha Beach and the other Normandy beaches because the RAF and our army air forces had beaten down the German air forces to such an extent that they had very little left with which to attack us. I do recall only one air raid against us during the time we were off the Omaha beaches and that was entirely ineffective. There may have been more but I can't recall. It was a period of a month or six weeks.

I don't remember when I left the Omaha beaches. It was when Admiral Wilkes came over and set up his headquarters within Cherbourg. Admiral Stark had talked about having me promoted to vice admiral and standing by to go into Germany and command the naval end of it when Germany folded up. I told him that I would far rather go to the Pacific and continue my work in joint operations.

Admiral Wilkes took over the naval support of the army in Europe after I left but he had no command position in the Normandy operation itself other than logistic support. Admiral King had been particularly positive about this in his letters to Admiral Kirk and me. But we did have to submit our recommendations for awards to Admiral Stark, Commander of Naval Forces in Europe.

Shortly after the attack on the Normandy beaches Admiral Wilkes and Admiral Flannigan (on Admiral Stark's staff) came over from London to see me in the *Ancon* off the Normandy beaches. They were the ones to first tell me that Admiral Kirk was being ordered back to Plymouth to

Admiral Moon's former headquarters and given a month to write up his report of the operations. I was to be placed in command of the entire American naval end of the operation. That was maybe two or three weeks after D day. I left on October 1, 1944, with a small section of my staff to fly to the Pacific to report as Commander, Amphibious Group 12, in the Pacific. I sent my flagship back to Charleston for refitting, overhaul, and I flew with a small section of my staff to Washington and then, after ten days, on to Pearl Harbor and Okinawa.

I must say that one of the most important highlights of the operation was the joint training and joint planning that we had, all the way from General Eisenhower's headquarters to the attack forces echelons. All of us were pioneers really in joint operations right at the start of World War II and perhaps even as late as 1944. We were exchanging information with the amphibious commands in the Pacific, we got their orders, their instructions, their literature just as they got ours. We learned together, I think. We learned the hard way.

Another highlight was the fine support that Mr. Churchill saw that we got and that the British Admiralty saw that we got through the availability of all the ports and port facilities and naval dockyard repair facilities of England all the way from the Clyde around the southern coast to the Thames. It was very splendid help in keeping perhaps 90 percent of our ships ready for operation at all times.

GETTING THE D DAY NEWS OUT

HANSON W. BALDWIN

HENRY CHANG

HANSON WEIGHTMAN BALDWIN was born in Baltimore, Maryland, 22 March 1903. His preparatory education was in the Boys' Latin School in Baltimore. He is a graduate of the U.S. Naval Academy in the class of 1924.

As an ensign in the navy he served aboard battleships and a destroyer on the East Coast, in the Caribbean and in a European squadron, attaining the rank of lieutenant, j.g. He resigned from the naval service in 1927 and turned to a career in journalism. His first assignment was as a police reporter on the *Baltimore Sun;* he became a general assignment reporter in 1928–29. He joined the staff of the *New York Times* in 1929 and served as military and naval correspondent from 1937 to 1942.

In 1942 Mr. Baldwin was awarded a Pulitzer Prize for a series of articles on the South Pacific situation. In that same year he was designated military editor and analyst for the *Times* and served in that capacity through 1968.

Mr. Baldwin has maintained his association with the U.S. Naval Academy through the years. He served as president of the Naval Academy Alumni Association from 1969 to 1971.

He is the author of many books and articles, primarily on military subjects. His home is now in Roxbury, Connecticut.

We landed in Liverpool and I went around various parts of England to see some of our forces before the invasion. I went down to Bristol where General Bradley had his headquarters and then went up to London and waited there after getting all the British accreditation, which you had to do, as well as our own for D day. We knew, or we assumed, we were pretty sure it was going to be sometime around the first of June, but we didn't have any date. There were various kinds of accreditation, those who were accredited to the navies, the various navies; those who were accredited to the army and the air force; and we were all strictly kept apart like sheep and goats.

I remember that after some effort and some discussion, particularly with John Mason Brown, who was, as you know, with Admiral Kirk, I had gotten assigned to the *Augusta*, which was one of the things I very much wanted. I wanted to get the whole ringside picture, if I could. I was accredited to the navy, and I guess I was the only full-time correspondent of a daily paper aboard the *Augusta*. There was a photographer, I know there was, and I believe a radioman aboard. I think there were only three of us, three or four, and John Mason Brown, of course, and General Bradley had his headquarters on the ship, which was the flagship of U.S. Navy forces under Admiral Kirk.

While we were waiting we suddenly got this word from press headquarters. In those days the *New York Times*'s headquarters was in the Savoy Hotel. It had been bombed out of its old office, which was farther down on Fleet Street, so we were all in the Savoy Hotel. I got a call one afternoon to report with all equipment—which meant the helmet and your clothes, whatever you were going to carry with you, cameras—at the Admiralty next morning. A great crew of us, including, I guess, all those who were accredited to both navies, the British and the American, appeared there with all this gear, which was of course certain to attract attention. They were right out in the street near that bomb shelter that they had built for Churchill, right by the Admiralty Arch, and we waited there fairly prominently for some minutes, then were ushered into cars and got on a train. We hadn't been told where we were going along the south coast. Then the escort officer broke down and told us that this was just a trial run. We were out to try to fool the Germans and the known German spies, and it was part of a deception technique for D day, and the press had been roped into the various deceptive measures.

We were taken down to this little port of Fowey in Cornwall that happened to be right near the estate of Daphne du Maurier, whose husband, General Browning, was head of the British paratroopers. He was not there, but we stopped in Fowey, which was a very picturesque port in those days, a little Cornish fishing village. In the morning I visited some of our landing craft. We had a lot of LCIs there. I don't think there were any LCTs, certainly not as we know them now. They were all relatively small craft, but a lot of LCIs. There were no craft that could—well, they could get up on the beach but they weren't adapted for beaching like the LST is.

We visited them and I found one or two officers I was looking for and then in the afternoon we were all taken up to Daphne du Maurier's house, you know, the writer? Then we got our train and went back to London and waited for the real D day!

We were all fairly cheerful, although we were sort of on tenterhooks like everybody else, and we were anxious to get the things started.

We finally went down on the real D day; I guess it was two nights ahead of time, yes, it must have been because the day was postponed once.

I think the groups were separated this time. Those who were going to one port went together. We were going to Plymouth. The *Augusta* was in Plymouth, so I went with all those who were assigned to ships in Plymouth, which was a fairly sizeable group but not too big. The others went on some other trains in some other direction.

We boarded the *Augusta* after some brief delay. I remember I think it was late at night. I think, too, that this time we assembled outside the Admiralty in the evening. It was either after dark or just before dark. It wasn't quite as conspicuous as before.

We were aboard the *Augusta* and all set for the next day, and in the morning we woke up to find that the D day announcement had more or less leaked, at least we thought it had because the radio had carried some word about a big storm in the bay and about a postponement in plans and another bulletin said invasion imminent. It got everyone aboard the *Augusta* rather jittery and sore, and the few newspapermen who were aboard were rather irate. Whether one of our colleagues had leaked this we didn't know or whether anyone had done it. Later on, I think, it came out that all this came from—not from England at all and not from any correspondents involved but presumably from a misreading of something in the United States or from German radio. I don't know. It didn't do any harm in the event but at the time it seemed ominous, an ominous start to the proceedings, particularly since we had all been briefed very thoroughly after we got aboard the *Augusta*. A few of us had even read, or were reading, the plans, the detailed plans, not only for the landings but also for what was to transpire after that. General Bradley had told me that he expected thousands of casualties and the airborne troops were sort of sacrificial troops. So we were all fairly jittery. We didn't know what was going to transpire.

Incidentally, in the plans, which I never see mentioned now, Patton and his Third Army were supposed to land in Brittany, not where he actually came across later, into Normandy. But Patton was shifted, not at the last minute, but shifted, I guess, just after the first few days when our beachhead was obviously being hemmed in. Originally, Patton's Third Army was supposed to be landed at Lorient and, I think, Saint-Nazaire.

In any case we proceeded after the one-day postponement on schedule to France. On the actual invasion night I was up all night. I may have had an hour's sleep at the beginning of the night just as we were pulling out of Plymouth. It was a pretty fresh sea and we were bobbing a little. The small craft, you could see as you passed them, were making fairly heavy weather of it. It was choppy in the Channel and there was a fairly brisk wind, and there was not very good visibility, but it was a very impressive sight to see this great flotilla, or what you could see of it, as you passed it.

The spirit on board was good. It was determined. Nobody knew what to expect. As I said, there was a slight sense of, I wouldn't say dread, but of worry, as there was bound to be for an operation like this.

Admiral Struble was chief of staff to Kirk then. He was an irascible little guy, a nice fellow in many ways.

I remember getting up on the bridge with John Mason Brown very, very early—it must have been about eleven o'clock or midnight—as we steamed in toward the beaches. Then I remember first, I guess, you couldn't see very clearly because there was still a pretty heavy overcast, you could hear what sounded a little bit like thunder, the bombs back of the invasion beaches. Then as we got in closer and as the hour grew later, you could see an occasional flash. Then I remember vividly as we were coming in to our assigned position (of course the *Augusta* moved up and down the beaches, but she had an anchorage), one plane that had been over the invasion beaches was obviously hit, and it came out flaming toward the *Augusta* like a shooting star or fireball and it crashed into the sea some distance from us. You couldn't tell whether it was one of ours or a German, but we were almost sure it was one of ours. There weren't many Germans, if any, around at that time of night. As we got in closer to our assigned places, you could see more and more of the fireworks on shore, the antiaircraft, and the great flash of the bombs bursting.

Then, as we got into the transport anchorages and saw them starting to unload their troops, climb down the cargo nets into these bobbing craft, we saw that in some instances the sea was going to give a good bit of trouble. It was quite rough, and many of these men being unloaded had great difficulty getting into the landing craft. There were quite a few delays from the set hours of departure. We saw quite a few pieces of artillery and other equipment dropped into the drink, of course by error.

Then as I recollect it, we opened up a couple of times with antiaircraft and once the entire invasion fleet seemed to open up. They were probably just either firing at their own planes or at a "ghost." They had that trigger-happy feeling, which is understandable. We moved then round the American invasion beaches a little. I don't know how long we remained anchored, but we did for a while.

Kirk was virtually incommunicado this whole time. He was so busy. He was up on the bridge. I saw Struble occasionally, but not often. I saw Bradley much more often. He had his headquarters on the main deck and an office had been put there for him, a large map room. He would say, "What's going on?" He didn't know what was going on himself, absolute blank. Neither did Kirk really, because those first hours information was delayed and there was a sort of ordered chaos, if indeed it was ordered.

I remember vividly in the middle of the afternoon that Bradley still hadn't had any word from the beaches at all. He really didn't know anything directly from the beaches. He had reports from the area commanders, still aboard ship, Omaha and the rest, but he didn't have anything direct from the beaches except that he'd heard rumors that it was tough going on Omaha, and he was a little nervous himself at that time. That was in the middle of the afternoon.

During this time I was talking chiefly to John Mason Brown, who was carrying on his famous descriptions over the loudspeaker system. He'd tell whatever he could see or find out about. There was a Colonel Jeschke, I think his name was, of the Marine Corps, who was assigned to the *Augusta*, and he and I hung around a good bit together. I was taking notes of anything and everything during this whole period.

D day passed in this way with a paucity of information. There was very, very little hard news. We just saw what went on around us, the ships unloading and more ships coming in.

At the end of D day I got some sleep. I've forgotten what time it was but I remember being waked up by a burst of antiaircraft fire that night, probably about 10 o'clock or something like that. I think I was up most of the rest of that night. Gradually a few pieces of information filtered back and we saw flotsam and jetsam. By that I mean lifejackets, gas masks, one or two sunken small craft, the small landing craft, not the ships, drifting by. We didn't see any bodies actually at that time. This was the kind of atmosphere, and it was becoming more tense in some ways because things obviously weren't going according to preconceived plans, especially on Omaha Beach, where there were supposed to be a certain number of troops well inland, and they weren't. The British hadn't taken Caen, which should have been taken very early on in the game and various other things like this. Tempers were a little irascible.

I remember drinking copious quantities of extremely hot tea, which helped me to stay awake that way.

I think it was the second day that I got into a slight tiff with Admiral Struble. They were going to send one of the ship's boats to the beach to try to find out, I guess for Bradley and Kirk, exactly what was going on at

Omaha, and I said I wanted to go. Struble said, "You can't. Your accredited to the navy and you can't go ashore." So I said nonsense, or words to that effect. We had quite an argument. I didn't go ashore that day, and I don't think they got very much information. But on the third day things were piling up on Omaha and elsewhere, and the army was blaming the navy for failure to get a lot of its supplies ashore. Admiral Hall was the naval commander concerned. So Admiral Kirk decided he himself would go and see, so I hooked a ride in with him. Kirk and Bradley and Hall met on Omaha Beach on D plus three. It was a rather grim scene because there was quite a heated debate between the three of them, standing there on the beach, because Bradley was insistent they had to get more army supplies, and Hall was sort of angry, and Kirk, you know how decisive he was and almost feisty in insisting that Hall get to it. There were quite a few heated words. I was trying not to listen, to stand out of earshot, but they were standing right next to a row of bodies of American GIs that had been brought down to the beach and covered with ponchos. I always felt this was most dramatic. Here they were, arguing, and here the dead are.

There was a lot of wreckage on the beach, landing craft destroyed, and so forth. I spent as much time there as I could, talking to all the officers and GIs I could find, getting the picture of the situation, how they'd gotten up the beach, and what they'd done. Then I went back to the *Augusta* and later—I think it was that day or the next day—went up to another American beach, the one farther up where we had not had great opposition, up on the Cotentin Peninsula, Utah Beach, and briefly got ashore there. Of course, there was not the same argument there because they were getting supplies ashore much more rapidly. There was less opposition and they had pushed inland rather fast.

There's one other point about the invasion itself which I should have mentioned before, a rather important one from the point of view of the press.

On those first three or four days of the invasion (I think I actually stayed aboard the *Augusta* the fourth or fifth day when our beachheads were secure), I wrote thousands of words. I literally wrote everything I could think of. I knew this was a tremendous story, and even though I didn't have direct information about a lot of it, I was with Kirk and Bradley and I could get what they said. We put these dispatches daily in a pouch. John Mason Brown would take care of them on the *Augusta*. I was about the only one who was filing daily on the *Augusta*. I think the radioman was sending in brief bulletins.

Then, going back to the old days of the British navy, you know how they arranged to collect these dispatches: they actually had a pinnace come around to each ship in the fleet that carried correspondents and take it back across the English Channel in this little tiny boat to Portsmouth, where it would then be put on the land wire to London, then censored, and then sent out. It was stormy weather, particularly after the first day, the wind increased and the waves increased. It was pretty rough. There were at least forty ships in this tremendous fleet along the miles of beachhead that carried correspondents and these little ships had to make interminable stops. They'd spend a whole day just visiting the ships that they were supposed to visit before they even started across the channel. Many of them sank. The copy disappeared. It got all fouled up. The biggest story I guess I ever covered, I think I got about eight paragraphs in the paper or something like that! All was lost, garbled, or arrived much too late to be any good. Very disorderly.

The British navy was ostensibly in charge of all the naval arrangements including press arrangements. Actually, there was a British admiral in command. Unfortunately, British public relations doesn't rate very high. Our people had protested but the Admiralty hadn't devised any modern way of getting this stuff out. This was in strong contrast to what later developed on the beach, where the army established a press wireless station for direct communications with the United States, a radio station which was financed by the papers.

So the navy again was the silent service and it never did get an awful lot of publicity at the time about its efforts in the invasion. It got very little actually because most of the interest was focused later on the army and by the time the dispatches got out, it was all a land war.

THE AFTERMATH—SALVAGE OPERATIONS

REAR ADMIRAL WILLIAM A. SULLIVAN*

As soon as I had time I went up to Base 2 (Scotland) to see about the salvage personnel and supplies that had been sent over from the States. A Lieutenant Commander Byron Huie, USNR, was in command of the salvage personnel.

A very considerable stock of salvage gear had been received, sorted out, and nicely stowed away. My only criticism was that there was too much of everything, particularly such consumables as explosives, lumber, cement, steel plate, and so on. There was much more than we could ever use in any one port or in fact in several ports.

I knew from what I'd heard about the war plans that our first job in harbor clearance was to be Cherbourg. Later we might have a second port. No arrangements had been made to move any of the salvage equipment or salvage personnel forward. Such developments had been deferred for my arrival.

In London I inquired about plans to move naval personnel and equipment forward, once a beach had been established. I found that the commander of landing craft and bases, Rear Admiral John Wilkes, had secured a Liberty ship to move all equipment and all personnel to be used in Cherbourg. Our salvage gear and personnel were to be included in this ship. I pointed out that we would undoubtedly need our salvage personnel and equipment at Cherbourg to open the harbor and prepare a berth before any Liberty ship could come in. Admiral Wilkes objected to my arranging for separate transportation for my salvage equipment and personnel. I

*For biographical information on Sullivan see pp. 295–296.

could not understand his objections until I realized he was engaged in some sort of a power struggle with Admiral Kirk. Wilkes had attempted to get Kirk to issue orders to me to report to Wilkes. Kirk wanted to keep me and the salvage facilities directly under him, particularly during the establishment of the beachhead. Wilkes told me I had no chance of getting any other transport. There was no possibility for me to get anything but space on his Liberty ship. So I went to see the British Admiral Dewar, who was head of the Salvage Department in the Admiralty. He had no position in the organization being developed for the Normandy landings, but he was a big help. He found a British coaster which had been used to transport animals for our use in transporting salvage gear to France.

This ship, the *Whitsable,* was quite satisfactory. I thought perhaps it would take 40 percent of the equipment stored at Base 2 which we would want. Then I worried about what would happen should the Germans so block Cherbourg and make the entrance so bad we might be delayed in bringing in the *Whitsable.* I decided to start moving equipment, supplies, and personnel down to the Channel coast, so we would have a reserve much more available than if it had been left at Base 2.

I had purposely been ignoring MacKenzie since the battle over tugs. I was afraid he would try to exercise some control over our operation. He felt this reluctance of mine and started to become helpful. What was I going to do if the Germans so thoroughly blocked the harbor entrance to Cherbourg as to make it an impossible job to open up? Of course this was a possibility and we had more than enough explosives on hand to do the job. However, MacKenzie had some wreck dispersal vessels he thought particularly suitable for this work, and he also thought that I should have them in the amphibious operation. He thought we might find it necessary to disperse a wreck of a ship that had been sunk off one of the beaches, instead of trying to salvage it.

It was a little different angle on salvage than we had had before. The value of the wreck-disposal ships to me was a question of the efficiency of the personnel manning them and their willingness to work in combat areas. A wreck-disposal vessel is just a little ship that carried explosives and some of them had horns in the bow for taking a bow lift of a section of a ship and moving it away.

While MacKenzie was in this friendly and helpful mood, I mentioned our lack of lifting craft. We were immediately assigned two lifting ships, two dumb lifting barges, and ten lifting pontoons. We were now in pretty good shape for any eventuality.

Admiral Kirk was to have command of all the U.S. naval forces in the operation. His flagship was to be the *Augusta.* I would ride the *Augusta* with him, and I was to command Task Group 122.2, which was the salvage harbor clearance and fire-fighting group.

As soon as possible after my arrival in London I contacted the army engineers and Army Transportation. I met the two officers who were to collaborate with me at Cherbourg. Colonel Cress of the engineers had been in the Army Engineers in World War I. I believe he was in the same class at West Point as Eisenhower. He had resigned after World War I and I understand had been operating an auto sales agency in Florida before he came back into the service. Colonel Sibley was a very young infantry colonel. He was a regular and a West Point graduate. He was to be the port commander at Cherbourg and to be in charge of transportation. He admitted having no previous experience at transportation such as he would encounter at Cherbourg.

I succeeded in getting my suggestions adopted for the rehabilitation of Cherbourg, to be undertaken under the direction of a committee consisting of Colonel Cress, Colonel Sibley, and myself and preparation of a joint priority list of items of work to be done. I particularly tried to get on the best of terms with the two colonels. I found this easy to do, and personally I liked both officers very, very much. Sibley, however, was very young. I found him quite ready to defer to others, especially to older officers on subjects with which he was not wholly familiar. Colonel Cress was an excellent administrator, was always most accommodating , and most cooperative, but was conscious of a lack of engineering experience and wouldn't take a strong position very often on any point.

I should have been alarmed more than I was about the possibility of trouble developing in the rehabilitation of Cherbourg. One sign—I could get no clear understanding of the command arrangements by either the army or the navy for the Cherbourg operations. Colonel Sibley was to be the port commander, but how much freedom of action was he to have and who exactly was to be his boss? There were indications that he was to have more than one boss. A similar trouble existed in the navy. Captain Norman Ives was to be the commanding officer of the naval base at Cherbourg but he was having trouble in making any plans or decisions. Rear Admiral John Wilkes was the commander of naval ports and bases in England. He resented anyone making decisions without his advance approval.

When I met Wilkes in London I learned that a British P-Party, a minesweeping unit trained for clearing mines in blocked harbors, was to do the minesweeping in Cherbourg. This unit would work from shore and from a couple of small minesweepers. The problem of who was to have general direction of this mine-removal party had not been settled. Intelligence reports said that Cherbourg had been heavily mined. The mines would have to be removed before we could start cleaning up the wrecks. The ships bringing in the base organization would not be able to enter the harbor until the mines were removed, and we cleared a path to the docks.

This was the first time Wilkes admitted that we would have salvage work to do before the base party came in. For some reason no one wanted Ives to take on this responsibility. Now, at a later date, I was asked to do so, and I was offered two LSTs to transport the party and anything else I could get on board.

I checked with the British and found two LSTs would not only carry the British P-Party but all of our motor transport and all of the personnel and salvage gear which had been assembled on the south coast. It would also carry a British hydrographic party, and much space left over which we could use to carry some of the engineers' heavy equipment. Colonel Cress had been telling me he still had a lot of equipment that he didn't know how he was going to get over. This deal was a good example of the shenanigans that went on in England before D day. No transportation for our salvage gear, unless we put ourselves under the base organization. Then we found our own transportation, except for motor vehicle lift. No possible space for motor vehicle transport. Then, when I agreed to be responsible for a relatively small port party—abundant transport was available!

A week before D day Admiral Kirk asked me to attend a test on the south coast of an obstacle which the Germans were known to be placing on the French beaches where we were to land. I should arrive early in the morning to see the test. I found it was being run by a British civil servant from some scientific office. He was most uncommunicative. Present, however, was a naval constructor on the British side who was a commander in the Polish Navy who had fled Poland and was working with the British. I found him very intelligent, and he gave me an understanding of the background of the test. Aerial photographs had shown the Germans were placing obstacles on the beaches in which we were interested. Starting just above the low-water mark, a row of obstacles which the photo interpreters had called Element C were placed end to end. We were to test one of those elements.

These were obstacles that were put just above the low water mark, to stop anything, any landing craft that was running in there. Then all the way up to the high water mark were more obstacles, different types. On these beaches there was a range of tide of about twenty feet between low water mark and high water mark, and in no place was the distance on the beach between these marks less than a quarter of a mile. In some places it was a half mile. The whole area was filled with these obstacles and they were wired together with barbed wire of various kinds; then there were contact mines tied into the whole business too. Element C was the first barricade. Now, in back of that they had piles driven in, with artillery shells lashed to the top of the piles, and contact fuses set into the artillery shells, so that if any boat ran into that it would set it off. Then they had concrete mines farther up, mines that they built right on the spot by pouring concrete.

The test we were to observe was what would happen to the obstacle—Element C—if it were hit by ramming it with an LCT at full speed? The model was to be tested at various stages of the tide. The Polish officer said he was quite sure that the plans for the landing included provisions for removing these obstacles. He had no information concerning how the obstacles would be removed or eliminated. He thought the test we were about to witness was being made to determine how serious one of these obstacles would be if any were overlooked or skipped by the arrangements which had been made to deal with all obstacles.

When the tests occurred the LCT was stopped cold. No damage was incurred except some dents on the bottom of the landing craft. The obstacle was rammed, with the landing craft running into it at various stages of the tide, at various angles and at various speeds. All results were the same.

I returned to London later in the evening and went straight to Admiral Kirk's hotel. I gave him a pessimistic report. I said I did not see how gunfire could eliminate these obstacles. The Element Cs might be wrecked by gunfire but the debris would still remain and would still be an obstacle.

The next day I saw MacKenzie and told him about the test I had seen the day before. He said that a rather large mixed group of naval and military personnel was to be landed at low tide to remove these obstacles by demolition. They were to cut paths for landing craft to pass through on D day. On subsequent days they were to completely clear away these obstacles to provide areas for the artificial harbors. He thought provisions had been made to take care of all eventualities.

Later in the day I found that another Element C test was about to be conducted in Scotland. I could not get away for this but alerted Wroten at Base 2 and asked him to witness the test. This test was delayed and Wroten only called me with his report as I was about to leave London for good. I passed his information on to Admiral Kirk, who surprised me with his indifference. From his attitude I felt sure that the information MacKenzie had given me about a force having been formed to take care of these obstacles was correct and that the tests Wroten and I had witnessed were to ascertain what would happen should any obstacles be skipped. In talking to Wilkes I mentioned the test of Element C and my concern over the possible difficulties that the removal of these obstacles might present. I was met with a blank wall of indifference.

On D minus one I left London, went to Plymouth, and reported on board the *Augusta*. The commanding officer of the *Augusta* was a very old and close friend of mine, Eddie Jones. I was assigned a cot in the cabin of

Watching the progress of the Normandy invasion from the bridge of the flagship USS *Augusta* are (left to right) Task Force Commander Rear Admiral Alan G. Kirk; Lieutenant General Omar Bradley, commanding general of American ground forces; and Rear Admiral A. D. Struble, chief of staff to Admiral Kirk. (U.S. Navy)

Admiral Struble, chief of staff to Admiral Kirk. I was to take my meals in Admiral Kirk's mess. Admiral Kirk was to have General Bradley, the army chief of staff; Admiral Struble, myself; and two or three others. Once on board the *Augusta* all communication with the shore ceased.

Soon the postponement of the landings for another twenty-four hours was announced. I could well have used the period for final check of the salvage arrangements on shore, but the rule of no communications ashore was still in force. I could only check the items in my mind. I had been making up the salvage plan. I'd assigned the officers I had earmarked for harbor clearance work in Cherbourg to remain behind on the south coast and come over when sent for. I spent most of the delay reading up on the war plans. All details of the plans were not available. I learned the details of the arrangements to eliminate the obstacles: a mixed military and naval party was to be landed at H hour at low tide and was to proceed to provide paths through the obstacles by demolition. As I thought about this job I wondered how well the men assigned to it had been trained. Did they know exactly where to put the demolition charges to obtain the desired results? Had they been supplied with an adequate amount of explosives? And so on. As I thought about all these possibilities I came to the conclusion that as far as I could see sooner or later we were going to have the whole thing dumped in our lap.

The *Augusta* pulled out of Plymouth on the evening of June 5. Late in the evening I went up on the bridge. It was a clear night. I could see the dim outlines of the minesweepers ahead and of other ships astern. Overhead was a constant stream of planes en route to France or returning. Sometimes very heavy formations passed, on the way to give some place a saturation bombing. Once we spotted a plane on fire some miles dead ahead, and apparently coming straight for us. A mile or so ahead it sheered off, passed us on our starboard side and crashed a mile or so astern. We arrived at the anchorage assigned to the *Augusta* in the early morning hours, long before daylight. Near us were anchored the attack transports, which at once started to lower away their LCVPs loaded with troops. A rather heavy swell existed, which made this operation very difficult. We were perhaps eight or ten miles from shore.

H hour had been set for around 6:30 A.M., an hour after low water. The first waves of infantry were sent in on LCVPs. At this time the demolition groups were sent in to blow paths through the obstacles for succeeding waves of assault troops. Some amphibious tanks were also landed at H hour. Heavy gunfire broke out ashore, and the navy guns went into action.

The first news of importance to me came at daybreak. Word was received that the destroyer *Curry* had been seriously injured by German gunfire off Utah Beach and was in danger of sinking. There was nothing I personally could do at the time. McClung had the combat salvage ships off Utah and Admiral Moon had apparently ordered one in to assist the *Curry*. Then we heard salvage assistance could not be sent to her until the German guns firing on her had been silenced. Almost at the same time we heard she had sunk. The *Curry* was our first casualty. There were to be more, almost all of which were caused by mines. The nature of the salvage work we had to undertake off Omaha and Utah was entirely different from the work we had performed in previous amphibious landings. Our firefighters had only one ship's fire to handle during the period.

There was considerable anxiety and tension on the *Augusta* on D day morning. All reports coming back from Omaha Beach were most discouraging. On the other hand, reports from Utah indicated progress better than anything anticipated. At noon word finally was received from Omaha Beach indicating progress was at last being made but casualties of both personnel and landing craft were heavy. A number of LCTs had run into mines. Altogether more than a dozen LCTs were lost from mines on D day, besides a half dozen LCIs. Most of the casualties were on Omaha Beach and were largely due to the inadequate provisions made for marking the entrances to the paths cleared through the beach obstacles and to the inadequate plans made to provide these paths.

The loss of life on many of these landing craft which ran into mines was very heavy. Nothing I could do at this time about the landing craft sunk by mines inshore. The depth of water was insufficient to send a fleet tug. Huie however found work to keep the tugs busy by making emergency repairs to landing craft which had sustained damage on the beach but which had been able to get back to deep water.

In the afternoon the gunfire support destroyers moved closer to the beach to silence the guns the Germans had stationed in caves and hills which covered the beaches where our men were landing. I shall always remember one concrete pillbox built into the side of a cliff, almost at the water's edge. It had a heavy caliber gun, which we could see firing on Omaha Beach. A destroyer was sent in to silence the gun. The destroyer's guns did not seem to have any effect at all on the concrete construction of the pillbox holding this gun. The destroyer finally lowered the aim of its guns to the bank below the pillbox. A minute or two rapid fire of all guns on the destroyer chopped away enough of the hillside under this pillbox to undercut the whole pillbox, and it came tumbling down the hill into the water. It was amazing to see it.

On the afternoon of D day I was able to get off the *Augusta* and in an LCVP to take a look around. I did not get in to the beach, as I had no responsibilities so far inshore.

Early the next morning I was notified that a troop ship, the *Susan B. Anthony,* had hit a mine. For some reason or other there was a delay in communications in connection with this casualty, but fortunately one of the fleet tugs was one of the first ships to learn of the situation. The damage to the *Anthony* was most serious. No chance to do anything to save the ship. It had over two thousand troops on board when hit. Fire broke out but the firefighters on the fleet tug kept this fire under control until the troops and crew could be taken off by a number of small craft which were in the vicinity and came to the rescue. This was the one time the firefighters fought a fire off Normandy. By the time the last of the men were taken off the *Anthony* the ship sank. I arrived about the time she sank.

Later that day Admiral Kirk told me that a very serious situation existed on Omaha Beach. The wreckage of landing craft, of motor vehicles, of obstacles was so great along the beaches that landing operations were being suspended. He was to meet Admiral Hall on the beaches and wanted me present. I went in at once and had a look around. It was very bad, the worst mess I have ever seen anyplace. I looked for the captain who was supposed to be in charge of beach salvage. He had remained behind in England. The beach salvage work was being done under the direction of a lieutenant junior grade who was working under the beachmaster.

The personnel engaged in this beach salvage work were carefully selected and skilled in the repair of landing craft. I saw an LCM which had been holed at the stern knuckle. The plating of the side of the transom and of the bottom bordering on this hole had been wrinkled. A man with an acetylene torch was cutting away the wrinkled plating, so that three flat steel plates could be welded to the side, the bottom, and the transverse plating, and make a new knuckle to cover the hole. A gasoline-driven welding machine was on the beach, and the work being done was first-class workmanship. It was exactly the same kind of a repair that would be done in any shipyard. I talked to the men. This was the only way they had been trained back in England to repair landing craft damaged on the beaches. It must be remembered that the beaches were still under gunfire.

It was the worst damned nonsense I had seen up to now. This work was being done under shellfire. Already the beach salvage parties had had some severe casualties. Although I was thoroughly disgusted with the officers responsible for this situation, I was full of admiration for the young officers and men who were carrying on as they had been told to do.

Most of the wrecked landing craft clinging to the beaches were LCVPs and LCMs, but there were some LCTs and LCIs. Mingled with the wrecked landing craft were wrecked motor vehicles of various kinds which had been damaged by gunfire or submerged by an incoming tide before they could get above the high water mark. There were still very many beach obstacles to be cleared. I was told that the obstacle demolition teams had sustained very severe casualties, some teams being entirely wiped out.

There was a very great deal of work to be done. It appeared to me that the army and navy personnel on the beach were quite sufficient in number to handle the work required. What was needed was someone to show them how to more quickly patch up the wrecked landing craft so that they could be floated out to deep water where more permanent repairs could be done beyond the range of German guns. They also needed someone of administrative ability to direct the operations. I did not believe that I should get involved very extensively in this job. I had to keep free for any major offshore job that might come up, and I must not jeopardize our preparations for Cherbourg. Consequently I could not offer to take over this situation or the salvage of these landing craft on the beach.

I decided to suggest sending in from the combat salvage ships a few young salvage officers and a few salvage men with supplies for making emergency patches, so that the landing craft could be removed and taken to an area beyond the range of the German artillery, where more permanent repairs could be done. I would send the electric welding machines back on board ship, where they could be more usefully employed. What was needed on the beach now was salvage work that could be done in one twentieth or so of the time now being spent with the welding of permanent patches. I would send for the two salvage vessels we had left on the south coast and anchor them offshore, beyond the range of the German guns, so that they could undertake to make emergency repairs on landing craft brought out to them. The fleet tugs were at the moment not needed for any major salvage operations and were being employed only on emergency repairs to landing craft. I suggested these fleet tugs be anchored offshore also and assigned the job of making more permanent repairs to landing craft removed from the beach. They could start this work at once and continue with it except when they had to be sent to major salvage jobs that might come up offshore.

I said I would have some buoys planted in the area to which the landing craft waiting for repairs could be secured. I pointed out to Admiral Kirk the way the work was being done, and how dozens of landing craft could be plugged up with temporary plugs, or even with some of the hundreds of life jackets which were lying around the beach, while one permanent steel patch was being fabricated and welded in place on the beach. I pointed out the hundreds of life jackets lying around. My suggestions and recommendations were approved, and I put Huie on the job with his group.

Temporarily patched landing craft started to stream away from the beaches. When I got out to where the two fleet tugs were anchored, here we had at least twenty landing craft lined up alongside each tug or secured to buoys astern. In the first three days of this arrangement the two fleet tugs had made repairs on sixty-three landing craft which had been salvaged from the beach so that they could be returned to service. A few of these repairs had been made by welding steel plates over the holes. But this type of permanent repair had only been done where conditions were such that it was as quick to put on a welded patch as any other kind of permanent patch. Most of the repairs done by the salvage vessels or the fleet tugs were the installation of concrete patches or the fitting of bolted wood or steel patches. Admiral Hall's report, I believe, contains a tabulated list of the landing craft repaired under this arrangement.

The beach was cleared sufficiently before the end of the afternoon of the first day to permit landing operations to be resumed. I believe it was at this time that Captain Arnold was sent in to start his work as beachmaster and the work ashore was done under his vigorous direction. On Utah Beach there had not been nearly as many obstacles and the beach obstacles had not been fitted with mines. Consequently the wrecked landing craft were not the problem they were at Omaha.

Now that we had the landing craft work well in hand, I really had nothing to keep me at Omaha Beach. In fact we were beginning to think we could release some of the personnel I had taken away from the group that Wroten was to take into Cherbourg. So Admiral Kirk released me from Omaha Beach to return to the United Kingdom and finalize operations for moving to Cherbourg.

I was happy to get back because there was a lot of correspondence I had to take care of before I became involved in another intensive job. I went back on the destroyer *Hambleton,* one of those employed in the destroyer screen off Utah. On the south coast I found everything in order but at the end of my second day there I received an urgent order from Admiral Kirk to return to the *Augusta* at once.

I learned that a terrific storm had created great destruction on Omaha Beach. I went back the next morning. There was a scene of great desolation. The floating breakwaters known as bombardons had been torn loose from the anchorage. Four out of every five bombardons had broken up. I believe they broke up when the structures bounced on the bottom as they were tossed up and down by the heavy seas. In my opinion the break-up of the bombardons was the most serious result of this storm. Fragments of them were all over the place. Lying on the bottom they were positive hazards to shipping until they could be fished out. At low water a Liberty ship could sit down on one of the fragments and puncture its bottom.

A number of Liberties had dragged anchor and grounded. This was no great problem. The sunken ships in the Gooseberries had started to break up as I had anticipated. The large old British battleship had ruptured amidships, and another rupture had started at a quarter length. In general this breakwater served a very useful purpose during the storm for the hulks had remained in place and so had provided a badly needed shelter for many small landing craft.

The Mulberries, the concrete phoenixes, had not taken the storm well. Many of the phoenixes had broken up and large chunks of concrete had broken off and obstructed the movements of craft in what had been the artificial harbor before. None of the floating piers or their pontoon causeways were serviceable. Many of the pontoons and causeways had filled up and sunk.

I went around with Captain Clark, who had been up and around since the start of the storm. He was yelling for salvage to come and rebuild his harbor for him. I lost patience with him and we had quite a set-to. There were dozens of his men hanging around not doing anything. There was a great deal of work which could be done at once to save the situation but no officer seemed to have the slightest idea of doing anything, only waiting for salvage to come in and take over. I called Clark's attention to the fact that the pontoon we were standing on was filling up because the manhole plates were not in place although they were lying alongside the manholes. Nearby were some pumps which could have been put to use, to pump the water out—water which had splashed in through the open manholes—and the manhole plates could have been put back on. The water was splashing over the deck and running into these holes. Already the tanks in the pontoon were at least half full. One man in half an hour with a wrench could easily have saved this pontoon. Clark's reply was that he was not a salvage officer. He was physically exhausted and should have been relieved.

The beach and the areas of harbor between the floating causeways were filled with a jumble of wrecked landing craft, concrete fragments of the phoenixes, obstacles, all sorts of things. I tried to discuss the situation calmly with Clark and show him how he could get a great deal done if he'd only get to work. He just had one thing on his mind: would salvage take on the job?

I spent the remainder of the day looking the situation over. Huie filled me in on much that had happened. I thought we should start first on cleaning up the debris of the bombardons. If we did not get much of this wreckage out of the way quickly we would have some Liberties to salvage or the Liberties would have to anchor much further offshore where the water was deeper. The two new salvage vessels were quite suitable for this work with the bombardons, for they had heavy lift booms. So were the British wreck-disposal vessels that I had not found to be any use until now. We could also use the fleet tugs, but perhaps we might need these to continue with repairs and the salvage of landing craft. I could not see how anything could be done to salvage the artificial harbor. Water was pouring through the gaps in the breakwaters where the concrete phoenixes had broken up. With the current sweeping across the harbor it would be difficult if not impossible to operate LSTs at the floating piers, even if these piers were rebuilt. By cannibalizing one of the causeways perhaps we could very quickly put two causeways back in use. But how would we close the gaps in the breakwaters, to permit any LSTs to use the pierheads?

All I could see that we could do, besides picking up the fragments of the bombardons, was to clear up the mess of landing craft, and perhaps by demolition remove some of the larger chunks of concrete lying around from the break-up of the phoenixes.

That night I talked to Admiral Kirk. I told him I considered the most important thing to be done was to pick up the fragments of the bombardons, then to salvage and repair the damaged landing craft. I thought the beach party should go to work on a section of the beach outside of the artificial harbors and prepare an area for grounding our LSTs. It was my strong recommendation that no attempt be made to fix up the artificial harbor for further service, only to get rid of the debris. I thought the whole conception of the artificial harbor was a terrific mistake. I explained the phenomenon of scouring and how it had resulted in the breakdown of the phoenixes and how it was breaking up the ships in the Gooseberry.

I went the next morning with Admiral Kirk to the beach where a conference was to be held with Admiral Hall and army representatives. As I was junior to any of the army representatives and really only there to furnish advice if requested, I stood to one side. I listened to what was said. I had never discussed the artificial harbor with Admiral Hall. I was therefore very surprised to hear him say everything I would have said if I had been asked to express my views. I wondered if Admiral Kirk ever thought I had primed Admiral Hall on what to say for Hall's ideas were exactly the same as mine: the artificial harbors were a complete and colossal waste of money.

The conference ended without my being consulted. The recommendations I had made to Admiral Kirk the previous evening were approved. It was at this conference that I learned that the army expected to enter Cherbourg in a few days. Admiral Kirk told me to get the work of clearing up the debris organized at once so that I could start operations in Cherbourg as quickly as possible. I had already started Huie on the job so I only had to tell him my tentative plan had been approved, so he could go ahead full speed. I arranged for McClung to transfer men and equipment to Huie, keeping only one fleet tug off Utah. I never realized the magnitude of work required to clean up the wreckage of the storm. I do not now remember the details, but Huie was kept very busy with this work for another five or six weeks. Most of the time he spent picking up fragments of the unwieldy bombardons. He had from six to eight shifts all this time, just picking up that damned nonsense!

AND NOW—THE TOUGH JOB AT CHERBOURG

REAR ADMIRAL WILLIAM A. SULLIVAN*

One of Admiral Kirk's staff brought me a resident of Cherbourg who had succeeded in getting through the German lines to bring us a chart of Cherbourg Harbor. It had been marked up to show where the Germans had planted mines inside the harbor. The chart had been prepared by a pilot and his friend. Both lived in houses a mile or so apart. Each house had windows overlooking the harbor. The two had compared watches and from each of their houses had watched the Germans dropping mines, noting the time of each mine and the angle and the direction of the mine from their house. Later they got together and prepared the chart. A resistance worker brought the chart through the lines. It showed that the Germans had dropped nearly ninety mines in the water and outer harbor. They were in addition to the buoyed mines at the entrance, which were controlled mines that had been put down years ago by the French.

The chart turned out to be quite accurate but it did not show all the mines planted by the Germans. I think altogether we found some four hundred. Of course the other thing they did not show on the chart were the types of mines. The Germans were planting half a dozen different types.

Just before I left Omaha Beach for Cherbourg, General Eisenhower arrived with a group of staff officers from London on an inspection tour. He asked me to drop him a note just as soon as I had formed any idea of the situation at Cherbourg and give him any estimate I could of the clearance work that was required.

Captain Norman Ives, who was to be the commanding officer of the

*For biographical information on Sullivan see pp. 295–296.

naval base at Cherbourg, arrived at Omaha from the U.S. He and I decided to drive into Cherbourg Harbor together. We left Utah Beach early on the morning that we had word that the army was beginning to enter Cherbourg. It was a slow trip for we were stopped for various reasons quite often. Once we came under sniper fire as we rounded a turn in the road. A couple of jeeps ahead of us had pulled off the road, and some army officers who had been riding in them had taken cover. I went over and talked to them. They had a walkie-talkie and said they had notified a tank unit nearby and the tank was coming to clear the road.

Ives, I found, was a very impatient man. He borrowed an army rifle and walked out in the open to get a better shot at the snipers. He had seen three or four Germans around a farmhouse. When Ives walked out the Germans took cover. There was no more shooting. The Germans left the farmhouse and disappeared over the top of a hill. We resumed our journey before the tank arrived.

We had to take quite a zigzag course in approaching the town. Everywhere there were signs of heavy fighting: burned-out tanks, trucks, autos, dead horses, cattle, and some dead Germans, parts of military gear, rifles, uniforms, pots and pans, ammunition all over the place. As we passed what had been a German fortification we stopped to see some military personnel extinguishing a fire. In the small building which had burned was a huge pile of French currency, much of which was smoldering but some of which was unburned. Our chauffeur got a thousand-franc note as a souvenir.

When we descended a long grade that took us into the town we came to what had been a wine shop the day before. A military guard had been posted to protect the premises. We stopped to get instructions. We were told that this wine shop had been looted by German civilians just before our troops entered the city. It was a mess. The windows had been broken. Even the furniture had been pulled out on the street. There were bottles all over the place.

On the way to the waterfront we passed a street where apparently there had been heavy fighting only a few hours before. There must have been at least twenty dead Germans lying on the sidewalks, and German rifles were strewn all over the place. We arrived at the waterfront just before sunset. I found Wroten had already arrived with Colonel Cress. Ives had sent a small advance party and they had also arrived. His party had found a house which had just been evacuated by German military personnel and had been reserved for Ives. He invited me to stay with him. Colonel Cress had temporarily taken a place around the corner. Wroten had arranged to stay with him for a few days.

Everywhere there was evidence that the town had been pretty well looted by the Germans before surrender. We were told later that most of the looting had been done by the TODT (foreign labor force made up of Poles, Russians, and so on), who ran wild when the German officials left for the Channel Islands.

The street outside the house reserved for Ives was littered with furniture. In the house we found one room, just to the right of the entrance, which was completely empty. A stairway leading upstairs was choked with furniture that had apparently been thrown down from the topside. The hallway leading to the remainder of the house was full of furniture and it was too late at night for us to do anything so we set up two cots in this one empty room and stayed there. We found a bathroom in a little house in the garden. It was quite a nice bathroom and we wondered how come there was a bathroom out there. For a few days, until we got somebody in to clean up the place, we had an idea that was the only bathroom in the house, but actually it was an extra one. There were two inside.

For two or three blocks around the streets were full of furniture. Now, why were these fellows looting the place? Why were they taking all this furniture out when they knew the Americans were coming in the next day? It's one of those crazy things that happen in wartime. You can't understand why people do some things. Apparently the Germans had occupied all these houses around and they had just been swapping furniture around from one house to another. "Oh, I just like that chair, I want that chair—you can have one from my place."

We were to have no rest that first night. The U.S. Army went on one big drunk. The Germans had gathered great quantities of Hennessy's brandy and Benedictine in Cherbourg. Every German billet, pillbox, military establishment of any kind had large quantities hidden away. Our troops found it. Some mixed the brandy with French wines. There were drunken voices singing, rifle shooting, all night, mixed with frequent detonation of hand grenades. Colonel Cress couldn't sleep because of the racket outside of his place. He got up during the night and went out to the front door to see if he could chase away some noisy drunks. When he left the room he had been sleeping in somebody tossed a hand grenade through the window into the bunk that he'd been using and blew it up.

The next morning Wroten and I started to take a look around. We found one of our groups had arrived. This was Hutch and three of his men in a jeep. He had gone directly to the waterfront and found explosives planted by the Germans in the locked gates to the commercial port. These explosives had not been detonated. Hutch cut the wires and saved the gates. This was a big help.

The most important facility in Cherbourg Harbor had been the Quai de France, which was quite a modern installation. Alongside this pier was the Darse Transatlantique, a large slip which the transatlantic passenger ships that had visited Cherbourg had used—such ships as the *Normandie,*

Queen Mary, Bremen, and so on. The Germans had run a few freight cars loaded with sea mines onto the pier and had blown up the whole place. Two large ships had been capsized and sunk to block the entrance to the Darse Transatlantique. It was clearly evident that a great amount of work would be required to do anything that would permit either the Quai de France or the Darse Transatlantique to be used again. We passed this by and looked around the two small harbors and the commercial port, which we found to be suitable for use by small boats, landing craft, barges, and so forth; noted several dozen small craft sunk in these basins.

Wroten and I then went to the arsenal area, which contained three large basins and which was clearly the part of the harbor most suitable for unloading military cargo. We were stopped by a military sentry at the entrance to the arsenal area. He said he would allow no personnel to enter unless he had a pass signed by General Barton, the general who commanded the division that had taken Cherbourg. He was adamant in his refusal to recognize me or my rank. There was no officer of the guard to whom I could appeal.

I went back to the waterfront building which Ives had taken over as naval headquarters. Ives knew about the sentry and was furious. He said the army had found a huge stock of liquor left by the Germans and had put sentries all over the place to stop anyone from entering until they could cart the booze away. He was looking for the general. I told him to tell the general I was under orders from General Eisenhower to survey the arsenal immediately, and that I would have to send him a report. I wanted quick action.

Wroten and I then drove around the arsenal area to the outer breakwater. There's a town there, but I've forgotten its name. We thought that by walking out on this breakwater we could get a bird's-eye view of the situation. We could only drive in the jeep to the end of the breakwater. We proceeded on foot to the main entrance of the outer harbor, which the French call La Grande Rade. Here our view of much of the harbor that we wanted to see was blocked off by an old French fortification built on an island in La Grande Rade. I had my glasses with me and took a good look around. There were a few wrecks to be seen in La Grande Rade, but whether they were so situated that they would be or should be moved, or how difficult they would be to move, we could not at that distance make any estimate. I had been told that the French had controlled mines at the entrance to La Grande Rade and that these mines were connected by submerged cables to a nearby French fort. I'd also been told that it was believed that the Germans had laid new cables to these mines so that they could also be controlled in another place. As long as I was at the harbor entrance, I thought I would look around for any indication of cables to these mines. Sure enough, we found an armored cable a couple of inches in diameter, which led from the face of the breakwater and then went back into the water, leading off at an angle that would take it across the harbor at this point. I felt that this was probably a cable controlling the mines, for I could not account for any other reason for a cable at this point. The breakwater itself had a nice promenade along the top.

Our British P-Party had not arrived. The minesweepers that were to sweep the waters approaching Cherbourg were being held up by German coastal batteries which had not been silenced, and which controlled all the waters off the harbor.

Wroten and I then drove back to town. There was nothing I could do until Ives could arrange to get the sentry removed from the arsenal area. He had not been able to get a pass to the arsenal. There were in fact two commanders to the port—Ives for the navy and an army commander—but neither one was allowed in that particular area because they didn't have a pass from General Barton.

I decided I could perhaps do a little useful work and cut the cable to the mines at the harbor entrance. This would perhaps prevent anyone from blowing the mines until the P-Party arrived and could take care of the situation. Wroten and I procured a length of rope, a hacksaw, and a few miscellaneous tools. We went to the outer breakwater. As we arrived at the place where the breakwater connects to the shore I met General Collins and General Roosevelt. Collins said I was just the person he was looking for. He wanted some small boats to land an assault party on the fort. He thought the navy should provide that transportation. He said there were Germans still in the fort. He had been told that the fort fired on U.S. planes passing overhead the night before. I questioned the accuracy of this report and said I'd spent an hour out on the breakwater that morning and had seen no signs of life anywhere. Anyway we had no boat to get out there at the moment, but I was now going out to cut the mine cables.

Collins thought I was taking a chance. He had a platoon of soldiers standing by and wanted to know if I wanted an armed guard. I said I saw absolutely no reason for any such protection. When I asked how did he know that this fort had fired on the planes he said someone in his troops reported it. I then asked if he did not realize the army was drunk last night? Didn't some drunk perhaps make up the yarn about the fort shooting at the planes? I offered my glasses to the general. He decided after looking at the fort that probably I was right. But he and General Roosevelt decided to come along and watch us cut the cable. We all walked out to the end of the breakwater. We saw no signs of life anywhere. Wroten and I lay down on the breakwater and by reaching over the side made rope slings fast to the cable so that the end would not slide away after we had made our cut. Suddenly we heard a commotion, something like hail splattering on the pavement. We looked up. The two generals were legging it

414

down the breakwater. On the fort a dozen Germans were firing at us with rifles. More were coming up from some hatch on the roof. Wroten and I got up and took to our heels. The bullets followed us as we ran, splashing all around us on the pavement but hitting no one. The infantry platoon had drawn up along the shore and was returning the fire. The generals were now furious. They sent for reinforcements but it was late in the day to do much before sunset.

The next day I saw the battle. The army brought up a piece of heavy artillery and started firing at one place in the side of the old fort. After several rounds a hole was made in the masonry. The Germans raised a white flag. Collins sent word to them to get inside the fort and to take shelter. He had arranged with the army air force to bomb the fort. Planes were sent from England to do the job. When the white flag was raised General Collins asked the air force to cancel the bombing. He got back word over the radio at once, the planes were en route and could not be called back for they were not fitted with radio. They arrived very soon and dropped their bombs but they did not bomb the fort General Collins had asked to have bombed. They bombed an abandoned fort on the other side of the harbor. Most of the bombs missed that fort and dropped into the water anyway.

Then the problem developed—how to get someone into the fort to accept the surrender and how to get the Germans out. Ives found a small sailboat the Germans had overlooked when they smashed up the craft in the harbor. He went out and brought some of the officers back. Then he arranged to have the garrison removed several at a time. He took the officers to the building he was using as naval headquarters. We questioned them about delayed-action mines planted on shore. They refused to talk about mines planted in the harbor, in the water, but were quite ready to talk about mines planted ashore, for they said that mines planted ashore were an oriental barbarism; that on their honor as German officers they would have nothing to do with it. They knew about the mines that had been planted in Naples and admitted they had been ordered to plant such mines in Cherbourg but had said they considered such mines to be disgraceful and below the dignity and honor of a German officer. Mines in the harbor were a military practice.

With all the excitement of the day I had forgotten about trying to get a pass for the arsenal area. Ives had taken it up with the army and had been assured that the sentry would be taken away that night. He was pacified by the navy getting a truckful of brandy. That night, after questioning the German officers, he and I had a drink of this brandy. It was the last we were to have for the load disappeared during the night. I always thought that the sailors in Ives's outfit were the thieves but nothing could ever be proved.

The next morning I went to the arsenal. The sentry had been withdrawn but a new sentry had been posted. Passes signed by General Barton were no longer valid. His troops had gotten all the liquor they could get. Another division had moved in. I looked up Colonel Sibley and raised hell. He promised to get me a pass. Finally I got in for a look around. I still have a copy of the report I drew up after I had a chance to look the whole harbor over. It was the report I drew up essentially for Admiral King. With all the damned nonsense that happened I never got around to sending one to General Eisenhower. He finally sent a man up and then he came up himself later.

The outer harbor at Cherbourg is a very extensive area. It is inside an outer breakwater which is at least three miles in overall length, and it is outside an inner breakwater. The French, as I have said previously, called it La Grande Rade. It was used for anchoring ships in heavy weather. Over on the very western corner of La Grande Rade the French had facilities for receiving petroleum from tankers. In this area about a dozen small craft were sunk, where the tankers normally moored. These were removed at a later date. We could see masts and topside structures of two ships projecting above the surface of the water. The French said that these ships had been sunk four years previously. They thought it possible that two large harbor tugs that were missing were also sunk in the outer harbor and were wholly submerged. They also had a list of thirteen small harbor craft which were missing and which might have been taken by the Germans to the Channel Islands or might have been sunk some place in the harbor, perhaps even in the inner harbor.

Many mines had been placed by the Germans in the outer harbor, and the removal of these mines was made extremely difficult because the Germans had planted several different types of mines. There were, besides the conventional moored mines which were detonated either by contact or by distant controls, magnetic mines, oyster mines, acoustical mines, and delayed-action mines. There were mines which could be made inactive for a certain predetermined time up to a maximum of eighty-five days. When inactive these mines remained on the bottom in the mud and could not be swept up by any kind of a sweep. Once activated, if they were of the contact variety, they would rise up to a predetermined depth. If magnetic or acoustical, they would remain on the bottom but would detonate upon receiving the necessary magnetic or acoustical impulse. However, to make the situation more complicated, these mines were fitted with a second delayed-action control. Say a mine had been set to be activated in eighteen days. On the eighteenth day after the clock mechanism had unwound, before releasing the device which activated the mine, a second delaying device came into play. Instead of permitting the mine to detonate when it became subjected to the first magnetic or acoustical

416

influence necessary for detonation, it would wait until these influences had been repeated to the certain predetermined number of times required by the second delayed action device. This could be as many as eight times. Consequently, until eighty-five days had passed since the Germans had departed from Cherbourg, it was necessary each morning to give the entire inner and outer harbor of Cherbourg eight acoustical sweeps and eight magnetic sweeps.

In our work on the waterfront on the arsenal area we had found a place where the Germans had been working on a large number of concrete boxes. There were a few completed boxes, but there were indications that quite a large number had already been made and taken away. We could not account for the purpose of these peculiar boxes until a landing craft was blown up at low tide in shallow water, inshore, in the outer harbor. The mine removal party found, when they investigated this casualty, that the landing craft had settled on a mine which had been made out of concrete. Checking around, we found that these boxes that were being made were indeed cases for an improvised sort of mine. A great many of these were scattered in the mud in shallow water portions of both the inner and outer harbor, just where a ship might settle. These mines were about three feet by a foot and a half wide, and probably about a foot deep. They had a place on top for a detonator, but then they also had an arrangement where you could screw a pipe into the top and put the detonator on top of the pipe, so although this mine might be on the bottom, a ship could settle on the pipe six or eight feet above and set it off. It was a homemade type mine and was pretty clever.

It was several days after the U.S. occupation of Cherbourg before the minesweepers could approach the entrance because of the coastal forts that still held out. By the time the minesweepers did arrive the British P-Party had come in over the road and had deactivated the controlled mines at the entrance. The minesweepers then started with the conventional circular sweeps in the outer harbor. However, the Pluto people started putting pressure to clear a path so that the gas pipeline from England could be run ashore in France. Everything had to make way for Pluto, which I thought and still think was a scandalous waste of time and effort. As soon as the sweepers had satisfied Pluto they resumed work on the outer harbor but were again diverted to other specific jobs, none of which I considered to be so urgent as to warrant upsetting the schedule which had been planned and agreed to for clearing the harbor.

The British minesweeping party which was doing this work was a splendid organization. I could not help siding with them when they objected to the interferences from the topside, trying to show that if the minesweepers were allowed to continue without interference the entire harbor would be made available for work by all activities very soon.

However, if the practice of designating certain spots to be cleared immediately continued, the work of opening up Cherbourg for receiving military supplies would be greatly delayed. Furthermore, the practice was placing the minesweeping personnel in what I considered unnecessary and unwarranted jeopardy. My objections and warnings were ignored, however, and so I asked to be relieved from any further responsibility for the minesweeping part of the harbor clearance. Admiral Wilkes, who had come over from the U.K. by that time, then relieved me.

At various times we had to salvage barges and landing craft that had settled on concrete mines in shallow water in one section of the eastern portion of the outer harbor. This salvage work was not difficult, but I wondered why the army kept putting landing craft, barges, and floating cranes in this particular section when we had already had several casualties there. Finally I found out that this area of the harbor was not visible from the windows of Admiral Wilkes's office. Wilkes was continually looking out on the ships unloading. If he saw any barge which was not alongside a ship being unloaded or unloading alongside a dock, he was on the phone to some general or other reporting the transportation authorities for inefficiency. He would listen to no reasonable explanation. If he was not making trouble with the military authorities in the port he was making trouble with me or with the French. When I found out why the army was moving idle barges and the like into this section of the harbor I did not complain but only asked the colonel to try and keep the craft in a little deeper water or in areas in which we had already salvaged one craft so we knew that the mines in that particular place had been detonated.

One day a gale developed and a sea sweeping in through the entrance washed a number of the craft moored on this side ashore. Before we could get the mess cleared up, Wilkes became cognizant of the strandings and he asked all sorts of embarrassing questions as to how come the army had so many craft tied up in this area.

I never sent General Eisenhower the report he desired. For the first few days I was kept from the arsenal area. I could make no report. When I did get an idea of the extent of the harbor clearance work involved I had become conscious of the extensive mine field in the inner harbor. About this time, Commander Butcher, naval aide to General Eisenhower, came to Cherbourg and looked me up. I found him pleasant and agreeable; told him of my difficulties in getting into the arsenal, and the number of mines in the harbor, and that the minesweepers were about to start work but first had to prepare a way for the pipeline Pluto. Our harbor clearance work was not extensive, compared to other places that we had worked in; I believed that there was much less than had been anticipated. However, as we had not been able to make a real survey I would not like to say that there were no complicated jobs. From what I was able to see, I could see nothing complicated. But if the speedy opening of the port was as important as it seemed to be, it would be better to forget Pluto and other things and let the minesweepers get going. I did not know how much of this message sank in, and how much was passed on to General Eisenhower. Butcher was not an engineer. He had no naval or maritime experience before he got his commission. He was just a nice guy at a poker party.

Some time later, about the time I was really disgusted, General Eisenhower paid a surprise visit to Cherbourg. No advance notice was given of his coming. He was such a considerate person, he did not want to discommode anyone by sending advance word but he wanted to see me so badly that he walked up the three long flights of stairs to our records office. He left his card, with regrets that I was not in my office. That day Wroten had left an enlisted man on watch. He had no idea where I was, and perhaps no idea who I was. Anyway, it was not until the next day that I got the card and the message. I thought it was unfortunate at the time, for I was fully prepared to give some very frank comments on the situation and on the many reasons for the unnecessary delays. This was at the time when there was general concern about the inadequate flow of supplies to the front. The general concern was responsible for increasing the delays in the reconstruction of Cherbourg. Every half-informed staff officer who was becoming interested was offering his two bits worth of suggestions. Perhaps it may have been fortunate for me that I did not blow off as I would have done if I had met General Eisenhower. I might have gotten myself in further difficulties.

A long time before D day, a joint British and American logistics study estimated that within a week after the capture of Cherbourg, about 4,000 tons of supplies a day should be landed in this port, and that a maximum daily tonnage of 7,200 tons should be obtained within two months after occupancy.

The mine problem knocked the estimate of 4,000 tons at the end of the first week out the window. The way higher authority interfered with minesweeping made a very serious delay in starting any harbor clearance work, but once we were able to start work, we opened the port quickly. On our thirtieth day of occupancy, 5,930 tons were landed, against a preinvasion estimate of 6,300 tons. Ten days later, the tonnage handled was 6,740 tons, and in another ten days the daily tonnage had grown to 7,200 tons, which was approximately the maximum daily tonnage considered possible in the preinvasion study. In another month the daily capacity of the port was raised to 9,000 tons.

The condition of the roads and the railroads out of Cherbourg could not handle more tonnage. The U.S. had to open other ports for the advance into Germany.

The invasion of southern France (Anvil/Dragoon) in August 1944 is considered in naval history as an example of an almost perfect amphibious operation. This degree of excellence involved most of the basic elements: training, timing, the cooperation of the army, navy, and air force and indeed, the fulfillment of military purpose. It puts one in mind of Admiral Harry Hill's amphibious operation on the island of Tinian in the Pacific in World War II except that Anvil/Dragoon was on a much larger scale. Admiral Cunningham, CinC Mediterranean, recognized that in his signal to Admiral Hewitt in his flagship: "All convoys have passed at the planned moment. An operation so well organized must succeed." Hewitt's assault force included a total of 880 ships, from battleships to small naval vessels while some 1,370 beaching craft were carried on decks with davits to land the military might on the beaches.

For the first time in the Mediterranean area the U.S. Army allowed the navy to lay on an extended prelanding bombardment and to land assault waves in daylight. There were 396 transport planes carrying more then five thousand paratroopers that landed at five in the morning on D day to be followed at 9 A.M. by 71 aircraft, towing in a fleet of gliders with reinforcements.

To be sure, enemy opposition could not be compared with that met on the beaches of Normandy. German U-boats and the Luftwaffe had been almost completely eliminated in the Mediterranean. The German ground forces put up no defense in depth and attempted no counterattacks. Admiral Ansel, in his oral history excerpt that follows, gives some evidence of this in his account of the surrender of some nine hundred Germans from the three islands near the port of Marseilles. It was they who gave a blinker signal that they were ready to surrender and then sent a German boat with two officers to negotiate, one flying a white flag. The French general de Lattre de Tassigny understandably was anxious to share in the initial assault on his German-occupied homeland, but Admiral Hewitt persuaded him that there was often enough confusion in any amphibious operation without adding a language difficulty. However a token French tank and motorized infantry brigade was joined to the army's sixth Corps.

Yet such achievement of a successful assault landing was not accomplished without some stubborn determination and disagreement by both American and British sides of the planning. It is difficult to discover in the long history of Anglo-American planning in the European/ Mediterranean theater a more determined resistance on both sides. General Eisenhower proved to be consistently unmovable in his insistence that the operation shall go on. Prime Minister Churchill seems to have been doggedly determined that the operation shall not go on *unless* it met with his intentions and they were at great variance with those of Eisenhower. President Roosevelt was sometimes vacillating—or perhaps wavering is the more likely term—at one time even enlisting the backing of Stalin at the Teheran conference to withstand the arguments of Churchill. Eisenhower finally won the day. He was consistently imbued with the thought that Anvil would help with the Normandy action and perhaps even more convinced that the capture of the major French port of Marseilles would prove of immense value to him as a port of entry for American troops, supplies, and equipment of all kinds. This conviction was amply rewarded.

Churchill on the other hand seemed never to appreciate the points upon which General Eisenhower stood. He wanted only, if the landing was accomplished, to veer off to the Adriatic in the direction of Vienna and the Balkans. It was only at the last moment, five days before the date set for D day, which was 15 August, that the British chiefs of staff gave their approval for advance. Even then Churchill was not happy. He had made his final appeal to Eisenhower on 9 August and was turned down by the general with a blunt "no." But, as Admiral Hewitt states in his account that follows this introduction, Churchill did appear on the deck of the HMS *Kimberley* on the afternoon of the D-day landings to smile and give his V sign for the benefit of the invasion troops and the hundreds of naval craft as they passed by. As has been quoted, "Churchill had at least done the civil to Anvil."*

In July Churchill had said he wanted the Americans to know "that we have been ill-treated and are furious." And the British chiefs of staff informed the Americans that neither the British government nor the chiefs considered the pending operation to be "correct strategy."

Churchill had made it known when the plans for Anvil began to be discussed that he had indeed shown some interest in Anvil at the Teheran conference but he also wanted the American combined chiefs to realize that the situation had now changed greatly. The British had high expecta-

*Samuel Eliot Morison, *History of United States Naval Operations in World War II*, vol. 11, *The Invasion of France and Germany, 1944–1945* (Boston: Little, Brown, 1975) 232.

tions when they invaded the Italian peninsula for they had expected that Rome would be captured in short order, but it had not fallen and General Wilson's troops were stalled at Anzio. There was an acute shortage of assault shipping, namely, LSTs.

General Eisenhower was concerned with the success of Overlord, and in order to guarantee that success he wanted added divisions of troops and landing craft. And there was a problem here. Eisenhower viewed Overlord and Anvil as a double envelopment but both were dependent on added LSTs. The general was willing to delay the operations for a month or so to allow for the U.S. production of these craft. Churchill was irritated by the delay and by the insistence of the U.S proposal for the southern France invasion. It was this set of circumstances that caused a typical Churchillian growl at one of the discussions: "The destinies of two great empires seem to be tied up in some God-damned things called LSTs."*

*Ibid., 28. A detailed discussion of the problem is to be found in chapter 13 of the same volume, "High-level Wrangling," p. 221ff, covering the period from October 1943 to August 1944.

A WARM WELCOME IN THE SOUTH OF FRANCE

ADMIRAL H. KENT HEWITT*

Some time before we made the move of headquarters from Algiers to Casablanca, Admiral King had been to a conference in London. He came back through Casablanca and I flew down to join him and have a conference. We went up to Port Lyautey to look at the airfields and then we had a chance to discuss further developments in the plans for the Anvil operation. That was the last time I saw him before we actually carried out the Anvil operation in August.

The plan must have been discussed in the combined chiefs of staff first. They wanted of course not only the liberation of southern France but to get the port of Marseilles and the railroad system up the Rhone Valley, which was of tremendous value in support of the armies operating in northern France—and particularly as it turned out that the French ports, the western ones and Cherbourg, were much more badly damaged than they had thought they would be. They weren't able to use them to full capacity for some time. Marseilles was almost a lifesaver from that point of view.

General Eisenhower was adamant as to the importance of that landing. He fought on that thing. But actually we didn't know until the very last whether we were going to be able to carry out that operation or not. It took Franklin D. Roosevelt himself to insist on it.

Churchill did everything possible to change the plan. But once it was decided upon, like a good soldier, he went along. He was in Naples when we set sail with our big convoy, and he passed in as we were steaming out.

*For biographical information on Hewitt see pp. 156–157.

424

He came in a British admiral's barge. We recognized him. He waved to us and held up his V finger signal and he was a very good sport about it. Then he flew over to Corsica and came out in a British cruiser and took a look at us again as we went by.

I would like to be able to confirm the story, which I believe is friendly, that Sir Winston renamed it Dragoon operation because he was dragooned into it. (Churchill himself says it was renamed because they didn't want to take the risk that the Germans had discovered the meaning of Anvil.)

Planning for the operation began in January 1944 in Algiers, very shortly after Anzio. The planning section of my staff and that of General Patch and his planners were established together in Algiers. Also an air force general was assigned to the planning and stayed with us right along. That is the first time we ever had any air planning at all, along with the naval and military planning. Before they just didn't seem to be particularly interested in it.

Let me add some little human interest remarks. When we went into Sicily we strove to get the air to join with us in making plans. They never did and so we put to sea without knowing what the air force plan was. We made preparations. General Patton came to me. We had had naval air support for the landing in Morocco, so General Patton said: "Admiral, I wish you'd get one of your navy carriers to back us up on this landing. I can't get that blankety-blank air force to do anything." We were all fighting the same war, but they were interested in long-distance bombing of enemy airfields and things of that sort, and anything like the supporting of a landing or supporting the troops on shore seemed to be a sort of side-show for them. Later on, that condition improved.

Well, I told Patton that I wished just as much as he did that we had some navy air behind us, but that with the land bases so close, I didn't feel I'd be justified in asking for it, and also if I did ask for it I wouldn't get it because all our carriers were badly needed in the Pacific at that time.

The landing in southern France was actually carried out on the fifteenth of August (D day for that operation). I think it was about the twelfth or thirteenth we sailed with the big transports from Naples. The other ships, the smaller landing craft, had to be sent earlier from various places, some of them from Corsica. All these details had to be worked out, and they were worked out very carefully, with the result that everything worked almost perfectly. We didn't know until we actually sailed whether we were really going to carry out the operation or not. We were threatened with having to take the same troops around and land them on the Bay of Biscay somewhere. This wouldn't have been so good. We would have to replan and reload and do most everything over.

The troops which were going to make the landing had to be withdrawn from the Italian front a little ahead of time, to retrain. There were ten divisions eventually, including the French army. There were three American divisions and seven French. There was also an airborne outfit which was British—the only British troops that took part in the operation. I don't think it was division strength.

The French—and you couldn't blame them—were very, very anxious to be the first to land on their own soil. General Delan was very strong for that. He was a very fine man, very pleasant, very volatile. I had to convince him—General de Gaulle too—that it was hard enough to get soldiers and sailors working together in the same boat in the first place, but with the language barrier it would be absolutely impossible. It would be chaotic. Fortunately, I had my friend Admiral Lemonnier to back me up on that completely. So they agreed to it finally. As it worked out, the American troops took the beachhead and then the French army landed in behind them and started inland.

For this operation we had a considerable naval force. We had two or three of our battleships, a large number of destroyers. We had British battleships, a number of British cruisers, a number of British destroyers, minesweepers, as well as some of the transports and landing craft. We had everything in the French navy that was available.

We had forces divided up between the different assault groups so that each group had their own force—battleships, cruisers, and so on—to call on for gunfire. Thinking things over from the political point of view, we carefully assigned at least one French ship to each of those units because we felt that if some honest citizen on shore got his house shot up during the operation we didn't want him to be able to blame the Yankees or the British for it. It might be one of their own ships.

Some of the small craft, the LCTs, had to be moved up ahead of time because they were very slow and they couldn't go too far. The craft were dispatched according to their speeds, rather than by the final force to which they were attached, so the slow ones went first, then the next ones, then finally the fastest ships came. As they approached the general attack area, they split up and the different crafts went to their own assault forces. We had to do the same thing in Sicily and Salerno, as a matter of fact.

It was all a great responsibility, the coordinating of these movements. I felt the responsibility, naturally. But I always had the feeling we had worked things out as well as we could. I had a very fine staff on whom I could rely, and naval commanders, subordinate commanders, on whom I could rely. I didn't worry. I mean that. I had the attitude—we've done our best and I hope that everything will be all right. I'm one of these double-acrostic addicts. It's a great relaxation. But sometimes some of my staff would have a fit because we'd be going into one of these landings and I'd be sitting up on the bridge, ready to take action if anything unexpected came up, and working out some of these puzzles. I had to concentrate my mind on that. It took it off other worries.

We met with some real opposition, particularly on the right, in the Golfe de Fréjus. We were supposed to land first up toward the Cape Geramo at a very steep shelving beach there and then get some of the army ashore so they could advance along the coast towards Saint-Raphael because the big beach was at the head of the gulf where we really wanted to land most of our forces. But that was flanked, on the shore, by the enemy force at Saint-Raphael so we'd try to make a sliding thing in there.

They landed at 6 o'clock in the morning. The other landing was supposed to be made at 12 o'clock. By this time the army was supposed to have been able to flatten those defenses. We made the landing on time. The boats went in, with the scout boats ahead and the slow minesweepers and what not. They were immediately taken under fire by the guns, not French, but German guns from Saint-Raphael.

Admiral Lewis (Rear Admiral S. S.), who had been my chief of staff, had taken over the command of that group. On his own he made the decision to hold that landing up and to land those troops in behind where the others were. That was very fortunate because there would have been very heavy losses if they'd continued to land.

When I first heard that landing was held up (the orders were to carry it out regardless) I was—and so was the general—somewhat annoyed. But when Lewis explained the situation to me I agreed with him. He'd done absolutely the right thing. And so did the division commander (Major General John E. Dahlquist) commanding the Thirty-sixth Division. He was already ashore and not in a position to make that decision himself.

There was some resistance at other points, but it was not too heavy. That was the main thing. Compared to what we'd been faced with before it wasn't bad. I think it was more or less a surprise landing. Of course they were ready for it. They had put up a lot of beach obstacles and the beaches were mined, but they didn't concentrate everything right at that point to meet it. I think they were looking for some landings maybe further east, along towards Cannes.

We received an amazing welcome, perfectly wonderful, on the part of the French people. I went ashore with General Patch the first day to go around and see what was going on. We took Admiral Lemonnier with us. He had begged to be taken along. He had no part, no command in the operation, but he went about with us. He was the junior, but we all stood aside and said he was to be the first one to land on his own soil. We went around in a jeep. He had a marvelous reception everywhere. We'd go through a little town and crowds would rush out from cafés with wine glasses and bottles of wine held up to us to partake.

I remember the first five or six hundred yards in this jeep after we landed. We went along on the road towards St. Raphael and there was a French girl riding a bicycle ahead of us with her skirts ballooning out. We overtook her and the admiral said something to her. I don't know what he said but she was so surprised that she promptly fell off her bicycle. We stopped and she came rushing up to the jeep and gave the admiral a kiss. That was his first welcome to France.

The French there in the south of France, when they recognized Admiral Lemonnier as a French admiral, just went wild. They had never been told anything. They didn't know whether France still had a navy. So he got a royal welcome and as soon as he told the crowd who General Patch and I were we got an equally warm welcome. This is another one of the things that the landing in the south of France did. It liberated that part of France immediately and gave a tremendous boost to French morale.

There were other important results of course. In addition to having a very valuable port, the port of Marseilles, as well as Toulon, a valuable naval base, was the fact that the western Mediterranean was practically cleaned up. The Strait of Gibraltar by that time had been pretty well sealed against movement through by enemy submarines because of the employment of U.S. Navy blimps, combined with the British surface forces at Gibraltar. No enemy submarines were passing through then and the ones which had been basing themselves in France had been destroyed or captured. There were no airfields now available to the enemy. Consequently we were able to sail shipping into the western Mediterranean independently, unescorted, and even with burning lights, navigation lights, at night. This resulted in tremendous saving in shipping.

THE ENEMY SURPRISES AND SURRENDERS

REAR ADMIRAL WALTER C. ANSEL

WALTER CHARLES ANSEL was born on 25 August 1897 in Elgin, Illinois. A member of the class of 1919 at the U.S. Naval Academy, he graduated on 6 June 1918 and proceeded to sea at once on convoy escort duty in the Atlantic during the closing months of World War I. After several sea and shore assignments he developed an interest in amphibious warfare while a student at the Naval War College and at the Marine Corps School in Quantico, Virginia, in 1930–31. This involved the study and development of naval doctrine for amphibious warfare, at that time a relatively unknown subject in the navy.

When World War II began Ansel was on duty in the office of the chief of naval operations but was soon ordered to command the *Winooski,* a fleet oiler of the Atlantic Fleet. Later he was transferred to the staff of Commander, Amphibious Forces, North African Waters, and took part in the invasions of North Africa and Sicily. In the landings at Algeria on 8 November 1942 he commanded the advance party that entered the small port of Arzeu, secured the shipping, and prepared the port for unloading operations. In October 1943 he took command of the cruiser USS *Philadelphia* in the Mediterranean. In 1944 the *Philadelphia* supported the operations at Anzio and Formia and in the summer of 1944 took part in the invasion of southern France where, with the aid of Marines from the *Philadelphia* and one other cruiser, Ansel accepted the surrender of the islands off Marseilles.

Ansel had later service in the office of the chief of naval operations, had duty as chief of staff to Commander, Cruiser Division One, in Japan and a final assignment as a member of the U.S. Naval Mission in Brazil. He was retired on 30 June 1949 and settled in Annapolis. In 1951 Ansel was named a Forrestal Fellow at the Naval Academy and used this award to write two books: one a study of why Germany did not attempt to invade England during World War II, and a second on the German invasion of Crete. In both cases he undertook research in Germany where he had access to German documents of the war and where he could use his facility in the German language.

Admiral Ansel died on 26 November 1977 in Annapolis, Maryland, and was interred in the Naval Academy cemetery.

The chief planning for Dragoon was done in Naples. The commander in chief was in Naples; Admiral Cunningham had moved over from Algiers. Admiral Hewitt and his staff were established there too. We found that we were to join up with battleships under Rear Admiral Carlton Bryant in Taranto, Italy, then to proceed to our fire-support jobs in southern France. It must have been early August by this time, or the end of July. On hand at Taranto were the *Nevada, New York, Arkansas,* and *Philadelphia.* We exchanged ideas with the British, read our plans, got ourselves squared away, and just waited until it was time to join the parade towards southern France.

It was thought to be a major operation. Sicily alone was almost of the same dimension as southern France. Our job was to support the landing at Saint-Tropez, which is on the west edge of the fine Riviera ports. It has a good little harbor with plenty of yachts. We had little information on what the opposition might be. Having learned at Anzio about hooking up in tight communication with the army people we were supporting, we put our radio gear in good shape and practiced with it. Our bombarding position, rather than on flank, was right to seaward of our troop transports. This landing took place in daylight. Now we did fire neutralization barrages ahead of the landings. We were in good touch with our people ashore. The day was 15 August (Quinze Août) 1944. A great day!

An element of surprise wasn't attempted, probably because we knew that the Germans were not very strong—not strong enough to mount a counteroffensive to drive us out. Our area was on the approaches to Toulon, the largest French naval base in the Med; it lay to the west of Saint-Tropez. Direct landing support lasted only two days; then came assignment to the task force on the left (western) flank of the landing front. The mission was to support the advance of our landed forces toward Marseilles in the west—the largest French port. As *Philadelphia* moved west in pace with army advances she took under fire defending guns on shore. She was screened by the French destroyer leader, *Le Malin,* commanded by our friend Captain Ballande. He joined our shoots; always was anxious to get in close and let them have it. The heaviest opposing fire came from 15-inch guns of Saint-Mandrier defending Toulon. They made big splashes but no hits. Off the Giens Peninsula we ducked in and out making smoke and shell fire. On 21 August we lost radio contact with one of our own spotting planes (*Philadelphia* alone had planes). Two were in the air. The second one soon reported seeing his mate struck by a shell and burst into flame. We lost Lieutenant Cahill, the pilot, and Radioman Ryan.

Marseilles's approaches and those to Port de Bouc on the Gulf de Fos just to the west in the delta of the Rhone River's mouth are guarded by three offshore fortress islands. We wanted to get access to these ports cleared of mines and gunfire. Ships had been shooting at the defending islands for days. The USS *Quincy* and *Philadelphia* entered the swept channel off Carro and steamed into the Gulf de Fos. The *Quincy* fired at the islands and silenced their shelling of minesweepers all around us. They were working hard, exploding mines as they went. Our plane flying surveillance reported French flags hoisted on the island target. It was growing dark; both ships stood out. On approaching the end of the swept channel near Carro the plane reported PT-boat 555 mined closer to Carro; then a rescue boat from there struck another mine. The plane landed to receive a hand message from the boat 555 but was unable to get close enough; attempts to get the message by blinker light likewise failed. It could have been a message on the shore situation, something that we needed badly.

On the following morning, 25 August 1944, PT 555 was still afloat near Carro. To clear up her status and that ashore, it was decided to establish a direct communication channel on shore. Ensign W. M. Pitcher, who knew French, and Aviation Radioman Hogg were flown in with a spotting radio set to friendly Carro. The plane landed them without any trouble; the radio at once established contact with the ship, which directed Pitcher to report on 555 and establish contact with the French Forces of the Interior for information on the military situation, especially as to the possibilities of opening Port de Bouc. The 555 he found holed in the stern but being towed into Carro. Five of the crew were missing (one with a broken leg was evacuated to the *Philadelphia* by plane). Medical stores and food were flown into the boat.

Command on up the line heard Station Pitcher—it became very popular. All kinds of questions were asked; most of them Pitcher couldn't answer. He did report three thousand German troops gathered in pockets to the northward of Target D-06. This was a target close to shore that our

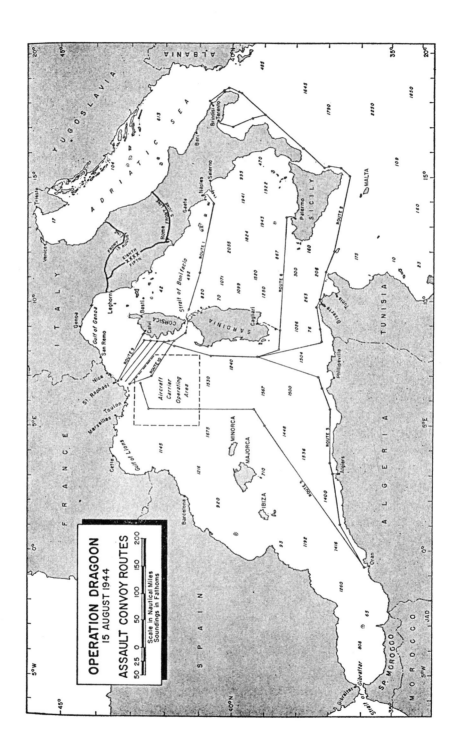

OPERATION DRAGOON
15 AUGUST 1944

ASSAULT CONVOY ROUTES

Scale in Nautical Miles
Soundings in Fathoms

50 25 0   50   100   150   200

432

destroyer escort had taken under fire during our first entry into the gulf. The trouble was we had run off to the west of our gridded map-chart and could not therefore locate the ships for ranging position with respect to the target. Feverishly the navigator tried to extend the map-chart with drawing instruments. The shore area was wooded; our planes could not find the enemy. Pitcher continued, there were but five hundred French troops (Forces of the Interior) to hold the Germans under surveillance. A plan was proposed—that the *Philadelphia* with shell fire should interdict the road out that the Germans would have to use if pressed by the French. The French then explained that U.S. engineers were already working on the road farther back and that it would be best not to stir the Germans but to take them later. That the engineers were this far along was good news.

Minesweepers under Commander Martin made progress. The *Philadelphia* fueled, watered, and provisioned them and flew their commander around to supervise. They kept at it. By 27 August LSTs and LCIs could go forward in the channel to help rehabilitate Port de Bouc. By 30 August a U.S. port party had de Bouc in hand: three ships of twenty-five-foot draft could be docked at one time. Station Pitcher was recalled. On 29 August the ship rendezvoused off Marseilles with the *Augusta* and Admiral Davidson, our commander support force. Throughout, the *Philadelphia* planes had proved themselves indispensable, and so they continued on 29 August when Captain Ansel accepted the surrender of the three defense islands: Ratonneau, Pomegues, and Château d'If.

As the ship approached the *Augusta* it was noted that a blinker signal light on the nearest island was signaling to the destroyer *Madison* lying off. The signal said that the three-island command was ready to surrender.

Thinking that a facility with German might help (I had taught it at USNA) I proposed to Admiral Davidson that I go in to the island headquarters and see to the surrender. He agreed at once, designated me his deputy for the job and sent me on my way, armed with his concept of terms and his blessing. A surrender party was whacked together.

All three islands are steep, bare, rocky masses jutting out of the sea. Château d'If of storybook fame, is the smallest but a real rock bastion; a lump from shore at the south end of Marseilles pushes westward toward Château d'If, two miles off. Another mile west is Ratonneau, the main island. With the help of a breakwater it shelters the small harbor Frioul. From its western edge a breakwater causeway runs south to hook up with Pomegues, stretching two miles south.

In support of the party were the USS *Madison,* three minesweepers to transport the marine detachments of the *Philadelphia* and *Augusta,* and three LCIs to take off POWs. Accompanied by Lieutenant Nuelson of Admiral Davidson's staff, and his yeoman, Jim Boylan, Captain Ansel boarded the *Madison* and stood in toward the inlet of Port Frioul. The story follows the chronological record kept by Boylan. The Germans were told by signal light to send a boat toward *Madison;* this was done. The party boarded Minesweeper 83 and went toward the boat accompanied by *Madison's* motor whaleboat. Overhead, *Philadelphia* planes covered and tried to guide the German boat out to the whaleboat, in which the party was by now embarked. It was 1500, 29 August 1944.

The German boat, flying a white flag, was motioned alongside; its two officers were told to shift to the whaleboat. One of the officers identified himself to me as the commanding officer, Kapitaenleutnant Fuellgrabe, Coast Artillery, and his companion as the CO of Château d'If. We went into Frioul harbor and disembarked at its breakwater quay. I asked if it was mined for demolition and Fuellgrabe said it was. We made note to have it defused before entrance of our vessels. At my request John Nuelson checked my directions; he was a German scholar. During the long boat trip in, he and I had gone over the terms carefully. His name seemed familiar to me. It turned out his father was Bishop Nuelson of the church my father's family belonged to. His Swiss father had visited our home in Illinois, I could recall. That he and I should meet here in a boat off Marseilles was a reassuring pleasure. With Fuellgrabe guiding, we walked off the quay to a shot-up headquarters building. What escaped my notice was that our ship's photographer, Lagatuta, had sneaked into the party and was walking along beside Boylan, shooting right and left.

This surrender group was a German coast artillery organization run by the German Navy. It was headed by a senior lieutenant at this time, the more superior officer having gone over to the mainland. Fuellgrabe with about 900 men had apparently been left to take the rap. We went into the little port named Frioul on the largest of the three coastal defense islands, which had a concrete breakwater quay protecting it. The Germans were using land demolition mines that could be exploded only by throwing the demolition switch. They were not seagoing underwater mines. Fuellgrabe led the way from the landing to the Ratonneau headquarters building, which had been partly destroyed by bombing. As we stepped off the quay on either side of the walkway, German officers were at attention to receive us, six naval officers on the left and two army officers on the right. The latter gave the Nazi salute with the outstretched right hand; two of the naval officers gave the normal military greeting. I did not respond to either. We sat down on the verandah of this partly demolished building. There was a table. Fuellgrabe sat on my right; to his right were his immediate subordinates, young naval officers. One officer, who had been a teacher, commanded the Château d'If; he had been in the boat with us. John Nuelson sat on my left, my yeoman Boylan back of both of us.

I identified myself as the CO of the USS *Philadelphia* in the offing, and gave my authority as the senior naval officer present to accept their surrender. The proceedings were conducted in German. Fuellgrabe in turn again identified himself and we proceeded with reading the terms that had been made into one, two, three, four paragraphs. There were very few interjections, except for some conditions with time limits that they considered impossible or impracticable. We changed a few in minor places, eased them a little, maybe, and tightened them in other places, and he, Fuellgrabe, affixed his signature. I signed my name and gave him a copy. He was accompanied back to the landing. In the meantime I had told him to assemble all of his men in a place where I could see them. We passed them on the way to the landing. The minesweepers had landed the Marine detachments from the USS *Philadelphia* and the USS *Augusta,* and they had established a perimeter enclosing these men. All this took longer than the telling does, of course. There were some small hold-ups. Fuellgrabe asked me if he could have an hour and a half or so to go up and look after the burial of some of his late casualties. He also had casualties from air bombing. His request was granted, and my concern now was to get the LCIs in to take the prisoners of war out and turn them over, down the coast, to the army. Also I wanted to report to Admiral Davidson on the *Augusta* as soon as possible.

It was almost dark. En route to *Philadelphia,* I was able to make the *Augusta* and give a short report. The next day a full report was made. Our own marines from the *Philadelphia* under Lieutenant Thompson were sent to Château d'If where there were ninety-nine Germans. The *Augusta* marines under Captain Schlesinger remained in Frioul. Captain Schlesinger was placed in charge of the whole operation on my departure. He later reported a few minor troubles. There were strays from the mainland: a few French women who claimed they were nurses or laundresses, and such. When he proposed returning them to Marseilles two threatened to do away with themselves. He let them stay.

The Morison account lists a Lieutenant Henry D. Reck as my interpreter and as source. He may have come in with the *Augusta* marines. He was not present at the surrender proceedings. No one interpreted for me. Only John Nuelson and I worked together in explaining our terms to the German command.

Pitcher at Carro had touch with French Forces of the Interior. From them he was able to pass on valuable shore information. Later in Toulon we met some members of the underground—it was mostly social storytelling, nothing that contributed to the things that we were doing militarily. Of course, we had stories to tell each other, but this was only in passing the time, rather than arriving at who did what or why.

The army had a POW system, and we, as we had in Arzeu and other places, made use of that. They had burial plans, too, for casualties. Those are side problems of war. We had no agencies or outfits that could handle the prisoners, and it had been agreed that the army would. In this instance we sent them by small craft to a collecting place down the coast and they were kept under guard by the army. As to their food and clothing, they had to go hungry until they got down to the POW compound. By and large they were well cared for. We had seen some on the African coast, even as many as 275,000 that the army took care of. No problem arose about them in this instance.

I will give you my views on Operation Dragoon. From my personal participation and study of that operation I thought it should have come earlier. It was effective when it did come; it helped a great deal—just how much I'm unable to judge. I have read the German records on it; their reactions and their thoughts on the thing supported my own, which I had already discussed with Admiral Hewitt. The Germans said that they weren't ready, that they had no adequate defenses to meet us down there in the Rhone Valley, had we made it earlier. Some of us, including myself, went so far as to say that the Med would have been the best place to make the main effort, rather than on the Channel coast.

I'm not aware of a specific British thought that wanted to make the Mediterranean the main effort. I'm only aware of the disagreement about going into the Adriatic and so on later that Mr. Churchill wanted very much and Mr. Roosevelt didn't. Being a Mediterranean sailor, I think it was wrong on our part. We could have gone. We had things open for us there. We wouldn't have some of the troubles we have now, had we done that.

My personal experience came out in agreement with some colleagues that the Mediterranean effort should have come earlier. We speculated about why the main effort wasn't made from the Mediterranean rather than on the Channel from England. Some senior officers that we discussed this with were also taken with the idea. Of course this was hindsight, but from the beginning, having been in England when the Dieppe raid was on, having been confirmed in the toughness of the job because of the tides alone in which LSTs would be left high and dry way out from the shore, and having become a Med sailor, I favored that area for the main effort. In the Mediterranean we had only about a foot and a half, or max of three feet, of tidal range. All those items that you live with in landing operations seemed to add up that it would have been easier to make the Mediterranean a main base and to have gone up the Rhone Valley on Mr. Churchill's original concept of the soft underbelly.

I had talked with Admiral Hewitt about this idea. He registered surprise and said he had never thought that through, that it was almost a new thought to him. He was so engrossed in the thing the way it was laid out, anyhow, that he had accepted it as was. He did grant that it looked practicable and perhaps it would have been a better plan. We weren't trying to judge the two, we were just looking back and thinking about how this could have been done better and easier. In general, he was favorably inclined.

TARGET PRACTICE ON THE MEDITERRANEAN

COMMANDER ALBERT K. MURRAY

NAVY COMBAT ART

ALBERT KETCHAM MURRAY was born in Emporia, Kansas. He studied at Cornell University and at the College of Fine Arts, Syracuse University, where he received a B.F.A. cum laude. He carried on additional study in England and France and later came under the tutelage of the noted portrait painter Wayman E. Adams in New York and Mexico. By the late 1930s Murray was exhibiting his works in such prestigious shows as that of the Carnegie Institute and the Corcoran Gallery in Washington, D.C.

In March 1942 Murray received a commission as a lieutenant in the United States Naval Reserve and was initially assigned for duty as a line officer. Six months later the navy recognized his artistic talents and reassigned him to the navy's newly created art program and had him paint portraits of the navy's general board of senior admirals. In December 1942 he went to the Philadelphia Navy Yard, where he recorded the heroes of the USS *Boise* (CL 47), one of the first ships to suffer battle damage in the war, damage received at Guadalcanal and Cape Esperance. The *Boise* again took part in naval battles, especially in the Allied landings in Sicily and Salerno. She and her battle-hardened crew had an immense impact on the young combat artist.

Murray was next attached to the Fourth Fleet in the South Atlantic, where he produced a large number of watercolors showing naval activities in the British West Indies, Brazil, and Puerto Rico. This sometimes quiet theater of the war was a major planning and training area. In 1943 the war correspondent of the

New York Times, Hanson W. Baldwin, said in *The Navy at War: Paintings and Drawings by Combat Artists:* "Lieutenant Murray's brush epitomizes this period of strain—of furious labor, endless watchfulness, unceasing training."

Murray was later assigned to the Eighth Fleet in the Mediterranean, where he manned combat stations and sketched with dedicated application. In his assignments with amphibious units and smaller vessels he sometimes shared in landings with the fleet. The account of his experiences on the southern coast of France in the summer of 1944 is told most vividly in the following excerpt from an interview. Here was an example of the artist under enemy fire, sharing the experiences of his fellow sailors and learning to depict reality in his countless sketches of World War II.

Immediately after the war, Al Murray was retained by the navy to paint many of the official portraits of the men who had led the battles and fought to win the war at sea. Among the greatest is a portrait of Fleet Admiral Chester W. Nimitz shown signing the Japanese surrender for the United States aboard the USS *Missouri.* This is hung permanently in the Pentagon. Another one might mention is his moving portrait of James Forrestal, the beleaguered secretary of the navy who had a sad ending. Many of his portraits of the various chiefs of naval operations were authorized by the U.S. Naval Institute in Annapolis, Maryland, and painted in the artist's study in Manhattan—a studio that in itself is a museum, with paintings lining the walls, some finished, some only half-finished—an inspiring place to visit.*

Today Albert K. Murray is among the nation's leading portrait painters. He has painted not only portraits of the secretaries of the navy, chiefs of naval operations, and commandants of both the U.S. Marine Corps and the U.S. Coast Guard, but more recently leaders of business and industry. As the U.S. Naval Academy Museum noted in the brochure for an exhibit of Al Murray's works: "From the battle front to the portrait studio, Albert K. Murray has excelled in his highly talented use of brushes, paints, and palette to capture the reality of the events and men of our time."

*The editor had the privilege of carrying many of these portraits of the chiefs of naval operations from New York to Annapolis. Collectively they are a study in human characteristics, as portrayed by a master hand.

Interested parties might be stirred to visit the Combat Art Gallery of the Navy Combat Air Collection in the Washington Navy Yard. More than 4,000 original works of art documenting the navy from World War II to the present are to be found there—the work of many combat artists like Al Murray who plied the oceans and stormed the beaches in World War II to document the navy in action on the battlefronts.

I came in on the third wave of the assault on southern France. Incidentally, I have been told that we had over one thousand combatant ships there, which is considerably in excess of what they had at Normandy.

The landing was reasonably easy in my opinion. Some new episodes were involved. Churchill had invented a scheme of putting a bulge on a Sherman tank like the old Eastman Kodak cameras that had a bulge arrangement when you pulled the thing out and before you take the pictures. On the tank that would allow about eighteen inches of freeboard for the tank to come off from an LST in deep water with a French 75 in it. So you didn't have to take a DukW (an amphibious tank) to hoist these things out, and when you got to the beach it would give you artillery fire support right away, in addition to what my story is about, so as to breach these antitank walls.

Well, anyway, the walls were successfully breached and I soon ran into my boss, Admiral Rodgers (Rear Admiral Bertram J. Rodgers), and he said: "Well, how are you making out? What do you think about it?" And I said, "Well, things are a little bit quiet." "Quiet!" he said, "Well, I'll tell you what you can do. There is a Special Service Force, the Raiders, down here, and they're trying to get to a fort that's harassing us badly right in back of Monaco. You go down there and see what you can dig up in a pictorial way. We've lost all contact with these people." I'm a combat artist and supposed to cover this thing pictorially as best I could.

So when I get to this place, it's out in back: it's between Nice and the casino of Montecarlo. There's a considerable mountain there called Mont Argil. After you got up there's a town called La Turbie. There is an old Roman aqueduct there and a fort—a medieval fort with a moat and a drawbridge, all dry of course, and with lance windows in there for archers, bows, and arrows—a real antique. The bridge was still down over the moat and it had parapet walls. The Raider Special Service Force had been assigned to get the Germans out of that place for harassing our troops because you could look over the parapets down into the town of Monaco. There were ten thousand German troops down there and they're going around out this way and we were not allowed to assault them because Monaco was neutral territory, and if we were apprehended down there we'd be imprisoned for the rest of the war as prisoners of war in neutral territory. So we were sure we didn't get down there and leave the troops alone there. But finally these special service guys got the Germans out of there about three in the afternoon and we came in. I discovered we were at an elevation of three thousand feet. There's a wonderful view of the whole coastline all the way down to Mentone on the Italian border, and the casino of Montecarlo, Cap Ferrat and all. I'd been sailing around Cap Ferrat every night in the PT boats that were sent out to give slim coverage to our fleet of considerable size there, both support units, combatant ships, and the whole works for the invasion. But down in front of me in this afternoon sun in August was the French light cruiser *Montcalm* having a duel with a 10-inch German cannon in a submerged dry swimming pool on the beach there at Monaco.

While I was observing this thing the special services squad was trying to get lunch ready. We had got in there around three o'clock and we hadn't had anything to eat. We had only five gallons of water for the whole company of men and what turned out to be cold beans. I wasn't interested in lunch because all of a sudden a big volume of smoke came up off the fantail of the *Montcalm* and I thought the German battery had made a direct hit. So I got out my watercolor business and started making some drawings of what I was looking at. The *Montcalm* sent a signal to two destroyers down there. She was trying to get away further to sea. She was only about two miles from shore at the time of this assault and was now trying to get into deeper water. She sent for the destroyers to come up and make a smoke screen for cover. I could see the whole episode like sitting in the number one box at the opera where you can see the prompter and both sides of the scenery at the same time and you're right up at the proscenium arch there.

And that's about where I was, watching this dramatic episode as these two destroyers (one was a French destroyer and the *Woolsey* was the American destroyer) that responded to the call from the cruiser under attack, black smoke pouring out of these destroyers and a tremendous wake as they're coming up with all the speed they can get to get up there and surround the *Montcalm* and give her smoke cover to hide her from the beach. I'm so excited with what's going on that I'm not aware I'm under observation. The Germans, when they left Mont Argil, retired to the summit that was five thousand feet and we were at three thousand. They had dragged up some of their artillery and the first thing there was a tremendous explosion in the courtyard. I wasn't aware of any of that because it wasn't what I was looking at. Then there was a second explosion. Then there was a third one. And then it dawned on me that these things are timed. Just as the fourth one was coming I figured I'd bug out from the fourth.

The only other fellow outside with me was a fire-control officer from one of the destroyers. There had been some change in the rules. Ordinarily if we up there in the fort needed some artillery support from the beach we would have to go through the chain of command and it would take a little bit of doing before the ship would respond to give us the gunnery support that we wanted. They changed the rules so that they had a fire-control officer on board the ship and we could get what we needed instantly. They spied this German battery up on the summit, and they wanted the fire directed up there to knock off that attack on us down below. What these explosions were was eighty-eight cannon shells exploding in the courtyard. Fortunately their fuses were a little bit long so they didn't explode on the fort itself. Then for some reason or other the gunnery officer disappeared and went back inside the fort where everybody else was getting their lunch ready.

Then it dawned on me. It was hot and in August, my shirt was open, my helmet was over on the grass, and I was dealing with this watercolor business. I had just bought some wonderful watercolor called Bleu Verdat (blue-green) and it was great, just right for August weather on the Mediterranean. Like a mother looking after her kids when the house is on fire, you do some foolish thing. I was thinking more about that paint than I was about what was really going on so I leaned over to get the paint and close up the box. One of these fellows popped up in the dugout back of the terrace where I was behind these parapets and he yells over to me: "For God's sake, Captain (I was a two-striper in the navy), come inside. Don't you realize you're the target out there?" So I leaned over to shut the paint box and get that Bleu Verdat and then get the hell out of there when the next round came. And the prize! That's when the shrapnel came. My dog tag was hanging down from my neck and one of the pieces of shrapnel cut the dog tag off. I still have one but the shrapnel got the other piece. That really alerted me that I was in a hot spot and had better get out of there in a hurry. The shrapnel that took the dog tag away went right between my chest and my arm.

So I got back inside the fort and there was complete silence in there until some voice said, "Well, damn you!" and I said, "What's the matter?" He said, "Well, look at it." They're down on their hands and knees, picking up bean after bean right in the dirt, dust, and debris that the Germans had left when they departed. What had happened was that they put some planks up on the cement on some ammunition boxes, put the planks down for the table to put the mess kits on for their beans. The concussion of the explosions in the moat knocked the table and the ammunition boxes down. All the beans are now on the floor. But you can't be choosers so you wipe the dirt off before you eat them and that's what they were all doing. I didn't get any lunch that day because I was the cause of it all, so I was spanked by no chow and also I had to be apologetic to these guys because if I hadn't been out there, they wouldn't have been in the fix they were in right now. I was very lucky to have been there at all in the circumstances.

The origins of the Yalta Conference are for most people lost in the mists of time. But in truth they are firmly embedded in the dreams and ambitions of three powerful men: Roosevelt, Churchill, and Stalin. Altruism was a factor perhaps, cultural influences were another, and selfish desires for power can't be overlooked.

President Roosevelt began to make a list of his reasons for a meeting of the Allies as early as September 1944. His list was long. No agreement had been established in their earlier meetings on the fate of Germany after her defeat and that was now almost certain; if and when she was defeated, what decision was to be made on reparations? The Soviets had some months before laid claim to 50 percent of what might be determined; was there to be a dismemberment of the Reich or was a central government to be permitted? What was the decision on war criminals? Were there to be zones of influence established for the several powers, and was the insistent voice of France to be heard and granted a zone of influence too? What about a world security organization and how would it be formed? What would be the fate of martyred Poland? When the Nazis invaded in 1939 the British could hardly come to her rescue and the United States was greatly shocked. They resolved on her resurrection when peace came once again. Now there were disturbing signs that the Soviets had their own plans for Poland and they didn't seem to indicate room for the views of either the United States or Great Britain. It was a sensitive moment and resentment was mounting in both countries—not a happy sign for amity between allies. And finally there was the question of Japan. She was waging a bloody war in the Pacific. Russia had given her pledge to enter on the Allied side. When was that to be and where would her help be manifest?

Roosevelt struggled over the selection of a place of meeting. His health was poor. Stalin gave notice he would not journey out of the country. Churchill, also for medical reasons, wanted a warm climate. But finally it became apparent that the Crimea was to be the location. This pleased Roosevelt in a sense because he had never been to that part of the world. Yet something tangible was thrown on the table. His presidential election was getting hotter when October came around. His attention to that was badly needed, and his advisors, not readily pleased with Russia in many ways, were against the Crimea and worried for the president's health but were also fearful that a conference in Russia might have some influence on the American electorate, not known to be filled with love for the Soviet state. So the president dropped the subject until after the November elections.

Winston Churchill by October felt that a meeting of the three leaders must be held immediately. His vision was focused as always on the map of postwar Europe. His strong political sense warned him of an uncertain fate for southeastern Europe. The Red Army had occupied Bulgaria and Finland, had advanced into Hungary and Yugoslavia, had reached the frontiers of Greece and Turkey and farther to the north had advanced over Estonia, Latvia, and Lithuania and across Poland to the Vistula. Churchill felt a conference of the three must be held without a moment's delay. But the political campaign in the United States stood in the way and Churchill thought the Soviets would not wait for the counting of ballots in the great democracy of the Western Hemisphere. So he proposed that he go to Moscow at once with his Foreign Secretary, Mr. Eden, and talk with Stalin. Perhaps he could speak for Roosevelt on questions they both knew well and had discussed in previous meetings.

The president seemed to agree, at least for the moment. He prepared a message to Stalin, wishing the conferees well and vaguely suggesting that Churchill would represent his views. Harry Hopkins, the president's close advisor, learned of this message, rushed to the White House war room where it was to be dispatched, and stopped the message from going out. Then he went immediately to the president's bedroom and reported what he had done and why. Hopkins felt this was a dangerous thing to have done and convinced the president of that. It seems that Roosevelt had been thinking of other pressing matters when he composed the message to Stalin and had not considered the possibility that Hopkins now raised: that this might be construed by Stalin as a lack of interest in postwar European matters. So Roosevelt now composed another message to Russia wishing both men good luck in their proposed deliberations and stating plainly that he was indeed concerned with all they discussed, and made the point that any decisions by the two men could only be implemented after Roosevelt had been with the others and agreed on what measures were to be taken.

Other minor disagreements arose between positions taken by Churchill and Roosevelt but they were ironed out without any permanent scars. But another problem did arise that had serious possibilities for both America and Britain. It was over the military strategy General Eisenhower was following on the western front near the Rhine. The British felt that Eisenhower should concentrate his forces on one front; the Americans, on the other hand, approved of his plan for a double advance into Germany, one north of the Rhine and a second towards Frankfurt. Field Marshal Alan Brooke, chief of the Imperial General Staff, disagreed flatly with Eisenhower and accused him of violating principles of the concentration of force and pointed out the impossibility of a double invasion with the limited forces he had. It was discovered that Eisenhower did not hope to cross the Rhine before May of 1945. This too was a blow to the British. Their government had recently announced a new military call-up and that meant a corresponding loss in war production. After six years of war with a higher proportion of her population mobilized than any other belligerent, Britain had reached the bottom of the barrel, and delays on the front made matters crucial.

Meanwhile the fuehrer had decided to stake everything on a single throw—to win or lose it all. It was in effect another blitzkrieg such as he had developed in 1940. His aim was to drive a wedge between the two main halves of the Anglo-American forces, which Eisenhower had aligned on either side of the Ardennes. Hitler's forces would strike at the point of maximum potential confusion where the American and British forces joined, to reach Brussels and Antwerp in the latter's rear, encircle, and destroy them. Then he would deal with the remaining Americans in the south as he had dealt with the French after Dunkirk. To allow for manpower Hitler made a drastic autumn call-up of men for this second blitzkrieg. The call-up age for men was reduced from age seventeen and a half to sixteen.

Hitler struck on 16 December and by the next morning the panzers were pouring through a fifty-mile gap; by evening their spearhead troops were twenty miles inside Belgium. Fortunately, Hitler's effort failed eventually, as his military advisors had feared it would. It was a desperate attempt. The Russians on the other hand had some great victories in the fall and had opened up the gates to the Balkans. Now in December 1944, only about three weeks before the Yalta Conference, their armies had swept westward for nearly three hundred miles and were now only forty miles from Berlin and in possession of almost the whole of East Prussia and Silesia as well as Hungary and Slovakia. They were in a state of elation and they meant to use the opportunity given them by the delays on the western front to drive the hardest bargain possible at the conference table. No longer concerned only with the defeat of Germany, they now aimed at the domination of as much of Europe as possible.

This point is made also by Vice Admiral John Victor Smith in his oral history interview that follows. Smith was aide to Admiral Leahy, chief of staff to President Roosevelt. Leahy was with the president at all the discussions. As a result Smith knew through Leahy about the thinking of the U.S. military and probably shared their opinions on the Russian designs.

Rear Admiral Clarence Olsen, an excerpt from whose oral history interview also follows, was U.S. naval attaché in Moscow. He had been delegated by Ambassador Harriman to go down to Yalta very early in 1945 and supervise the preparation of quarters for the American delegation at the conference. His actions reveal the circumstances under which the delegates worked.* His problems were gigantic but the reader will see that he achieved a modern miracle in whipping things into shape before the arrival of the president and all the generals and admirals.

I do not presume, in this preface, to deal with the conference itself. There are many records available to the interested party. There were accomplishments in number, there were promises made, especially by the Russians, and never fulfilled. Sometimes it seems the verdict is still out on what was truly accomplished at Yalta. When one dwells on the fate of many small European countries today one is likely to have some negative thoughts. On the other hand, the founding of the United Nations as a vital force in the world is less likely to be challenged in these latter days of the twentieth century.

*Just before the Yalta Conference Harry Hopkins called on Churchill in London and he quoted the prime minister as saying that from all the reports he had received on present conditions at Yalta, "we could not have found a worse place for a meeting if we had spent ten years on research." (Quoted in Robert E. Sherwood, *Roosevelt and Hopkins: an Intimate History*) (New York: Harper and Brothers, 1948), 847.

REPAIRING THE CZAR'S PALACE

REAR ADMIRAL CLARENCE E. OLSEN*

Plans for Yalta started before Christmas in 1944 when Roosevelt was asking Stalin about a meeting and Stalin said he would meet him any time, any place. Roosevelt didn't want to do it until after January and where would he like to have it?

Roosevelt's first dispatches to us indicated we should make preparations for a group of about thirty-five, a very small select group with himself and the joint chiefs of staff, and wanted to know where Stalin would meet him. So Stalin told the ambassador that he would meet in Odessa. Well, we all got rather excited about that because Odessa was within easy bombing range of the German front lines and also Odessa was one of the most heavily mined areas in the Black Sea. We felt that if we were going to have any kind of a conference (all of us having attended several at various times before and knowing what heavy demands for communications and supplies and so forth there are at that time), we figured we were going to have to have a communications ship in there. So we told the ambassador that Odessa looked like a very poor place: that the Germans were within striking distance; that we couldn't get a communications ship in there; and that in winter weather with the cold winds coming across the steppes toward Odessa it was no place to put Roosevelt in his weakened condition.

Stalin wouldn't go out of Russia. We tried to get him to go to Malta but he wouldn't go out of Russia. He suggested any place on the Black Sea Russian shore. Stalin said his doctors would not allow him to go outside of

*For biographical information on Olsen see pp. 232–233.

Russia because of the long flight time. I also think he feared going out of Russia for security reasons. Again, their natural suspicion of everything and everybody. So Harriman told me to make a study and work with the Soviet navy to select a better place. It was a pretty hard job because all I had was a Baedeker guide to go by on the climate down there. I finally took it up with Admiral Kuznetsov and he agreed that Yalta would probably be the best alternate place, but they wanted time. He didn't know where they could actually get together at Yalta because it had been heavily bombed and destroyed by the Germans.

You see they would not allow any of our communications and we had no over-air way of bringing communications systems in adequately to meet the demands of the conference. So we wanted a ship if possible. We finally agreed on Yalta. It was past Christmas then. So Harriman told me to take three officers—General Hill from the air force; and Ronnie Allen, my interpreter, as secretary; and Lieutenant Chase—and the four of us should go down there. Allen and Chase spoke fluent Russian, Hill and I just a few smatterings of it. Stalin and Molotov approved of our going down. We were to assist them in planning this thing. Then they wouldn't give me any transportation. Day after day I appealed to them about giving me transportation down, and meanwhile the dispatches indicated that instead of having 35 they would have about 85. The next thing we knew they had about 125. In the end the maximum number went up to 330.

I found out afterwards that all the buildings they were going to use were in such complete disrepair after the German evacuation that they needed time to make any of them habitable in any form. I suppose the same would have been true in Odessa if we had gone there. It was certainly true in Yalta. The place they chose was the palace of Czar Nicholas, Livadia, which had three main buildings and several minor buildings in a large compound. It had been occupied by the Germans. In fact, the Germans used the ground floor for stables for their horses, and when they pulled out they wrecked everything they could. They dug up the floors, they pounded down the walls, they broke all the glassware, the windows and everything. Fortunately they did not break up the heating system. So the Russians were busy trying to resurrect the two main buildings and needed time. One of them they weren't planning to resurrect until I got there and persuaded them to. By the time I got there, the second week of January, they had relaid all the floors, plastered up all the walls, repaired all the windows, and the heating system was operating. They were still working night and day. They had about five hundred Roumanian prisoners around the grounds, repairing and planting shrubbery, making the grounds presentable, in addition to several hundred working on the buildings.

When I got there everything was a horrible mess, but I got working with General Gorlinski, who was their senior man in charge of the recon-

448

struction down there, and we made daily tours of all the buildings and the rooms and made lists of all the things we felt were going to be needed— furniture, equipment and things like that. We also had a member of the diplomatic staff, commissar, who was overseeing and trying to stick his nose into everything. He did more to retard progress than anybody else they could have sent down there: Mr. Chavakin.

The British were to be elsewhere. The Russians were elsewhere, and this was only for the American delegation and the meeting area. In the main building, we had to prepare a large meeting hall. It was the old ballroom. We had to prepare private rooms for the president and the senior members of his staff, and then in all the other rooms we had to prepare double-up bunks set military style row by row for generals and admirals on down. We had seven senior officers in one room—a little bit unheard of.

On the twenty-fourth of February, Mike Reilly, White House security service head, and several of his men left to meet Mr. Big (the president) at Malta. I had a nice little set-to with him the night before when he proposed we should put Mrs. Boettiger (the president's daughter, Anna) into a separate room instead of with Kathy Harriman, the ambassador's daughter. Under the crowded conditions and the fact both of them were joy riding, I was damned if I could see it and Mr. Harriman backed me up later, so the two were set up in one room—and not a very big one at that! After all, when State Department people, admirals, and generals were doubled up even four deep I could see no reason why two girls, the only two in the party, could not live together.

Admiral King had his own space, of course, the czarina's boudoir. A commissar came up at one time and insisted he wanted the room right next to Roosevelt's room. I told him nothing doing, but he had been sent down, he said, by Stalin to supervise this deal and for his own security reasons to protect the president he had to have the room next to his. I said I'm very sorry but we have a room reserved for you over here, and it was at the farthest corner on the second floor of the barracks and office building. That is where you and your two men are going to stay whether you like it or not. And he said, "I'm going to stay down next to the president." "If you make a move to do that," I said, "I'm going to send a dispatch to Mr. Molotov immediately and have you recalled for interfering with the operations." At Molotov's name, of course, he blanched a little bit. So we finally compromised. He decided he didn't want that room down there, he wanted the room over where I was going to put him.

Every night after we had made a tour of the buildings, a Russian convoy would set out over the peninsula—all over Yalta. They would scavenge from all the old buildings, the farmhouses, the schools, the hotels, any place that had furnishings, and pick up the things that we needed to fill our list and bring them in. The next morning they would put them into the rooms. When we got through we not only had those buildings completely rebuilt and furnished but planned with the allocation of all the officers who were coming.

We had them stuffed in like a barracks. We even had a barracks up on the third floor where all the guards and the enlisted men who came were lodged. We had two big restaurants, junior and senior ones, where they moved in all of the staff of the Hotel Splendide, the National Hotel, and the Moscow Hotel: the whole staff and all their equipment, complete with maître d's, chefs, waiters, equipment, and food and wines. The office building was separate. That was another problem because the Russians couldn't understand why people couldn't work on their bunk or on a chair beside their bunk—why they needed an office. I had a hard time explaining but we finally got all the offices laid out that we wanted.

And the communications building, they had no place for that at all—that was the third building with the floors completely gutted out. So I looked it all over and said, "Well, if you'll get the planks—it doesn't have to be a finished job—if you'll just get planks and cover these big holes here and make the floor safe, we can arrange this." They were so relieved that I did not want a complete renovation that they agreed at once.

Now going back a little bit, when I first got up there, we had arranged for the *Catoctin,* one of our communications ships, to come into the Black Sea with four minesweepers, and they came over to Sevastopol and tied up there. Immediately after I'd visited them and told them what our requirements were, they sent a communications team in trucks over and they laid land wires out over the thirty miles of land coming up to Yalta and began to establish the communications link between Yalta and Sevastopol—and of course from Sevastopol back to the fleet. Until that time we were talking by one little land wire between Sevastopol and Yalta on which I had to send all my coded dispatches down to them and then up to Moscow and answer back down there. I found nothing was coming through so I made an early trip to Sevastopol and found they had them all stacked up while they were trying to break them down and analyze them before delivering them. Since we had one of these single-pad, one-time codes that we rigged up ourselves it was almost unbreakable unless you knew the book you were taking it from. We were not concerned about that. What we were saying wasn't important anyway, but they just wanted to break it down and find out. I sent several in plain language because I wanted them to know.

Up in Moscow we knew perfectly well that they were taking advantage of every opportunity to set up hearing devices, even in the telephones. We were always conscious of this and were very careful about where and how we talked. I had an electrician up there who was briefed on all this equipment and we had him making inspections at Spasso House and the embassy all the time. Actually he pulled a listening device right out of the light up above the ambassador's desk in his own office, which shows how brazen they became in putting those things in. But down in Yalta with their people doing all the resurrection work and so forth we had no knowledge at any time of any activities such as that. We never found them, anyway.

When we got this thing completed we had the best first-class hotel in Russia, staffed by the best Russian staff available in Russia. Our troops meanwhile—the people who were coming from Washington—had no idea what they were in for and some of them came with a personal supply of C-rations, a bedroll or a sleeping bag, and that sort of thing. They couldn't believe it when they found themselves set up in a first-class hotel, even though the living conditions were quite crowded. We had to establish our own security guards all around the place. The Russians had guards also around the place. Security as far as the Russians were concerned was very, very deep. The road was open between there and Sevastopol, and we had daily convoys going over there bringing enlisted men over for their guard duty and supplies and that sort of thing. We were pretty well fixed as far as our general living conditions were concerned—much more so than the British. They were out in another building. They came over and couldn't believe that we had got in as much as we had. They wanted to move in with us. Stalin was in another broken-down castle and I don't think even he had as much as we had.

It probably was their intention to make it as pleasant as possible for us and for Roosevelt. He was a very sick man when he came over. As a matter of fact, when they had their first joint meeting in the big ballroom—in the center of the room they had a big round table with spaces for the Americans and for the British and the Russians—we were all in there and we were asked to stay on the sidelines and line the two walls. First Churchill came in the door and marched right down the center with his cigar and the little bulldog look he always had. He was definitely on display. With his staff following he went and sat down. Then Roosevelt came in in his wheelchair with a big shawl over his shoulders and looking very, very tired and drawn. He had a big negro, Pleasant I think was his name, pushing him. He was a great big burly, husky fellow and this little old man (Roosevelt) looked like a dried-up old lady sitting there. He was taken from his wheelchair and put in his other chair. And then Stalin came down, just glaring and looking as if he was expecting to have knives thrown at him at any minute from either side. The contrast between the physical fitness of Churchill and Stalin and that of Roosevelt was very striking. Of course, all through the conference we had the feeling that Roosevelt was not holding up our interests, that he was giving way, giving in to the Russians on almost everything. The comments made by Chip Bohlen when he came out sometimes indicated that was what was going on.

Hopkins, his main adviser, was not much stronger than Roosevelt. He died shortly afterwards. In fact, I thought Roosevelt was going to pass out the night he spent on the *Catoctin* right after the conference, because under darkened ship conditions and with the closed ports and everything, the cabin space was quite stuffy. I understand that he complained considerably, and they opened the doors and ports but kept everything dark. But when we saw him on the field the next day going down the line in a jeep, he didn't look like he had long to live. They told me they were really scared in the *Catoctin* that he was not strong enough to go through with the trip. I can't believe that a man in that physical status could be so strong-minded as to carry a point with people like Stalin and Churchill, and apparently he didn't.

FROM BANDITS TO BEDBUGS

VICE ADMIRAL JOHN VICTOR SMITH

JOHN VICTOR SMITH was born in Seattle, Washington, on 24 May 1912, the son of General Holland M. Smith, USMC. He graduated from the U.S. Naval Academy with the class of 1934 and was commissioned as an ensign on 31 May of that year and served for a year aboard the battleship USS *Oklahoma*. From there he was assigned to the USS *Perry* (DD 340) on a three-year tour of duty after which he had cruiser duty on the USS *Honolulu*. There followed another year with destroyers and in June 1940 he entered the Postgraduate School at Annapolis for instruction in ordnance engineering. In 1942 he joined the staff of commander, Service Force, Atlantic, and then served as executive officer on the USS *Shubrick* (DD 639), becoming that ship's commanding officer late in 1943.

Early in 1944 Admiral Smith became aide to Admiral W. D. Leahy, chief of staff to President Roosevelt, and served the admiral until after the Yalta Conference in February 1945. He followed that with command of a destroyer with the fast carrier task forces in the Pacific, going on to service at the Naval Proving Ground at Dahlgren, Virginia, as head of the Armament Department, where he remained until August 1949. There followed a year of instruction at the Armed Forces Staff College in Norfolk, Virginia.

From 1950 to 1952 he saw duty on the staff of commander, First Fleet, and then the staff of commander, Seventh Fleet, serving in Korean and Japanese waters. He then took command of Destroyer Division 112 in Korean waters, remaining in WESTPAC until July 1953.

There ensued another year of study, this time at the National War College in Washington, D.C. That was followed by duty in the strategic plans division of the chief of naval operations.

In 1957 Admiral Smith returned to the Naval Academy for nine months as head of the Department of Ordnance and Gunnery, followed by ten months as academic aide to the superintendent. In June 1959 he left the academy to take command of the USS *Newport News* for a year, after which he was sent to the Bureau of Naval Personnel for duty as special assistant to the chief of naval personnel for leadership.

Admiral Smith was promoted to rear admiral on 1 July 1962 and then served in the office of the chief of naval operations as director of the Foreign Military Assistance Division until July 1963, when he became commander of Cruiser Destroyer Flotilla Eight. He then returned to the office of the CNO, where he served in several capacities until December 1966, when he became assistant chief of naval operations for plans and policy. In October 1967 he became senior member of the United Nations Military Armistice Commission in Korea. This involved daily contact with the North Korean delegation and proved to be a most frustrating assignment, for the communist delegation from the north seemed unwilling to arrive at any solution. In April 1968 the admiral assumed command of the amphibious force of the U.S. Pacific Fleet. In August 1970 he became commandant of the Industrial College of the Armed Forces in Washington, D.C., where he served until relieved of active duty upon retirement on 1 August 1973.

Admiral Smith lived in Annapolis, Maryland, for some time and then moved to La Jolla, California, where he died in 1989.

We were under great pressure from Stalin. He had a great deal of influence over the president, much more than he did over Churchill, of course. Roosevelt didn't realize that Stalin was a bandit. Churchill of course did. You can word it in different ways. The word "bandit" was never used, but Russia is supposed to be a mystery wrapped in an enigma. That's Russia.

Several times Roosevelt practically said: "I've given my word to Stalin as a gentleman and we're going to go through with it"—things like that. You see, there was that difference. Churchill had Greece, Yugoslavia, and some of those things to consider. From that point of view, he was right in that the Russians did take over the Balkans and we might have been able to prevent it. At the Yalta Conference one of the few concessions we got out of them was a promise to hold free elections in the Balkans, which, of course, they had no intention of doing, and which they didn't do.

454

One must remember that Roosevelt had recognized the Russians as far back as 1933 and that many of his international actions vis-à-vis the Russians were such as to tie him, historically speaking, to their fortunes. He was forced, in this case, to get agreement with the Russians at the Yalta Conference; someone else might not have. Truman didn't feel compelled to reach agreement when he went to Potsdam, but Roosevelt's position in history seemed to depend on getting the best agreement he could with the Russians, and any agreement was better than nothing.

He didn't want to face up to the fact that they might not honor the agreement, or even face up to the few agreements they had honored. He was very much concerned over whether he could sell this rather poor agreement to Congress and was distressed that Harry Hopkins was not well enough to help him argue the case. Actually I believe there was less trouble than Roosevelt anticipated and even less trouble than I would have anticipated. There were secret agreements formulated at Yalta, but what had been said and what the implications were had not really come to light. We didn't know there was going to be an iron curtain. It's too bad we had poor leadership at Yalta. The president was dying. Harry Hopkins was dying. He never got out of bed the whole time he was there. One thing I looked askance at was that after every head of state meeting, Hopkins would send for Chip Bohlen, our interpreter, and talk to him for hours about what had happened at the meeting. There was a time when Hopkins would have been in a position to give good advice to the president, but sick as he was, I don't think any of that information imparted to Hopkins by Bohlen bore fruit.

The military delegation was not really in a position to exert much influence over there. They hardly got in to see the president. The liaison that was conducted was done through Admiral Leahy. The president had a habit of staying up late at night and rising late the next morning. Thus the joint chiefs of staff didn't see him before the next meeting with Stalin.

I want to bring out some points that I remember rather vividly. At the time the conference was about to get under way, the U.S. and British forces were just recovering from the Battle of the Bulge. We were fighting in a way that was designed to save lives and get the war over with. We had extended our forces to the point where the Germans were able to mount this secret push and drive us back. So we entered the conference with a psychological disadvantage of having almost committed a boo-boo, almost been thrown back, lost Antwerp, and so on. The Russians on the other hand had played this politically. For the longest time they had been saving their forces and not committing them to action, building up tremendous stockpiles of ammunition for artillery and tanks. They were very good at the use of massed artillery. They would expend much more artillery in battle than U.S. forces, with all our national wealth. Much of this material was obtained from us, but nevertheless they were much more lavish in its use. It wasn't necessary for the saving of Russian lives. They were more interested in achieving overwhelming striking power to ensure tactical victory.

What they were doing then was using this artillery and the cumulative supplies, having been through a suitable rest period, and they were advancing hundreds of miles a day through the plains of central Europe, north central Europe particularly. So the nearly defeated Allies in effect met the obviously victorious Russians, who seemed to be able to outperform us on the battlefield with a great margin of advantage. This was indeed a psychological disadvantage to us because the Russians chose to make much of it. In one of the early meetings there the chairman of their joint chiefs of staff pointed out the glorious victories that they were having and claimed that they had borne the brunt of the war for a very long time and this must be reckoned with.

The gist of their argument was we had not landed as soon as we had undertaken to land in Normandy or anywhere in Europe and we were behind and had held back, and now it was proof that the glorious Russian forces were winning the war and here we had come to a conference. It would be the last conference during the war and we didn't have a very good record.

This was prepared and rather convincing, and I read the minutes almost breathlessly wondering what would happen next, and my recollection is that General Marshall was forced to undertake an extemporaneous defense of our position, which he did fairly well. Of course he couldn't accuse them of the base motives which they had indeed used, but he was able to point out that in spite of what they claimed, the British, the French, and the Americans (I call them Allies even though we were allied with Russia in a way) were engaging at least half of the German troops and the German military effort. Of course Marshall mentioned the supplies that we were making available and providing around the North Cape and through Iran, and he did a fairly good job. Nevertheless the obvious results on the battlefield gave the Russians a great psychological advantage. On top of that the U.S. was just one of two partners. Churchill was there for the British and their views; the Russians spoke with one voice. We had to agree. And in addition, our president was in poor health. I think the poorness of his health is underestimated by those who weren't there and didn't see him day by day, nor see how he acted.

I think the people like General Marshall were having second thoughts long before we got to Yalta. Perhaps we should not have invited the Russians into the war. Perhaps at that time the bomb looked more promising. Perhaps it was obvious that we really held the balance of power. Had we cut off aid to the Russians the Germans right up to pretty close to the end could have defeated the Russians. But anyhow—the president— "having given his word"—that sort of thing was the prevailing attitude.

I stayed in the former palace with the rest of the American delegation. We had a tremendous staff there. I'm sure we took three times as many people as the czar ever took down from St. Petersburg. But my closet was a pretty-good-sized closet. There was room for two of us and so the JCS aide, a Captain Clark, roomed with me. It was his duty to grab every JCS paper that came in for Admiral Leahy to work on. Clark would make a one-page brief of it and it was often my duty to take that and read it to Admiral Leahy, who might be too busy to see Captain Clark. The admiral would read the summary all right, but if he had to eat a sandwich for lunch or shave instead of reading the paper he would listen while I read it. Clark and I, sharing our closet, were able to compare notes and keep up to date and so better serve the admiral. I had flown in with the Secret Service in advance of the conference while Clark had accompanied the president in the cruiser so that he could get the papers that came in and be ready to brief them.

I was really the bedbug man to get the bedbugs killed before Admiral Leahy got there. Those of us who got to the palace before the presidential party knew there were bedbugs. We had been bitten and we were using all kinds of sprays. It didn't seem anachronistic to have bedbugs in the summer palace of the czar. They probably had them when he was there years before. I got a lieutenant commander, a doctor, to spray Admiral Leahy's bunk to be sure that there was no chance of a bedbug because Admiral Leahy might say, "Off with his head!" or send me home or something drastic like that. So by golly, the admiral finally arrived and took over his quarters. When he was ready to see me the next morning I walked into his quarters and said, "Good morning, Admiral. I trust you had a quiet night." And he retorted, "Well, I wasn't bitten but look at this thing on my pillow." And there was a bedbug! I should have slept in that bed myself the night before the Admiral arrived. Just as the captain of a flagship would be well advised to spend the night in the admiral's quarters before the admiral reports on board to be sure the shower works, that no springs have become loose that will stick him, that the hot water is turned on, and the telephones work. Such things can be checked in advance, but the actual living in the quarters is the surest way.

Immediately after the end of the conference I was detached from duty with Admiral Leahy with orders to proceed to the Pacific, where I took command of a 2,200-ton destroyer. Admiral Leahy returned to Washington with the president.

APPENDIX

The following is a list of names that appear in the excerpts in this volume. For information on the individuals who have given their oral histories, see the biographies that precede their respective pieces.

ADAMS, CHARLES FRANCIS
Former secretary of the navy.

ALEXANDER, GENERAL HAROLD, BRITISH ARMY
Senior army commander under General Eisenhower at the invasions of Sicily and Salerno.

ALLEN, RONNIE
Interpreter for naval attaché in Moscow.

ANDREASON, LIEUTENANT, USNR
Scout for reconnaissance of Normandy beaches.

ANTONOV, MARSHAL ALEXIS I., SOVIET ARMY
Deputy chief of staff.

ARCHER, CAPTAIN STEPHEN MORRIS, USN
Assistant naval attaché, London, 1940.

ARNOLD, GENERAL HENRY H., USA
Head of the U.S. Army Air Corps during World War II.

ARNOLD, CAPTAIN J. E., USN
Beachmaster at Omaha Beach, Normandy invasion.

ASTOR, LADY NANCY
Member of British House of Commons and mayor of Plymouth.

BIERI, ADMIRAL BERNARD, USN
As rear admiral, a U.S. naval representative to planning activities in London.

BLANDY, REAR ADMIRAL W. H. P., USN
Head of U.S. Navy Bureau of Ordnance.

BOETTIGER, ANNA ROOSEVELT
Daughter of President Franklin D. Roosevelt; attended Yalta Conference.

BOHLEN, CHARLES
Foreign service officer; first secretary at American embassy in Moscow from November 1942 to January 1944. He accompanied President Roosevelt to the Yalta Conference and served as interpreter there.

BOISSON, GENERAL PIERRE, FRENCH ARMY
Governor at Dakar.

BOLSTER, CALVIN, USN
Aeronautical engineering duty officer in Bureau of Aeronautics.

BONESTEEL, MAJOR GENERAL C. H., USA
In 1941 arrived with Army units for defense of Iceland.

BRADLEY, GENERAL OMAR N., USA
In the rank of major general, commanded the U.S. First Army at the invasion of Normandy.

BROWN, JOHN MASON, USNR
Aide to Admiral Kirk at Normandy invasion.

BUNDY, LIEUTENANT McGEORGE, USA
Army aide to Admiral Kirk at Normandy invasion.

BUSH, VANNEVAR
While president of the Carnegie Institution of Washington, D.C., he was named by President Roosevelt to the National Defense Research Committee out of which grew the Office of Scientific Research and Development.

BUTCHER, COMMANDER HARRY, USN
Naval aide to General Eisenhower at the Normandy landings.

CHAVAKIN
Soviet commissar, named to diplomatic staff at Yalta for arrangements.

CLARK, LIEUTENANT GENERAL MARK, USA
As deputy to General Eisenhower, in command of North African landings.

COCHRAN, REAR ADMIRAL EDWARD (NED), USN
Head of U.S. Navy Bureau of Ships in World War II.

COLLINS, CAPTAIN HARRY, USN
Head of procurement, U.S. Treasury Department.

COLLINS, GENERAL JOSEPH LAWTON, USA
In command of U.S. First Army during advance into France after Normandy invasion.

CONANT, JAMES B.
President of Harvard University. With Vannevar Bush directed the Office of Scientific Research and Development.

COOKE, REAR ADMIRAL CHARLES M., USN
Chief planning officer on Admiral King's staff. In spring 1944 he attended a special conference in London on the prospective Normandy landings.

CRANDALL, ELIZABETH
Early WAVE officer, previously in charge of women's residence at Stanford University.

CRESS, COLONEL, USA
Army engineer at clearance of Cherbourg harbor.

CUNNINGHAM, ADMIRAL OF THE FLEET A. B., RN
Commander in chief, Mediterranean, at the time of the North African landings.

DALRYMPLE-HAMILTON, ADMIRAL SIR FREDERICK, RN
At the Admiralty in London during World War II.

DARLAN, ADMIRAL JEAN, FRENCH NAVY
Minister of Defense and vice premier of Vichy France under Pétain.

DAVIDSON, REAR ADMIRAL L. A., USN
Commander of the support forces at the Allied landings in southern France.

DE GAULLE, GENERAL CHARLES, FRENCH ARMY
Leader of the Free French during World War II.

DELAN, GENERAL, FRENCH ARMY
In command of Free French troops to land in southern France.

DEWAR, ADMIRAL, RN
Head of Salvage Department, British Admiralty.

EISENHOWER, GENERAL DWIGHT D., USA
Supreme Allied commander at the Normandy invasion; Allied commander at earlier landings in North Africa.

ERSKINE, GENERAL GRAVES B., USMC
Head of Retraining and Reemployment Administration after World War II.

FAIRBANKS, DOUGLAS, JR., USNR
Attached to Admiral Kirk's staff; at the Normandy landings he prepared feints and false information in counterintelligence activities.

FAYMONVILLE, MAJOR GENERAL PHILIP R., USA
Army member of lend-lease mission to Russia; he was a close friend of Harry Hopkins. He was later recalled since he was thought to be too pro-Soviet.

GILDERSLEEVE, DR. VIRGINIA
Dean of Barnard College; adviser on women in military service.

GILBRETH, DR. LILLIAN
Professor at Purdue University; management specialist.

GIRAUD, GENERAL HENRI, FRENCH ARMY
He was considered by the Allied leaders as a possible head for the French armed forces of resistance, but this did not materialize.

GLASSFORD, VICE ADMIRAL WILLIAM A., USN
In charge of mission to Dakar, North Africa, to survey naval and merchant ships available there.

GOLOVKOV, ADMIRAL ARSENT G., SOVIET NAVY
Commander of Northern Fleet at Polyarny.

GORLINSKI, GENERAL, SOVIET ARMY
He was in charge of the reconstruction of buildings at Yalta to prepare for the conference there in 1945.

GUINGAND, MAJOR GENERAL SIR FRANCIS DE, BRITISH ARMY
Chief of staff to General Bernard L. Montgomery.

HARRIMAN, W. AVERELL
U.S. ambassador to Moscow during Yalta Conference in 1945.

HARRIMAN, KATHERINE
Daughter of Ambassador Harriman; attended Yalta Conference.

HELEN, ROBERT, USNR
Member of U.S. salvage team under Commodore Sullivan.

HENCKE, WERNER, GERMAN NAVY
One of the U-boat aces in the German Navy.

HILL, GENERAL, U.S. ARMY AIR CORPS
Member of the U.S. military mission in Moscow at the time of the Yalta Conference.

HILLENKOETTER, ADMIRAL ROSCOE, USN
In the rank of commander he was naval attaché in Paris in 1940. He was later director of the Central Intelligence Agency.

HOBBY, COLONEL OVETA B., USA
Director of Women's Army Auxiliary Corps (later Women's Army Corps).

HOLCOMB, GENERAL THOMAS, USMC
Commandant of the U.S. Marine Corps in 1943, retired in 1944.

HOLMES, GENERAL JULIUS, USA
Political adviser to General Eisenhower for North African campaign.

HOPKINS, HARRY
Special and confidential adviser to President Franklin D. Roosevelt.

HORROCKS, GENERAL SIR BRIAN, BRITISH ARMY
Part of the command structure at the landings at Salerno.

HUIE, CAPTAIN BYRON S., USNR
As commander, one of the salvage officers at the harbor of Cherbourg.

IVES, CAPTAIN NORMAN, USN
Commander of naval base at Cherbourg, under the overall command of Admiral Wilkes in England.

JACOBS, VICE ADMIRAL RANDALL, USN
Chief of naval personnel.

JOHNSON, HOWARD
Owner of chain of restaurants in the United States.

KAUFFMAN, VICE ADMIRAL JAMES L., USN
Commander of destroyers and cruisers, Pacific Fleet, 1944.

KING, ADMIRAL ERNEST J., USN
Commander in chief, U.S. Navy.

KNOWLES, KENNETH, USN
In the rank of commander, responsible for submarine estimates for COMINCH; in charge of Tenth Fleet (intelligence).

KNOX, FRANK
U.S. secretary of the navy during World War II.

KNUDSEN, WILLIAM O.
With Sidney Hillman, in charge of War Production Board in the United States during World War II.

KUZNETZOV, ADMIRAL NIKOLAI G., SOVIET NAVY
Navy commissar for the Baltic region.

LEAHY, FLEET ADMIRAL WILLIAM D., USN
As admiral, chief of staff to President Franklin D. Roosevelt.

LEE, COMMANDER P. E., USN
Senior technical officer, office of the U.S. naval attaché, London, 1940.

LEMNITZER, GENERAL LYMAN, USA
Chief of plans on General Eisenhower's staff, for North African invasion.

LEMONNIER, CONTRE-AMIRAL, FRENCH NAVY
Present at the Allied landings in southern France.

LEWIS, REAR ADMIRAL SPENCER S., USN
In command of a landing group at Saint Raphael in southern France.

LLEWELLYN, CAPTAIN, RN
Commanding officer of a British bomb disposal unit.

LLOYD, VICE MARSHAL HUGH PUGH, RAF
In command of fighter command for North Africa.

McCAIN, ADMIRAL JOHN S., USN
As vice admiral, in Admiral King's office, dealing with supplies to Russia.

MARSHALL, GENERAL OF THE ARMIES GEORGE C., USA
In the rank of general, chief of staff, U.S. Army.

MASON, GEORGE
Head of Nash Kelvinator; took on manufacture of propellers and later worked with Vought and Sikorsky on helicopters.

MAST, GENERAL CHARLES, FRENCH ARMY
Chief of staff to General Giraud in North Africa.

MEADE, GEORGE
Member of National Advisory Committee for Aeronautics; chief engineer for Pratt and Whitney; assistant to William Knudsen.

MICHELIER, VICE ADMIRAL F. C., FRENCH NAVY
Naval commander at Casablanca in 1942, loyal to General Pétain; resisted Allied forces at Casablanca landings.

MIKOYAN, ANASTAS A.
Member of Soviet Politburo and Ministry of Foreign Trade.

MONTGOMERY, MARSHAL BERNARD L., BRITISH ARMY
Commander of land forces for Sicilian landings; Allied commander under General Eisenhower for Normandy landings and campaign.

MOON, REAR ADMIRAL DON P., USN
Naval assault force commander at Utah Beach, Normandy landings.

MORGENTHAU, HENRY L.
Secretary of the Treasury in the Franklin D. Roosevelt administration.

MURPHY, ROBERT
Foreign service officer, State Department; liaison in North Africa in preparation for landings.

O'CONNOR, BASIL
Law partner of President Franklin D. Roosevelt.

PAPANIN, ADMIRAL, SOVIET NAVY
In charge of North Sea route to Murmansk.

PATCH, MAJOR GENERAL ALEXANDER M., USA
In command of the U.S. Seventh Army for the invasion of southern France.

PATTON, GENERAL GEORGE S., USA
Military commander for Moroccan landing; commands in subsequent landings in Sicily and Normandy.

PEARSON, DREW
U.S. journalist.

PHILIP, PRINCE, RN
Later duke of Edinburgh and consort of Queen Elizabeth II.

PLEVEN, RENÉ
French government negotiator for aircraft procurement from the United States.

PRATT, ADMIRAL WILLIAM V., USN
Retired chief of naval operations; wrote military column for *Newsweek* during World War II.

QUESADA, MAJOR GENERAL ELWOOD R., USAAC
Assisted naval operations off Normandy coast by gun spotting.

RADFORD, REAR ADMIRAL ARTHUR W., USN
In charge of aviation training program for U.S. Navy immediately after Pearl Harbor.

RAMSEY, ADMIRAL SIR BERTRAM, RN
Allied naval commander for Normandy landings.

RAMSEY, REAR ADMIRAL DEWITT C., USN
Head of Plans Division, Bureau of Aeronautics.

REILLY, MIKE
Head of White House Secret Service detail at Yalta.

RENTSCHLER, FREDERICK B.
Head of United Aircraft.

REYNARD, ELIZABETH
Professor at Barnard College; early WAVE officer.

RICHARDSON, COMMANDER L. B., USN
Procurement officer, Bureau of Aeronautics.

ROMMEL, MARSHAL ERWIN, GERMAN ARMY
Army commander in North Africa and at Normandy.

ROOSEVELT, FRANKLIN D., JR., USNR
In rank of lieutenant commander, executive officer of *Mayrant* at Palermo.

SABIN, CAPTAIN LORENZO S., USN
Replaced Admiral Wilkes for combat assault at Normandy invasion.

SALTONSTALL, LEVERETT
Governor of Massachusetts; later U.S. senator.

SCHLESINGER, DR. RICHARD, USN
Medical doctor attached to salvage team at Palermo and Cherbourg.

SELF, SIR HENRY
Civil servant in Air Ministry in Great Britain, charged with procurement.

SIBLEY, COLONEL, USA
Port commander at Cherbourg in charge of transportation.

SMITH, GENERAL BEDELL, USA
Chief of staff to General Eisenhower at Normandy operation.

STANDLEY, ADMIRAL WILLIAM H., USN
U.S. ambassador to Moscow before Averell Harriman.

STARK, ADMIRAL HAROLD R., USN
Chief of naval operations at outbreak of World War II; later special liaison in London.

STRUBLE, REAR ADMIRAL ARTHUR D., USN
Chief of staff to Admiral Kirk at Normandy operation.

TOLLEY, REAR ADMIRAL KEMP, USN
Assistant naval attaché in U.S. embassy in Moscow, 1942 to 1944.

TOVEY, ADMIRAL SIR JOHN, RN
Commander in chief, Home Fleet, 1942.

TOWERS, ADMIRAL JOHN H., USN
Chief of Bureau of Aeronautics early in World War II.

TRUSCOTT, MAJOR GENERAL LUCIAN K., USA
   With Third Infantry Division and two Raider battalions in Task Force 88 under the command of Rear Admiral Richard Conolly for Sicilian landings.

VAUGHN, GUY W.
   Head of Curtiss-Wright, aircraft engine manufacturers.

VICKERY, REAR ADMIRAL HOWARD L., USN
   Head of U.S. Maritime Commission, World War II.

VINSON, CARL
   United States representative from Georgia, chairman of the House Naval Affairs Committee.

WALSH, DAVID I.
   Senator from Massachusetts and chairman of Senate Naval Affairs Committee.

WELLINGS, CAPTAIN JOHN, USN
   Observer aboard British destroyers, 1940.

WELLINGS, TED, USN
   Operations officer on Admiral Kirk's staff before Normandy landings.

WILKES, ADMIRAL JOHN, USN
   Commander of landing craft and bases of the Eleventh Amphibious Force at Normandy.

ZONDORAK, CAPTAIN CHARLES J., USN
   Member of the military mission in Moscow.

BIBLIOGRAPHY

ORAL HISTORIES

The oral history memoirs from the Columbia University Oral History Collection are copyrighted by and used with the permission of The Trustees of Columbia University in the city of New York.

Anderson, Admiral George W., Jr. U.S. Naval Institute, 1975. Interviewed by the editor.

Ansel, Rear Admiral Walter O. U.S. Naval Institute, 1970. Interviewed by the editor.

Baldwin, Hanson W. U.S. Naval Institute, 1975. Interviewed by the editor.

Bucklew, Captain Phil H. U.S. Naval Institute, 1980. Interviewed by the editor.

Conolly, Admiral Richard L. Columbia University Oral History Collection, 1959. Interviewed by Donald F. Shaughnessy.

Duncan, Admiral Donald B. Columbia University Oral History Collection, 1964. Interviewed by the editor.

Dyer, Vice Admiral George Carroll. U.S. Naval Institute, 1971. Interviewed by the editor.

Felt, Admiral Harry D. U.S. Naval Institute, 1972. Interviewed by the editor.

Frankel, Rear Admiral Samuel B. U.S. Naval Institute, 1971. Interviewed by the editor.

Gallery, Rear Admiral Daniel V., Jr. U.S. Naval Institute, 1974. Interviewed by the editor.

Hall, Admiral John Lesslie, Jr. Columbia University Oral History Collection, 1963. Interviewed by the editor.

Hewitt, Admiral H. Kent. Columbia University Oral History Collection, 1963. Interviewed by the editor.

James, Rear Admiral Ralph Kirk. U.S. Naval Institute, 1972. Interviewed by the editor.

Kauffman, Rear Admiral Draper L. U.S. Naval Institute, 1979. Interviewed by the editor.

Kirk, Admiral Alan Goodrich. Columbia University Oral History Collection, 1961. Interviewed by the editor.

Murray, Commander Albert K. U.S. Naval Institute, 1988. Interviewed by the editor.

McAfee, Captain Mildred. U.S. Naval Institute, 1969. Interviewed by the editor.

Olsen, Rear Admiral Clarence E. U.S. Naval Institute, 1970. Interviewed by the editor.

Riley, Vice Admiral Herbert D. U.S. Naval Institute, 1971. Interviewed by the editor.

Rivero, Admiral Horacio, Jr. U.S. Naval Institute, 1975. Interviewed by the editor.

Smith, Vice Admiral John Victor. U.S. Naval Institute, 1976. Interviewed by the editor.

Stratton, Captain Dorothy C. U.S. Naval Institute, 1970. Interviewed by the editor.

Streeter, Colonel Ruth Cheney. Columbia University Oral History Collection, 1979. Interviewed by the editor.

Sullivan, Rear Admiral William A. Columbia University Oral History Collection, 1969. Interviewed by the editor.

Waters, Rear Admiral Odale Dabney, Jr. U.S. Naval Institute, 1971. Interviewed by the editor.

Whiting, Vice Admiral Francis E.M. U.S. Naval Institute, 1970. Interviewed by the editor.

Wilson, Commander Eugene Edward. Columbia University Oral History Collection, 1962. Interviewed by the editor.

Wright, Admiral Jerauld. U.S. Naval Institute, 1977. Interviewed by the editor.

BOOKS

Baldwin, Hanson W. *Battles Lost and Won: Great Campaigns of World War II.* New York: Harper & Row, 1966.

————. *The Crucial Years, 1939–1941.* Boston: Harper & Row, 1976.

Churchill, Winston S. *The Second World War.* Vols. 2, 3, 4, 5, 6. Boston: Houghton Mifflin, 1949–53.

Farago, Ladislas. *The Tenth Fleet.* New York: Ivan Obolensky, 1962.

Keegan, John. *Six Armies in Normandy.* New York: Viking Press, 1983.

————. *The Price of Admiralty.* New York: Viking Press, 1989.

Lewin, Ronald. *Churchill as Warlord.* New York: Stein & Day, 1973.

McJimsey, George. *Harry Hopkins: Ally of the Poor and Defender of Democracy.* Cambridge, Massachusetts: Harvard University Press, 1987.

Morison, Samuel Eliot. *History of United States Naval Operations in World War II.* Vols 1, 2, 9, 10, 11. Boston: Little, Brown, 1975.

Murphy, Robert. *Diplomat among Warriors.* Garden City, New York: Doubleday, 1964.

Salisbury, Harrison E. *The 900 Days: The Siege of Leningrad.* New York: Harper and Row, 1969.

Sherwood, Robert E. *Roosevelt and Hopkins: An Intimate History.* New York: Harper & Brothers, 1948.

Watson-Watt, Sir Robert. *The Pulse of Radar: An Autobiography.* New York: Dial Press, 1959.

Wilmot, Chester. *The Struggle for Europe.* London: Collins, 1952.

INDEX

ABOUT THE AUTHOR

John T. Mason, Jr., is a trained historian with an advanced degree from George Washington University. His further graduate work at Columbia University was interrupted by duty with the Office of Naval Intelligence in Washington, D.C., from 1940 to the end of World War II. He then obtained a graduate degree from General Theological Seminary and was ordained an Episcopal priest. From 1960 to 1969 he was associated with the Oral History Research Office of Columbia University under the guidance of the noted American historian Allan Nevins. He later established an office of oral history at the U.S. Naval Institute, where he developed one of the most extensive collections of naval oral history transcripts in the country. One of his most notable projects was a seven-volume compilation of interviews on the career of Fleet Admiral Chester W. Nimitz. He is also the editor of *The Pacific War Remembered: An Oral History Collection.*

The **Naval Institute Press** is the book-publishing arm of the U.S. Naval Institute, a private, nonprofit professional society for members of the sea services and civilians who share an interest in naval and maritime affairs. Established in 1873 at the U.S. Naval Academy in Annapolis, Maryland, where its offices remain today, the Naval Institute has more than 100,000 members worldwide.

Members of the Naval Institute receive the influential monthly magazine *Proceedings* and discounts on fine nautical prints, ship and aircraft photos, and subscriptions to the quarterly *Naval History* magazine. They also have access to the transcripts of the Institute's Oral History Program and get discounted admission to any of the Institute-sponsored seminars regularly offered around the country.

The Naval Institute's book-publishing program, begun in 1898 with basic guides to naval practices, has broadened its scope in recent years to include books of more general interest. Now the Naval Institute Press publishes more than forty new titles each year, ranging from how-to books on boating and navigation to battle histories, biographies, ship and aircraft guides, and novels. Institute members receive discounts on the Press's more than 375 books.

Full-time students are eligible for special half-price membership rates. Life memberships are also available.

For a free catalog describing the Naval Institute Press books currently available, and for further information about U.S. Naval Institute membership, please write to:

Membership & Communications Department
U.S. Naval Institute
Annapolis, Maryland 21402
Or call, toll-free, (800) 233-USNI. In Maryland, call (301) 224-3378.

THE NAVAL INSTITUTE PRESS

THE ATLANTIC WAR REMEMBERED

Set in Times Roman
by BG Composition, Baltimore, Maryland

Printed on 50-lb. Text White Opaque Decision
and bound in Holliston Kingston Natural Breakwater
with 80-lb., text-matching endsheets
by The Maple-Vail Book Manufacturing Group,
Binghamton, New York